AF829067

Studies in Economic Transition

Series Editors
Jens Hölscher
The Business School
Bournemouth University
Bournemouth, Dorset, UK

Horst Tomann
Department of Economic Policy and Economic History
Freie Universitaet (FU) Berlin
Berlin, Germany

This series brings together theoretical and empirical studies on the transformation of economic systems and their economic development. The transition from planned to market economies is one of the main areas of applied theory because in this field the most dramatic examples of change and economic dynamics can be found. It is aimed to contribute to the understanding of specific major economic changes as well as to advance the theory of economic development. The implications of economic policy will be a major point of focus.

Saul Estrin • Milica Uvalic
Editors

Collected Works of Domenico Mario Nuti, Volume I

Socialist Economic Systems and Transition

palgrave
macmillan

Editors
Saul Estrin
London School of Economics and Political Science
London, UK

Milica Uvalic
Department of Political Science
University of Perugia
Perugia, Italy

ISSN 2662-6675 ISSN 2662-6683 (electronic)
Studies in Economic Transition
ISBN 978-3-031-12333-7 ISBN 978-3-031-12334-4 (eBook)
https://doi.org/10.1007/978-3-031-12334-4

© The Editor(s) (if applicable) and The Author(s), under exclusive licence to Springer Nature Switzerland AG 2023
This work is subject to copyright. All rights are solely and exclusively licensed by the Publisher, whether the whole or part of the material is concerned, specifically the rights of translation, reprinting, reuse of illustrations, recitation, broadcasting, reproduction on microfilms or in any other physical way, and transmission or information storage and retrieval, electronic adaptation, computer software, or by similar or dissimilar methodology now known or hereafter developed.
The use of general descriptive names, registered names, trademarks, service marks, etc. in this publication does not imply, even in the absence of a specific statement, that such names are exempt from the relevant protective laws and regulations and therefore free for general use.
The publisher, the authors, and the editors are safe to assume that the advice and information in this book are believed to be true and accurate at the date of publication. Neither the publisher nor the authors or the editors give a warranty, expressed or implied, with respect to the material contained herein or for any errors or omissions that may have been made. The publisher remains neutral with regard to jurisdictional claims in published maps and institutional affiliations.

This Palgrave Macmillan imprint is published by the registered company Springer Nature Switzerland AG.
The registered company address is: Gewerbestrasse 11, 6330 Cham, Switzerland

Acknowledgments

We have been greatly helped in putting together these Collected Works by a large number of people, including Frances Nuti, Will Bartlett, Renzo Daviddi, Michael Ellman, Derek Jones, Susan Senior Nello, Jan Svejnar and Vela Velupillai. Our editor Wyndham Hacket Pain and his staff at Palgrave Macmillan offered every level of assistance and encouragement that we greatly acknowledge. Much of the burdensome work of transcribing the texts and obtaining permissions was done by Rachel Harris. We are most grateful for Ruth Martin's excellent index. Mario Nuti's portrait was photographed by Francesco Gnot. The Research Infrastructure and Investment Fund of LSE's Department of Management, administered by Nino Nizharadze and Emma Ward, provided generous financial support for the preparation of these volumes.

Contents

List of Figures

List of Tables

1

An Introduction to the Collected Works of Domenico Mario Nuti

Saul Estrin and Milica Uvalic

1.1 Domenico Mario Nuti's Life and Work

These two volumes bring together many of the most significant contributions to economic theory and policy of Domenico Mario Nuti (1937–2020).

Mario's remarkable professional career is intrinsically linked to his rich and eventful life. He was born and received a classical education in Arezzo (Italy) and grew up in the nearby Tuscan village Castiglion Fibocchi.[1] After having graduated at the University of Rome in 1961 with a thesis on "Problems and models of economic growth", he worked briefly at the Bank of Italy and at the Inter-Ministerial Committee for the Development

[1] Further details about Mario Nuti's life can be found in Chapter 2 of Volume 1, which contains his autobiography.

S. Estrin (✉)
London School of Economics and Political Science, London, UK
e-mail: s.estrin@lse.ac.uk

M. Uvalic
Department of Political Science, University of Perugia, Perugia, Italy
e-mail: milica.uvalic@unipg.it

© The Author(s), under exclusive license to Springer Nature Switzerland AG 2023

S. Estrin, M. Uvalic (eds.), *Collected Works of Domenico Mario Nuti, Volume I*,
Studies in Economic Transition, https://doi.org/10.1007/978-3-031-12334-4_1

of Southern Italy, seeing at first hand the problems of underdevelopment and poverty. A scholarship at the Polish Academy of Sciences took Mario to Warsaw in 1962–63, where he learnt Polish and was taught by Oskar Lange and Michal Kalecki, two giants of socialist economics. They both strongly influenced Mario's research interests and remained lasting intellectual influences. It was upon the recommendation of Kalecki that Mario was admitted in 1963 to King's College, Cambridge, to work under the supervision of Nicholas Kaldor and Maurice Dobb towards his 1970 PhD on "Problems of investment planning in socialist economies". Mario stayed at Cambridge University until 1979 as a Fellow of King's College and later as Lecturer in the Faculty of Economics. During those years, Mario was deeply involved in the debates among Cambridge economists which embedded Mario's understanding about macroeconomics, growth and the possibilities for widespread state intervention in the economy. These experiences led Mario to develop his own intellectual framework, combining his knowledge of the socialist economy with his understanding of macroeconomic issues and leavened with his own fierce logic and systematic analysis. Mario was appointed Professor of Political Economy and Director of the Centre for Russian and East European Studies at the University of Birmingham in 1979, where he continued to explore how to combine socialist ideals with elements of a market system.

In 1982, Mario left the UK to take up the position of Professor in Economics at the European University Institute (EUI) in Florence, where he stayed until 1990. The protracted economic crises in Eastern Europe during those years brought a number of important and controversial issues onto the research agenda, to which Mario made significant contributions. While at the EUI, Mario organized seminars and conferences on socialist economies, inviting the most prominent experts on Eastern Europe, both from the East (e.g. Tamas Bauer, Janos Kornai, Vladimir Dlouhy, Grzegorz Kolodko) and the West (e.g. Jozef van Brabant, Wlodzimierz Brus, Gregory Grossman, Kazimierz Laski, Marie Lavigne). Mario's interest in comparative economic systems led him to launch another project, on economic democracy, inspired by James Meade's early work on alternative ways of firm organization. The project focused on the labour-managed firm and Italian cooperatives and involved Saul Estrin, Derek Jones, Steve Smith, Jan Svejnar, Will Bartlett and Milica Uvalic. Soon after, Martin Weitzman's work on profit-sharing inspired new research on participatory forms in the European Community, which resulted in the publication of the PEPPER Report (an acronym coined by Mario that stands for Promotion of Employee Participation in Profits and Enterprise Results).

After the fall of the Berlin Wall, the European Commission lacked the expertise to deal with the momentous changes this event heralded, so Mario was invited to Brussels in 1990 as an advisor to DG-II (Economic and Monetary Affairs, as it then was called), with responsibility for relations with transition economies. He returned to his alma mater, the University of Rome *La Sapienza*, as Professor of Comparative Economic Systems in 1993, a position he held until his retirement in 2010, alongside other appointments. Thus, during 1993–2005, Mario was also Visiting Professor at the London Business School (LBS) working closely with Saul Estrin, head of the Centre on CIS and Middle Europe, jointly running a seminar on transition economics. Mario's engagement with policy went even deeper after 1994, when he was appointed Economic Advisor to the Polish government—under Grzegorz Kolodko from 1994 to January 1997; Marek Belka until September 1997; and again, Kolodko in 2001–02, during the final stage of Poland's successful accession negotiations with the European Union. Mario's deep knowledge and expertise on socialist economies brought him other important assignments. He was consultant to the World Bank with a number of missions to Poland and work on post-communist economies; economic adviser to President Lukashenko of Belarus under World Bank sponsorship (1998); consultant to the IMF, ILO, NATO, UNDP, OECD; and Specialist Adviser to the House of Lords European Communities Committee (1993–1994).

Mario Nuti became an Emeritus Professor of the University of Rome *La Sapienza* in 2010 and also remained an Honorary Senior Research Fellow of the Centre for Russian and East-European Studies at the University of Birmingham. His retirement did not interrupt his research, production of papers and commentaries (including his blog, "Transition") and active involvement in various projects. In October 2017, he presented one of his last papers on "The Rise and Fall of Socialism" at a conference in Berlin published in 2018 (see Volume 2).

Mario made significant intellectual contributions across many fields, inspiring generations of students and colleagues for more than fifty years.

However, he is fairly difficult to classify as an economist, not least because in order to get to the heart of complex ideas, he played the role of an iconoclast. Much of his work was centred on trying to understand actual socialist and capitalist systems, conceptually and in practice, as well as, later, the paths from socialism to capitalism.

Our purpose in these volumes has been to select from Nuti's papers so as to make his best works, including his policy contributions, readily accessible. Moreover, in bringing his work together for the first time, we hope as well to elicit the underlying intellectual framework. Mario made contributions across a variety of topics that have resonance and significance today. In particular, he brought an original and distinctive intellectual vision to bear on some of the grand issues in economics: what drives growth and development; what is the most efficient economic system; can socialism be combined with markets; how should firms be organised; and how should economies be managed? To these questions, he provided answers which continue to have contemporary relevance. His was also a powerful intellectual voice for a more radical theoretical and policy framework to analyse the economic problems in his homeland, Italy, in the UK, and in various transition and developing countries.

Much of Mario's published output is fragmented across a variety of scholarly and policy outlets, while some of his most significant works are only available in publications that are neither readily accessible or simple to find. We have tried to select papers that cover the whole range of his ideas and contributions, including some unpublished papers. In some cases, we have chosen versions of his papers different from those actually published, because in our judgement, they more clearly present his analysis and arguments. Moreover, we have left the papers as written with no editorial intervention (although minor errors in subediting of texts have been corrected), so that Mario's voice can be heard as he intended through his own words.

Mario had a coherent intellectual vision which was well understood by his colleagues and close associates, and which we hope to transmit to a wider audience by publishing these volumes. Mario never produced an integrated account of his contributions, except, partly, through the blog "Transition" where he made available most of his papers written after

2009. Mario also did not produce a full bibliography of his own work. A more complete bibliography is provided at the end of each volume.

1.2 Structure of the Two Volumes

We have organised our selection of papers into five areas spread across the two volumes. The first volume entitled *Socialist Economic Systems and Transition* is concerned with Mario's writings about socialist economic systems, their growing problems in the 1980s and their abrupt demise at the end of that decade. The papers in the first volume are organised into two sections: Socialist economic systems and the Transition to a market economy respectively. The second volume entitled *Economic Systems, Democracy and Integration* is more wide-ranging and includes papers in three areas: Evolution of economic systems; Economic democracy; and East—West integration and globalisation. The papers in the first part of Volume 2 are more theoretical, and concern Mario's analysis of the functioning of capitalist and socialist systems. The papers in the second part focus on Mario's lifetime concern with alternative ways to organise production and the possibilities of bringing economic democracy into the workplace. In the final section, we bring together Mario's recent writings about some topical issues in the new EU member states in the 2000s, as well as his concerns about globalization, the state of the world economy and the problems of the European Union. We provide brief Forewords for each of the five sections to integrate the arguments across the papers.

In organizing these sections, the classification of Mario's writings into distinct research areas has been a heroic task, since there is a substantial overlap of underlying themes across his writings. This should be of no surprise, since a handful of fundamental concerns have been at the basis of Mario's research throughout his life, from his early days in Cambridge to his more recent work on the transition in Eastern Europe and globalisation. Perhaps the major concern that inspired much of his life-long research revolves around the quest for a more just and more egalitarian economic, social and political system. Indeed, the search for a more democratic economy and society can be found at the basis of many of his papers. As well expressed by Michael Ellman in his memorial article,

"Nuti considered that economics should be about understanding the world and using that understanding to help improve the life of its population." (Ellman, 2021, p. 1363).

Thus, Mario's reflections on socialist economic systems closely overlap with some of his writings on the evolution of economic systems, but also anticipate themes related to economic democracy. Similarly, the themes addressing the transition to a market economy are closely inter-related with those covered by topics on integration and global economic issues, while reflections on the evolution of economic systems are intrinsically linked to the broad area of comparative economic systems.

While he held a variety of prestigious academic positions, Mario was never just an ivory tower economist. We have seen that he was closely involved in analysing and advising international organizations about policies during transition in Central and Eastern Europe. His rigorous training in economic theory combined with his long practical experience meant that his papers on transition, as well as his more recent work on global economic issues, bring a unique perspective and provide long-lasting lessons from his analysis of what were then contemporary issues. Mario continued to reflect on major economic topics throughout his life, in his later years through his blog site, and we include few of these writings in order to indicate his thinking on these more contemporary issues.

In the remainder of this Introduction we will briefly present the five areas of Mario Nuti's opus following the classification adopted in these two Volumes.

1.2.1 Socialist Economic Systems

The section on Socialist Economic Systems includes Nuti's work on the functioning of the Soviet-type centrally planned economies and variants that developed during the post-Second World War period in Central and Eastern Europe. Mario's interest in this topic no doubt was strongly influenced by his early studies in Warsaw and the economic discussions at Cambridge University in the 1970s. The topics he addressed reveal his deep Keynesian (and Kaleckian) influences, focusing on investment, trade cycles and growth in socialist economies.

Mario was primarily interested in the functioning of actual socialist economies, 'realised socialism', from Soviet planning through market socialism in Hungary to the self-managing socialism of Tito's Yugoslavia. He always favoured clear definitions and careful categorisation. He was not in sympathy with the traditional Soviet variant of socialism, which he described as 'Rugged … the bestselling type of socialism', but was more positive about the Yugoslav and Hungarian reform variants, though not entirely convinced by either. In particular, he described Yugoslav socialism as an 'ingenious and peculiar system'. More generally, he was intrigued by market socialism which he viewed as a capitalist system improved by embodying socialist features.

Mario addressed the question of why socialism everywhere collapsed in 1989 only in his later papers, but many of his writings offer important insights about the key contributors to its demise. In addition to the protracted economic and political crises, he stressed the positive role of Gorbachev's Perestroika and Poland's trade-union movement *Solidarność*. He noted that none of the reform systems had traction in their own right; when the Soviet Union withdrew and then fell, they all fell too; even the Yugoslav variant disappeared at the same time as systems based on central planning. He felt this was because the socialist systems were unable to reform themselves further and the Party was unwilling to give up its monopoly of power, even when this might have helped the long run survival of the system. In Mario's view, the collapse of the Soviet Union did not invalidate the socialist model: it was the failing of one (unattractive) variant of it. He argued that Soviet-type socialism suffered greatly from the belief that economic laws would not operate at all in the socialist economy.

1.2.2 The Transition from Socialism to Capitalism

Given his deep understanding of socialist economic systems, Mario was well placed to analyse questions of the transition to a market economy. In the absence of blueprints at that time, his innovative ideas on how to implement radical reforms of the socialist economy were important in defining the main objectives, speed, and sequencing of economic reforms;

suggesting desirable macroeconomic stabilization and exchange rate policies; and explaining the specific supply inertia behind the deep recession of the early 1990s. He was also deeply involved in analysing the advantages and disadvantages of different privatization methods, arguing in favour of a multi-track approach. He warned against the glorification of mass privatization 'as a method for implementing instant, irreversible, politically self-supporting, large-scale capitalism'. He also warned against simplified interpretations of dominant insider ownership, a frequent yet unexpected consequence of privatization in many countries across Eastern Europe.

Mario was also among the first to emphasize the flaws of the transition to a market economy. These included the high social costs of transition: the persistence of unemployment, the rise of inequality and of poverty. These phenomena were particularly serious because they meant a drastic reversal of earlier conditions of full employment, greater equality and low poverty incidence. He was also a fierce critic of hyper-liberal economic policies, arguing that excessively restrictive monetary and fiscal policies are detrimental for economic growth.

1.2.3 Evolution of Economic Systems

A related area of Mario's work is about how economic systems evolve. Most economists have for years regarded capitalist systems as inherently superior to socialist ones though the latter may have some potentially attractive features in terms of income distribution and other values. Mario's analysis was more nuanced, pointing to developments in general equilibrium theory that might invalidate such claims of inherent superiority. To quote, 'I believe the neoclassical picture of the capitalist economy is fantasy because markets are both incomplete (where are the future markets for manufactured goods, or the contingent commodity markets?) and, most importantly, sequential. Hence resource allocation is ruled by price (and quantity) expectations as much as by actual spot prices, and therefore from [the] Arrow-Debreu [model] we instantly fall into a Keynesian world of expectations—whether self-fulfilling or false—of underemployment equilibria and economic fluctuations' (see chapter 2,

Volume 1). There is little doubt that his thinking was strongly influenced by both the Cambridge School, including his supervisors Kaldor and Dobb, but also mathematical socialist economists from Eastern Europe including Kalecki, Lange and also Dmitriev, whose work he introduced to the Anglo-Saxon world with an Introduction to the English translation of his Essays.

Mario's papers in this area were largely theoretical papers including work which criticises, from a Kaleckian perspective, the Kaldor-Mirrlees model of growth, and contributions to the lively debate between the followers of neoclassical economics and those in the Keynesian, Marxian and Ricardian traditions about the measurement of capital and the use of aggregate production functions. Further, Mario developed a critique of traditional capital theory that developed a 'flow-input flow-output' model, inspired by Kalecki's investment criteria and compared Kalecki and Keynes in their approaches to demand-determined income.

Mario was also concerned about the evolution of economic systems in practice. He sought to analyse from a comparative perspective a variety of models, including recent variants of the socialist economic system—such as that of China. Some of the included papers also provide comparisons over time of the evolution of economic systems.

1.2.4 Economic Democracy

Mario had a profound interest in industrial and economic democracy, alternative forms of enterprise that assure workers' participation in decision-making and in enterprise results. His work was inspired by the practice of workers' cooperatives, profit-sharing and co-determination in western market economies and the self-management experience in Yugoslavia. He was also interested in the experiences of employee ownership in western market economies as well as in workers' share-ownership in many East European countries as a result of privatizations in the 1990s.

His research interests did not preclude his open criticism of some of the most influential works. Mario considered Martin Weitzman's Share Economy, that proposed giving workers a share in profits in addition to a fixed wage and leading to full employment resilient to deflationary shocks, 'a Catch 22' based on 'claims and overclaims'. Similarly, Mario was a great admirer of James Meade's work, but he questioned the assumptions of Meade's capital-labour partnership due to the violation of the principle of equal pay for equal work. Through his critical analysis of existing models, Mario tried to elaborate his own, that would offer more viable participatory solutions.

With the start of transition in Eastern Europe, Mario raised his voice against simplistic generalisations regarding the negative implications of diffused employee ownership. In countries that had to privatise entire economies but had no domestic capital and lacked the major interest of foreign investors, privatizations had often led to the sale of shares under privileged conditions (or free distribution) to workers. Hence, insiders often became the dominant shareholders 'by default'. Mario was well aware of the drawbacks of the insider-controlled firm, but he formulated the conditions under which the expected adverse effects would be avoided, showing how the outcome depends on the worker's short-term interests as a wage-earner and his/her longer-term interest as a shareholder. Inefficiencies would arise only if employees as shareholders had a lower share in company equity than they had in labour supply as workers. Mario also correctly anticipated that enterprises in which insiders held a controlling interest might be institutionally unstable. He further considered that employee participation in enterprise results encourages higher labour productivity, not so much via greater individual effort (given that the employee only gains a fraction of the extra product due to his/her greater effort), but through the greater intelligence and cooperation with which any given effort is exercised and through mutual employee monitoring. He argued that employee ownership creates a sense of identity with the company, improves channels of communication and the chances of avoiding and resolving conflicts.

1.2.5 East-West Integration and Globalisation

Mario's research interests included issues related to integration between Western and Eastern Europe, and therefore also the policies of the European Union. He stressed the benefits of fast Western support of the countries of Central and Eastern Europe after 1990 and contributed one of the first in-depth analyses on the impact of the transition on the European Union. He was also involved in examining the benefits and costs of adoption of the Euro by the new EU member states. Another concern regarding the new EU member states was that most had adopted social models based on the liberal approach, with weak trade unions and a minimal role of the welfare state, thus contributing to the 'dilution' of the European Social Model. When the global financial crisis hit the European Union in 2007–2008, Mario drew an interesting parallel between the underlying causes of the crisis in developed market economies and those in Eastern Europe, pointing to the common features of subprime loans in the West and East.

Mario was an attentive observer of the challenges posed by increasing integration and by the unregulated nature of many global processes. He noted, in 2009, that globalisation is equally as spectacular in its progress as in its incompleteness, in addition to being distorted and unfair. In his view, globalisation was incomplete because of the maintenance of many forms, often intense, of protectionism and the proliferation of free trade agreements. He also viewed it as distorted, unfair, and asymmetric in favouring the international mobility of capital rather than labour and financing global imbalances instead of investment and growth in poorer countries. He therefore considered essential to create and strengthen redistribution agencies at all levels—of nations, commercial blocks, the global economy. He was prescient in pointing out that failure to govern globalisation and to correct its impact on poverty, inequality, and redistribution, would breed increasing opposition to its further progress.

Additional challenges are faced regionally by the member states of the European Union and especially the Eurozone, given the disintegration trends resulting from their dysfunctional construction. Mario particularly condemned the persistence of austerity policies, showing that fiscal consolidation can actually increase, instead of decreasing, the public debt/GDP ratio. He believed there were remedies in line with the original European design—such as a common asylum acceptance regime to reduce the migration crisis, or excluding public investment from the permitted public deficit, that would loosen austerity; but he was also aware that these remedies may not be consistent with what he saw as the dominant hyper-liberal perspective.

1.3 Concluding Remarks

Mario always stressed that no theoretical paradigm in economics should be accepted *a priori*, but its use should depend on the problem to be solved. This was in line with his own approach. In his autobiography, he wrote: 'I am not fond of labels; like all aggregates they destroy information and are potentially misleading. If pressed, I would choose a handful of them. I would call myself a keynesian-kaleckian-kaldorian-robinsonian when modeling the macroeconomics of the capitalist economy; a "left-wing monetarist" … when modelling the macroeconomics of the socialist economy; a consumer of Marxian techniques when studying the dynamics of economic institutions and systems, but ready to turn them against Marx-inspired systems with a vengeance; a neo-classical in micro-economics, convinced of the importance of prices and a strong supporter—though very critical—of markets as homeostatic mechanisms, indispensable no matter how crude or imperfect. What approach is best depends on the question you ask (Oskar Lange); you choose a model as you would choose a map, according to the nature of your journey (Joan Robinson)' (see chapter 2, Volume 1). In these Volumes, we have tried to illustrate the richness of models and frameworks he applied as his eye roamed across a wide variety of economic issues over half a century.

Mario Nuti had many students, collaborators, colleagues, close friends. On the occasion of his 70th birthday, a Festschrift was prepared by his colleagues to honour his work, with contributions, in addition to the editors, by M. de Cecco, L. Csaba, S. Commander, P. Desai, J. Eatwell, M. Ellman, M. Keren and G. Ofer, V. Popov, S. Godoy and J. Stiglitz, J. Prasnikar and J. Svejnar, and V. Tanzi (Estrin et al., 2007). Mario taught his students to be critical, rigorous, thorough, substantiating every sentence they wrote; in this, his own papers served as the best example to follow. He transmitted to his students the passion for research and thorough analysis, as he was never satisfied with simple explanations. Nor was he always an easy interlocutor, especially regarding issues about which he had strong beliefs, but he was always ready to enter a discussion about alternative views. As these volumes show, he was an intellectual of a special kind, with a critical mind and great knowledge in many fields that extend far beyond economics.

Bibliography

Ellman, M. (2021). Tribute to Domenico Mario Nuti. Cambridge Journal of Economics, 45(6), 1361–1372.

Estrin, S., G. W. Kolodko and M. Uvalic (eds) (2007). Transition and Beyond – Essays in Honor of Mario Nuti, Palgrave Macmillan.

2

Domenico Mario Nuti (1937-)

Domenico Mario Nuti

I am flattered at being classed as a rebel but I regard myself more as an omnivorous eclectic (of "catholic" tastes, I would say, if that label were not so potentially confusing when applied to a non-practicing atheist). I am not fond of labels; like all aggregates they destroy information and are potentially misleading. If pressed, I would choose a handful of them. I would call myself a keynesian-kaleckian-kaldorian-robinsonian, when modelling the macroeconomics of the capitalist economy; a "left-wing monetarist" (as Peter Wiles recently actually called me) when modelling the macroeconomics of the socialist economy; a consumer of Marxian techniques when studying the dynamics of economic institutions and systems, but ready to turn them against Marx-inspired systems with a

Mario Nuti's contribution to the *Dictionary of Dissenting Economists* edited by Philip Arestis and Malcolm C. Sawyer, Elgar Publishing, London, 1992. Domenico Mario Nuti passed away on 22 December 2020.

D. M. Nuti (✉)
La Sapienza, University of Rome, Rome, Italy
e-mail: milica.uvalic@unipg.it

© The Author(s), under exclusive license to Springer Nature Switzerland AG 2023

S. Estrin, M. Uvalic (eds.), *Collected Works of Domenico Mario Nuti, Volume I*,
Studies in Economic Transition, https://doi.org/10.1007/978-3-031-12334-4_2

vengeance; a neo-classical in microeconomics, convinced of the importance of prices and a strong supporter—though very critical—of markets as homeostatic mechanisms, indispensable no matter how crude or imperfect. What approach is best depends on the question you ask (Lange); you choose a model as you would choose a map, according to the nature of your journey (Joan Robinson).

I was born in the Tuscan town of Arezzo in 1937 and grew up in a small village, a poor agricultural centre of fewer than 1000 souls, with 50–50 sharecropping the only form of land tenure, two latifundia, a usurer and two shopkeepers, and only one car even in 1950; now a polluted, overgrown industrial centre. I had a classical education. My interest in economics was generated by both personal and social circumstances. My father—a teacher and journalist—was a small landowner financially ruined by post-War Italian hyperinflation (he honoured a pre-war debt as if it were indexed, which it was not, while his savings were decimated by inflation) and by the pig cycle. I still remember his astonishment when, many years later, I explained to him the cobweb theorem. A self-supporting student of Law, at Rome University in the mid-fifties, I got in touch with Danilo Dolci, a practitioner of self-help and non-violent action for civil rights, working in Sicilian mafialand. A stay in Palermo and Trappeto in 1958, and the sight of road-building by voluntary workers asserting their right to work guaranteed on paper by article 4 of the Italian Constitution, made a great impression on me. Helping to organise and attending a Conference on "Planning from below" arranged by Dolci in Palermo did the rest, i.e. gave me the motivation and contacts to do my degree dissertation in development economics and to get a research post with the Inter-Ministerial Committee for the Development of Southern Italy. The job took me to field visits throughout the Mezzogiorno, with a team whose task was identifying suitable locations for concentrating industrial infrastructures, following the "growth poles" approach of Albert Hirschman, Gunnar Myrdal and Francois Perroux. This early personal and social background vaccinated me for good against economic theories relying on malleable capital, voluntary unemployment and rational expectations.

Graduating "cum laude" I was placed in a queue for a Bank of Italy scholarship to study abroad. Waiting to go to Cambridge, England, I obtained a fellowship of the Polish Academy of Sciences; I wanted to see socialism and central planning in action, and I knew that in Warsaw I would find outstanding economists. I joined a course for planners from developing countries at the Warsaw School of Planning and Statistics, where I was fortunate to be taught by Oskar Lange, Michael Kalecki, Wlodek Brus, Kazimierz Laski and others. I also learned Polish and attended Lange's lectures at the University. Poland at that time was the most liberal Eastern European country; there were no food shortages; the arts were thriving; there were obvious inefficiencies and in many ways the place was uninspiring but there were also expectations of early improvements and of further progress towards a better, market oriented model of socialism. In addition to my modest zloty grant I turned a couple hundred dollars into a very large sum at a vast multiple of the official exchange rate—openly and legally—by importing from Switzerland a small amount of a crucial scarce input used to make scent and sold it to a cooperative producing for the Soviet market; I lived comfortably, demonstrated the twist to Polish teenagers, and learned a great deal.

From Warsaw I went to King's College, Cambridge, as a research student; I was to remain there in various capacities for the next 17 years. I was taught first by Nicky Kaldor, a most inspiring teacher and "maestro", a challenger of orthodoxies whose main amusement was to turn established theories on their head, but who had a deep understanding of how both government and business actually worked in reality. I shone in the Cambridge Tripos and I began work on a PhD thesis on "Problems of investment planning in the socialist economies". Soon Maurice Dobb—by virtue of being a leading specialist in my chosen field—replaced Kaldor as my supervisor. My first research output on socialist economies—three essays on enterprise incentives, investment criteria, and inflation—gained me the Stevenson Prize 1965 and a Research Fellowship at King's, followed by a tutorship, teaching lectureship and Directorship of Studies accompanied, from 1970, by a parallel appointment at the Faculty of Economics.

At Cambridge in the 1960s a lively debate was taking place between the followers of neo-classical approaches to production, distribution and growth, and those seeking alternatives in the Marxian and Ricardian tradition. A major issue was the measurability of capital (historical cost, capacity, replacement cost, present value, physical indices, other aggregates?), capital malleability and substitutability, the shape and very existence of aggregate production functions. The questions may seem highly esoteric but have devastating policy implications: an innocent looking assumption of a Cobb-Douglas aggregate production function implicitly leads to the assertions that income distribution is given by "god and the engineers" (Joan Robinson) and cannot and should not be altered; that unemployment is not due to keynesian deficit demand but to excessive high real wages; that investment mistakes can be costlessly rectified, almost as if agents had perfect foresight, so that market failures do not matter. Like me, many knew that this was not and could not be the case and clung to the promises of any seemingly plausible alternative approach, like Piero Sraffa's cryptic "Production of commodities by means of commodities", neo-marxian and neo-ricardian cost-based prices, neo-keynesian propositions about income distribution and their possible microeconomic extension.

As it turned out, these were dead ends, not viable alternatives. Production prices, i.e. cost-based prices embodying a uniform rate of profit, are relevant under special conditions: constant returns to scale, only one primary factor i.e. labour, no joint production; then demand—if correctly anticipated by producers—will have no influence on relative prices. In those conditions production prices are part of every economist's education and are not controversial, as they correspond to the prices of Paul Samuelson's dynamic non-substitution theorem. Sraffa never conceded the necessity of constant returns, and fudged the questions of land and joint production by referring to marginal land and equi-profitable joint-production techniques: to establish which land is marginal and which equi-profitable techniques to look at one needs to know precisely those demand conditions that Sraffa claimed to dismiss. Wage bargaining has no connection whatever with his "standard commodity", nor can it or should it because, for a start, in a world of technical alternatives such a composite commodity must differ for different real rates of wage or profit. Production prices could be expressed as "transformed" values but there is no general way of preserving the total surplus value-total profit equality postulated by Marx. Outside distribution theory capital aggregates are inaccurate but harmless; ironically the conditions under which

Marxian labour values can be used as prices are virtually the same as those needed for treating capital as if it were homogeneous. True, there have been countless useless mathematical and econometric studies of aggregate production functions but on the other side one also finds equally useless, if fewer, similar exercises as well as a frequent obscurantist rejection of mathematical methods (I learned as much maths as I could and never found I had enough). Neo-keynesians express the extreme implications of constant behavioural parameters (such as propensities to save or to import, technical coefficients) whose invariance cannot be justified and is at odds with their findings; they have no alternative microeconomics (Kaldor's "representative firm" is a macroeconomic devise). These exercises had great pedagogical value, but ultimately could not provide new and unorthodox answers. Neo-classical theorists moved on to discuss important questions such as temporary equilibria, transaction costs, the nature of money, exhaustible resources, uncertainty, information, principal-agent relations, games; they replaced malleable capital with equally implausible constructs such as rational expectations but also gained new insights and, whether right or wrong, had something to say. Most practitioners of the alternative approaches—with notable exceptions such as my good friend Bob Rowthorn - remained silent on crucial old and new questions, stuck as they were in their grooves. I do not mind that this kind of dissent has made me somewhat unpopular.

A by-product of my research on socialist investment planning was an analysis of intertemporal allocation in a steady growth, flow-input flow-output model in the "putty-clay" tradition (i.e. with ex-ante but not ex-post substitutability). The model produced the desired re-switching of techniques and capital-reversal and a crop of other results (consumption-growth wage-profit duality, golden rules of accumulation, etcetera); they were interesting negative results as even in a steady state the time dimension of production ruled out the conventional treatment of capital. But I over-claimed, asserting that capital measurements were redundant (which they are not, out of a fully anticipated steady state), and that socialism would yield a better consumption performance than capitalism (which it would in such a model but in the real world this claim was soon to be contradicted by events). The paper, inspired by Kalecki's project selection rules, developed what John Hicks labelled a "Neo-Austrian" approach (not to be confused with later Neo-Austrian ultra-*laissez-faire* theories) and was published in the *EJ* (Nuti 1970); I beat Hicks to print, which goes to his credit because he later told me he had actually refereed that paper (lesser men might have been less generous). I played with Marx's Transformation Problem (in an essay in J. Schwartz, Ed., The Subtle Anatomy of Capitalism, Goodyear, Santa Monica, 1977, though written much earlier), following Marx's gross neglect of the importance of entrepreneurship and of price adjustment. I developed the "neo-Austrian" approach further to handle truncation of production flows and unsteady states (still fully anticipated, *Kyklos*, Nuti 1973) but I soon realised—alerted by Jack Hirschleifer's book on Investment, Capital and Interest - the limits of both the so-called Cambridge School and of neoclassical theory. My change of mind is already clear from my article in *Kyklos* (Nuti, 1974b) and my edition of the Economic Essays by V.K. Dmitriev (Nuti, 1974a), an anti-Ricardian pioneer. Of course I would not renege a single word of what I have ever written: *habent sua fata libelli*, i.e. writings have a life of their own, and are there to be judged within their context and on their own terms. I never thought one has to be consistent over time. But my views on alternative approaches and on economic systems naturally have changed.

Ultimately, I believe the neoclassical picture of the capitalist economy is fantasy because markets are both incomplete (where are the future markets for manufactured goods, or the contingent commodity markets? they cannot be replaced by asset markets) and, most importantly, sequential: you do not have to transact in future or forward markets to secure the delivery of future goods, you can always do it later in spot transactions. Hence resource allocation is ruled by price (and quantity) expectations as much as by actual spot prices, and therefore from the Arrow-Debreu world we instantly fall into a keynesian world of expectations, whether self-fulfilling or false, of under-employment equilibria and economic fluctuations. It is precisely the essence of Keynes that saving decisions do not signal demand for future goods, and that money balances can be a bottomless pit draining purchasing power no matter how low the money interest rate. As Joan Robinson used to put it, most neoclassical macroeconomics is "pre-keynesian economics after Keynes". Hence the absolute advantage of Keynesian and Kaleckian macroeconomics, and of the macro-dynamics of Dick Goodwin with his insights on capitalism as a symbiotic system of profits and wages and therefore capitalists and workers, producing a growth cycle through profit-linked accumulation.

If the claim that a private ownership and market economy is the best of all possible worlds cannot be supported by neoclassical theory, this does not mean that markets can be dispensed with, that individual agents (both households and firms) do not respond to relative prices as neoclassical microeconomics predicts, or that central planning is necessarily superior. Markets are automatic self-regulating mechanisms (as Dick Goodwin taught me), they produce some of the economic anarchy stressed by Marx but also some order—in due course, too fast or too slowly, imperfectly, mercilessly for the poor, the unemployed and the bankrupt, but surely. Lack of such an automatic response is one of the reasons why the Soviet-type socialist model failed: through the inertia of central planners' inaction in the face of a changing world, i.e. of changing technology, domestic demand, world trade opportunities. Anybody who has ever gone on a diet—as I often have—cannot possibly doubt that prices matter: confronted with the relative calorie content of alternative dishes and a calorie constraint instead of relative money prices and a money budget constraint one does alter drastically one's eating habits—regardless of socio-economic systems. Individuals and firms may or may not optimise their behaviour, but sooner or later they will learn to respond to relative prices—hence the neoclassical dominant role in this—but only in this—area, i.e. microeconomics.

The other main economic drawback of the centrally planned socialist system of Soviet-type is overambition, aiming at an impossible set of targets, for collective consumption, social welfare, living standards, investment and growth, defence, space research. This is the spirit of Soviet planning from the First Five Year Plan onwards, the pretence that 2+2=5, that there is no fortress that the Soviets cannot storm, that planning is like an act of war and tight plans mobilise resources, that socialism marks the end of economics, whereas socialism cannot bend the laws of economics any more than it can those of arithmetics or thermodynamics. Thus the passive adjustment of monetary flows to impossible targets and the parallel commitment to price stability—to avoid one of the evils of capitalism—set up a lethal time bomb, as inflationary gaps piled up over time to construct an inordinate monetary overhang (see *Contributions to Political Economy*, Nuti 1986b). Socialist planners would have fared much better by following Friedmanite policies of a steady and slow growth of the money supply (profligacy is also, I believe, the main cause of decline of the Scandinavian alternative). Instead the misguided commitment to price stability in the face of persistent monetary indiscipline, and planners' inertia—rather than the informational and coordination problems usually investigated by economists working on planning—aggravated by communist party political monopoly have made Soviet-type production relations and infrastructure—in Marxian parlance—inadequate to the level of development of productive forces. As a result, economic and political fluctuations have been generated since the mid-1950s, which I have tried to analyse using Marx's own approach to the dynamics of "modes of production" (see Nuti 1979; EUI Working Papers 85/156, Nuti 1985b; and my New Palgrave entry on cycles in the socialist economy, Nuti 1987a).

From Cambridge I moved to Birmingham to direct the Centre for Russian and East European Studies (1980–83), where I was in a much better position to monitor East European developments and learned much from my colleagues, especially Bob Davies, Phil Hanson, Ron Amann, Julian Cooper. I was much encouraged by the rise of Solidarity and Polish "party renewal" (see my Inaugural Lecture on "Socialism on Earth", Nuti 1981a) but I correctly predicted Polish military rule (in the *New Left Review*, Nuti 1981b). With British university cuts, I sold my chair back to Thatcher and retired to the ivory tower of the European University Institute at Florence, where I was able to pursue my research on the dynamics of socialism (1983–1990; see for instance *Contributions to Political Economy*, Nuti 1986b; *Economic Policy*, Nuti 1988; EDI-World Bank, Nuti 1989). I set up a working group on comparative economic systems, to whose members and visitors (including many East Europeans now holding ministerial posts) I am much indebted, and watched in disbelief the collapse of the Soviet type system.

Protracted and obtuse procrastination by communist leaders—including also, indeed especially, Mikhail Gorbachev—brought about the Soviet economic catastrophe of 1990, disintegrated the Union and CMEA, freed Eastern-Europe, justified the restoration of private property and re-switching to capitalism (see my contribution to the OECD Volume, Nuti 1990d). The tasks of stabilisation, restructuring and systemic transition are massive and provide an exciting field of research; I have been particularly interested by the questions of appropriate sequencing, speed and credibility of economic reform, the role of foreign trade liberalisation, the routes to convertibility. I believe in the primacy of stabilisation, preferably fast; the need to demonopolise and restructure before large scale privatisation, avoiding undue appropriation or dilapidation of state property; the need for commercial banking and financial markets immediately afterwards; the possibility of instant improvements but of slow completion of trade liberalisation and convertibility (see the OECD paper (Nuti 1990d) and my Louvain article (Nuti 1990b), and other forthcoming papers on these subjects).

The Soviet economic catastrophe restored a great deal of democracy throughout the area and, therefore, can be regarded as a blessing in disguise. But it also set back by twenty or perhaps fifty years the possible construction of an alternative social-democratic market-oriented and participatory model, which would have been easier to achieve by reforming the Soviet-type model than by reforming Western capitalism.

Yet market socialism has not failed: it was never fully designed or even imagined, let alone implemented (see my piece in Aslund, Ed., Nuti 1991b); today it is still literally a utopia, but is well worth exploring. I always liked to investigate utopias (and cacotopias, see my paper on Orwell, in *Coexistence*, Nuti 1985a); "Progress is the realisation of utopias" (Wilde). As the Eastern European economic crisis unfolded I turned my interest to economic institutions that might make up such a market socialist model: cooperatives and similar Yugoslav-type self-managed firms, profit-sharing, wage-earners' investment funds, leasings of state assets, workers participation à la Mitbestimmung, basic income schemes, labour-capital partnerships, neo-corporatist institutions. I found that cooperatives were microsocialist, almost monastic institutions with defective incentives (*Advances* ..., Nuti 1990a); that profit-sharing does not have the employment enhancement properties believed by Martin Weitzman (*Industrial Relations*, Nuti 1987b) and—another byproduct of my capital theory explorations—for proper incentives profit must be defined to include capital gains (i.e. as dividends plus all increments in an enterprise's capital value, see the "profit-sharing" entry in Szell,

Nuti 1991a); that workers' investment funds cannot be the painless nationalisation machines hoped for by Rudolf Meidner, except for the brief period while they are being set up, before they pay out dividends and redemptions; that democracy in the workplace is an essential concomitant of profit-sharing; that the guarantee of a basic income is a luxury that few economies can afford. None of these steps on its own would make much difference, but all of them together could add up to a coherent alternative model, where dependent workers would genuinely transform themselves, to the extent that they wished, into entrepreneurs (in G. Szell Ed., Nuti 1991a). This model is very close to James Meade's Agathotopia (Aberdeen UP, 1989)—a better utopia than most (see *Advances...*, Nuti 1990a). I also explored Kalecki's version of vertically integrated, self-managed planned socialism (*CJE*, Nuti 1986c) and possible new instruments and institutions, such as the replication of financial markets without private ownership (EDI-World Bank, Nuti 1989), contingent policy commitments, possible state agencies undertaking the role of Employer (or Investor, or International Trader) of Last Resort (in Nolan-Paine, Eds., Nuti 1986a). The need for a better system will be intensified once lessons are drawn from the collapse of both the Soviet-type and the Scandinavian model, and after the unavoidable disappointment with the restoration of crude capitalism in Eastern Europe, as excessive doses of the IMF medicine are taken (as in Poland in 1990, see *European Economy*, Nuti 1990c) and incomplete and out of sequence reforms (see my paper on Soviet reform sequencing, Nuti 1990b) fail to yield the expected results. Capitalism will bring improvements but will not solve the problems of Central Eastern Europe; it will transform them into other problems, i.e. the unemployment, open inflation, market turbulence and social conflicts with which we are only too familiar. The search is still on.

I am glad I never joined any political party. For all my penchant for utopias I never was an armchair economist. Beside my spell in the Mezzogiorno I worked in Egypt for FAO, helped to set up the Italian Trade Union CGIL research department, worked in Zambia on a large scale irrigation and resettlement scheme at Mpongwe. I helped the Zambian Ministry of Power to regain control over their share of Kariba electricity, leading to much higher prices for electricity exports to

Rhodesia; I was nearly napalmed in a Rhodesian raid on Lusaka and was held at gunpoint in the bush, but I cost Ian Smith the equivalent of a few dozen helicopters. I was then involved in undoing what I had contributed, and helped to restore cooperation between Zambia and Zimbabwe. I joined three World Bank and one UNDP missions to Poland, and one to Algeria (a disconcerting Mediterranean cross between Poland and Hungary) in the late 1980s. I wrote published reports for ILO, OECD, the League of Italian Cooperatives, the IMF, NATO and the European Commission. I directed various research projects on Poland (SSRC), on East-West relations (CEC and EUI) and on workers participation (EUI). A project on profit sharing (CEC-DG-V) produced the PEPPER Report (by Milica Uvalic, Brussels 1990), my acronym for Promotion of Employee Participation in Profits and Enterprise Results; the Report has been used for the implementation of the European Social Charter. I joined a "task force" of Western and Soviet economists under Wassily Leontief and Ivan Ivanov (of the Soviet State Committee for Foreign Economic Relations), sponsored by George Soros, on the opening up of the Soviet economy. I am now—while on leave from the University of Siena—an economic adviser on Central Eastern Europe at the Commission of the European Communities in Brussels, where I am pleased to work with some former students of mine (needless to say, my views should not necessarily be associated with the Commission). I know no better way of doing economics.

I have been very fortunate in having good teachers, many good colleagues, good secretaries, students, friends, opportunities. I used to reproach myself for not doing enough work, for I only regarded research as true work, but I now regret not having spent more of my time on a beach.

Brussels, December 1990.

Bibliography

D. M. Nuti (1970). Capitalism, socialism and steady growth. *The Economic Journal*, Vol. LXXX, 32-57, March.

D. M. Nuti (1973). On the truncation of production flows. *Kyklos*, Vol. XXVI, No. 3, 485-496.

D. M. Nuti (1974a). An edition of V.K. Dmitriev's Ekonomicheskie Ocherki, under the title: *Economic Essays on Value, Competition and Utility*, with notes and an Introductory Essay, Cambridge, Cambridge University Press.

D. M. Nuti (1974b). On the rates of return on investment, *Kyklos*, Vol. XXVII, No. 2, May, 345-369.

D. M. Nuti (1979). The contradictions of socialist economies - a Marxian interpretation, in R. Miliband and J. Saville (Eds.), *Socialist Register 1979*, The Merlin Press, London, pp. 228-73.

D. M. Nuti (1981a). Socialism on earth (Inaugural lecture). *Cambridge Journal of Economics*, Vol. 5, No. 4, December, 391-403.

D. M. Nuti (1981b). Poland: socialist renewal and economic collapse, *The New Left Review*, I/130, November-December, 23-36.

D. M. Nuti (1985a). A critique of Orwell's oligarchic collectivism as an economic system, *Coexistence: A Review of East-West and development issues*, Vol. 22, July, 151-163.

D. M. Nuti (1985b). Political and economic fluctuations in the socialist system, EUI Working Paper No. 85/156, European University Institute, Florence.

D. M. Nuti (1986a). Economic planning in market economies: scope, instruments, institutions, in Nolan-Paine (Eds), *Rethinking Socialist Economics*, Croom Helm, London, pp. 83-98.

D. M. Nuti (1986b). Hidden and repressed inflation in Soviet-type economies: definitions, measurements and stabilisation. *Contributions to Political Economy*, Vol. 5, 37-82; reprinted in C. Davis & W. Charemza (Eds) (1989). *Models of disequilibrium and shortage in centrally planned economies.* Chapman and Hall, London, pp. 101-146.

D. M. Nuti (1986c). Michal Kalecki's contributions to the theory and practice of socialist planning, *The Cambridge Journal of Economics*, Vol. 10, 333-353.

D. M. Nuti (1987a). Cycles in socialist economies, in John Eatwell, Murray Milgate and Peter Newman (Eds), The New Palgrave: A Dictionary of Economics, Vol. I, Macmillan, London, 1st edition, 1987, pp. 744-746.

D. M. Nuti (1987b). Profit-sharing and employment: claims and overclaims, *Industrial Relations*, Vol. 26, No. 1, Berkeley, Winter, 18-29.

D. M. Nuti (1988). Perestroika: transition between central planning and market socialism, *Economic Policy* Vol. 3, No. 7, October, 353-389.

D. M. Nuti (1989). Feasible financial innovation under market socialism, in: Christine Kessides, Timothy King, Mario Nuti, Kathy Sokil (Eds), *Financial Reform in Centrally Planned Economies,* EDI-World Bank, Washington, pp. 85-105.

D. M. Nuti (1990a). On traditional cooperatives and James Meade's Labour-Capital Discriminating Partnerships, in D. Jones and J. Svejnar (Eds.), *Advances in the Economic Analysis of Participatory and Labor-Managed Firms*, Vol. 4, JAI Press, Greenwich and London.

D. M. Nuti (1990b). Stabilisation and reform sequencing in the Soviet Economy, *Recherches Economiques de Louvain*, Vol. 56, No. 2, 169-180.

D. M. Nuti (1990c). Internal and international implications of monetary disequilibrium in Poland, *European Economy*, CEC Brussels, No. 43, March, 169-182.

D. M. Nuti (1990d). Privatisation of socialist economies: general issues and the Polish case, in Hans Bloomenstein and Michael Marrese (Eds), *The Transformation of Planned Economies*, OECD, Paris, 1990.

D. M. Nuti (1991a). Profit sharing, in G. Szell (Ed.), *Concise Encyclopedia of Participation and Co-management,* de Gruyter, Berlin and New York.

D. M. Nuti (1991b). Market socialism: the model that might have been - but never was, in Anders Aslund (Ed.), *Market Socialism or Restoration of Capitalism?,* Cambridge, CUP.

Part I

Socialist Economic Systems

Foreword to Part I: Socialist Economic Systems

Saul Estrin and Milica Uvalic

This first section of Mario Nuti's *Collected Works* is devoted to one of the central themes of his lifetime research agenda: the functioning, performance and reform of socialist economic systems. Much of Mario's early career was spent in trying to understand the functioning of socialist economic systems, both at a theoretical level and based on a deep practical knowledge of the functioning of socialist economies from the 1960s to the late 1980s. The selected papers were written mostly during the 1980s, before the revolutionary changes in Central and Eastern Europe and the fall of the Berlin Wall, although drawing heavily on Mario's earlier work on socialist economic systems (e.g., Nove and Nuti, eds, 1972). The papers reflect simultaneously a number of interests and skills which developed in his formative years.

The first chapter (Chap. 3) addresses key issues concerning the categorisation of socialist economic systems. Mario wanted to understand the strengths and weaknesses of the models that actually operated in the Soviet Union, countries in Central Eastern Europe, Scandinavia, Yugoslavia, addressing the question of which form of socialism is preferable. Mario does not make a choice himself, but only provides the pros and cons of each option and evaluates the possibilities for improvements. While highly critical of the traditional centrally planned economy, he was more hopeful of other variants of socialism such as the one developed in Poland.

The next five chapters (Chaps. 4–8) explore specific characteristics of socialist economic systems. In Chap. 4, Mario builds on Kalecki's work to present one of the few coherent theoretical models of the functioning of a socialist economy in a dynamic context, emphasising constraints to growth and accumulation policy. Drawing on the Keynesian concept of aggregate demand, he shows how socialist economies tend to over-invest and how this breaches the so-called golden rule that sets a maximum limit to the accumulation share. Nuti shows how consumption sacrifices for the sake of higher investment that Kalecki strongly opposed were neglected by Polish leaders, with negative political and economic consequences.

These themes are picked up in Chap. 5, where Mario considers the impact of excess demand in the context of fixed prices—one of the key systemic features of socialist economies—distinguishing between hidden and repressed inflation and suggesting how to define and measure them. Chapter 6 represents a further Keynesian analysis in the context of a socialist economy, looking at socialist trade cycles. Mario argues that contrary to the popular view, socialist economies did display cyclical behaviour, though in a very different form to capitalist economies. Chapter 7 shows how, in the traditional socialist economy, money was primarily an accounting instrument for monitoring and controlling plan implementation. Chapter 8 raises one of the fundamental dilemmas for socialist economies: can capital markets, which play such a fundamental role in the growth process, be reconciled with socialism?

The last three chapters of this section extend these ideas but also presage some of the themes of Mario's later work on the economic transition from socialism (covered in the next section of Volume 1). In Chap. 9, a paper written a few years before the fall of the Berlin Wall, Mario asks what financial innovations would be required in order to permit a market socialist economy to function more efficiently. How to allow a role for money or a capital market in a system in which prices are fixed, there is systemic excess demand and central allocation of investment, and firms are not privately owned? Mario's entrée to the issues of reform is through the analysis of market socialism, an attempt to reconcile markets and socialist systems developed previously by economists such as Lange. Since market socialism is often seen as a contradiction in terms, Mario seeks to define and identify the model in Chap. 10. The final paper in the section (Chap. 11) presents Mario's thinking about how to integrate entrepreneurship with socialism, an idea which he takes and develops from the Hungarian economist Tibor Liska.

Taken together, the nine chapters in this section represent a systematic analysis of the socialist system under which a significant proportion of the world's population lived between 1917 and 1989, as well as an evaluation of the prospects for successful reform.

3

Socialism on Earth

Domenico Mario Nuti

My understanding of an inaugural lecture is a cross between sermon and sales talk, an occasion for inflicting one's research and world view on to a well-disposed, yet watchful audience.

The title is deliberately cryptic. Why on earth socialism? Down to earth socialism? Socialism on earth as opposed to socialism in heaven? Is this an extension of 'Life on Earth', or 'Peace on Earth'? Is it a threat or a promise? In fact, all these would be correct interpretations of the content of this lecture. I shall look at socialism as we know it, as it actually exists and affects one third of the land, population and wealth of our planet. In common parlance the area is often labelled as 'communist', but technically the term designates a stage (Marx 1891; Lenin 1917) no country has ever reached; thus I will be talking of 'socialism'. East Germans have

Inaugural Lecture delivered by Domenico Mario Nuti, Professor of Political Economy and Director of the Centre for Russian and East European Studies in the University of Birmingham, on 28 April 1981, published in *Cambridge Journal of Economics* Vol. 5 (4).

D. M. Nuti (✉)
La Sapienza, University of Rome, Rome, Italy
e-mail: milica.uvalic@unipg.it

© The Author(s), under exclusive license to Springer Nature Switzerland AG 2023

S. Estrin, M. Uvalic (eds.), *Collected Works of Domenico Mario Nuti, Volume I*,
Studies in Economic Transition, https://doi.org/10.1007/978-3-031-12334-4_3

coined an expression, 'realised socialism',[1] which I could use as an alternative title, as long as it is not taken to imply that existing types of socialism actually succeed in realising an ideal. They do not. Indeed many dispute whether the countries of Eastern Europe, the Soviet Union, China and all the others usually grouped with them actually deserve the label of socialist. I believe they do, just as Thatcher's Britain deserves the label of capitalist. British pragmatism has prevailed over my continental intellectual upbringing; I believe that in political economy there is no room for utopias, 'nowhere' to be found. The empirical study of socialism, as it actually exists, is also a tradition firmly established by my predecessor, Professor R. W. Davies, at the Centre for Russian and East European Studies, and the main reason for its successes in the eighteen years of its life. By looking at socialism on Earth, warts and all, I wish to pay tribute to, and to reassert, this tradition.

I will try to provide a kind of *Which?* Report on the existing brands of economic systems based on the socialist blueprint. The emphasis will be on economic more than social and political features of systems. Following the Consumers Association practice for new products, a brief sketch of the merits and drawbacks of existing competition—*capitalism*—is in order. This will also provide a convenient reference point for comparative purposes.

Capitalism is one of the greatest social inventions of mankind. The combination of wage labour, private property, market monetary exchange and free enterprise, has liberated a fantastic amount of human potential and led to the industrialisation, urbanisation, scientific progress and unprecedented prosperity of a large part of the globe for many generations since the mid-eighteenth century. By 1848 two distinguished political economists could write:

> The bourgeoisie, during its rule of scarce one hundred years, has created more massive and more colossal productive forces than have all preceding generations together. Subjection of Nature's forces to man, machinery, application of chemistry to industry and agriculture, steam-navigation, railways, electric telegraphs, clearing of whole continents for cultivation,

[1] 'Realised Socialism', or 'actually existing socialism', is the expression used for instance by R. Bahro (1978).

> canalisation of rivers, whole populations conjured out of the ground—what earlier century had even a presentiment (of) such productive forces…
>
> The bourgeoisie, by the rapid improvement of all instruments of production, by the immensely facilitated means of communication, draws all, even the most barbarian, nations into civilisation.

Yet it is no accident that this high praise should be contained precisely in the document that did most to undermine the capitalist system; as you may have realised, the two political economists in question are Dr. Karl Marx and Frederick Engels, and the quotes are from the *Communist Manifesto* (Marx and Engels 1977, pp. 47 and 48).

In the capitalist blueprint, individual agents in pursuit of their self-interest—firms maximising profit and consumers maximising utility—freely producing and exchanging, are supposed to bring about a general equilibrium by the most desirable properties of full employment of resources, efficiency and stability, so long as competition prevails and the government does not interfere, in the best of all possible worlds. This rationalisation of capitalism from Adam Smith to Walras, Arrow and Debreu, still permeates undergraduate textbooks and the policies of Western governments, but is blatantly contradicted by realised capitalism today. Three hundred and sixty four leading British economists know better. There is also a distinguished tradition in economics that stresses the importance of expectations about the future—as much as current prices and quantities in present markets—for the actual allocation of resources. This tradition is well represented in different strands of modern theory, by economists as diverse as Lord Kaldor and Professor Frank Hahn, Professor Joan Robinson and Sir John Hicks. People's expectations differ; even if they were the same they would not necessarily be correct, or even 'rational' in the limited sense of events not generating surprises, and even if people acted on correct expectations they would not necessarily bring about the cosy and simplistic picture of the textbook capitalist blueprint. Fluctuations, unemployment, bankruptcies, crises are only too familiar features of realised capitalism, common to the Keynesian as well as the Marxian picture of capitalist economic anarchy. Not to mention the persistence of poverty and inequality and the power of corporations over sovereign governments. Capitalism today is so sick an organism as to be in the hands not of doctors but of Friedmanite faith-healers.

Signs of capitalist breakdown were already present in the last century, which is why a socialist blueprint was gradually developed. The word 'socialism' first appeared in English writings in the 1820s. A century later, an English social scientist could list over 260 definitions of Socialism (Griffiths 1924); though at that time only one country called itself socialist. Today Socialism is a combination—in varying proportions—of social ownership, economic planning, equality and participation in decision-making. Thirteen countries follow Marxian-inspired socialism, and are uneasily and euphemistically labelled as 'centrally planned economies' in United Nations publications; Yugoslavia boasts a special brand of 'associationist' or 'self-managed' socialism, and is non-committally labelled as an 'advanced market economy' in UN documents; another brand prevails in Scandinavia and is partially adopted or imitated in other Western countries; a number of countries in the Third World also call themselves socialist or adopt socialist policies. All in all, today there are not more than half a dozen brands of realised socialism. These I will now review, and you may be relieved that my purpose is not to try to sell you any of these brands. You can choose for yourself. Besides, socialism, unlike Christianity, is not a product that you acquire individually; you can only acquire it collectively, either through majority rule or by force. Until then, individual attempts at living according to socialist principles can only result in misguided self-denial; it is no good pretending that socialism is here, and my considered advice to you is that while in a capitalist environment you live as capitalistically and comfortably as you possibly can.

I will not even consider Third World-type socialism outside the socialist commonwealth. These are rather inferior brands superimposing elements of central direction, possibly also nationalism or humanism or egalitarianism, onto what remains essentially the old capitalist product. The socialist label in this case contravenes the Trades Descriptions Act.

I will start from Scandinavian-type socialism. This is basically an improved version of the capitalist product, embodying many elements of the socialist blueprint: namely, a large nationalised sector not only in public utilities but also in manufacturing; egalitarianism under the guise of progressive taxation and generous redistributive policies; relatively large public consumption, with ample provisions for social insurance; and attempts at directing centrally the course of economic events, though with full respect for private ownership and free enterprise. Scandinavian socialism is the collectivisation not of private property but of private risk; both the individual risks of being poor, unhealthy, disabled, or blessed with a large family, and the social risks of being unemployed, ill-educated or socially inadequate. It is capitalism with a human face. It is, of course, highly desirable, if you want to keep private property. But social insurance, like all services, has a cost, and the free state provision of such services on the scale required to make a difference is extremely costly. It can only be provided at the expense of lower individual consumption than would otherwise be feasible. Thus this extremely attractive product can only be recommended in conditions of very considerable national affluence; otherwise it is bound to disappoint, leading to frustrations and inflationary pressure, as other private and social demands conflict with the provision of large-scale social insurance. The verdict is: very good, but extremely pricey—the Rolls Royce of socialism. Few can afford it, or need it, and for some to have it other peoples must tighten their belts.

A British home-made social-democratic imitation is being currently marketed on attractive credit terms by a new British firm, SDP. Produced on a low budget, it is not the real article. There is also a Eurocommunist product, of Italian, French or Spanish design. A planned co-production between local rulers and Communist parties, its specifications -judging from advance publicity—are quite attractive, but it is unlikely ever to be delivered. Waiting lists run into millions.

Next is Yugoslav-type socialism. This is a market economy with free enterprise and without central planning, with additional special features. The bulk of the means of production does not belong to private individuals or the state, but to co-operative enterprises which pay little or nothing for their use but have the duty to preserve them. Subject to this minimum obligation, which is the only vestige of the public nature of ownership, the members of the co-operative enjoy the direct fruits of their labour and the social assets entrusted to them; through organs of self-management they decide how much of the co-operative revenue should be reinvested and how much should be distributed among members according to a strict job-evaluation code. Accumulated revenues, like their original endowment of assets, belong to the co-operative as a collective whole and not to its individual members, who lose any entitlement to the fruits of the co-operative capital by leaving, while any new member has equal automatic entitlement. Strictly speaking, wage labour is eliminated, and workers' incomes are shares in entrepreneurial gross profits. The system amounts to the generalised diffusion—among the workers of an enterprise—of the entrepreneurial risk which in the capitalist system is vested in owners or shareholders. It is socialism as lottery, in that—predictably—workers' incomes vary greatly not only by occupation and skill but by sector, region and enterprise, according to the relative endowment of capital, the past history of enterprises and the vagaries of markets (Estrin 1981).

This is an ingenious and peculiar system. It came about not as a result of a slow evolution under the pressure of objective needs of industry, like joint-stock companies, nor as a result of workers' demands, like trade unions; it was imposed from above, by President Tito, as a delayed response to Yugoslav expulsion from Cominform in 1948, as a gimmick to show to the world the Yugoslav independent course and to appeal to the international labour movement.[2] Giving factories to workers was not the Marxist-Leninist view of socialism, as witnessed by Lenin's polemics with Kautsky; orthodox Marxists look at this as an anarcho-syndicalistic deviation. I prefer the label of 'micro-socialism', not to belittle the socialist commitment of Yugoslavia, but because a basically capitalistic environment embodies all socialist principles at the micro-level of enterprises.

It is a peculiar system, of which some people here will have first-hand experience, perhaps without realising it. One does not have to go far to come across it, for the Yugoslav micro-socialist enterprise is typified by the Oxbridge college. All the features are there: in a capitalist environment we find an endowment capital entrusted to the college fellowship, self-management organs, control over the distribution of revenue. I know it well from seventeen years at King's, one of the richer co-operative enterprises selling education at Cambridge, where well into the 1970s I

[2] For a candid account of the circumstances in which self-management was introduced in Yugoslavia, see M. Djilas (1969).

received 'dividends' from college revenue but could not take with me when I went—alas—my share of college assets. Nice work if you can get it, but the drawbacks are the large number of unemployed dons who cannot join, inequality between colleges, their restrictive employment policies, the tendency for colleges to turn into financial holdings, and output-restricting oligopolies. The same is true of the Yugoslav co-operative enterprise. Unemployment, inflation, income inequalities, emigration, monopolies, internal and external imbalances, devaluations, indebtedness, have marred the Yugoslav system since its inception, reproduced the flaws of the capitalist system, and set in motion tendencies to revert to it: wages and prices policies, redistributive policies, the protection of workers from the adverse effects of their entrepreneurial risk-taking, have effectively obliterated—or at any rate very substantially reduced—the specific features of the Yugoslav system. As in Yugoslavia, in Cambridge colleges today self-management is nominal, dividends are no longer paid and dons are simply salary earners, with tenure no longer the rule.

In sum, the Yugoslav brand of socialism is beautifully designed, but performs as poorly as capitalism. It contravenes safety regulations, in that the dangers of the market economy are there, without due warning. A poor rating all round; its importation into Western countries is not to be recommended.

We now come to the best-selling type of socialism, the rugged Soviet-type centralised model, established after the October Revolution of 1917. This model was developed from scratch, without a blueprint, along the lines of the capitalist war economy, in a large, labour-abundant underdeveloped country with an autocratic, despotic tradition, ravaged by a world war and civil war and operating in a hostile international environment. These birthmarks remained very deeply imprinted in the finished product which after the experiments of War Communism (1918–21) and the so called New Economic Policy (1921–28) was established in a form that remains almost unchanged to date. The model was successfully 'marketed' by the boot-in-the-door technique of the Red Army in Eastern Europe, and exported to the rest of the socialist world. It is also the system towards which China is presently tending, after a long detour, together with North Korea, Vietnam and Albania.

In Soviet-type socialism, the whole economy is managed as a single, giant firm. The economy is partitioned into sectors, each run by a Ministry, connecting the Central Planning Commission *(Gosplan)* to the enterprises operating in each sector. Horizontal links between enterprises are scant, or absent altogether; vertical links prevail, enterprises transmitting information to and receiving orders from the centre. The enterprise is basically a one-man-managed administrative unit, executing within narrow margins of discretion a detailed and ambitious plan determined centrally. Formally it has legal personality and *khozraschot* (economic accounting) but practically this means no more than a separate accounting identity. Planning is done in physical terms, Gosplan and Ministries trying to balance beforehand, by successive approximations, resources and uses for thousands of products and factors. Money exists but is passively adjusted to physical flows—a monetarist paradise where, however, there is no scope for monetary policy, in that money is automatically available to enterprises to enable them to fulfil their plans. Performance is measured by physical—or at any rate 'gross'—indicators of success, and prices play more of an accounting than an allocational role. Distribution is according to work, and to some extent rewards depend on enterprise success in fulfilling and over fulfilling the plan. Normally people can choose what they do, and buy what they like, within what is available.

Early critics of this model (von Mises 1920; Hayek 1935) argued that economic calculus, that is a *rational* allocation of resources, was either impossible or impracticable in the centralised socialist economy. Without owners of and markets for production goods, central choice was bound to be arbitrary and inefficient. The problem, however, had already been considered and solved by two Italian economists of impeccable bourgeois extraction, long before the storming of the Winter Palace. Enrico Barone and Vilfredo Pareto at the turn of the century demonstrated the equivalence of socialist central planning and the perfectly competitive solution of a capitalist system of resource allocation (Barone 1908; Pareto 1897). The immanence of economic categories—price, profit, rent, wage, etc.—in all systems ensures the possibility of economic rationality in socialist planning. As to its practicability, the Polish economist Oskar Lange—one of my Warsaw teachers—demonstrated that all the central planner needs to do is to simulate the competitive process, by trial and error.

Prices, whether or not they are actually paid, are very convenient devices; the central planner can start from old prices, or choose them at random, tell firms what they are and ask them to draw a provisional plan of production where marginal cost equals the price of their product. If the accounts do not square, the centre raises the prices of deficit goods and lowers that of excess goods, until an equilibrium is reached in an optimum plan (Lange 1938). In the sixties the growth of mathematical methods and computers led Lange to suggest the replacement of 'perfect competition' by 'perfect computation', in the words of Professor Wiles (Wiles 1962). The market being no more than a social mechanism for solving millions of economic equations, its job conceivably could be done by modern computers (Lange 1967; Ellman 1973; Cave 1980; Shenfield 1981). The applicability of mathematical methods in socialist planning today is investigated prominently at the Central Mathematical Economic Institute of the Soviet Academy of Science, led by Academician Nikolai Fedorenko (1969). The subject was pioneered by Academician V. S. Nemchinov at Moscow, and at the Centre for Russian and East European Studies in the University of Birmingham by Professor T. O. M. Kronsjö (1972), who has contributed algorithms for the solution of large scale computational problems. Whether by computer, quasi-markets, or trial and error, the management of the centralised socialist economy is no problem at all. Or is it?

Experience has shown that socialist planning is not always as easy to practise as it is to theorise, though not because of the absence of private property, the reason given by von Hayek. Mathematics and computers have greatly assisted our understanding of planning, and the solution of specific problems such as the optimisation of transport flows, but we are nowhere near the 'perfect computation' solution. As to markets, prices and profits, and the enterprise autonomy theorised by Lange, successive waves of economic reform—notably in the mid-sixties in the Soviet Union and elsewhere in Eastern Europe before and since—have tried to introduce them with little success. With the exception of Hungary economic reforms have remained no more than short-lived experiments.

The drawbacks of Soviet-type planning are well documented (Wiles 1962; Nove 1970; Kaser 1970). Directors are human; rewarded by degree of plan fulfilment, they conceal reserves, overestimate requirements, grab all they can, monitor and strive to implement success indicators regardless of quality and cost, obtain what they need by informal exchange, connections and 'pull'. Bureaucrats know this, discount it, and make their life harder; they breathe down their neck, penalise success by raising tasks further above achieved levels, and nip entrepreneurship in the bud. The centre is out of touch with popular wishes. 'Democratic centralism' is in theory the central execution of decisions democratically reached, but in practice turns into 'voluntarism', the arbitrary pursuit of the wishes of the leadership of the day, as each new leader reveals to have been the case with his predecessor.

This picture too is familiar. In many respects, a miniature version of the Soviet-type system can be found in any large-scale organisation, and this University is no exception. We also use physical indicators, such as staff-student ratios, regardless of quality; we measure 'full-time student equivalents', painfully reminiscent of Soviet wheat 'biological yields'. A bureaucracy exercises what the Russians call 'petty tutelage' over Heads of Departments; a small elite prevails over a formally democratic structure. A move from Cambridge to Birmingham is in some ways—*mutatis mutandis*—like a trip from Belgrade to Moscow.

In spite of these drawbacks, Soviet-type planning obtained massive achievements: the industrialisation of a backward country (Carr and Davies 1969; Davies 1980), the build-up of military power, survival in a hostile environment, victory in war; impressive improvements in standards of education, health, social and private consumption; full employment of labour (Ellman 1979) and (since the mid-fifties) price stability (Portes 1977); the development of natural resources, and the development of science and technology (Amann et al. 1977; Amann et al. 1982). Since the mid-fifties, however, the drawbacks have grown in scope and intensity and have adversely affected Soviet economic performance. The system has allowed the Soviet Union to retain its international power position and to keep sending 100 satellites a year into space, but growth rates have been falling steadily (Hanson 1979, 1980), in spite of the continued massive accumulation of capital and parallel sacrifices of current consumption—willy nilly—by the population. These trends are partly due to demographic slowdown, which raises the cost per head of defence and most social infrastructure; partly to the exhaustion of labour reserves at very high activity rates for both men and women; partly to the increasing cost of tapping natural resources both for further expansion and exports to the West. These problems have been alleviated, but not solved, by Soviet access to raw materials from less developed countries under the same type of international division of labour practised with them by Western industrialised economies; by increasing reliance on the importation of Western technology and machinery (Sutton 1973; Hanson 1978), and by a process of economic integration within the Comecon countries. In the rest of Eastern Europe, however, the same problems have prevailed. Indeed the drawbacks of the Soviet-type model have been felt sooner and more deeply in the socialist countries of Eastern Europe, which, by comparison with 1917 Russia, had already reached a generally higher level of economic development, social diversity, and growth of democratic institutions (Brus 1975). Externally, the deterioration of economic performance throughout the area has manifested itself in a growing economic dependence on the West for the supply of foodstuffs, technology and finance, with a mounting indebtedness currently of the order of $75 billion. The world-wide recession of the mid-seventies aggravated East European decline and dependence, restricting policy options further. Internally, this deterioration has disappointed the plans and expectations of leaders and people; in the last years consumption standards have stagnated in most of the area; 'repressed' inflation has appeared under the guise of a permanent state of excess demand and mounting shortages of many necessities as well as luxuries; open inflation also appeared in the late seventies outside the Soviet Union; an informal sector has developed—a second economy with various shades of black to grey markets, with semilegal transactions and straight economic criminality.

In response to these economic pressures, in the last twenty-five years three alternative models of economic organisation have been produced in Eastern Europe.

The first is the 1957 Soviet model of regional decentralisation. Industrial Ministries—overcentralised and prone to autarkic tendencies within the sector—were abolished, and the Soviet economy was partitioned into regions run by *sovnarkhozy* (regional economic councils). These new institutions were expected to be closer to local needs and more efficient, but in practice they reproduced and indeed enhanced at regional level all the problems of the centralised Soviet system, substituting *mestnichestvo* (localism) and regional autarky for the autarky of the abolished Ministries. The reform was—as Alec Nove put it—'not a step forward, but a step sideways' (Nove 1968). The model was dismantled and scrapped after eight years.

The second is the East German model, developed in the seventies and still extant. It consists of almost total *sectoral* decentralisation and vertical integration. In other words, each industry is a centrally planned economy in its own right, producing not only a product for final use but also most of its own components and intermediate products (Metzler 1981). Instead of correcting the autarkic tendency of Soviet-type industrial Ministries, the East German model has pushed it to its extreme limits. The economic reform has given a measure of autonomy to enterprises within an industry and by reducing the volume of inter-industry transactions it has reduced the *size* of the informational and organisational problems of central planning. Since these problems increase with the square, or even the cube, of the size of the system, this reorganisation has had some success in rationalising production and normalising supply, maintaining East German performance above the average. This model, however, affords only a modest improvement on the Soviet-type system, in the special circumstances of a heavily industrialised, diversified and relatively small economy. It is a palliative, not a viable general alternative.

The third reformed model is the more extensively decentralised model along the lines theorised by Oskar Lange. It is a model of socialism as capitalism without capitalists. Central planning is restricted to broad macroeconomic guidance, and enterprises are relatively free to decide output quantities and prices, employment and investment, responding to the signals of internal and international prices, subject to financial viability and credit discipline. Managers and workers are rewarded according to enterprise success measured by profits and profitability, both by means of personal bonuses in addition to wages and by the retention of finance for the further expansion of their firm. The model was first attempted in Poland in 1956, enhanced by forms of workers' participation in the management of industry; it lasted for only eighteen months (Zielinski 1973). Later it was attempted in other socialist countries, including the Soviet Union in 1965 when Kosygin endorsed the ideas associated with Yevsei

Liberman but widely debated among Soviet economists and managers; implementation however was slow and soon came to a standstill before the end of the decade. Alec Nove dubbed it 'the reform that never was' (Nove 1972). The only country to implement this model successfully has been Hungary, where it was introduced in 1968 under the name of 'the New Economic Mechanism', and has performed relatively well since then (Hare et al. 1981). Its advantages are a greater mobilisation of entrepreneurship and initiative, a more satisfactory degree of market equilibrium, economic efficiency and flexibility in responding to changes in technology, tastes and international factors. Its performance, however, depends on very careful and fine tuning, on the achievement of a delicate balance between markets and plans—the right mix of market decentralisation and social control, appropriate to actual changing circumstances.

Three fundamental questions arise. How can we find the 'correct' degree of decentralisation that can make this system viable? How is social control to be exercised? Why is Hungarian-type decentralised socialism so difficult to transplant to the rest of the socialist bloc? In trying to answer these questions I shall be drawing on my own research on socialist accumulation, since the theory and practice of investment decision making is crucial here. All three questions involve not only economic but political issues.

Maurice Dobb, my supervisor and mentor at Cambridge, said that 'No clear cut, logically defined frontier line can be drawn between the province of centralised and decentralised decision' (Dobb 1969, p. 127); he suggested a blend of central decisions in capital investment, and enterprise discretion about current output decisions (Dobb 1969, p. 140; Nuti 1978). Professor Wlodzimierz Brus also taught the necessity of keeping investment decisions, affecting the general direction and pace of development, outside the sphere of market decentralisation (Brus 1972). Non-socialist economists such as Maynard Keynes—who stated unequivocally that the class war would find him on the side of the educated bourgeoisie (Keynes 1952a, p. 324)—believed too that investment should be planned, subjected to what he called 'a coordinate act of intelligent judgment' (Keynes 1952b, p. 318). If decisions about investment and growth were left to socialist enterprises, a much wider range of economic institutions would be needed in the socialist economy, such as financial intermediaries, shares, bonds, stock markets, takeover bids etc. The socialist economy would lose its identity, though this is beside the point; in truth it is naïve to expect that markets, prices and profits could always do, in the socialist economy, what they so blatantly fail to do in the capitalist one—take Britain today. Expectations are just as important in socialist as in capitalist markets; in any system, an uncertain future defies even the proper definition of 'profit'. Profit is an ambiguous signal, which may indicate superior managerial abilities, or above-average hard work by enterprise workers, or under-provision of productive capacity, or indeed any number of factors totally external to the enterprise; thus the presence of profit is not necessarily a case for either reward or expansion. The decentralisation to enterprises of as many decisions as practicable has distinct political advantages—the reduction of the size and the power of central bureaucracy, the participation of a larger number of people in decision-making and the mobilisation of initiative and entrepreneurship. But it seems desirable to retain a greater degree of social control over investment and growth than envisaged in the Langean economy.

The trouble is that centralised investment planning *per se* does not guarantee *social* control over accumulation and growth. Paradoxically, the actual experience of socialist countries follows exactly the pattern envisaged by Marx for the capitalist mode of production: a tremendous urge to accumulate, an imbalance between means of production and consumption, an investment cycle, even a tendency for the rate of profit and growth to fall over time. Instead of the chronic underinvestment and unemployment of labour experienced by capitalism, socialism has produced chronic over-investment and unemployment of capital. Spontaneous unplanned processes have emerged in centrally planned economies, and have led to accumulation rates consistently of the order of 25–35% of national income, and more. These are high by any standard, and too high in many respects: they are higher than those centrally planned, consistently overfulfilled, excessive with respect to both the interests of maintainable consumption levels and to the availability of labour and other resources. For historical reasons deriving from the Soviet experience, there is a tradition and inertia of accelerated accumulation, justified perhaps in the Soviet case between the Wars but not since and elsewhere; this is deeply ingrained into the system. Central planners have a long time horizon, are concerned with the survival of the system, the overtaking of capitalist countries and the reaching of full communism; they are not constrained by the need to present alternatives to the population and to seek its consent, and thus they push accumulation to its limits. State enterprise managers add to investment pressure: their salary, bonuses, career opportunities and job satisfaction—like those of their capitalist counterparts—depend on the size and growth of their operations, without being subject to stock-market discipline and other constraints; thus they use their discretion in pressing for accumulation and growth. The same pressure is exercised by local authorities and Ministries. In the game played by socialist managers and planners, overambitious tasks are set from above, are countered by managers' claims for increases in plant; competing for scarce investment resources, managers make their projects look attractive, they 'hike themselves onto the plan' and then let investment costs escalate, adding to investment pressure (Bauer 1978; Kotowicz-Jawór 1979; Nuti 1980b). The whole system is stuck in low gear, working at high revs without picking up enough speed after initial acceleration, the engine wastes fuel, overheats and often breaks down. Inefficiency ensues, as more capital is accumulated than the economy can absorb; fluctuations occur, as the economy moves from overextending its 'investment front' with new projects to concentrating on the completion of those already started; income grows, but so much of that growth is needed to keep the machine going that gains in consumption are postponed into an indefinite future (Nuti 1979). Another teacher of mine—the Polish economist Michal Kalecki—stressed the limits set to accumulation by foreign balance, consumption, labour and natural resources supply (Kalecki 1969), but his warning went unheeded. Indeed Poland is a macroscopic example of what happens when the system is driven so hard: central planning simply collapses. *Economic* reform on its own can do little to correct these trends. The solution can only be *political.*

It is now clear why the implementation of economic reform in the Soviet Union and Eastern Europe has been so slow and short-lived. Overaccumulation creates glaring inefficiencies and disruption, and mounting pressure for reform, but also creates an environment of shortages and imbalances in which no reformed system can have a fair run. The leadership—within the Party, State and military apparatus—fears the loss of economic and hence *political* power and clings on to central control. As long as overaccumulation persists, any reform project must either be shelved or be doomed to fail. The Hungarians were both wise—at stockpiling and eliminating imbalances before they embarked on reform—and lucky—at timing their move at a time of world boom; other countries were neither. The result today is a widespread compromise between markets and plans, based on the emergence and development of very large state corporations throughout the area, a trend which I have researched in Poland (Nuti 1977), but is present everywhere—only names change. Many believe, mistakenly, that this trend, and parallel changes in East and West, indicate a *convergence* (Tinbergen 1961; Bornstein 1971; Ellman 1980) of systems, towards a uniform model with a mixed economy, broad state intervention and a large government budget, markets dominated by large corporations, with wages and incomes control. On the contrary, there is considerable *complementarity* between the drawbacks of different systems—with the creation of wealth being prevented *here* by lack of demand, *there* by structural problems, *here* by too little investment, *there* by too much—complementarity which should provide a fresh opportunity for mutually advantageous trade and cooperation (Nuti 1981b), *if* common sense prevails. Again, it is political will, not economic formulas, that will provide the solution: without this the only thing that different systems will converge to is an unpleasant crisis.

This view may be regarded as pessimistic—but then, as the Russians say, 'a pessimist is a well-informed optimist'. In socialist countries economic disappointment has led to popular demoralisation, resentment at unequal access to goods for different sections of the population, and has somewhat eroded the 'legitimacy' of the regime. Industrial workers are to a great extent 'incorporated' (Lane and O'Dell 1978) into the system in the Soviet Union, but they are less so elsewhere, and the frustration of economic aspirations has bred opposition and dissent. The product of what Isaac Deutscher called 'The Unfinished Revolution' (Deutscher 1967) is less attractive now that it can no longer boast a superior economic performance.

In the circumstances, I cannot recommend to you a 'best buy'. Models of realised socialism have solved—to varying degrees—the problems and contradictions of capitalism, at the expense of generating their own.

There is not, or not yet, an absolutely superior product, but different ones, which may or may not appeal to you according to taste. Besides, a crucial factor in the choice between systems is the consideration of their respective social and political merits, which I have broadly neglected. If you want socialism, you might either join do-it-yourself enthusiasts—like Tony Benn —or wait for a New Improved product.

Since last summer, an experimental model has been in the making—in a chaotic fashion—in Poland. The Poles have been first in driving a centrally planned economy—in first gear—to total collapse. They have tested the model to destruction. An excessively high degree of overaccumulation, coupled with exposure to a world recession, has pushed inflation, shortages and foreign indebtedness beyond people's forbearance. This, more than any national vice or virtue, has brought about two fundamental political changes in Poland: an independent Union and the revival of Party democracy, on top of the usual proposals for economic reforms. The Poles are rediscovering the political equivalent of gears. There are still many dangers ahead. The new Union has almost wrecked the already ailing economy with strikes and impossible economic demands, but has also obtained important concessions in civil and political rights. The Party has initiated a process of internal renewal, with secret ballot elections, unprecedented and extensive personnel changes in the leadership, apparatus and bureaucracy. These changes could provide precisely those political processes needed to improve the Soviet-type system and complete the Unfinished Revolution. The changes, however, could also destroy it, and are perceived—rightly or wrongly—as a potential threat by other socialist leaders, who might bring the experiment to an abrupt end. Also, unless a new Social Pact is struck between the Party and the Union, sanctioning both economic austerity and political rights, the state of the Polish economy can only worsen, tempting a domestic authoritarian solution and ruining any chance the economic reform may otherwise have (Brus 1980; Kolankiewicz 1981; Nuti 1980a, 1981a, pp. 39–62 and 157–59, Nuti 1981c). It is still too early to judge. But I would like to end expressing my belief that a new, better model of socialism can be achieved in Poland, and that, whatever happens to it, the system—indeed the systems, including our own—will never be the same again. The Polish experience will in any case contribute to enlarging and improving the range of systemic choice. I may be an optimist, but then, as the Russians say, 'an optimist is simply a pessimist who has been well-indoctrinated'. Socialism may yet bring good will, to all men, on earth.

Bibliography

Amann, R., Cooper, J. M. and Davies, R. W. (1977). *The Technological Level of Soviet Industry,* New Haven and London, Yale University Press.

Amann, R. *et al.* (1982). *Industrial Innovation in the Soviet Union,* forthcoming.

Bahro, R. (1978). *The Alternative in Eastern Europe,* London, New Left Books (originally published 1977 as *Die Alternative: zur Kritik des realexistierenden Sozialismus,* Europaische Verlagsanstalt).

Barone, E. (1908). Il ministro della produzione nello stato collectivista, in F. A. Hayek (Ed.) *Collectivistic Economic Planning,* London, 1935.

Bauer, T. (1978). Investment cycles in planned economies, *Acta Oeconomica,* Vol. 21 (3).

Bornstein, M. (1971). East European economic reforms and the convergence of economic systems. *Jahrbuch der Wirtschaft Osteuropas,* Band 1.

Brus, W. (1972). *The Market in a Socialist Economy,* London.

Brus, W. (1975). *Socialist Ownership and Political Systems,* London.

Brus, W. (1980). Lessons of the Polish Summer. *Marxism Today,* November.

Carr, E. H. and Davies, R. W. (1969). *Foundations of a Planned Economy.* Macmillan.

Cave, M. (1980). *Computers and Economic Planning: the Soviet Experience,* Cambridge, CUP

Davies, R. W. (1980). *The Industrialisation of Soviet Russia: Vol. 1: The Socialist Offensive: the Collectivisation of Soviet Agriculture 1929-1930; Vol 2: The Soviet Collective Farm, 1929-30,* Macmillan

Deutscher, I. (1967). *The Unfinished Revolution,* London

Djilas, M. (1969). *The Unperfect Society: Beyond the New Class,* Harcourt, Brace and World

Dobb, M. H. (1969). *Welfare Economics and the Economics of Socialism: Towards a Common Sense Critique,* London, CUP

Ellman, M. (1973). *Planning Problems in the U.S.S.R.: the Contribution of Mathematical Economics to their Solution, 1960-71,* Cambridge, CUP

Ellman, M. (1979). Full employment-lessons from state socialism, *De Economist,* No. 4

Ellman, M. (1980). Against convergence, *Cambridge Journal of Economics,* Vol. 4 No. 3, September
Estrin, S. (1981). *Self-management: Economic Theory and Yugoslav Practice,* CUP, forthcoming
Fedorenko, N. P. (1969). The role of economic-mathematical methods in the planning and management of the economy of the U.S.S.R., *Journal of Development Planning,* No. 1
Griffiths, D. F. (1924). *What is Socialism? A Symposium,* London, Richards
Hanson, P. (1978). Soviet imports of Western technology, *Problems of Communism,* November–December
Hanson, P. (1979). *Quarterly Economic Review of the U.S.S.R.,* No. 4
Hanson, P. (1980). *Quarterly Economic Review of the U.S.S.R.* Nos 1, 2, 3 and 4.
Hare, P. G., Radice, H. K. and Swain, N. (1981). *Hungary: A Decade of Economic Reform,* London.
Hayek, F. A. (Ed.) (1935). *Collectivistic Economic Planning,* London.
Kalecki, M. (1969). *Introduction to the Theory of Growth in a Socialist Economy,* London, Blackwell.
Kaser, M. (1970). *Soviet Economics,* London, OUP.
Keynes, J. M. (1952a). Am I a liberal (1925), *Essays in Persuasion,* London.
Keynes, J. M. (1952b). The end of laissez-faire (1926), *Essays in Persuasion,* London.
Kolankiewicz, G. (1981). The politics of 'socialist renewal', paper presented to the annual conference of the British National Association for Soviet and East European Studies, Cambridge, 21–23 March.
Kotowicz-Jawór, J. (1979). Presja inwestycyjna w rozwoju gospodarczym, *Gospodarka Polanowa,* No. 3.
Kronsjö, T. O. M. (1972). A decentralised economic planning system based on decomposition into only master problems, *Jarbuch der Wirtschaft Osteuropas,* Band 2, Teil 1, Munich.
Lane, D. S. and O'Dell, F. (1978). *The Soviet Industrial Worker-Social Class, Education and Control,* London, Martin Robertson.
Lange, O. (1938). *The Economic Theory of Socialism,* University of Minnesota Press (originally published in a slightly different version in the *Review of Economic Studies,* Vol. 3, 1936-37.
Lange, O. (1967). The computer and the market, in C. H. Feinstein (ed.), *Capitalism, Socialism and economic growth - Essays in Honour of Maurice Dobb,* Cambridge.
Lenin, V. I. (1917). *The State and Revolution,* English edition Moscow 1949.

Marx, K. (1891). *Critique of the Gotha Programme,* English edition London 1933.
Marx, K. and Engels, F. (1977). *Communist Manifesto,* Moscow, Progress Publishers.
Metzler, M. (1981). Combine formation and the role of the enterprise in East German industry, in I. Jeffries (Ed.) *The Industrial Enterprise in Eastern Europe,* London, Praeger.
Mises, L. von. (1920). Economic calculation in the socialist Commonwealth, in F. A. Hayek (Ed.), *Collectivistic Economic Planning,* London, 1935.
Nove, A. (1968). An *Economic History of the U.S.S.R.,* Penguin.
Nove, A. (1970). *The Soviet Economy,* London.
Nove, A. (1972). Economic Reforms in the U.S.S.R. and Hungary, a study in contrasts, in A. Nove and D. M. Nuti (Eds), *Socialist Economics,* Penguin.
Nuti, D. M. (1977). Large corporations and the reform of Polish industry. *Jahrbuch der Wirtschaft Osteuropas,* Band 7, Munich.
Nuti, D. M. (1978). Investment interest and degree of centralisation in Maurice Dobb's theory of the socialist economy. *Cambridge Journal of Economics,* June.
Nuti, D. M. (1979). The contradictions of socialist economics – a Marxian interpretation, *The Socialist Register,* London, Merlin Press.
Nuti, D. M. (1980a). Pay now, live later, *New Statesman, vol.* 100, no. 2591, 14 November.
Nuti, D. M. (1980b). Socialist overaccumulation. A paper presented at Nuffield College, Oxford, November.
Nuti, D. M. (1981a). Industrial enterprises in Poland, 1973-80: economic policies and reforms and Postscript on Poland, in I. Jeffries (ed.), *The Industrial Enterprise in Eastern Europe,* London, Praeger.
Nuti, D. M. (1981b). Prospects for trade between economies in crisis: Britain and Poland. A paper presented at the CREES-IKC Conference on Polish trade and development, Birmingham University, 26-27 March.
Nuti, D. M. (1981c). Banks not tanks, *New Statesman,* Vol. 101, No. 2612, 10 April.
Pareto, V. (1897). *Cours d'Economie Politique.*
Portes, R. (1977). The control of inflation—lessons from Eastern European experience, *Economica,* No. 2.
Shenfield, S. (1981). The flow of economic information in the U.S.S.R., is computerisation a myth? CREES Seminar paper, March.
Sutton, A. C. (1973). *Western Technology and Soviet Economic Development 1945-1965,* Stanford, California.

Tinbergen, J. (1961). Do communist and free economies show a converging pattern? *Soviet Studies,* April.
Wiles, P. J. D. (1962). *The Political Economy of Communism,* Oxford.
Zielinski, J. G. (1973). *Economic Reforms in Polish Industry,* London, OUP.

4

Michal Kalecki's Contribution to the Theory and Practice of Socialist Planning

Domenico Mario Nuti

4.1 Introduction

Michal Kalecki's contributions to the economics of socialism—less widely known but no less important than his pioneering contributions to the economics of capitalism – span the period 1946–1970 and are affected by the development and performance of the Polish system, as well as coloured by his views on capitalist dynamics. They consist of a coherent model of the socialist economy and its functioning, characterised by centralised

Published in *Cambridge Journal of Economics* December 1986, Vol. 10, No. 6, pp. 333–353. An earlier longer version under the same title was published as *EUI Working Paper* No. 227, European University Institute, Florence, 1986. The paper was reprinted in Malcolm C. Sawyer (Ed.), *The Legacy of Michal Kalecki*, Intellectual Legacies in Modern Economics 5, Vol 2. Edward Elgar, Cheltenham 2000, pp. 137–157.

Paper presented at the Conference on Michal Kalecki's economics, held at the Economics Department of Perugia University, 22–24 April 1986. I am grateful to Alberto Chilosi, Jerzy Osiatynski, Ferdinando Targetti and, in particular, to the discussant Lynn Mainwaring for useful comments.

D. M. Nuti (✉)
La Sapienza, University of Rome, Rome, Italy
e-mail: milica.uvalic@unipg.it

© The Author(s), under exclusive license to Springer Nature Switzerland AG 2023
S. Estrin, M. Uvalic (eds.), *Collected Works of Domenico Mario Nuti, Volume I*, Studies in Economic Transition, https://doi.org/10.1007/978-3-031-12334-4_4

economic planning and political decentralisation with a limited role for markets; a well-developed theory of socialist dynamics, emphasising exogenous constraints to growth and accumulation policy, which were neglected by Polish leaders with dramatic consequences; and a number of planning procedures and guidelines of practical use, for the selection of investment projects, consumption planning and the construction of long-term plans.

4.2 Kalecki's Model of the Democratic Planned Economy

By 1942, in connection with British discussions on economic planning, Kalecki had already sketched the main features of his approach to economic planning: nationalisation of the most important enterprises (financial, industrial and public utilities); coordination and direction of their activity by a central institution of economic planning, responsible to Parliament; full public control over the banking and financial system, investment and foreign trade as well as, if possible, allocation of the main materials and products. Private enterprise would still play an important role in industrial sectors of secondary importance, in the production of consumption goods, and in the distributive services. Central planning of investment would ensure full employment of labour; Workers' Councils, representing workers, technical personnel and managers of each enterprise, now freed from the threat of unemployment, would maintain support for economic planning and exercise control over the development of their enterprises. Public control from below, together with the initiatives of a socialist government from above, would protect the system from regressing towards monopoly capitalism (Kalecki 1942).

Kalecki's international reputation and his known socialist sympathies gave him instant access to the new rulers of People's Poland: in 1946 he was already—in a brief visit and from a distance—giving advice to the Polish Minister of Reconstruction on rationing (which he regarded as equivalent to but, practically, slightly superior to income subsidies), on monetary circulation and on the 1946–47 financial plans, which he analysed at great length (see respectively Kalecki 1946a, 1946b, 1946c, first published in Kalecki 1982, and editorial comments on pp. 308–310), checking the consistency of real and financial flows and using the budget as the primary instrument of macroeconomic planning. Kalecki's return to Poland in early 1955, as adviser to the Prime Minister, marked the beginning of a ten-year-long involvement in the shaping of the Polish economic system and policies: as a Vice-Chairman of the Economic Council advising the Council of Ministers from 1957 to its disbanding in 1963, and as head of the perspective plan division of the Central Planning Commission, in charge of drawing up the 1961–75 plan, until increasing disagreement with the government put an end to his advisory activity in 1964. Meanwhile, and until the end of his life, he continued to make important intellectual contributions to the economics of socialism; his papers on the organisation and functioning of the socialist economy, however, are concentrated in the period 1955–58.

Kalecki's socialist model retains, next to a dominant centrally-planned state sector, a liberalised cooperative sector and private handicrafts, as well as state small-scale production operating on similar principles: purely indicative plans in value terms, contractual cooperation with state industry and distribution network (though contracting can be made compulsory); free purchases and sales of non-contracted output in the market (though sales to the state not contracted in advance ought to take place below the market price); profit sharing (oddly enough, only applicable to technical personnel and managers and not to workers in the case of cooperatives); investment self-finance except for small-scale state enterprises where investment is also funded by local authorities; employment limits for artisans (e.g., five workers excluding apprentices); local controls. Kalecki recognises the practical difficulties and the disproportionate administrative effort of attempting to control production in small-scale units characterised by highly diversified and rapidly changing composition, and the counterproductive nature of price and other control (Kalecki 1956a; there is no mention of agriculture in that paper, produced for the Polish Prime Minister and first published in Kalecki 1982).

Large-scale state enterprises, on the contrary, in Kalecki's view should be given physical targets for both total employment and the larger investments in new capacity, as well as targets for the net value of production, its main composition, the wage fund and distribution of main inputs; they should also be subject to price controls for both their purchases and sales (1956b, 1957c, 1957d, 1958a, 1958b). With respect to employment the model is centrally planned more tightly than the traditional Soviet-type model: against strong opposition from most of his colleagues Kalecki was adamant that enterprises should not be free to set the level of employment; he knew only too well how enterprise autonomy and labour unemployment went hand-in-hand in the capitalist economy and was not prepared to leave state enterprises any discretion in this matter. 'In England for so many years they paid me to liquidate unemployment, and here you want to pay me to generate it'—was his cry at the suggestion that enterprises should only be subject to a limit on their total wage fund, at a memorable session of a special Committee on enterprise organisation set up by the Council of Ministers (see editorial notes, Kalecki 1982, p. 324). In other respects, however, Kalecki's model of socialism is more 'liberal' than the conventional Soviet-type model (to which the Polish actual model has adhered broadly to date).

First, Kalecki laid emphasis on the *net* value of output (1957d; this notion was actually implemented in Poland in the 1974 reform; see Nuti 1977) and neither on the physical nor the gross value indicators of Soviet-type planning. Second, he also envisaged, next to centralised investment, some decentralised investments out of own funds and interest-bearing but non-returnable loans, both to allow for enterprise initiative and to reduce the pro-investment bias associated with free investment funds (1957d).

Third, Kalecki strongly recommended the restructuring of industrial organisation along vertical lines (1957b): large-scale associations of vertically integrated enterprises largely, though not fully, self-sufficient (along the lines later adopted by the GDR: see Granick 1975; Melzer 1981) would cooperate in the reciprocal supply of semi-finished products and in the distribution of essential materials. Enterprises would retain autonomy as members of the association, so that each *koncern* would be responsible for a given finished product (or group of similar products) without introducing monopolistic tendencies. Central authorities would be concerned only with the group performance in the supply of finished goods without interfering in their internal organisation. Mutual interest of member enterprises in the overall performance of the group would secure their cooperation; actual orders and incentives regulating enterprise activity would be decentralised to *koncern* level and the central authorities would only have to deal with a small number of agencies, simplifying and de-bureaucratising economic administration, especially in the distribution of centrally-allocated materials. (Large-scale industrial associations were revamped in Poland in the 1974 reform but member enterprises were more tightly merged than envisaged by Kalecki, and the element of vertical integration was the exception, not the norm, which emphasised horizontal concentration; see Nuti 1977).

Fourth, Kalecki envisaged in his model—in place of economic decentralisation—generalised political decentralisation under the guise of Workers' Councils which, in every enterprise, would take decisions about the organisation of production (work conditions, overtime pay, etc.), oppose the excessive bureaucratisation and centralisation tendencies which appear when the enterprise director answers only to central powers, and exercise initiative under the stimulus of material incentives (Kalecki 1956b). At the time Oskar Lange regarded enterprise autonomy extending to prices and investment as a precondition of workers' self-management: without greater enterprise independence Workers' Councils—wrote Lange in the same issue of the Party monthly *Nowe Drogi*—'... would be a fiction, since they would not have anything to decide...' (Lange 1956). But Kalecki was much too concerned with the maintenance of full employment to push enterprise autonomy further, and regarded Workers' Councils as a political countervailing power holding central government in check.

Kalecki's distrust of the market and his reliance on planning have perhaps been underplayed in subsequent literature. Brus, for instance, writes: 'He did not ... oppose the idea of utilising the market-mechanism, but considered it a subordinate element in the running of an economy which should be planned centrally as far as the main lines of development were concerned' (Brus 1977; also quoted by Sawyer 1985). I believe the example of inter-war Poland, the experience of capitalism as he knew it and his overall theoretical background led Kalecki to hold stronger views. Under no circumstances should firms be allowed to set prices, except local small-scale enterprises (see Kalecki 1958b, with the significant title 'Centralised price formation as an essential feature of the socialist economy'). Reliance on market signals leads to economic stagnation, whereas the fully-employed socialist economy needs to grow *via* investment; purely indicative planning can lead to even worse mistakes than detailed centralised planning; profit is a synthetic indicator of performance but this is a disadvantage as well as an advantage, because there is no point in raising profits at the cost of unemployment (Kalecki 1956b, 1957a, 1957c, 1957d and editorial comments on the account of a March 1957 discussion within the Economic Model Commission, Kalecki 1982, pp. 336–339). How, then, should the time-honoured question of price determination be solved in the socialist economy? Just as under capitalism, by charging a mark-up on current costs, except that the mark-up should be related to the needs of investment finance (1958b; also making allowances for import-intensity, Kalecki and Polaczek 1957a, 1957b). Full costs should provide a basis also for intra-CMEA trade (Kalecki 1962). Markets are left to determine quantities, rather than prices, and in the event of disequilibrium the adjustment process takes place through planned quantity adjustment rather than through prices. Kalecki simply did not believe in short-term substitutability in either production or consumption and this set him apart from the neoclassical tradition, even if Marxist-inspired (e.g. Oskar Lange), and from the whole tradition of 'market-socialism'.

In brief, Michal Kalecki's model of the socialist economy is a cross between the GDR (vertical groupings subject to central planning, a liberalised private sector) and Yugoslavia (cooperative sector, self-management) but with roles for markets, plans and self-management intermediate between the two. It is a very topical model, corresponding to what IMF officials today call 'the modified centrally planned economy' (Wolf 1985), no longer corresponding to the classical Soviet-type model but still a far cry from full-fledged market socialism. It is also the furthest Gorbachev's reform can go in the USSR if it succeeds, at any rate within the foreseeable future. Kalecki was aware that the model he outlined was far from ideal, but he knew also that there is no point in replicating capitalist markets and capitalist plans—a lesson which most East European reformers less acquainted than Kalecki with 'realised capitalism' still have to learn. Between piecemeal improvements and general change of principles, Kalecki favoured the first (1958a, in 1982, p. 88). He was aware that his proposed improvements would not put an end to the conflictual aspects of socialism: he was prepared to pay for Workers' Councils the price of possible disruption and growth deceleration, and only too aware, prophetically, of the strength of central opposition to their effective operation. Referring to his proposed 'synthesis of central planning and Workers' Councils' he wrote:

> We should not delude ourselves that such a system is free of contradictions and easy to steer. There is no doubt that always there will exist tendencies towards the erosion of the prerogatives of Workers' Councils through greater centralisation, as well as towards the weakening of central plan discipline through Workers' Councils. On the one hand there will be the danger of weakening Workers' Councils and bureaucratising the whole system of management, on the other hand Workers' Councils, through their pressure, can lead to situations where it is necessary to reduce the pace of growth or to become dependent on foreign aid, or where after a period of chaos 'order is restored', returning to the system of bureaucratic centralism (Kalecki 1956c, in 1982, p. 99; my translation).

An important element of Kalecki's approach to the formulation of a model of viable socialism, finally, is the strong weight given to actual *economic policies,* as well as to systemic questions; indeed one of his 1957 articles bears the significant title 'The role of the model should not be overestimated' (1957a)—a message which should be repeated *ad nauseam* for the benefit of all East European reformers and counter-reformers alike.

4.3 Investment and Growth Policies

A high and rising share of capital accumulation in national income has been the policy adopted by the Soviet Union since the inception of its First Five Year Plan (1928) and imitated by the other countries where a Soviet-type system was introduced after the war.

This policy, raised to the status of official dogma as a 'law of faster development of department I' (producing production goods in Marx's reproduction schemes) or priority for heavy industry or for 'group A', was plausible in a country like the Soviet Union in the late twenties: rural, industrially undeveloped, labour-abundant, capital-constrained and practically closed yet wishing to accelerate growth. Its soundness has been well theorised by the Soviet economist Feldman (1928, 1929) under precisely these assumptions. These were not, however, the conditions of the European countries which joined the Soviet bloc, with the exception perhaps of Bulgaria and Romania. Michal Kalecki was the first outspoken opponent of this official dogma; his criticism, originally raised in a paper presented to the Second Congress of Polish economists (1956c, in Kalecki 1984) was further developed (see for instance 1958c) and became the main theme of his 'Theory of growth of the socialist economy', devoted precisely to the study of exogenous constraints limiting the feasibility and plausibility of ambitious investment policies (1963a).

In Kalecki's approach the economic growth of a full-employment economy above its 'natural' growth rate (determined by the growth of the labour force and technical progress) has increasing costs in terms of a lower share of consumption. These costs are lowered by international trade but reassert themselves because of the necessity of balancing foreign trade over time and set an upper limit to the share of investment that can be gainfully undertaken. Within this limit, which is seen as a maximum, set not by political but by technical considerations, central powers can exercise their political discretion according to the strength of their political concern for current consumption and careful consideration of the actual trade-off between the share of consumption and faster growth—a trade-off which worsens with the acceleration of growth.

Kalecki's notion of maximum investment share is best analysed with the help of a simple model (similar to that of Kalecki 1963a). Consider a socialist economy where all savings are invested or, rather, savings are generated *via* financial planning to match planned investment; labour is fully employed and labour reserves (e.g. agricultural underemployment) have been exhausted. There is a range of alternative production techniques whereby output is produced by labour and capital, and technology is embodied in capital equipment of constant productivity and uniform lifetime. Provisionally assume that technical progress does not occur. The economy is closed (or, which is the same, foreign trade is balanced at a given level). The following symbols are introduced:

Y = national income	C = total consumption
L = labour force	n = growth rate of L
g_n = natural growth rate of income = n	g = actual growth rate of income
K = capital stock	y = labour productivity Y/L
k = capital per man K/L	v = capital/output ratio K/Y
s = share of investment in national income	
t = lifetime of equipment	

The following identities hold:

$$v \equiv K/Y = (K/L)/(Y/L) = k/y \tag{4.1}$$

$$s \equiv g.v \tag{4.2}$$

$$C \equiv (1-s)Y \tag{4.3}$$

At time 0 let the labour force be L_0. For a given technical choice that has prevailed for the previous t years, corresponding to given values of k_0, y_0, the three identities above identify also v_0, s_0 (since $g = g_n$ is also known) and C_0. For an unchanged technical choice after t years income Y_t and consumption C_t would be given by:

$$Y_t = Y_0(1+g_n)^t \tag{4.4}$$

$$C_t = (1-s_0)Y_0(1+g_n)^t \tag{4.5}$$

Suppose planners considered switching to a more capital intensive technique with parameters k_1 and y_1. Of course, since $k_1 > k_0$ there must be also $y_1 > y_0$, otherwise the new technique is absolutely inferior and should not be considered at all; and $v_1 > v_0$ otherwise the original technique is absolutely inferior and should have not been chosen in the first place. Define

$$p \equiv (y_1 - y_0)/y_0 \tag{4.6}$$

If the economy switched to technique 1, after t years the whole capital stock would be of the new kind and the values of Y_t and C_t would be given not by 4.4 and 4.5 but by 4.4′ and 4.5′:

$$Y_t = Y_0\left(1+g_n\right)^t\left(1+p\right) \tag{4.4'}$$

$$C_t = \left(1-s_1\right)Y_0\left(1+g_n\right)^t\left(1+p\right) \tag{4.5'}$$

At time t income with the newly adopted technique 1 would be greater than with former technique 0 by a factor of $(1 + p)$ but the share of investment would also be higher for the more capital intensive technique because of 4.2 and the fact that $v_1 > v_2$; hence $(1-s_1) < (1-s_0)$ and C_t is not necessarily higher than with the previous technique. For consumption to be higher after the switch the condition must be satisfied (from 4.5 and 4.5′):

$$\left(1-s_1\right)\left(1+p\right) > \left(1-s_0\right) \tag{4.7}$$

Otherwise, consumption is sacrificed not only throughout the transition to the new technique for t years but ever after if the new technique is maintained. While other writers (for instance Horvat 1958) had stressed the existence of a limit to the economy's absorption capacity of investment from the viewpoint of income, beyond which investment would not raise *income,* Kalecki introduces a stricter limit, beyond which investment does not raise *maintainable consumption* levels.

Kalecki's condition 4.7 appears as a kind of golden rule of accumulation; in fact it can be proven that *it is the same thing as the golden rule of accumulation* familiar from Western literature on the theory of economic growth (Hahn and Matthews 1964), except that it is a rule about *maximum* and not about desirable accumulation. For two techniques to be equally eligible from the viewpoint of the maximum sustainable consumption per head, the inequality (4.7) should turn into an equality, or

$$\left(1-s_1\right)\left(1+p\right)-\left(1-s_0\right)=0 \tag{4.8}$$

from which, substituting for the values of s from 4.2,

$$g_n = p/\left(v_1+v_1.p-v_0\right) \text{is obtained.} \tag{4.9}$$

For any given wage rate, the profit rate on the switch to the more capital intensive technique—regardless of whether such a profit rate is actually monitored, calculated (which Kalecki does not) or is even a concept ideologically allowed—is

$$r = (y_1 - y_0)/(k_1 - k_0) \tag{4.10}$$

from which, substituting from 4.1 and 4.6, we have:

$$r = \frac{p}{v_1 + v_1.p - v_0} = g_n, \text{Q.E.D.} \tag{4.11}$$

This proposition [which can be obtained from Kalecki's model but was not fully drawn out by him beyond the expression of (4.7)] holds also when there is technical progress, as long as this is *neutral* in Kalecki's sense of the rate of progress being uniform regardless of capital intensity of output (therefore identical to Harrod-neutrality, whereby progress is uniform regardless of capital/output ratios; see Chilosi 1971). If progress was faster the higher the capital intensity of output (Kalecki's capital-intensity-encouraging progress) it might pay to invest beyond the limits indicated by (4.7), because the benefits of higher capital intensity are underestimated by *p*, whereas if productivity growth and capital intensity of output were inversely related condition (4.7) would hold *a fortiori.* Foreign trade does not alter the approach, though it may shift temporarily the investment costs of growth acceleration at full employment and, therefore, the attractiveness of alternative rates of accumulation.

In fact Kalecki's notion of a maximum limit to the share of accumulation should not necessarily be approached, let alone met. Kalecki introduces a supply function of savings on the part of the planners, which he calls the planners' 'decisional curve' (to stress its non-technical nature) but which is simply a special form of 'objective function': instead of expressing preferences about dated consumption levels, per man or overall, Kalecki's planners compare the falling growth acceleration dg/ds obtained by higher investment shares at higher levels of growth rate g, with the increasing growth acceleration which they would require to

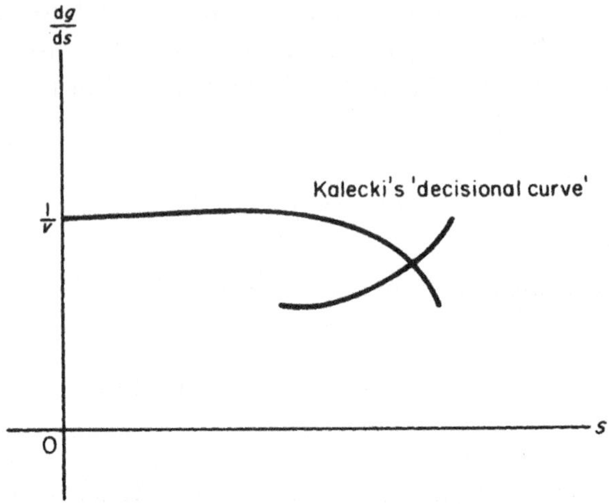

Fig. 4.1 Kalecki's 'decisional curve'. Note: *v*: marginal capital/output ratio, *g*: growth rate of income, *s*: share of investment in national income

induce them to squeeze consumption further at higher growth rates. A balance is struck when the sacrifices demanded for acceleration (by the economy as a whole) are equal to the price that planners are willing to pay (see Fig. 4.1).

The objective lesson of this exercise is not optimisation *per se,* which Kalecki stresses is a pure pedagogical device, but the notion that planners' investment policy should not only stay within the golden rule limit but also demand a greater acceleration of income for every percentage sacrifice in the share of consumption associated with it.

This lesson was quickly absorbed, popularised and developed by Kalecki's pupils (in particular, Laski 1965; Jozefiak 1971; and many others) but was coldly received in most other circles. Polish leaders had already reacted in 1964 to Kalecki's theories and his application of those theories to Polish long-term planning by dismissing him from his advisory role. Accumulation policies throughout the sixties (and well into the seventies) remained as much based on high and rising investment shares as ever before, throughout Eastern Europe. In the Soviet Union, the book (Kalecki 1963a) was published with a misleading and patronising introduction by Academician Khatchaturov (Polish translation in Kalecki

1984), who praised the mathematical approach while lamenting the neglect of socio-political factors (what could have been more socio-political than Kalecki's concern for the plausibility and the intelligent use of people's sacrifices?). The Polish academic establishment at first appeared to accept, or at least not to reject, Kalecki's approach, which found its way into textbooks on the economics of socialism. But in 1968 an attack was launched by party hacks in writings and at two meetings at the Central School of the Party and at the Central School of Planning and Statistics (SGPiS). Kalecki was accused of being a 'prisoner of capital fetishism' (by W. Iskra), of 'smuggling bourgeois economics' (by B. Rudowicz), of organising a 'cult of his theory and personality' among his followers (by D. Sokolow), of plagiarism of Harrod and Domar (though Kalecki had long acknowledged the connection and stressed the differences), of excessive formalism, neglect of the human factor and other inanities (by J. Gorski, who in earlier writings had expressed appreciation). Kalecki replied and, later, resigned (see Osiatynski's account of those meetings in Kalecki 1984); official condemnation did not prevent Kalecki's critics from continuing to use his work in their texts, but deleting the source (see Nuti 1973).

In truth, *Kalecki's contentions about either the golden rule limit or the planners' increasing supply price of savings have no general validity; yet he was right in the specific conditions* of Eastern Europe at the time and with reference to the policies followed there by socialist leaders, and he was proven right, with a vengeance, by the recurring Polish crises (from 1970 to 1980 through intermediate stages), the generalised decline to date and the policy reversal of the early 1980s.

The adoption of more capital-intensive techniques than those which satisfy condition (4.7) cannot be regarded as *necessarily* mistaken: in principle—as long as the new technique is not absolutely inferior, which has been ruled out in the analysis above—that policy can always be reversed and will lead to higher consumption than with the less capital-intensive technique throughout the period of transition back to that technique. This gain in consumption may be considered as insufficient to compensate for the sacrifices incurred during the transition to the more capital-intensive technique and before the policy is reversed; but this is a political judgement, not a technical one as Kalecki would have us believe. His neglect of potential gain from policy reversal is something of a sleight of hand; we know from optimum saving theory that golden rule growth is a crude benchmark against which to assess accumulation policy and that maximisation of maintainable consumption per head is not necessarily the best course. Yet if, in principle, it cannot be said that East European planners were inefficient simply because of their disregard of golden rules, it is right to put on them the burden of proof: what conceivable reason might there have been to shift consumption from today to tomorrow, if tomorrow's gain can only be a temporary blip? Speeding up the achievement of full communism is not a good enough answer, since nobody ever said that communist bliss had to be prepaid. No other possible reasons—as far as I know—have been given. In practical terms, therefore, Kalecki stood on firm ground.

Theoretical weakness and practical strength is a characteristic also of Kalecki's 'decisional curve'. The notion that planners should require faster acceleration of growth to be induced to invest higher shares of national income may seem harmless enough. This is, for instance, how the level of expenditure (and therefore its share in a given income) behaves with respect to quantity demanded for any demand function whose price elasticity falls with the quantity demanded, as happens, for instance, for any downward sloping linear demand function for any commodity. But suppose that demand is, at some point, fairly inelastic to price increases and elastic to price decreases: total revenue beyond that point will be rising with quantity at an *increasing* rate; hence, progressively *smaller* increases in quantity will be required to induce the consumer to raise the share of that good in his total expenditure beyond that point. The economic meaning is that there is a target minimum quantity below which a commodity's demand price rises steeply. Is there any reason to exclude, in principle, the possibility that growth-minded planners might likewise price additional growth more highly, in terms of consumption forsaken, at lower than at higher growth rates, at least over a certain range? This time the burden of proof is on Kalecki, and there is nothing in his work, or in the theory of demand or of optimum saving, to justify the need for a monotonically rising 'decisional curve' as a *general* case. Yet the notion that at some point demand for growth becomes less elastic down to unity or less must be correct since some current income must be consumed even if growth becomes inordinately cheap; i.e., there will be maximum share of accumulation and *in its neighbourhood* the decisional curve must be rising as Kalecki supposed. If it is accepted that golden rule growth sets a maximum limit to the accumulation share, why should planners choose a minimum growth close to that limit? When the economy is close enough to the limit of sustainable consumption, Kalecki's argument applies. The question becomes one of fact: in the 1960s were Polish planners overstepping the limits of people's forbearance in their trading off of current for future consumption, or the (related) limits of the planners' own ability to deliver the consumption goods promised with the payment of wages? If they had not been, the Polish crises would have been averted. That Kalecki was right is shown by Gomulka's fall (within months of Kalecki's death), by the mounting excess demand for consumption goods at official prices and the inability of authorities to make price increases acceptable to the population, by the greater emphasis on consumption in the plans for the 1970s, the mounting external debt and deteriorating performance. The consumption sacrifices opposed by Kalecki were not worth undertaking. The lesson should not be lost on the rest of the socialist bloc where repeatedly investment policies have neglected the constraints of full employment, natural resources and foreign balance, and have often generated not higher income, let alone higher consumption, nor sufficiently higher consumption with respect to *some* preference system, but only excess capacity. Kalecki was fighting a dogma and could not afford to dilute his case with too many qualifications; that he glossed over some of them does not mean that he was unaware of their existence.

4.4 Shadow Interest Rates and Technical Choice

The choice of techniques was investigated by Kalecki not only in a macroeconomic context (as seen in the previous section) but also at the micro-level, in the selection of investment projects. There is a link between his macro-analysis and his micro-findings, which were co-authored with Mieczyslaw Rakowski, an officer of the Polish Planning

Commission. Their joint efforts (Kalecki and Rakowski 1959) became almost verbatim the official handbook on project selection (KPpRM 1962).

Since the mid-fifties in Poland the choice between alternative projects had been following informally the Soviet practice: (1) the scope of selection was limited to alternative ways of producing the same kind of capacity (decided by the centre or by enterprise associations), and not extended to the choice between plants producing alternative products; (2) investment funds were made available to enterprises from the government budget at no cost; (3) investing enterprises confronted with alternative ways of producing identical capacity were instructed to choose a more investment-intensive alternative only if it led to operating costs economies sufficient to recover the associated *additional* investment cost within a maximum number of years, a statutory 'standard recoupment period' fixed by the centre. The codification of this informal practice in 1962 was profoundly influenced by the work of Kalecki on his own and with Rakowski.

The basic rule adopted by the Polish Planning Commission in their 1962 *Instrukcja Ogolna* (General Instruction) issued to all industrial enterprises required investors to aggregate costs into investment and yearly operating costs, reject inferior alternatives (costlier in both investment and operation) and minimise the sum of operating costs and a fraction of investment costs given by the inverse of the standard recoupment period:

$$C + \frac{1}{T} I = \text{minimum} \tag{4.12}$$

where C now stands for yearly operating costs, I for the investment costs associated with C, and T is the standard recoupment period. In the Polish practice T was fixed at six years for new plants and five years for modernisation investment; these rates were uniform throughout the economy. Clearly the recommended procedure is tantamount to a shadow capital charge of $1/T$; in a market economy, where an interest rate r prevails and capital is competitively rented, equipment of expected lifetime t would command a capital charge equal to a fraction $r(1 + r)^t/((1 + r)^t-1)$

of its purchasing price (here we abstract from the complications of inflation accounting, because there was price stability in that decade in Poland and because in any case inflation should not affect competitive rentals other than through its impact on the nominal interest rate *r*). Hence there is an implied relation between *T* and an *implicit* interest rate, i.e.

$$\mathrm{T} = \frac{(1+r)^t - 1}{r.(1+r)^t.} \tag{4.13}$$

For $T = 6$ and an investment lifetime of 20 years (regarded in the *Instrukcja* as the average lifetime of equipment in Poland at the time of issue) there was an implicit interest rate of about 15.7%, which is rather high in view of price stability. The same rate applied to investment in modernisation, which was shorter-lived and required a shorter standard recoupment period: five years was an approximation.

Polish practice here differed from that of the Soviet Union and Czechoslovakia, where the standard recoupment period was different in different sectors (ranging from 3 to 10 years according to the ranking of each sector in national policy; the more favoured, the longer the period over which additional investment could be recouped) and straight-line amortisation was added to $1/T$ to calculate the shadow investment charge. This departure had been advocated by Kalecki on the grounds of efficiency: seeing that these calculations affected not capacity expansion but only its form there was no reason to favour capital intensity in favoured sectors (Kalecki 1965), while durability differences between plants could be accounted for in other ways than through amortisation (Kalecki 1958d; see below, this section).

There are three main innovations introduced into this practice by Kalecki and Rakowski: (1) a link between the uniform standard recoupment period in the economy and labour-saving investment opportunities in modernisation; (2) the compounding of output losses due to the 'freezing' of investment resources in incomplete projects during their gestation period; (3) the correction of investment and operating costs to account for differences in expected lifetime of projects, based on the hypothetical comparison of steady-state balanced stocks of those projects (for a more detailed discussion, see Nuti 1971).

The rationale behind the value of T recommended by Kalecki and Rakowski for the Polish economy (in other East European countries following the same practice no rationale is given) is concern over the possibility of a labour shortage. Given full employment of labour, new plants would be operated by a number of workers equal to the natural increase of the labour force, plus workers formerly attached to equipment now come to the end of its lifetime, plus workers freed by investment in modernisation. The lower the standard recoupment period, the higher the labour requirements of new plants (labour forming the bulk of operating costs) and the lower the investment in modernisation and therefore the lower the number of workers freed from scrapped plants. Given the non-regulatory nature of wages policy with respect to the relative scarcity of labour, and the lack of actual investment charges, the shadow capital charge implicit in the value of T is used to prevent labour shortage. Kalecki and Rakowski had estimated that there existed ample labour-saving opportunities in the Polish economy through modernisation investment which could be recouped in five or six years. Hence, as long as labour could be drawn from this source, it would be wasteful to undertake more investment-intensive projects unless their additional cost could be recovered in less than the same period (the differential T adopted in the end for new investment and modernisation is a rough way of accounting for the longer expected life of new versus modernised plant; for a more formal analysis see Nuti 1971). The high shadow charge therefore simply reflected the low technical level of Polish industry and the high profitability of investment in its modernisation. In view of this rationale, one would have expected the standard recoupment period to have varied over time; the shadow capital charge, however, proved just as rigid as actual prices and was not altered for as long as the *Instrukcja* remained in force, i.e. until 1969, when a specific shadow capital charge of 0.12 (corresponding to roughly $T = 8$) replaced T.

Kalecki's keen eye for planning malpractices had identified the dangerous propensity to open a wide 'investment front', starting more projects than could be finished on schedule, and he alerted the planners to the social cost involved in locking up resources during the gestation period of projects. To favour quick-yielding projects and discourage the unnecessary prolongation of gestation periods, Kalecki introduced a 'coefficient of immobilisation' by which investment costs had to be compounded during the corresponding immobilisation period (Kalecki 1958d). Kalecki and Rakowski assume that if one unit of investment were to be 'unfrozen' it would yield an amount of national product of an average pattern equal to $1/v$ where v is the gross capital/output ratio. Allowing for depreciation of fixed capital at a yearly rate d, the net product would be $(1/v-d)$ per annum. At full employment, in order to release the manpower necessary to man this unit of investment some additional investment must be undertaken elsewhere in the economy, given by $a.T$, where a is the labour cost of the production of one unit of gross output and T is the standard recoupment period. The yearly net product of one unfrozen unit of investment is then reckoned as:

$$q = \frac{1}{v + a.T} - d. \tag{4.14}$$

It is difficult to see why the locking up of investment resources in the form of a longer gestation period should be treated any differently from the locking up of investment resources in the form of a higher investment intensity. Consistency would require $q = 1/T$, and it is no accident that the Soviet, Czechoslovak and Hungarian investment choice methodologies of the 1960s all use $1/T$ as the fraction of investment costs to be added to actual costs during gestation. As it happens, the value of the relevant parameters estimated by Kalecki and Rakowski for the Polish economy are $v = 2.5$, $a = 0.5$, $d = 0.03$, which give a magnitude of q, subsequently codified in the *Instrukcja*, of 0.15, i.e. comfortably close to 0.157 (corresponding to $T = 6$). When I put this question to Michal Kalecki he insisted that $1/T$ and q were different concepts and could differ; the only way I could accept this was by looking at them respectively as linked to notional long term and short term interest rates. Kalecki insisted that their near-identity was a mere coincidence, but seeing that they were so close he saw no point in discussing the question further.

A third implicit interest rate, one moreover equal to the growth rate of investment (i.e. complying with the golden rule of the previous section), is implicit in Kalecki and Rakowski's treatment of plant lifetime. Instead of gearing the shadow capital charge to plant durability as in a competitive rental market, or adding straight line amortisation to $1/T$ as the Soviet and Czech planners, Kalecki and Rakowski proceeded from a detailed analysis of the costs and benefits of plant durability.

A longer-lived plant has the relative advantage of producing a given stream of output for a longer period, but also the disadvantage of being tied to a given technical form for a longer period, therefore remaining excluded from the benefit of technical progress of the embodied kind. The balance between the two effects in the comparison of two alternative lifetimes depends on the difference in durability, the rate at which operating costs decrease every year in the new plants, and the growth rate of investment in the production of the output considered. Suppose that investment in plants of durability of n years grows at a rate g per year, and the capital output v is constant over time. If investment at a time t is indicated by I, in the preceding year it was $I(1 + g)^{-1}$ and $(i-1)$ years back it was $I(1 + g)^{-(i-1)}$. The stock of fixed capital operating in a given year (expressed at historical cost at constant prices) is the sum of gross investment carried out in the last n years; since the flow of output per unit of investment is constant through time this gives a convenient index of output capacity, M_n:

$$M_n = \sum_{i=1}^{n} I\left(\frac{1}{1+g}\right)^{i-1} = I\left(1-\left(\frac{1}{1+g}\right)^{n}\right)(1+g)/g \qquad (4.15)$$

Since the capital-output ratio is v, the output of this stock of capital is F_n, or

$$F_n = \frac{M_n}{v} = I\left(1-\left(\frac{1}{1+g}\right)^{n}\right)(1+g)/g.v. \qquad (4.16)$$

In order to make this technical alternative comparable with that of plants of durability n_s, which is taken as 'standard', the same procedure is applied to a hypothetical stream of investment with identical I and g but with lifetime n_s and with investment/output ratio v_s. Other things being equal, the output flow of an investment process with parameters v, n, will be equal to that of an investment process of standard durability n_s and investment output ratio v_s if

$$v / v_s = \left(1-\left(\frac{1}{1+g}\right)^n\right) / \left(1-\left(\frac{1}{1+g}\right)^{n_s}\right) = z_n \qquad (4.17)$$

Thus Kalecki and Rakowski and the Polish *Instrukcja* recommend that the comparison of projects should be made not minimising actual and shadow costs for the actual capacity, but the ratio between costs and z_n times actual capacity. For a standard durability $n_s = 20$ and $g = 7\%$, for instance, z_n is 0.86 for $n = 15$ and 1.10 for $n = 25$: in other words planners should prefer a 25-year-long project to a 20-year one, given $g = 7\%$, if the investment-output ratio is less than 10% higher than for the 20-year-long project; while $n = 15$ can be preferred to standard durability n_s if its investment output ratio is lower by more than 14%.

The effect of durability over the introduction of technical progress is accounted for in a similar way. It is assumed that, for investment growing at a rate g per year, total operating costs of production in the *new* investment increase at a rate $c < g$, because of technical progress advancing at a rate approximately equal to $g-c$. Following the same method used for output, the relation between total costs G_n for a stock of plants of durability n and total costs G_{ns} for a stock of plants of durability n_s is given by

$$y_n = \frac{G_n}{G_{ns}} = \frac{\left(1-\left(\frac{1}{1+c}\right)^n\right)}{\left(1-\left(\frac{1}{1+c}\right)^{n_s}\right)}. \qquad (4.18)$$

If we call C the operating costs in a stock of plants of durability n, the operating costs in an identical stock of plants of durability n_s would be y_n C, a longer lifetime of plant involving a flow of costs larger by a factor of y_n. For instance, for $g = 7\%$ and $c = 3\%$ (with technical progress advancing at a rate of 3.9%) and $n_s = 20$ years, y_n will be 0.80 for $n = 15$ and 1.17 for $n = 25$. Instead of minimising the expression given in (4.12) above, investors are instructed to select projects so that:

$$E = \frac{I(1/T)(1+q.z)+C.y_n}{X.z_n} = \text{minimum} \tag{4.19}$$

where z is the average period of freezing of investment resources during the gestation period and X is the capacity target.

A final refinement was introduced to take into account the possible differences between the rate at which labour costs and other costs (raw materials, semi-finished products, fuel, energy and capital maintenance) fall in time, but the basic approach remained unchanged: tables for alternative values of y_n and z_n were attached to the *Instrukcja* for the use of investors. Basically, for each project of given technical durability, first the lifetime for which the expression above reaches a minimum is found and this is taken as the optimum economic lifetime of the project; then the project is chosen for which that expression, taken for the optimum economic lifetime of each project, is lowest.

The comparison of projects with reference to the characteristics of hypothetical balanced stocks is very ingenious; it inspired my treatment of more complicated time patterns of input and outputs (Nuti 1970); it is not, however, immune from criticism. The optimum economic lifetime of plants might vary with the reference durability n_s, which is arbitrary; the optimum lifetime of a plant should be assessed without reference to a standard durability. The treatment of durability differs from that of gestation, whereas gestation and durability are both aspects of the time profile of inputs and outputs and should be treated in the same way. If the growth rate of investment is slowing down, the advantage of a longer lifetime is higher than if the growth rate is constant, and the reverse is true for an accelerating growth rate; the opposite applies to the disadvantages of longer lifetimes. What is most interesting, however, is that in an economy where investing firms obtained funds free of charge from the state budget no less than *three* shadow rates were introduced, *implicit* in T, q and in the use of g to calculate y_n and z_n. Shadow rates were fairly close (15.7% for T, 15% for q, 7–15% for g) but the approach was untidy and messy. Why did Kalecki become so involved in it? Presumably the answer is that he would have liked to introduce an actual interest rate in investment selection (see Sect. 4.2 above) but was operating within a system dominated by a Soviet practice (that of recoupment period) difficult to change; he also specifically did not want to introduce interest and profitability in the selection of the areas of capacity expansion (except in the long run); at the same time he wanted to improve the existing planning system, practice prevailing over theory in his concern.

4.5 The Perspective Plan

Kalecki's ideas about socialist planning reviewed in the previous sections are brought together in the procedure he devised for the construction of a perspective plan, i.e. a plan for the long-term development of a socialist economy (see Kalecki 1958e, 1963c, 1963d). What follows is a generalisation and formalisation of Kalecki's procedure.

The perspective plan covers a time span of 15 to 20 years; the planning horizon is actually longer, in that investment expenditure in the last few years of the plan is laid down on the assumption that the broad lines of development of the economy outlined in the plan will also continue after the end of the plan period. It is a 'sliding' plan; the first five years become the starting point for drawing a medium-run plan for the economy, especially the investment plan and, as time goes by, the terminal date of the perspective plan period is shifted forward, say, by five years every five years, so that a picture of the perspective development of the economy is kept, brought up to date as past and current experience produces more accurate projections. The plan is drawn at constant prices and is, therefore, designed basically to check the consistency of physical flows, while financial flows and the price level are adjusted later, with the drawing up of short-run financial balances and balances of the income and expenditure of the population.

The first stage in the construction of the perspective plan is the choice of a preliminary target for the average growth rate during the period, which we can call $\bar{g}_0$. The main constraints on average growth are: (1) the expected growth rate of the active population and the growth rate of its average productivity (partly dependent on technical progress and, partly, on the rate of investment itself); (2) the minimum growth rate of consumption of the population and the share of accumulation associated with it, constraining $\bar{g}_0$ for the preliminary coefficients, at the prices and the sectoral composition of the base period; (3) the balance of foreign trade. These constraints can be summed up as:

$$\bar{g}_0 \leq n_0 = h_0 \tag{4.20}$$

$$\bar{g}_0 \leq \frac{s}{v_0} \tag{4.21}$$

$$\bar{g}_0 \leq \frac{g_x}{e_m} \tag{4.22}$$

where $\bar{g}_0$ is the preliminary target for the average growth of income over the period, n_0 and h_0 are preliminary estimates of population growth and of average productivity growth; s is the maximum share of accumulation corresponding to the minimum consumption requirements of the population, and v_0 is a preliminary estimate of average investment intensity; g_x *is* the expected growth rate of the value of exports, and e_m is the estimate of the elasticity of imports with respect to income (given the planners' expectations about world demand and relative internal and international prices). Ideally, all these constraints should be simultaneously met so as to have the equality sign in Eqs. (4.20–4.22); if one of the constraints bites first, to some extent it might be possible to ease whatever is the bottleneck by bringing the right side of the other equations closer to $\bar{g}_0$: for instance, to raise h_0 or lower e_m or raise g_x at the expense of raising v_o, but there might be limits to the possibility of trading off one constraint for another and the most stringent constraint will determine the highest $\bar{g}_0$

which is tentatively considered feasible. However, even if the tentatively chosen growth rate does not quite meet all constraints one might pass to the second stage of the calculations, since the purpose of this stage is only that of ruling out blatantly unrealistic variants of the plan checking the internal consistency of expectations. The estimates are aggregates of different sectors, and it is not granted that the subsequent breakdown of these variables will give aggregation weights consistent with the provisional calculations.

The second stage is a tentative estimate of the output structure of different sectors required for final uses in each year. The changes in the pattern of final private consumption are predicted (by means of calculations of consumption elasticities, the analysis of family budgets, available time series of consumption data, the pattern of consumption of countries at similar stages of development, etc.) or planned (on the basis of consumption norms). Public consumption of the product of each sector can be added directly, but the requirements of the net output of each sector for investment and exports will depend in turn on the targets for gross output expansion in the different sectors, so that only preliminary estimates can be inserted at this stage, to be checked later for consistency with data obtained at the next stage. These operations can be summarised as the drawing of a set of provisional vectors of final demands in each period,

$$\mathbf{y}_{t+j} = \mathbf{c}_{t+j} + \mathbf{u}_{t+j} + \mathbf{s}_{t+j} + \mathbf{f}_{t+j}, j = 0,1,\ldots,20; \quad (4.23)$$

where **y** is the vector of final demand, **c** is the vector of private and **u** of public consumption, **s** is the provisional investment vector estimate and **f** the export vector.

The third stage consists of the attempt to estimate the sectoral breakdown of demand for intermediate products corresponding, in each period during the plan, to the provisional estimate of final demand obtained in stage two. This is done by means of either input-output analysis, or the material balances of resources and uses usually drawn in planned economies for the main commodity groups. In either case allowance has to be made for technical progress so that *ex ante* planning matrices **A** of technological coefficients have to be used rather than *ex post* tables. An estimate of the gross output targets **x** consistent with the final output targets of the perspective plan is thus obtained:

$$\mathbf{x}_{t+j} = \mathbf{A}_{t+j}\mathbf{x}_{t+j} + \mathbf{y}_{t+j} \; j = 0,1,\ldots,15-20. \qquad (4.24)$$

The fourth stage consists of a reassessment of the provisional estimates, for investment and foreign trade, on the basis of the supply constraints on the growth of each sector. Productive activities are divided into two main categories, of 'supply determined' and 'demand determined' activities (Kalecki 1963b and his Preface to Rakowski 1963). The first category includes those activities which are subject to a ceiling for their long-run growth rate, for technical or organisational reasons, which cannot be removed even at the expense of higher capital expenditure. The technological and organisational limits are given by limited natural resources, or by the time necessary for the introduction of new technological processes, or for the training of workers or technicians of different skills, or by difficulties in recruiting manpower for certain trades (mining, for instance). Demand-determined industries are the industries which, within the relevant range of the growth rate of national income, are not subject to such ceilings in their growth rates. The comparison between the estimates of gross output requirements and the ceilings limiting the growth of supply-determined industries will give a first assessment of import requirements, to which non-competitive imports have to be added, to obtain total import requirements. In order to meet import requirements with exports, the targets for the final output of the industries which are not supply-determined has to be raised, following the indications of foreign trade agencies, as long as higher amounts of output marketed for exports are not counterbalanced by more unfavourable terms of trade. Once the net trade balance and the actual targets for the increase of gross output are known, a more accurate estimate of investment requirements can be obtained and checked against the provisional estimates adopted at stage two. If the divergence between the initial estimates of the net trade balance and investment requirements and the estimates obtained at stage four is not acceptable the process of plan construction will have to start again, from stage two, until the two estimates are sufficiently close and the relations hold:

$$\mathbf{x}_{t+j} + \mathbf{m}_{t+j} = \mathbf{A}_{t+j}\mathbf{x}_{t+j} + \mathbf{y}_{t+j}\ j = 0,1,\ldots,15-20; \tag{4.25}$$

$$\mathbf{x}_{t+j} \le \tilde{\boldsymbol{x}}_{t+j} \tag{4.26}$$

$$\mathbf{s}_{t+j} = \mathbf{B}_{t+j}\left(\mathbf{x}_{t+j+1} - \mathbf{x}_{t+j}\right) \tag{4.27}$$

$$\mathbf{p}.\mathbf{f}_{t+j} = r.p_i.\mathbf{m}_{t+j} \tag{4.28}$$

where $\mathbf{m}$ is imports, $\tilde{\mathbf{x}}_{t+j}$ is the capacity constraint of x_{t+j}, $\mathbf{B}_{t+j}$ is the matrix of projected investment requirements on a sector-to-sector basis; p and p_i are internal and international prices and r the exchange rate.

The choice of the technical form of investment is undertaken at this stage. Whenever alternative ways of achieving given targets for output expansion in different sectors are available the procedure for technical choice is usually that of minimising the sum of perspective operation costs and a shadow charge for investment, according to the methods discussed in Sect. 4.4 above. Alternative ways of earning foreign currency, and the alternative between import and domestic productions, are treated as any other technical choice, in the same way (Kalecki 1971b).

After these stages are performed the disaggregated data can be aggregated to recompute the aggregate targets for the growth of national income, investment intensity and import requirements, in order to check them against the preliminary estimates. In case of inconsistency the plan is revised and a new variant is worked out through the stages described above.

> The variant finally adopted should be distinguished by the highest possible rate of growth at which there is a realistic possibility of balancing foreign trade and at which the relative share of productive investment plus the increase in inventories in the national income is considered tolerable by the authorities from the point of view of the impact upon consumption and unproductive investment in the short run (Kalecki 1963b).

This procedure proposed by Kalecki has a number of shortcomings. Computations undertaken at constant prices can at most ensure the *consistency* of plans in physical terms (as long as aggregation weights within sectors do not change too drastically) but there is nothing to ensure that the relative prices deriving *from the plan* should be consistent with the relative prices assumed *in the construction of the plan.* On the side of production goods, the relative scarcities of inputs caused in the very process of planning might diverge from initial relative prices and, if this divergence is neglected, opportunities for substitution among alternative inputs might be lost. For consumption goods, the relative long-run production costs of consumption goods over the plan period might diverge from the pattern of relative prices of consumption goods initially assumed for the purposes of forecasting consumption patterns over the period, inducing, therefore, the neglect of opportunities for substitution among alternative consumption goods. Finally, since the calculations for investment choice are carried out for given output expansion targets, the procedure implies that the quantity of material inputs in the operation of the plants after construction and the proportion in which material inputs are required to make the investment goods considered are not affected by the technique eventually chosen; technological choice, in other words, is assumed to take the form of the substitution between labour and an aggregate notion of investment measured at constant prices, instead of more complex alternatives.

These shortcomings can be summed up as the possible *inefficiency* resulting from the neglect of three main feedbacks of the plan on the system of prices (and hence, whenever alternative consumption and production choices are available, on the pattern of planned quantities). These feedbacks are: (1) the choice of the technical form of investment on the physical composition of the sectoral targets for output expansion; (2) the feedback of the investment plan on the prices of investment goods to be used as the basis of plan construction; (3) the feedback of relative costs of consumption goods resulting from the plan on the relative prices to be used as the basis of the consumption plan. The extent of the divergence between the plan obtained following the stages outlined and an 'ideal' plan, which should be constructed taking into account also the feedbacks mentioned here, and the practical importance of this divergence are questions open to discussion. According to Michal Kalecki the drawbacks of performing calculations to choose techniques measuring the value of investment (per unit of output or per labour employed) at constant prices are of the same nature as all index number problems and can be reduced, in the framework of investment planning, by using chain indexes of the volume of investment (Kalecki 1963a, ch. 1). He recognises that the crude recoupment period approach and the other rules put forward for investment choice are only a first approximation to a complex problem (Kalecki 1963c) but regards more sophisticated approaches as not necessarily representing an improvement, given the inaccuracy of initial data and the uncertainty about the future. The necessity of checking the consistency between the relative prices of consumption goods at which future consumption is being forecast and relative costs anticipated in the calculations of 'investment effectiveness' has been stressed by Kalecki himself, although his own treatment of the problem does not seem to provide a satisfactory solution.[1]

In handling these problems in Poland in the early 1960s Kalecki rose to the challenge of 'realised' socialism and favoured approximate procedures of practical use to rigorous solutions without application. Even with hindsight, nobody could say that he was wrong.

4.6 Summary and Conclusion

Kalecki's contribution to the theory and practice of socialist planning—as distinguished from the wider aspects of socialist economy and society—are discussed in this paper under four headings:

1. *Kalecki's comprehensive and coherent picture of the organisation model of the socialist economy as an alternative to the Soviet-type model different from the 'market socialism' of Lange and other reformers.* In Kalecki's model prices are fixed, as in his picture of the capitalist economy, by mark-up pricing, with the average mark-up on actual and shadow costs related to the requirements of investment finance; markets are

[1] This question will be treated in a future paper.

used but market signals are quantity signals determining quantity adjustments in the use and expansion of capacity; firms performance is assessed using net value indicators but within wage guidelines and employment targets; investment is kept in check by interest payments deducted from performance indicators; but neither investment nor employment is guided by enterprise profitability considerations; central planning is made easier by grouping enterprises in vertically integrated sectoral associations. The countervailing power *vis-à-vis* central planners is not the market but Workers' Councils: in Kalecki's reform scheme therefore democratisation takes the place of marketisation.

2. *Kalecki's approach to the external and political limits to the accumulation policy of central planners.* Labour force growth and technical progress set a limit to the accumulation that can be usefully undertaken from the viewpoint of *maintainable* consumption growth (golden rule accumulation of Western texts being regarded not as an optimum but as a maximum accumulation policy). Within this maximum limit, planners' concern for short-term consumption *should* (following from a rationality postulate in Kalecki but really embodying a plausible but special preference system on the part of planners) stop well short of that maximum.
3. *Kalecki's innovations in revamping the Soviet-type approach to investment project selection based on the notion of 'standard recoupment period' in place of interest rates.* Kalecki and Rakowski linked this period to the marginal labour-saving opportunities in modernisation given the full employment constraint of the socialist economy, introduced an alternative implicit rate of interest in dealing with the immobilisation of resources during investment gestation, and used investment growth rates in discriminating between projects of different lifetimes. Theoretically the use of multiple implicit shadow rates of interest can be questioned; in practice their values were close and these improvements of current practice must have seemed to Kalecki as more easily acceptable to Polish leaders than actual interest rates, and more desirable than an unqualified use of actual interest rates for the choice of investment levels and structure instead of just technical choice.
4. *Kalecki's procedure for the construction of a perspective plan of the development of the socialist economy, as a foundation for medium-run and*

investment planning. This brings together all the previous points and leads to a practical solution of plan formulation, which in theory can be regarded as possibly inefficient because it neglects a number of feedbacks in plan construction, but in practice is of considerable use especially if compared with the alternative Soviet-type methods using material balances alone.

This critical but positive assessment leads to some reconsideration of Kalecki's overall contribution to socialist economics. Accused of not being a Marxist he was more Leninist than his critics (with his emphasis on workers' control). Accused of neglecting social and political factors he had the most perceptive feeling for precisely these factors, with his emphasis on democratisation and on the political limits to investment policies and other work (not reviewed in this paper) on subjects ranging from economic criminality to peasant behaviour, from systemic influence on labour productivity to income distribution between manual and non-manual workers (see Kalecki 1984, Part III). For a man revered as a great theoretician, his propositions often lack generality, though the qualifications are not significant in practice for Eastern Europe in the 1960s. In this Kalecki is in a position similar to that of Keynes, who also claimed generality for a theory deeply grounded in the time and place of his theorising, Britain in the 1930s, and requiring some practically plausible qualifications which reduce generality without reducing policy relevance. Keynes was really a high Tory believing in markets, as Kalecki was a high Socialist believing in planning, and the theoretical and political stance of both has been frequently misunderstood. The world is not in the best of possible states, not because of qualification required for the general validity of their theories, but because of the pursuit of pre-Keynesian and pre-Kaleckian policies in both West and East.

In one respect Kalecki's contribution to socialist economics has not yet been tested, i.e. the viability of his model of socialist organisation, since the combination of central planning and workers' control has not been realised anywhere. That model was more the product of Polish conditions in the 1960s than perhaps anything else produced by Kalecki; it may be no accident that he decided to include almost none of his papers on the subject in his *Selected Papers* on socialism (Kalecki 1972), though pessimism on workers' powers, which was justified in 1968 Poland, might not be justified today, after the explosive effects of workers' discontent in 1980–81 Poland, and in the reform climate set up by Gorbachev. Kalecki's qualms about market prices, the risks of unemployment associated with decentralisation and the risks of central planning without workers' control, however, remain as valid and relevant today as ever.

Bibliography

Brus, W. (1977). Kalecki's economics of socialism, *Oxford Bulletin of Economics and Statistics,* Vol. 39, No. 1, February (Michal Kalecki Memorial Issue).

Chilosi, A. (1971). The theory of growth of a socialist economy of M. Kalecki, *Economics of Planning,* Vol. 11, No. 3.

Feinstein, C. (Ed.) (1967). *Socialism, Capitalism and Economic Growth, Essays in honour of Maurice Dobb,* Cambridge, CUP.

Feldman, G. A. (1928). K teorii tempov narodnogo dokhoda (On the theory of growth rates of national income), *Planovoe Khoziaistvo,* No. 11 and 12, November and December; English translation from Russian in Spulber (1964).

Feldman, G. A. (1929). O limitakh industrializatsii (On limits to industrialisation), *Planovoe Khoziaistvo,* No. 2, February; English translation from Russian in Spulber (1964).

Granick, D. (1975). *Enterprise Guidance in Eastern Europe,* Princeton, Princeton University Press

Hahn, F. H. and Matthews, R. C. O. (1964). The theory of economic growth: a survey, *Economic Journal,* December.

Horvat, B. (1958). The optimum rate of investment, *Economic Journal,* Vol. LXVIII, No. 272, December.

Jeffries, I. (Ed.) (1981). *The Industrial Enterprise in Eastern Europe,* London, Praeger.

Jozefiak, C. (1971). *Optimum techniczno-renowacjine w gospodarce socjalistycznej* (Optimum technical choice in the socialist economy), Warsaw, PWN.

Kalecki, M. (1942). Basic preconditions for a democratic planned economy, *Labour Discussion Notes,* No. 35, September, The Socialist Clarity Group, London (Polish version in Kalecki, 1982).

Kalecki, M. (1946a). Uwagi o racjonowaniu i systemie cen (Observations on rationing and the price system), first published in Kalecki (1982).

Kalecki, M. (1946b). Uwagi o oszczednosciach i obiegu pienieznym w Polsce (Observations on savings and monetary circulation in Poland), first published in Kalecki (1982).
Kalecki, M. (1946c). Plany finansowe na II polrocze 1946 r. i na I polrocze 1947 r. (Financial plans for the second semester of 1946 and the first semester of 1947), first published in Kalecki (1982).
Kalecki, M. (1956a). Liberalizacja zarzadzania drobnym przemyslem (Liberalisation of management in small-scale industry), first published in Kalecki (1982).
Kalecki, M. (1956b). Rady robotnicze a centralne planowanie (Workers' councils and central planning), *Nowe Drogi,* No. 11-12, November-December; also in Kalecki (1982).
Kalecki, M. (1956c). Dynamika inwestycji i dochodu narodowego w gospodarcze socjalistycznej, *Ekonomista,* No. 5.
Kalecki, M. (1957a). Nie przeceniac roli modelu (The role of the model should not be overestimated), *Trybuna Ludu,* No. 33, 3 February; also in Kalecki (1981).
Kalecki, M. (1957b). Koncern pionowy? *Polityka* No. 8, 17-23 April, Warsaw; also as, Koncern pionowy jako element nowego modelu gospodarczego (Vertically integrated enterprise groups as an element of the new economic model), in Kalecki (1982).
Kalecki, M. (1957d). Schemat nowego systemu bodzcow i nakazow (Scheme of the new system of incentives and orders), *Zycie Gospodarcze,* 21 July 1957, No. 29; also in Kalecki (1982).
Kalecki, M. (1958a). Bodzce zainteresowania materialnego w gospodarce socjalistycznej (Material incentives in the socialist economy), in the proceedings of a conference on the same subject in January 1956, *Szkice Ekonomiczne,* ZNE PAN, Warsaw; also in Kalecki (1982).
Kalecki, M. (1958b). Centralisticko odredivanje cena kao bitni elemenat socijalisticke economije (Centralised price formation as an essential element of the socialist economy), *Medjunarodni Problemi,* No. 3, Belgrade; Polish translation in Kalecki (1982).
Kalecki, M. (1958c). Czynniki okreslajace tempo wzrostu gospodarki socjalistycznej (Factors limiting the growth rate of a socialist economy), *Gospodarka Planowa,* No. 8.
Kalecki, M. (1958d). O wspolczynniku zamrozenia (On the freezing coefficient), *Ekonomista,* No. 6.
Kalecki, M. (1958e). Plan perspektiwyczny na lata 1961-75 (The perspective plan for 1961-75), *Nowe Drogi,* No. 8, August; English translation in *Polish Perspectives,* No. 3, 1959.

Kalecki, M. (1962). Problemy wlasnej bazy cen krajow RWPG (Problems of the own price basis for CMEA countries), first published in Kalecki (1982).

Kalecki, M. (1963a). *Zarys teorii wzrostu gospodarki socjalistycznej* (Outline of a theory of growth of the socialist economy), Warsaw, PWN, English translation in Kalecki (1972).

Kalecki, M. (1963b). Zagadnienie optymalnej struktury spozycia (The problem of optimum consumption structure), *Gospodarka Planowa,* July, also in Kalecki, 1984; English translation in *Mathematical Studies in Economics and Statistics in the USSR and Eastern Europe,* Vol. I, No. 4, 1966.

Kalecki, M. (1963c). An outline of a method of constructing a perspective plan, in SGPiS, 1963.

Kalecki, M. (1963d). O podstawowych zasadach planowania wieloletniego (On the general principles of long-term planning), *Zycie Gospodarcze,* No. 24; in Kalecki, 1982.

Kalecki, M. (1965). Krzywa produkcji a rachunek efektywnosci inwestycji (Production curve and the evaluation of investment effectiveness), *Ekonomista,* No. 1; English translation in Feinstein (Ed.), 1967.

Kalecki, M. (1971b). Zakres stosowania rachunku efektywnosci inwestycji w gospodarce socjalistycznej (The scope of the evaluation of investment efficiency in a socialist economy), *Gospodarka Planowa,* No. 5; English translation in Kalecki, 1972.

Kalecki, M. (1972). *Selected Essays on the Economic Growth of the Socialist and the Mixed Economy,* Cambridge, CUP.

Kalecki, M. (1982). *Dziela, tom 3: Socjalizm – Funkcjonowanie i wieloletnie planowanie* (vol. 3 of Collected Works on 'Socialism – Functioning and Long-Term Planning', edited by J. Osiatynski), Warsaw, PWN.

Kalecki, M. (1984). *Dziela, tom 4: Socjalism – Wzrost gospodarczy i efektywnosc inwestycji* (Vol. 4 of Collected Works on 'Socialism – Economic Growth and Investment Effectiveness', edited by J. Osiatynski), Warsaw, PWN.

Kalecki, M. and Polaczek, S. (1957a). Uwagi w sprawie metody ustalania cen surowcow podstawowych (Notes on a method for fixing the prices of basic raw materials), *Gospodarka Planowa* No. 4; also in Kalecki (1982).

Kalecki, M. and Polaczek, S. (1957b). Dyskusja o cenach surowcow podstawowych (The debate on the prices of basic raw materials), *Gospodarka Planowa,* No. 9; also in Kalecki (1982).

Kalecki, M. and Rakowski, M. (1959). Uogolnienie wzoru ekonomicznej efektywnosci inwestycji (A generalised formula of investment effectiveness), *Gospodarka Planowa,* No. 11; English translation in Nove and Zauberman (Eds), (1964).

KPpRM-Komisia Planowania przy Radzie Ministrow 1962. *Instrukcja ogolna w sprawie metodyki badan ekonomicznej efektywnosci inwestycji* (General instruction on the methodology for determining the economic effectiveness of investment), Warsaw.

Lange, O. (1956). Budowa nowego modelu gospodarczego musi oprzec sie na dynamice klasy robotniczej i socjalistycznej inteligencji (The construction of the new economic model must be based on the dynamics of the working class and the socialist intelligentsia), *Nowy Drogi,* No. 11-12.

Laski, K. (1965). *Zarys teorii reprodukcji socjalistycznej* (Outline of a theory of socialist reproduction), Warsaw, PWN.

Melzer, M. (1981). Combine formation and the role of the enterprise in East German industry, in Jeffries (Ed.) 1981.

Nove, A. and Zauberman, A. (Eds) (1964). *Studies on the Theory of Reproduction and Prices,* Warsaw, PWN.

Nuti, D. M. (1970). Capitalism, socialism and steady growth, *Economic Journal,* vol. LXXX, March.

Nuti, D. M. (1971). The evolution of Polish investment planning, *Jahrbuch der Wirtschaft Osteuropas,* Band 3.

Nuti, D. M. (1973). The political economy of socialism – orthodoxy and change in Polish texts, *Soviet Studies,* Vol. XXV, October.

Nuti, D. M. (1977). Large corporations and the reform of Polish industry, *Jahrbuch der Wirtschaft Osteuropas,* Band 7.

Rakowski, M. (Ed.) (1963). *Efektywnosc Inwestycji* (Investment efficiency), Warsaw, PWN, English translation 1966, Warsaw, PWN.

Sawyer, M. C. (1985). *The Economics of Michal Kalecki,* London, Macmillan.

Spulber, N. (Ed.) (1964). *Foundations of Soviet Strategy for Economic Growth - Selected Soviet Essays 1924-1930,* Bloomington.

Wolf, T. A. (1985). Economic stabilisation in planned economies, *IMF Staff Papers,* Vol. 32, No. 1, March.

5

Hidden and Repressed Inflation in Soviet-Type Economies: Definitions, Measurements and Stabilisation

Domenico Mario Nuti

5.1 Introduction

Official price trends in the USSR and in the Soviet-type economies have changed markedly through time but have followed a roughly uniform general pattern: hyperinflation at times of war, systemic transition and

Published in *Contributions to Political Economy*, 5, 1986, pp. 37–82. An earlier version of the paper was published as *EUI Working Paper* No. 200, European University Institute, Florence, 1985. Republished in Christopher Davis and Wojciech Charemza (Eds), *Models of Disequilibrium and Shortage in Centrally Planned Economies,* London and New York, Chapman and Hall, 1989, pp. 101–146.

Paper presented at the III World Congress for Soviet and East European Studies, Washington DC, 30 October–4 November 1985. An earlier draft was presented at the AISSEC Conference (Turin 25–26 October 1984), the EUI Working Group on Comparative Economic Systems (Florence, 22 November 1984), and the Department of Economics of Warsaw University (19 April 1985); acknowledgements are due to participants in these events for useful comments. This research is part of an EC funded project on 'East—West Trade and Financial Relations in the 1980s conducted by the author at the EUI.

D. M. Nuti (✉)
La Sapienza, University of Rome, Rome, Italy
e-mail: milica.uvalic@unipg.it

© The Author(s), under exclusive license to Springer Nature Switzerland AG 2023

S. Estrin, M. Uvalic (eds.), *Collected Works of Domenico Mario Nuti, Volume I*,
Studies in Economic Transition, https://doi.org/10.1007/978-3-031-12334-4_5

reconstruction; inflation at times of accelerated industrialisation; stabilisation through currency reform and fiscal measures, followed by modest deflation and a record of substantial price stability, recently broken by the spreading—with fewer and fewer exceptions—of renewed open inflation. This general pattern is due to fairly uniform trends in both policy stances and objective conditions: in theory central planning of both physical and financial flows should enable Soviet-type economies to achieve price stability; in practice the persistence of downward rigidity of money wages, the ambitious growth and accumulation targets, as well as adverse exogenous and systemic factors, have frequently necessitated planned or unplanned price increases.

What is particularly striking, however, is not the frequent departure of Soviet-type economies from price stability, since by and large their price record has been comparatively creditable and often even impressive, but *the persistence of unsatisfied demand at the official prices (especially but not only for consumer goods) regardless of whether these prices were being kept stable, or falling, or rising at slow, fast or very fast rates.*

Market clearing at official prices has been a rare and short-lived phenomenon in the economic life of socialist countries, where *shortage* of both production and consumption goods has been the norm (Kornai 1980), while access to goods and services at the official prices has been the privilege of priority sectors and elite groups. Shortages have taken one or more of the following forms: long searches; queues and waiting lists (including sometimes queues to join waiting lists and waiting lists to join queues); transactions at prices higher than official norms even in state shops (sometimes disguised by nominal changes in product or labels) but more often in alternative black, grey and multicoloured markets; forced substitution of available for unavailable goods; inventories below norm held by distributors and above norm by consumers; extensive holdings and use of foreign exchange; excess liquidity; rationing; barter (which through effective demonetisation suggests the existence of hyperinflationary excess demand). The difference between countries and between periods has been one of degree, ranging from market near-clearing at stable and even falling prices in the early 1950s almost throughout the area after the tough measures of post-war stabilisation, to the simultaneous and dramatic occurrence of shortages in *all* the guises listed above *together with* high official open inflation in post-1980 Poland.

These manifestations of shortage, i.e. excess demand at official prices, are often discussed in Western literature under the heading of 'hidden' and 'repressed' inflation. In Eastern Europe they are rarely discussed, mostly in Hungarian literature as 'shortage' (Kornai 1980, 1982) and in Polish literature (e.g. Herer and Sadowsky 1981), including official documents (Raport 1981), as 'inflationary gap' *(luka)* between the value of available goods and intended purchases out of income, and inflationary 'overhang' (*nawis*, or the cumulated gaps over time). This terminology requires two important qualifications. First, current usage in the literature has been inconsistent but it seems useful and appropriate to define in general 'unofficial inflation' or more precisely 'inflation other than open official', as including both 'hidden' open inflation, i.e. *higher price indices than officially recorded* and 'repressed inflation', i.e. *rising excess liquid balances in the hands of the population with respect to what they would wish to hold if markets cleared at official prices* (see below, Sect. 5.4 on definitions). Second, concepts of hidden inflation require the presence not just of shortage but of *increasing shortage* over time (i.e. increasing excess demand); if excess demand was constant a once-and-for-all increase in official price would be sufficient to eliminate it, and we would not call 'inflation' a once-and-for-all price rise (Portes 1977; though there is inconsistency in usage, even by the same author in the same year, see Portes and Winter 1977, who define repressed inflation as 'the existence of excess demand in the consumption goods market' p. 352). Thus endemic and large shortages at official prices are consistent with falling rates of hidden and repressed inflation (if shortages are increasing at a decreasing rate) or even negative rates (if shortages, though large, are falling).

This paper deals primarily with hidden and repressed inflation in the consumption goods market; it will consider inflationary pressure in general (whether or not it takes the form of open official inflation) with special reference to system-specific sources (Sect. 5.2); discuss briefly the Soviet and Eastern European record of open official inflation (Sect. 5.3); propose a set of definitions for alternative forms of unofficial inflation (Sect. 5.4); review critically a number of existing estimates of 'hidden' (Sect. 5.5) and 'repressed' inflation (Sect. 5.6); sketch an alternative model for analysing repressed inflation (Sect. 5.7) and draw policy implications relevant for the possible paths towards stabilisation (Sect. 5.8), desirable in view of the costs of unofficial inflation (Sect. 5.9). The main propositions of the paper are summarised in Sect. 5.10.

5.2 Inflationary Pressure in the Socialist Economy

The Soviet-type socialist economy is a monetarist paradise where the quantity theory of money applies in its strictest traditional form, but where there is no scope for monetary policy because the quantity of money is automatically adjusted by monetary authorities to planned physical flows (given planned prices) and to the degree of their actual implementation (see Lavlan 1973; Garvy 1977; Zwass 1979; Portes 1981a). There are two monetary circuits, separate in principle and to a broad extent also in practice. The first consists of cash and cash-convertible accounts for the payment of incomes to households (wages, salaries, scholarships, pensions, state purchases from the private sector; liquid assets of the population) who use them for their purchases primarily of consumption goods and services (and also of some physical and financial assets) from the state sector, as well as for all transactions within the private sector. The second monetary circuit consists of bank-money which enterprises can use for transactions within the state sector but not for the payment of personal incomes. The separation of the two circuits, and the planners' *a priori* attempts at balancing incomes and expenditures of the population through wages policy and control (Adam 1979) is the foundation of the traditional claim that inflation can be eliminated under socialism. The instruments for the *a priori* balancing of incomes and expenditures, however, are fiscal instruments and direct controls of wages and of consumption supply; if institutional or physical constraints in the use of these instruments leave an extant inflationary gap the planners have only one instrument of domestic monetary policy, namely the net sale of financial assets to the population,[1] which is however blunted by

[1] Net of government debt redemptions and increases in bank lending to the public; private loans however are modest and do not give banks tangible opportunities of coping with inflationary pressure by means of a credit squeeze.

the traditional ideological resistance to the payment of attractive enough interest rates for fear of creating a new rentier class. Hence the justification for the neglect of monetary *policy* (as distinct from the behaviour of some monetary aggregates such as money incomes and cash balances of the population) in the analysis of inflationary pressure in the Soviet-type economy (on Soviet-type banking and credit see also: Podolski 1972; Lavlan 1973).

Since the last war, in Soviet and East-European countries price stability has been such a major policy commitment that traditionally victory over inflation is regarded as a systemic feature of socialism and one of its claims to superiority over the capitalist system. For instance Kronrod (1960) claims that 'inflation has been eliminated in a socialist society' (p. 364); Dudinsky (1976) lists lack of inflation as one of the features of socialism (together with full employment, steady economic growth, confidence in the future and social justice) which are most attractive to workers in capitalist countries. Glushkov (1982) claims that 'in the developed socialist society' ... 'prices are planned in accordance to the demands of objective economic laws. Planned production and unplanned prices in the market would be incompatible with one another. Stability of the system of prices is assured by the unified and centralised plan for economic development' (p. 24). Similar claims abound. There have been times, however, when open inflation has been the planned instrument for expropriating the private sector or financing investment and defence, or the unplanned result of below-plan economic performance (see next section).

As in the case of capitalist countries, the source of inflationary pressure in Soviet-type economies is to be found in cost factors or in the shortfall of supply with respect to demand, except that these factors (1) exercise a direct influence on market imbalance and neither affect nor are affected by monetary policy; and (2) are influenced by the specific systemic features of the Soviet-type economy.

On the supply side, inflationary pressure can arise from rising costs or from quantity shortfalls. Rising costs may be due to the exhaustion of accessible natural resources, wage growth outstripping labour productivity growth, or imported inflation. Quantity shortfalls arise from: (1) the systematic underplanning (except for the present decade) and underfulfilling of the production of consumption goods and services, built into the traditional principles of Soviet planning, of priority to heavy industry (or also to the so-called A-sector producing means of production, as opposed to the B-sector of consumption goods); (2) the failure to recognise the existence of downward trends in both labour and capital productivity growth (including occasional negative growth) which have been recorded in Soviet-type systems since the mid-1960s, and which are associated partly with the rising costs caused by exhaustion of labour and natural resources reserves, partly with the failure to adjust the centralised allocation system to these changed circumstances; (3) slow growth of agricultural production due to system-specific neglect of investment in agriculture and the adoption of organisational forms (large state and collective farms) which are ill suited to a spatially-diffused and effort-responsive economic activity such as agriculture. These adverse systemic supply factors are sometimes made worse by random supply shocks such as adverse terms of trade (e.g. those experienced by East European countries over the last decade, with the exception of the oil-exporting USSR), world recession depressing export below plans; natural conditions (draught or flood, heat or frost) affecting especially agriculture, building and transport.

On the demand side, inflationary systemic factors include: (1) pressure on wage rates (under the guise of job classification, career structure, and other discretionary decisions of enterprises causing wage drift) because of full employment of labour, through high labour turnover and informal plant bargaining; (2) over-ambitious investment plans exceeding the absorption capacity of the economy (i.e. its ability to finance, install, operate all the new plant and to import necessary inputs, sometimes investment plans at the lower operational levels adding up to more than the overall centrally planned investment target, and also being systematically overfulfilled); (3) the increasing demands of all other items of expenditures (which like investment might crowd out private consumption), such as public consumption and defence.

Cost-push pressures can be and frequently have been absorbed in Soviet-type economies by means of subsidies from the state budget, either boosting the revenue side of enterprise accounts with subsidies on the goods produced or distributed (e.g. foodstuffs) or relieving the expenditure side of enterprise accounts with grants for investments or other costs.

A typical instrument of price stability in this respect is the 'price equalisation' subsidy (or tax, in the case of deflationary trends; see Wolf 1980) for imported commodities, absorbing into the state budget the effects of imported inflation; Wiles (1973, 1974) advocated its introduction as an anti-inflationary measure in Western countries. All these subsidies, however, do not eliminate inflationary pressure but simply transform a cost-push into a demand-pull; to avoid inflation the subsidy component of the state budget will raise the government borrowing requirement or crowd out alternative items of expenditure. Thus subsidies can be a convenient instrument of inflationary control when cost-push pressures are of a cyclical nature, but are ill-suited to deal with permanent shifts (for instance in terms of trade) and even less with sustained trends (such as rising costs of natural resources, especially in the USSR).

The appearance of a shortfall of supply with respect to demand at constant prices—whether due to demand or supply factors, or the transformation of cost-push into demand-pull through state subsidies; whether planned or unplanned—leaves the planners with a very narrow range of choices: additional external finance, *and/or* inventory falls below normal levels *and/or* open inflation, recorded or unrecorded, in state sales or in secondary markets *and/or* additional cash holdings in the hands of the population over and above what would be held if markets cleared at official prices.

5.3 Open Official Inflation in the USSR and Eastern Europe

Open official inflation in the USSR and the Eastern European countries has occurred at hyperinflationary rates at times of war and reconstruction, especially during the transition to the new system, and at lower but still high rates at times of accelerated industrialisation. For instance in the USSR the official price index, which had risen from 100 in June 1914 to 630 in November 1917, had risen to 6200 in July 1918, 60,500 in July 1919, 129,000 in July 1920 and 1,290,000 in January 1921 (Pindak 1983). This was partly due to the destruction of productive capacity and transport, partly the result of a deliberate monetary policy—theorised among others by Preobrazhensky —aimed (especially during war communism 1918–21) at gaining state access to real resources, protecting the workers from inflation (whose full blast was felt by the bourgeoisie and the kulaks) through higher wages which fuelled further inflation, and abolishing money through demonetisation of the economy. The New Economic Policy (1921–28) restored a measure of price stability through conventional fiscal and monetary policies, but a further inflationary wave was brought about by accelerated industrialisation and the need to finance it in spite of downward rigidity of money wages, as well as by collectivisation of agriculture (through its adverse impact on agricultural output) and full employment of labour (which caused high labour turnover and wage drift). Table 5.1 indicates retail price indices from official sources and Western reconstructions for the period 1928–47, at a yearly rate of the order of 17–21% *vis-à-vis* a parallel increase of 12.8% in average nominal wages (the implied trend in real wages grossly underestimating average standard of living growth due to the parallel growth of wage labour employment during the period at a rate faster than population growth), wholesale prices of basic industrial goods remaining much more stable thanks to state cross subsidies from consumption to production goods, to supplement the revenue of enterprises producing production goods. 1947 was an anomalous year, with peak prices and a monetary reform aimed at confiscating much of the purchasing power of the population through a change of the currency that converted prices, wages, savings and cash at rates diversified so as to favour wages and saving deposits with respect to cash (Holzman 1955).[2]

The East European countries that joined the socialist bloc after the last War experienced a similar pattern: inflation at a fast and occasionally hyperinflationary rate during the period of transition to the new system and reconstruction and the early stages of Soviet-type ambitious investment policy (for instance, retail prices in Poland increased by 62.4% between 1946 and 1949, and again by 78.5% in 1950–53; in Czechoslovakia by about 64% between 1948 and 1953; the GDR

[2] In the Soviet Union in 1947 all roubles in circulation were withdrawn and replaced with new roubles at a 10 to 1 ratio, while for bank savings and state bonds the conversion ratio was more favourable. On the day after the reform workers were paid their two-weekly wage in new roubles, at a one-to-one ratio (see Holzman, 1955, p. 232 *et seq.)*.

Table 5.1 Prices and nominal wages in the USSR, 1928–47

	Average percentage annual increments				
	Retail prices in state and co-operative shops			Wholesale prices of basic industrial goods	Average nominal wages
	Official	Chapman	Holzman		
Period	(1)	(2)	(3)	(4)	(5)
1928–47 of which:	17.2	16.2–17.4[a]	21.3	5.6	12.8
1928–37	20.5	22.5–26.3	24.0	12.2	17.6
1938–40	5.9	8.0–9.7	13.0	6.5	10.3
1941–47	18.1	11.5–12.3[a]	21.4	0.8	8.0

Sources: Average percentage annual increments were computed from the following data:

Col. (1): Chapman (1963, p. 157) for 1928–40; Malafeyev (1964, p. 258) for 1940–47.

Col. (2): Chapman (1963, pp. 81 and 87) for 'all commodities'; her two sets of indices in col. (2) reflect different weights, 1928 and 1937 respectively.

Col. (3), (4), (5): Holzman (1960, pp. 168 and 169); for 1940 his January retail price index—and not that of July—was employed.

From: Pindak (1983, pp. 5–6).

[a]Chapman's data refer to 1948 instead of 1947; they do not comprise, therefore, the peak price 1947.

experienced early hyperinflation), followed by monetary stabilisation mainly through Soviet-type currency conversion at diversified and progressive rates. In Poland in 1950 all prices, wages and saving deposits were converted at a rate of three new to 100 old zlotys, while cash was converted at a 1 to 100 rate, thus confiscating two thirds of the cash in the hands of the population (see Montias 1962, pp. 69–70). In 1952 in Rumania and Bulgaria cash holdings were reduced to one fifth and one fourth respectively of their previous value; conversion rates were progressively unfavourable with respect to the amount converted[3]; a similar reform took place in Czechoslovakia in 1953 (see UN-ECE 1953, p. 32).

[3] In 1952 in Rumania prices, wages and state funds were converted at the rate 100 to 5; cast at a progressive rate ranging between 100 to 1 and 100 to 0.25, savings at progressive rates ranging between 100 to 2 and 100 to 0.50. In Bulgaria in the same year the conversion rate was 100 to 4 for prices, wages and state funds, 100 to 1 for cash, while savings were converted at progressive rates ranging between 100 to 3 and 100 to 1.

There followed, throughout the area, three distinct periods (see Table 5.2), a period of falling prices from the time of stabilisation roughly to the late 1950s; a period of remarkable price stability until after the first oil shock and often well beyond it into the late 1970s (thanks to the delayed impact of oil price rises within CMEA trade, the initial absorption of imported inflation through state budget subsidies, and the rise of external borrowing); and a period of open inflation, fuelled by the gradual diffusion of oil price rises, the mounting cost of price subsidies, the slowdown and occasional fall of external finance and the rising pressure of wages. This tendency has become much clearer in the last couple of years, but (see Table 5.3) has not reached two digit rates with the exception of Rumania in 1982 and Poland in 1980 to date (primarily due to the accelerated growth of money wages in conditions of falling labour productivity, the external credit squeeze and its negative cascade effects on supplies through the curtailment of essential imports, the excessive weight of over-ambitious investment plans ineffectively executed, as well as exogenous factors; see Nuti 1981, 1982). By 1983, when major price increases have been recorded even in Bulgaria, though their impact is still not officially assessed, the GDR is the only East European country that can claim an uninterrupted quarter century spell of price stability.

5.4 Definitions: Unofficial, Hidden and Repressed Inflation

Inflationary pressure which does not take the form of open official inflation (including official open inflation in the collective farm market) can express itself through the market in the form of *open non-official (unrecorded)* and therefore *hidden* inflation and/or be *repressed* and remain at the purely potential state of unused liquid assets in the hands of the population over and above their desired level. Both types of inflation are 'hidden' until they are reconstructed from the inconsistencies of official records, fragmentary direct observations and indirect evidence.

Unrecorded—and therefore *unofficial*—*open but hidden inflation* can occur for three different reasons. *First, because of price rises above the official level,* either in state shops or in private markets. Official price lists

Table 5.2 Retail prices and nominal wages in USSR and Eastern Europe, 1948–80 (Average percentage annual rates (+ increase / – decrease)

	USSR	GDR	Cze	Pol	Hun	Bul	Rum
1. Deflationary period:	1948–1957	1951–1960	1954–1961	1954–1961	1954–1956		
Retail prices	–8.2	–6.0	–3.5	–3.9	–1.0	–	–
Nominal wages[a]	+ 3.3[b]	+ 2.9	+3.1	+7.2	+ 6.7[c]		
2. Period of 'retail price stability':	1958–1976	1961–1978	1962–1973	1957–1972	1957–1968	1958–1972	1961–1972
Retail prices	0.0	–0.2	1.0	1.3	0.6	0.5	0.4
Nominal wages[a]	3.6	3.2	4.0	5.2	2.7[d,f]	5.4	–
3. Period of open inflation:	1977–1979	1979	1974–1980	1973–1979	1969–1980	1973–1979	1973–1979
Retail prices	0.7	0.2	1.7	5.3	4.1	1.1	1.0
Nominal wages[a]	2.6	3.0	2.9	10.7[e]	4.8[d]	4.5[d]	5.0[d]
Of which: retail prices in 1979	1.1	0.2	3.8	7.1	8.9	4.6	2.0
In 1980	–	–	3.4	–	10.9	–	–
Nominal wages[a] in 1979	2.2	3.0	2.5	8.8[d]	5.8[d]	5.5	4.8[d]
In 1980	–	–	2.4	13.5[d]	2.6[d]	–	–

Sources: Computed from official data of national statistical yearbooks, various issues; International Labour Office, *Yearbook of Labour Statistics*, various issues, and International Labour Office, *Supplement 1981*, April 1981.
From: Pindak (1983, p. 10).
[a] Gross nominal wages in the socialist sector, unless otherwise stated.
[b] Instead of the non-available average nominal wage in 1947, A. Nove's estimate—550 rubles—was used.
[c] Average rate of 1955 and 1956.
[d] Wages in non-agricultural sector.
[e] Net wages.
[f] Average rate for 1958–1968.

Table 5.3 Retail prices in the USSR and Eastern Europe 1974–83 (average annual percentage growth rates)

Country	1971–75	1976–80	1981	1982	1983
All items[a]					
Bulgaria	0.2	4.0	0.5	0.2	N.a.
Czechoslovakia	0.1	2.1	0.8	5.7	0.9
East Germany	-0.3	0.1	0.2	0.0	0.0
Hungary	3.0	7.1	5.0	6.6	7.2
Poland	2.5	6.8	21.2	101.0	25.0
Rumania	0.5	1.4	2.0	16.0	5.7
Soviet Union	-0.1	0.7	1.4	3.4	N.a.
Food[b]					
Bulgaria	0.6	6.2	0.3	0.2	N.a.
Czechoslovakia	-0.1	1.2	0.0	10.6	0.3
East Germany	0.2	0.0	0.0	0.0	0.0
Hungary	2.2	7.3	3.1	8.2	5.6
Poland	2.9	7.5	30.3	125.0	26.0
Rumania	1.1	1.0	1.7	N.a.	N.a.
Soviet Union	0.3	0.4	1.9	3.8	N.a.
Non-food items[c]					
Bulgaria	-0.1	2.4	0.7	0.1	N.a.
Czechoslovakia	0.2	2.8	1.5	1.5	1.5
East Germany	-1.0	0.2	0.5	0.0	0.0
Hungary	3.7	6.9	6.6	5.5	8.8
Poland[d]	2.5	6.5	13.1	85.0	19.0
Rumania	-0.3	0.6	2.3	N.a.	N.a.
Soviet Union	-0.3	0.8	1.6	2.3	N.a.

Sources: 1980–82: official East European and Soviet statistics. 1983: estimates prepared by the Centrally Planned Economies Service of Wharton Econometrics on the basis of preliminary official statistics published in 1983 plan, fulfilment reports and other official East European statistical sources.

From: Vanous (1984)

[a] In most cases including services.

[b] In most cases including prepared food in restaurants and enterprise cafeterias. Alcohol is included in this category (even in the case of Poland).

[c] In most cases, this item does not include services. It covers primarily prices of industrial consumer goods.

[d] Excluding both services and non-consumption goods.

may lag behind actual prices charged by retailing organisations within their discretionary powers (e.g. for new products, including pseudo-novelties). Quality may deteriorate at constant prices. State goods may be sold at prices higher than state prices by dishonest retailers charging a premium to customers or by buyers reselling in a private market; private producers may supply additional consumption goods and services also at a price higher than the official price (of course profits from private production or redistribution should then be included on the income side of household accounts). When these price premia appear or rise, actual open inflation is higher than officially recorded.

Second, unrecorded open inflation can arise from *quantity weights in official* price indices understating the relative weights of goods whose actual market prices (whether or not equal to the official price) rise relatively faster. In principle quantity weights different from those appropriate to actual prices could lead to a price index bias either way, but systematic official understating is the likely result of cosmetic data manipulation by the authorities, information lags and higher than official price rises. *Third,* unrecorded open inflation can arise from *progressive forced substitution* by consumers of goods which are available at their official price for goods which are not available; usually higher priced substitutes replace cheaper (often subsidised) goods. The use of actual quantity weights instead of dubious and conveniently changing official baskets captures both the possible understating of inflation with respect to equilibrium weights and the inflationary effect of forced substitution over time (though not the loss of consumer surplus involved in the limited access to shortage goods, implicit in forced substitution). As Nove puts it, 'In any system, when price controls exist and the product mix can be varied, the price index will *always* understate price rises ...' (Nove 1981a, p. 145).

If, directly or indirectly, a price index is constructed reflecting actual prices and actual (Laspeyres or Paasche) quantity weights, the actual open inflation rate p can be decomposed into its recorded and unrecorded components, respectively p_r and p_u, given the relationship $(1 + p) = (1 + p_r)(1 + p_u)$. Rates of unrecorded open inflation calculated for each period putting the previous period's index equal to 100 are cumulative over time, but unrecorded open inflation is not 'repressed' in any conceivable sense, as it is an effective outlet for inflationary pressure, and therefore is not cumulative in the sense of contributing to inflationary pressure in the following period through accumulated pent-up demand, as in the case of excess liquid assets of the population (inflationary gap and overhang).

Repressed inflation is rising excess demand which does not take the form of higher prices but remains in the hands of the population as excess liquid assets over their desired level. Thus its definition and measurement requires the prior definition and measurement of 'desired' liquid assets. *In a trivial sense all liquid assets could be considered as desired* because asset holders can always convert any surplus holdings into any good in the free (legal or black) market or into non-shortage goods in the official market. Therefore in the strictest sense there could be 'excess' asset holdings only for inflexibly law-abiding citizens with zero storage facilities, or for people deterred from transacting in the markets to the full extent of their intended purchases because of particularly high transaction costs (in the state market because of abortive searches, queues and waiting; in the free market because of legal and moral restraints, its thinness and inconvenience). Otherwise liquid asset holders will have expressed effective demand up to the point where the marginal utility of current purchases of higher-priced goods in the free market or of forced substitution goods in the state market is equal to the discounted marginal utility of future prospective purchases of goods at official prices (weighed by the probability of their future availability) or at expected free prices, or of additional leisure at the going wage (at least within the period obtainable through voluntary unemployment in between jobs). By and large, any intended purchasing power which cannot satisfy itself in the state market will push up prices in the free (legal and black) market where goods purchased from the state market are re-traded and newly produced goods from the private sectors may be sold, up to the point where demand for liquid assets for transaction and speculation purposes is raised to the level of existing liquid assets; barring extreme hyperinflationary situations where the economy is effectively demonetised, monetary equilibrium in the economy as a whole will be reached or (within the limits set by high transaction costs) approached. *Nevertheless, a significant part, if not all, of liquid assets held by the population in a situation of imbalance in the state market at official prices will be excessive with respect to the assets which the population would wish to hold if it could convert them into goods in that market at those prices.*

Government internal and external borrowing can ease inflationary pressure but the size (and growth) of debt cannot be properly included in excess demand (and repressed inflation), except for the component of debt (and its growth) on which the government may have defaulted.

Once excess demand in the state sector at official prices rises above a critical threshold, repressed inflation steps in; open inflation in free markets can lead to overall monetary equilibrium in the economy as a whole but this is consistent with persistent disequilibrium *in the state sector.* In fact the entire excess of liquid assets over the level which would be desired at the given state price level if the state market had been clearing for a long time, *plus* the liquid assets which the population—having experienced market imbalance instead—would wish to convert speculatively into goods if supply suddenly became infinitely elastic at state prices, at any moment of time is pressing on the state market backing intended purchases with the necessary spending power. Moreover, any unsatisfied demand (overhang) existing at the beginning of a period plus any inflationary gap (intended purchases out of disposable income not matched by goods at official prices) will be carried over into the next period; a sequence of small gaps therefore can cumulate over time to a serious overall level of excess demand. While it is correct to define as repressed inflation, strictly speaking, only the growth rate of this excess demand, past repressed inflation is cumulatively pressing in current markets and would have to be added to current open inflation *in its cumulative entirety* if it were to be transformed into open inflation (its additional contribution to open inflation of course depending on the length of the period over which it was made open). A zero or negative current rate of repressed inflation is therefore consistent with the possibility of massive current imbalance in the state market, which would require an injection of goods, or a tax on liquid assets or a higher rate of open inflation than would otherwise be the case, at rates inversely proportional to the period of time over which the stabilisation is attempted.

There is a connection between unofficial/unrecorded inflation, *plus* officially recorded inflation in non-state markets (such as kolkhozian markets), and repressed inflation. Namely, if the sum of the first two types of inflation is zero (or small), it can be conjectured that the monetary magnitude of excess demand has not grown (much) relatively to money income; however excess demand can still be large, and—following this line of argument—it will have grown approximately as fast as money income.

5.5 Estimates of Hidden Inflation

Three basic methods have been used to estimate inflation rates over and above official levels (including official inflation in recorded legal markets): the direct computation of price indices from available information about quantities and prices of individual categories of goods; the calculation of deflators implicit in indices of monetary and real magnitudes; the purchasing power parity approach to black market exchange rates.

Western economists started recomputing their own price series in the early 1960s: Michal (1971) for Czechoslovakia, Nutter (1962) and Chapman (1963) for the Soviet Union. Michal, for instance, found that retail prices rose in Czechoslovakia by about 64% between 1948 and mid-1953, instead of the officially reported stability depicted in Table 5.2; Chapman's estimates for Soviet retail prices in 1928–47 diverge less from official indices but are also higher than them (except for 1941–47 due to non-comparability of periods; see Table 5.1). The long duration of the price stability achieved in the mid-1950s somewhat lessened interest in independent computations of this kind. When the reliability of official statistics began to be suspect again, after incidents such as Polish under-recording of the 1970 price increases and similar *prima facie* cases for challenging official data, convenience and lack of data led Western economists to use indirect methods.

It is well known that dividing an index of expenditure at current prices by a Laspeyres quantity index one obtains an implicit Paasche price index. Howard (1976a, 1976b) used real consumption estimates independently constructed by Bronson and Severin (1966) and current consumption expenditure indices to calculate lower and upper limits for Soviet state retail and general consumer 'true' or 'actual' price indices. The lower limit is calculated by assuming that there was no hidden inflation in the food sector; the higher limit by assuming that the hidden inflation in food is equal to that in durables and 'soft' goods (see Table 5.4). Howard found

Table 5.4 Howard's estimated and official indices for prices and sales, USSR 1955–72

	State retail price index			General consumer price index			Real sales index on state and co-operative retail market		
	Official	Minimum estimate	Maximim estimate	Official	Minimum estimate	Maximim estimate	Official	Minimum estimate	Maximim estimate
1955	100.0	100.0	100.0	100.0	100.0	100.0	100.0	100.0	100.0
1956	100.0	101.9	102.5	98.8	100.9	101.5	108.7	106.4	107.0
1957	100.0	104.8	108.7	98.4	103.3	106.9	124.0	114.6	118.8
1958	102.2	106.7	107.8	101.0	105.4	106.4	131.7	125.2	126.4
1959	101.4	106.1	107.3	100.1	104.7	105.8	142.3	133.5	135.1
1960	100.7	106.0	108.0	99.6	104.7	106.5	156.7	144.9	147.6
1961	100.0	104.5	105.7	99.7	103.7	104.8	162.5	152.8	154.6
1962	101.4	107.2	108.0	101.7	106.8	107.5	172.6	161.0	162.2
1963	102.2	108.7	108.9	102.9	108.6	108.8	180.8	167.7	168.0
1964	102.2	108.3	108.9	103.3	108.5	109.0	190.4	176.3	177.3
1965	101.4	109.6	111.6	101.6	108.9	110.9	209.1	187.0	190.4
1966	100.7	108.7	110.4	100.4	107.7	109.3	227.4	203.9	207.1
1967	100.7	109.5	112.2	100.4	108.4	110.9	248.6	219.4	224.8
1968	100.7	110.1	113.5	100.5	109.1	112.2	269.2	235.5	242.8
1969	100.7	111.3	115.3	101.4	110.9	114.5	288.9	249.5	258.5
1970	100.7	112.3	117.3	102.0	112.2	116.7	310.6	263.6	275.3
1971	100.7	114.1	120.5	101.4	113.4	119.3	331.7	273.8	289.1
1972	100.7	115.1	122.6	102.1	114.8	121.7	354.3	286.7	305.4

From: Howard (1976a), p. 607

'true' price indices substantially but not devastatingly higher than the official indices, 'true' inflation still being contained within 0.8–1.2% per annum in 1955–72; Howard also found that state and co-operative retail sales have not increased as much as suggested by official indices over the period.

Howard's approach was severely criticised by Rosefielde (1980) and further debated by the two authors (Howard 1980; Rosefielde 1981a). The main point of the debate is the legitimacy of using, for the calculation of an implicit deflator, a quantity index which does not embody the same weights used to construct the monetary expenditure index, and therefore the reliability of Howard's estimates. Admittedly the 'true' price index calculated by Howard is, as Rosefielde contends, a quantity/price 'hybrid'; it remains to be shown, however, that the use of more accurate weights would yield drastically different results. As a 'rough estimate', in Howard's words, the 'true' price index provides an interesting check to the hypothesis of a close-to-true Soviet official index. (Similar rates were computed by Schroeder and Severin 1976, at the yearly rate of 1.3% in 1955–75).

The same line of reasoning followed by Howard is implicit in Portes (1977), who compared directly average increases in money wages (which nobody ever suggested are under-recorded) and real consumption (which he takes from official data, regarded as reliable) in order to obtain indirect confirmation of the thesis that officially recorded inflation was by and large correct in the 1955–75 period. Alton et al. (1979) used their own independent estimates of real consumption growth for the CMEA Six to establish the 'true' inflation rates for 1970–78, which are substantially higher (though still modest by Western standards and in the one-digit range) than official rates except for Hungary (see Table 5.5; for a discussion of Alton's results see also Kohn 1980). Presumably Rosefielde's objection to Howard applies with the same strength to Alton's estimates.

If the purpose of the 'true' indices was that of assessing the truthfulness and efficiency of statistical offices in recording prices and relative quantities of all goods leaving the state shops and all those exchanged in the official non-state sector, then the use of own recalculations or implicit

Table 5.5 East European alternative consumer prices indices

	Price indices 1970 = 100		Average annual change (%)			
	1975	1978	1971–75	1976–78	1978	1979
Bulgaria:						
Official: state retail trade[a]	100.9	102.8	0.2	0.5	1.2	[b]
Official: co-operative market[a]	123.6[c]	137.6	4.3[d]	5.5	[b]	[b]
Alternative	116.0	129.1	3.0	3.2	2.5	[b]
Czechoslovakia:						
Official: consumer retail prices[a]	100.7	103.6	0.1	0.9	0.9	2.5
Alternative	111.4	116.2	2.2	1.6	1.8	[b]
German Democratic Republic:						
Official: consumer retail prices[a]	98.4	98.2	-0.3	0.0	0.0	[b]
Alternative	103.3	108.6	0.7	1.3	0.6	[b]
Hungary:						
Official consumer prices[a]	114.5	130.8	2.9	4.3	4.6	9.0
Alternative	122.4	139.8	4.1	4.4	4.5	[b]
Poland:						
Official: consumer retail prices[a]	113.3	134.1	2.5	5.9	8.1	[b]
Alternative	131.8	168.5	5.7	8.0	8.9	[b]
Rumania:						
Official: commodity prices and service tariffs	102.6	105.4	0.5	0.7	1.5	2.5
Alternative	[b]	[b]	[b]	[b]	[b]	[b]

Source: Alton *et al.* (1979).
[a] The official price indices are described in detail in Alton (see source).
[b] Not available.
[c] 1977
[d] 1976–77

deflators could be good enough. But for discussing hidden and repressed inflationary processes, however, these indices have a major defect. A 'true' price index in fact ought to record ideally the price actually paid *by ultimate users,* both for goods originally purchased in state shops and for goods which private producers might supply. At the same time, 'true' income indices ought to include the total increment that the value of state goods acquire in the (legal or illegal) process of redistribution, and the total value added in private production, so as to make price and income indices mutually consistent.[4]

The existence of a two-tier market, consisting of controlled and (legal and illegal) free segments (see Katsenelinboigen 1977; Morton 1980; Bauer 1983), is fully recognised and modelled in the literature on the 'second economy' (e.g. G. Grossman 1977, 1985; O'Hearn 1980) but is not fully modelled and measured in the literature on unofficial inflation, where the dominant model is that (exemplified by Barro and Grossman 1974) of the 'rationed' quantity-constrained consumer (and firm) and the measurement of market phenomena excludes both the private retrading of state goods and non-state production outside the collective farm sector (which is played down anyway in view of its small relative weight in total consumption expenditure, e.g. by Portes 1979, p. 329). Yet consumers in Soviet-type economies are not at all technically 'rationed' in their *overall* budget constraint; they are only 'rationed' (whether through coupons or at random) in their purchases from state shops at official prices. Their position is that of a consumer facing a two-part tariff with a high marginal price, and with an option on purchases at the lower price of the first part of his tariff—an option which however is not being honoured and which he relentlessly seeks to realise ready to switch all his higher part tariff expenditure and buy more if he only could at any time. Such a consumer would not be regarded as quantity rationed, nor should the consumer in Soviet-type economies. The thinness of the free (legal and illegal) market where state goods are retraded and non-state goods are sold—if that market *is* thin—makes its quantitative impact on hidden inflation small, but the very fact that consumers can, if they wish, convert liquid assets into goods and services in free markets has a major implication also for the definition and measuring of repressed inflation, because the opportunity of transacting in secondary and primary non-state markets naturally makes all liquid assets 'desired'.

[4] Nove's guess-estimate of Polish hidden inflation at 8% in 1975 (Nove 1979) is rejected by Portes because, given official estimates of nominal incomes and consumption price index, would imply 'that real incomes actually fell that year!' (Portes 1984). Yet if, say, half the hidden inflation was due to transactions in private and secondary markets, nominal incomes would also be higher, by 4%, and Nove's assertion – though unsupported – would at any rate be perfectly plausible.

Table 5.6 Culberston and Amacher's estimated average annual rates of inflation, 1963–70 (purchasing power parity method)

Country	Officially reported open inflation (%)	Culbertston and Amacher's estimates (%)
Bulgaria	1.1	3.4
Czecholsovakia	1.2	5.0
East Germany	0.0	3.4
Hungary	0.9	4.1
Poland	1.2	5.5
Rumania	0.4	6.3
USSR	0.1	8.6

Source: Culbertson and Amacher (1972). Estimated actual inflation is equal to US rate of inflation plus domestic currency depreciation with respect to the US dollar in the black foreign exchange market.

Culbertson and Amacher (1972) apply the purchasing power parity theory of exchange rates to black markets for foreign exchange in CMEA countries and estimate actual inflation rates by comparing changes in the black rate of the US dollar—regarded as an equilibrium rate—with trends in the US consumer price index. Any depreciation of the national currency *vis-à-vis* the US dollar is attributed to differential inflation with respect to the US. Their estimates are summarised in Table 5.6; like the other estimates reviewed here, actual inflation is estimated at a substantially higher but still one-digit level. If it worked, this method of indirect estimate of actual inflation rates would reflect trends in the marginal cost to consumers of acquiring goods in free markets, i.e. the inflation rate in those markets rather than in the average cost of living. This method, however, is subject not only to the customary reservations applicable on the purchasing power parity approach to market economies (the neglect of capital flows, the choice of weights, the use of average instead of marginal concepts, etc.) but also to system-specific reservations: (1) no black market price in a two-tier black/white market can be regarded as an equilibrium price; it is usually higher than the equilibrium price but not necessary by the same proportion at different times; (2) black market rates are affected by a number of variable demand and supply factors, which have nothing to do with underlying trends in hidden inflation, such as remittances from abroad, degree of foreign tourist surveillance, toughness of penalties, foreign travel opportunities, official attitude towards emigration, etc.; (3) black market rates have a floor below which the dollar will not fall, given by the ratio between the domestic price of goods (like vodka and cigarettes) widely consumed and with semi-monetary qualities in personal exchange, and their dollar price in special state shops (Beriozka, Pewex, Cedok, etc.) for sales in hard currencies. Thus if the dollar price of a bottle of vodka in a Pewex shop is $1 and its zloty price in ordinary shops is zl. 700, the black market rate for the US dollar will not fall substantially below zl. 700. Thus trends in black market exchange rates reflect the vodka purchasing power parity in domestic ordinary and special state shops, or the equivalent rate for other goods supplied in both kinds of shop at more advantageous rates if supplied and demanded in sufficiently high quantities to make them the marginal rate, rather than any comparison of generalised purchasing power parity. Vanous (1984) suggests the same approach with reference to the Deutschemark, but the same reservations apply; since arbitrage in black markets for foreign currency is far from perfect, cross rates and therefore inflation estimates will differ with the hard currency actually used in the comparisons.

A more interesting and imaginative use of purchasing power parities, which does not lend itself to the criticisms raised here, is made by Askanas and Laski (1985) who, starting from a bilateral comparison of consumption levels in Poland and Austria in 1964, 1973 and 1978 (estimated by the Central Statistical Offices of the two countries in the currencies of either country) calculate the implicit price indices for both countries. They find that implicit indices differ from official statistics and infer that over the period considered either Austrian actual inflation has been over-recorded and has taken place at 3.0% per year instead of the official 5.3%, or Polish actual inflation has been at 5.2% instead of the official under-recorded 2.9%. Since this kind of problem does not arise in similar comparisons among Western countries, and the authors have no reason to believe that Austrian inflation—lowest among market economies in Europe—has been overvalued, they conclude that Polish inflation has been 5.2% instead of 2.9% over the period.

In general, there is an ‘informal consensus of experts’ that ‘official inflation statistics are most reliable for Hungary, followed by Czechoslovakia, East Germany, Bulgaria, Poland and Romania’ (Vanous 1984). When inflation is officially understated, if this is due to actual prices in state markets being higher than official price lists no policy measure is required except official admission that prices are higher than previously claimed; a once-for-all uplift in official inflation (which can be substantial due to the cumulative effects of even small discrepancies over time) will suffice without altering the population's purchasing power. If official understatement of inflation is due to free (black and legal) markets being under recorded, the case for closing the gap between the two price levels is made stronger. Even the total coincidence of 'true' and 'official' inflation rates does not rule out the existence of a possibly large inflationary overhang, already in existence at the beginning of the period for which the comparison is made and growing through time at the same pace as income and expenditure.

The existence and measurement of hidden inflation outside the sphere of consumption goods has also been widely debated (see for instance Becker 1974; Nove 1981a, 1981b; Cohn 1981; Rosefielde 1981b, 1983; Steiner 1982, 1983). The question is interesting for the overall assessment of economic performance in Soviet-type economies, and in particular of the actual size and growth of investment and defence outlays. Inflationary pressures outside the consumption goods sector are bound to spill over into it through direct competition between consumers and firms for some goods and through substitution processes; non-open inflation for non-consumption is likely to take more the form of repressed than hidden inflation, in view of greater restrictions and easier monitoring of financial transactions between firms with respect to redistributive transactions between consumers.

5.6 Estimates of Repressed Inflation

Visible signs of frustrated spending intentions, such as queues, are not by themselves conclusive evidence of repressed inflation. They are not necessary, because spending intentions may be so totally frustrated that queueing is not worth one's time.[5] They are not sufficient, because queues may

[5] 'Do you often have queues as long as these?' 'No, not very often. Only when there are goods in the shops' (Polish humour).

be due to the inefficiency[6] or the under provision of distributive services (Turcan 1977), or to *relative* prices (instead of the overall price index) differing from market-clearing prices (Delhaes 1978; Podkaminer 1983[7]), and not necessarily to the presence of excess demand at official prices. Even if there are visible signs of frustrated spending intentions, they can be misleading for the measurement of excess demand and above all of its rate of change (only which is, strictly speaking, repressed inflation): declared demands may be greater than intended purchases, because they discount a scaling down process (just as in an expectedly oversubscribed share issue in a market economy; a household may be queueing in more than one queue for a single intended purchase); queues may get longer because of an improvement rather than a worsening of the state of supplies.

By itself the increase (even if substantial) of liquid balances in the hands of the population, relatively to income or sales, is also neither necessary nor sufficient as an indication of repressed inflation. Liquid balances may be accumulated because of systemic lack of access to less liquid forms of holding wealth (land, plant, non-state bonds, shares, etc.). Open (official or unrecorded) inflation might require the accumulation of liquid assets to raise transaction balances whose real value has been lowered by inflation. Cash requirements relative to purchases may increase because of the increasing share of transactions taking place in the second economy (Grossman 1977). A more erratic pattern of supply, without any alteration in the overall balance between supply and demand, may raise required cash holdings, desired for speculative purposes; Green (1978)

[6] Often simply moving few people from the queue to behind the counter would eliminate queues and save time all round. Turcan (1977) suggests that in Poland in the mid-1970s queues were due to 'organisational and human factors' more than to shortages (p. 136). Under provision of distributive services is of course by definition excess demand but only for the services, not the goods; a small excess demand for distributive services may appear as large excess demand for goods, because these goods must be jointly purchased together with the distributive service associated with their sale.

[7] Comparing Polish with Italian and Irish data, Podkaminer estimates excess demand for commodity groups and the price changes necessary to eliminate them in Poland in the period 1965–78. He claims that food demand would have been consistently *lower* than supply had it not been for spill-over demand (forced substitution) due to excessively low prices in the 'rent' and 'rest' commodities. To eliminate imbalance food prices should have been *lowered* by 15%, provided that other low-price goods were made correspondingly dearer (Podkaminer 1983, p. 179).

likens this phenomenon to 'the demand for cash balances among New York drug addicts' —or, one might add less dramatically, among antique dealers everywhere.

Nevertheless, the *coexistence* of visible officially recognised signs of frustrated spending intentions *and* the parallel accumulation of increasing substantial liquid assets relative to incomes and sales had been widely taken as a *prima facie* case for presuming excess demand and repressed inflation, or at any rate for considering it as a hypothesis worthy of testing and measurement.

Pindak (1983) is typical of a simple and direct approach to repressed inflation (another instance is Cassel 1984). First indirect evidence of excess demand is considered, such as the falling share of goods officially recognised as not experiencing 'supply difficulties' (for Czechoslovakia in the 1970s, for instance, see Table 5.7); then the ratios of cash and non-cash financial assets to other variables are regarded as indicators which 'express the processes of repressed inflation' ... 'Even if the exact level of forced savings remain unclear ...' (p. 33). These indicators are the average saving propensity, the ratio between cash increments and total income, and especially the income velocity of financial assets (which is reproduced from Pindak in Table 5.8). However as we have just noted there is no systematic necessary relation between these indicators and repressed inflation; moreover Pindak's conclusion that 'the GDR emerges as the country with the most virulent repressed inflation' is contrary to casual observation and other evidence (Flaetgen 1985; see below). Birman (1980a) claims that 'an overwhelming part of all savings is forced' (p. 88),

Table 5.7 Share of goods without supply difficulties in Czechoslovakia, 1972–78

Period	Foodstuffs (%)	Industrial products (%)
1972	58.5	52.0
1973	72.5	43.2
1974	75.0	36.6
1975	66.7	28.2
1976	47.1	28.7
1977	27.9	20.7
1978	35.9	19.0

Source: *Politicka ekonomie*, Prague 1979, Vol. XXVII, p. 458.
From: Pindak (1983), Table 4.

Table 5.8 Pindak's income velocity of household financial assets, 1955–79 (for Czechoslovakia, the GDR, Hungary, Poland and the USSR)

	Ratio between income and household cash				Ratio between income and household non-cash financial assets				
Year	Cze	GDR	Hun	Pol	Cze	GDR	Hun	Pol	USSR
1955	7.4	4.7	–	10.7	15.0	8.5	–	834	10.1
1956	6.1	4.1	9.9	8.1	11.1	7.1	119.8	58.2	9.2
1957	5.5	3.7	10.3	7.9	8.6	5.2	60.5	32.0	7.8
1958	4.7	3.9	9.3	7.3	7.0	4.5	36.6	26.3	7.7
1959	4.3	3.0	7.6	6.9	6.1	3.9	23.3	19.0	7.2
1960	4.2	2.6	6.8	5.5	5.7	3.3	17.0	13.6	7.1
1961	3.9	2.4	6.4	5.5	5.2	2.9	14.6	13.6	7.2
1962	3.6	2.3	5.9	5.0	4.8	2.7	11.7	11.0	7.1
1963	3.5	2.1	5.1	4.6	4.5	2.5	9.0	8.7	6.9
1964	3.2	2.0	4.5	4.2	4.2	2.3	7.1	7.6	6.7
1965	3.1	1.8	4.1	4.0	3.9	2.1	6.1	6.9	6.0
1966	2.9	1.7	3.9	3.8	3.7	1.9	5.8	6.2	5.4
1967	2.7	1.6	3.9	3.5	3.5	1.8	5.8	5.5	4.9
1968	2.7	1.5	3.6	3.3	3.5	1.7	5.3	5.2	4.5
1969	2.8	1.4	3.3	3.1	3.6	1.6	4.8	4.7	4.0
1970	2.5	1.3	3.0	3.0	3.2	1.5	4.9	4.4	3.6
1971	2.3	1.3	3.0	2.9	2.9	1.5	4.3	4.2	3.3
1972	2.1	1.3	2.9	2.8	2.6	1.4	4.1	3.9	3.1
1973	2.0	1.2	2.7	2.5	2.4	1.4	3.9	3.6	2.9
1974	1.9	1.2	2.6	2.3	2.3	1.4	3.8	3.2	2.7
1975	1.8	1.2	2.5	2.3	2.2	1.3	3.6	3.2	2.4
1976	1.8	1.2	2.4	2.2	2.2	1.3	3.4	3.2	–
1977	1.7	1.1	2.3	2.3	2.1	1.3	3.2	3.3	–
1978	1.7	1.1	2.2	2.2	2.1	1.2	3.0	3.2	–
1979	1.7	1.1	–	2.2	2.1	1.2	–	3.2	–

Sources: Computed from the following data:

(a) For Czechoslovakia, the GDR, Hungary and Poland for 1956–75, Rudcenko (1979). The corresponding data for 1976–79 were taken from national statistical yearbooks, various issues.

(b) For the USSR, the data on savings deposits of the households from *Narodnoe khoziaistvo SSSR*, various issues; estimates of household incomes from Schroeder and Severin (1976) (years 1956–59 and 1961–64 were extrapolated).

From: Pindak (1983), Table 5.

talks of 'the colossal surplus of money' and the 'crisis in the circulation of cash' (p. 90; see also 1980b).

Official recognition of excess monetary balances of the population in Soviet-type economies first came in the 1981 official report by the Polish government on the state of the economy (from which Table 5.9 is taken;

Table 5.9 Fundamental magnitudes illustrating the formation of market equilibrium in Poland, 1970–80 (current prices, *zl. bn*)

	1970	1971	1972	1973	1974	1975	1976	1977	1978	1979	1980	Second half year 1980	First quarter 1981
1	2	3	4	5	6	7	8	9	10	11	12	13	14
Sales of goods to the population	395	429	482	544	625	713	813	920	1000	1102	1207	630	309
Sales of services	70	75	82	92	104	119	134	150	162	175	192	98	48
Total goods and services	465	504	564	636	729	832	947	1070	1162	1277	1399	728	357
Dynamics (previous year =100)	—	108.4	111.9	112.8	114.6	114.1	113.8	113.0	108.6	110.0	109.5	108.0	111.2
Total net incomes	489	543	626	717	824	933	1040	1169	1271	1397	1535	797	447
Dynamics (previous year =100)	—	111.0	115.3	114.5	114.9	113.2	111.5	112.4	108.7	109.9	109.8	109.6	119.4
Monetary balances of the population													
Total (zl. bn)	171	198	239	300	370	435	486	538	600	675	766	766	843
of which—savings	117	137	170	213	264	307	339	376	415	464	500	500	542
—cash	54	61	69	87	106	128	147	162	185	211	266	266	301

Source: Raport (1981) p. 127.

Raport 1981), echoing the approach developed by Polish economists (for instance, Herer and Sadowsky 1981) who carefully distinguish inflationary gap *(luka),* i.e. the share of current personal incomes not covered by consumption goods and services at official prices, and inflationary overhang *(nawis,* or current demand out of liquid assets built out of past inflationary gaps and carried over from previous periods). The sum of the two adds up to more conventional 'excess demand'; the distinction between the two components is notional and arbitrary, but it is useful in discussing time processes and *trends.* Without reference to additional evidence, however, or without the support of models and estimates of demand for financial assets, both notions of gap and overhang are also arbitrary and so are their measurements. The same applies to calculations embodying an allowance for an arbitrarily estimated growth of desired financial holdings with respect to a period of market balance and tranquillity (Gomulka 1979).

The first attempt at building an index of repressed inflation is by Holzman (1960) who interprets the ratio between free market price (in the kolkhozian market) and state price for foodstuffs, weighted by the share of output sold in the free market, as an indicator of overall excess demand (which he identifies with repressed inflation); Holzman's series have been updated by Garvy (1977) and Dirksen (1981; see Table 5.10, where the value of the index in 1955 is made equal to 100; see also Portes 1977, 1981b). The index suggests a fall in excess demand (i.e. negative repressed inflation) between 1955 and the early 1970s in the USSR,

Table 5.10 Holzman's indicator of repressed inflation for the USSR, 1955–79 (1955 = 100)

Year	Indicator	Year	Indicator	Year	Indicator
1956	59	1964	39	1972	23
1957	40	1965	28	1973	25
1958	41	1966	24	1974	23
1959	32	1967	24	1975	27
1960	30	1968	22	1976	30
1961	38	1969	25	1977	30
1962	37	1970	22	1978	34
1963	36	1971	22	1979	34

Sources: Holzman (1960), Garvy (1977), Dirksen (1981).

followed by a modest positive rise in the rest of the decade. The notion that, if there is excess demand at state prices and some of it is repressed, the amount of repressed excess demand will be directly related to the impact of non-repressed excess demand on free prices is ingenious and appealing. If this is the underlying rationale of Holzman's original approach, an even better indicator would be provided by the ratio between 'true' price indices such as those discussed in the previous section, and official price indices in state shops (i.e. excluding the kolkhozian market from the official price index) because in that way the varying intensity of excess demand in non-food as well as food intended expenditure is taken into consideration. If the reasoning is accepted, the constancy of the index from one year to the next indicates the constancy of *relative* excess demand with respect to current sales, i.e. the growth of *absolute* excess demand by the same rate as sales—which is convenient for preserving the possibility of multiplying indices of true open inflation and repressed inflation to obtain total inflation.[8] Zero repressed inflation, however, simply means the preservation of the relative excess demand existing in the base period, and if this is large it is hardly a consolation for the planners facing the task of markets stabilisation. Holzman's index, unfortunately, does not indicate the *size* of that excess demand, only its time trend.

Kornai claims that in a situation of *chronic* shortages '... aggregate excess demand is not an operational category ...' (1980, p. 477) and proposes a composite 'shortage index' (Kornai 1982). Partial indicators of shortages are identified: the orders refused by the building industry, unfilled orders for cars, building materials shortage, deviation of household savings from the trend; a macroindex of shortage is then constructed on the basis of time series for the partial indicators (see Table 5.11 for Hungary 1965–78). Like Holzman's index, Kornai's macroindex indicates the dynamics of the phenomenon under investigation, not its absolute size at any time; also, it combines consumption and production goods; these appear as advantages from Kornai's theoretical stance, since

[8] As in the analogous relationship between the recorded and unrecorded components of open inflation, see above. Dirksen contends that the validity of Holzman's indicator rests on state prices having a zero rate of open inflation (1981, p. 307, footnote 1); this is unjustified and would violate the multiplicative relation required by consistent accounting.

Table 5.11 Kornai's macro-index of shortage (based on Hungarian data, 1965–78)

Year	Index based on 14-year time-series	Index based on 9-year time-series
1965	0.412	—
1966	0.430	—
1967	0.429	—
1968	0.544	
1969	0.600	—
1970	0.548	0.548
1971	0.498	0.486
1972	0.400	0.404
1973	0.401	0.401
1974	0.456	0.447
1975	0.508	0.496
1976	0.505	0.503
1977	0.553	0.531
1978	0.496	0.479

From: Kornai (1982).

they avoid the notion of aggregate excess demand and the problem of netting out positive and negative excess demands in different sectors, and allow for the generalised spreading of shortage, when it occurs, across sectors; they seem, however, drawbacks with respect to the observer" and the planner's task of assessing both performance and the difficulty of tasks ahead. Moreover, the particular version of macroindex constructed by Kornai—which shows shortage to be a cyclical phenomenon rather than a trend—may reflect the choice of savings deviation from trend as a partial indicator of shortage, which already *presumes* consumer shortage to be cyclical without a long-run trend.

Attempts at measuring excess demand and the implicit repressed inflation, as well as testing the hypothesis of its existence at the same time, have been developed in econometric studies, and recently have grown considerably with the application of disequilibrium econometrics. Soviet household savings were found to conform to patterns well explored for market economies in early attempts by Volkonskii et al. (1976) using a Houthakker-Taylor savings function and by Pickersgill (1976) using the permanent income hypothesis (see also Pickersgill 1977, 1980a, 1980b). Portes and Winter (1978) provided an estimate of household demand for money and saving functions well tried for market economies (log-linear function for desired balances with a stock-adjustment process; and savings functions based on the absolute income hypothesis and on the Houthakker-Taylor function); they reported successful estimation and found '... no evidence of abnormal behaviour that might suggest sustained disequilibrium ...' (p. 17). Green (1978) replicating a slightly modified version of the same analysis for the GDR reached similar conclusions but found that the attainment of equilibrium appeared to depend upon the availability of food sold at official retail prices, since households accumulate fewer financial assets when food supplies are tight in the GDR (which therefore indicates greater consumption disequilibrium in spite of lower savings when that occurs).

In a subsequent paper Portes and Winter (1980) apply techniques of disequilibrium econometrics to the same problems, applying a discrete-switching disequilibrium model with a household demand equation for consumption goods, a planners' supply equation and 'min' condition stating that the actual quantity transacted is the lesser of the quantity demanded and supplied; they reject 'the hypothesis of sustained repressed inflation in the market for consumption goods and services since the mid-1950s in our four CPEs' (1980, pp. 155–156); indeed, excess supply is regarded as the most probable dominant regime in three out of the four countries (1980, p. 149). A further development of this model was based on the approach of Charemza and Quandt (1982) who postulated the adjustment of planned quantities instead of actual prices; Portes et al. (1983) used new data about plan fulfilment to model an elaborate (plausible though arbitrary) objective function for socialist planners which include plan response to plan fulfilment, and applied the model to Poland in 1955–80. Alternative models are generated, according to slightly different ways of defining and computing excess demand terms; average simulated excess demands for Poland in 1957–80 using the four best performing variants of the model are reproduced in Table 5.12. The startling result is the persistence of low estimates of excess demand (and of the average rates of repressed inflation which are implicit in them over the period), even for the country and the years where indirect evidence suggests that excess demand and repressed inflation were at their peak. Thus in 1980 Poland simulated excess demand for the best four models

Table 5.12 Average simulated excess demands (%), Poland 1957–80

	Model I	Model IIa	Model III	Model Vb
1957	3.0	3.7	0.7	-3.6
1958	-4.1	-1.8	-2.5	-3.9
1959	0.8	0.7	-0.8	1.0
1960	-6.8	-5.5	-5.2	-4.4
1961	5.1	2.2	1.7	1.4
1962	-4.1	-3.1	-2.8	-2.0
1963	-0.3	-1.5	-0.8	-0.6
1964	-4.2	-2.5	-3.1	-1.6
1965	-1.1	-0.8	-1.0	1.8
1966	-3.5	-2.0	-3.0	1.0
1967	-3.0	-1.1	-2.1	-0.7
1968	0.4	1.8	0.5	2.5
1969	-0.9	1.6	-0.8	0.2
1970	-0.2	0.9	0.1	-1.0
1971	4.5	3.8	2.2	2.5
1972	0.7	5.0	0.9	7.0
1973	-3.0	1.8	-2.3	2.7
1974	-0.9	3.6	-0.3	1.2
1975	1.0	2.2	-0.4	2.8
1976	-1.0	-0.8	-2.4	-2.9
1977	-1.5	-1.3	-2.6	-0.1
1978	-10.7	-7.1	-7.2	-8.7
1979	1.5	0.4	0.4	1.2
1980	1.2	-0.1	0.5	1.2

From: Portes et al. (1983).

ranges from a maximum of 1.2% in two of the models to -0.1% (i.e. excess *supply*, though at a negligible rate).

Charemza and Gronicki (1982, 1984) and Charemza (1984) apply the 'rational' expectations hypothesis (pioneered by Muth 1961) to a disequilibrium model *à la* Barro and Grossman (1976), embodying households demand for consumption and money and supply of labour; wages adjust to workers' expected excess demand and primary plans drawn on enterprises' expectations of labour shortages and aggregated and adjusted to labour supply by central planners. Estimated excess demands for consumption and labour, absolute and relative to the quantities transacted, are included in Table 5.13; rising trends can be observed for all variables, with a U-shaped pattern for percentage excess demands (with turning

Table 5.13 Charemza and Gronicki's estimates for absolute and percentage excess demand for consumption and labour

	Absolute estimates		in % of quantity transacted	
Year	Consumption in bn zl.	Labour in ml. of employees	Consumption	Labour
1960	15.1	0.373	6.20	3.01
1961	16.6	0.351	6.29	2.79
1962	16.1	0.532	5.74	4.15
1963	13.2	0.234	4.43	1.79
1964	15.2	0.309	4.82	2.35
1965	17.2	0.140	5.04	1.03
1966	20.3	0.089	5.53	0.64
1967	20.2	0.365	5.07	2.54
1968	19.6	0.265	4.51	1.80
1969	16.2	0.428	3.54	2.84
1970	13.9	0.269	2.84	1.77
1971	30.8	0.039	5.81	0.25
1972	48.4	0.261	8.08	1.65
1973	62.8	0.971	9.30	6.01
1974	79.7	0.919	10.34	5.58
1975	81.4	2.273	9.27	7.68
1976	86.0	1.313	8.48	7.93
1977	87.6	0.826	7.72	5.00
1978	80.4	1.169	6.51	7.03
1979	92.1	1.985	6.81	12.00
1980	117.7	2.133	7.74	12.93

From: Charemza and Gronicki (1984), Table 2, p. 82.

points in 1970 for consumption and 1971 for labour).[9] Charemza and Gronicki also define 'balancing price' p_B as the price level which would have equated the value of actual purchases to the value of intended purchases at actual prices. The difference between the p_B index and the actual price index p_{60} obtained by putting 1960 = 100 is regarded as a measure

[9] From the data reproduced in Table 5.13 Charemza and Gronicki calculate an index of 'degree of repressed inflation' (RID) defined as the difference between the excess demand index evaluated in constant 1960 prices and the price index for particular years (Charemza and Gronicki 1984, p. 88). The RID index has the drawbacks of comparing indices (of excess demand and of prices) not weighted by their respective volumes of transactions, of not possessing the multiplicative properties of price indices (differences between indices being very rough approximations to the trend of their ratios for the large relative changes recorded) and of measuring *changes* in excess demand with respect to the base year and not its degree. The Charemza and Gronicki index for the 'degree of repressed inflation' (1984, Table 4) is therefore meaningless.

Table 5.14 Charemza and Gronicki's balancing and observed price indices for consumption goods, Poland 1960–80

	PB	P60	
Year	1960 = 100-0		PB-P60
1960	106.2	100.0	6.2
1961	107.6	100.9	6.7
1962	109.4	103.5	5.9
1963	108.9	104.3	4.6
1964	111.1	106.0	5.1
1965	113.0	107.6	5.4
1966	114.6	108.6	6.0
1967	116.0	110.4	5.6
1968	117.4	112.3	5.1
1969	118.0	114.0	4.0
1970	118.8	115.5	3.3
1971	123.4	116.6	6.8
1972	126.2	116.8	9.4
1973	131.7	120.5	11.2
1974	141.6	128.3	13.3
1975	144.2	132.0	12.4
1976	151.3	139.5	11.8
1977	158.2	146.9	11.3
1978	169.0	158.7	10.3
1979	180.8	169.3	11.5
1980	200.6	186.2	14.4

From: Charemza and Gronicki (1984), Table 5, p. 91.

of excess demand (Table 5.14), better than that indicated in Table 5.13 in that it conveniently peaks in 1980 as direct observation would have suggested.[10]

There are a number of criticisms and reservations which could be raised against the econometric estimates of excess demand and its rates of change reported here, to try and reconcile the generally low estimates with the more widespread impressions of large scale and growing imbalance. Thus, for instance, the use by Portes et al. (1983) of deviations from

[10]As in the RID index, mentioned in the previous footnote, differences between indices only approximate trends in the ratios between them; even accepting the proposed approach the appropriate measure of the proportional excess of P_B over P_{60} is $(P_B/P_{60}-1)$ and not $(P_B - P_{60})$, which here systematically over-estimates excess demand. When properly calculated excess demand still peaks in 1974 at 10.4%, later falls to 6.5% in 1978 and rises again to 7.7% in 1980. Cumulative rates of repressed inflation can be calculated as the growth rates of these excess demand indices.

trend in households' financial assets could be thought to rule out from the outset the possibility of a trend of increasing excess demand and explain the closeness of their results to Kornai (1982) who does the same. Labour supply negatively responding to market imbalance (Charemza and Gronicki 1984) in spite of constraints in workers' choice of working time may have over-estimated excess demand in the labour market and under-estimated it for consumption goods.

Rational expectations—which many would regard as inappropriate to model market economies, let alone centrally planned ones—leaving hardly any room for the unexpected might have been crucial to the results reported by Charemza and Gronicki (who specifically use them) and Portes et al. (who approximate them in two of their model variants).

Even without this kind of criticism, however, it is perfectly possible to reconcile estimates of low excess demand and repressed inflation with the widespread concern for market imbalance expressed by many observers and officials alike: consumers may be quantity rationed in their purchases from the state sector at state prices, but are not rationed in their purchases in the non-state sector where non-state goods may be supplied and state goods may be retraded at higher prices. Excess demand at state prices is channelled into the non-state sector driving prices there up to the point where liquid balances for transactions plus those speculatively held are voluntarily demanded by the population. This point is made strongly and persuasively by Gregory Grossman: '... it would seem that the very presence of a large secondary economy, and in particular of a black market, in a sense does away with repressed inflation, despite fairly rigid control of official retail prices. In the second economy, prices tend to be high enough to eliminate any overall 'monetary overhang' (that is, excess of purchasing power over the total supply of goods and services at effective prices) and to forestall a repressed inflationary situation in relation to the controlled and non-controlled sectors taken together' (1977, in Tanzi 1982, p. 259). Hartwig (1983) also stresses that involuntary real money balances are removed already in the short run for their overwhelming part, 'partly by increasing prices in the second economy, partly by a renewed rise in the demand for liquid assets'; the rise in transaction costs (queueing, bribes, information costs, etc.), growing informal transactions and 'the desire to possess liquid assets in order to take advantage of unexpected opportunities cause economic agents to convert involuntary into voluntary money balances' (Hartwig 1983, p. 104). Brus and Laski (1983), though concurring with this general view, regard the speculative element in money holdings as dependent on the maintenance of lower state prices and therefore properly classified under excess demand; this is an important condition for the stability of the free market which, however, does not make speculative cash holdings any less voluntarily held. By and large, except for temporary excess balances due to time lags in adjusting to monetary shocks, 'enormous amounts of involuntary liquid assets in the private sector seem very implausible'[11] (Hartwig 1983, p. 105).

If there is no hidden or open hyperinflation, and no differential transaction costs in the free and the controlled market, a properly constructed and specified econometric model *should* give zero excess demand all the time and therefore zero repressed inflation. Since we know from direct evidence that there was no hidden or open *hyper*-inflation in the period and countries considered, estimates of positive excess demand must be due to factors such as the use of price indices different from the 'true' indices, consumer restraint from transacting fully on free markets (out of Party loyalty, fear of penalties or lack of storage space) and more generally differential transaction costs. However information costs and any other inconvenience in the free market cannot be much greater than the cost of searching and queueing in the controlled market; Party-loyal citizens are likely to have privileged access to goods and large storage space, while less enlightened citizens are likely to be less deterred by penalties and to be willing to go to great lengths to realise their purchasing power (within the

[11] With the existence of an extended second economy, postulated generally for the CPEs of Eastern Europe, growing cash and savings bank deposits do not indicate forced saving, but only show that private households are unwilling to pay the higher prices on the different types of markets outside the public sector, to pay bribes, or to incur other forms of transaction costs. They prefer liquid assets. Likewise queueing does not indicate that people cannot buy what they wish and therefore cannot spend their money, as is often argued. Queueing only shows that private households evaluate the disutilities of queueing less than the disutilities arising from higher prices in the second economy or from paying bribes. Every economic unit can choose to spend its money outside the public sector and obtain goods more rapidly, but at higher costs, or to wait for a favourable occasion. The respective behaviour is determined by various expectations. However, the decision to accumulate money and near-money under these circumstances is voluntary (Hartwig 1983, p. 104).

limits set by expected future prices, probability of supply and time preference, as indicated in the previous section): excess demand *in the economy as a whole* is likely to be small.

This is the good news. The bad news is that *most and possibly all* of the liquid assets in the hands of the population are pressing at any time onto the lower priced and quantity constrained state sector.[12] Intended purchases at *state prices* will be equal to the quantity which would have been demanded at those prices if no market imbalance has been experienced recently, *plus* speculative demand[13] expressed on the reasonable expectation that recent market imbalance at those state prices might reoccur in the near future (within the constraints set by storage opportunities and by expectations about likely appreciation at future free prices relative to interest foregone plus physical depreciation and other storage costs). Excess demand *in the state sector* is equal to these intended purchases minus actual supplies, and *this* can be large and increasing fast even if excess demand in *the economy as a whole* is constantly held at zero by inflation in the non-state sector whether or not officially recognised. In the presence of this phenomenon, which has very considerable economic costs to the economy (not to count political costs to the regime), claims about the absence or low incidence of excess demand sound somewhat frivolous and the rough and ready estimates of experts in the field (whose main fault is that of not distinguishing between the state sector and the whole economy) appear more credible, as an indication of the existence and size of market imbalance and the gravity of the problem confronting central planners, than the spurious precision of advanced econometrics, which almost tautologically defines imbalance out of existence.

---

[12] '... repressed inflation (excess demand in our terminology) *in the state goods market* persists even when the collective farm market clears' (Gardner and Strauss 1981, pp. 392–393). These authors, however, infer from this the existence of excess (involuntary) money balances in the economy as a whole, which as we have seen is not necessarily the case. See also Wimberley (1981) on the 'involuntary' nature of most transactions in the second economy.

[13] In the summer of 1985 water authorities facing drought in Florence did not ration water in spite of water reserves gradually falling to zero because they expected the introduction of rationing would raise current demand over the normal level through consumers building up their own reserves, filling up their bath tubs and therefore demanding more water than usual at the same price. In the same way, once supply of any good falls substantially below equilibrium at the going price, consumers will demand at that price more than the normal equilibrium level, lowering their liquid asset holdings below the normal equilibrium level.

5.7 An Alternative Model

Let us consider a Soviet-type economy in a state of persistent equilibrium: consumption markets clear and have cleared without inflation for the last *h* years of relevant consumer memory (*h* being of the order of magnitude of, say five years), at a uniform price level in state and non-state sectors. Money (i.e. liquid financial assets) is demanded both to finance current transactions and as a component of consumers' portfolio, i.e.

$$M_{\mathrm{d}} = M_{\mathrm{T}} + M_{\mathrm{K}} = M(Y,P,K) \tag{5.1}$$

$$M_{\mathrm{S}} = 0 \tag{5.2}$$

where:
M_{d} = consumers' demand for money,
M_{T} = consumers' demand for transaction purposes,
M_{K} = consumers' demand for money as an asset,
Y = money incomes,
P = the price level,
K = the money value of consumers' total assets,
M_{S} = consumers' speculative demand for money.

Differences between money incomes and current expenditure add to (or diminish) the stock of money held by consumers adjusting it to the desired level over time. In the position considered here equilibrium has prevailed for *h* periods during which

$$P = P^{*} \tag{5.3}$$

$$M = M^{*}\left(Y,P^{*},K\right) \tag{5.4}$$

where M is the money in existence and the asterisk indicates equilibrium magnitudes in conditions of persistent equilibrium. These are the conditions which prevailed, or were approximated, in the Soviet Union and Eastern Europe roughly in the second half of the 1950s, after the experience of price stability and mild deflation.

Next we can imagine the appearance at time t of *creeping repressed inflation,* i.e. excess demand at prices P^*_{t-1} prevailing previously. The price level is held at P^*_{t-1} but $P^*_t > P^*_{t-1}$. An excess demand appears and may even grow over time, but the following conditions are fulfilled: (i) excess demand appears and remains at below a critical fraction of current consumption supplies (or, which is the same, the value of excess demand is below a critical fraction of M_T); thus excess demand grows no faster than consumption; (ii) no open inflation appears (whether officially recorded or unrecorded); (iii) shortages are sporadic, not persistently concentrated always in the same sectors; they are accompanied by excess supply in other sectors and shortages of individual commodities can fall as well as increase. Welfare is reduced because of the absolute shortfall and because of forced substitution, but the persistent expectation of availability of goods in the future at constant prices and at a small but positive real interest rate leads consumers to hold speculatively any surplus money over and above desired transaction and asset demand. Within the bounds of the three conditions listed here, there is infinitely elastic demand for money on the part of consumers for speculative purposes, a kind of liquidity 'trap' which however in the circumstances of the Soviet-type is not at all a 'trap' (catching the economy on its way to full employment) but rather a shelter protecting it from open inflation.

$$M_S = M - (M_T + M_K) \text{ subject to conditions (i)–(iii).} \quad (5.5)$$

These conditions prevailed, or were approximated, in Eastern Europe in the 1960s, and well into the 1970s for the Soviet Union and especially the GDR (thanks to its special relation with the FRG which transforms structural imbalances into a less intense overall imbalance, preventing spill over effects of concentrated shortages).

The acceleration of the relative weight of shortages, their concentration, or generalised upward trend, lead to *open inflation,* whether hidden or officially recorded. When inflation first appears, or when it accelerates, if the price increase is initially calibrated to respond to the scale of the shortfall of consumption with respect to current income there will remain residual inflationary pressure because at least some of the former M_S will be switched towards current purchases. This is why higher prices, when decreed after a spell of creeping repressed inflation, are either pitched at too low a level with respect to equilibrium in current markets or, if prices are pitched at the equilibrium level, they will have to be higher than the long-term equilibrium level consistent with the given flow of real consumption and of monetary income, in which case they are perceived as an unwarrantedly drastic cut in the standard of living and strongly resisted.

Open inflation may and often does lead to the establishment or rapid growth of a two-tier market: the state sector where price P_1 prevails, and price P_2 in the second economy where a fraction of the goods originally supplied by the state sector are retraded and additional goods are supplied. Thus (for each commodity, though here we assume for simplicity that there is a homogeneous single consumption good) we have:

$$P = P_1 C_{S1} + P_2 \left(C_{S2} + C_K \right) \quad (5.6)$$

where C_K is the consumption supplied by the non-state (kolkhozian and other) sector, C_{S1} and C_{S2} are the parts of state-supplied consumption C_S respectively consumed directly and retraded in the second economy. Retrading and non-state output raise income by the same amount of the value added by these activities, i.e.

$$Y = Y_S + \left(P_2 + P_1 \right) C_{S2} + P_2 C_K . \quad (5.7)$$

Therefore the second economy does not eliminate excess demand by its *direct contribution* (if any) to the reduction of supply shortfalls. It may contribute to the absorption of excess demand through its higher transaction requirements of cash per value of turnover; this is likely to be the case but is not necessary to the equilibrating role of the second economy. Ultimately, excess demand is eliminated by P_2 rising high enough to raise the demand for money for transaction purposes and (given time preferences, expected free prices, and expected state prices times the likelihood of their availability at those prices) speculative demand for money. An equilibrium is reached at prices P_2^{**} such that:

$$M = M_{\mathrm{T}} + M_{\mathrm{S}} = \tilde{M}\left(Y, P_2^{**}, \bar{P}_1\right) = M^{**}. \tag{5.8}$$

The process through which equilibrium is reached is similar in the capitalist and the Soviet-type economy. In a capitalist economy with a full-fledged monetary and financial system there cannot be 'too much money' in the sense of excess liquid assets in the hands of the public with respect to their desired level. Any excess bonds can be converted into cash; any excess cash can be spent on goods driving up their price (which reduces the excess also indirectly by raising cash requirements for transactions); any remaining excess cash can be used to reduce outstanding debt or raise net credits *vis-à-vis* the banking system, any excess cash within the banking system can be deposited with the Central Bank; the interest rate and its structure will be influenced by all these moves, but in this way 'excess' liquid assets ultimately will be eliminated and can only appear as a temporary phenomenon due to the length and structure of lags involved in the adjustment process. In the Soviet-type economy there are constraints affecting this process: price controls lead to price rises only outside the formal sector, the interest is kept at low levels to prevent the rise of rentiers and the existence of two monetary circuits slows down both the transmission of shocks and the adjustment process; the two-tier formal and informal price system causes queues and other transaction costs but otherwise the adjustment process is the same.

It follows from the temporary and unlikely character of *overall* excess demand, and from the existence of a second economy where state goods are retraded and possibly additional goods supplied, that the consumer-rationing model *à la* Barro and H. Grossman is not at all suitable for Soviet-type economies outside the extreme case of distribution exclusively through actual ration coupons without retrading, i.e. war communism. While Barro and H. Grossman specifically stress their assumption that there is no secondary trading in a two-tier market, and do not claim their results to apply outside their model's assumptions, Howard's use of that model in spite of his recognition of 'the uncontrolled or free consumer goods market' (which, moreover, is restricted to the kolkhozian market) is illegitimate. The same consideration applies to Portes' theoretical (1979, which considers not only current consumption but also expectation of future consumption as quantity-rationed) and empirical work (Portes et al. 1983), Charemza and Gronicki (1982, 1984) and others. Consumers are indeed quantity-rationed in the state sector but they are not subject individually to overall quantity constraints since they can always spend their money in the secondary market. It follows that the 'supply-multiplier', i.e. the rounds of reduction in labour supply (and therefore consumer goods supply) which are alleged as a consequence of quantity constraints, do not necessarily occur and can only be expected to be present in the same circumstances in which labour supply would respond negatively to open inflation. Moreover, demand functions in the presence of *persistent* and large quantity-rationing must differ from the case of sporadic, occasional and small rationing.

Under-recording of the actual price level faced by consumers (whose actual average income is inclusive of second economy value added) is due to four possible causes:

1. P_1 being higher than its recorded level;
2. P_2 being higher than its recorded level;
3. the relative weights of C_K with respect to C_S being under-recorded;
4. the neglect of C_{S2} being ultimately purchased by consumers at P_2 instead of P_1 (though, for the purpose of calculating consumers' total purchasing power income is also under-recorded unless Eq. (5.7) is used to restate it).

In the extensive literature on 'hidden' inflation considered above (Sect. 5.5) the first three sources of under-recording are discussed and attempts are made for their estimate; while demand for money and the income to which demand for money is related should depend on P as defined in Eq. (6) and not on $P_1\ C_S + P_2\ C_K$ as in standard work (Howard, Alton, Askanas and Laski etc.). The same, more comprehensively defined, price level should be used in econometric work *à la* Portes. Once hidden inflation is properly accounted for, any residual excess demand which might be detected must be due to adjustment not being instantaneous, because of lags in stock adjustment behaviour or to storage capacity constraints (restricting effective demand) and similar factors unlikely to be large.

Hence it is not surprising to find econometric studies estimating it to be small, as in the literature surveyed above (in the previous section). Money which, in view of the opportunities afforded by the second economy, is voluntarily held by consumers is, however, involuntarily held in so far as consumers would only too willingly unload on to the state sector at state prices their entire cash holdings except for $\tilde{M}(Y_S + P_2 C_2, P_1)$. Hence the alarmed assessment and the admittedly rough estimates of observers who claim there is large imbalance is also correct, and indeed has greater merit if the question is 'do Soviet-type economies face a large-scale stabilisation task?' instead of 'are there forced savings?' or 'are official authorities lying?'. Cumulative hidden inflation can be dealt with at a stroke simply by updating official price lists and/or recalculating official price indices with the appropriate weights; but the quantification of the stabilisation task, the policy measures and the alternative *paths* towards the restoration of market clearing at a uniform price and of price stability is much harder both to theorise and to implement.

There are very few *a priori* propositions which we can make about the size of the task and the price trends which would restore equilibrium:

1. The price level which would restore equilibrium is not a single valued magnitude but an inverse function of the period over which equilibrium is to be restored;
2. The range of prices over which this re-equilibrating price would have to be pitched, as a function of the period of transition to equilibrium, presumably has a maximum level of P_2 because, once consumers have to pay prices higher than P_1 in the state sector, their real income is reduced and they could not afford to pay P_2 for the rest of their purchases. However, an awkward complication is created by the possibility of consumers, formerly willing to hold cash balances in the expectation of future purchases at given expected state and free prices, now revise upwards their price expectations and unload at least some of their balances into the present market, possibly driving the range of re-equilibrating prices above the current P_2;
3. The re-equilibrating price will be greater than P^*, i.e. the price which would preserve equilibrium if it had been in force for the last h years;

4. The re-equilibrating price being a function of the period of transition to equilibrium, it cannot be identified with current P, which is *a* weighted average of P_1 and P_2, but not necessarily the average corresponding to the selected period of transition.

These propositions may not provide much assistance for actually assessing the gravity of the problem faced by planners, but at the same time are strong reasons for rejecting measurements of hidden and repressed inflation put forward in the literature reviewed above. Estimates of hidden inflation can be rejected because they neglect the weight of secondary transactions involving state goods, and because the actual price index relative to the official one does not indicate the 'true' extent of current excess demand, or the 'true' price level which if prevailing in the state sector would restore equilibrium. Diverging estimates of repressed inflation—whether crude or based on advanced econometric methods—can be reconciled in so far as crude pessimistic assessments can be referred to policy propositions and optimistic econometric assessments can be referred to a much stricter (and policy-irrelevant) definition of the problem; both approaches, however, neglect the problem's time dimension (being instantaneous measurements) and complexity (i.e. the difference between the equilibrium level which would *preserve* equilibrium and the time path of prices which would *restore* it). Both features of the problem have strong policy implications.

5.8 Implications for Market-Clearing and Stabilisation

In market and Soviet-type economies the availability of monetary instruments is radically different. In the market economy the measures available include: direct controls over bank lending, raising of reserve requirements, special (compulsory and unprofitable) deposits to be held with the Central Bank by commercial banks, funding of government debt, open market operations, raising of the bank rate, etc. In the Soviet-type economy some of these monetary instruments can be used *if the economy has got out of planners' control* to reinstate that control and restore planning: controls over bank lending, interest rate policy for firms. Once the economy is back in the grip of planners, however, none of these instruments can be used. In the household sector the interest rate cannot be raised and net issues of government bonds at low interest rates do not find buyers unless an element of formal or informal compulsion is introduced in which case they become just a form of taxation. In the firms sector, if financial flows have already been dovetailed to plans for output, any sales of bonds, additional interest rate payment, direct control of credit, would have to be matched and therefore neutralised by a government subsidy to firms to enable them to fulfil plans. Thus money can be an instrument of monitoring plan execution (the 'control by the rouble' of Soviet textbooks), not a policy instrument. The same applies to taxation in the firms sector. The burden of market adjustment will fall on firms under the guise of changes in output plans, in which case financial adjustments can be made.

In the Soviet-type economy, therefore, once money incomes in the state sector have been fixed, market stabilisation, understood as the restoration of a single market-clearing price will take one or a combination of three policies which do not involve monetary means: (i) price rises; (ii) taxation of wealth (not income tax because, if after-tax income could have been lowered, money incomes would have been fixed at a lower level); (iii) supply rises. Both in academic and official circles the discussion of effective stabilisation policies in a search for *the* equilibrium price *level,* or the once-and-for-all capital levy (mostly in the form of a currency conversion at diversified rates, see Sect. 5.3 above), or the level of the once-and-for-all or recurring increase in supplies which must take place to stabilise the market. The problem, however, is more complex and has a time dimension.

It is more complex because the price level at which markets would clear if they had been clearing for the last *h* years of consumers' relevant memory will only preserve market equilibrium, if everything else remains unchanged, *after* equilibrium has been reached and maintained for *h* years. That price level, however, will be too low to *restore* equilibrium even given all the time in the world. The time dimension is involved not only under the guise of h (a parameter of the formation of consumers' expectations, which is influenced not by economic but by political factors, i.e. the credibility of governments and of their commitment to market clearing) but as the length of the period over which first market clearing is to be achieved, and then a transition to equilibrium ratios between assets, income and sales is to be implemented. In fact the price level necessary to absorb all excess demand will be inversely related to the length of time over which such absorption takes place. For instance, if the liquid assets which the population would like to convert into goods in the state sector are equal to six months of state sales at current prices, it will take a price level twice the current level to reach equilibrium in six months, six times the current level to reach it in one month, fifty per cent higher to reach it in one year and only 10% higher to reach it in three years, with disequilibrium persisting at gradually falling levels during the period of transition. Once market clearing at a uniform price is reached, consumers having exhausted their excess liquid reserves will not be able to maintain their real purchases at the going price; the price level will have to *fall*. After h periods consumers will be persuaded that market clearing will persist and they will begin to replenish their liquid assets and reduce their inventories of goods towards their long-run equilibrium levels. For markets to clear at a constant rate of supplies and constant money incomes prices will have to fall again for a period of time V'' equal to the ratio of the difference between equilibrium and current money holdings ($M^* - M_{V+h}$) to the decrease in the market value of the constant supply of goods (per unit of time) caused by the price fall. After a time V'' has lapsed, consumers will have reached their long-term equilibrium holdings of liquid assets M^* but further cyclical perturbations will follow unless the authorities promptly decree a price increase that brings prices to their equilibrium P^*. At that point, and not before, market clearing is associated with price stability. The process is illustrated in Fig. 5.1.

Planners do not know beforehand the value of h, M^{**} or M^*; they need to know these values in order to complete the process neither later nor sooner than they intend, but they do not have to know them to execute a stabilisation programme. As long as the planners set a price level at which consumers cannot afford to buy up current supplies out of income

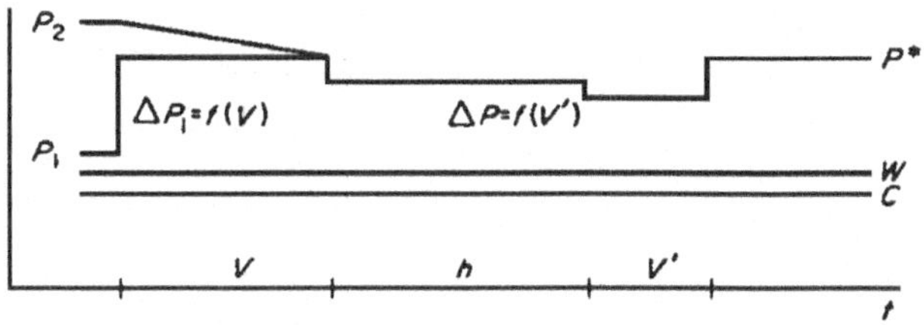

Fig. 5.1 Stabilisation through price policy

alone, sooner or later they will complete the first stage of market stabilisation after a time V corresponding to the price increase and whatever $M - M^{**}$ is. If, as is likely, the strictest constraint on the stabilisation programme is the rate at which the excess liquid assets can be depleted, i.e. the highest state price level the population is prepared to put up with, planners' ignorance of M^{**} does not matter at all. They will know that the length of time V has been completed when they experience a generalised rise in inventory levels. At that point they can let prices find their own level; they will know the second stage of stabilisation is completed and the hth period has arrived after V when at those prices they will see a further generalised rise in inventories. Again they can let prices find their own level but after a while they will experience lower than normal inventories. The authorities will know from this sign that they have just overshot the end of the further V' periods. They will have to raise prices but if they let the market find its level a dampened fluctuation around the long-run equilibrium level of liquid assets and prices will follow; this might be preferable to attempts at guessing what the equilibrium level is, which might cause disturbances worse than dampened fluctuations. At the end of the V periods after an initial mild price fall, which is desirable in itself to penalise speculative hoarding of goods and stabilise expectations, it may be preferable and more expedient to raise incomes instead of lowering prices further, in order to allow consumers to replenish their cash holdings. The trouble is that the lower prices cannot be maintained after the end of period $V + h + V'$ when consumers have replenished their cash holdings; for the higher income level to be maintained, prices would have to undertake a final hike, to the P^* equilibrium level. This policy variant mixing prices and incomes measures is illustrated in Fig. 5.2.

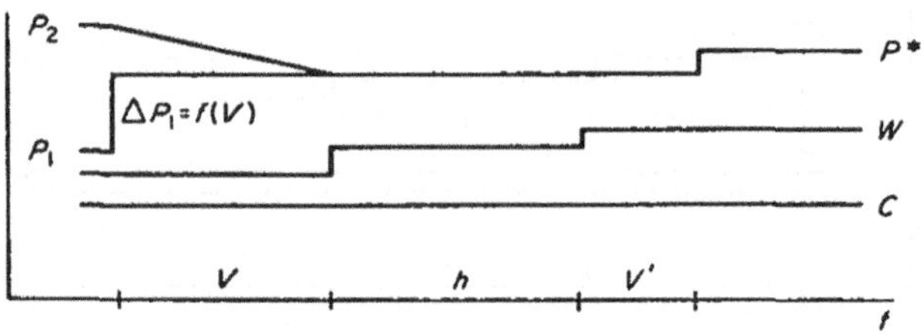

Fig. 5.2 Stabilisation through prices and incomes policy

Reliance on a wealth tax or on increased supplies to restore equilibrium can now be easily illustrated by highlighting the differences with respect to the previous case during the three stages of stabilisation, of lengths *V*, *h* and *V'*. A conversion of the currency confiscating the excess part of real value of liquid assets would shorten period *V* to zero. Beside the advantage of speeding up the stabilisation process, the conversion has other enormous advantages: it can confiscate purchasing power at progressive rates; it confiscates totally those liquid assets which originated from illegal profits to the extent that they cannot be laundered; even if a constant (i.e. non-progressive) part of liquid assets are confiscated, the measure is not *regressive,* as a generalised price increase which forces greater consumption cuts on people who do not hold liquid assets would be. The only disadvantage of a confiscatory currency conversion is that it takes longer to print the new currency and execute the manoeuvre than to decree higher prices; there is a greater chance of a leak, in which case all liquid assets would become instantaneously 'surplus' in the whole economy (including the non-state sector): serious market disruptions and social disturbances might be set in motion unless the manoeuvre is swiftly and efficiently executed. Also, there may be—without real justification—greater *odium* for the government in a single large-scale confiscatory move than in an equally confiscatory price rise diluted over a period of time *V.* If the conversion is pitched at the 'right' rate, equivalent to M^{**}/M units of the new currency for one old, market-clearing will be instantaneously reached and from that point onwards the story will continue as in the previous case: prices will fall for *h* periods, fall further for another *V'* periods, after which equilibrium can be attained (see Fig. 5.3), or approached through dampened fluctuations (or incomes may

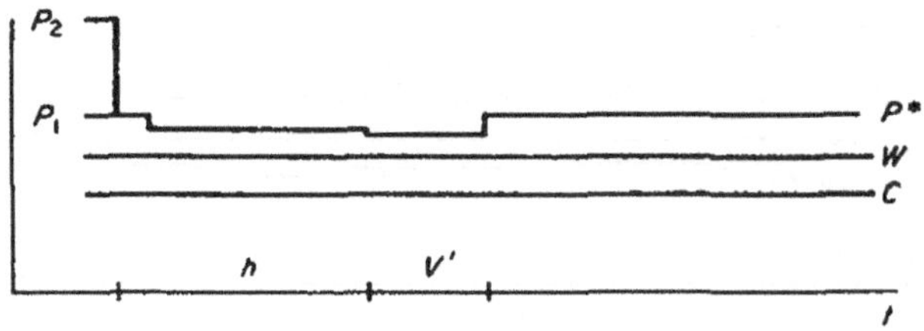

Fig. 5.3 Stabilisation through currency reform

undertake compensatory inverse changes, as in the previous case). The period of mild open deflation experienced by the Soviet Union and other East European countries after the currency conversions at the turn of the 1950s (see above, Sect. 5.3 and Table 5.2) can well be attributed to the necessary overshooting implicit in achieving market-clearing, whether instantly or through a period of confiscatory inflation. The experience of those conversions suggest that the conversion had been pitched at rates which were either correct or slightly lower (i.e. more confiscatory) than necessary. If the conversion is not pitched at the appropriate rate, because planners do not know the value of M^*, other instruments (prices, incomes, income taxes or supply changes) will have to be used, rather than making further clumsy attempts at currency reform.

If stabilisation were to be achieved through changes in supplies the corresponding path is the parallel of stabilisation through price changes. Namely, incomes and prices remain unchanged while supplies must rise over and above what consumers can afford at current prices out of income, for a length of time V inversely related to the improvement in supplies, until liquid assets reach M^{**}. At that point, signalled by inventories rising above normal levels, supply could fall below the previous level for h periods, fall further for V periods and then be pitched at the long-run equilibrium level exactly when consumers reach asset holdings M^*. The path is illustrated in Fig. 5.4.

An infinite number of alternative paths can be generated by mixing in different proportions the three policy alternatives. The best course would be the following: (i) smooth the course of real consumption, switching resources from accumulation to consumption if this can be done without reducing growth—as it probably can if the structure of investment is more

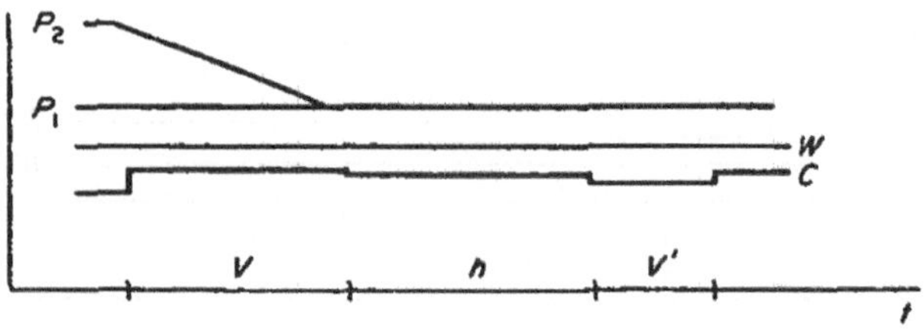

Fig. 5.4 Stabilisation through supply policy

efficiently planned and executed—or at any rate without a growth cost greater than the value put on market stabilisation; (ii) maintain the existing level of money incomes, or if necessary raise them at any time as little as possible consistently with the maintenance of social peace (or at least of law and order without extreme measures); (iii) execute a currency reform aimed at instantly obtaining market clearing at a uniform price level within and outside the state sector; (iv) aim at the maintenance of the price level during the *h* periods of the second stage of stabilisation, lowering income tax rather than raising incomes or lowering prices (if social pressure imposes higher incomes than required by the manoeuvre, then maintain the increase as low as possible and allow prices to increase so as to preserve market-clearing); (v) continue with this kind of policy during the *V*″ periods of the third stage of stabilisation; (vi) raise income tax and if necessary hike the price level once and for all at the end of the period to make current incomes and liquid assets consistent with the consumption flow. Others might prefer other courses; the choice is political, but one thing is sure: the path to market-clearing and to stabilisation is more complex than the simplistic pitching of an equilibrium price level as usually suggested in discussions about repressed inflation and in policy documents.

5.9 The Cost of Hidden and Repressed Inflation

If overall excess demand in a two-tier Soviet-type economy is supposed to be small, in the limited sense that a sudden and extensive 'flight out of money' with hyperinflationary consequences is highly unlikely, the question might be asked whether hidden and repressed inflation have a cost for the economy which is high enough to warrant the effort of reaching and maintaining market clearing and stabilising prices.

Hidden inflation has a distorting informational effect, if people actually believe official indices, but since consumer choice will be guided by actual prices the unreliability of official indices is likely to have little effect (except perhaps in wage negotiations). Excess demand at state prices, however, through queueing, informal exchanges and a two-tier price system, does have considerable costs. Queueing time is a direct and sizeable loss of leisure; it is also a transaction cost which, together with the other additional costs of the two-tier market (which often has three or many more tiers, neglected here for simplicity) reduce consumer welfare. There are illegal and immoral implications of two-tier markets and the non-state production sector (pilfering to supply inputs in the non-state sector, etc.). Short of actually rationing supplies with coupons, distribution of real consumption acquires an element of chance which cannot be reduced by fiscal measures; it is as if money consisted of lottery tickets, a system which nobody has ever sponsored. Speculative stockpiling by consumers instead of shops can be wasteful. The persistence of a sellers' market depresses quality of goods and keeps producers out of touch with consumers' wishes, leading to unnecessary inefficiency; persistent excess demand is the main obstacle to the introduction and to the effectiveness of economic reforms, which is a considerable cost in itself. It is doubtful—or at any rate controversial—whether inflation has a real cost in a capitalist market-economy; apart from adverse distributional effects (which can be mitigated or eliminated by compensatory payments to the needier and weaker sections of society) the only tangible drawback being the restriction that inflation poses on the scope of division of labour and therefore welfare. These costs of open inflation are bound to be even smaller in a Soviet-type economy, where redistribution measures can be taken even more swiftly than in a market economy, and the degree of 'division of labour' can be planned regardless of inflation. Open inflation, therefore, is undoubtedly a better alternative than persistent excess demand.

It may or may not be the case that an environment of generalised abundance will make it possible to reduce the scope of markets (of 'commodity production' in Marxian parlance) without adverse effects on labour supply, moral hazards, etc., but it is absurd to pretend that abundance has been achieved already when it has not. As long as markets are used for the distribution of at least some consumption goods, there can be no doubt that the restoration of equilibrium in those markets at a single price is a desirable, indeed essential task for the socialist planner. Markets may be rightly distrusted in their role in investment allocation, and even in the allocation of current resources (for the neglect of externalities, inability to deal competitively with increasing returns, etc.), but remain unrivalled systems of distributing whatever amounts and kinds of consumption goods and services a socialist economy of the Soviet-type makes available to its citizens, apart from public goods (and possibly saturated needs). There is nothing 'socialist' or even 'Marxist-Leninist' about excess demand. There is nothing in the original design or in the philosophy of socialism that justifies the distribution of consumption goods and services to the population through the inefficient, unfair and degrading mechanisms of queueing, informal exchanges and barter. Marx had incited his followers to change the world, not to pretend that they had changed it: if socialism, through a combination of bad luck and ill judgement, has failed to deliver price stability it is better to recognise it than to ignore this failure or treat it as a passing temporary self-regulating minor phenomenon. The persistence of excess demand, indeed the elevation of shortage to a systemic feature, leads to a *prima facie* case for suspecting that it is maintained primarily because it conceals the privileges of the elite through exclusive access to luxuries and necessities at abnormally low prices, while market-clearing prices would reveal and quantify privilege, as its maintenance would require drastically more unequal incomes and wealth.

5.10 Summary and Conclusions

In a centrally planned economy of the Soviet-type, inflationary pressures may arise due to planning error, unfavourable exogenous factors and downward inflexibility of money wages (Sect. 5.2). These pressures do not always take the form of open official inflation (Sect. 5.3) in view of systemic commitment to the maintenance of price stability; in this case inflationary pressures take the form of hidden and/or repressed inflation.

Hidden inflation is a differential between official (state and non-state) price indices and the actual cost of living to consumers; it arises from understatement of actual prices (in the state and non-state sectors) and/or of the relative weight of the more inflationary goods or sectors. Repressed inflation is *rising* excess demand for goods and services at the actual prices in the state and non-state sectors, i.e. rising excess liquid balances in the hands of the population (often the very existence of excess demand is defined as 'repressed inflation'; see Sect. 5.4).

Estimates of hidden inflation in the recent literature (reviewed in Sect. 5.5) are based on direct recomputation of indices, the calculation of implicit deflators and international comparisons of purchasing power parities. These estimates neglect the impact on the price level of the retrading of goods originally supplied in the state sector and other production and distribution activities outside the state sector (except the collective farm market), i.e. they understate the price differential in the controlled and uncontrolled (legal and illegal) market. Also the *actual* price level, being an average of prices in a two-tier system, cannot be identified with an 'equilibrium' level.

Excess demand and its rate of change (i.e. the rate of repressed inflation) are the object of wildly diverging estimates (Sect. 5.6). These range from alarmed outcries of impending financial catastrophe, based on the visible growth of financial (cash and non-cash) assets with respect to income and expenditure, to cool dismissive counterclaims that excess demand is negligible, based on the observation of uncontrolled transactions in the second economy and on econometric testing and quantification. Econometric models based on quantity-rationing consumer behaviour models seem inappropriate in view of uncontrolled-price transactions where individual consumers are *not* rationed, and therefore the postulated adverse feedback on labour supply is not necessarily present. By and large excess money holdings in the economy as a whole (i.e. with reference to the two-tier market) can be deemed to be small regardless of reliance on econometric evidence, except for the presence of lags and other minor factors which might slow down the adjustment of money balances to the actual two-tier price level. However, the small size or even absence of excess money holdings (and therefore of repressed inflation) is consistent with large-scale imbalance *in the state sector*, since consumers who—given the two-tier market—voluntarily hold liquid assets, do not refrain voluntarily from converting most or all of them into goods in state shops where they *are* quantity-rationed.

A simple model has been presented illustrating the complexity and time profile of the problem under discussion, due to the difference between the price level which would *preserve* equilibrium if it had been prevailing for a sufficiently long period, and the price levels (depending on the speed of adjustment) and their time paths which can *restore* market clearing at single prices starting from a two-tier market in a state of imbalance (Sect. 5.7). The model has been used to analyse states of persistent equilibrium; creeping repressed inflation (i.e. excess demand growth being tolerated because it remains diffused, fluctuating and not exceeding a critical average threshold); hidden inflation (as defined above in this section) and excess demand/repressed inflation which, when referred *to the state sector*, is large and endemic in Soviet-type economies.

Alternative stabilisation paths and their combinations have been investigated, using as policy instruments the price level, a liquid wealth tax (or currency conversion) and supply improvements (Sect. 5.8). All paths have three stages: transition to market clearing at a single price (instantly reached only with a currency conversion at the 'right' rate) which implies overshooting with respect to long-run equilibrium, restoration of market-clearing habits on the part of disillusioned consumers, and eventually the replenishing of liquid asset holdings by reassured consumers.

Finally, the costs of hidden inflation and above all of excess demand (and repressed inflation) in the state sector, and the two-tier market associated with excess demand at state prices, are discussed (transaction costs, misallocations and hindrance of economic reform, random distributive effects, etc., see Sect. 5.9) and are found to be greater than the cost (if any) of open inflation. In sum, the task of stabilisation in Soviet-type economies is seen as large-scale, time-consuming and complex, and its implementation imperative.

Bibliography

Adam, J. (1979). *Wage Control and Inflation in the Soviet Bloc Countries,* London, Macmillan.

Alton, T. H. *et al.* (1979). Official and alternative consumer price indexes in Eastern Europe, selected years, 1960-78, *Working Papers,* L.W.I.F.R., New York, September.

Askanas, B. and Laski, B. (1985). Consumer prices and private consumption in Poland and Austria, *Journal of Comparative Economics,* Vol. 9, No. 2, June, 164-177.

Barro, R. and Grossman, H. (1974). Suppressed inflation and the supply multiplier, *Review of Economic Studies,* Vol. 41, 87-104.

Barro, R. J., and Grossman, H. I. (1976). *Money, Employment, and Inflation.* Cambridge University Press: London.

Bauer, T. (1983). A note on money and the consumer in Eastern Europe, *Soviet Studies,* Vol. XXXV, No. 3, July, 376-384.

Becker, A. S. (1974). The price level of Soviet machinery in 1960, *Soviet Studies,* Vol. XXVI, July, No. 3, 363-373.

Birman, I. (1980*a*). The financial crisis in the USSR, *Soviet Studies,* Vol. XXXII, No. 1, January.

Birman, I. (1980*b*). A reply to Professor Pickersgill, *Soviet Studies,* Vol. XXXIII, No. 4, October.

Bronson, D. and Severin, B. (1966). Recent trends in consumption and disposable money income in the USSR, *New Directions in the Soviet Economy,* U.S. Congress, JEC, Washington, pp. 495-530.

Brus, W. and Laski, K. (1983). Repressed inflation and the second economy under central planning, Conference on 'The Economics of the Shadow Economy', Bielefeld.

Cassel, D. (1984). Inflation in socialist planning economies – causes, effects and policy options of inflation in Soviet-type command economies, Working Paper No. 64, Fachbereich Wirtschaftswissenschaft Universität Duisberg-Gesamthochschule.

Chapman, J. G. (1963). *Real wages in Soviet Russia since 1928,* Cambridge, Mass.

Charemza, W. (1984). The centrally planned economy in the international crisis: Poland 1974-80, CREES Annual Conference, Cumberland Lodge, Windsor, July.

Charemza, W. and Gronicki, M. (1982). Rational expectations in a disequilibrium model for centrally planned economies: the case of Poland, Discussion paper on econometrics and statistics, No. 14, University of Gdansk, March.

Charemza, W. and Gronicki, M. (1984). Simultaneous consumption-labour-money analysis in disequilibrium framework: Poland 1960-1980, CREES Discussion paper, University of Birmingham, March.

Charemza, W. and Quandt, R. E. (1982). Models and estimation of disequilibrium for centrally planned economies, *Review of Economic Studies,* Vol. LXIX, 109-116.

Cohn, S. H. (1981). A comment on Alec Nove 'A note on growth investment and price indexes', *Soviet Studies,* Vol. XXXI II, No. 2, April, 300-301.

Culbertson, W. P. and Amacher, R. C. (1972). Inflation in the planned economies: some estimates for Eastern Europe, *Southern Economic Journal,* Vol. 45, No. 2, 380-393.

Delhaes, K. V. (1978). Mis-allocations as cause of inflationary processes in centrally administered economic systems, analysis of a model, *Jahrbuch für Socialwissenschaft,* Vol. 29, 282-286.

Dirksen, E. (1981). The control of inflation? Errors in the interpretation of CPE data, *Economica,* Vol. 48, August, pp. 305-308.

Drewnowski, J. (Ed.) (1982). *The Polish Disease,* London, Croom Helm.

Dudinskiy, I. (1976). Ekonomicheskie zakonomiernosti mirovoi sistemy sotsialisma, *Voprosy ekonomiki,* No. 9, 23-33.

Flaetgen, S. (1985). Monetary Stability in a Centrally Planned Economy – the case of the GDR, PhD dissertation, European University Institute, Florence.

Gardner, R. and Strauss, J. (1981). Repressed inflation in the Soviet Union: a temporary equilibrium approach, *European Economic Review,* Vol. 16, No. 2-3, 387-404.

Garvy, G. (1977). *Money, Financial Flows and Credit in the Soviet Union,* Cambridge, Mass., Ballinger.

Glushkov, N. T. (1982). Tsenoobrazovanie i khoziaistvennyi mekhanizm, *Ekonomika i organizatsiia promyshlennogo proizvodstva,* No. 9, 3-33; also in *Problems of Economics,* August 1983, 24-56.

Gomulka, S. (1979). Poland's economic situation in the second half of the 1970s, *Osteuropa Wirtschaft,* Vol. 24, 13-23.

Green, D. W. (1978). Household expenditures and the demand for money in the German Democratic Republic (mimeo).

Grossman, G. (1977). The second economy of the USSR, *Problems of Communism,* September-October, 25-40; also in Tanzi (1982) pp. 245-269.

Grossman, G. (1985). The second economy in the USSR and Eastern Europe: a bibliography, Paper No. 1, Berkeley-Duke Occasional Papers on the Second Economy in the USSR.

Hartwig, K. H. (1983). Involuntary liquid assets in Eastern Europe: some critical remarks, *Soviet Studies,* Vol. XXXV, No. 1, January.

Herer, W. and Sadowsky, W. (1981). Nawis inflacyjny: I: Zjawisko i mechanizmy; II: Reforma cen, *Zycie Gospodarcze,* No. 32 and 33.

Howard, D. H. (1976*a*). A note on hidden inflation in the Soviet Union, *Soviet Studies,* Vol. XXVIII, No. 4, October.

Howard, D. H. (1976*b*). The disequilibrium model in a controlled economy: an empirical test of the Barro-Grossman model, *The American Economic Review,* Vol. 66, No. 5, 871-879.

Howard, D. H. (1980). Hidden inflation in the Soviet Union: a reply to Professor Rosefielde, *Soviet Studies,* Vol. XXXII, No. 4, October.

Holzman, F. D. (1955). Financing Soviet Economic Development. In *Capital Formation and Economic Growth* (pp. 229-287). Princeton University Press.

Holzman, F. D. (1960). Soviet inflationary pressures, 1928-1957: causes and cures, *Quarterly Journal of Economics,* Vol. LXXIV, No. 2, May, 167-188.

Katsenelinboigen, A. (1977). Coloured markets in the Soviet Union, *Soviet Studies,* Vol. 29, January, pp. 62-85.

Kelly, A. C., Sanderson, W. C. and Williamson, J. G. (1983). *Modelling Growing Economies in Equilibrium and Disequilibrium*, Duke Press Policy Studies, Durham, N.C.

Kohn, M. J. (1980). Consumer price developments in Eastern Europe, US Congress, JEC.

Kornai, J. (1980). *Economics of shortage* (2 vols), Amsterdam, North Holland.

Kornai, J. (1982). *Growth Shortage and Efficiency – A Macrodynamic Model of the Socialist Economy,* Oxford, Blackwell.

Kronrod, Ya. A. (1960). *Den'gi v sotsialisticheskom obschestve,* Gosfinizdat, Moscow.

Lavlan, Y. (Ed.) (1973). *Banking, money and credit in Eastern Europe,* Brussels.

Malafeyev, A. (1964). *Istoriya tsenoobrazovaniya v SSSR,* Moscow.

Michal, J. M. (1971). Price Structures and Implicit Dollar-Ruble Ratios in East-European Trade. With Special Reference to Czechoslovakia. *Weltwirtschaftliches Archiv*, 159-180.

Montias, J. M. (1962). *Central Planning in Poland,* Yale University Press.

Morton, H. W. (1980). Who gets what, when and how? Housing in the Soviet Union, *Soviet Studies,* Vol. XXXII, No. 2, April, 235-259.

Muth, J. F. (1961). Rational expectations and the theory of price movements, *Econometrica,* Vol. 29, pp. 315-335.

Nove, A. (1979). Inflation in communist countries, in *Political Economy and Soviet Socialism,* London, Allen and Unwin, pp. 178-191.

Nove, A. (1981*a*). A note on growth, investment and price-indexes, *Soviet Studies,* Vol. XXXIII, No. 1, January, 142-145.

Nove, A. (1981*b*). A reply to Stanley Cohn, *Soviet Studies,* Vol. XXXIII, No. 2, April, pp. 300-301.

Nuti, D. M. (1981). The Polish crisis: economic factors and constraints, *The Socialist Register 1981,* Merlin Press, London; reprinted in Drewnowski (1982).

Nuti, D. M. (1982). Open and repressed inflation in Poland 1975-1981, NASEES Annual Conference, Cambridge, 27-29 March.

Nutter, G. (1962). *Growth of Industrial Production in the Soviet Union,* Princeton.

O'Hearn, D. (1980). The consumer second economy: size and effects, *Soviet Studies,* Vol. XXXII, No. 2, April, 218-234.

Pickersgill, J. (1980a). A long-run demand function for money in the socialist economy, *Journal of Money, Credit and Banking,* No. 1, February.

Pickersgill, J. (1976). Soviet household saving behavior, *The Review of Economics and Statistics,* Vol. 58, May, No. 2.

Pickersgill, J. (1977). Soviet inflation: causes and consequences, *Soviet Union/Union Soviètique,* Vol. 4, 297-313.

Pickersgill, J. (1980b). The financial crisis in the USSR, a comment, *Soviet Studies,* Vol. XXXII, No. 4, October, 583-585.

Pindak, F. (1983). Inflation under central planning, *Jahrbuch für Wirtschaft Osteuropas,* Vol. 10/2, reprinted in SUERF Reprint Series, No. 29, Tilburg, 1984.

Podkaminer, L. (1983). Estimates of the disequilibria in Poland's consumer markets (1965-1978), in: Kelly, A. C. *et al.,* 1983.

Podolski, T. (1972). *Socialist Banking and Monetary Control,* Cambridge, CUP.

Portes, R. (1977). The control of inflation: lessons from East European experience, *Economica,* Vol. 44.

Portes, R. (1979). Internal and external balance in a centrally planned economy, *Journal of Comparative Economics,* Vol. 3, No. 4, December, pp. 325-345.

Portes, R. (1981*a*). Central planning and monetarism: fellow travellers? Working paper No. 782, NBER, Cambridge, Mass., October.

Portes, R. (1981*b*). Reply to E. Dirksen, 'The control of inflation? Errors in the interpretation of CPE data', *Economica* Vol. 48, August, pp. 309-311.

Portes, R. (1984). The theory and measurement of macroeconomic disequilibrium in centrally planned economies, (mimeo), CEPR, October.

Portes, R., Quandt, R., Winter, D. and Yeo, S. (1983). Macroeconomic planning and disequilibrium estimates for Poland, 1955-1980, *Working Paper* No. 1182, NBER, Cambridge, Mass., August.

Portes, R. and Winter, D. (1977). The supply of consumption goods in centrally planned economies, *Journal of Comparative Economics,* Vol. 4, December, 351-365.

Portes, R. and Winter, D. (1978). The demand for money and for consumption goods in centrally planned economies, *Review of Economics and Statistics,* Vol. 60.

Portes, R. and Winter, D. (1980). Disequilibrium estimates for consumption goods markets in centrally planned economies, *Review of Economic Studies,* Vol. 47, 137-159.

Raport o stanie gospdarki (cited as 'Raport') (1981). Nakladem Trybuny Ludu, Warsaw, July.

Rosefielde, S. (1980). A comment of D. Howard's estimate of hidden inflation in the Soviet Union retail sales sector, *Soviet Studies,* Vol. XXXII, No. 3, July.

Rosefielde, S. (1981*a*). Hidden inflation in the Soviet Union: a rejoinder to David Howard, *Soviet Studies,* Vol. XXXIII, No. 4, October.

Rosefielde, S. (1981*b*). Are Soviet industrial-production statistics significantly distorted by hidden inflation? *Journal of Comparative Economics,* Vol. 5.

Rosefielde, S. (1983). Disguised inflation in Soviet industrial sector: a reply to J. Steiner, *Journal of Comparative Economics,* Vol. 7.

Rudcenko, S. (1979). Household money income, expenditure and monetary assets in Czechoslovakia, GDR, Hungary and Poland, 1956-1975, *Jahrbuch der Wirtschaft Osteuropas,* Vol. 8, pp. 431-450.

Schroeder, G. E. and Severin, D. (1976). Soviet consumption and income policies in perspective, US Congress, JEC, *Soviet Economy in a new perspective,* USGPO, Washington D.C.

Steiner, J. E. (1982). Disguised inflation in Soviet industry, *Journal of Comparative Economics,* Vol. 6, September, 278-287.

Steiner, J. E. (1983). Disguised inflation in Soviet industry: a final reply to Steven Rosefielde, *Journal of Comparative Economics,* No. 4, December, 449-451.

Tanzi, V. (Ed.) (1982). *The Underground Economy in the US and Abroad,* Lexington, Mass., Lexington Books.

Turcan, G. (1977). Some observations on retail distribution in Poland, *Soviet Studies,* Vol. XXIX, No. 1, January, 128-136.

UN-ECE (1953). *Economic Survey of Europe since the War,* Geneva.

Vanous, J. (1984). Macroeconomic adjustment in Eastern Europe in 1981-83, *Wharton Centrally Planned Economies Current Analysis,* Vol. III, No. 28-29,23 April.

Volkonskii, V. A., Solovyev, J. P. and Semenova, I. V. (1976). Voprosy modelirovaniya denezhnykh sberezhenii naseleniya, *Ekonomika i matematicheskiye metody,* No. 3.

Wiles, P. J. D. (1973). Cost inflation and the state of economic theory, *Economic Journal,* Vol. 83.

Wiles, P J D. (1974). The control of inflation in Hungary, January 1968-June 1973, *Economie appliquée,* No. 1, Paris.

Wimberley, J. (1981). The Soviet financial crisis? A comment, *Soviet Studies,* Vol. XXXII I, No. 3, July.

Wolf, T. (1980). On the adjustment of centrally planned economies to external economic disturbances, in Marer and Montias (1980).

Zwass, A. (1979). *Money, Banking and Credit in the Soviet Union and Eastern Europe,* London.

6

Cycles in Socialist Economies

Domenico Mario Nuti

In the Marxist-Leninist project of socialist economy the elimination of cycles in economic activity is the expected result of central planning replacing the 'anarchy' of capitalist markets. *Ex-ante* coordination of the activities of government, households and firms according to a consistent, feasible and efficient plan should, in principle, ensure the continued full employment of labour and other resources along smooth growth paths instead of the recurring bouts of booms and recessions and persistent unemployment characteristic of capitalism.

The experience of those capitalist countries which, especially since World War II, have tried to implement a social-democratic version of this

This chapter was originally published in John Eatwell, Murray Milgate and Peter Newman (Eds), *The New Palgrave: A Dictionary of Economics*, Vol. I, Macmillan, London, 1987, 1st edition, 1987, pp. 744–746.

D. M. Nuti (✉)
La Sapienza, University of Rome, Rome, Italy
e-mail: milica.uvalic@unipg.it

© The Author(s), under exclusive license to Springer Nature Switzerland AG 2023

S. Estrin, M. Uvalic (eds.), *Collected Works of Domenico Mario Nuti, Volume I*, Studies in Economic Transition, https://doi.org/10.1007/978-3-031-12334-4_6

project while maintaining free enterprise does not differ significantly, at least qualitatively, from that of more conventional capitalist economies. Built-in stabilisers and anticyclical management of demand may have reduced the amplitude of fluctuations and the depth of unemployment (though some government intervention has been deemed cyclical because of leads and lags); the individual cost of fluctuations and unemployment has been partly collectivised by the welfare state; but the undesired phenomena have persisted. The same is true for Yugoslavia, a country which has implemented an associationist form of socialism introducing self-management on a large scale but has retained enterprise initiative and markets.

Other countries attempted to implement the Marxist-Leninist project—state ownership, central planning, equalitarianism, 'democratic centralism' under the leadership (and practical monopoly of power) of the communist party, such as the Soviet Union, the East European Six, Mongolia, China, Cuba and the other countries loosely classed as centrally planned economies or CPEs. These countries have been successful in eliminating fluctuations in the degree of labour employment. Full employment of labour was reached in the Soviet Union at the inception of the First Five-Year Plan (1928) as a result of full-scale mobilisation of labour and in the other countries in the course of reconstruction after the wars that brought about the new system. Ambitious accumulation policies maintained full employment; the wage pressure generated by labour shortage itself, combined with government commitment to price stability, added sustained excess demand for consumption which contributed further to full employment stability, without any need for specific policies to support it. Full employment has been the by-product of growthmanship. In view of the persistent microeconomic inefficiency of central planning and the under-fulfilment of labour productivity targets it can also be said, in a sense, that full employment of labour has been achieved 'by default'. If, however, the decentralisation process currently undertaken in most centrally planned economies were to reproduce unemployment tendencies no doubt specific policies would be adopted to restore and stabilise full employment.

Outside labour employment the performance of socialist planning has been less satisfactory than originally expected. In the Soviet Union, since the completion of reconstruction and the launching of accelerated industrialisation in 1928, and in the other socialist countries since the corresponding dates in their economic history, fast growth of all performance indicators in peacetime until *circa* 1960 has smoothed small-scale cyclical phenomena, reducing them to fluctuations of positive growth rates rather than of levels of income and consumption. Since then, partly because of the gradual exhaustion of labour reserves and of easily accessible natural resources, partly because of the systemic microeconomic inefficiency exacerbated by the lack of such reserves, a discernible slowdown of growth trends has been accompanied by the appearance of negative rates, i.e. fluctuations of levels as in capitalist countries. Instances range from the early minor case of Czechoslovakia in 1963 to the large-scale income drop of one third in three years in Poland 1980–82.

These phenomena are only partly attributable to exogenous shocks and their echoes, whose persistence in the socialist economy was recognised by Oskar Lange (1969), or to adjustment processes such as accelerator-type movements, whose persistence in the socialist economy had been anticipated by Aftalion already in 1909 (see Aftalion, 1909) and recognised by Notkin (1961) and Cobeljic and Stojanovic (1969). Partly—indeed mostly—these phenomena are caused by systemic factors which could be classed under three groups: (1) the lack, or at any rate the slowness, of automatic adjustment feedbacks in the economic life of centrally planned economies; (2) the acceleration of economic activity towards the end of the planning period—be it a month, a year or five years—to avoid the formal and informal penalties of under-fulfilment of targets and to obtain the rewards associated with fulfilment and over-fulfilment, followed by slackening at the beginning of the next period; (3) the presence of political feedbacks, such as popular discontent and unrest resulting from deteriorating economic performance, the changes in political centralisation induced by manifestations of unrest, the economic management changes associated with political changes; these phenomena adding up to a systemic mechanism of economic/political cycles.

Markets, like all servomechanisms or homeostatic (self-regulating) devices, are neither costless nor instantaneous but are automatic in their operation; at the cost of unemployment and possibly with a considerable lag, for example, an unexpected contraction in world trade can be gradually accommodated through lower wages and prices than would otherwise have prevailed, lower exchange rate and higher interest rates regardless of government intervention, capital flows etc. Central planning, like manual control, may or may not be faster and cheaper, or more accurate, than automatic servomechanisms, depending on the relative quality of alternative controls and the actual circumstances, but is never automatic. The experience of centrally planned economies has shown repeated and sometimes glaring instances of inertia and sluggish response to exogenous change, such as persistent accelerated accumulation in the face of rising labour shortages, wage and price stability administratively enforced in spite of rising excess demand for labour and goods, systematic underpricing of imported materials and of exportables in spite of sharpening external imbalance. Reliance on monetary budget constraints and the continued presence of consumers' discretion (if not sovereignty) and some managerial room for manoeuvre make these forms of inertia and delayed response an important handicap for central planners trying to outperform market adjustments. It is precisely inadequate central response to a changing environment (including inadequate ability to innovate institutions and technology) that has given impetus to repeated attempts at reform in the last two decades.

The incentive system typical of central planning, strongly and discontinuously geared to the degree of fulfilment of physical targets, leads to frantic speeding-up of activity (*shturmovshchina* in Russian, literally 'storming') towards the end of the planning period. For monthly plans this haste leads to frequent quality deterioration; for yearly plans 'storming' leads to output being overestimated, or 'borrowed' from the subsequent period (i.e., made up through subsequent unrecorded additional output); so much so that the ratio of December output to that of the following January can be regarded as an index of economic centralisation (Rostowski and Auerbach 1984). For five-year plans, 'storming' implies a concentration of investment project completions towards the end of the period and a spate of new starts at the beginning, with corresponding fluctuations. Moreover, the generalised growthmanship and emphasis on capital accumulation typical of the centrally planned economy leads usually to the inclusion in investment plans of more projects than can be completed on schedule, through 'investors' (local authorities, ministries, enterprises) underestimating true requirements in order to get a place in the plan and later escalating their demands, and through central planners systematically overestimating capacity and especially labour productivity prospects. Sometimes investment ambition leads to additional investment projects being added after or outside the plan balance (as in Gierek's Poland). As they say in East European literature, 'the investment front widens'. Sooner or later specific or generalised bottlenecks of productive or import capacity slow down implementation and reduce or block new starts. Efficiency falls due to investment resources being frozen for periods longer than economically and technically justified, and possibly because of disruption elsewhere in the economy due to resources being sucked in by investment projects given priority over current operations (a 'supply-multiplier' effect). Capital—i.e. in Marxian terminology 'dead labour'—is made unemployed instead of live labour. The cyclical pattern of starts and completions of projects, mostly within the plan period but sometimes overstepping it, leads to cyclical patterns of capacity and output endogenously generated by the system and not justified by exogenous factors. These processes have been investigated theoretically and empirically by Olivera (1960), Goldmann (1964 and 1965), Bajt (1971), Bauer (1978), Dallago (1982) and above all by Bauer (1982, in Hungarian, forthcoming in English).

Political factors induce cycles in socialist economy directly, through successive leaders trying to reinforce the legitimacy of their rule by appeasing their subjects with short-lived but significant spurts of consumption before the standard growth and accumulation-oriented policy typical of socialist governments is resumed and comes up against the constraints discussed in the previous paragraph (Mieczkowski 1978; Hanson 1978; Bunce 1980; Lafay 1981). The association of economic and socio-political factors is investigated by Eysmontt and Maciejewski (1984), who apply discriminant analysis to a large number of indicators of such factors over time in order to identify—and anticipate—periods of crisis; they do not, however, have a model of the actual interaction of political and economic factors. An attempt at constructing such a model is made by Nuti (1979, 1985): a critical relationship is assumed between political centralisation and popular unrest, inverse up to a threshold level and direct beyond it; economic centralisation is directly related to political centralisation and affects—through its impact on investment policy—the level of shortages and inefficiency which in turn fuel political unrest. A recursive model with lagged variables is shown to simulate the kind of recurring rounds of reform attempts and accumulation drives observable in actual socialist economies. Screpanti (1985) has modified such a model applying catastrophe theory and obtaining a political/economic accumulation cycle similar to that of capitalist economies.

The further progress of economic reform in centrally planned economies towards market socialism is bound to attenuate and ultimately eliminate the systemic types of economic cycles discussed above. However, as Maurice Dobb had already anticipated in 1939 (see Dobb, 1939), the diffusion of markets instead of solving the instability problems of the centrally planned economy transforms them into those typical of capitalist economies.

Bibliography

Aftalion, A. (1909). La réalité des superproductions générales. *Revue d'Economie Politique* 23(3): 201-229.

Bajt, A. (1971). Investment cycles in European socialist economies: A review article. *Journal of Economic Literature* 9(1): 56-63.

Bauer, T. (1978). Investment cycles in planned economies. *Acta Oeconomica* 21(3): 243-260.

Bauer, T. (1982). *Tervezès, beruchàzàs, ciklusok*. Budapest: KJK.

Bunce, V. (1980). The political consumption cycle: A comparative analysis. *Soviet Studies* 32(2): 280-290.

Cobeljic, N., and R. Stojanovic (1969). *The theory of economic cycles in a socialist economy*. New York: IASP.

Dallago, B. (1982). *Sviluppo e Cicli nelle Economie Est-Europee*. Milan: Angeli.

Dobb, M.H. (1939). A note on saving and investment in a socialist economy. *Economic Journal* 43: 713-728.

Eysmontt, J. and Maciejewski, W. (1984). Kryzysy spolecznogospodarcze w Polsce – ujecie modelowe (Social-economic crisis in Poland-a model approach). *Ekonomista*.

Goldmann, J. (1964). Fluctuations and trends in the rate of economic growth in some socialist countries. *Economics of Planning* 4(2): 88-98.

Goldmann, J. (1965). Short and long term variations in the growth rate and the model of functioning of a socialist economy. *Czechoslovak Economic Papers* 5: 35-46.
Hanson, P. (1978). Mieczkowski on consumption and politics: A comment. *Soviet Studies* 30(4): 553-556.
Lafay, J.-D. (1981). Empirical analysis of politico-economic interaction in East European countries. *Soviet Studies* 33(3): 386-400.
Lange, O. (1969). *Theory of Reproduction and Accumulation*. Oxford: Pergamon.
Mieczkowski, B. (1978). The relationship between changes in consumption and politics in Poland. *Soviet Studies* 30(2): 262-269.
Notkin, A. (1961). *Tempy i proportsii sotsialisticheskogo vosproizvodstva (The rate and proportions of socialist reproduction)*. Moscow: IEL.
Nuti, D. M. (1979). The contradictions of socialist economies: A Marxian interpretation. *Socialist Register*. London: The Merlin Press.
Nuti, D.M. (1985). *Political and economic fluctuations in the socialist system*, Working Paper No.85/156. Florence: European University Institute.
Olivera, J. (1960). Cyclical growth under collectivism. *Kyklos* 13(2): 229-252.
Rostowski, J. and Auerbach, P. (1984). Storming cycles and central planning. Discussion Paper in Political Economy No.52, Kingston Polytechnic.
Screpanti, E. (1985). *A model of the political economic cycle in centrally planned economies*, Working Paper No.85/201. Florence: European University Institute.

7

Socialist Banking

Domenico Mario Nuti

A moneyless socialist economy, outside the remote prospect of full communism, has been rarely suggested or practised; instances of its suggestion such as Neurath's *Naturalminschafi* (1919), or its practice, such as Soviet War Communism (1918–21) at its peak or Cambodia in the early 1970s, were exceptions. Lenin had understood the importance of banks as an administrative structure; his intuition and the necessary implications of central planning are reflected in the role of money in the traditional socialist model, which took shape in the USSR at the turn of the 1930s and was fully imitated in the other central eastern European countries (see Arnold 1937; Garvy 1966; Grossman 1968; Nuti 1986).

Published in Peter Newman, Murrey Milgate and John Eatwell (Eds.), *The New Palgrave Dictionary of Money and Finance*, Vol 3, The Macmillan Press and Stockton Press, London and New York, 1993, pp. 474–479.

D. M. Nuti (✉)
La Sapienza, University of Rome, Rome, Italy
e-mail: milica.uvalic@unipg.it

© The Author(s), under exclusive license to Springer Nature Switzerland AG 2023

S. Estrin, M. Uvalic (eds.), *Collected Works of Domenico Mario Nuti, Volume I*, Studies in Economic Transition, https://doi.org/10.1007/978-3-031-12334-4_7

In the traditional centrally planned socialist economy the production side of the economy is organized as a single giant firm, a monopolistic corporation entirely owned by the state. Individual production units are administrative subdivisions dependent on branch Ministries and acting exclusively on central instructions. Production tasks are worked out at a central level for the whole economy and stated in a national plan, then broken down by branch and by enterprise as a result of a few (at most half a dozen) iterative rounds of two-way consultations between the centre and the productive units.

Workers are employed by state enterprises at a money wage and have a right/duty to work; in practice they have an entitlement to keep their post or to be redeployed within or by their enterprises. Private enterprise is forbidden or restricted to the use of small amounts of owned or state-rented land or capital goods, with the assistance of family labour and perhaps a few employees, in minor sectors. Prices are centrally fixed, on the basis of average production costs plus actual or implicit subsidies and taxes reflecting government preferences. Once fixed, money prices change infrequently and only through administrative decisions.

In such a system money is primarily an accounting instrument of aggregation and control; financial flows are compartmentalized between enterprises and households, with a bank money circuit for inter-enterprise transactions and cash (or cash convertible accounts) for transactions involving households as buyers or sellers. These financial flows are adjusted passively to planned physical flows and to the degree of their implementation by a single bank monopolizing the functions of commercial as well as central banking (therefore dubbed 'Monobank' in Western literature).

Households are free to convert cash into available consumption goods, a small range of durables including some production goods, or save it as cash or a limited range of financial instruments (deposits, bonds, insurance, lottery tickets, etc.). The balance of revenues and expenditures of the population is closely monitored and ideally balanced *ex ante* through price and incomes policy; it forms the basis of cash issues. Enterprises can only use finance for purposes specified in plan documents; in this sense Berliner (1976) talks of 'documonetary' economy. Since both quantities supplied and prices are state-fixed, markets do not necessarily clear.

Investment is centrally decided and allocated in real terms while finance is provided automatically and interest-free from the state budget to investors, who are subject to straight-line amortization charges on the historical cost of their investments, and to statutory criteria for investment project selection (such as the necessary recoupment of additional investment outlays through current cost savings within a maximum 'recoupment period', equivalent to the application of a shadow capital charge. Enterprises transfer back to the state budget any surplus which they may realise over and above the financing requirements of their centrally approved investments (or rely on further transfers from the budget to cover their planned losses and necessary investment finance).

Credit is mostly short term and is also automatically available to enterprises to finance their working capital requirements necessary to fulfill their planned tasks; it is granted by the Central Bank at an almost symbolic interest rate desired to cover banks' administrative costs. Trade credit between enterprises is forbidden, so that the central bank is not only the lender of last resort, but the only lender: there is no quasi-money.

Fiscal policy takes the form primarily of diversified turnover tax rates or subsidies on commodities; income tax is spurned as an unnecessary internal transfer within the state sector; a modest government surplus is the customary budgetary stance; government deficits are effectively instantly monetized, in view of the small absorption capacity for government bonds; sales of bonds to the population often have a compulsory nature—that is, are a form of taxation.

Thus money in the traditional, centrally planned, socialist system is a unit of account, a two-tier medium of exchange conditionally to plan conformity, and a store of value in competition with inventories of goods rather than with alternative financial or productive assets. It is an instrument for monitoring and controlling plan implementation ('control by the rouble' is emphasized in Soviet literature), not an instrument for economic management, except when planners lose control over financial balances, in which case monetary policy can be an important instrument for restoring that balance.

Traditionally centrally planned economies are regarded as having a propensity for autarkic or quasi-autarkic structure (Wiles 1968). In the process of plan construction first the necessary import requirements of planned levels of gross output are estimated by commodity groups, then export plans are adapted to the foreign currency requirements of the import plan; if a deficit emerges, over what can he financed out of reserves or fresh borrowing, unless import substitution can fill the gap, output plans are scaled down. Exports are regarded as a 'necessary evil', as a withdrawal from the domestic market. Planned trade is undertaken through large import-export state enterprises, specialized by commodity group, not on behalf of producers but on their own account. Domestic currencies are not convertible into commodities (outside the sphere of consumer purchases by nationals), let alone other currencies; exchange rates have a purely accounting role, with equalization subsidies and taxes tending to make all planned exports equally profitable to producers and imports competitive with domestic substitutes whenever they are available; the economy is effectively insulated from the fluctuations in international prices and exchange rates. As the result of the coordination of national plans, there was planned trade integration within the socialist trading bloc—CMEA or Council of Mutual Economic Assistance (also called Comecon in Western literature; it was founded in 1949 and, at the time of its dissolution in September 1991, it included the USSR, the East European Six, Mongolia, Cuba and Vietnam). Even within CMEA, however, trade flows tended to be bilaterally cleared (moreover within groups of hard and soft commodities), and there was no common currency, balances in the so-called transferable rouble being neither convertible into Soviet commodities nor transferable to countries other than the Soviet Union without prior mutual agreement; intra-CMEA trade prices were usually indexed to a moving average of international prices in convertible currencies. Like national banking institutions, CMEA financial institutions would pay only a symbolic interest rate on outstanding balances. All in all, foreign trade transactions in this kind of system are administratively determined and there is no automatic mechanism transmitting to producers signals about trade opportunities and inducing them to take advantage of any such opportunities (see Wiles 1968; Marer 1972; van Brabant 1973).

It is conceivable that gold and hard currency reserves might allow such a system to introduce and maintain convertibility of the domestic currency, and indeed plans for the introduction of convertibility were considered in the USSR even at the height of central planning. However such convertibility would only be applicable to capital transactions, as the practice of central planning would have to restrict the convertibility of domestic currency into domestic purchases of goods and services, in order not to disrupt the pattern of planned inter-enterprise transactions (moreover, the insulation of domestic from international prices might have led to inefficient trade flows). Such convertibility into specific commodity groups would have to be fitted into the national plan — that is, multilateral trade clearing could not be automatic, it would either have to be negotiated or lead to hard currency settlements. Hence the nature of the so-called transferable rouble described above.

This system of real and monetary management of the economy was expected to yield price stability, domestic and external macroeconomic balance, full employment of labour and economic growth. In practice—apart from roughly 1950–70—it was broadly characterized by widespread excess demand at controlled process (i.e. repressed inflation visible through generalized shortages), generating full and overfull employment as a by-product, and/or external imbalances financed through external debt; growth performance, impressive until the 1960s though possibly overstated, subsequently deteriorated, and by the end of the 1980s turned into decline.

This disappointing performance is usually attributed to the built-in inefficiency of a system that disregarded, due to administrative prices, substitution opportunities both in production and consumption; and to the informational complexity of planned coordination. An element of strength and weakness was the built-in economic inertia of the centrally planned system, involving both the ability to reproduce itself and the inability to adjust to exogenous shocks, to changes in technology, tastes and world trade opportunities. Probably an even more important factor in the deteriorating performance of these economies was the combination of monetary indiscipline and a misguided commitment to stable prices in the face of excess demand, which, having started variously in 1975–85, by the end of the 1980s had cumulated to significant degrees of monetary overhang throughout the area (less so in Hungary and Czechoslovakia).

Endemic excess demand was due to both macro- and microeconomic factors. The first took the form of a generalized overambition in planning investment, collective consumption, defence and other desirable targets, and the money wage push unavoidable at overfull employment — all claims validated by an accommodating monetary policy, but incompatible at constant prices. The microeconomic aspect of these policies was the 'soft budget constraint' to which state enterprises are subjected, that is, their ability to replenish their financial resources in the pursuit of planned tasks whenever needed, for instance in the face of higher prices (Kornai 1986; constraints were never infinitely 'soft', but sufficiently flexible to recreate excess demand for the small range of price increases considered by central planners). As a result, the centrally planned economy over time became typically a 'shortage economy' (Kornai 1980), with adverse implications for both consumer welfare and production efficiency.

The actual size and presence of monetary overhang in the 1970s have been the object of controversy, since measurement presumes a reliable estimate of what the demand for money would be if current prices were market clearing (see for instance Portes and Winter 1980); but there is generalized consensus both about its presence in the 1980s and on its significant size, as witnessed by large price differentials between the official level and that prevailing in secondary retrading ('black' or grey markets). Alternative indicators of true inflationary pressure have been attempted, such as the direct recomputation of price indices, the calculation of implicit deflators, the purchasing power parity approach to black market exchange rates, the share of goods officially regarded as 'without supply difficulties', the ratio of cash and non-cash financial assets to income and composite indicators of excess demand (see Nuti 1986).

The opportunity to convert money into goods at higher prices in the 'secondary' economy in a trivial sense made all monetary holdings voluntary, but equilibrium in this limited sense was still consistent with large-scale imbalances at the official price level, as witnessed by the large-scale price increases usually occurring at times of partial or total price liberalization (as in the stabilization programmes of 1990–91 in central eastern Europe).

The monetary regime of an economy affected by endemic monetary overhang can be characterized as one in which money is a peculiar kind of lottery ticket, with a recurring probability p of a prize consisting of access to purchase at official prices at face value, where p is equal to one minus the ratio between monetary overhang and total money supply

(Nuti 1991a). Clearly this peculiar regime—never suggested by anyone for any system—has nothing to do with socialism as such, but was the result of historical accidents and bad policies.

The traditional model was the subject of repeated reform attempts, especially in 1965–89. At first the aim was that of improving central planning, through the use of international prices, actual interest rates and rentals for scarce resources; the use of value instead of physical indicators, including profit and profit rates; and enterprise autonomy and inter-enterprise direct links, government contracts instead of orders or quality controls. Then reform attempts were directed at constructing a model of 'market socialism', which might combine dominant public ownership and macroeconomic management with the benefits of full-fledged markets, to be used as instruments of resource allocation instead of solely for the distribution of centrally decided outputs. This kind of 'radical reform' (in Mikhail Gorbachev's words) included the dismantling of central planning and of administrative supply channels, the replacement of branch Ministries by a single Ministry, sectoral ministry of firms, anti-monopoly legislation, performance related managerial incentives and freer access to foreign trade. In these repeated reform attempts, money recovered an important role (see Brus 1964: for a pioneering detection and analysis of the early stages of this process in the 1900s consolidating the currency; financial flows become fully connected, commercial banking is separated from central banking (as was done in Britain with Sir Robert Peel's Act of 1844, which abandoned the principles of the banking school in favour of those of the currency school) and exercised by competing banks (as had been the case already in the USSR in the early stages of NEP; see Arnold 1937); investment is funded by bank credits, inter-enterprise loans and self-finance; credit is provided not automatically, but at the discretion of banks on a contractual basis and at an interest which is supposed to balance the market; enterprises which are not deemed creditworthy can be forced into liquidation and bankruptcy; and there is a wide range of financial instruments available to households and enterprises. Money becomes an unconditional and therefore more liquid means of payment, and a less attractive store of value because of a wider range of alternatives. The way is paved for active monetary policy, using standard instruments such as reserve and liquidity ratios, rediscounting scale and rates, open-market operations, etc.

This design for reform was partially implemented early on in Yugoslavia, where for a long time, and especially since 1971, banking and credit have been major instruments of macroeconomic management: there is a plurality of commercial banks, investment banks and other financial institutions, and enterprises can lend to or have a share in other enterprises or even found new banks, or sell bonds to the public including individuals (see Dimitrijevic and Macesich 1983). However, in Yugoslavia these developments may have been due to its specific systemic features, since income-sharing by self-managed enterprises is expected to favour financial intermediation at the expense of direct reinvestment of enterprise income (self-financed assets, unlike distributed income, cannot be appropriated by workers; see for instance Pejovich 1976 and Furobotn 1980). Moreover, an enterprise in which another enterprise has a direct share investment can pay that investment back at historical cost, so that what appears as equity is effectively a loan (see Uvalic 1989). Yugoslav banks tended to channel private savings to the enterprises that owned them, on favourable terms, acting as a decentralized form of collectivization of enterprise losses, thus raising similar problems to those of less developed monetary systems elsewhere in central and eastern Europe (see Uvalic 1992). The first full implementation of monetary reform along the lines illustrated above took place in Hungary in 1984–9 (see Blejer and Sagan 1991). In 1984 a government decree authorized the issue of bonds to the public by government, local authorities, financial institutions and all enterprises. On 1 January 1987 the National Bank of Hungary hived off its credit activities by transforming its lending directorates and some local branches into associated but separate bank, soon joined by other banks with substantial foreign participation. An obligatory reserve ratio of 20% was established for demand deposits and 10% of time deposits; the discount rate, which until the end of 1984 was decided by the government, was put under the control of the President of the Central Bank. A law on bankruptcy (1986) gave initiative to creditors and established rapid proceedings. A market for share issues by private and state enterprises to the general public was set up from 1 January 1989.

By the end of the 1980s similar measures were being contemplated and had begun to be implemented in other central and eastern European countries (China had been an early starter and a slow mover along this road). However the 1989 revolutions switched the target model from the construction of 'market socialism' to the restoration of capitalism, that is, of a market economy with prevalent private ownership and enterprise. This involved privatization (as well as re-privatization, i.e. restitution to earlier owners), including privatization of financial institutions. In Hungary, again leading the reform process, the 1988 Law on the Transformation of Enterprises and subsequent legislation laid the foundation for the privatization of state enterprises (which had been occurring spontaneously since the mid-1980s); in June 1991 a bank privatization plan was announced, which may permit foreign ownership of up to 20% of even the largest commercial banks. The growth of the private sector, especially in banking and financial activities, has proceeded mostly through new institutions rather than through privatization of the state sector. Throughout central and eastern Europe, including the former Soviet Union (from the end of 1991 a smaller and looser Commonwealth of Independent States), privatization is in progress; by 1992 the old style system is surviving in a precarious form only in a few Asian countries and Cuba.

There are many reasons for the failed implementation of an alternative market socialism project. First, a consistent theoretical model of market socialism, different from a capitalist economy governed by socialist principles and policies, was never fully developed. In particular, the monetary and financial arrangements that might characterize such a model were never satisfactorily addressed, let alone resolved, in either literature or reform projects. Pareto (1902) stressed the immanence of economic categories such as capital and interest regardless of economic system (vol. 1, ch. 6); criticized socialist thinkers for confusing the capitalist and the entrepreneur (vol. II, ch. 10) and Proudhon's monetary and banking scheme (vol. II, ch. 11) which, providing money automatically for productive undertakings at virtually no interest, closely resembles the monetary system of a traditional centrally planned economy. Barone (1908) expected the Minister of Production of his Collectivistic State to finance investment exclusively through loans at an equilibrium interest rate that matched the marginal return on investment. None of the proponents of *Marktsozialismus* worked out any system-specific arrangement for money and finance. The list includes, beside Heimann (1922, 1934), who coined this term, Taylor (1929), Landauer (1931), Dickinson (1933) and Lange (1938) (for a comprehensive survey of prewar literature, see Landauer 1959). The same is true of more recent literature on socialist blueprints, except perhaps Brus's stress on the importance of money in the decentralized model of socialism (Brus 1964). Nove's 'feasible socialism' (1983) only mentions money to say that it must be there and never mentions financial markets. The development of monetary and financial institutions in the 'reformed' socialist economies has simply imitated without change a few capitalist institutions (arguably not even the most appropriate among capitalist financial institutions; see Corbett and Mayer 1992).

Even within the old ideological restrictions on private ownership of means of production and of enterprises it might have been possible to simulate the functions of a competitive market for capital goods and for enterprises as going concerns, and the functions of a stock exchange (see Nuti 1989; this relies on a challengeable self-assessment of capital values by state enterprise managers, and private loans and deposits indexed to the value of chosen state enterprises). However, any such scheme would involve private enrichment through saving and good judgement, and therefore would have represented a needless detour from establishing actual financial markets. Probably the financial arrangements appropriate to market socialism should be accompanied by forms of employee ownership and participation in decision making, like Tibor Liska's 'entrepreneurial socialism' (Liska 1963; Nuti 1991b) or James Meade partnerships (Meade 1989), as well as other extensive forms of economic democracy (basic or citizen income, etc.). Thus to a great extent, the failure to implement market socialism has been a failure of the imagination.

Second, the transformation of the old system has been taking place at an excessively slow pace, subject to experimentations and reversals, leading to an incoherent and contradictory partly planned, partly market-oriented system, or rather non-system, which performed as badly as the old system, if not worse. Such is still (in 1992) the economic system in the former Soviet area.

Third, with the partial exception of Hungary, monetary overhang persisted, while the political class was either unwilling to handle the problem or lacked the necessary political legitimacy to impose the austerity measures necessarily associated with monetary and fiscal discipline, price liberalization and trade opening. Moreover, the old political and economic regime would not have commanded the kind of international solidarity enjoyed by its successors. Thus the former political class could not have undertaken the stabilization programmes which were implemented in 1990–91 by Poland, Czech and Slovak Federal Republic, Romania and Bulgaria, and have been envisaged in Russia and Ukraine in 1992, with the full backing of the IMF, the World Bank, Western countries and the international financial community (including forms of debt relief as well as grants and loans).

For these reasons, by 1990–92 the only course left was a return to capitalism. The feasibility of an alternative model of market socialism—which arguably would have been easier to implement starting from the reform of centrally planned socialism than from that of advanced capitalism—remains an open question, unlikely to be resolved or even posed in the near future.

Bibliography

Arnold, A. Z. (1937). *Banks, Credit and Money in Soviet Russia.* New York: Columbia University Press.

Barone, E. (1908). II Ministro della Produzione nello stato collettivistico. *Giornale degli Economisti,* September-October; reprinted as 'The ministry of production in the collectivist state', *in Collectivist Economic Planning,* Ed. F. A. von Hayek, London: Routledge & Kegan Paul, 245-90.

Berliner, J. S. (1976). *The Innovation Decision in Soviet Industry.* Cambridge, Mass.: MIT Press.

Blejer, M. and Sagari, S. (1991). Hungary: financial sector reform in a socialist economy. Policy Research and External Affairs Working Paper WPS 595, World Bank, Washington, February.

Brus, W. (1964). Ogolne problemy funkcjonowania gospodarki socjalistycznej. Warsaw: PWE; trans. into English under the title *The Market in a Socialist Economy,* London: Routledge & Kegan Paul, 1972.

Corbett, J. and Mayer, C. (1992). Financial reform in Eastern Europe: progress with the wrong model. *Oxford Review of Economic Polity*, forthcoming.

Dickinson, H.D. (1933). Price formation in a socialist community. *Economic Journal 43, June.*

Dimitrijevic, D. and Macesich, G, (1983). *Money and Finance in Yugoslavia.* New York: Praeger.

Furobotn, E.G. (1980). The socialist labor-managed firm and bank-financed investment: some theoretical issues. *Journal of Comparative Economics,* 4(2): 184-91.

Garvy, G. (1966). *Money, Banking and Credit in Eastern Europe.* New York: Federal Reserve Bank of New York.

Grossman, G. (Ed.) (1968). *Money and Plan.* Berkeley and Los Angeles: University of California Press.

Heimann, E. (1922). *Mehrwert und Gemeinwirtschaft* (Surplus Value and the Communal Economy). Berlin: H.R. Hengelmann.

Heimann, E. 1934. Planning and the market system. *Social Research* 1, November: 486-504.

Kornai, J. (1986). The soft budget constraint. *Kyklos* 39(1): 3-30.

Landauer, C. (1931). *Plantwirtschaft und Verkehrswirtschaft* (Planned economy and market economy). Munich and Leipzig: Duncker and Humblot.

Landauer, C. (in collaboration with E. Kridl Valkenier and H. Stein Landauer) (1959). *European Socialism:A History of Ideas and Movements from the Industrial Revolution to Hitler's Seizure of Power.* Westport, Connecticut: Greenwood Press.

Lange, O. (1938). The economic theory of socialism. In Lippincott (1938); originally published in a slightly different version in *Review of Economic Studies* 3, 1936-37.

Lippincott, B. (Ed.) (1938). *On the economic theory of socialism.* Minneapolis: University of Minnesota Press.

Liska, T. (1963). Kritik as koncepcio. Tezisek a gazdasa.gi mcchanizmus reformiahoz. (Critique and construction. Theses for a reform of the economic mechanism). *Kozgazdasagi Szemle* 9.

Marer, P. (1972). *Soviet and East European Foreign Trade 1946-69. Statistical Compendium and Guide.* Bloomington: Indiana University Press.

Meade, J.E. (1989). *Agathotopia - The Economics of Partnership.* Aberdeen: Aberdeen University Press.

Neurath, O. (1919). *Durch die Kriegswirtchaft zur Naturalwirtschaft* (From the war economy to the natural economy). Munich: Georg D. W. Callwey.

Nove, A. (1983). *The Economics of Feasible Socialism.* London: Allen and Unwin.
Nuti, D. M. (1986). Hidden and repressed inflation in Soviet-type economies: definitions, measurements and stabilisation. *Contributions to Political Economy.* 5: 37-82.
Nuti, D. M. (1989). Feasible financial innovation under market socialism. In *Financial Reform in Socialist Economies,* Ed. C. Kessides, T. King, M. Nuti and K. Sokil, Washington, DC: EDI-World Bank, 35-105.
Nuti, D. M. (1991a). How fast should convertibility be introduced? A Comment on Friedrich Levcik and Jacques J. Polak. In *Currency Convertibility in Eastern Europe,* Ed. J. Williamson, Washington, DC: IIE, 48-55.
Nuti, D. M. (1991b). On Tibor Liska's entrepreneurial socialism. In *The Legacy of Karl Polanyi —Market, State and Society at the end of the Twentieth Century,* Ed. M. Mendell and D. Salee, St. Martin's Press, New York.
Pareto, V. (1902, 1903). *Les Systèmes Socialistes.* 2 vols, Paris: Giard and Briere.
Pejovich, S. (1976). The labor-managed firm and bank credit. In *EconomicAnalysis of the Soviet-type System,* Ed. J. Thornton, Cambridge: Cambridge University Press.
Portes, R. and Winter, D. (1980). Disequilibrium estimates for consumption goods markets in centrally planned economies. *Review of Economic Studies* 47: 137-59.
Taylor, F. M. (1929). The guidance of production in a socialist state. *American Economic Review* 19 (1), March; reprinted in Lippincott (1938).
Uvalic, M. (1989). Shareholding in Yugoslavia: theory and practice. In *Financial Reform in Socialist Economies,* Ed. C. Kessides, T. King, M. Nuti and K. Sokil, Washington, DC: EDI-World Bank, 106-25.
Uvalic, M. (1992). *Investment and Property Rights in Yugoslavia.* Cambridge: Cambridge University Press.
van Brabant, J. M. (1973). *Bilateralism, and Structural Bilateralism in Intra-CMEA Trade.* Rotterdam: Rotterdam University Press.
Wiles, P. J. D. (1968). *Communist International Economics.* Oxford: Blackwell.

[illegible]

8

Remonetisation and Capital Markets in the Reform of Centrally Planned Economies

Domenico Mario Nuti

8.1 Introduction

Since the mid-1950s there have been repeated attempts at reforming the Centrally Planned Economy (CPE) of the Soviet Union and other Soviet-type economics, i.e. decentralising economic decisions, activating markets to replace plans, using incentives geared to performance at market values. The frequency of these attempts and their reversals indicates both the intense pressure for reform and the difficulty of its successful

Published in *European Economic Review*, Vol. 33, 2–3, March 1989, pp. 427–438, a *Paper and Proceedings* issue that contains invited lectures and invited papers presented at the Third Congress of the European Economic Association in Bologna. Among the twelve topics chosen was *Opening up Capital Markets in Eastern Europe* within which the present paper was published. An earlier version was published as *EUI Working Paper* No. 361, European University Institute, Florence 1988.

D. M. Nuti (✉)
La Sapienza, University of Rome, Rome, Italy
e-mail: milica.uvalic@unipg.it

© The Author(s), under exclusive license to Springer Nature Switzerland AG 2023

S. Estrin, M. Uvalic (eds.), *Collected Works of Domenico Mario Nuti, Volume I*, Studies in Economic Transition, https://doi.org/10.1007/978-3-031-12334-4_8

implementation. The current round of economic reform involves the Soviet Union, with the 'perestroika' launched by Gorbachev on his accession to power in March 1985; Hungary, where the process started in 1968 has entered a new phase in the last three years; Poland, in spite of a spell of military rule; Bulgaria and from a higher achieved degree of marketisation—Yugoslavia. Reform appears to have restarted, more recently and slowly, in Czechoslovakia; in Eastern Europe the only countries without signs of reform are the GDR, where pressure for change is reduced by its privileged relationship with the FRG and by its more flexible vertically integrated structure, and Romania which is regressing towards the Albanian model. However significant reforms are also taking place in socialist countries outside East Europe, notably in China and Algeria.

The current round of reforms differs from earlier attempts in several respects. This time the lead comes from the Soviet Union; it is accompanied often by political renewal (see Soviet emphasis on *glasnost*); it is more widely understood that a technological and sectoral restructuring of the economies to be reformed is necessary, and that reform implies abandoning traditional policies of overambitious investment, unconditional commitment to price stability and protection of job rights (and perhaps full employment itself); there is greater opening to direct foreign trade with other economic systems and to foreign investment, while the burden of servicing a large external debt forces the maintenance of these conditions. However the most visible, sometimes spectacular aspect of the current round of economic reform is the revamping of money and monetary policy, followed or to be followed by more or less developed capital markets.

This paper characterises the traditional CPE monetary and financial system (Sect. 8.2), illustrates the extent of current changes (Sect. 8.3) which will be discussed further in the papers presented at this session by Zsigmond Jarai and Ales Vahcic; retraces the steps in the argument for and the actual sequencing of monetary and financial reform (Sect. 8.4); discusses some systemic constraints and their impact on feasible further developments (Sect. 8.5). The paper by Wlodzimierz Brus and Kazimierz Laski considers whether the full-fledged model of market socialism might be able to avoid labour unemployment or handle fluctuations in the level of economic activity; Richard Portes considers the international aspects of introducing capital markets in Eastern Europe.

8.2 Money and Finance Under Central Planning

In the traditional CPE money is primarily an accounting instrument of aggregation and control; financial flows are compartmentalised between enterprises and households, with a bank money circuit for inter-enterprises' transactions and cash (or cash-convertible accounts) for transactions involving households as sellers or buyers, i.e. wage payments and consumption purchases. These financial flows are adjusted passively to planned physical flows and to the degree of their implementation by a single bank monopolising the functions of commercial as well as central banking (therefore dubbed 'Monobank' in Western literature). Households' savings (whether voluntary or, when intended purchases exceed supply at centrally fixed prices, involuntary) can take the form of a small range of durables including some production goods, or cash or a limited range of financial instruments (deposits, bonds, insurance, lottery tickets); the balance of revenues and expenditures of the population is closely monitored and forms the basis of cash issues; ideally it is balanced *ex ante* through price and incomes policy. Enterprises can only use finance for purposes specified in plan documents; in this sense Berliner (1976) talks of 'documonetary' economy.

Investment is centrally decided and allocated in real terms while finance is provided automatically and interest-free from the state budget to investors, who are subject to straight line amortisation charges on the historical cost of their investments and transfer back to the state budget any surplus which they may realise (or rely on further transfers from the budget to cover their planned losses; however official regulations for investment selection imply a shadow capital charge, see Nuti 1971). Credit is mostly short term and is also automatically available to enterprises to finance their working capital requirements necessary to fulfil their planned tasks; it is granted by the Central Bank at an almost symbolic interest rate designed to cover banks' administrative costs. Trade credit between enterprises is forbidden. Thus money in the traditional system is the unit of account, a two-tier medium of exchange conditionally to plan conformity, a store of value in competition with inventories of goods rather than with alternative financial or productive assets. Money is an instrument for monitoring and controlling plan implementation ('control by the rouble' is emphasised in Soviet literature), not an instrument for economic management, except when planners lose control over financial balances, in which case monetary policy can be an important instrument for restoring that balance. Fiscal policy takes the form primarily of diversified turnover tax rates or subsidies on commodities, and is indistinguishable from profit; income tax is spurned as an unnecessary internal transfer within the state sector; a modest government surplus is the customary budgetary stance; government deficits are effectively instantly monetised.

Traditionally CIEs are regarded as having a propensity for autarkic or quasi-autarkic structure (Wiles 1968). In the process of plan construction first the necessary import requirements of planned levels of gross output are estimated by commodity groups, then export plans are adapted to the foreign currency requirements of the import plan; if a deficit emerges, over what can be financed out of reserves or fresh borrowing, unless import substitution can fill the gap output plans are scaled down. Exports are regarded as a 'necessary evil', as a withdrawal from the domestic market. Planned trade is undertaken through large import-export state enterprises, specialised by commodity group, not on behalf of producers but on their own account. Domestic currencies are not convertible into commodities (outside the sphere of consumer purchases by nationals), let alone other currencies; exchange rates have a purely accounting role, with equalisation subsidies and taxes tending to make all planned exports equally profitable to producers and imports competitive with domestic substitutes whenever they are available; the economy is effectively insulated from the fluctuations in international prices and exchange rate. There is planned trade integration within the socialist trading bloc—CMEA or Council of Mutual Economic Assistance (also called Comecon but only in Western literature; at present includes the USSR, the East European Six, Mongolia, Cuba and Vietnam) as the result of the coordination of national plans. Even within CMEA, however, trade flows tend to be bilaterally cleared (moreover within groups of hard and soft commodities) and there is no common currency, balances in the so-called transferable rouble being neither convertible in Soviet commodities nor transferable to countries other than the Soviet Union, without prior mutual agreement; intra-CMEA trade prices are usually indexed to a moving average of international prices in convertible currencies. All in all, foreign trade transactions are administratively determined and there is no automatic mechanism transmitting to producers signals about trade opportunities and inducing them to take advantage of any such opportunities (see Brown and Neuberger 1968; Holzman 1974, 1976; van Brabant 1973).

In theory the CPE's Monobank is the custodian of economic equilibrium; in practice it presides over a regime of almost permanent excess demand, internal and external, to the point of leading to the identification of the economics of socialist planning with 'the economics of shortage' (Kornai 1980, 1982, 1986); this is the result of overambition at all levels and price upwards inflexibility but is ultimately made possible by the acquiescence of the banking system. Hence the move towards market discipline, including credit discipline instead of automatic credit.

8.3 The Extent of Monetary and Financial Reform

Monetary and financial reform presupposes the prior dismantling of central planning as a set of detailed physical commands to enterprises and sectors, and the implementation of a degree of enterprise autonomy and financial identity, subject to government policy exercised through indirect instruments. Thus the monetary and financial institutions of Yugoslavia, which first moved away from central planning, are the most developed in Eastern Europe (see Dimitrijevic and Macesich 1973, 1981); but especially in the last two years the pace of monetary and financial reform has been fast and accelerating.

The Yugoslav banking system includes—besides the central bank NBY plus the national banks of the federation members—166 basic banks and the associated banks formed by basic banks, other financial institutions such as the Post Office Savings bank, the Yugoslav Bank for International Economic Cooperation YBIEC and internal banks (i.e. closed financial institutions internal to enterprises accepting deposits from enterprise workers and Basic Organisation of Associated Labour—BOALs). NBY controls commercial banks through liquidity ratios, reserve requirements, credit ceilings and refinancing. In 1972 the commercial banking structure changed from one consisting of commercial banks and investment banks to a mixed bank system engaged in both short- and long-term operations. Basic banks are formed by enterprises, internal banks of enterprises, and other non-government institutions; they are regulated by organs composed of representatives of founding enterprises; until recently founding members of banks had unlimited liability. Associated banks formed by basic banks pool resources and usually handle foreign exchange operations and tend to operate along regional lines.

In 1985 a new law was introduced, with which banks were to comply before the end of 1986. The new law raises capital requirements of commercial banks, defines the limited liability of banks shareholder enterprises, requires the build-up of reserves and encourages inter-regional competition. A new accounting law from 1 January 1987 eliminated the possibility of deferring current foreign exchange losses in enterprise budgets. The purpose of these reforms is that of eliminating the drawbacks of the Yugoslav banking system to date: the financial indiscipline in the enterprise and banking sectors, the taking over by the NBY of foreign exchange risk on enterprise foreign borrowing, the negative interest rates, the lending to enterprises at rates lower than the cost of finance, the socialisation of enterprise losses all round.

In Hungary, with effect from 1 January 1987, first commercial banking has been separated from central banking by the Monobank (as it was done in Britain with Sir Robert Peel's Act of 1844, which abandoned the principles of the banking school in favour of those of the currency school); then competition has been introduced in commercial banking by turning the Monobank lending directorates and some regional departments into autonomous banks and creating additional commercial banks (competing commercial banks were already present in the USSR in the early stages of NEP, see Arnold 1937; Carr and Davies 1969). Three of the new banks have been set up with the participation of Western capital, namely Citibank Budapest, the Central European International Bank and Unicbank; commercial banks however do not yet compete for households' deposits, reserved to the National Savings Bank. The change implies the gradual integration and connection of all financial flows, and the replacement of budgetary grants and automatic credit by contractual relations with banks based on credit-worthiness, and at an interest which is supposed to balance the loans market. Central Bank control of credit expansion is exercised through indirect instruments such as reserve and liquidity ratios, rediscounting scale and rates, open market operations (initially consisting of primary issues of short-term securities); the way is paved for active monetary policy. At present it is felt that both the scale of refinancing and reserve ratios are high by international standards, two elements offsetting each other but perhaps adding up to a higher degree of direct central control than desirable or intended. A thorny question is the verification and treatment of the portfolio inherited by banks, some of which consists of doubtful loans made under the earlier financial regime. Another is the organisation of housing finance, which is precondition for the unification of the two monetary circuits of households and enterprises.

Hungarian style monetary reform has been adopted in Poland and Bulgaria (see Daviddi 1987), and its necessity has been maintained in the Soviet Union by leading reformers; a first step in the USSR has already been made with the setting up of six new specialised banks, decreed in July 1987. Credit-worthiness and financial discipline requires strict procedures for the recovery, liquidation and bankruptcy of non-financially viable enterprises; such procedures are now in force in Hungary, Yugoslavia, Poland and the Soviet Union, and a handful of bankrupt firms mostly in construction are proudly listed by reformers as a major achievement.

In Hungary since 1983, i.e. already before the banking reform, a bond market has operated with primary issues and secondary trading, for both enterprises (non-state guaranteed) and households (guaranteed), with issues growing by over thirty times (100 times for households) in five years to almost 30bn Forint in 1987. Shares have also been issued and re-traded though until now exclusively within state enterprises. The next tasks of the financial reform are the development of the role of financial investors (insurance companies, pension funds, savings association etc.) and of an integrated money market with a unified interest rate structure, and the development of an equity market extended to households (announced for 1 January 1989); this will require a parallel development and generalisation of joint-stock companies, at present limited in number and scope.

Similar financial facilities have been available since 1986 on an experimental basis in China, where commercial banking has developed and the first stock exchange was opened on 1 September 1986 in Shanghai, followed by Guangdong and other provincial initiatives; there are eight 'over the counter' centres in Shanghai and Shenyang (in the Liaoning Province; by November 1987 the value of bonds quoted had reached Yuan 300mn, or US$85mn at the official exchange rate; see Ellman 1987, on early experiments see Xu Jing'an 1987). Shares are still illiquid, having to be held for substantial minimum periods, and do not carry a vote. At China's 13th Party Congress in October 1987 it was agreed that stocks and bonds have a positive role to play in the Chinese economy at its present stage of development (Ellman 1987).

In Algeria, following liberalisation measures for enterprises and banks (maintained in existence by the 1962 nationalisation but otherwise operating as in a traditional CPE model), January 1988 legislation has decreed the financial restructuring of state enterprises, which have been given new capital and turned into state-owned joint stock companies; their shares are given a value calculated and revised by accountants and government officials. In May 1988 eight state-owned but independent Trust Funds ('Fonds de Participation') were established, partly but not completely specialised by sector (mining, investment goods, construction, petrochemicals, electronics, food processing, miscellaneous industries, services); they have the function of managing state ownership. In the Algerian approach funds managers, rewarded according to the financial performance of their portfolio, which they can alter by trading with other funds, are expected to effectively simulate the functioning of capital markets.

In mid-August 1988 a special Yugoslav commission headed by Mr. Branko Mikulic, the Prime Minister, proposed a radical reform of enterprises and of socialist ownership, which would allow Yugoslav and foreigners to buy shares in them; the proposal will be considered in the autumn by the Federal Assembly (FT, 17 August).

Other countries have been more cautious in developing capital markets, but some have been bolder in other directions: for instance, since September 1987 once a fortnight the Polish Export Promotion Bank has been auctioning foreign exchange worth millions of dollars, to importers on behalf of exporters, at a realistic rate of exchange increasingly close to the black-market rate.

In the Soviet Union joint-stock companies are reported to have been set up 'spontaneously' by state enterprises or agencies, seeing that inter-enterprise agreements of this kind are not actually forbidden by law. For instance, in Leningrad there are now two 'commercial joint stock' banks, set up by the Ministry of Chemical Equipment (Minkhimash) and that of Energy Technology (Energomash) to finance export promotion and domestic ventures, apparently empowered to issue bonds and accept deposits in foreign currencies as well as in roubles (FT, 12 August 1988). At the end of July 1988 Vneshekonombank—the Soviet Bank of Foreign Economic Affairs—and the Eurocard/Eurocheque and Mastercard organisations signed a licencing agreement extending credit card and cheque facilities first to foreigners (in competition with Inturist which has signed a similar agreement with Visa) then, in the second year of operation, to 150,000–200,000 Soviet diplomats, business executives and technicians with convertible rouble accounts at the Foreign Economic Affairs Bank. Savings banks also have been involved in discussions about issuing credit cards on their own account—a step towards a cashless society but definitely not moneyless society. At the signing ceremony of the licencing agreement Mr. Viktor Gerashchenko, the Soviet Union first deputy chairman, took delivery of a three by five foot Eurocard (FT, 1 August). This is *perestroika.*

8.4 The 'Sequencing' of Reform

The importance of money in the reformed socialist model was stressed by Brus (1964); a pioneering detection and analysis of the early stages of this process in the 1960s can be found in Garvey (1966) and Grossman (1966, 1968); a great deal of attention has also been paid to monetary imbalance and the definition and measurement of 'repressed inflation' (see for instance Portes 1983; Nuti 1986). Otherwise the role of money and financial institutions under market socialism has been conspicuously neglected both in the classical literature on market socialism and—until very recently—in the blueprints for economic reform in Eastern Europe. Yet there is a compelling logical sequence in the argument for monetary and financial reform, which can also be identified as an actual and indeed normative sequencing in reform implementation. It bears out Maurice Dobb's contention that elements of different economic systems cannot be mixed in just any proportions, as one can with a cake vary ingredients to taste: once limited markets for products are introduced, the argument escalates in favour of further extensions.

The starting point is the inefficiency of central allocation of production targets and given physical resources to enterprises in the consumption goods sector: it soon becomes apparent that it is more efficient to let consumers indicate their preferences for the kind of goods that can be produced with those resources, by signalling demand prices, instead of leaving output structure to a central decision (even socially desirable and undesirable goods can be regulated by taxes and subsidies instead of direct commands). The second stage is the extension of this reasoning to inter-enterprise allocation of current inputs, still within an overall allocation of intermediate inputs to consumption; the third stage is the redeployment of a given amount of planned investment, allocated to consumption goods, between different sectors and enterprises. Gradually, in the fourth and fifth stages, both the level and the structure of investment are argued to be best decentralised to the level of enterprises. A parallel development opens enterprise purchases and sales to international suppliers and purchasers.

These piecemeal extensions of the basic efficiency of market redeployment of scarce resources towards their most productive uses trace a natural path and sequencing of economic reform of the CPEs. First the market for consumption goods, then for production goods, demand remonetisation, i.e. the use of value indicators to measure enterprise performance and to take the given resources to their most productive uses. Then the market for factors of production, i.e. for labour, land and capital, both financial capital and productive assets; financial capital first between enterprises, then between enterprises and their own workers, then between enterprises and households as sectors; first for loan capital, then for risk capital. There is a tendency towards a cascade or domino effect from the acceptance of markets as (i) automatic (ii) self-regulating mechanisms (iii) raising the productivity of resources. Of course the extension from micro to macro of the argument in favour of markets is not watertight; taking investment out of the planning sphere raises the possibility of labour unemployment; indeed some labour unemployment becomes necessary to accommodate the structural change produced by decentralisation. This problem, tackled by Brus and Laski in their paper at this session, is often easily forgotten, since the comparative macroeconomic performance of socialist countries in recent years has been so poor as to tip the balance in favour of markets even in the macrosphere; or at least experience has shifted the burden of proof.

In an economy such as Yugoslavia, where workers are entitled to a share of their enterprises' value added after deductions for interest, amortisation and reinvestment, the introduction of shares makes it possible to recognise by means of free share issues—workers' contributions to self-financed investment and to entrepreneurial success (Uvalic 1987). Without such a recognition, the Yugoslav-type enterprise seems subjected to a propensity to under-employ labour and respond perversely to short term price changes (Ward 1967; Vanek 1970), as well as underinvest in self-financed projects (Furobotn and Pejovich 1972; Furobotn 1980). Shares also enable the cooperative-style Yugoslav enterprise to tap outside risk capital, without which it is permanently dependent on central capital or relegated to small-scale labour-intensive sectors.

8.5 Systemic Constraints and Reform Alternatives

Once the necessity of remonetisation and some kind of capital market is accepted two problems arise: (i) systemic identity, i.e. whether a fully reformed market socialism is reconcilable with the systemic and ideological premises of socialism; (ii) feasibility, i.e. whether it would be possible to develop further financial institutions while still satisfying systemic or ideological restrictions.

Can capital markets or quasi-markets be reconciled with socialism? The boldness of the Hungarian or the Chinese projects may suggest that this is an idle question. Yet we must take into account the small scale, experimental nature and unfinished implementation of these projects, which may still be opposed, suspended or reversed precisely in the name of systemic orthodoxy.

The question has a qualified positive answer. In all socialist economies there is a possibility of appropriating consumption goods for postponed consumption; why not then let people save in the form of money rather than hoarding goods, so that there is more to go round for those who wish to consume or for the state to undertake more productive investment or more social consumption. If there is money, there is a positive nominal interest to induce people to part with their liquidity-yielding cash (too much liquidity in the hands of the population is potentially unstable); in all socialist economies there are also lotteries. If private shareholding was diffused, as in the capitalist ideal of a 'property owning democracy', and if shareholders' voting powers were restricted or removed, private shareholding would be no different from a combination of fixed interest savings and lottery tickets, except that its yields would be more justifiable than those of a pure game of chance. If shares were regarded as conflicting with socialist principles then the very ability to save would have to be challenged on the same grounds. But suppose a further restriction—which will certainly remain at least for some time in a number of socialist countries—that shareholding should be public not private. Would it be feasible to replicate the functioning of capital markets under these restrictions?

There seem to be two readymade solutions. The first is the development of a German-type banking involvement in the management of enterprises; the second is the more specialised use of Algerian-type Fonds de Participation.

Banks' control over companies is exercised in Germany through the appointment of representatives to the boards of borrowing firms, through direct shareholding [found to be 9 per cent of share capital in a study of 74 representative quoted companies, Eckstein (1980)] and above all through proxy voting on behalf of those shareholders (by and large the majority) who have lodged their shares with their banks see for instance Cable (1985a, b). This institutional pattern was introduced as a consequence of the underdevelopment of capital markets in late nineteenth century Germany and is naturally suited to the rudimentary capital market of a reforming socialist country. Public shareholders, possibly also private shareholders without voting rights, could entrust competing commercial banks with the task of overviewing their companies and monitoring and promoting their profitability. However, the merits of German-type supervision of industry by banks are controversial and the system has come under strong criticism recently, especially in Germany (Gessler Kommission 1979; Eckstein 1980; Vittas 1983). The system is widely regarded as a second-best option; the dominating role of banks in the stock exchange is resented, especially in view of conflicting interests vested in different functions of banks as lenders, shareholders and advisors to investors, their emphasis on short term performance and the dangers of monopolistic practices [which have attracted the attention of the Monopolkommission, see Cable (1985a)]. Moreover the German system generates a certain insulation between the real world of production and the world of financial values, which prevents the fulfilment of one of the main functions of a capital market, that of stimulating efficient redeployment of assets. More to the point, the German system coexists with a full-fledged stock exchange and cannot possibly be expected to function as a substitute for a stock exchange.

The second feasible development involves exclusively state holding companies in market-making and the management of state investments; it is the Algerian solution. The establishment and the mode of operation of Fonds de Participation are very ingenious and original means of administering state ownership and simulating the operation of the wanted capital markets. Three problems can be anticipated, however: (i) the arbitrary and necessarily accounting-oriented valuation of enterprise assets, which remains an administrative act divorced from market verification; (ii) the understatement of profits if only cash flows are considered, ignoring the component of enterprise profits which is made up of capital gains brought about by enterprise success, with resulting conflicts between Fonds and enterprises as to the distribution or reinvestment of profits;

(iii) the incentive structure of individual administrators of the Fonds raises a dilemma: individual benefit can be seen as undue participation in the returns to national savings; yet without some form of participation the incentive/penalty structure of Fonds administrators is defective, and only too likely to be dominated by ministerial presence in their shareholders' assemblies, leading to a perpetuation of central administrative control on enterprise capital.

A third possibility can be imagined, of relying on a competitive valuation of enterprise assets, generated within the state sector, as a basis for an implicit valuation of enterprise shares, with individuals barred from ownership but able to take risks and associated rewards and penalties by means of loans and deposits indexed to the performance of shares of their choice (or by means of bets such as can be taken today in capitalist economies on a share index). Such competitive valuation of enterprise assets would start from a self-assessed valuation by enterprise managers. Realistic valuations of assets would be obtained if managers were forced to sell them to other enterprises that might wish to buy them at the declared prices or to revise prices so as to make such transactions unattractive [capital taxation being used to avoid overvaluation by managers; for a more detailed description and account of the possible mode of operation of such a scheme see Nuti (1987a, b)].

Such simulation of capital markets would not violate any of the systemic-ideological restrictions indicated above, yet would have no side effects other than those of a true capital market. Although the effects on efficiency and distribution of such a simulated market would be qualitatively similar to actual capital markets with private shareholdings, the impact of individual gambling on share valuations would be regulated at will by government policy through the agency or agencies entering indexed transactions or taking bets with private individuals. The basic equivalence of actual and proposed capital markets has an important corollary; if capital markets can be replicated without violating the strictest systemic/ideological constraints, in this way or in some other way they ought to and most probably will be implemented.

Bibliography

Arnold, A. Z. (1937). Banks, credit and money in Soviet Russia (New York).

Berliner, J. (1976). The innovation decision in Soviet Industry (MIT Press, Cambridge, MA).

Brown, A. A. and E. Neuberger (Eds.) (1968). International Trade and Central Planning (University of California Press, Berkeley and Los Angeles, CA).

Brus, W. (1964). Ogolne problemy funkcjonowania gospodarki socjalistycznej (PWL Warsaw). English trans. The market in a socialist economy (Routledge and Kegan Paul, London).

Cable, J. R. (1985a). The bank-industry relationship in West Germany: Performance and policy aspects, in: Schwalbach ed., Industry structure and performance (Edition Sigma, Berlin 1985).

Cable, J. R. (1985b). Capital market information and industrial performance: The role of West German Banks, *The Economic Journal*, March, 118-132.

Carr. E.H. and R.W. Davies (1969). Foundations of a planned economy (1926-29, Vol. I), (Macmillan, London).

Daviddi, R. (1987). Monetary reforms in Bulgaria. Conference paper (EUI, Florence).

Dimitrijevic, D. and G. Macesich (1973). Monetary finance in contemporary Yugoslavia (Praeger, New York).

Dimitrijevic, D. and G. Macesich (1981). Money and finance in Yugoslavia (Praeger, New York).

Eckstein. W. (1980). The role of the banks in corporate concentration in West Germany, Zeitschrift fur die gesamte Staatswissenschaft 136, 465-482.

Ellman, M. (1987). China's OTC markets, Conference paper (SSEES, London), forthcoming in ACES.

Furobotn, E.G. (1980). The socialist labor-managed firm and bank-financed investment: Some theoretical issues, Journal of Comparative Economics 4, No. 2, 184-191.

Furobotn, E.G. and S. Pejovich (1972). Property rights and economic theory: A survey of recent literature, Journal of Economic Literature, 10, No. 3, 4, 1137-1162.

Garvey, G. (1966). Money, banking and credit in Eastern Europe, New York (Federal Reserve Bank of New York).

Gessler, Kommission (1979). Bericht der Studienkommission - Grundsatzfragen der Kreditwirtschaft, Schriftenreihe des BMF No. 28 (Report of the Study Commission: Basic questions of credit economics, BMF Series No. 28), Knapp, Frankfurt.

Grossman. G. (1966). Gold and the sword: Money in the Soviet command economy, in: H. Rosovsky (Ed), Industrialization in two systems: Essays in honor of Alexander Gerschenkron (Wiley, New York).

Grossman. G. (Ed.) (1968). Money and Plan (University of California Press, Berkeley and Los Angeles, CA).

Holzman. F. D. (1974). Foreign Trade under Central Planning (Harvard University Press, Cambridge, MA).

Holzman. F.D. (1976). International Trade under Communism: Politics and Economics (Macmillan. London).

Kornai. J. (1980), The Economics of Shortage, Vol. I and II (Amsterdam, North-Holland).

Kornai, J. (1982). Growth, Shortage and Efficiency (Blackwell. Oxford).

Kornai, J. (1986), The soft budget constraint. *Kyklos*, 39, No. 1, 3-30.

Nuti, D. M. (1971). The evolution of Polish investment planning, Jahrbuch der Wirtschaft Osteuropas, Band 3, Munich and Vienna, 395-483.

Nuti, D. M. (1986). Hidden and repressed inflation in Soviet-type economies: Definitions, measurements and stabilisation. Contributions to Political Economy. Vol. 5, 37-82.

Nuti, D.M. (1987a). Financial innovation under market socialism, EUI working paper No. 87/285, EUI Florence).

Nuti, D.M. (1987b). Competitive valuation and efficiency of capital investment in the socialist economy, *European Economic Review,* 32, 2-6.

Portes, R. (1983). The theory and measurement of macroeconomic disequilibrium in centrally planned economies (Birkbeck College. London), Discussion paper, No. 161, October.

Uvalic M. (1987), Shareholding in Yugoslavia: Theory and practice, Conference paper, EUI, Florence.

van Brabant, I. M. (1973), Bilateralism and Structural Bilateralism in Intra-CMEA Trade (Rotterdam University Press. Rotterdam).

Vanek, J. (1970). The General Theory of Labor-managed Market Economies (Cornell University Press, Ithaca, NY).

Vittas. D. (1983). Banks' relations with industry (CLBC Research Group, London).

Xu Jing'an (1987). The stock-share system: A new avenue for China's economic reform, *Journal of Comparative Economics* 11. No. 3. September.

Ward, B. (1967). The Socialist Economy. A Study of Organizational Alternatives (Random House, New York)

Wiles, P. J. (1968). Communist International. Economics, 247.

9

Feasible Financial Innovation Under Market Socialism

Domenico Mario Nuti

Published in Christine Kessides, Timothy King, Mario Nuti and Catherine Sokil (Eds), *Financial Reform in Socialist Economies,* Economic Development Institute (EDI) - World Bank Seminar Series and the European University Institute, Florence, The World Bank, Washington, D.C., 1989, pp. 85–105. The volume includes revised papers presented at a workshop on Financial Reform in Socialist Economies at the European University Institute, Florence, in October 1987, which originated from discussions between Timothy King, then a World Bank country economist working on Hungary and Poland, and Mario Nuti of the Economics Department of EUI, then a consultant to the Bank in its work on Poland, about the parallel movements toward financial reform taking place in the Bank's socialist member countries and the interest of the international financial institutions in this process. An earlier version of the paper under the title "Financial innovation under market socialism" was published as *EUI Working Paper* No. 285, European University Institute, Florence, 1987.

This paper is part of an EC-funded research project on "East-West trade and financial relations in the 1980s" directed by the author at the EUI and has benefited from the author's collaboration with the World Bank. Earlier drafts of this paper were presented at the EUI Working Group on Comparative Economic Systems on November 20, 1986 and at the LSE Seminar on Comparative Economics on February 25, 1987. Nonincriminating acknowledgments for useful comments and suggestions are due to participants in both seminars and in particular to Renzo Daviddi, Saul Estrin, Felix FitzRoy, Donald George, Staszek Gomulka, Jacek Rostowski, Francis Seton, Milica Uvalic and Peter Wiles, as well as to Marcello de Cecco, Bob Davies, Manuel Hinds, and George Suranyi.

D. M. Nuti (✉)
La Sapienza, University of Rome, Rome, Italy
e-mail: milica.uvalic@unipg.it

© The Author(s), under exclusive license to Springer Nature Switzerland AG 2023

S. Estrin, M. Uvalic (eds.), *Collected Works of Domenico Mario Nuti, Volume I,* Studies in Economic Transition, https://doi.org/10.1007/978-3-031-12334-4_9

Over the last 30 years centrally planned economies, also known as Soviet-type or socialist economies or as instances of realized socialism, have often undertaken and to some extent implemented reform projects for the progressive expansion of the scope of markets at the expense of direct central allocation. From Yugoslavia to China, from Hungary to Poland and the Soviet Union, none of these economies with the possible exception of Albania has escaped this process; the very frequency of reform attempts indicates both the necessity and difficulty of changing the principles of operation of socialist planning, rather than simply introducing marginal improvements. Reform projects have included varying degrees of enterprise decisional autonomy, contractual relations instead of central allocation of materials and foreign exchange, direct access to foreign trade, workers' self-management, and reprivatization.

Economic reform in each case has implied also, sooner or later, a certain remonetization of the socialist economy. This paper reviews monetary reform, its latest developments and its systemic limits, and then considers the following questions. Take an imaginary closed economy where socialist central planning has been successfully reformed and converted to market socialism, but where the system's economic or ideological premises still preclude financial institutions such as private ownership of voting equity shares or a full-fledged stock exchange. Are there important functions in such an economy that might have been performed by the missing financial institutions? Could these functions be performed by already existing, permitted financial and other institutions? What kind of financial innovation might replace or simulate the functioning of the missing institutions? I will argue that the customary restrictions do not affect the possibility but hinder the efficiency of financial intermediation, and that secondary equity markets importance also under market socialism; that, nevertheless, market socialism could, in principle, replicate or simulate those functions without relaxing systemic restrictions. A three-stage proposal is put forward for financial innovation which ought to replace the missing institutions; here financial innovation is understood not only in the general sense of new markets, instruments, and institutions, but also in the technical sense in which it is used in current debates on capitalist financial developments, that is, of "banks' disintermediation" and of the economy's "securitization." The final section of the paper summarizes the arguments for and against the proposal.

It should be stressed that this is a purely intellectual speculation about the feasibility of potentially useful institutions, not a firm statement about desirable change. No market socialist model, however, can be deemed complete unless it considers and settles one way or another the questions raised by the missing financial institutions.

9.1 Reform and Remonetization

A moneyless socialist economy, outside a distant full communism, was rarely suggested or practiced; Neurath's Naturalwirtschaft (1919), Soviet War Communism (1918–1921) at its peak, or Cambodia in the early 1970s were exceptions. Lenin had understood the importance of banks as an administrative structure; his intuition and the necessary implications of central planning are reflected in the role of money in the traditional socialist model, which took shape in the USSR at the turn of the 1930s and was fully imitated in the other Eastern European countries (see Garvey 1966).

In the traditional centrally planned model money is primarily an accounting instrument of aggregation and control; financial flows are compartmentalized between enterprises and households, with a bank money circuit for interenterprise transactions and cash for transactions involving households as buyers or sellers. These financial flows are adjusted passively to planned physical flows and to the degree of their implementation by a single bank monopolizing the functions of commercial as well as central banking (therefore dubbed "monobank"). Households are free to convert cash into available consumption goods, a small range of durables including some production goods, or save it as cash or a limited range of financial instruments (deposits, bonds, insurance, lottery tickets, etc.); the balance of revenues and expenditures of the population is closely monitored and ideally balanced ex ante through price and incomes policy; it forms the basis of cash issues. Enterprises can only use finance for purposes specified in plan documents; in this sense

Berliner (1976) talks of "documonetary" economy. Investment is centrally decided and allocated in real terms while finance is provided automatically and interest-free from the state budget to investors, who are subject to straight-line amortization charges on the historical cost of their investments and transfer back to the state budget any surplus which they may realize (or rely on further transfers from the budget to cover their planned losses). Credit is mostly short term and is also automatically available to enterprises to finance their working capital requirements necessary to fulfill their planned tasks; it is granted by the Central Bank at an almost symbolic interest rate designed to cover banks' administrative costs. Trade credit between enterprises is forbidden. Thus money in the traditional system is a unit of account, two-tier medium of exchange conditionally to plan conformity, a store of value in competition with inventories of goods rather than with alternative financial or productive assets. It is an instrument for economic management, except when planners lose control over financial balances, in which case monetary policy can be an important instrument for restoring that balance.

In the reformed socialist model (which still is not fully realized in any actual socialist economy) money recovers an important role (see Brus 1964, for a pioneering detection and analysis of the early stages of this process in the 1960s; and Grossman 1968). Financial flows become fully connected. Commercial banking is separated from central banking (as it was done in Britain with Sir Robert Peel's Act of 1844, which abandoned the principles of the banking school in favor of those of the currency school) and exercised by competing banks (as had been the case already in the USSR in the early stages of NEP; see Arnold 1937; Carr and Davies 1969). Investment grants are replaced by bank credits, interenterprise loans, and self-finance. Credit is provided not automatically but at the discretion of banks on a contractual basis and at an interest rate which is supposed to balance the market. Enterprises which are not deemed creditworthy can be forced into liquidation and bankruptcy. There is a wide range of financial instruments available to households and enterprises. Money becomes an unconditional and therefore more liquid means of payment, and a less attractive store of value because of a wider range of alternatives. The way is paved for active monetary policy, using standard instruments such as reserve and liquidity ratios, rediscounting scale and rates, open market operations, etc.

The role of financial markets and their possible features in a socialist system have been conspicuously neglected both in the classical literature on market socialism and in the blueprints for economic reform in Eastern Europe. Pareto (1902, 1903) stressed the imminence of economic categories such as capital and interest regardless of economic system (Vol. I, Chap. 6; a point made also by Bohm-Bawerk 1909, Vol. I); criticized socialist thinkers for confusing the capitalist and the entrepreneur (Vol. II, Ch. 10) and Proudhon's monetary and banking scheme (Vol. II, Ch. 11) which, providing money automatically for productive undertakings at virtually no interest, closely resembles the monetary system of a traditional centrally planned economy. Barone (1908) expected the Minister of Production of his Collectivistic State to finance investment exclusively through loans at an equilibrium interest rate that matched the marginal return on investment. None of the proponents of "Marktsozialismus" worked out any system-specific arrangement for money and finance. The list includes, besides Heimann (1922, 1934), who coined this term, Taylor (1928), Landauer (1931), Dickinson (1933), and Lange (1938; for a comprehensive survey of pre-War literature see Landauer et al. 1959). The same is true of more recent literature on socialist blueprints, except perhaps Brus' stress on the importance of money in the decentralized model of socialism (Brus 1964). Nove's "feasible socialism" (1983) only mentions money to say that it must be there and never mentions financial markets. In the latest volume on "Rethinking socialist economies" (Nolan and Paine 1986) financial innovation only goes as far as a new State Investment Bank. The development of monetary and financial institutions in the "reformed" socialist economies has simply imitated without change a few capitalist institutions.

9.2 Recent Developments in Socialist Economies

Monetary and financial institutions perhaps are most developed in Yugoslavia where for a long time, especially since 1971, banking and credit have been major instruments of macroeconomic management;

there is a plurality of commercial banks, investment banks, and other financial institutions; and enterprises can lend to or have a share in other enterprises or even found new banks, or sell bonds to the public including individuals (see Dimitrijevic and Macesich 1973, 1983). However, in Yugoslavia these developments may be due to its specific systemic features, since income-sharing by self-managed enterprises is expected to favor financial intermediation at the expense of direct reinvestment of enterprise income (self-financed assets, unlike distributed income, cannot be appropriated by workers; see for instance Pejovich 1976; Furobotn 1980). Moreover, an enterprise in which another enterprise has a direct share investment can pay it back at historical cost, so that what appears as equity is effectively a loan (see the Associated Labor Act, and Uvalić 1987).

Leaving aside Yugoslavia, the most developed monetary and financial institutions can be found in Hungary, especially since the inauguration of the new banking system on January 1, 1987. The National Bank of Hungary has hived off its credit activities by transforming its lending directorates and some local branches into associated but separate banks, such as Innofinance, the National Commercial and Credit Bank, and the Credit Bank of Budapest (Budapesti Itelbank). These and other commercial banks are or soon will be operating, including the Hungarian Foreign Trade Bank, the General Banking and Trust Company, and three banks with substantial foreign participation (the older Central-European International Bank and Citibank Budapest as well as the new 45-percent foreign-owned Unicbank). There is an obligatory reserve ratio of 20 percent for demand deposits and 10 percent for time deposits. "To avoid multiple creation of outstanding reserves, deposits taken over from other financial institutions are exempt from the obligatory reserve requirement" (NBH 1986). The discount rate, which until the end of 1984 was decided by the government, is now decided by the President of the Central Bank.

Bonds were first issued experimentally in Hungary in October 1981 for local authorities and are now regulated by a decree of the Minister of Finance of 1984, no. 28. Government, local authorities, financial institutions and enterprises (state, cooperative, and joint) can issue bonds subject to the approval of the Ministry of Finance. The State Development

Bank is playing a major role in financial intermediation and operates a primary and secondary market for bonds issued by public utilities and other state enterprises.

There are two types of Hungarian bonds: those for sale to the population and those to state agencies. The first are guaranteed by the state (which defeats one of the purposes of financial intermediation, that is, the discrimination between different classes of borrowers with respect to risk), and are tax-free—the latter are not guaranteed and are taxed. The State Development Bank does about one-half of the underwriting. Prospectuses are available to investors and advertised. Bonds for the population are sold for cash over the counter, have bearer form, and can be retraded; most of them are listed daily by the State Development Bank to whom they can be resold. Dealings take place in a trading room in the Budapest headquarters of the State Development Bank, but there are facilities also in the provinces. The range of maturities at issue is 1–15 years, with yields of 7–15 percent, and an average of 11 percent on an average maturity of 7 years. There has been at least one case of performance-linked bonds, with interest of 9 percent increasing to 13 percent subject to the borrower's profit performance. These bonds are traded at various premia or discounts with respect to the price of issue. Average yield is presently 10–10.8 percent, compared with an interest rate of 11 percent paid by enterprises and of 9 percent paid on time deposits of comparable length. The typical investor (accounting for 80 percent of investment) is 50–60 years old. Bonds represent under 1 percent of the population's stock of savings; yearly turnover is about 10 percent the stock of bonds.

After Hungary, the socialist economy most advanced in its monetary and financial reform is perhaps China, where commercial banking has developed and the first experiments with financial markets are taking place (see Naughton 1986). Most of the enterprises issuing shares are collectives or private enterprises whose employees buy the stock, but a few state enterprises are also experimenting with stock. Joint-stock companies are regarded as a mixture of the other three forms of ownership (state, private, and collective; see Sensenbrenner 1987). A first stock exchange is reported to have been opened on September 1, 1986, in Shanghai. The official press has published regulations for bond and share trading in the southern province of Guangdong, where more than 1000 companies have issued such securities. According to the official Economic Daily: "Buyers of shares will be the working public."[1] However this is still no more than a small-scale local experiment; in any case, shares are still illiquid (having to be held for substantial minimum periods) and do not carry a vote. It is significant that the Shanghai Stock Exchange had to be closed for weeks after its opening because all the bonds and shares had been "sold out"[2]; if that market had been functioning properly, oversubscription should have led to intensive retrading.

The Polish reform project of 1981, which is still the official blueprint endorsed by the Party Congresses in 1981 and 1986, envisaged the creation of new, specialized, and fully independent credit institutions. Enterprises are to enter contractual relations with any one bank of their choosing, while the Central Bank is to acquire a new major role as institution of refinancing for other banks (KPZdsRG 1981). Implementation to date in principle does away with automatic credit and relies on contractual relations between banks and enterprises. However, the National Bank of Poland still combines central and commercial banking functions and has virtual monopoly of credit, in spite of the birth (again on the fated date of January 1, 1987) of an Export Development Bank for the state sector. Legislation on state enterprises (September 1981) simply refers to "the bank." However, recently the chief Polish government spokesman, Mr. Jerzy Urban, is reported to have announced that Poland will soon offer shares to private citizens in several state companies: "Plans to start a classic stock market like London's have not been included in existing projects, but if there is a demand for it and if it proves necessary or suitable for the good of the Polish economy, we would not refrain from it."[3]

Recently it has been announced that Bulgaria is to follow the Hungarian monetary and financial reform by mid-1987.[4] If Gorbachev's economic

[1] *Financial Times,* October 15, 1986.

[2] *Handelsblatt,* November 27, 1986.

[3] *Financial Times,* April 7, 1987.

[4] *Financial Times,* February 10, 1987, and *East European Markets,* February 20, 1987.

reforms get off the ground in the Soviet Union, similar monetary and financial changes would have to be introduced, but so far there have only been unofficial intimations of such a possibility.[5]

9.3 Restrictions on Equity Ownership, Control, and Exchange

The introduction of monetary and financial institutions, instruments, and markets in the socialist model so far has not developed anything new, or system-specific. Well-tried capitalist practices simply have been grafted onto the socialist model, only on a smaller scale and subject to three important systemic limitations:

- the exclusion of national individual ownership of equity stakes in state enterprises, with the possible exception of China;
- in any case, the even stricter lack of provisions for shareholders' voting rights to influence managerial appointments, dismissals, and policies; and
- the lack of a developed secondary market even for the equity shares owned by state agencies.

It might be argued that these three restrictions on individual ownership, voting, and secondary exchange do not derive from the system's economic features but are purely ideological. From a purely economic viewpoint, the big divides are:

- whether or not individuals are allowed to save[6];
- the payment of an interest on savings;

[5] Witness an interview with Leonid Abalkin in East European Markets, February 20, 1987, where specific reference to the Hungarian and Bulgarian model is made, and an interview with Abel Aganbegyan on Italian TV on March 15, 1987. See also Petrakov (1987), who specifically indicates the replacement of automatic credit with enterprise creditworthiness, a time structure of interest rates, and profit-oriented and competing "special purpose" banks, though still subject to the "leading role" of Gosbank.

[6] Joan Robinson used to say that the reward of abstinence is first of all the ability to keep what one abstains from consuming.

- the opportunity to take risk and the reward or loss associated with it; and
- whether or not private individuals or agencies are allowed to own means of production and to hire labor.

All extant models of socialist economy encourage individual savings, pay more than symbolic interest, hold lotteries, and pay profit-linked premia. Private enterprises—including joint enterprises also with foreign capital and even with a majority interest—are allowed in many socialist economies, such as Hungary and Poland. Once these systemic limits are exceeded, restrictions on individual ownership and control and the lack of secondary retrading of equities appear to be rooted in the ideological rather than economic principles of the socialist system. Nevertheless, regardless of their causes these restrictions are an integral part of "realized socialism" everywhere; they are hardly dented by the Chinese experimental reform, and given the usual implementation lags they can be expected to continue to apply for the foreseeable future.

The rest of this paper considers:

- the implications of these three restrictions on equity ownership, control, and exchange for the efficiency of market socialism; and
- the possibility of performing or simulating, in that model, the functions which in a capitalist economy are performed, or at any rate should be performed, by capital markets with unrestricted ownership, control, and trading of equity shares.

9.4 Financial Intermediation and Secondary Markets

It is useful to distinguish between the functions of direct (that is, primary) financial intermediation and of secondary trading in securities (which is thin or partly missing for shares under market socialism). Financial intermediaries basically match lenders and borrowers, the short- and long-term ends of the market, and pool or share risks. The issue of new bonds and shares pertains to these functions and can be performed regardless of the existence of a stock exchange as a secondary market, though of course the anticipation of after-issue prices in such a market when it exists is an important determinant of issue prices. In the absence of secondary retrading, financial intermediation would consist exclusively of the issue of new bonds and shares which, as Keynes once advocated out of concern for speculatory instability and the liquidity trap, would be tied to their purchasers in an indissoluble marriage-like contract. Financial intermediation could still be performed, but with two major disabilities. First, over time on average, the resulting illiquidity of financial assets would make them less attractive to potential lenders/investors so that intermediation would take place presumably on a smaller scale and at higher cost to borrowers/issuers—that is, less efficiently than if a secondary market were allowed. Second, speculatory instability would be replaced by yields instability in a thinner market where old stocks are not substitutes for new issues. Borrowing on the security of nontransferable bonds and shares, or small-scale retrading as in the case of unlisted securities, reduces but does not eliminate completely these disabilities and the ensuing inefficiency.

Thus, the first function of secondary markets is that of continuously "liquidizing" both bonds and the real assets embodied in shares, which would otherwise remain illiquid, introducing the possibility of divorcing investors from their long-term investment. This represents a considerable financial inducement to save and to place savings in bonds and shares rather than in inventories and cash, which would be otherwise a more liquid alternative in spite of their actual (storage) or opportunity (forsaken interest) cost. This is an important function in present-day socialist economies, reported to be in a semipermanent state of excess demand (Kornai 1980; see also Nuti 1986), not only for individuals if shares were to be made available to them, but for enterprises which could be cured at least partly of their hoarding habits and of their "soft budget" syndrome (diagnosed by Kornai 1980). An enterprise with access to liquid investment in other enterprises, in fact, would find hoarding of both materials and cash more costly than without such an access.

Another function of secondary markets for shares and bonds is that of providing a current valuation of enterprise financial liabilities and above all a valuation of sorts of any listed company as a going concern—that is, a current valuation of enterprises' net physical and financial assets in their current use and under the existing management and the actual policies pursued. Together with the dividend record of a company, this valuation and its trend give an indication of past performance and prospects. A corollary, which could be viewed as a separate function, is that of bringing the current valuation of an enterprise as a going concern close to the maximum value, net of liabilities, that the enterprise's productive assets could have if redeployed elsewhere in the economy or employed in the same activity under a different management and/or policy. If this were not the case, an incentive would appear for another company or group to acquire a controlling interest and gain from a change of management and/or policy or even the liquidation of the company regardless of the wishes of the existing management. This function, which the stock exchange in capitalist economies often does not perform sufficiently or performs only too well (as witnessed by factory closures, asset stripping, and insider trading as well as turbulence in financial markets) is very important for bringing managerial capitalism somewhat closer to the traditional capitalist model in spite of the separation of ownership and control (Marris 1964; see however the reservations expressed by Stiglitz 1985).

There can be no doubt that these functions, whether or not they are well performed in a capitalist economy, if at all, are extremely important in a "market socialist" economy where production and trade are decentralized to enterprises, and "monetization" has been introduced successfully. A continuous evaluation of assets is needed to assess performance by adding to (deducting from) current distributed profits the increase (decrease) in the value of capital assets used by enterprises; this is preferable to arbitrary and debatable (especially if there is inflation) accounting conventions for the determination of an appropriate capital amortization allowance to be subtracted from gross profits. Such valuation is also necessary in order to assess the prospective profitability of enterprise activity, as opposed to profitability calculated on the historical cost (even if properly corrected for amortization) of the enterprise's capital assets. If the ratio of prospective profitability to the current value of assets is lower than interest rates applicable over the period, there is a case for considering enterprise liquidation and redeployment of assets even if prospective profits are sufficiently high with respect to the historical cost of the enterprise's capital assets. These functions are particularly important at times when a productive structure that has become inappropriate to current conditions is being "restructured" in order to indicate the desirability of continued operation versus redeployment and to put all enterprises on an equal footing when performance indicators are used to determine managerial and staff bonuses, profit retentions, and creditworthiness. Polish planners, for instance, have expressed a preoccupation for giving all enterprises "equal chances" with the introduction of economic reform, whereas historical valuations of enterprise assets normally are a biased basis for calculating profitability as an indicator of current and prospective performance, except in the unlikely case that *ex post* profit rates happen to be uniform and equal to their planned levels throughout the economy.

Suppose an enterprise expects to be able to use the assets of another more productively if it could take them over and use them in a different sector or simply change its policies or pursue the same policies with greater efficiency. Suppose also that the first enterprise has the financial means to acquire the second, or it can persuade other enterprises or credit institutions to lend the means to acquire it. The ability of the first enterprise to take over the second simply descends from competitive entrepreneurship and not from capitalism as a system of ownership. Once state enterprises are transformed—as reform projects state to be the intent—from administrative agencies into competing profit-minded and decentralized agencies, it makes no sense to give them a de facto monopoly in the use of the productive assets which they happen to possess. That monopoly is already broken when a loss-making enterprise is liquidated or goes bankrupt (for instance in current Polish legislation), as in that case its assets and liabilities can be taken over by another enterprise or be dispersed among a number of enterprises. At present, however, managers of state enterprises—both in capitalist and socialist systems—are protected from "unfriendly" takeovers by groups acquiring a controlling share interest. Yet without this potential threat managers can afford to be inefficient and monopolistic, and there is no competitive mechanism which might redeploy efficiently existing assets, in view of the rarity and at any rate the imperfection of markets for used productive assets.

The question is, therefore, how can these functions be performed in economies which, rightly or wrongly, do not allow individual shareholders to have a vote or possibly even to exist, and which do not, in any case, wish to recreate the large-scale logistic apparatus of a stock exchange.

9.5 Existing Instruments and Institutions

The valuation of capital assets could be undertaken as a centralized task or market service within the framework of the respective model. We could imagine a State Committee of Experts for the Current Valuation of Capital, enlisting accountants, economists, and engineers, sitting in the capital city and issuing an official valuation of all plants, buildings, and land in the whole country, officially applicable from January 1 of the base year, revised periodically or on request. Information costs and "moral hazard" make this impracticable; we can presume that if central planning were capable of performing this kind of task speedily and accurately, it would not need reforming, since the information required for such task is the same as that required for the efficient management of the planned economy—that is, data about current and future resource allocation and prices.

Alternatively, we could imagine a private or state brokerage agency (as suggested by Manuel Hinds) which, for a fee, would seek better uses for existing capital equipment and locate redundant equipment to fill existing needs. Such an agency, or a number of them in competition, however, would be limited to consensual redeployment of existing assets, and would not perform any disciplinary role on enterprise management.

Starting from a Hungarian-type environment—that is, public shareholders and commercial bank competition—perhaps the most promising development which could be imitated from Western experience is that of German bank involvement in the management of enterprises. The special feature considered here is not the mixed nature of German banks, operating both at the short and long end of the market, but their intimate involvement in the management of industrial companies: through the appointment of representatives to the Boards of borrowing firms, through direct shareholding (found to be 9 percent of share capital in a study of

74 representative quoted companies by Eckstein 1989) and above all through proxy voting on behalf of those shareholders (by and large the majority) who have lodged their shares with their banks (see for instance Cable 1985a, b). This institutional pattern was introduced as a consequence of the underdevelopment of capital markets in Germany in the late nineteenth century and is naturally suited to the rudimentary capital market of a country like Hungary. Public shareholders, possibly also private shareholders without voting rights, could entrust competing commercial banks with the task of overviewing their companies and monitoring and promoting their profitability.

However, the merits of German-type supervision of industry by banks are controversial. The system has come under strong criticism recently, especially in Germany (Gessler Kommission 1979; Eckstein 1989; Vittas 1983). The system is widely regarded as a second-best option; the dominating role of banks in the stock exchange is resented, especially in view of conflicting interests vested in different functions of banks as lenders, shareholders, and advisors to investors; their emphasis on short-term performance; and the dangers of monopolistic practices (which have attracted the attention of the Monopolkommission, see Cable 1985a). It is no accident that German bank legislation explicitly prohibits any transmission of inside information by bank representatives on company boards to their own bank or primary employer, or to any other party.[7] Werner (1981) suggests that bank officials are well aware of their sensitive position and comply with these prescriptions; Lutter (1981) emphasizes that bank appointees on company boards are subject to the mandate to exclusively promote the interests of the company supervised. Thus the kind of board behavior that is supposed to give banks direct control over their borrowers is actually illegal; control must rely on banks' shareholding and proxy-voting. (Fitzroy and Kraft point out that the main role of bank representatives in the supervisory board, or Aufsichtsrat, is to approve annual financial statements and to appoint members of the management board (Vorstand); only at times of crisis, such as the recent near-collapse of AEG, is there any direct

[7] See Articles 93 and 116 of the Aktiengesetz. Article 404 treats any break of confidentiality by bank representatives as liable to prosecution as a criminal offence. I am grateful to Felix RitzRoy for drawing my attention to these norms and for providing the next references quoted from an unpublished paper by FitzRoy and Kornelius Kraft.

involvement by bank representatives, while a strong bank presence in the Aufsichtsrat of AEG did not help reveal the build-up of the crisis until it was almost too late.) Moreover, the German system generates a certain insulation between the real world of production and the world of financial values, which prevents the fulfilment of the function discussed above, of stimulating efficient redeployment of assets.

For these reasons, and as an end in itself, let us explore further the range of permissible financial institutions under market socialism. What follows is an intellectual experiment understood as an exercise in consistency between the premises and existing models of market socialism, not a statement about the relative merits of markets versus plans, private versus state ownership, or of alternative models of socialism.

Stage I: Capital Evaluation and Interfirm Mobility

Imagine a successfully reformed and remonetized socialist economy where enterprises are engaged in production and trade through contractual relations with other state agencies, while planning is confined to macroeconomic policies and truly parametric (that is, non enterprise-specific) instruments for the central manipulation of market signals. Sectoral policies can be undertaken by the government, but sector-specific subsidy or tax differentials must be applied by the government consistently and predictably. Suppose the following steps are implemented:

1. Enterprise managers are asked to assess the current value of their productive assets, as a whole and for specific components (such as individual plants) exceeding a certain ceiling, and to register it with a central public record office. If managers do not provide such a valuation by a given date, the central record office automatically enters the book value of enterprise assets. (Yearly book values are already publicly available in Poland for the top 500 manufacturing enterprises and the top 300 state farms.)
2. At any subsequent time any other state enterprise can bid for the enterprise's productive assets, as a whole or for a specifically listed plant or other large item. When this happens, either the challenged enterprise

revises upward the valuation of its assets to the point that the request to purchase is withdrawn, or has to sell at the highest valuation offered. If the bid is for a section of the enterprise assets, the enterprise can link it to other sections but has to prove that there is a technological connection between the two sections. If there is a sale, sale revenue is first used to satisfy creditors; any remainder is retained by the enterprise unless it has sold all its assets, in which case any net residual value is transferred to the enterprise's shareholders. (In their absence, Branch Ministries, defined as "founders" in Polish law, could take this role.)

3. At any time the enterprise can alter its capital valuation registered with the public records office, raising it as new capacity comes on stream or as the profitability of its products increases, or lowering it in consideration of wear and tear, obsolescence, or falls in the profitability of its products.
4. Any increase in the valuation of the enterprise's productive assets recorded spontaneously by the enterprise, or as a result of a bid for its assets (whether failed or successful) in any fiscal year, net of any change in its financial assets and liabilities, is regarded as part of net profit (and any fall as a loss) to be added to (or deducted from) the enterprise's distributed profits. (Any deduction for amortization becomes a purely internal reallocation of funds in compliance with accounting conventions, but no deduction for amortization is needed to calculate net profit once the change in the current value of enterprise assets has been estimated and added to dividends. Whether profits distributed to workers should or should not be included in this notion of profit depends on whether the workers' profit share is or is not regarded as part of workers' basic income.)
5. Unsuccessful bidders are paid by the enterprise a small commission on their raise over the last previous bid (or over the initial value for the first bidder).
6. A tax is charged on any increase in the value of the enterprise's net assets due exclusively to a revaluation of existing assets, at a tax rate higher than the tax on operating profit. Alternatively, or at the same time, any profit-rate-linked bonus for managers and staff is calculated at a lower rate for that part of the enterprise profit which is due to the revaluation of existing assets.

Enterprise managers have an incentive to understate the value of their assets to avoid paying tax on capital gains or to obtain in the future higher profit-rate-linked bonuses; but a limit to their wish to understate is set by the positive though weaker impact of capital gains on current bonuses and, above all, by the danger of encouraging other enterprises to consider taking them over. The two opposite incentives do not necessarily cancel out, inducing managers to reveal their true assessment of capital values, but their deliberate distortions will be contained within a range which can be narrowed by manipulating bonuses and tax parameters.

The arrangements outlined under Stage I have the advantage of providing:

- a continuous, nonbureaucratic, decentralized, and automatic evaluation of enterprise capital, necessary to assess past performance and guide current allocation;
- a mechanism for intersectoral and interfirm mobility of physical capital, necessary to ensure its efficient use; and
- an incentive for enterprises to use their capital equipment in the way that maximizes their valuation and a disincentive to invest in ventures which might reduce the net value of their assets.

Thus some of the tasks usually expected of a capital market are performed here without a bureaucracy and with a minimum of financial innovation without touching at all the systemic constraints of "realized socialism."

Stage I is similar to a proposal by the Hungarian economist Tibor Liska (see Liska 1963, 1986a, b; MacRae 1983; Barsony 1982). In Liska's "entrepreneurial socialism," however, individuals use the guaranteed income out of their share of social capital to bid for the rental of production goods, renting them if successful or encashing from successful bidders the amount of their unsuccessful raises, surrendering at death their original capital stake and its accretion. Here state and private enterprises bid for the purchase of larger chunks of productive assets, if unsuccessful keeping nothing or at most a small percentage on their raises. The differences between the two schemes are substantial; ultimately they only have in common the permanent state of insecurity of enterprise managers, continuously exposed to the challenge of potentially better users of their enterprise's assets. Kornai criticizes Liska for exposing managers to this kind of insecurity (Kornai 1982) but no competitive behavior and profit-mindedness—and therefore no hardening of Kornai's alleged "soft-budget constraints" (Kornai 1980)—can be expected of managers without introducing precisely this kind of insecurity.

A limitation of Stage I is that it forces managers to utilize their assets as profitably as they could be used in their best alternative use outside their firm and not up to the maximum profitability that could be obtained in the firm, and which only they are likely to know. Stage I can, at most, bring the valuation of an enterprise's capital up to its maximum value obtainable outside the enterprise. If enterprise capital is not easily redeployable elsewhere, that is, if it is highly specific or immobile, the possibility remains of its management using it inefficiently undisturbed or exploiting monopolistic power. The same snag would apply to Liska's proposals. Stage II is designed to overcome these difficulties by introducing voting shares but maintaining the systemic constraints of excluding private individuals from share ownership and voting control and of avoiding a large-scale secondary market.

Stage II: Share Capital Evaluation, Exchange, and Control

Stage II is composed of the following steps, preferably but not necessarily taken after Stage I is completed:

1. State enterprises are requested to declare and record in a public register the current market value of their physical assets (hence the desirability of Stage I to ensure a realistic assessment of current value), financial assets, and liabilities (which could be audited and evaluated at the time of the declaration, subject to the same external bidding in case of divergent views about interest rate trends), and thereby their estimated net worth.
2. The enterprise founders (branch ministries if there are no others) are then issued a number of shares, each of a nominal value of, say, for

Poland, 100,000 zlotys with a total capitalization equal to the enterprise's estimated net worth.

3. Thereafter the enterprise can, at any time on its own initiative, raise or lower the valuation of its net worth, thereby altering the current value of its shares. In practice the enterprise simply announces publicly a revised value of its shares, without reference to its founders as initial shareholders or to subsequent shareholders.
4. As long as they are shareholders, founders can *ex officio* raise or lower the valuation of the enterprise shares. However, founders must sell the shares in their possession to any state agency (productive enterprises, banks including the central bank and financial institutions, pension funds, insurance companies, etc.) wishing to buy them at the price decreed by enterprises or revised by themselves. The shares so acquired by state agencies are managed by them as owners and not by their own founders; the government can repurchase those shares if they are offered for sale but it can only do this via the central bank or through a special State Holding Company, not through the original branch ministries as founders. In this way share transfers implement automatically a decentralization process which progressively divests ownership and control away from central sectoral bodies, however without violating the principles of public ownership since the transfers do not involve the private sector or private individuals. Founders transfer the proceeds of their share sales to the state budget; government policy can affect share prices in such a way as to reduce or raise the liquidity of state enterprises, as it happens in capitalist economies as a result of open market operations.
5. State agencies wishing to purchase or to sell the shares of an enterprise at the price published by enterprises or revised by shareholding founders address their request to the enterprise itself (hence the avoidance of a large-scale centralized market). If a net excess demand or supply of shares arises at those prices, if it is small relative to turnover—say, 20 percent—it is handled through proportional rationing (as in the case of oversubscribed issues of capitalist companies). If it is large relative to turnover but small relative to the total stock of the enterprise—say, 1 to 5 percent—a waiting list is used. Otherwise, alternative procedures are followed for excess demand or supply.

6. If, once the enterprise founders hold no more shares, a net excess demand appears, the enterprise must either accept the surplus bids and issue additional shares at the published price, or raise the valuation of its shares upward by small predetermined discrete steps until the excess demand disappears. (If at some point excess demand turns into excess supply, the price last quoted is regarded as an equilibrium price though bidders are rationed, regardless of the size of the latest excess demand relative to either turnover or total stock.)
7. If at the self-assessed share price of an enterprise there is a net excess supply of shares, beyond the tolerance limits indicated above, the enterprise may choose to reimburse the excess shares at that price but is highly unlikely to do so unless it is particularly liquid and the management is far more confident of the enterprise's profit prospects than existing shareholders. Alternatively the enterprise can and, more probably, will lower the value of its stock until the excess supply of its shares disappears or turns into a small excess demand, at which point as in the previous case bidders either are in equilibrium or are rationed at a price treated as the equilibrium price.
8. Each share carries a voting right, exercised at yearly meetings of shareholders, or more frequently at special meetings if they are called by a substantial fraction of total shareholders. At those meetings the performance of existing managers is discussed; current policies and future plans can be revised and limits imposed on management or distribution to shareholders; and managers can be dismissed and appointed. If shares are sufficiently dispersed, a controlling interest can be acquired with a fraction substantially lower than the majority of shares. The potential threat of hostile bidders taking over a controlling interest will exercise some restraining influence on managers otherwise tempted to stray from the straight and narrow development path of efficiency and concern for shareholders' interests. In general, there can be no effective market or quasimarket for shares without the attachment of voting rights to shares, because otherwise there is no shareholders' protection against managerial inefficiency or simply lack of initiative or imagination; at a time of transition from centralized commands to decentralized enterprises the voting provision is even more necessary.

9. As in Stage I, the change in the market valuation of the enterprise is an element to be added to distributed profits for the assessment of managerial performance. In Stage II, however, the possibility of managers deliberately overstating the value of their assets is ruled out by market discipline (that is, by the appearance of excess supply of shares at artificially inflated asset values) so that there is no longer a need for a tougher tax treatment of the appreciation of enterprise assets.
10. The operation of this kind of secondary market for shares is not only fragmented and decentralized to each enterprise, but is also intermittent to a greater extent than the capitalist stock exchange as we know it. The secondary market envisaged here is best thought of as opening and shutting once a day, or a week, or even a month, to handle the bids received since the previous closure. To iron out the effect of this type of discontinuity (qualitatively no different from the closure of capitalist stock markets outside opening hours and working days), it is best to conceive buying and selling bids not as single-valued quantities at the previously announced price, but as indications of alternative quantities bought or sold at alternative prices in the neighborhood of that price; or more simply as indications of reserve prices below or above which the bid is revoked.

The combined outcome of all these arrangements is a kind of "slow motion" stock market, however, with all the features necessary for its vitality, namely: competitive bidding, negligible indivisibilities, and restraint of managerial discretion. Stage II can be introduced gradually. It does not violate the principles of public ownership. It does, however, dissolve the sectoral centralization built into branch ministries, thus preparing the ground for their abolition, but it preserves instruments of central government policy, both macroeconomic (through open market operations of the central bank) and sectoral (through the activities of a new State Holding Company). In principle, it cannot be said to be potentially better or worse than the capitalist stock exchange as we know it, except for the exclusion of private individuals. This matters not only because of individual exclusion from a range of enrichment opportunities, which is bound to have a discouraging effect on personal savings, but because the exclusion makes the secondary market described unresponsive to information, beliefs, and expectations diffused throughout society at large. The additional provisions introduced in Stage III are designed to remove this limitation.

Stage III: Individual Indirect Participation Without Ownership or Control

The exclusion of private individuals from direct ownership of shares in productive and financial state enterprises (investment trusts, common funds, and so forth) is not an insurmountable obstacle to individual participation in either risk-bearing or control. Risk-bearing without ownership is already present in capitalist financial markets through options trading as well as "bets" on the movements of major financial indices; with appropriate modifications these institutions could be grafted onto market socialism. One could also add a new institution, namely the indexation of deposits and loans to the cumulative performance of a share inclusive of the reinvestment of dividends, which would produce the same results without the leverage effect and therefore speculative dangers of options and "bets." The idea is that one or more state agencies should buy and sell options, take bets, make loans or take deposits, at prices/odds/rates such that individuals could gain from spotting above average and below average performing enterprises or lose from their failure to do so, if they wish and on the scale they wish to expose themselves to risk. If, in addition, a mechanism was introduced to ensure that individual "investment" choices had an impact on share prices, individuals would be exercising, indirectly, some influence both on managers (threatened by takeover if policies unwanted by the public depress share prices) and on investment allocation (since enterprises popular with the public will register higher share prices, thus facilitating their raising of capital through share issues). Let us consider first the three alternative modes of risk-sharing without ownership and the pricing formulas associated with each, then the question of indirect control.

1. An option is the right to buy (call option) or sell (put option) shares (or anything else) at a specific price (the striking price) before a specific date at which the option expires. Normally, however, when an option is exercised by its buyer/owner it leads to a payment by its seller of an amount corresponding to the difference between the striking and the spot price of the amount of shares involved, rather than to the actual purchase/sale of that amount of shares at the striking price (especially if a share purchase had to be followed by an actual sale for the realization of profit from the operation). The option transactor thus incurs risk and is exposed to uncertain benefits or losses without acquiring ownership (see Cox and Rubinstein 1985).
However, a share option market is not enough for a market socialist economy where Stage II of financial innovation has been realized: options trading in capitalist markets is not purely speculative but plays a major hedging role for share owners, so that nonshare-owning individuals would not be present in large numbers on that market. But suppose that a state agency, possibly the State Holding Company that actually owns shares on behalf of the government, is given the statutory obligation of issuing or buying call or put options. Let us say that call options are traded for a striking share price equal to the current share price and are sold at a price equal to the market rate of interest which would mature over the period on the current value of the shares involved, while dividends, if any, paid before the option expires accrue to the buyer of the call option. In this way the individual "investor" buying the option, in spite of having no access to the secondary market for shares, breaks even if the rate of return (including distributed and reinvested profits plus capital appreciation) is equal to the interest rate, gains exactly to the extent that the enterprise shares perform better, and conversely loses up to 100 percent of his investment, if the enterprise shares perform worse than the going interest rate. Or, for example, let us say that the price of put options is set at the same level as for a call option, but the striking price is made equal to the current value of shares plus twice the market rate of interest over the period. Here the option buyer will lose up to 100 percent of his investment, if the selected enterprise performs better than normal, but will gain to the full extent that the enterprise performs worse than the market rate

of interest. (Discipline of individual transactors might require that any option price paid by the State Holding Company for options sold by the public should be deposited into a special account as a guarantee to cover the investor's possible losses.) Thus, from the point of view of individuals, access to options trading is as good as access to share trade and ownership.

2. An alternative or additional provision enabling nonowner individuals to participate in stock value gains and losses is the ability to bet fixed amounts of money on a share, or an index of share prices, moving in a specified (upward or downward) direction within a prearranged time. In the simplest version of this game, the stake would be either lost or doubled, according to whether or not the share or the index moves in the predicted direction; more interestingly, losses and gains could be made proportional to actual price changes. For instance, someone betting 1000 forints that a given share will rise would lose his stake if the share does not move (within small bounds), will gain 1000 forints for every percentage point increase, or lose 1000 forints for every percentage point fall registered (outside the same small bounds) at the time the position is closed by the betting individual within the stipulated time. This type of opportunity is available to investors in capitalist economies, and is indeed favored by tax treatment being more lenient for betting wins than for capital gains on share trading. For instance, one can bet on the Financial Times index of London share prices, or on the rate of exchange between dollar and sterling. The extension of this facility to enterprise shares would, as in the case of options trading, give individuals the opportunity to benefit fully from their ability to predict movements in share prices in spite of their lack of access to share trading.
3. The only disadvantage of options and bets on enterprise shares, from the viewpoint of the socialist economy, might be the leverage involved in both institutions, which enables individuals to notionally move masses of shares at a fraction of their market value. To discourage the speculative implications of options trade, which very often rightly or wrongly come under strong criticism also in capitalist economies, it might be necessary to stipulate that individual traders should, simultaneously with their options transaction, deposit with the Central

Bank or with a specialized bank an amount corresponding to the total value of the shares on which they are trading options. The combination of compulsory deposits with either options trading or share bets, however, is equivalent to lending and borrowing operations indexed to the price of shares, with reinvested dividends computed into the index. If, as is likely in socialist economies, speculative opportunities are not encouraged, this type of indexation is the simplest financial innovation necessary to expose individuals to the effects of a stock exchange in which they are not allowed to trade shares. Taking a loan indexed to the price of a share and depositing the amount at the normal rate of return; betting that the share price will fall; purchasing a put option or selling a call option—all are equivalent strategies, given the pricing criteria selected above for these alternatives for individuals believing that the share of a particular enterprise will perform below the going rate of return. Conversely, a deposit indexed to the price of a share; a bet that its price will increase; the purchase of a call option or the sale of a put option—again are equivalent strategies for individuals convinced of the above-average performance prospects of a particular enterprise share.

All three systems, which could even coexist, presume the existence of one or more specialized state agencies respectively issuing or buying options, or taking bets, or taking or making loans indexed to share performance. If these agencies acted passively they would only undertake those transactions requested by individuals and suffer or gain from the accidents of the aggregate good or bad judgment of individual investors; the obstacle of no individual ownership of shares would be overcome but individuals would have no influence on share market values. The share trade of state agencies would be totally insulated from individual beliefs, information, and preferences. This confirms that the envisaged financial innovation is compatible with total retention of state control—through state enterprises and specialized agencies—over the economy. At the same time, if the public at large disagreed with the government about the relative merits of specific sectors and enterprises, and the public were right, as long as compensatory subsidies and tax changes were prevented the government would be specifically penalized—through the net losses of its agencies transacting options, bets, or indexed loans with individuals—for having disregarded the indications coming from the household sector. What is more, the government would be penalized precisely in proportion to the intensity of disagreement between its agencies and the public, measured by the volume of transactions in share options, bets on share price trends, and loans indexed to enterprise performance. Therefore, even a passive position on the part of the state agencies transacting with the public would produce information, penalties, and rewards and therefore an incentive to respond to the public's convictions.

At the other extreme of possible responses, the new specialized agencies could respond instantly and fully to the individuals' choices as investors, offsetting their net exposure in transactions with individuals through balancing purchases and sales of shares, which they, unlike individuals, are allowed to undertake. In this way, the specialized agencies would make neither profits nor losses from share movements, covering their running costs on average out of commissions on their transactions, but would transmit speedily and fully to the exclusively public trade of shares the wishes, beliefs, and convictions of the public at large.

9.6 Summary and Conclusion

The recurring attempts at reforming central planning in socialist countries have been accompanied by measures of remonetization of their economies. This process has gone furthest in Hungary, with the separation of commercial from central banking functions of the National Bank, the establishment of competition in commercial banking, primary and secondary trading in bonds issued by state agencies and enterprises and available to the public, and equity shares tradable among state agencies. However, the development of financial institutions has found everywhere, in practice, three systemic constraints, namely the lack of private ownership of equity shares or, in any case, of voting rights associated to them, and the inadmissibility of a large-scale secondary market for the retrading of equity shares. This paper considers the implications of these constraints for the efficiency of market socialism and the possibility of producing the same effects with existing instruments and institutions.

Restricted ownership, control, and retrading do not impede completely financial intermediation under market socialism: lenders and borrowers, short and long ends of the markets can still be matched, and risks can be pooled or shared. The systemic constraints, however, prevent the exercise of three important functions of a stock exchange: the liquidity of investment in equity shares, the lack of which is a disincentive to save; the valuation of enterprises as going concerns, which is needed to assess past performance and to plan future allocation; and the ensuing mechanism for redeployment of productive assets via mergers and takeovers, which in a capitalist economy does not even require the consensus of the managerial groups involved (for instance, in the case of hostile takeovers).

These functions, which are important also for market socialism, could be performed by existing types of institutions: a centralized State Committee, which however would reproduce the drawbacks of central planning; a brokerage agency, which could only operate if there were consensus among different managerial groups; a German-type banking involvement in the management of firms (through membership of boards, direct shareholding, and proxy-voting), which however is subject to criticisms for its internal conflict of interests and monopolistic tendencies. For these reasons, and for its own sake, the possibility is explored of alternative and innovative financial instruments and institutions.

A three-stage scheme is outlined. In Stage I, state and private enterprises are allowed to bid up the valuation of existing productive assets—a challenged enterprise having to either release or revalue its assets—thus ensuring the potential mobility of resources toward their most productive uses outside the enterprises that possess them. Tax and bonus provisions would encourage truthful reporting of asset values; indivisibilities are dealt with by introducing joint bidding for technically joint productive assets.

At Stage II, an intermittent stock exchange is suggested, decentralized to individual enterprises and with share ownership reserved to state agencies, also on the basis of the "challengeable self-assessment" principle. The valuation of underlying assets and liabilities associated with Stage I provides a practical underpinning of market valuation of shares, but Stage II could also function on its own, with enterprises and institutional investors (insurance companies, pension funds, etc.) as shareholders.

At Stage III, individuals are allowed to benefit from their ability to identify above- or below-average performing enterprises in spite of being excluded from ownership and control. This is done by means of loans (equivalent to a "bear" stance) and deposits (equivalent to a "bull" stance) indexed to the cumulative performance of any enterprise share, on any scale; it could also be done by a system of options and/or bets, though these would have the disadvantage of speculative leverage. Stage III is compatible with any degree of government interference with the economy, as long as this is consistent and predictable. That is, the government could pursue its own industrial policy regardless of the indications of individuals' positions in the market for options/bets/indexed loans—and be penalized if individuals are proved right in the aggregate—or transmit fully individual positions to the limited stock exchange of Stage II, thereby simulating much more fully the operation of a conventional capital market.

The simulation of a stock exchange in a "market socialist" economy of course would expose that economy not only to potential efficiency gains but also to potential drawbacks such as instability, unemployment of labor, insider trading, and adverse distribution of income and wealth. If these illnesses appeared, antidotes would have to be found. Apart from the insulation between individual behavior and real allocation, potentially still open in Stage III, other system-specific remedies could be suggested. For instance, if there is unemployment the pricing of assets and the principles of bidding could be altered, any unused asset being compulsorily released by enterprises to whoever can provide the highest employment at whatever price is offered, unless the enterprise possessing the asset undertakes to match the additional employment offered. Workers' self-management organs could be given or take a lead in the proper valuation of assets (that is, stamp on insider trading by diffusing relevant information) and in their redeployment. Undesirable distributional effects could be handled by means of taxation.

If the scheme proposed here is deemed unworkable or unsuitable, some other scheme will have to be devised. Once traditional central planning is replaced by competitive entrepreneurship, it is necessary that monetary and financial institutions also be altered to match. Unless socialist reformers intend to reproduce a capitalist economy without or with fewer capitalists, it is imperative that they invent and introduce financial innovations suitable to the systemic premises of their brand of market socialism.

Bibliography

Arnold, A.Z. (1937). Banks, Credit and Money in Soviet Russia. New York.

Barone, E. (1908). Il Ministro della Produzione nello stato collettivistico. (The Minister of Production in the Collectivistic State). Giornale degli Economisti. English translation in Hayek (1935), pp. 247-290.

Barsony, J. (1982). Tibor Liska's Concept of Socialist Entrepreneurship. Acta Oeconomica. Vol. 28, No. 3-4.

Berliner, J.S. (1976). The Innovation Decision in Soviet Industry. Cambridge: MIT Press.

Bohm-Bawerk, E. (1909). Positive Theorie des Kapital (Positive Theory of Capital). Innsbruck.

Brus, W. (1964). Ogolne problemy funkcjonowania gospodarki socjalistycznej. PWE, Warsaw. English translation title: The Market in a Socialist Economy. Routledge and Kegan Paul. London 1972.

Cable, J R. (1985a). The Bank-Industry Relationship in West Germany: Performance and Policy Aspects. In Schwalbach (ed.), 1985.

— (1985b). Capital Market Information and Industrial Performance: The Role of West German Banks." The Economic Journal. March: 118-132.

Carr, E H. and R.W. Davies. (1969). Foundations of A Planned Economy, 1926-29. Vol. 1. London: Macmillan.

Cox, J.C. and M. Rubinstein. (1985). Options Markets. London: Prentice Hall.

Dickinson, H.D. (1933). Price Formation in a Socialist Community. The Economic Journal. Vol. XLIII, June.

Dimitrijevic, D. and G. Macesich. (1973). Monetary Finance in Contemporary Yugoslavia. New York: Praeger.

— (1983). Money and Finance in Yugoslavia. New York: Praeger.

Eckstein, W. (1989). The Role of the Banks in Corporate Concentration in West Germany. Zeitschrift fur die gesamte Staatswissenschaft. 136: 465-482.

Furobotn, E.G. (1980). The Socialist Labor-Managed Firm and Bank-Financed Investment: Some Theoretical Issues. Journal of Comparative Economics. Vol. 4, no. 2: 184-191.

Garvey, G. (1966). Money, Banking and Credit in Eastern Europe. New York: Federal Reserve Bank of New York.

Gessler Kommission. (1979). Bericht der Studienkommission - Grundsatzfragen der Kreditwirtschaft. Schriftenreihe des BMF N. 28. (Report of the Study Commission: Basic Questions of Credit Economics, BMF Series no. 28). Frankfurt: Fritz Knapp Verlag.

Grossman, G. (1968). Money and Plan. Berkeley and Los Angeles: University of California Press.

Hayek, F.A. (1935). Collectivistic Economic Planning. London.

Heimann E. (1922). Mehrwert und Gemeinwirtschaft (Surplus Value and the Communal Economy). Berlin: H.R. Henglemann.

— (1934). "Planning and the Market System." Social Research: I, November.

Kornai J. (1980). The Economics of Shortage. 2 vols. North Holland.

— (1982). On Tibor Liska's Concept of Entrepreneurship. Acta Oeconomica. Vol. 28: 455-460.

KPRdsRG (Party Government Commission for the Questions of Economics Reform). (1981). Kierunki reformy gospodarczej - projekt. (Directions of Economic Reform - A Project). Warsaw: Nakladem Trybuny. July.

Joint Economic Committee, U.S. Congress. (1986). China's Economy Looks Toward the Year 2000. Vol. 1: The Four Modernizations. Washington, D.C.: U.S. Government Printing Office.

Landauer, C. (1931). Planwirtschaft und Verkehrswirtschaft. (Planned Economy and Market Economy). Munich and Leipzig: Duncker and Humblot.

Landauer, C. E., Kridl Valkenier and H. Stein Landauer. (1959). European Socialism: A History of Ideas and Movements from the Industrial Revolution to Hitler's Seizure of Power. Westport, Connecticut: Greenwood Press.

Lange, O. (1938). The Economic Theory of Socialism. In Lippincott (1938). Originally published in a slightly different version in the Review of Economic Studies. Vol. 3: 1936-37.

Lippincott, B. (1938). On the Economic Theory of Socialism. Minneapolis: University of Minnesota Press.

Liska, T. (1963). Kritik es koncepcio. Tezisek a gazdasagi mechanizmus reformiahoz (Critique and Construction. Theses for a Reform of the Economic Mechanism). Kozgazdasagi Szemle 9.

— (1986a). "Un mercato più sviluppato di quello capitalistico" (A Market more Developed than Capitalist Market). In Morley-Fletcher (1986), pp. 85-100.

— (1986b). Molto più di un accordo (Much More Than an Agreement). A Rejoinder to Kornai. In Morley-Fletcher (1986), pp. 140-147.

Lutter, M. (1981). Bankenvertreter im Aufsichtsrat. Zeitschrift fur Handelsrecht. Vol. 145: 224-251.

Macrae, N. (1983). Into Entrepreneurial Socialism." The Economist. 19 March, pp. 23-31.

Marris, R. L. (1964). The Economic Theory of Managerial Capitalism. London: Macmillan.

Morley-Fletcher, E. (1986). Cooperare e competere (Cooperation and Competition). Milano: Feltrinelli.

The National Bank of Hungary (1986). The New Banking System in Hungary 1987. Budapest.

Naughton, B. (1986). Finance and Planning Reforms in Industry. In JEC-US (1986), pp. 604-629.

Neurath, O. (1919). Durch die Kriegswirtschaft zur Naturalwirtschaft (From the War Economy to the Natural Economy). Munich.

Nolan, P. and S. Paine. (1986). Rethinking Socialist Economics. London: Polity Press.

Nove, A. (1983). The Economics of Feasible Socialism. London: Allen and Unwin.

Nuti, D.M. (1986). Hidden and Repressed Inflation in Soviet-type Economies: Definitions, Measurements and Stabilisation. Contributions to Political Economy. Vol. 5: 37-82.

Pareto, V. (1902 and 1903). Les systèmes socialistes. Two vols. Paris: Giard and Briere.

Pejovich, S. (1976). The Labor-Managed Firm and Bank Credit, in J. Thornton, 1976.

Petrakov, N. (1987). Soviet Pricing and Fiscal Credit System. Mimeo. Moscow: TsEMI.

Schwalbach, J. (1985). Industry Structure and Performance. Berlin: Edition Sigma.

Sensenbrenner, J.S. (1987). The Evolving Enterprise. The China Business Review. Vol. 14, No. 2: 35-38.

Stiglitz, J. E. (1985). Credit Markets and the Control of Capital. Journal of Money, Credit and Banking. Vol. 17, No. 2: 133-152.

Taylor, F. M. (1928). The Guidance of Production in a Socialist State. Reprinted in Lippincott (1938).

Uvalic, M. (1987). Shareholding in Yugoslavia: Theory and Practice. Paper presented at Workshop on Financial Reform in Socialist Economies. Florence.
Vittas, D. (1983). Banks' Relations with Industry. London: CLBC Research Group.
Werner, W. (1981). Aufsichtsratstatigkeit von Bankenvertretern. Zeitschrift fur Handelsrecht. Vol. 145: 252-270.

10

Market Socialism: The Model that Might Have Been—But Never Was

Domenico Mario Nuti

History punishes those who are too late.
(M.S. Gorbachev, 1989)
'It's a poor sort of memory that only works backwards,' the Queen remarked.
(Lewis Carroll. *Through the Looking Glass*)

A previous version of this paper has been published in *Russia and the World* no. 18, 1990, pp. 12–16, 38–39. This version of the paper was published in Anders Aslund (Ed.), *Market Socialism or the Restoration of Capitalism?* Cambridge: Cambridge University Press, 1992, pp. 17–31. The Italian version was published in Alberto Chilosi (Ed.), "Il socialismo di mercato: Il modello che avrebbe potuto esserci, ma che non c'e' mai stato", *L'economia del periodo di transizione—Dal socialismo di tipo sovietico all'economia di mercato,* Il Mulino, 1992, pp. 143–158.

D. M. Nuti (✉)
La Sapienza, University of Rome, Rome, Italy
e-mail: milica.uvalic@unipg.it

© The Author(s), under exclusive license to Springer Nature Switzerland AG 2023

S. Estrin, M. Uvalic (eds.), *Collected Works of Domenico Mario Nuti, Volume I*,
Studies in Economic Transition, https://doi.org/10.1007/978-3-031-12334-4_10

10.1 The Moving Target of Economic Reform

The ultimate model for the wave of economic reforms attempted in Central Eastern Europe over the last thirty-five years has been a moving target. At first, reform aimed at improving Soviet-type central planning, replacing central commands with contractual relations, using net value instead of gross physical indicators of enterprise performance, credit instead of budgetary grants, material incentives instead of campaigns, and gearing the system to some market signals, especially to world markets (e.g. Poland, 1956; USSR, 1965; Hungary, 1968; Czechoslovakia, 1981).[1]

In a second stage the target was a fuzzy notion of a radically new model, 'market socialism'. Initially, there were talks of a 'socialist market', an expression coined by Gorbachev which was rightly criticized: 'We want sausage', said Gavril Popov, not socialist sausage'; 'A market is a market is a market', added Czechoslovak Vice-Premier Valtr Komarek soon after coming to power. Clearly only the institutional environment in which markets operate, and the policies followed by governments, can be socialist or non-socialist, while markets cannot be so labelled; thus, there can be market socialism but not socialist markets. A 'socialist' market may be understood as an egalitarian market where participants have equal income and wealth and 'vote by the ruble' in a genuine economic democracy; however, money, unlike votes, can always be lent and borrowed, and the position of households and enterprises is in any case asymmetric; a market cannot be equalitarian; only policies can be equalitarian. A 'socialist' market may also be understood as a 'regulated' market; however, either the regulation takes the form of price control, in which case we are outside a market system, or it takes the form of state transactions in the open market, in which case there is a perfectly ordinary market. The same objection could be raised against the expression 'social market' familiar from Erhard's Germany, in that government policies implement social concerns; however 'social market' is an

[1] On this characterization, see Bauer (1990a, b): he distinguishes among the improvement of the old system, its reform into a new system, and the transition to capitalism. However, Bauer regards the 1968 reform as already an attempt at reforming rather than improving the system. See also Nuti (1988b); on Czechoslovakia, see Drabek (1989).

established shorthand for a mixed economy with moderate state intervention and social policies. 'Social market' is a label now widely used also with reference to Central Eastern Europe by social-democratic as opposed to liberal reformers.

A notion of market socialism was soon understood as a mixed economy still with prevalent public ownership and a dominant communist party but with generalized market exchange, regulated by public policy, and with a form of political pluralism.[2] The model was not completely developed in its final form, but was rather defined by radical moves in its direction; the lack of a clear and accepted ultimate model did not seem to matter, as the first steps would be the same regardless of the final target (Hewett 1989). Especially in Hungary, Poland and the Soviet Union, substantial and unprecedented changes took place, such as the dismantling of mandatory planning; the gradual remonetization of the economy and establishment of financial discipline of enterprise activity (including procedures for enterprise recovery, liquidation and bankruptcy); the introduction of bonds, shares, and capital markets for their primary and secondary trading; the gradual exposure of enterprises to international competition, through greater access to foreign trade and foreign exchange transactions; the development of non-state economic activities, i.e. by individuals, cooperatives, joint ventures and sometimes even wholly private enterprises, domestic or foreign; the connection of incomes and enterprise performance, and greater mobility of labour; last but not least, some relaxation of the party's grip over political, economic and social life. (for an up-to-date account of economic reform in eastern Europe see UN-ECE (1989,1990)).

Both kinds of reform attempts—at improving the old model and at constructing a new one—failed to cure the inefficiency, inertia and instability of the old system. At present, most of these countries (the GDR through merger with the FRG; Poland, Hungary, Czechoslovakia) are in transition back to multi-party democracy and a full-fledged capitalist

[2] According to Kornai (1990), 'market socialism = state ownership + market coordination' (p. 58): however this seems to be an unduly restrictive definition, in that market socialism is increasingly understood as including even substantial private ownership and enterprise.

economy; the evolution of Bulgaria, Romania and the USSR in theory is still open but in practice no alternative has been developed.[3] No 'Third Way', distinct from a capitalist economy with social democratic policies, has been implemented or even conceived in Western countries either.[4]

It is usually inferred from these developments that the Soviet-type economic system is doomed and that 'market socialism' has failed.[5]

Clearly the rejection of communist monopoly of political power can be regarded as a precondition of any systemic improvement, whether minor or major; otherwise the system's drawbacks are bound to be perpetuated by direct political interference in economic affairs, adverse selection in nomenklatura appointments, lack of political feedbacks, the use of economic weapons in political life, the inability of non-elected government to enforce the austerity needed by economic adjustment processes. However, both minor and major attempts at systemic improvement are likely to have failed not because of the presumed impossibility of the attempted task but because of other factors. These include: the dogmatic unwillingness and political inability to stabilize the economic environment in which reform was to take place and to maintain financial discipline thereafter; the failure to sever the links between the centre and enterprises, to unleash competition, to expose enterprises fully to market rewards (including some appropriation of capital gains) and penalties (without enterprise-specific *ad hoc* and *ex post* compensatory subsidies and taxes, amounting to indirect instead of direct centralization); the

---

[3] The closest to a blueprint for the new model is contained in the Abalkin Report (1989), but even that is incomplete, out of sequence, and has been further diluted. 'Even in outline, the Soviet model of socialism for the twenty-first century has not yet emerged' (Davies 1990: p. 27).

[4] The recent manifesto by the British Labour Party (1988), for instance, is a vague picture of traditional social democratic policies, listing 'a genuine free society ... real stake in and real democratic influence over the industries and services in which [workers] are employed ... freedom to choose ... redistribution ... extension of democratic control'. 'Democratic socialists believe in market allocation—but market allocation guided by agreement that the competitive system should pursue the objective of greater freedom, greater equality and greater choice'. The picture of 'market socialism' discussed in the Le Grand and Estrin volume (1989) simply makes a case for markets and mentions egalitarian policies, some planning to obviate coordination and information failure of markets, some profit sharing, cooperatives, and some workers ownership.

[5] For a sharp criticism of attempts at market socialism see Keren (1989), Kornai (1990); on the eve of such attempts, Abram Bergson expected market socialism to perform moderately better than central planning though he questioned its ability to improve over the capitalist competitive solution; see Bergson (1967).

failure to undertake reform measures according to an efficient operational sequence instead of meandering, always following the line of least resistance; the lack of a clear cut, coherent and detailed blueprint for the target model; the frequent aimless revisions and sudden reversals under the pressure of interest groups and political currents.[6]

In these conditions, the reform of the old system was and is doomed, and the only viable course is its total rejection. Does this mean that these are the only conditions that the traditional Soviet-type model can generate for its own reform? It may well be that this is the case, i.e. that no socialist economy is capable of following financial discipline (i.e. of sticking to 'hard budget constraints'), of recruiting profit-minded managers to whom devolve economic decisions, of using economy-wide instruments of economic policy, of de-politicizing the economy. It is true that, to date, socialist leaders have proved to be incapable of learning not only from other people's mistakes (which is true wisdom) but also from their own; is this to be regarded as an immutable and permanent state of affairs? Learning being an essential perquisite of the human condition there is something awkward—to say the proof should rest on those who entertain such presumption.[7] If so, it is neither futile nor trivial to consider what a model of 'market socialism 'might begin to look like, if it is to differ from a mixed economy under an elected social democratic government: this is the purpose of this chapter.

It should be stressed that speculation about a possible alternative model of 'market socialism'—a 'Third Way'—is a purely intellectual exercise, the exploration of a utopia. It cannot possibly involve claims to superiority over the capitalist system but it might well have been an improvement over the half measures taken in the name of reform. However, market socialism today cannot be regarded as a blueprint for action in Central Eastern Europe: obtuse procrastination on the part of past and present socialist leaders (including also—indeed, especially—Mikhail Gorbachev) has made it impossible for anything but a version of capitalism to be the target model for Central Eastern European countries: when a boat is

[6] On sequencing, see Nuti (1990a, b).

[7] Indeed, Hewett (1989) finds that 'What is most impressive about Mikhail Gorbachev and those around him is their ability to learn ... mistakes are not important, but learning from them is. Soviet leaders are learning.'

sinking, it is no time to experiment with the floating properties of alternative rafts.

Nevertheless, it is facile to quip, with the Czechoslovak Finance Minister Vaclav Klaus, that 'The Third Way is the quickest road to the Third World'. The exploration of a model that might have been should be of interest to socialists and non-socialists alike, also in the West.

10.2 Market Socialism

Economic literature does not provide a comprehensive model of 'market socialism'. Usually Oskar Lange is regarded as the originator of the concept of market socialism, in spite of the fact that he never spoke of market socialism and would not have been the first if he had. In fact, Lange's model involves only a partial market simulation for the trial-and-error iterative construction of a central plan, and belongs to the set of decentralization procedures in central planning. The term appears to have been coined by Heimann (1922, 1934) who first spoke of *Marktsozialismus;* other proponents usually associated with market socialism include Taylor (1928), Landauer (1931), Dickinson (1933), Lange (1938; for a comprehensive survey of pre-War literature, see Landauer et al. 1959). Even before Heimann, Barone (1908) had discussed the activity of the Minister of Production of his Collectivistic State in terms of actual markets, but only to show the basic equivalence of the two systems. Post-Lange literature on market socialism ranges from Brus (1964), whose work actually influenced Czech and Hungarian reforms and gradually developed more and more decentralized schemes in the light of experience (see Brus 1985), to Nove's 'feasible socialism' (1983) and the statements produced by the more enlightened East European reformers and Commissions for Economic Reform. Nove proposes really an 'efficient socialism, no more 'feasible' than traditional central planning, undistinguishable from the capitalist mixed economy; while the others seem stronger on criticism than on positive propositions.

A major question is whether 'market socialism' should be understood as a set of specific policies (e.g. full employment, social consumption, social insurance and equalitarian redistribution of income) in a mixed, market economy, or also a set of specific institutions beside those of such an economy. The characterization proposed here includes both policies and institutions.

Kornai (1990: pp. 22–3) contrasts 'market socialism' with what he calls 'the free economy ':

> A free economy is, of course, a market economy, but the concept is richer and refers not only to the fact that the main coordinator of economic activities is a specific mechanism, namely the market. A free economy is one that allows unhampered entry, exit and fair competition in the market. The notion of a free economy also implies a certain configuration of property rights and a certain institutional and political structure. The system promotes the free establishment and preservation of private property and encourages the private sector to produce the great bulk of output. It is a system that encourages individual initiative and entrepreneurship, liberates this initiative from excessive state intervention, and protects it by the rule of law. A free economy is embedded in a democratic political order, characterized by the free competition of political forces and ideas.

However, we might imagine a model of market socialism that includes all the features of Kornai's free economy but also exhibits additional features strictly related to the socialist project; namely, the privatization of the management of state assets instead of their property; the payment of a national dividend or citizens' income; the transformation of workers—at least on a part-time basis—into entrepreneurs; the use of open-market operations (instead of controls) in all markets on the part of the government as instruments of economic policy, instead of planning; the use of contingent policy commitments, and of state agencies subject to strict budgetary constraints and acting as Employer (or Investor, or Foreign Trader) of last resort.

10.3 Markets: Competition and Balance at Single Prices

The necessity of markets rests on several strong arguments. First, one can view 'The market as a procedure for discovery and conveyance of inarticulate knowledge' (which is the eloquent title of a paper by Lavoie (1986)). Secondly, and perhaps more importantly, markets are servomechanisms, homeostatic automatic devices that adjust price, output and capacity in response to excess demand (respectively, the Walrasian, Marshallian and capital-stock adjustments). Thirdly, markets constrain economic agents to income and wealth budgets.

In order to play these roles, markets have to be competitive on the side of both demand and supply, yield single prices and always clear. Competition requires the splitting of the large enterprises and their associations, currently dominating Eastern Europe in all sectors including agriculture, as well as their total freedom to diversify their output and to move into and out of any sectors. Market clearing is essential to avoid unjustified and inefficient rents otherwise implicit in access to purchase or outlet; the frequent presence of excess demand in socialist countries (see Kornai 1980; Nuti 1986a) is the result of a tragic misunderstanding, a confusion of aspirations and potentials with actual achievements; there can be no market without market clearing at the ruling prices. This means there can be no room for 'price criteria' and 'price formulas' or for intermittent 'price reforms': any price policy should take the form of quantity policies, or income policies; if need be in a passing emergency actual rationing might be considered, instead of the indignity and inefficiency of the kind of queuing where supplies end before all queue members are satisfied. Market clearing should normally happen at single prices, i.e. at uniform conditions for all transactions.[8] Markets as feedback mechanisms ought to be direct and automatic, i.e. not mediated by an intermediate administrative body and depending on its reactions; they are often slow, or unstable, or costly, and in many circumstances they may function worse than plans, but with respect to plans they have the advantages of being automatic where plans may exhibit inertia, and of generating and transmitting information to market transactors. There would have to be market not only for commodities and services but also for productive factors, money[9] and foreign exchange (i.e. currency convertibility). This gives economic agents the opportunity to 'optimize' their behaviour, adjusting it to external parameters and their changes, unimpeded by administrative bodies.

[8] There may be exceptions in motivated special cases, such as multi-part tariffs for electricity, which is produced under increasing returns to scale and is not retransferable.

[9] See Nuti (1989a, b).

10.4 Pluralist Ownership

Mises (1951) argued that private ownership of means of production was a precondition of markets, because only ultimate owners have the incentive to control their efficient use. Hence, for Mises there was the dilemma: either socialism or markets, and there could not be such a thing as market socialism.[10] I believe he was both right and wrong. He was right in that the appropriation of all or a sizeable fraction of the capital gains deriving from successful enterprise seems a necessary precondition for the mobilization of entrepreneurial initiatives; but he was wrong in that this is all that is needed. We can imagine an economy where the ownership of all means of production and their further reproduction is in the hand of the state, but these means are leased in competitive leasing markets to private entrepreneurs who retain a residual claim to both income and capital gains and are able to transfer those claims. Capital leasings—present on a small scale under NEP—have reappeared widely in the recent reform, unfortunately also on too small a scale. But there is a model of 'entrepreneurial socialism' by the Hungarian economist Tibor Liska (1963) based precisely on the competitive leasing of state assets and their compulsory surrender to the highest bidder (however, with the additional bids belonging to bidders, not to the state), all citizens having a capital stake to invest or to use to exercise entrepreneurship (see Barsony 1982; Nuti 1988a, c). Leasings, instead of privatization, are worthy of greater consideration than they have attracted in economic reform to date.

Another form of privatization of management is the maintenance of a large state stake in national capital through state shareholdings in private companies. Thus there can be a large but not exclusive or even necessarily predominant public ownership of productive capacity (state, local and cooperative) coexisting and competing on equal terms with a non-public sector. State and local authorities property is not entrusted to enterprises controlled by administrative agencies, but is sold to independent enterprises in exchange for bonds or equities held by specialized state holdings acting as independent shareholders. There would no longer be any role for so-called

[10] He argued that capital markets cannot be simulated; Kornai (1990) concurs: 'We are fed up with simulation' (p. 72).

'founding organs' i.e. Ministries (whether branch Ministries, or a single Ministry for Industry, or functional Ministries) or other central agencies: the 'petty tutelage' of central organs over enterprises would have to be abolished.

The expectation that cooperative enterprises might supplant state enterprises within the public sector, through the leasing of state assets to workers' cooperatives, is probably far-fetched; the spectacular hyper-growth of Soviet cooperatives (see Nuti 1989c) is not indicative of this sector's potential because those cooperatives are not subject to traditional limitation of earnings and return on capital. In general, for cooperative members to be fully-fledged entrepreneurs it would be necessary to give them a share of the capital value increments in the assets of their enterprises; this, however, would transform cooperative into private partnerships (see below).

10.5 Political and Economic Participation

There would have to be generalized participation in economic and political decision making at all levels, moving away from bureaucratic power and what Wlodzimierz Brus calls the party's 'mono-archy'. After all, originally this kind of participation was to be exercised through the Soviets' power, and it is an aberration that today 'the Soviets' should be liable to being used—in American and now also in English practice—as a citizenship label, as we might for instance refer to 'the British'. Participation would be necessary, in a phase of transition to the new system at a time of crisis, as a non-resource-intensive good which could be used as a counterpart for austerity in a social pact between the government and society (the other non-resource-intensive goods, i.e. alcohol and drugs, have undesirable side effects).

10.6 Supplementary Nature of Government Activity

There would have to be active use of a wide range of policy instruments to implement government policies; however, only government activity would be planned; it would have to be additional, i.e. supplementary to what else happens by itself in the economy and not totalitarian (i.e. not embracing the whole economy); it would be contingent on the economy not following unaided a course judged as desirable by a government subject to frequent electoral verification of popular support. Government activity consists in steering the spontaneously existing economic motion, not in actually providing the engine of the economy's motion.

10.7 Socialist Policies Through the Market

In the envisaged model of 'market socialism' commitment to socialist values such as equality, social consumption, social security, and full employment of labour, would be maintained. However, these objectives are not pursued at all costs, or right down to the level of saturation of private or government demand, but only to the extent that their cost at the margin is specifically regarded by the government as commensurate with their achievement. Hence, there are no open-ended (i.e. soft-budget) commitments, but only hard-budgeted allocations to specific targets, directly from the state budget or through independent agencies responsible for their achievement and accountable for their cost-effectiveness. The government policy is asserted primarily through the market, i.e. through budgetary expenditure and the sale of goods and services, physical and financial assets. Provision of social consumption out of the budget would be recognized to be crowding out alternative individual consumption or public targets, and regarded as a good thing not in absolute but in competition with other good things; it would be provided perhaps less generously than previously expected, both in terms of the number of people entitled and of individual entitlement. The commitment to full employment is accompanied by high labour mobility, across firms, regions and occupations; there is no 'job right protection' (a feature of the traditional model theorized by Granick 1987), only a general entitlement to 'a' living job, or rather to a guaranteed income (see below). In a paper on 'Plan and Market' (Nuti 1986b), I envisaged the possibility of a State Agency for Labour hiring at the prevailing wage all unemployed who wish to be employed, and either leasing its labourers at whatever spot price it can get from enterprises, or using their labour for local social needs (especially environmental). This would absolve the government of any duty to look after those unwilling to be so employed; in order to stop enterprises from replacing their labourers with labour from the Labour Agency, usually cheaper, no enterprise reducing its current employment would be eligible for the scheme. A similar principle of government budgeted intervention through the market could be applied to investment policy, or to trade policy (see below). The cutting of social consumption short of saturation, the acceptance of labour mobility and of budgetary limits are partly lessons to be learnt from Thatcherism, especially in view of its popular support; however, market socialism would attach greater weight than Thatcherism to the importance of social consumption and other social values, and would consistently raise tax revenue from capital and capital income (including capital gains) to an extent much greater than Thatcherism.

An Open Economy

The market socialist economy is open to foreign trade in order to ensure competition in domestic markets and the utilization of efficient opportunities for international division of labour and factor transfers (including technology). This does not prevent the government from undertaking designs of planned economic integration such as those which might arise from the continuation of CMEA, but forces the government to pursue such a design through the market, i.e. assigning tasks to enterprises on a contractual basis for the fulfilment of possible medium and long-term international obligations, and reselling in spot markets the deliveries obtained in return; in such a way the efficiency of planned integration is visible through the transparency of related transactions.

No Indirect Centralization

Just as prices normally ought to be uniform for all transactions for markets to be efficient, so fiscal and other parameters must be uniform, and there must not be enterprise-specific or even budget-specific subsidies or *ex-post ad hoc* compensatory payments or withdrawals aimed at equalizing the ultimate position of enterprises regardless of their market performance (the large scale of such redistributive cross-subsidization is documented by Kornai 1986 for Hungary). Anything else amounts to indirect or parametric centralization, which perpetuates many familiar disadvantages of central planning (neglect of efficiency, lack of incentives, targets bargaining, etc.).

Minimum Guaranteed Income

There is some guaranteed income, in lieu of product subsidies which may distort consumption structure; a minimum income is guaranteed also in lieu of some consumption earlier provided as free social consumption, for consumers to be able to exercise some choice even in areas such as medical care or education.

Profit Sharing

There is profit sharing by workers of all enterprises, necessarily by statute in cooperatives and optionally by contract in other enterprises (this practice is spreading rapidly in Western Europe, and is the object of further development in spite of British opposition within the implementation of the European Social Charter; see Uvalic 1990). This link gives those workers who wish to take on the risk of entrepreneurship the opportunity—not the obligation—of doing so to the extent that they so desire. The guarantee of a minimum income, and of productive employment, makes this form of risk-taking more approachable by workers. The link ought to have some, sizeable if not dramatic, effect on labour productivity. Possible inequalitarian effects ought to be dealt with through normal taxation; in any case, equality of opportunity should matter more than actual equality of achievement.

Neo-corporatism

The market socialist economy is bound to require neo-corporatist institutions, to move away from what Paul Marer calls the 'atomization of society' towards organized interest groups, and to handle group conflicts which markets are not capable of resolving as well as they handle microeconomic trade-offs, if at all; a social pact seems essential to achieve price stability at full or near-full employment. Neo-corporatist institutions are all the more important if the Party were to retain a special role (as it still might in Romania, Bulgaria and perhaps the USSR).[11]

10.8 Conclusion

In brief, economic reform in Central Eastern Europe, which has failed to significantly improve the old system and to generate a new 'market socialist' model, is now leading to the restoration of versions of the capitalist system. This development seems both unavoidable and desirable in view of the dogmatic unwillingness and political inability to stabilize the economic environment and to maintain financial discipline, of the failure to complete essential elements of the reform project and to follow rational sequencing of reform steps. While there is no ready-made alternative at present, it is interesting to explore a course that might have been taken instead, of market socialism understood as a 'free economy' plus a continued commitment to socialist aims and values, if the obstacles to reform had been surmounted.

The implications of such commitments, summarily discussed in this paper, are a combination of policies and institutions, such as the privatization of the management of state assets instead of their property; the payment of a national dividend or citizens' income; the transformation of workers—at least on a part-time basis—into entrepreneurs; the use of open-market operations (instead of controls) in all markets on the part of the government as instruments of economic policy, instead of planning; the use of contingent policy commitments, and of state agencies subject to

[11] It has been argued (for instance by Marer) that an implicit social pact between the government and workers was always there; this hypothesis is consistent with the observation of official price stability and labour full employment but is not conclusively proven, as there is no positive evidence of this unobservable pact; observations may be the effects of sequential strategies, whereas here we postulate a formal, institutionalized and somewhat guaranteed social pact. Of course, nobody is really bound, individually, by the existence of a social pact, but there is a difference in culture and economic climate and expectations.

strict budgetary constraints and acting as Employer (or Investor, or Foreign Trader) of last resort; the promotion of neo-corporative institutions.

The 'market socialist' alternative path is not necessarily 'better' than capitalist restoration, but it would have been 'better' than both the old system and the unfinished reform, preferable from the viewpoint of the old leadership, and interesting for the Western social reformer seeking new solutions for the problems of the capitalist system.

Bibliography

Abalkin Report [All-Union Conference and Workshop on Problems of Radical Economic Reform, chaired by Vice-Premier Leonid Abalkin] (1989). Radical economic reform: top-priority and long-term measures (material for discussion), Moscow.

Barone, E. (1908). Il Ministro della Produzione nello stato colletivistico (The Minister of production in the collectivistic state), *Giornale degli Economisti.* English translation in Hayek 1935: pp. 247-90.

Barsony, J. (1982). Tibor Liska's concept of socialist entrepreneurship, *Acta Oeconomica,* 28, Nos. 3-4.

Bauer, Tamas (1990a). Hungary on the way towards a market economy, NATO colloquium on 'The Central and East European economies in the 1990s: prospects and constraints', April, Brussels.

— (1990b).From limits to reform to brakes to transition, Conference paper. London School of Economics, London.

Bergson, Abram (1967). Market socialism revisited, *Journal of Political Economy,* Vol. 75, No. 5, October, pp. 655-73.

British Labour Party National Executive (1988). *Democratic Socialist Aims & Values,* London.

Brus, W. (1964). *Ogolne problemy funkcjonowania gospodarki socjalistycznej,* Warsaw, PWE, translated into English under the title: *The Market in a Socialist Economy,* Routledge & Kegan Paul, London, 1972.

— (1985). Socialism — feasible and viable?, *New Left Review,* No. 153, pp. 43-62.

Davies, R. W. (1990). Gorbachev's socialism, *New Left Review,* No. 179, pp. 5-27.

Dickinson, H. D. (1933). Price formation in a socialist community, *The Economic Journal,* 43, June.

Drabek, Zdenek (1989). Czechoslovak economic reform: the search for a minimum market approach, Ms., Washington.

Granick, David (1987). *Job Rights in the Soviet Union: Their Consequences,* Cambridge, Cambridge University Press.

Hayek, F.A. (Ed.) (1935). *Collectivistic Economic Planning,* London, Routledge & Kegan Paul.

Heimann, E. (1922). *Mehrwert und Gemeinwirtschaft* (Surplus value and the communal economy), Berlin, H.R. Hengelmann.

— (1934). Planning and the market system, *Social Research,* 1, November.

Hewett A., Ed. (1989). Is Soviet socialism reformable?, Sturc Memorial Lecture, Johns Hopkins School for Advanced International Studies, 11 November.

Keren, Michael (1989). The New Economic System, the New Economic Mechanism, and Gorbachev's perestroika: bureaucratic limits to reform, conference paper, Jerusalem, November.

Kornai, Janos (1980). *The Economics of Shortage,* 2 vols., Amsterdam, North Holland.

— (1986). The Hungarian Reform Process: Visions, Hopes and Reality, *Journal of Economic Literature,* 29, No. 4, pp. 687-737.

— (1990). *The Road to a Free Economy — Shifting from the Socialist System: the Example of Hungary,* New York and London, W.W. Norton & Co.

Landauer, C. (1931). *Planwirtichaft und Verkehrswirtschaft,* (Planned economy and market economy), Munich and Leipzig, Duncker and Humblot.

Landauer, C. E., Kridl Valkenier and H. Stein Landauer. (1959). *European Socialism: A History of Ideas and Movements from the Industrial Revolution to Hitler's Seizure of Power.* Westport, Connecticut: Greenwood Press.

Lange, O. (1938). The economic theory of socialism, in Lippincott (1938), originally published in a slightly different version in the *Review of Economic Studies,* 3,1936-37.

Lavoie, Don (1986). The market as a procedure for discovery and conveyance of inarticulate knowledge, *Comparative Economic Studies,* 28, no. 1, pp. 1-19.

Le Grand, Julian and Saul Estrin (Eds.) (1989). *Market Socialism,* Oxford, Clarendon Press.

Lippincott, B. (ed.) (1938). *On the Economic Theory of Socialism,* Minneapolis. University of Minnesota Press.

Liska T. (1963). Kritik es koncepcio. Tezisek a gazdasagi mechanizmus reformiahoz (Critique and construction. Theses for a reform of the economic mechanism), *Kozgazdasagi Szemle,* No. 9.

Mises, Ludwig von (1951). *Socialism - An Economic and Sociological Analysis,* trans. J. Kahane, Indianapolis, Liberty Classics.

Nolan, P. and S. Paine (Eds.) (1986). *Rethinking Socialist Economics*, London, Polity Press.

Nove, A. (1983). *The Economics of Feasible Socialism*, London, Allen and Unwin.

Nuti, D. M. (1986a). Hidden and repressed inflation in Soviet-type economies: definitions, measurements and stabilisation, *Contributions to Political Economy*, 5, pp. 37-82.

— (1986b). Economic planning in market economies: scope, instruments, institutions, in Nolan and Paine (1986), pp. 83-98.

— (1988a). Competitive valuation and efficiency of capital investment in the socialist economy, *European Economic Review*, 32, pp. 2-6.

— (1988b). Perestroika: transition between central planning and market socialism, *Economic Policy*, October, pp. 353-89.

— (1988c). On Tibor Liska's entrepreneurial socialism, *Proceedings of the Second International Polanyi Conference*, Montreal, 10-13 November 1988, on 'Market, State and Society in the Late -20th Century' (forthcoming, St Martin's Press).

— (1989a). Remonetisation and capital markets in the reform of centrally planned economies, *European Economic Review*, 33, Nos. 2/3, March, pp. 427-38.

— (1989b). Feasible financial innovation under market socialism, in Christine Kessides, Timothy King, Mario Nuti and Kathy Sokil (Eds), *Financial Reform in Centrally Planned Economies*, Washington, EDI-World Bank, pp. 85-105.

— (1989c). The new Soviet cooperatives: advances and limitations, *Economic and Industrial Democracy*, special issue on Eastern Europe, Vol. 10, pp. 311-27.

— (1990a). Stabilisation and reform sequencing in the Soviet Economy, *Recherches Economiques de Louvain*, 56, No. 2, pp. 1-12.

— (1990b). Stabilisation and reform sequencing in the reform of Central Eastern Europe', in Simon Commander (Ed.), Washington, EDI-World Bank.

Pareto, V. (1902/3). *Les systèmes socialistes*, 2 vols., Paris, Giard and Briere.

Taylor, F. M. (1928). The guidance of production in a socialist state, reprinted in Lippincott (1938).

UN-ECE (1989). *Economic Bulletin for Europe, Economic Commission for Europe*, Geneva.

UN-ECE (1990). *Economic Bulleting for Europe, Economic Commission for Europe*, Geneva.

Uvalic, Milica (1990). *The PEPPER Report: Promotion of Employee Participation in Profits and Enterprise Results in the Member States of the European Community*, Florence and Brussels, EUI and CEC.

11

Tibor Liska's Entrepreneurial Socialism

Domenico Mario Nuti

11.1 Premise

There are interesting links to be drawn between Tibor Liska's model of entrepreneurial socialism and Polanyi's explorations of alternative economic systems. Liska's model is also an original version of what 'market

Published in M. Mendell and D. Salee (Eds.), *The Legacy of Karl Polanyi. Market, State and Society at the End of the Twentieth Century*, St. Martin's Press, New York, 1991, pp. 215–230.

Much of Liska's work is available only in Hungarian; this paper has relied on English and Italian translations of published work (Liska 1956, 1986a, b), as well as unpublished translations kindly provided by Liska, surveys (Barsony 1982; Macrae 1983; Matyaszovski 1986a, b), critics (Kornai 1980) and discussion with George Sorany and other Hungarian colleagues. I have greatly benefitted from several discussions with Tibor Liska on the occasion of his visits to the EUI, Florence, in 1987 and 1988, but this should not imply his agreement with the presentation of his views or any part of this paper. An earlier version was presented at a seminar of the EUI Working Group on Comparative Economic Systems on 14 May 1987; acknowledgements for useful suggestions are due to seminar participants, in particular Jozef van Brabant, Alberto Chilosi, Renzo Daviddi, Mario Ferrero, Felix FitzRoy and Silvana Malle.

D. M. Nuti (✉)
La Sapienza, University of Rome, Rome, Italy
e-mail: milica.uvalic@unipg.it

© The Author(s), under exclusive license to Springer Nature Switzerland AG 2023

S. Estrin, M. Uvalic (eds.), *Collected Works of Domenico Mario Nuti, Volume I*,
Studies in Economic Transition, https://doi.org/10.1007/978-3-031-12334-4_11

socialism' might look like, if it is to differ from the model of a capitalist society pursuing socialist policies. This is important in its own right at a time when many centrally-planned economies within and beyond Eastern Europe are undertaking radical reforms, while social democratic parties in the West—whether in power or in opposition—have no alternative system to propose other than a moderately and temporarily improved capitalism. While Tibor Liska may not provide an ideal alternative—indeed it is claimed in this paper that he does not—his ideas are a very useful starting-point for debating the questions of initiative, efficiency and equality that are so crucial to the feasibility and viability of a distinct model of market socialism; moreover, some practical lessons can already be drawn from his model.

This paper introduces a brief profile of Tibor Liska; discusses his model of entrepreneurial socialism; and compares it to a somewhat similar scheme recently proposed by James Meade (1988). A number of ambiguities and inconsistencies are considered, which appear to have been neglected by Liska but which can be remedied or regarded as special cases, without altering the nature of his system; and a few general and major objections are raised. Some practical lessons and alternative suggestions are considered, i.e. the scope for leasing state capital, the need for recognizing the entitlement to net capital increments on the part of cooperative members, and the need for a challengeable self-valuation of capital.

11.2 Tibor Liska

Tibor Liska is a flamboyant and controversial sixty-four-year old Hungarian economist, an early and vigorous supporter of economic reform and the author of a highly original and intriguing blueprint of socialist economy. A professor at the Karl Marx University of Economics in Budapest, he served a short prison sentence in 1956. Unpopular with the authorities, he attracted publicity in the early 1980s, when he organized an Entrepreneurial Research Group holding meetings for which an entry ticket was sold at a price which was raised as the meeting got closer, up to a $40 spot price. His ideas have influenced small-scale experiments. After an extended visit to the United States in 1986–1987, he returned to Budapest where his earlier work has now been published and his ideas have received renewed attention. In spite of serious illness and heart surgery, Tibor Liska continues to be a productive and enthusiastic scholar and social reformer.

Liska's main contributions to economic theory are as follows. First, in the areas of international trade, he wrote a 1954 article with Antal Marias (translated and reproduced extensively in the *UN-ECE Economic Bulletin for Europe* and later in *East European Economics* in 1963, and other articles 1956, 1960) advocating unrestricted free trade, convertibility and floating exchange rates. Second, there is an early book entitled *Econostat* (meaning the economic homeostat or self-regulating mechanism of socialist commodity production), published after a long delay in 1988, which stresses the importance of markets in the socialist economy (see Liska 1986a, where he complains that the book could not find a publisher in Hungary; Barsony 1982; Matyaszovski 1986a, b). Third, Liska has contributed a study of the housing market (1979) in which he advocates the abolition of housing subsidies and the charging of market clearing rents, using rent increases, however, to supplement wages. He has also discussed ecological problems (1973). Liska's most important and controversial contribution, however, is his organizational model of entrepreneurial socialism (1963, 1986a, b), locally implemented on a small scale (see Varga 1982).

Liska's work has been provocative and controversial. Reviewing Liska's theories, one commentator wrote:

> Tibor Liska is undoubtedly a peculiar personality of Hungarian economic science, who searches passionately for the uncommonly new. He is a fanatic in his intentions to improve and in his agility; due to extremeness stemming from his convictions and his agitative zest he may be called a prophet and a daredevil at the same time, who is often—groundlessly—not being taken seriously. Even if his proposals seem utopic, his opinion always gives rise to thoughts and points to the essence (Barsony 1982: p. 422).

Liska himself reacted to being called a 'miraculous healer' by commenting that 'as a miraculous healer I may still achieve more than as a graduate physician who considers the patients only treatable but not curable' (Barsony 1982: p. 422).

In 1983 Norman Macrae, editor of *The Economist* at the time, devoted a long article entitled 'Into entrepreneurial socialism' to Liska which he subtitled, 'A spectre is stalking Hungary'. In this piece, he referred to Liska as a 'socialist Friedmanite', a 'most aggravating socialist and yet also an Adam Smithian economist, whom the Hungarian authorities periodically ponder whether they should put back in jail'. In Macrae's view, Liska's entrepreneurial socialism 'is the only socialism that will work' (Macrae 1983: pp. 23, 31). Janos Kornai, though critical, expresses very high appreciation for Liska's works which he sees as 'outstandingly important milestones in Hungarian economic thought'. Kornai writes:

> I cannot fully identify myself with the content of any of his works; I have some reservations and objections to all of them. Nevertheless, in all of them many important—often extremely significant—ideas can be found. Liska's spiritual independence, his moral courage and perseverance, the depth of quite a few of these thoughts are worthy of respect (Kornai 1982: p. 455).

11.3 Entrepreneurial Socialism

The setting of Liska's model is a market socialist system, i.e. a competitive market economy open to international trade and with little state intervention in the economy, where most or even all the means of production are state-owned; state capital is either used by state enterprises employing wage labour or leased out to individuals and cooperative firms. Private ownership of the means of production, indeed of anything, is subject to confiscatory inheritance tax. Any individual is entitled, by birthright and for life, to a share of the nation's net capital; he receives a guaranteed minimum income as a return on his share, paid out of the revenue collected by the state budget from state and private enterprise taxes and from capital leasings. Individuals spend their guaranteed income partly to purchase goods that in other socialist models are provided as public consumption, and in that way they are able to exercise choice even in areas such as education and medical care, through market purchases. However, the main purpose of the 'national dividend' is that individuals can use it to bid competitively for the rental of state-owned capital goods.

At the time of transition to this system, and when new capital goods are produced, state-owned capital goods are leased by state authorities through auctions, starting from a base rental fixed by those authorities. However, anybody can secure the lease of any set of capital goods owned by the state at any time by out-bidding current users, forcing them either to release the capital goods in their possession or to match the higher rental offered by the challenger.

Individuals can bid for rentals on their own account or jointly with other individuals to form a cooperative enterprise. If successful in securing the required capital goods, the enterprise (individual or group) organizes production freely, may hire additional workers as new members or as wage labour; receives and distributes according to previously agreed rules, or retains any value added net of the lease and other contractual payments. Unsuccessful bids, however, are not fruitless. All bids, whether successful or not, reveal an ability to do better than the previous bidder or the present user or, for newly-produced goods, to do better than anticipated by the state authority originally setting the starting price at capital goods auctions. In any case all bids reveal that the goods could be used yielding a productivity higher than that currently imputed to them, and for both successful and unsuccessful bids, the additional rental associated with each bid does not go to the state but to the challenger as a reward for the additional ability revealed and the informational function of the bid: 'the overbid belongs to the bidder'.

Out of the rental successfully bid by an individual or team, therefore, the basic rate initially set by the state authority goes to the state budget; incremental bids by other than the current user are paid to them, while the difference between the successful bid and the previous bid is not actually paid, or is deemed to be paid by the successful bidder to himself in recognition of his own quasi-rent in using the capital goods which he has secured.

Individual income is made up of the minimum guaranteed income, plus a wage if the individual is hired at a fixed rate or an agreed share (100 per cent if the individual is self-employed) of any of the value added, net of contractual payments made by the enterprise to which the individual is associated (including as income of any successful or unsuccessful overbid or overbids, whether on the goods actually used by the enterprise or on capital goods used outside), plus any other overbid or share in overbids unsuccessfully made by the individual or by enterprises with which he has been associated, and to whose income he still has a share entitlement.

Individuals unable to earn at least that part of the agreed rental that has to be paid to the state and to others must pay out of their other income, i.e. their entitlement to interest out of their current capital share (which is the sum of original capital savings plus the capitalization of unsuccessful overbids).

In this world, anybody who has the know-how and loves risk-taking can be an entrepreneur; others will prefer fixed wages, or mixed contracts to be stipulated with the entrepreneurs or entrepreneurial teams. An enterprise will have a capital value, equal to the capitalization of capital productivity over and above rentals, so that shares could be issued, tentatively priced at the share price implicit in that capitalization, but transacted at an equilibrium price in order to facilitate the turnover of cooperative membership. Income could be freely spent or accumulated; the capitalization of overbids could also be part of individual budgets (to control current expenditure out of capital the interest rate used in capitalizing overbids could be raised if total withdrawals are excessively inflationary). At death, all of one's capital—the national share out of which an interest is paid as minimum guaranteed income, and any accretion during one's lifetime—would revert to the state, and become part of the general pool out of which individual stakes are determined and, presumably, periodically adjusted.

This construction, which differs from any known model East or West, has a considerable appeal. On the one hand, it has familiar socialist connotations: (1) state ownership, with private ownership playing a quantitatively small and qualitatively restricted role because of confiscation at death; (2) equality of minimum consumption standards through guaranteed minimum income; (3) equality of opportunities, through equal access to social capital at birth (or rather at maturity), which turns unemployment—if any—into a voluntary phenomenon. On the other hand, this model also has features typical of a competitive market economy: (1) it restricts the role of state enterprises, leading to the direct socialization of the use of means of production, without an intervening bureaucracy;

(2) it activates rampant competition, encouraging the efficient redeployment of capital goods throughout the economy; (3) it sets up incentives for individuals who wish to exercise entrepreneurship and to retain the rewards, including a lifelong interest in future expected rewards; all members of society have a reciprocal relation with capital goods and between themselves, of exasperated reciprocity as continuous bidders and counter-bidders; (4) it subjects former public consumption to the scrutiny of choice.

The model is slightly reminiscent of Fourier, in its claimed superiority and in the undertones of sexual liberty which colours some of the Liskian experiments in Hungary (a photograph of a man marrying two women at Szentes figures prominently in the *Economist* feature of Liska) (see Macrae 1983). These experiments have been short-lived and have had more the nature of holiday camps than of alternative enterprises or societies.

11.4 Liska's Model and Meade's 'Agathotopia'

The suggestion of a minimum guaranteed income is not new and in recent years has been gaining increasingly widespread support in diverse circles: from Alexandre Marc to Michel Rocard, from Sam Brittan to James Meade. In particular Meade (1986a, b, 1988), like Liska, proposes a minimum guaranteed income financed out of the revenue from a substantial state share (say, half) of national ownership, and supplemented by profit-sharing. These elements are complementary and self-reinforcing, because without state ownership, minimum income guarantee would be 'hideously expensive', requiring self-defeating attempts at raising confiscatory and incentive-destroying taxes on income other than the guaranteed minimum; while without a minimum guaranteed income, the introduction of extensive profit-sharing would be otherwise unattractive to workers unable to spread labour-income risk in the way capitalists can by selecting a diversified portfolio.

The similarity between Meade and Liska ends here. In Meade's system (which he calls 'Agathotopia', i.e. a 'Good Place' rather than a 'Utopia' which is a place nowhere to be found) state ownership is financial, not real; it is not leased but invested in unit trusts, holding shares of ordinary companies managed by managers who are private employees of private enterprises (except for the usual sectors of public utilities, state administration and defense).[1] Thus there are no auctions of real capital; what is more, in Meade, there is no suggestion or possibility of the overbidder's claim on overbids. Meade's enterprises are not cooperatives but partnerships between private capitalists and profit-sharing workers; workers' shares lapse with the end of their employment, but capitalists' shares are a permanent claim (see Nuti 1988c).

Liska's state ownership consists of physical capital whose lease is auctioned off to the best potential users. The financial system is not developed and its rise rests on the marketability of cooperatives' shares, which, however, represent a fuller claim on entrepreneurship rewards than Meade's workers shares. Liska's guaranteed minimum is the seed corn expected to turn everybody into a socialist entrepreneur (everybody bidding for the rental of state capital out of their guaranteed income); his partnerships are short-lived as workers group and regroup themselves incessantly.

Meade's scheme, which deserves separate treatment and cannot be fully discussed here, is a modification of really existing capitalism, while Liska's is a modification of really existing socialism. The two proposed systems are closer than the actually existing systems but do not converge to a common standard.

11.5 Ambiguities and Minor Problems

The characterization of Tibor Liska's scheme given above is a reconstruction of his model from various texts and an attempt to establish a coherent picture. Liska's model, however, has a rich texture developed over a

[1] It should be stressed that in Meade the acquisition of a large portion of national capital is advocated not as the result of instant nationalization without compensation, but as the gradual result of a sequence of state budget surpluses on current account, which would first wipe out the national debt, then gradually bite into national private wealth. These budget surpluses, incidentally, would not be deflationary because they would be offset by the state purchase of private capital, and because monetary policy would be used to maintain full or full-enough employment.

number of different texts and is not a clear-cut and totally consistent proposal. There are a number of linguistic liberties[2] which unnecessarily mislead and irritate the reader and which are not worth repeating; there are ambiguities and variations—some of them slightly inconsistent with other aspects of the model—which ought to be considered. There is occasional confusion, or change of mind, as to whether individuals actually have some command over their share of capital (their 'social inheritance'), i.e. whether or not they can use it directly or indirectly as a guarantee for their entrepreneurial operations; and whether individuals are entitled to income or/and to a credit corresponding to their capital share. In the version given above, income has been preferred to a claim on capital because otherwise the possibility of private consumption of national capital might have arisen, with individuals recklessly gambling their capital stake on risky ventures in the expectation of being able to keep the gains while socialising the possible loss.

Another difference between alternative versions of the Liska model is the scope for private ownership, sometimes excluded, sometimes permitted as a life interest; the possibility has been retained in the version given here. However, if this life interest can be extended by transfer to others, this is a loophole in extending the scope of private ownership; while if it is not, it introduces short-sight in private transactions. If capital accretions are subject to a life interest earnings only, would a successful entrepreneur not transform his winnings into a life annuity, so as to be able to transfer back to the national pool no more than he has received from it? Regardless of whether or not private ownership of the means of production is allowed, ownership of savings out of income must be allowed in some form, or the incentive to consume would be overriding; without the ability to transfer at least part of one's savings and capital accretions to others at death, the incentive to exercise entrepreneurship and take risks must be all that much weaker.

There is some ambiguity about the nature of Liska's minimum guaranteed income. If it is to guarantee a minimum standard of living, surely it should not be available for gambling on risky ventures? Is the

[2] For instance, an unconventional use of 'real capital' and 'moral capital' to indicate respectively the original individual share of national capital and its subsequent accretions.

unsuccessful entrepreneur to be completely unprovided for against ill health and old age; are rotten teeth the price of socialist entrepreneurship? And if the minimum guaranteed standard is an inalienable right, how high must this guaranteed income be to leave room also for the provision of risk capital to any bidding entrepreneur? And can such a high minimum guaranteed income be afforded by most societies? We can, however, leave these problems aside at least temporarily, by imagining that the Liska economy is rich enough to guarantee minimum living standards and still provide all with the seed corn of socialist entrepreneurship.

If individual entrepreneurs are not allowed to bequeath their investments, why invest at all? Moral hazard arises; we must imagine an institutional investor, or investors, who would probably be subject to direct government control. Presumably there would be banks; would their assets then be hired out on the same basis as physical assets? Unlike physical assets, whose material deterioration can be protected by insurance, banks' assets are subject to non-insurable risks. What would then ensure the preservation of the value of their assets? Banks could finance bidders to the extent of the capitalization of their guaranteed income and overbids, but could they go further? Could they go further to the extent of the capital paid up by shareholders? If so, banks' capital basis must be thin, since shareholders can only use their guaranteed income, to start with, to fund banks' capital; unless the state itself is a shareholder, in which case bureaucratic or etatist power creeps back. In any case, can banks finance the production of capital goods for sale in the market? But who would demand capital goods in that market, and how would these purchases be financed? Or would capital goods producers also rent out their capital goods in competition with state agencies?

Surely a state agency must exist with the responsibility to take over or at least supplement capital accumulation, given the constraints on private capital ownership? For the sake of argument, let us suppose that such a state agency is either not needed (say, there is a near-stationary state), or it operates responding to market signals as if it was a consortium of private investors. Presumably the value of national capital, and the state income obtained from it (which is only a fraction of national profit, much of which consists of overbids paid out to overbidders) will vary over time. Individuals will receive yearly adjustments. In a recession, the national dividend may well have to go down. Yet individual rental bids are guaranteed by the national dividend. Is the guarantee fixed, in which case new entrants are at a disadvantage and some of the entrepreneurial risk is borne by the state; or is it a variable guarantee, in which case the guarantee is somewhat uncertain? But let us suppose that the economy is rich enough and tranquil enough for these problems not to arise and matter.

11.6 Major Objections

If these complications can be assumed away as arising in special—though possibly frequent—circumstances, there are also major objections of a general nature. The first is the medium-long term nature of bids, and therefore the necessity of a 'validation' process of the credibility of bids similar to financiers' endorsement of investment projects in a capitalist economy. Bidders will not and should not make a bid only in a spot market for capital goods rentals: production commits entire sets of capital goods over time, and bidders should be able to secure the fixed inputs they need on long leases if they wish. Presumably bids of different length or time pattern are compared on their present value; but whenever bids are made for more than the current period, bidders pledge more than their known-current command on resources and their bids have to be scrutinized and compared. The highest bid will not necessarily be also the most credible, or be credible at all.[3] A state endorsement of multi-period bids would reintroduce bureaucratic control by the back door; yet it is hard to see how this role could be performed on the required scale by private undertakings without the kind of concentration of financial resources that the model is seeking to avoid.

[3] In the sale of tobacconist licences by the Italian State Monopoly for Salt and Tobacco, bids take the form of estimates of potential sales, to which there corresponds a percentage revenue for the State Monopoly; the licence is not allocated to the bidder predicting the highest level of sales, but to the one closest to the State Monopoly's own forecast of the sale potential of the given sale outlet. By being closest to that expert forecast, the bidder displays his own competence and understanding of the market in which he is to operate.

A second major problem is represented by capital intensive activities. My own capital stake will give me, by definition, at the very most, command on the average capital per man in the economy. To exercise entrepreneurship outside a narrow category of activities (such as personal services, handicraft, petrol stations, taxi driving, gardening or small-scale catering) a mechanism is necessary for people using less than average capital per man to make available funds to people using higher than average capital per man. Would shares be issued? But the available funds are a flow out of people's minimum guaranteed income; would a flow of shares be issued to fund a flow of rentals in undertakings with above average capital? Would schemes for contractual savings have to be started for the orderly funding of capital intensive activities over time? And if part of the state income out of capital rental is going to be used for funding education, health care and retirement, who is going to make up for that withdrawal by adding a corresponding amount to the level of rental expenditures? Again, will it be a state agency or agencies in charge of investment?

A third major problem arises from the model's implication for the size and scope of firms. There is a vast literature (exemplified by Oliver Williamson, or Harold Demsetz) on why firms' boundaries are what they are, and why firms exist at all in place of a network of *ad hoc* contracts. Ordinary firms as we know them in market economies are mostly long-term, encompassing activities within their boundaries so as to balance the benefits of certainty, derived from integrating a group of related activities over a long term, with the actual or potential costs of such longer-term commitments. Liska's firms cannot be anything of the kind: they rather suggest themselves as small bands of workers, continuously grouping and splitting and regrouping themselves, as capital goods and sets of capital goods are continuously reshuffled around the economy by bidders. In fact, bidding teams cannot be managerial teams, as is often the case in the reshuffling of capital assets in ordinary market economies; they must be complete teams of managers and workers, backing their bid with their own personal minimum guaranteed income and subsequent accretions. For the system to work at all it must operate through marauding bands of workers successfully taking over, reorganising and operating sets of capital assets, displacing incumbent teams. This is at odds with the reasons of efficiency as investigated in the Williamson-Demsetz literature. The system will either be somewhat inefficient, or not work as envisaged.

Finally, problems are raised by the principle that 'overbids belong to the bidders'. If a capital asset is on offer at 100 monetary units and I can break even offering 150, I can safely bid, say, 400 units knowing that the 300 units overbid will belong to me and I will not have to pay it, that I will have the undisturbed use of the asset until somebody comes along and offers over 400 units, in which case I will turn into a rentier to the tune of 300 units over the period for which I was committed to pay a rental for that asset. Thus bidders can protect themselves from competition by exaggerated bids, at the cost of only missing the higher probability of turning into a rentier for more modest overbids. There is little effort involved in bidding: rewarding that kind of effort would encourage a lot of wasted effort for abortive bids; the same competitive access to capital goods might be achieved by overbidders keeping only a small fraction of their overbids, say of the order of 2–4 per cent such as might be paid to any intermediary or broker. This avoids the dead weight of a layer of rentiers over the back of those who actually do the work; Liska seems to be unaware of the unpleasant aspects of generalized rent-seeking, and the unnecessary rise of a rentier class, however large.

11.7 Practical Lessons

The minor and major reservations raised above would have to be satisfactorily answered, before the 'Socialist' system can be regarded as a viable, efficient and desirable system. Nevertheless, as is often the case with utopian models—such as pure capitalism or pure central planning might also be considered—there are a number of practical lessons and suggestions which can be drawn from Liska's model, which is best seen as an exercise, or a source of potential partial and not total solutions. There are at least three such practical and partial lessons:

1. The first is the importance of capital leasings to workers and teams of workers, as opposed to privatization, in the process of radical reform of socialist economies and in the restructuring of declining sectors and inefficient states enterprises. This lesson was already understood, at least partly under the influence of Liska's proposals, in the early stages of Hungarian reform, and now in the Polish reform. From the sectors of public catering and retail establishments (to which the leasing principle was first applied in these reforms), this principle has recently been extended to land-leases to family groups by Kolkhozy in the USSR: on 5 October 1988 Ligachev's successor, Vadim Medvedev, indicated the importance of extending the leasing principle not only to manufacturing but also to heavy industry *(Financial Times,* 6 October 1988). This seems a promising way of breaking up excessively large production units, gaining acceptance for otherwise unpopular redeployment of labour, restoring incentives and responsibility, as long as it is not the exclusive mode of organization in the whole economy or even only in industry.
2. The second is the understanding of the need to recognize the entitlement of cooperative members to the capitalization of the reinvestment and the success of their enterprises. In truth Liska seems to recognize less than this full entitlement, still bound by the institutional constraints of traditional socialism, since he suggests something closer to bonds with a performance clause, than to true shares as now accepted in China (since September 1987) and Hungary (since 1 January 1989; see Nuti 1988d). Nevertheless, the principle of attributing to worker-members of cooperatives a share of capital value increments of their cooperative is a necessary step to counteract the well-known tendencies towards inefficiency and instability exhibited by the traditional cooperative, where members only share in the cash flow of their enterprise. Moves in this direction are exemplified by Yugoslav discussions on issuing shares to members of their enterprises (Uvalic 1987), Soviet new legislation on cooperatives (Nuti 1989), and the attempt by Italian cooperatives to establish a new role for capital members ('Socio sovventore'; Nuti 1988b).
3. The third, and perhaps most important suggestion to be drawn from Liska is that of a self-assessed and challengeable valuation of capital. However, what is needed is not a valuation of current capital rentals

but of capital values, which implicitly involves an assessment of both future capital rentals and of appropriate discount rates.

Capital assets are notorious for the difficulties associated with their evaluation, other than in the case of brand-new machines in an equilibrium market, or in the case of land and buildings for which there are established criteria and markets. Such difficulties impede the redeployment of assets to the best possible uses, reduce the tax basis of possible capital tax, and prevent the full recognition of the capital claims of cooperative members. Imagine a system whereby owners of assets, or firms, are forced to announce the value of their assets (broken down by main components, together with liabilities), while any economic agent (individual, enterprise or government agency) is able to challenge that valuation by announcing a higher bid. Let us stipulate that in this case the challenger either secures the ownership of the asset at the higher price bid for it, or forces the owners to revalue upwards their self-assessed valuation and to pay the overbidder a small commission on the unsuccessful overbid. Such a system has untold potential in establishing a basis for capital tax collection, forcing redeployment of capital assets even in the absence of a stock exchange, and adequately rewarding cooperative enterprise members for their entrepreneurship through an issue of shares matching the increase in capital values from the time of their joining the cooperative. This scheme (outlined in Nuti 1988a) seems to deliver many of the advantages sought by Liska without any of the drawbacks or its idiosyncracies.[4]

[4] It was the Hungarian economist George Suranyi, to whom I outlined this procedure in June 1986 during a World Bank Mission to Poland as a solution to the problems of capital redeployment in an economy without a stock exchange, who pointed out to me the similarity with Tibor Liska's scheme. However, in Liska's 'entrepreneurial socialism', individuals use the guaranteed income out of their share of social capital to bid for the rental of production goods, renting them if successful or obtaining from successful bidders the amount of their unsuccessful raises, surrendering at death their original capital stake and its accretion. Here state and private enterprises bid for the purchase of larger chunks of productive assets. If unsuccessful, they keep nothing or at most, a small percentage of their raises. The differences between the two schemes are substantial, but the spirit is the same; ultimately they have in common the permanent state of insecurity of enterprise managers, continuously exposed to the challenge of potentially better users of their enterprise's assets. Kornai criticises Liska for exposing managers to this kind of insecurity (Kornai 1982) but no competitive behaviour and profit-mindedness—and therefore no hardening of Kornai's alleged 'soft-budget constraints' (Kornai 1980, vol. I, Chap. 13)—can be expected of managers without introducing precisely this kind of insecurity.

Bibliography

Barsony, J. (1982). Tibor Liska's Concept of Socialist Entrepreneurship. *Acta Oeconomica,* Vol. 28, No. 13-14, 424-455.

Kornai, J. (1980). *The Economics of Shortage* (Amsterdam: North Holland Publishing Co.).

Kornai, J. (1982). Comments on Tibor Liska's Concept of Entrepreneurship. *Acta Oeconomica,* Vol. 28, No. 13-14, 455-60.

Liska, L. (1956). Experimental calculations on the efficiency of our participation in investment and international labor division programs (in Hungarian), *Kőzgazdasági Szmele,* 3.

Liska, T. (1960). Problems connected with calculations of export efficiency (in Hungarian), *Kőzgazdasági Szmele,* 12.

Liska, T. (1963). Critique and concept. Theses for the reform of the economic mechanism (in Hungarian), *Kőzgazdasági Szmele,* 17.

Liska, T. (1973). The critique of human ecology (in Hungarian), *Valoság,* 3.

Liska, T. (1979). The concept of the buying and selling of rented dwellings (in Hungarian), *Valoság,* 1.

Liska, T. (1986a). A market more developed than capitalist market (in Italian), in Morley-Fletcher (1986), 85-100.

Liska, T. (1986b). Much more than an agreement (a rejoinder to Kornai, in Italian), in Morley-Fletcher (1986), 140-7.

Liska, T. (1988). Econostat (in Hungarian, available since 1965 as unpublished typescript).

Liska, T. and Antal Marias (1954). Effectiveness and the international division of labor (in Hungarian), *Kőzgazdasági Szmele,* 1; English translation in *Eastern European Economics,* (4), 1953, 215.

Macrae, Norman (1983). Into Entrepreneurial Socialism: A Spectre is Stalking Hungary. *The Economist,* 19 March.

Matyaszovski, V. (1986a). Tibor Liska: an introductory note (in Italian), in Morley-Fletcher, 1986.

Matyaszovski, V. (1986b). Tibor Liska and the debate on economic reforms in Hungary (in Italian), in Morley-Fletcher, 1986.

Meade, J. E. (1986a). *Alternative Forms of Business Organization and of Workers' Remuneration* (London: Allen & Unwin).

Meade, J. E. (1986b). *Different Forms of Share Economy* (London: Public Policy Centre).

Meade, J. E. (1988). The Partnership Economy, paper for a Conference on Co-entrepreneurship held by the LICM (League of Italian Cooperatives), Rome, 14-15 March.

Morley-Fletcher, E., (1986) (Ed.). *Cooperare e competere* [Cooperation and competition] (Milan: Feltrinelli).

Nuti, D. M. (1988a). Competitive Valuation and Efficiency of Capital Investment in the Socialist Economy, *European Economic Review*, Vol. 32, 2-6.

Nuti, D. M. (1988b). Progetto per un Fondo Mutualistico per la promozione e lo sviluppo di imprese cooperative [Project for a Mutual Fund for the Promotion and Development of Cooperative Enterprises], paper for a Conference on Co-entrepreneurship held by the LICM (League of Italian Cooperatives), Rome, 14-15 March 1988.

Nuti, D. M. (1988c). On Traditional Cooperatives and James Meade's Labour-Capital Discriminating Partnerships, *EUI Working Paper*, Florence.

Nuti, D. M. (1988d). Remonetisation and Capital Markets in the Reform of Centrally Planned Economies, EUI Working Paper No. 88/361; forthcoming in the *European Economic Review*.

Nuti, D. M. (1989). The Soviet Cooperatives: Advances and Limitations. *Economic and Industrial Democracy*, 10, 3 (August).

Uvalic, Milica (1987). Shareholding in Yugoslav Theory and Practice, *EUI Working Paper*, Florence.

Varga, Gy (1982). The Experiment of Szentes, *Acta Oeconomica*, 28, No. 13-14, 460-5.

Part II

Transition to a Market Economy

Foreword to Part II: Transition to a Market Economy

Saul Estrin and Milica Uvalic

Mario Nuti's knowledge about the functioning of socialist economic systems stood him in good stead when the cracks in the socialist economic monolith began to show, first in Poland in the 1980s, turning to a flood across Central Europe, leading to the fall of the Berlin Wall in 1989 and the disintegration of the Soviet Union and several federations. Most countries had been centrally planned for decades and with almost entire enterprise capital stock owned by the state. With these unpromising preconditions, each country embarked on its own uncharted path of economic transition to a market system. Mario was exceptionally well placed to analyse the trials and tribulations, as well as to reflect on the successes, of this process, both as a scholar of economic systems and as an active participant in policy making.

As with his work on socialist economic systems, Mario's approach to economic reforms was eclectic, drawing on his training in macroeconomic and growth theory as well as his growing understanding of the transition process itself. The papers in this section cover the transition to a market economy in Central and Eastern European countries between

1990 and 2013. When reading each paper it is important to be aware of the date when it was written, because issues, and economists' understanding of their implications, were evolving throughout. Thus, for example, some of the chapters written in the early 1990s involved Mario's understanding of the context to devise appropriate policies for transition, at a time when there were no blueprints on what should be done. Though this was a period of great uncertainty and experimentation, this section reveals how Mario combined merciless logic and great depth of understanding to provide his virtually instantaneous judgements about the profound policy dilemmas of transition, especially during the first half of the 1990s.

Chapters 12, 13, and 14 are primarily concerned with broad questions about overall transition programmes, defined by Mario to comprise macroeconomic stabilisation, both internal and external; restructuring at the microeconomic level primarily through enterprise privatisation; and institutional reforms in different areas—including the setting up of social safety nets, the creation of capital markets, and other fundamental institutional changes. In Chap. 12, written in 1991, Mario provides an overview of the issues taken together because they all were to be addressed simultaneously, and indicates their appropriate sequencing. Mario could draw on his unparalleled understanding of socialist economies and how they functioned until 1989 to consider the pitfalls that lay ahead. His knowledge often made him more aware of the potential dangers ahead than some other Western analysts and policy advisers. For example, because he understood that a fundamental characteristic of planned socialist economies was that prices were fixed at disequilibrium levels, he argued that price liberalisation had to be rapid and would initially lead to high inflation. At the same time, because, under socialism, trade was conducted on the basis of planned exchanges at fixed prices, convertibility and exchange rate management would also be a major challenge. Other important issues he considered included how to replace state owned by private firms, and how to reform the financial system so as to allow the emergence of the capital market. By the time that Chap. 13 was written, in 1992, there were already some preliminary experiences of stabilisation programmes and initial transition reforms, and for the most part the outcomes were not very positive, since all transition countries had gone through a period of deep recession and high inflation. Mario critically reviews what happened in those early years in a number of countries including East Germany, Russia, Hungary, Yugoslavia and especially Poland and goes on, in Chap. 14, to reflect on some of the deeper causes of the massive dislocations that had occurred. These he links to a much slower reaction to the dramatic changes in relative prices by households and firms than had been anticipated by policymakers, along with much slower than expected reforms of the underlying incentives, for example through privatisation. In these early reflections on transition, Mario made a particularly important contribution to the issue of "sequencing" of the transition process, pointing to those objectives that must be accomplished immediately—such as price liberalisation and stabilisation—and those that would necessarily require time—primarily institutional reforms.

The next few chapters address in depth particular topics in the transition process. In Chap. 15, Mario reflects on the appropriate timing of currency convertibility. His analysis is built upon his understanding of the role of money in a socialist economy, from which he derives the preconditions for the successful introduction of convertibility. Chapter 16 examines internal and external macroeconomic balances and their interaction in countries undertaking transition to a market economy. The paper pins down how the initial freeing of exchange rates in a situation of disequilibrium will lead to the overvaluation that we observed in most economies. On the other hand, Mario considered currency convertibility as one of the principal achievements of the transition process—indeed, a fundamental distortion of the socialist economies, the separation of domestic and foreign relative prices, was resolved by these transition reforms. In Chap. 17, Mario takes the discussion further, evaluating the variety of exchange rates regimes that operated in Poland in the previous decade and using the diversity of experience as a sort of natural experiment to draw policy conclusions.

Chapters 18–21 look at the conceptual issues that arose in the process of privatisation. This was also at the heart of the transition because the vast majority of firms in Eastern Europe were state or socially owned. Chapter 18 was written much before privatisation had taken place, in 1991, and provides Mario's rather unique view of the challenges involved in transforming an economy from state to private ownership. The chapter is partly conceptual, assessing the key function of private ownership in an economic system and evaluating what might be its legitimate scope and limits. He also reflects on whether private ownership is a necessary precondition for the existence of a capital market (an argument of Von Mises), something he rather doubts. However, by the time Chap. 19 was written, in 1995, we have rather more experience to evaluate, and Mario can consider the large gap between ambition and outcomes in privatisation programmes. A key section of the paper is entitled "delays and diversions" and looks into their impact on corporate restructuring and enterprise performance. He returns to the theme in a 2000 paper (Chap. 20, coauthored with Saul Estrin and Milica Uvalic), on whether privatisation would actually improve firm performance in transition economies, especially if the process entailed a significant element of free distribution of property (mass privatisation). The chapter evaluates in detail the institutions set up in the Czech Republic, Poland and Slovenia to provide external corporate governance to former state-owned firms, namely Investment Funds and the prevalently disappointing outcomes of these innovative solutions. Finally, Chap. 21 brings many of these themes together in considering the issues involved in the privatisation of financial institutions, and therefore in the creation of a capital market.

Chapter 22 provides one of Mario's discussions of transition in Russia, through the device of asking what would have been required for Gorbachev's *perestroika* to have succeeded. He presents the actual reforms that were introduced, explains why they failed, and then offers in the light of what we had learnt about transition a set of policy initiatives that might have succeeded, not only in reforming the economic system but in keeping the Soviet Union united. Finally, in Chap. 23, written in 2001, Mario looks back at the transition process recalling its undoubted achievements and numerous failures. It is remarkable how often the judgements Mario made at the time, as reflected in this Section, yielded profound insights into the transition process across the East European region.

12

Stabilization and Sequencing in the Reform of Socialist Economies

Domenico Mario Nuti

The countries of Central and Eastern Europe, including the Soviet Union, are currently facing three major economic tasks at the same time: macroeconomic stabilization, both domestic and external; microeconomic and sectoral restructuring; and the transition from central planning to a mixed market economy. Political reform is also being attempted throughout the area, away from "democratic centralism" namely, Communist Party monopoly of power in the state and the economy, toward forms of democratic pluralism. This chapter considers the appropriate order in which governments might introduce changes in economic policy and institutions in these transitional economies. The state of economic reform is shown in Table 12.1.

Published in Simon Commander (Ed.), *Managing Inflation in Socialist Economies in Transition*, EDI Seminar Series, The World Bank, Washington DC, 1991, pp. 155–174. French version: 1992.

D. M. Nuti (✉)
La Sapienza, University of Rome, Rome, Italy
e-mail: milica.uvalic@unipg.it

© The Author(s), under exclusive license to Springer Nature Switzerland AG 2023
S. Estrin, M. Uvalic (eds.), *Collected Works of Domenico Mario Nuti, Volume I*, Studies in Economic Transition, https://doi.org/10.1007/978-3-031-12334-4_12

Table 12.1 Economic reform in Central and Eastern Europe as of January 1991

Reform	Poland	Hungary	Romania	Czechoslovakia	Bulgaria	ex-GDR[a]	Yugoslavia	USSR
Abolition of imperative planning	Yes	Yes	No	Yes	Discussed	Yes	Yes	Yes
Reduction in number of ministries	One ind. min	One ind. min.	No	Yes	In progress	Yes	Yes	No
Reduction of government contracts	Yes	Yes	No	Yes	In progress	Yes	Yes	No
Smaller scope of centrally fixed prices	Free prices	Yes	Somewhat	Yes	Somewhat	Yes	Free prices	Small
Laws promoting genuine cooperatives	No need	No need	No	No need	Yes	No need	Yes[b]	Yes (hypergrowth)
Laws promoting the private sector	Yes	Yes	Yes	Yes	Yes	Yes	Yes	Yes
Laws promoting joint ventures	Yes	Yes	Yes	Yes	Yes	Yes	Yes	Yes
Labor mobility	Yes	Yes	Yes	Yes	Yes	Yes	Yes	Yes
Splitting of large enterprises	Some	Some	No	Some	No	Yes	Some	No
Anti-trust and competition laws	Yes	Yes	No	Yes	Discussed	Yes	Yes	No

Unemployment: current	1.2 m	200,000	No	50,000	No	700,000[c]	16%	4 m
Unemployment: forecast end 1991	2 m	Increasing	No	6–10%	Expected	Increasing	Stable	Increasing
Sectoral restructuring	Yes	Yes	Not yet	Yes	Not yet	Yes	Yes	No
Stabilization program	Yes	Yes	Expected	Yes	Yes	*de facto*	Yes	No[d]
Privatization of state assets	Yes	Yes	Some land	Yes	Expected	Yes	Yes	Some
Banking reform	Yes	Yes	No	Yes	Some	*de facto*	Not needed	Some
Financial market for bonds and shares	Yes	Yes (1987, 1990)	Discussed	In progress	Discussed	Yes	Yes	Yes, limited
Liquidation and bankruptcies	Yes	Yes	Expected	Yes	Expected	Yes	Yes	Yes, rare
Foreign trade liberalization	Yes	Yes	No	Yes	Some	Yes	Yes	Licensing
Direct access to world market	Yes	Yes	No	Yes	In progress	Yes	Yes	Yes, controlled
Hard currency auctions	Convertibility	Not needed	No	Convertibility	Yes	Not needed	Convertibility	Monthly

[a]*De facto* transformation into market economy from July 2, 1990 through monetary union with the Federal Republic of Germany.
[b]The social property enterprises were self-managed and considered to act as cooperatives; mid-1990 privatization laws are transforming self-management rights into partial property rights.
[c]Plus two million part-time employees.
[d]Destabilization due to preannounced and postponed price increases and to partial confiscation of large denomination notes.
Source: Prepared by the author for the European Commission; based on memoranda submitted by individual countries and other official documents.

12.1 Stabilization

Domestically, macroeconomic stabilization means the elimination of inflationary pressures, whether open or "repressed" under the guise of domestic currency overhang. There was open hyperinflation in Poland (740 percent a year in 1989), and in Yugoslavia (2500 percent a year in 1989), prior to their stabilization plans of January 1990 and December 1989, respectively. Repressed inflation is difficult to quantify because it involves an estimate of demand for money in equilibrium, but its presence is signaled by persistent shortages, as in the ex-German Democratic Republic (GDR), where the monetary overhang at end 1989 was estimated at 30–40 billion ostmarks, and was rising rapidly due to the reduced demand for money on the part of recent and prospective emigrants, and above all in the Soviet Union, where in mid-1990 the overhang was officially estimated at 160–200 billion rubles just in the household sector, or about one quarter of the national income. In Romania, Czechoslovakia (until the stabilization plan of January 1, 1991), and Bulgaria a grossly undervalued currency in black market transactions reveals the presence of some overhang, while in Hungary, the current rate of open inflation in 1989 was about 20 percent per year despite wage controls, rising to 30 percent in 1990.

Most of these countries also need external stabilization, that is, they need to achieve net exports adequate to service, now or at some definite time in the future, an external debt that has exceeded the limits of viability or prudence. At one extreme Romania, under Ceausescu's dictatorship, succeeded in repaying US$10 billion in external debt—including World Bank and IMF loans repaid before maturity despite favorable terms—at the cost of brutal deflation that compressed consumption beyond the population's endurance. Czechoslovakia can cope despite stagnation, and is the most creditworthy. At the other extreme Poland, with over US$45 billion in external debt, and Yugoslavia, with US$18 billion, have lost their creditworthiness: their commercial debt is retraded in secondary markets at a fraction of its face value (150 and 500, respectively, on the dollar at the end of 1990). Hungary, with US$20 billion in external debt following a 1989 upward revision of over US$2 billion, began to show a small discount in early 1990 and was retrading at 800 at the end of 1990. In between is the USSR, with a net debt around US$30 billion or more according to a recent pronouncement by Prime Minister Ryzhkov. Bulgaria (also revised upward to over US$10 billion) is no longer in a position to rely on positive net transfers to offset income stagnation or outright decline. (The ex-German Democratic Republic had US$10 billion debt in mid-1990 at the time of unification.)

12.2 Restructuring

The task of microeconomic and sectoral restructuring is to renew capacity structure, which is currently inappropriate:

- With respect to domestic demand, given its excessive emphasis on heavy industry (especially metallurgy), shipbuilding, and machinery, and its lack of focus on consumption durables, high technology industries, services.
- With respect to opportunity costs, for example, the higher price of energy and materials, the presence of diffused labor shortages, and the heavy costs of environmental destruction.
- With respect to best practice technology; many industries employ obsolete techniques and produce poor quality output. For example, Poland is the most energy-intensive country in the world; Romania's latest five-year plan did not contemplate any computer plants. The share of services in employment and output, material intensity, and labor productivity compare most unfavorably with countries at a similar level of development.
- With respect to international division of labor until 1990–1991 much trade has been taking place within the CMEA (except for Yugoslavia which has only associated membership), with a bilateral bias and Soviet dominance, at prices reflecting not today's opportunity costs, but at outdated international prices averaged over the last five years. (Only since January 1, 1991, has this been replaced by trade at international prices and settlement in hard currencies.)

Incapacitated by a "petrified" capital structure and paralyzed by excessive concern about inflation, the countries of Central and Eastern Europe have suffered from progressive slowdown, stagnation, and economic decline (especially per capita, and relative to similar countries). The realization that economic crisis had systemic roots has led to a renewed wave of reforms aimed at introducing some features of a market economy into the centrally planned economy, first in Poland and Hungary, then in the GDR through monetary union and unification with the Federal Republic of Germany, then Czechoslovakia, while in the Soviet Union progress has been illusory despite repeated apparent attempts.

12.3 Developing a Market Economy

Economic reform has not followed a uniform pattern in Central and Eastern Europe because of the varying degrees of political and economic pressure, as well as the lack of precedents (see Table 12.1). Pre-1990 reform measures have included:

- Replacing imperative planning and physical targets for enterprises and ministries by purely indicative macroeconomic targets (in Hungary, Poland, the USSR, and Yugoslavia). Planning commissions have been transformed into planning offices (Hungary, Poland), accordingly, the number of branch ministries has been reduced (Hungary, Poland).
- Developing the nonstate sector, including cooperatives, especially in the Soviet Union where they have increased 20-fold in two years; private enterprises, especially in Hungary and Poland; joint ventures; and foreign enterprises.
- Permitting greater income disparity than in the past when justified by relative performance, and greater labor mobility, not only across regions, but often also across borders (most spectacularly in the ex-German Democratic Republic in the months running up to unification).
- Accepting unemployment, which in 1990 reached 200,000 in Hungary and 1.2 million in Poland.

- Undertaking price liberalization and stabilization programs implemented in Yugoslavia in December 1989, in Poland in January 1990, in Czechoslovakia in January 1991, and soon even in Bulgaria.
- Privatizing state assets, already under way in 1990 in Hungary and Poland, and now in Czechoslovakia, accompanied by the transformation of state enterprises into joint stock companies, and to a small extent (housing, leasing of land and state plants) even in the USSR.
- Undertaking a generalized commitment to sectoral restructuring.
- Separating commercial from central banking and establishing new and competing commercial banks, often with joint or foreign capital, in Hungary, Poland, Bulgaria, and to a lesser extent in the Soviet Union. The automatic granting of credit by a monobank is being replaced by contractual relationships based on creditworthiness, and procedures for the liquidation and bankruptcy of nonviable enterprises have been activated in Yugoslavia, Poland, Hungary, and even the Soviet Union.
- Introducing financial markets for bonds and shares, first in Hungary, then in Poland, and to a smaller extent the USSR, and now in Yugoslavia and Czechoslovakia.
- Liberalizing foreign trade and permitting enterprises to have direct access to world markets, especially in the USSR, Poland, and Hungary.
- Holding hard currency auctions in Bulgaria, Poland, Czechoslovakia, and the Soviet Union and then establishing internal convertibility for current transactions in Yugoslavia (1989), Poland (1990), and Czechoslovakia (1991).

All the countries concerned have either renounced or challenged the Communist Party's so-called "leading role," that is, its power monopoly. The party has been forced either to change its name, surrender its assets, "refound" itself, share power with other political groups, and relinquish its power altogether. Most countries have also dismantled their special security contingents and created new parties, free trade unions, other organized groups, and countrywide non-Communist fronts. In all the countries, elections with genuine multi-party options have taken place in 1990.

12.4 A Naive Approach to Economic Reform

Until recently, a naive, orthodox approach has dominated the reform movement in Central and Eastern Europe. Within this approach, decentralizing economic decisions and activating markets has an instant, or certainly very rapid, effect on resource mobilization and efficiency, which is enhanced by reduced defense expenditure (10 billion rubles in the USSR in 1989, or 14.2 percent of the defense budget, followed by proper cuts in 1990) and restructuring from heavy industry to light industry and technologically advanced sectors. This supply response (Gorbachev's *uskorenie* or acceleration effect) will, during a short time, take care of existing excess demand without substantial price rises, although an initial injection of additional imports may be necessary. Of course, relative prices will have to change, but—within this approach—the government can do this once the economy has recovered by a price reform to fix prices and price criteria on the basis of international prices and long-run domestic costs.

Enterprise independence from the center can be achieved by abolishing branch ministries and, as in Hungary, replacing them with a single ministry for industry. Banks will monitor credit extended to the enterprises and will not grant it automatically, but base it on their creditworthiness. Competitive behavior, even by large specialized firms, can be induced through international competition, hence the importance of trade liberalization and an early convertibility of the domestic currency.

Ideally, the reforms should be implemented simultaneously, but this is impractical, therefore the process has to take a couple of years. Any single step toward the reformed model is an improvement regardless of its timing and sequential position. Governments can make parallel progress on different fronts, starting where resistance is weakest, or at some other obvious point, for instance, ruble convertibility into foreign exchange will be realized first domestically, then within CMEA, then worldwide (Aganbegyan 1988). The Abalkin Report on Soviet reform (1989) recognizes that: "We had no concept or theory of the transitional stage, no idea of the sequence of how to implement our reforms." The stages of economic reform as envisaged by the government are no more than a bunching of measures according to increasing difficulty of implementation rather than a well-reasoned sequence.

This approach, a sort of "meandering toward reform," is naive for three reasons. First, just any step toward reform is not necessarily an unambiguous improvement. An incomplete reform is as useless as an incomplete railway line, which goes nowhere. Yevgeni Yevtushenko makes this point forcefully in his poem "'Half Measures". What is worse, some measures without others can be pernicious, for example, enterprise autonomy without competition, foreign exchange liberalization without prior stabilization, privatization without markets. In particular, markets cannot be expected to yield any benefit if prices are not market clearing; if enterprises are still subject to the tutelage of central government bodies (whether a sectoral branch ministry, a single industrial ministry, or any other administrative agency) instead of being free to respond to market incentives and disincentives; if large enterprises and their cartel-like associations have a monopoly position; and if the enterprises' income is not strictly residual, without enterprise-specific compensatory subsidies and taxes, individually negotiated ex post.

Second, the reform must be completed on a scale sufficient for the emerging system to have the minimum critical mass.

Third, in any case an immediate supply response large enough to stabilize the economy in the course of economic reform and to finance restructuring is unlikely. The only known instances of such a supply response were in Chinese agriculture and, in the last two years, in the Vietnamese economy, which is also largely agricultural. In general, economic reform is likely to cause a temporary deterioration in current performance, to be compensated for by improvements only later. Reform is best seen as an investment; a good one, but still an investment.

The recognition of these difficulties with gradual but unstructured reforms has led to two variations of this "naive" approach: one is the global shock therapy approach; the other is sectoral or geographical gradualism, combined with the idea of a parallel, new, domestic hard currency. Neither is satisfactory.

12.5 Global Shock Therapy

Instantaneous and simultaneous progress on all fronts was recommended for Poland in a plan announced in mid-June 1989 at a press conference in London held by George Soros (the Hungarian-born American millionaire and fund manager) and Solidarity spokesman Bronislaw Geremek. They proposed a global shock therapy ("big bang" or "cold turkey") approach, consisting of implementing price liberalization and zloty convertibility; transforming state enterprises into joint stock companies and privatizing them through share distribution and sales in a new stock market; and introducing debt-equity swaps, debt relief, and other forms of Western assistance. This action of global shock therapy should not be confused with speedy stabilization, like the Polish or Yugoslav programs as they were actually implemented.

A global shock therapy program seems dangerous. There is no historical precedent for nor economic theory of the sudden, simultaneous opening of markets for goods, factors, financial assets, and foreign exchange, especially when starting from an overall imbalance. Previous liberalizations have affected one market at a time and started from uniform, market-clearing prices. The result of a primeval big bang is just as likely to be paralysis and stagnation as it is to be efficiency and growth. As in the recent Argentinian hyperinflation, shops might simply be "closed for lack of prices" (*cerrado por falta de precios*).

Significantly, for the Soviet economy George Soros and others have advocated a gradual approach, through the growth of an initially small "open sector" (see next section). Without prior stabilization, foreign exchange will be overpriced, as in the recent Soviet auctions of foreign exchange, while illiquid assets will be underpriced. The result of debt-equity swaps will be indeterminate without defining a monetary and an exchange rate policy.

In his 1989 plan for Poland, Jeffrey Sachs also appears to advocate shock therapy, but really stresses the need to operate on a wide front at the same time rather than do everything at once. "You do not cross a chasm in two leaps," he quotes from an unknown Polish economist; but it is more a case of discontinuity, of having to get to the other side before it makes a difference. It is better to crawl all the way down (to stabilization) and up again to the other side (reform, restructuring) rather than to jump.

12.6 Sectoral or Geographical Gradualism

Sectoral or geographical gradualism originated in the Soviet Union, probably because of the large size of its economy. The idea is that economic reform should be first implemented in a subsection of the economy, whether a sector (Belkin et al. 1988), a grouping of interlinked, independent, market-oriented enterprises (Soros et al. 1988), or a geographical area (one or more large free economic zones, similar to some of those in China) as favored by Ivanov (1989).

A new domestic currency, convertible into hard currencies and subject to disciplined monetary management by a new authority, would sustain transactions in the privileged sector or area and seal it off from the rest of the ailing economy. From the initial nucleus of economic activity, where an instantaneous supply response would be activated, reform would gradually spread, bringing about generalized stabilization and economic restructuring. In Belkin's approach enterprises that provided additional consumption output would be paid in special rubles that they could use to buy additional production goods from domestic producers and from the world market. Equilibrium in the consumption market would gradually be restored, contractual relationships would induce additional intermediate inputs, and the old currency would be strengthened and gradually withdrawn, leaving a healthy economy with a convertible currency.

The Soros project, discussed during the last year by several Soviet-Western working groups at the State Committee for Foreign Economic Relations and headed by Ivan Ivanov, advocates setting up an open sector made up of nonstate enterprises (private, cooperative, joint ventures) and state enterprises or their subsidiaries, but the latter only after they have shed surplus liquidity and cut their access to easy money. The open sector enterprises would use a convertible valutny ruble obtained through exports and loans, import freely, obtain any domestic input in short supply at international prices, export freely, and retain or sell freely all their export earnings. An open sector managing authority would monitor all their activities, especially their relations with the rest of the economy. The reform of the Soviet economy would be achieved by progressive expansion of the open sector. In the version the Soviets prefer, the open sector has a territorial basis, that is, it amounts to a set of special economic zones instead of a sectoral (Belkin) or functional (Soros and others) basis. The zones' successful growth and gradual extension to other enterprises would implement reform and bring about stability and economic restructuring.

The hidden assumption of these schemes is reliance on a large, positive supply response, larger than existing inflationary gaps so as to stabilize the economy, and large enough to generate and attract the finance necessary for restructuring. Again, there is no reason to expect such prodigious effects; indeed, partitioning the economy into different sectors or regions is bound to accentuate the already existing dualistic features of the centrally planned economy: households versus enterprises, different goods obtainable for domestic versus foreign currencies, dual access to consumption goods for the elite versus ordinary people, military versus civilian access to inputs (see McKinnon 1989).

12.7 A Parallel Currency?

Others, such as Nikolai Petrakov (1989) have suggested a new parallel domestic currency. In 1989, the government announced that Soviet farms that produced 10 percent more grain than the average taken over the last five years would be paid in dollars. Vice Premier Leonid Abalkin proposed a new parallel currency in the Soviet reform plan of November 1989. In February 1990, a parallel convertible ostmark (managed by the Bundesbank not the Staatsbank) was suggested as a possible transitional stage in the prospective German currency union.

There is neither theoretical nor historical justification for such a proposal. Theoretically the case for it implicitly rests on the presumption that economic reform results in a positive supply response that, moreover, is only available for a slow diffusion of reform measures via the growth of a parallel monetary circulation. However, a currency with a fixed parity would have the same effects as dollarization of the economy, while a floating currency would have a value determined solely by the monetary authorities. Admittedly, the state may derive some resources from the resulting seignorage, but before a successful stabilization, national monetary authorities will lack the necessary credibility. A one-to-one reserve backing for the new currency (or more, to cover possible fluctuations in the value of hard currency bonds, as used to be the case in the British colonies) may be necessary; higher interest may have to be paid to depositors than obtainable on hard currency investments. This is hardly a foundation for substantial seignorage. The only historical example of such an operation is the 1924–1926 issue by Soviet authorities of convertible 10 ruble units, the *chervonetz*, alongside ordinary rubles. However, this was preceded by the New Economic Policy (or NEP) and monetary reform, and in any case led to hyperinflation and the demise of the other ruble, the *sovznak*. There is no reason to suppose that this would not happen again today.

There is nothing that a new parallel convertible currency can do that cannot be done by directly using any already existing convertible currency. On the contrary, the road to stabilization of a domestic currency goes through de-dollarization or de-deutschmarkization of domestic transactions precisely to restore seignorage and domestic control of the money supply. Paying peasants partly in foreign exchange simply acknowledges officially the debasing of the domestic currency and secures its further debasement, while discussions of convertibility of any kind before stabilization are fatuous, even perverse.

12.8 Alternative Sequencing and Anchoring Patterns

In an ordinary open market economy experiencing domestic and external imbalance, the government usually gives priority to external stabilization and to the trade account before the capital account, while domestic stabilization may be the result of anchoring the economic system to a devalued nominal exchange rate and to fixed nominal wages. Traditionally economists distinguish between an "orthodox" approach based on monetary and budgetary deflation, and an "unorthodox" approach based on wages and prices policy (see Bruno et al. 1988).

In general, governments of highly inflationary countries lack credibility; hence the need for speedy implementation (or front-loading) and for a commitment to maintain the values of preannounced variables or anchors. Nominal wages and exchange rates are favorite anchors. The idea is that in an open market economy, a commitment to maintain a fixed rate of exchange after devaluation, made credible by the backing of a stabilization loan, is bound to bring the rate of domestic inflation down to the international level. Any departure of domestic inflation from that rate sets in motion offsetting tendencies, such as increases in imports and falls in real wages, which cool inflation and make stabilization possible. The experience of Latin American countries suggests that continued inflation and hyperinflation may rapidly lead to gross overvaluation of the real rate of exchange, and to such large falls in real wages that governments will eventually end up overcompensating for them, revamping inflation.

In Poland's January 1990 stabilization program the government chose the same nominal anchors. It selected a uniform nominal exchange rate close to the free rate in the earlier two-tier system, which therefore corresponded to an initial devaluation larger than the equilibrium level (since the free price in a dual free/controlled market is always higher than the equilibrium price that would prevail without controls). The government committed itself to keeping this rate unchanged and has succeeded in holding it to date (February 1991). Now, it is plausible to announce a fixed nominal rate of exchange anchor in the hope, perhaps optimistic, that domestic inflation may be abated, but it is unreasonable to enter such a commitment when hyperinflation is actually predicted and takes place over the period. The real rate of exchange has been left not to float in response to market pressures, but to be pulled about, around a strong upward trend, by the vagaries of hyperinflation, to levels that bear no relation to either purchasing power parities or to foreign trade policy.

The government also fixed nominal wage rates based on expected inflation lower than eventually materialized. Given an extremely weak indexation of actual wage levels, at 20 percent of price increases for January, 30 percent in February through April, and 60 percent for the rest of the year, real wages were also pulled about, around a strong downward trend, below any level consistent with the assumed real growth rates of output, employment, and the reversal of resource transfer abroad. Far more austerity was asked initially in 1990 of Polish workers than was strictly necessary for stabilization, thus reducing the chances of popular support for the program and revamping wage inflation in late 1990. This does not mean that the policies followed are absolutely inferior, because tenuous wage indexation and a strong domestic currency have stronger immediate braking effects on inflation. But the greater likelihood of bringing inflation under control sooner has been paid for by a deeper recession than strictly necessary, and by the danger of later inflation.

Other transitional governments may be better advised to anchor a stabilization program to real variables, such as the lowest real wage regarded as compatible with the required macroeconomic adjustment, and to a real exchange rate consistent with the required trade balance. This would imply the indexation of a lower initial real wage at a higher rate of purchasing power protection than implemented in the Polish stabilization plan. Naturally, any stabilization program needs at least one nominal anchor. This could be a nominal quantity of money path (a fixed nominal quantity is not sustainable because successful inflation control raises the demand for money; see Bruno and Piterman 1988), or the price level prevailing immediately after liberalization.

In general, in the transitional economy domestic stabilization must precede external stabilization for several reasons:

- The urgency of external stabilization is reduced by the dominant role of sovereign state borrowing and the automatic (*de facto* if not negotiated beforehand) rescheduling of debt and capitalization of unpaid interest.
- Starting from excess demand, domestic absorption should be reduced before adjusting the exchange rate, that is, before tackling external stabilization because if there is excess demand, a devaluation will not promote exports.
- In general, the elasticity of supply with respect to relative prices is low before a reform is undertaken. Low elasticities of demand for imports and of supply of exports make exchange rate maneuvers worsen rather than improve the terms of trade.

12.9 The Primacy of Domestic Stabilization

Most economists now agree that in the transitional socialist economy domestic stabilization should take priority. Here stabilization means the achievement of market clearing prices if not yet prevailing, and the defusing of open hyperinflationary or excessively inflationary pressure. Stabilization may come as a single package of simultaneous measures (shock therapy, not to be confused with the global shock therapy discussed earlier), or as a rapid sequence of steps.

Poland embarked on this course in January 1990, Yugoslavia in December 1989, Czechoslovakia in January 1991, Hungary has deleted it, and the GDR has achieved stabilization by economic integration with the Federal Republic of Germany. The most notable exceptions are the Soviet and Romanian leadership. The USSR, in December 1989, postponed price reform, and therefore domestic stabilization, to 1993; then brought them forward to 1991, but destabilized markets by prior announcements and further postponements. Romania also postponed price increases. With the passage of time monetary imbalances are bound to reach unmanageable proportions and explode into hyperinflation.

Even earlier supporters of global shock therapy, such as Soros (1989), recognized that economic stabilization was the highest priority. Only after stabilization could a more general strategy for opening to the world economy be considered. It was also recognized that "...If a special hard currency was to be introduced, all the existing and yet-to-be-created rubles would be converted into it, making the latent inflation manifest. Before a market-oriented open sector can be established, ...the ruble must be turned into a real currency."

The Soviet leadership's refusal to acknowledge this is ultimately responsible for the economic failure of *perestroika*. It is also at the root of centrifugal trends in the USSR and the CMEA: if the ruble could be turned into a sound currency, the various republics could be given a great deal of autonomy, and *perestroika* could proceed at different speeds in different places. Without stabilization Gorbachev will be forced either to quit or to engage in a policy of repression (Soros 1989).

The reasons for the primacy of domestic stabilization are:

- Without market clearing prices, markets cannot operate at all, since random access to goods and services is unfair, disruptive, and inefficient; leads to hoarding, excessive vertical integration, and forced substitution in production and consumption; reduces incentives; and requires the indefinite continuation of central controls (that is, the indefinite postponement of radical reform).
- Hyperinflation or excessive inflation impedes rational economic calculations, promotes hoarding rather than productive investment, shortens economic agents' time horizon, is time consuming, and has massive redistribution effects with no specific incentive role.

If the government feels that the difficult and unpopular course of stabilization is not politically feasible, then it should recognize that radical reform is impossible. Instead, it should concentrate all its efforts on eliminating the more glaring inefficiencies and on making minor, piecemeal improvements of traditional management methods. However, the experience of Poland, Hungary, and Czechoslovakia shows that for the old elites the ideological and political implications of what we could broadly label "sequential failure" can be disproportionally greater than the ideological and political preoccupations that may have led to that failure.

Stabilization involves generalized market clearing at nonhyperinflationary or not excessively inflationary prices. Thus, an austere social pact, budgetary balance, monetary discipline, and possibly a net inflow of external resources must accompany price liberalization.

12.10 Price Liberalization

Markets in centrally planned economies in transition are segmented into two-tiered or many-tiered price systems. The government needs to unify the price at a single market clearing level. If necessary, the government can introduce a price liberalization sequence, starting with consumption goods, continuing with intermediate goods given the derived demand, and the following up with capital equipment on the basis of demand derived from both consumption and intermediate goods. This is the opposite of the usual Soviet approach as confirmed in the Abalkin reform plan, where first the price of materials is to be raised over a period of time.

There can be no price reform other than price liberalization: cost-based price formulas must be accompanied by supply policies such that the formulas correspond to market clearing. Liberalized spot prices are bound to diverge from medium- and longer-run equilibrium, given the divergence of current capacity from the medium- and longer-run capacity structure. To prevent spot prices from diverging too much from longer-term equilibrium, and above all from giving the wrong signals to investment decisions, the economy must be opened to the signals, if not to the uncontrolled flows of imports and exports. Thus, even with restricted trade and rationing of traded goods, it is important to unify the rate of exchange (typically in the poorer system consisting of a basic rate converted through *ad hoc* multipliers into thousands of rates by country and commodity groups) at a rate intermediate between the official average level and the free rate. However, leading the stabilization process with a devaluation, as done in Czechoslovakia in mid-December 1989 and in Romania in mid-January 1990, is inadvisable without prior reduction of monetary overhang.

Price liberalization is compatible with large-scale government contracts (which in the European Community amount to about 16 percent of final output), as long as they are not accompanied by privileged access to inputs and foreign exchange. Liberalization might be followed by a temporary price freeze (as in Israel in 1985) to avoid the revamping of inflation and excessive real revaluation (as in Poland today or in the recent Chilean stabilization program).

Before liberalizing prices, exchange rate, and international trade, it is necessary to reduce open or repressed inflationary pressure by any means available. The range of instruments includes draining liquidity from both households and enterprises through greater fiscal pressure, switching from product to income subsidies and an overall subsidy reduction, and ensuring monetary discipline and an active monetary policy (higher interest rates, bond issues, reserve requirements, and so on).

If a gap remains after supply and demand conditions have been improved, market balance cannot be achieved in a single round of price increases. This is because the one time price increase that would eliminate excess money balances in the hands of the population and of enterprises (stock equilibrium) is usually greater than that consistent with the balance of current incomes and real supplies (flow equilibrium). If the government uses prices to achieve balance, then further rounds of compensatory increases—possibly through indexation of equilibrium real levels—are required to adjust flow equilibrium.

12.11 Fiscal Policy

Streamlining the old tax system is important. It is excessively based on turnover taxes, usually has a large number of charges and surcharges allegedly levied for specific purposes, and sometimes includes oddities (such as a tax amortization that was levied until recently in Poland). Most existing taxes could be replaced by income tax, which until fairly recently was regarded as a pointless transfer for state employees of money from and back to the state, and value added tax (VAT) at a uniform rate regardless of the state of supplies, that is, goods in short supply would not be taxed at higher rates. It is important not only to reduce the overall level of subsidies, but also to replace product subsidies with income subsidies in order to reduce price distortions, and above all to abolish *ex post* and *ad hoc* enterprise-specific subsidies and taxes, which insulate enterprises from market penalties and rewards.

The importance of balancing the budget is borne out by recent stabilization experiences in developing countries, both successful (such as in Mexico and Israel) and unsuccessful (as in Argentina). Several definitions of a budget deficit exist, whether on a cash or accrual basis; whether related to the change in public debt, the change in the government's net wealth, or the change in the public sector's borrowing requirements; and whether in real or monetary terms. All these definitions are relevant, but perhaps the most important aspect of the deficit is its link with monetary creation, which is particularly marked in socialist economies in view of the low degree of securitization, and therefore the large-scale monetization of budgetary deficits. During the stabilization process, the less strict definition of "balance" may be sufficient, especially in view of the low burden of internal debt that is mostly monetized. Current accounting procedures in central Eastern Europe are often misleading in that they tend to neglect important factors, such as the change in the value of hard currency debt, the presence of unpaid interest on that debt, and the losses of the banking sector and of many parastatal institutions.

Especially at inflationary times, new taxes may be required to compensate for the Tanzi Effect of the vanishing real value of delayed tax collections, for instance, taxing of excess wages above basic guidelines; or nominal capital gains above the rate of indexation of wages. In 1989, the Polish government introduced a tax on enterprises' net assess to drain liquidity, identify and penalize enterprises not earning a minimum profit, and to stress the state's claim to a return on its capital (which is why the tax was misleadingly called a "state dividend," which it is not). However, neither historical cost nor automatic accounting revaluation of assets (by an average factor of 14 in January 1990 in Poland) are a suitable tax basis. A competitive valuation of enterprise capital would be necessary, either through the market or through self-assessment of capital values by enterprise managers (see Nuti 1988).

A fiscal element is present is some aspects of monetary policy, not only in seignorage and in inflation tax, but in larger than usual reserve ratios and in the possible retroactive imposition of higher interest rates than contractually stipulated.

12.12 Monetary Policy

The very possibility of monetary policy presumes prior reform of the banking system, to do away with its traditional features: the automatic granting of credit to enterprises for fulfilling planned tasks, the monetization of the budget deficit, the commitment to a purely symbolic interest rate to cover banking costs, and the excessively large negative interest rates. Hungary and Poland, and now Czechoslovakia, have undertaken this transformation; Bulgaria, Romania, and the USSR are lagging behind.

The thorny question of the central bank's autonomy also arises in the transitional economy. Under the old system, the central bank was no more than a department of the ministry of finance, therefore reform should grant the central bank more independence. Ultimately, however, the government as a whole must be responsible for economic policy, and it cannot totally delegate monetary policy or the establishment of monetary targets to the central bank. The tendency in economic reform has been to err on the side of central bank independence, especially in those countries that are members of the IMF.

It has been argued that if the population and enterprises hold assets denominated in foreign exchange, this reduces the central bank's ability to control the money supply. The size of such holdings varies in different countries, but can be substantial. In Poland, for example, the population at end 1989 had hard currency deposits with state banks of some US$4.5 billion, plus cash estimated at between US$4 billion and US$8 billion, while enterprises have foreign currency credits and options of some US$2.5 to US$3 billion. In the German Democratic Republic before unification, Yugoslavia, and the Soviet Union, the holdings were smaller.

Here we should distinguish between two kinds of assets; namely, on the one hand cash and reserve-backed deposits and credits, and on the other hand hard currency credits toward the banking system that are not backed by reserves. The first kind does not prevent the central bank from controlling the money supply, because the bank can resell to the public any hard currency presented for conversion. The second kind does not provide this possibility of sterilization, and therefore hinders the central bank's ability to control the money supply. For instance, in Poland in January 1990, state enterprises appear to have converted about US$1 billion out of dollar credits. This liquidity injection must have put some strain on monetary policy.

McKinnon (1989) suggested that in a system like a transitional economy, with a thin market for bonds, reserve ratios should be substantially higher than in an ordinary market economy, say 20 or 30 percent. This kind of "reserve tax" seems most appropriate.

The level of interest rates, especially the real rate, is controversial. No doubt, in a state of economic tranquillity (fairly long-standing equilibrium), an economy capable of supporting self-sustained growth must have a positive real rate of interest. However, it is not equally clear that the real rate of interest should be positive during the transition to such a stable environment. Of course, the rise and acceleration of open inflation requires higher levels of money interest rates, but as long as the rates of return on alternative assets are sufficiently variable and reach into the negative range, there will be a demand for money as a safe asset, even though it is depreciating in real terms and yields a negative real interest rate. If this proposition is accepted, a corollary is that government bonds should not be indexed. In any case, higher interest rates should not be exempted from taxes, even on government bonds, and nominal capital gains should also be taxed at least on realization to reduce the attraction of a flight from money into alternative assets.

The introduction of commercial practices in bank lending requires standard procedures to monitor enterprises' financial viability and to enforce liquidation and bankruptcy when appropriate. However, the viability of existing enterprises cannot be properly assessed on the basis of the spot prices emerging from sudden liberalization. A longer-term view has to be taken on the basis of either international prices or independent views about domestic price trends.

A major problem in the transition is the existence of bad loans made by the previous banking system (these are probably largest in Yugoslavia, where in early 1990 their order of magnitude appeared to be close to that of the country's external debt; see OECD 1990). The transformation of the system requires substantial writing off of bad loans and recapitalization of banks.

McKinnon (1989) suggests that in the liberalization of a Soviet-type system, commercial banks should initially be confined to short-term, fully collateralized lending, according to the so-called "real bills" doctrine. This would mostly involve financing working capital, that is, the fund invested in inventories of finished and semi-finished goods, accounts receivable, and working cash balances. However, assigning priority to the security of these kinds of loans over investment credit would be difficult. Such a system would be limited to investing its own funds, and would therefore be small initially and very slow to develop.

12.13 A Confiscatory Currency Reform?

In an imaginary world without political constraints, a government can handle monetary overhang or inflationary pressure by means of a confiscatory and progressive replacement of the domestic currency by a new currency unit at a rate of conversion that might differ for prices, incomes, and monetary assets, and be progressive for different types of assets (cash, savings) and tranches of each type of asset, and perhaps also incomes.

The attractions of this instrument are first, the simultaneous achievement of stock equilibrium and flow equilibrium through diversified rates of conversion for money and for incomes relative to prices; the alleviation of distribution effects through progressive rates of conversion, and the destruction of those monetary assets that are not presented for conversion due to illegal or suspect provenance (the additional possibility of choosing a currency with reasonably large unit purchasing power is a secondary advantage). In the uncertainty about the precise size of the monetary overhang, it is better to avoid undershooting, which would revamp inflation, and rather incur some overshooting, immediately followed by incomes and/or wealth compensatory corrections or price falls.

This type of operation was undertaken in the Federal Republic of Germany after World War II, but it was managed by the Allied forces under conditions of multiple currencies and war devastation. It was also undertaken in the Soviet Union, Romania, Poland, Czechoslovakia, Bulgaria, and China shortly after the end of World War II. Precisely because it has already been used once, and also because of its Stalinist association, this measure is regarded as sufficiently unpopular as to be undesirable. There can be no doubt, however, that a decisive reform of this kind in Poland, say, in September 1989, may have been a less bitter pill than the package introduced in January 1990. On the contrary, the sole confiscation of large denomination banknotes, as in the half-hearted, half-baked measures of January 1991 in the Soviet Union, is a destabilizing measure because it promotes further the flight from currency.

12.14 Social Pacts

Austerity and the fall in the real purchasing power of wages (which in the presence of monetary overhang is greater than the actual fall in the effective consumption commanded by wages) require some form of an explicit or tacit social pact. The austerity involved can only be managed by governments willing and able to negotiate the consent of free trade unions.

The Polish experience shows that a democratically elected government can impose a much more drastic drop in real wages than military rulers under martial law, whereas unrealistically high wage claims are used to express opposition to a nondemocratic government. However, even democratic governments have a breaking point and their honeymoon period is short; a resource transfer may be necessary—in the absence of early supply effects—to implement stabilization. Today, Western countries understand this case for aid, which could be called "infant democracy protection," and which has led to calls for a new Marshall Plan and in 1990–1991 to large-scale loans and grants coordinated by the European Commission for the Group of 24.

12.15 Resource Transfer

An increase in supplies requires additional imports, financed by a reduced or reversed resource transfer, via rescheduling of debt service or fresh loans. The Soviet Union would need some US$25 billion to eliminate its overhang via additional imports, if imports could be sold at prices reflecting the free instead of the official exchange rate otherwise applicable to trade transactions. This may be an underestimate because it ignores the excess liquidity in the hands of state enterprises (R250 billion). The free (black) exchange rate would probably fall as a result of this operation, but this in turn would signal the reduction of the underlying overhang.

12.16 Factor Markets

A labor market, that is, redeployment and unemployment of labor, is already necessary at this stage when enterprises are subjected to harder budget constraints. The Abalkin Report suggests that in practice, a labor market has always existed, even during central planning; its existence simply has to be recognized. However, while labor supply and effort supply, and therefore labor deployment, may always have been affected by wage rates, enterprise demand has usually been larger than the available supply of labor and has not been very responsive to wage levels. The full activation of labor markets requires hard enterprise budgets and full-fledged enterprise reform, as well as the elimination of familiar rigidities in the labor market, such as those stemming from the availability of housing.

Capital markets for government bonds (including the issue of bonds possibly carrying the option of unrestricted access to subsequent privatization) and for the shares of new joint stock companies can play an important role during stabilization. In addition, a new capital market must be able to undertake its other functions: making financial assets liquid through secondary retrading, matching the time structure of lending and borrowing, evaluating the net assets of enterprises as going concerns, inducing redeployment of capital assets through mergers and acquisitions, and subjecting managerial discretion to market discipline through the threat of such mergers and acquisitions.

The very idea of a capital market may appear to run against the grain of a socialist or post-socialist system, but once the logic of markets has been accepted, these functions must somehow be performed. Their undertaking on a large scale, however, requires further substantial reform of state enterprises. The same is true of restructuring, which to begin in earnest needs not only a market clearing, nonhyperinflationary environment, with opportunities to redistribute labor and financial and physical capital, but also the transformation of enterprises from administrative agencies into genuine entrepreneurs undertaking the redeployment of existing resources and the reshaping of capacity structure.

12.17 Enterprise Reform

After stabilization and preparatory work on factor markets, the reform process—which cannot be expected to yield benefits before it is completed on a significantly large scale—must recreate a sufficient number of autonomous and competitive enterprises. These enterprises must be subject to financial discipline and rewards, capable of responding to market incentives, with managers chosen not for their political merits, but for their professional qualities.

Three major obstacles must be removed for this entrepreneurial function to arise. First, the monopoly power of large-scale, specialized enterprises and their associations must be eliminated, or at least reduced, not just by potential competition through international trade, but by the fragmentation of large, multiplant units, anti-trust legislation, and above all, access to markets for new small- and medium-scale enterprises.

Second, the link between enterprises and central administration must be severed. This link implies their dependence through managerial appointments, salary scales, and career structure; through allocations of scarce materials and foreign exchange; and through negotiated incentives and disincentives, formal and informal pressure. One way to ensure such independence is privatization, transforming state enterprises into joint stock companies whose shares are distributed or sold to employees, managers, and other investors. This is not, however, the only way to sever the link between enterprises and central administration. The shares can be held by a State Property Fund, as originally envisaged in Hungary and Poland, or, preferably, by a number of state holding companies (as in Algeria) and other institutional as well as private investors. Enterprise capital can be leased rather than sold out.

Third, the redistribution function of the state budget, which subsidizes loss making enterprises out of transfers from profitable ones and compensates net revenue changes after the event, must be eliminated so as to reinstate the residual nature of profits as net revenue after contractual fixed payments. Markets have not only an allocative function, but also a much neglected function of forcing economic agents to live within their means under penalty of bankruptcy. The budgetary validation of enterprise losses removes this kind of financial discipline without which the sound budgetary policies advocated above cannot be implemented.

These three obstacles must be removed simultaneously, because of the linkages between them. For instance, the existence of monopolies justifies central control over prices, supply, and capacity expansion, as well as some redistribution of profits. The removal of central control while maintaining monopolies is bound to involve a deterioration of market supply and economic efficiency.

The elimination of the "petty tutelage" exercised by the center (whether by many branch ministries or a single ministry) over state enterprises should not lead to the dissipation of state ownership, as seems to have been the case in Hungary with the 1984–1985 enterprise legislation, which removed central powers without vesting them elsewhere external to the enterprise. In the early stages of the Polish privatization in 1989–1990, similar cases of "self-appropriation" of state property by privileged insiders have also arisen.

12.18 Privatization

The transformation of state enterprises into joint stock companies presupposes the valuation of their net assets, their recapitalization (or, if necessary, the drainage of excess liquid resources), and at least some rationalization of their output structure and input costs (including labor).

In those countries where workers have gained a measure of self-management, enterprises may have to sell some of the new shares or grant them to their employees to trade off their management rights, incompatible with shareholders' rights, with ownership rights embodying a smaller voice in enterprise management. This is precisely the nature of the Yugoslav privatization laws of mid-1990. Enterprises may also sell shares to their workers to strengthen popular support and to promote a property-owning democracy. Forms of worker ownership abound in the capitalist economy: employee stock ownership plans, where workers acquire shares held collectively before they are distributed after a specified period or at retirement or departure; trusts, where workers are temporary co-owners and only enjoy a share of the revenue while they are employed; personal equity plans for regular savers that offer tax exemption up to a maximum limit; equity holding cooperatives; additional pension funds; Swedish-type wage earners' collective investors; and so on.

Selling off shares in state enterprises before stabilization and fiscal reform is inappropriate. Trends in product and input prices, and therefore in profitability, would be difficult to assess, assets would be underpriced, and yet unattractive under conditions of uncertainty. Thus privatization cannot really contribute directly to the stabilization process. However, the very decision to proceed with privatization can contribute to stabilization if the announcement is followed by the issue of special bonds at low or zero interest, but carrying an option to purchase without restriction any state asset that will subsequently be privatized, pending the definition of privatization terms. This instrument was used in Poland in September 1989, but bonds redeemable through privatization were indexed, thus costing the government much more than other forms of bonds finance, and yet being not so attractive to the public at the time of issue.

It has been suggested that shares could be sold to workers at a price below their market value, or even given away free to all citizens to speed up the transition and create an instant capital market. However, the needs of budgetary balance and monetary discipline should strictly limit workers' privileged access to shares. Free distribution of shares would add a wealth effect to consumption demand, worsening inflationary pressure, whether open or repressed.

The new shares can be partly managed by state holdings and new pension funds. State holdings are often regarded with suspicion as bearers of central interests dependent on and ultimately answering to the center. However, there is no reason why they should not respond to a policy commitment to make profits instead of being responsible for the achievement of government targets. For example, the Italian state holding company, IRI, has responded to policy changes and has rapidly turned from an endemic loss maker into a profit oriented and profit making entity presiding over privatization. Pension funds—new, for there are none—are also credible collective investors, but they should only be given as much stock holding as they can reasonably need to take over pension liabilities. There is no justification for funding the consumption of rentiers even if they are old age pensioners instead of using profits for self-financed investment.

The banking system's ability to administer state ownership should not be overestimated; the Nippo-German model of capital markets, which assigns to banks a central role over equity capital, relies on and does not replace a full stock exchange. Depending on the policy toward debt/equity swaps, credit may be granted on a large scale for the population to take part in privatization. As long as this credit is sterilized and is not recycled to government expenditure, it can create a useful buffer against possible subsequent loss of macroeconomic control.

Note the danger of privatization without publicity and competition, which would result in divestiture rather than sale, and in the appropriation of state property by a few well-informed people in positions of power.

12.19 Trade Liberalization

Trade liberalization can progress in parallel with domestic stabilization and reform. McKinnon (1989), referring to the Soviet economy, stressed that:

> Before any sector moves to virtually free trade with the outside world, the integration of market and production processes within the Soviet Union should be largely secured. Carefully considered liberalization of both foreign and domestic trade should proceed in parallel for many years. In the end, the whole economy—by then reasonably well integrated domestically—would be naturally open to international economics.

A full-fledged trade liberalization and the use of the rate of exchange as an instrument of trade policy require the preconditions of domestic stabilization and sizeable elasticities of both import demand and export supply; otherwise devaluation will lead to worsened terms of trade and inflationary pressures instead of promoting net exports. However, from the very beginning a uniform rate of exchange is necessary to transmit signals from the world market, and a fairly open trade policy is necessary to avoid large divergence of domestic spot prices from international prices. Exposure to international competition is needed to supplement domestic competition, which is bound to be weak initially.

The scope of convertibility can be gradually extended, following the Polish pattern: legalizing the black market, increasing the share of export earnings to be retained by exporters for their own use and for transfer to other enterprises at contractual rates, auctioning substantial amounts of foreign exchange, and unifying the official and free rates at an intermediate rate (not, however, as in the Polish case at the free rate, which implies excessive devaluation) supported by a stabilization loan.

The amounts that might be required to sustain convertibility for current trade transactions is relatively small because of the lack of foreign holdings abroad of large balances of domestic currency (such as the sterling balances that absorbed vast funds when the United Kingdom reintroduced convertibility).

The very last stage of a stabilization/reform/restructuring program is bound to be international convertibility for capital transactions. For those countries that are now insolvent, external stabilization requires either automatic rollover of existing debt and unpaid interest or debt relief on a substantial scale.

12.20 Debt Relief

Debt relief does not necessarily imply aid, but simply the realistic acknowledgment that some loans, most of which have already been written off in the creditors' books, are actually bad loans. This acknowledgment is actually overdue, in that it has long been made in secondary markets: whenever those loans are retraded, they are done so at a fraction of their nominal value. Now, if US$1 of debt trades at under 20 cents, as in the Polish case, if all creditors were to forgo four-fifths of their credits, they would lose nothing, because 20 percent is the market valuation of that fraction of the outstanding debt that can be serviced. Only the remission of more than four-fifths of outstanding debt could be regarded as aid. However, if such relief is not done collectively, an individual creditor remitting 80 percent of his credit will also lose 80 percent of the remaining 20 percent if nobody else remits.

Unfortunately, debt relief is still controversial. It is anathema to the IMF, though the attitude of World Bank officials is mellowing. It raises major concerns in banking and government circles in creditor countries (including the Soviet Union as a creditor of large-scale, uncollectable loans to developing countries) about other debtors, especially those in Africa and Latin America who are also demanding debt relief, about moral hazard and about the general deterioration of a creditor's credibility. The stumbling block is the need for collective action involving all debtors and all creditors for the operation to be truly costless. It should still be possible, however, for aid to take the form of debt relief, as long as it did not formally appear to be debt relief, and therefore did not lead to undue expectations of universal debt relief.

Suppose the European Community (EC) decided to give US$1 billion in cash aid to Poland, on condition that Poland used it to buy back Polish debt in the secondary market from EC banks, which currently trades at a substantial discount. This would have to be preceded by an agreement with commercial creditors allowing the parcelling out and retrading of syndicated loans in order to broaden the scope of secondary retrading of Polish debt. Poland would have a credit line without time constraints, and would be able to draw from it whenever it wanted to. These conditions would be necessary to avoid a fall in the discount at which Polish debt is traded in secondary markets the minute such an operation was announced.

This operation would be a transfer from the EC to EC banks, that is, it would have no net cost for the Community area as a whole, though undoubtedly the burden would have to be divided among EC member countries so as to fall on the richer and more exposed members. Why should Greece and Portugal pay? The operation would have a multiplier effect because it would reduce Polish debt by something like US$4–5 billion; it would bring nearer the day when Poland can obtain fresh funds from commercial lenders; it would be considered aid without creating generalized expectations of equal entitlement on the part of other countries; it would have the same global effect of debt relief without being direct debt relief; and it would not create a precedent even if everybody saw it as having exactly the same effects as debt relief.

More ambitiously, imagine Paris Club governments collectively granting US$6–7 billion to Poland on condition that it is used to repay official debt with individual Paris Club governments, at a rate equal to the price of Polish debt in secondary markets. To simplify things, Paris Club governments might transfer the management of their credits to their central banks or to other financial intermediaries. This would wipe out Poland's official debt, leaving Poland with only commercial debt to pay on a manageable scale, and opening up the possibility of a resumption of commercial credits.

Seeing that unlike commercial debt, official debt might never be repaid, this operation would not have a net cost for Paris Club countries as a whole. Again, this would be equivalent to total debt relief, and clearly seen to be such without formally being debt relief.

12.21 Conclusion

From the arguments developed above, a tentative sequencing pattern emerges.

(1) Governments must impose monetary restraint and budgetary discipline, strengthened by a wage and price policy preferably enshrined in a social pact, with some indexation guaranteeing living standards in exchange for their moderation.
(2) Market clearing balance must be obtained in existing markets, whether through supply effects (presumed modest if any), net imports (possibly with international assistance), or the issue of bonds (nonindexed) without a premature privatization of state assets.
(3) Competitive conditions must be ensured, not only in the output markets, but also in access to the existing capital stock, with compulsory surrender of assets by current users if others can employ those means more productively and bid more than them for their use.
(4) The redistributive function of the state budget must be abolished. The residual nature of entrepreneurial income must be guaranteed and enterprise and product subsidies replaced by income subsidies to alleviate adverse distribution effects.
(5) The hierarchical link between enterprises and central administration must be cut through leasings, state holdings, and privatization.
(6) Exposure to international trade signals and pressures can be gradually increased. The exchange rate must be unified to avoid trade distortions that might result in very low (or even negative) value added.
(7) Full-fledged convertibility may be attempted.

This proposed sequencing is not necessarily unique, let alone superior to others, but is offered as a starting point for discussion. It assumes that partial and out of sequence reforms are bound to be not just ineffective, but actually damaging, not only because of the continued and possibly worsened waste of resources, but also because they will have made the task of radical reform that much more difficult to implement. They will have generated and diffused false signals, both for quantities and prices, caused frustration and disillusionment of all economic agents ("reform fatigue"), and reduced the effectiveness of those measures already tried, misused, and reversed.

Bibliography

Abalkin Report [All-Union Conference and Workshop on Problems of Radical Economic Reform, Chaired by Vice-Premier Leonid Abalkin] (1989). *Radical Economic Reform: Top-Priority and Long-Term Measures (Material for Discussion).* Moscow.

Aganbegyan, A. (1988). *The Challenges: Economics of Perestroika.* London: Hutchison.

Belkin, Viktor, P. Medvedev, and I. Nit (1988). The Means of Radical Reform of the Circulation System. *Kommunist* (14, September). In Russian.

Bruno, M., and B. Piterman (1988). Israel. In M. Bruno, G. di Tella, R. Dornbusch, and S. Fischer, Eds. *Inflation Stabilization. The Experience of Israel, Argentina, Brazil, Bolivia, and Mexico.* Cambridge, Massachusetts: MIT Press.

Bruno, M., G. di Tella, R. Dornbusch, and S. Fischer (1988). *Inflation Stabilization. The Experience of Israel, Argentina, Brazil, Bolivia and Mexico.* Cambridge, Massachusetts: MIT Press.

Ivanov, Ivan (1989). On Creating Mutual Enterprise Zones in the USSR. Moscow: State Committee for Foreign Economic Relations.

Nuti, Domenico Mario (1988). Competitive Valuation and Efficiency of Capital Investment in the Socialist Economy. *European Economic Review* 32:2-6.

OECD (1990). Memorandum on Economic Reform in Yugoslavia and the Programme of Measures for its Implementation in 1990. Yugoslav Delegation to OECD, Belgrade. Processed.

Petrakov, Nikolai (1989). Ruble Convertibility. Moscow: Academy of Sciences. Processed.

Soros, George (1989). Can the Soviet Economy be Saved? *The Wall Street Journal* December 7.

Soros, George, Ed Hewett, Wassily Leontief, and Jan Mladek (1988). Working Paper for the International Task Force on Foreign Economic Relations. October 22-31. Moscow: Soros Fund.

13

Lessons from the Stabilisation Programmes of Central and Eastern European Countries, 1989–1991

Domenico Mario Nuti

13.1 Introduction

For a number of years before 1989 Central Eastern European countries had been facing, to various extents, severe domestic and external imbalances, economic slowdown or decline and the need to restructure production capacity, while attempting to reform their traditional central planning system (see Nuti 1988). These problems were less intensely felt in Hungary and Yugoslavia, both early starters on the road to reform, relatively free from endemic shortages and more open to trade with the West; but even there the same underlying trends were present.

Contribution to the 13th Arne Ryde Symposium, Rungsted Kyst, 11–12 June 1992, published in Laszlo Somogyi (Ed), *The Political Economy of the Transition Process in Eastern Europe*, Aldershot, Edward Elgar, 1993, pp. 40–66.

At the time of writing Mario Nuti was at University of Rome 'La Sapienza' and at the Commission of European Communities, DG-II, Brussels.

D. M. Nuti (✉)
La Sapienza, University of Rome, Rome, Italy
e-mail: milica.uvalic@unipg.it

© The Author(s), under exclusive license to Springer Nature Switzerland AG 2023

S. Estrin, M. Uvalic (eds.), *Collected Works of Domenico Mario Nuti, Volume I*, Studies in Economic Transition, https://doi.org/10.1007/978-3-031-12334-4_13

The first half of 1989 Gorbachev's *perestroika* and Soviet economic debacle led to Soviet acquiescence to the demise of the communist party in Poland; this in turn triggered off a cascade of political revolutions in the other Central-Eastern European countries in the second half of the year.

The 1989 revolutions had three immediate economic effects:

- the target model of economic reform switched from the search for a market-oriented version of socialism back to the restoration of a capitalist economy, with dominant private ownership and enterprise;
- the new governments, unlike their communist predecessors, enjoyed the kind of political legitimacy and popular support necessary to undertake unpopular measures of stabilisation;
- the end of Soviet rule throughout the bloc led to the speedy collapse of CMEA trade arrangements (with formal CMEA dissolution in September 1991), which greatly opened up Central and Eastern European economies, and the reorientation of their trade towards the West.

The new political conditions and the precarious state of these economies required urgent stabilisation plans, to put an end to shortages, open inflationary pressures and impending debt crisis. Radical institutional reforms were required including for the first time large-scale privatisation. The economies would also have to be opened up to international trade and finance. These were also preconditions for effective restructuring of productive capacity. Former political obstacles to these measures were no longer present. Thus a wave of stabilisation and reform programmes, supported by loans and grants from international organisations and Western countries, were introduced in rapid succession in 1989–1991. The exceptions were Hungary, which was able to continue with a gradualist approach because of a much earlier start; the ex-GDR, which rapidly achieved the same targets by virtue of German reunification; the Soviet Union, because of disastrous procrastination.

When, in the autumn of 1989, the first non-communist government in Poland started preparing its plan there was no precedent for the simultaneous undertaking of stabilisation, systemic transition and capacity restructuring, and on such a large scale. Therefore it was natural to proceed from first principles and to examine—because of the underlying hyperinflation—the experience of Latin American stabilisation plans in spite of their extremely poor record. Today, however, when exploring desirable economic strategies for the further progress of transition in the whole area, there is no justification for ignoring the performance of stabilisation plans to date, the experience of transitional economies which for one reason or another have not undertaken such plans (Hungary, ex-GDR, the Soviet Union before its disintegration at the end of 1991), as well as that of economies further east, such as those of Vietnam, China and the more successful South-East Asian countries. This paper is an attempt to draw certain lessons from the experience of Central Eastern European countries in 1989–1991 (on Vietnam see Kolodko 1990a, Kolodko et al. 1992; on China, Chen et al. 1990; on South-East Asian economies, Fry and Nuti 1992).

13.2 Gradualism Versus Speedy Transition: Hungary and the ex-GDR

Hungary and the ex-GDR represent unique, extreme, opposite patterns respectively of gradual and instantaneous 'transition', which could not be followed by other countries.

Hungary, by virtue of its early start with the 1968 New Economic Mechanism (NEM) and better economic conditions, was able to avoid a drastic programme in 1989–1991 and continued its gradualist strategy, now redirected towards the new target model. Its earlier achievements provided a model for the other countries in a number of areas: the transformation of the monolithic monetary and banking system into a multi-level, competitive and pluralist system; the liberalisation of trade and foreign investment; the development of an articulated tax system, replacing diversified *(ad hoc* and often enterprise-specific) tax and subsidy rates with uniform rates of income and value-added taxes, the development of financial markets first for bonds then for shares. The option of gradual transformation, however, by 1989–1991 was no longer open to the other countries: their domestic and (except for Romania) external imbalances had cumulated to unsustainable levels, the CMEA had disintegrated cutting them off from cheap Soviet supplies of oil and materials, and less favourable conditions prevailed in international trade and financial markets, with respect to Hungary's position in the first years of the NEM.

The ex-GDR achieved all the desired goals (stabilisation, systemic transition, opening of the economy) at once, by virtue of accelerated reunification with Federal Germany, first *de facto* then *de jure* in under a year (see Siebert 1990a, b; Jackson 1991a, b). The Ostmark overhang was partly confiscated, partly made good by instant replacement with a convertible currency. At a stroke, a complete new price system, body of legislation, and set of financial institutions were imported into the ex-GDR. The economy was not only opened but also joined to the European Community. All these factors facilitated privatisation.

The ex-GDR transition incurred additional costs, with respect to other countries, because of the rapid growth in real wages, which caused large-scale unemployment. This was not due to the one-to-one DM/Ostmark rate of conversion for wages and for part of the liquid assets of the population, as is often believed. The conversion of a limited amount of liquid assets at a favourable rate had only a once-and-for-all wealth effect which actually sustained demand and employment. DM wages in the Eastern region were bound to move towards the Western level regardless of the rate of conversion applied to wages, simply due to labour mobility, which started first with migration through Hungary then through the gaps in the Wall, and became totally free after unification. The additional costs of the consequent real wage rise, as well as the general costs of such a speedy transition and restructuring, were mostly borne by the Federal Budget and German financial markets, rather than by the ex-GDR population. While some aspects of the German experience are potentially repeatable in other countries (for instance, rapid privatisation through Treuhandanstalt), neither the ex-GDR transition model nor the speed of its implementation are repeatable anywhere else.

13.3 Stabilisation and Reform Plans, 1989–1991

The first stabilisation plan of 1989–1990 was introduced by Yugoslavia (1 December 1989; see Coricelli and Rocha 1990). This was, however, a fairly conventional plan (see Table 13.1), which could not provide a model for the other countries. At that time Yugoslava had virtually no overhang, and already had a considerable degree of economic decentralisation, fairly free trade and a nearly convertible currency, experience with restructuring and a sizeable pool of labour unemployment. Moreover, the Yugoslav programme was rapidly aborted in mid-1990, because of republican failure to comply with federal wage guidelines and resulting monetary indiscipline and pressure on the exchange rate; convertibility was suspended *de facto in* late 1990; the country precipitated into civil war in 1991.

The first comprehensive and innovative programme for stabilisation and reform was the Polish plan of 1 January 1990, associated with the name of Finance Minister Leszek Balcerowicz. It included broad price and trade liberalisation, nominal anchoring of the programme to money wages and the nominal exchange rate, targeting the real money supply and real interest rates, monetary and fiscal austerity, large devaluation; and internal convertibility, extreme fiscal pressure on the state sector, taxes on excess wage increases and, in the longer run, privatisation and capacity restructuring. The Polish stabilisation plan has provided a prototype for other transitional countries: in 1990–1991, similar plans were introduced in Romania (1 September 1990), Czechoslovakia (now known as CSFR, or Czech and Slovak Federal Republic, 1 January 1991), Bulgaria (1 February 1991).

Meanwhile, in 1989–1991 the Soviet Union continued its inexorable march towards repressed and open hyperinflation, economic disorganisation and supply disruption, republican disintegration and associated drastic falls in consumption and output. The end of the Soviet Union, accomplished by the August 1991 *putsch* failure, was formalised by the creation of a smaller and looser Commonwealth of 11 Independent States (CIS; SNG from the Russian initials), established by the Alma-Ata and Minsk treaties of December 1991 and excluding Estonia, Latvia, Lithuania and Georgia. This paved the way for the unilateral introduction by Russia of a stabilisation and reform programme on 2 January 1992. The programme had been announced by Boris Yeltsin on 28 October 1991 but would have been incompatible with the Draft Economic Union Treaty, which was then still under discussion, and excluded unilateral price increases by individual republics. Implementation was originally due in mid-December but was postponed at the request of other republics, notably Ukraine; further and more coherent rounds of measures followed in April and in June 1992.

Russian price liberalisation forced all the other ex-Soviet republics to follow, because of the continued use of roubles as legal tender not only within the CIS but also in the rest of the former Union. However the other republics, including Ukraine, are very much behind on their way to a new system. The Russian package has a great deal in common with the Polish prototype of January 1990, on which it is modelled. However, in view of the speed of developments, the special feature of the ex-Soviet area (such as size, the persistence of a rouble area and the introduction of republican currencies, inter-republican trade and payments regime) and of the Russian programme, and its implementation failures in 1992, we shall leave it out of this paper (see Nuti 1992; Nuti and Pisani-Ferry 1992).

13.4 The Polish Prototype

The Balcerowicz plan envisaged the following steps (see Kolodko 1990a, b; Nuti 1990a; Rosati 1991a, b):

(i) Instantaneous price liberalisation of 90 per cent of transactions and a reduction of government subsidies (from 17 per cent of national income in 1989 to 4 per cent in 1991); initially some budgetary support was retained for coal, electricity, gas, state housing rents, heating and hot water, transport and telecommunications, pharmaceuticals; support was reduced for energy in June 1990.

(ii) A balanced state budget for 1990, accompanied by a restrictive monetary policy aimed at restoring a positive real interest rate; interest rates were raised on old as well as new credit contracts. State enterprises assets were revalued on average by a factor of 14 (and again in 1991), at rates differing by type of assets but uniform throughout the economy, with a uniform capital tax (called a 'dividend', improperly because it bore no relation to either current profits nor reinvestment requirements of enterprises) levied on revalued state assets. Average turnover tax was raised from 10 to 20 per cent.

(iii) Wages policy; money wages were set for January on the basis of an expected monthly rate of inflation of 45 per cent in January, with maximum wage guidelines indexed to prices at a monthly pre-fixed rate for 1990: 20 per cent of price inflation in January, 30 per cent in February to April, 60 per cent in the rest of the year except for June (when energy prices would be raised) when wage indexation was at 100 per cent. A tax on wage increases over these guidelines (PPWW or 'popiwek') was levied, at progressive rates of between 200 to 500 per cent of excess wages, exclusively on enterprises with state majority capital.

(iv) Unilateral suspension of debt service from 1 January 1990, soon followed by formal rescheduling of foreign debt, with interest and debt amortisation due in 1990 postponed to 1991; large-scale debt relief was granted by official creditors in April 1991.

(v) Zloty convertibility for residents and for current account transactions; following the devaluations of 22 and 28 December, a further devaluation of the zloty by 31.6 per cent (43 per cent in ten days) on 1 January 1990 lifted the US dollar to 9500 zlotys, i.e. practically to the end-year free market rate (the black market for foreign exchange had been legalised already since March 1989). Domestic enterprises could buy freely at this rate to finance current imports; households could buy dollars for current purposes (i.e. not to invest in foreign assets) from licensed foreign exchange 'counters', at a floating rate which was maintained very close to the official rate. A $US1 bn loan was made available by the G-24 to support convertibility, in addition to a $US700 mn IMF standby, a $US300 mn structural adjustment loan from the World Bank (plus additional project loans totalling $US780 mn in 1990) and a substantial package of aid and loans from the EIB, the European Community, its member states and other members of G-24; there was an informal commitment to maintain the rate of exchange constant until May 1990, but this was not taken as a performance criterion. In the event the rate of exchange was maintained until mid-May 1991, when the zloty was devalued by 17.4 per cent and linked to a basket of currencies instead of the dollar; in October 1991 a crawling peg regime was introduced, with a maximum monthly devaluation of 1.8 per cent; further devaluations in October 1991 and February 1992 restored some of the competitiveness lost through inflation.

(vi) Trade liberalisation, with a new tariff system whose average incidence was 12 per cent, followed for most goods by a tariff reduction to 5 per cent (April) or outright suspension (July); the elimination of export quotas (in January and in October 1990) except for coal and a small number of items (though 20 commodities were still subject to licences at the end of 1991), and automatic authorisation to trade for all registered firms whether state or private.

(vii) An undertaking to implement further institutional reform in the direction of a private market economy, including the development of banking and credit institutions, competition, privatisation and the introduction of financial markets, accompanied by capacity restructuring in the medium term. A spate of new legislation was introduced in 1990–1991 to implement this part of the programme. Following extensive debate on privatisation, a new Law was adopted in June 1991 (Nuti 1990b); small-scale privatisation (housing, retail and catering establishments, land) was to be followed by large-scale privatisation of state enterprises; however this side of the programme was delayed mostly because of the technical difficulties of implementing mass privatisation (Grosfeld and Hare 1991). This was to take place through the free distribution to the whole adult population of entitlements to certificates in foreign-managed investment funds, but their establishment was postponed to late 1992; there were also delays due to the complexities of property restitution to old owners (so-called 're-privatisation', first introduced by Germany and followed throughout the area except by Yugoslavia).

13.5 Other Polish-Style Plans, 1990–1991

Table 13.1 summarises the main features of the Polish plan and the main differences with respect to the plans subsequently adopted by other countries.

Romania adopted a more gradual price liberalisation in three stages, beginning on 15 November 1990, 1 April and 1 July 1991; price increases

Table 13.1 Stabilisation and reform programmes in Central-Eastern Europe

Feature start	Yugoslavia 1.12.89	Poland 1.1.90	Romania 1.8.90	CSFR 1.1.91	Bulgaria 1.2.91
Price liberalization	Instant 90%	Instant 90%	3 stages	Instant 85%	Gradual
Subsidy reduction 1989/1991	Yes	17.4–4%	Partial	16.1–4.6%	16.7–3%
Fiscal squeeze	Temporary	Yes	No	Yes	Limited
Monetary restraint	Temporary	Yes	No	Yes	Limited
Currency devaluation	Yes	Yes	Yes	Yes	Yes
Foreign trade liberalization	Extensive	Extensive	V. limited	Extensive	V. limited
Internal convertibility for firms	Yes; aborted	Yes	End-1991	Yes; delayed	Yes
Internal convertibility for households	Yes; aborted	Yes	No	No	No
Wages policy	Yes; ignored	Fiscal	No	Yes	Yes
Small-scale privatization	Yes	Yes	Yes	Yes	Slow
Sale of state enterprises	Some	Some	Mostly land	Slow	Slow
Property restitution	No	Yes	Yes	Yes	Yes
Mass privatization through vouchers	No	Delayed	Delayed	Delayed	Delayed
Capacity restructuring	No	Little	No	Little	No
Real anchoring		M, r		M, r	
Nominal anchoring	W, i	W, e		W, e	M

Note: M = Money, r = real interest rates, W = wages, i = nominal interest rate, e = exchange rate

were subject to three months advance notice to be given to central authorities. The nominal anchor was fixed as a 15 per cent increase of the nominal money supply. A special fund financed out of a 10 per cent tax on enterprise profits was set up for the purpose of liquidating inter-enterprise arrears (400 bn Leu). There were no provisions for wages policy. Convertibility was supposed to be introduced on 27 September 1991 but was postponed in the absence of a government and implemented on 11 November under a 'managed float' regime (*Romania Economic Newsletter* 1, 2, 3, 1991).

In 1990, ahead of the stabilisation plan, the CSFR took preparatory measures that in Poland had followed the plan, such as major legislative changes, price increases, tax changes (Hrncir and Klacek 1991); announcements of price increases forced a devaluation already in September 1990. With the 1991 plan, convertibility was granted to enterprises, excluding households; even for enterprises access to foreign currency was subject in practice to considerable delays. Small-scale privatisation proceeded fast but large-scale privatisation, much more reliant on free distribution of assets to the population, was delayed until 1992. Inter-republican conflicts between the Czech and the Slovak Republics have characterised the CSFR experience, with the creation of duplicate Ministries and Agencies at the federal and the republican level, and the difficulties of coordinating fiscal policy, privatisation, and other aspects of stabilisation and reform. Inter-republican conflict, though not as sharp as in the Soviet Union/CIS, the Russian Federation or Yugoslavia, has put a brake on transition progress. A split now appears inevitable, only its form and modalities are under discussion.

The Bulgarian plan was perhaps the one closest to the Polish prototype, however with more gradual trade liberalisation, nominal anchoring to the money supply, slower privatisation of state assets (even small scale, except for land, where quick progress was made). The lower real wage reached after price liberalisation was stabilised and strongly indexed, unlike the Polish real wage guideline which was indexed much more weakly but was linked to the pre-stabilisation level (Angelov 1991).

13.6 Economic Performance

The main indicators of macroeconomic performance in the five Central Eastern European countries under consideration, immediately before and after the stabilisation plans, are summarised in Table 13.2; Yugoslavia is atypical, because of both plan abortion and civil war.

The programmes succeeded in establishing market-clearing prices, except of course for Romania during the intermediate stages of price liberalisation. Inflation predictably rose at first (Romania and Bulgaria are still at that stage) but was brought down fairly fast in Poland and even

Table 13.2 Key macroeconomic variables in Central-Eastern European economies (percentages)

	(1) Rate of GNP growth		(2) Overall government balance/GNP		(3) Inflation rate		(4) Rate of unemployment		(5) Current account balance/ GNP 1990	(6) Monetary overhang		(7) Net foreign debt/ hard currency exports	(8) Foreign exchange reserves/ imports
	1989	1990	1991	1990	1990	1991	1990	1991	1990	January 1990	June 1991	1990	1990
Bulgaria	-0.4	-11.8	-22.9	-12.7	19.3	574	1.0	12.0	-2.8	Small	Zero	497	31
CSFR	-0.7	-4.1	-15.9	0.2	10.0	45.3	1.0	6.6	-2.9	Small	Zero	116	26
Hungary	-0.2	-3.3	-11.0	0.1	28.9	35	1.6	8.0	0.4	Zero	Zero	328	19
Poland	-0.2	-11.6	-7.5	0.4	585	70.3	6.1	11.4	1.1	Significant	Zero	408	53
Romania	-5.8	-8.4	-13.0	1.2	40.2	222.8	1.5	4–5	-4.4	Small	Small	35	27
Yugoslavia	-6.6	-8.0	-20	n.a.	583	235	17.0	20.1	-7.1	Small	Significant	75	34

Note: This table has been compiled from official statistical sources and the *UN-ECE Economic Bulletin for Europe* 43, 1991. Inflation rates are point-to-point rates of change faster in the CSFR (price stability was reached already in the summer 1991) although it is still subject to sudden revamping. Fiscal deficits in 1991 (not shown in the table) have been higher than expected because of a lower tax basis for the state sector, lower tax rates and lower collection rate for the private sector, higher welfare expenditures made necessary by higher unemployment and poverty.

With the exception of Yugoslavia, the degrees of convertibility introduced with the stabilisation plans were maintained. Exports in convertible currencies rose, mostly because of diversion to trade to Western countries; imports were often cut drastically.

Everywhere the recession of 1989 accelerated in 1990 and continued in 1991 and 1992. The collapse of CMEA trade exacerbated the recession; this is generally regarded as an exogenous shock but was actually the result of a deliberate, concerted action on the part of Soviet trade partners, seeking economic independence in spite of the cost, and refusing to maintain CMEA even in a modified form, or to establish multilateral clearing arrangements among former members. Soviet economic decline was another contributory factor; indeed it is now clear that this would have led to trade collapse within the former CMEA area regardless of attempts to maintain a trade area. Thus persistent recession was at least partly unrelated to the presence or the intensity of the stabilisation effort.

There are ongoing debates on whether the depth of recession has been perhaps overestimated, due to the under-recording of the growth of private activities, including a 'black' or 'grey' sector. However, while under-recording may underestimate the current *level* of private activity, it must have surely decreased in the new conditions, thus actually *overstating the growth* of the private sector. In any case, given the initial low weight of the private sector, no plausible allowance for a possible underestimate of private activities is hound to make a difference to trends.

Unemployment, virtually unknown before the start of the plans (except for Yugoslavia), rose rapidly although not nearly as fast as output reduction but faster relatively to output than in Western countries at times of recession.

Prospects for 1992 are poor everywhere in the area: further output decline or stagnation, and further unemployment, is expected. According to the OECD the average GNP decline in the area was about 10 per cent in 1991 and is expected to continue at 2 per cent in 1992; in the autumn of 1992, this expectation appears to be over-optimistic.

A number of political and economic lessons can be drawn from these experiences to date.

13.7 Political Lessons

Economic austerity requires political legitimacy, and a formal or informal social pact. Under a communist government in Poland, a modest real wage cut of 8 per cent in early 1988 was followed by successful street protests and overcompensatory wage claims, ending up with the resignation of the Minister who had taken the initiative, Zdzislaw Sadowski, and an increase in the (statistical) real wage of 17 per cent; Balcerowicz got away with a real wage cut of one-third. In Bulgaria the stabilisation plan could only be introduced under a coalition government and a non-communist President, with a social pact with the Trade Unions, succeeding where the former government had failed. Hungarian stabilisation, though slower, also relies on a social accord through its Council for the Reconciliation of Conflicts, though its implementation leaves something to be desired. Romania, where the government lacks the necessary popular support, is lagging behind. The best contribution that a communist government can make to stabilisation is to follow Mieczyslaw Rakowski's example (August 1989) and to take unpopular decisions before resigning.

Political legitimacy needs a local (regional, republican) foundation. The 1989 revolutions were not only anti-communist but also anti-centralist. Centralisation of economic policy decisions, even in conditions of political pluralism and free elections, is no longer acceptable. This is demonstrated not only by Yugoslav, Soviet, Russian and Czech/Slovak separatist movements but also by the autonomy acquired *de facto* by large cities and small regions especially in the ex-Soviet Union.

Economic crisis is necessary—up to a point—to impose a consensus on drastic measures. Protracted and endemic shortages, inflation and hyperinflation are a great problem but also mollify the population and reduce popular resistance to the shock therapy of an austere stabilisation plan; thus governments should not be so reluctant to free prices even before a proper stabilisation plan. This is also confirmed by the Yugoslav experience; in the ex-USSR outside Russia, and perhaps in Romania, things may have to get worse before a Polish-style stabilisation plan can be fully implemented.

Popular support for austerity, even when undertaken by a legitimate government, is short-lived. Unpopular measures should not be spread over time but taken as quickly as possible. The population should soon be able to perceive a degree of improvement in living standards after the fall; if a positive supply response is too slow or too weak to allow an early reversal in consumption trends then one should deliberately induce a worse squeeze than strictly necessary in order to be able to deliver the expected and pre-announced improvement within the honeymoon period, after which the population will stop being cooperative. In Poland this period lasted roughly 200 days and in other countries the honeymoon is unlikely to last longer. The improvement has to be sustainable; 'double-dips' in consumption have adverse effects on expectations.

There is a great danger of populism in the course of stabilisation. Populist temptations should not be tolerated; on the contrary they should be discussed, identified, publicised and specifically rejected. For a start, the costs and risks of speeding up transition and especially trade liberalisation and convertibility should be recognised by the government. In particular, unemployment should not be underestimated and appropriate provisions should be made for it: belittling the costs of stabilisation, as was done in Poland, is as populist a practice as the making of impossible promises.

13.8 Domestic Macroeconomic Balance

Shock therapy stabilisation can bring an instant end to shortages, through a large but tolerable hike in prices, after which the rate of inflation can be brought down.[1] This may now seem obvious but at the time was not at all

[1] Shock therapy stabilisation should be distinguished from global shock therapy *à la* Dornbusch (1990), which would also include instant privatisation through free handouts of capital to citizens, debt for equity swaps, instant total liberalisation of trade and capital movements, and more; and from the actual global shock therapy followed in Polish-type programmes which include free trade and convertibility as well as stabilization.

clear in Poland at the end of 1989, in view of the unprecedented features of that stabilisation: disequilibrium relative prices and the unknown size of repressed inflation, which might have generated prolonged chaos instead of a relatively orderly bout of inflation; the combination of supply rigidities and the possible recreation of soft budget constraints, a potential recipe for protracted hyperinflation. Purely administrative price increases, below the market-clearing level, of the kind introduced by the Romanian government, and in the Soviet Union by Premier Valentin Pavlov on 2 April 1991, aroused popular resistance and discontent without eliminating shortages. They may have had some positive effect by inducing some supply response from farmers, reducing shortages, bringing down the ratio between black and official exchange rates, but otherwise are counterproductive in that they generate hostility against market reform.

There is another reason why all price increases (and compensatory payments) should he made all at one go: if price increases are diluted over time (as they were in Romania, through three stages of price liberalisation; to a smaller extent in Poland) the consequences are inflationary expectations, forward-looking inflationary wage settlements, and a secondary wave of inflation that may set in motion an inflationary spiral.

Stabilisation needs prior or simultaneous monetary and fiscal restraint. Budgetary and monetary discipline is indispensable, otherwise the round of price increases involved by stabilisation is wasted, and inflationary pressures are continually recreated. Again, this may seem obvious enough but it is a lesson which was lost, for instance, on Soviet or Romanian leaders. In this respect Janos Kornai has been proven both right and wrong: wrong in that state enterprise budget constraints can be hardened, right in that it requires a noncommunist government aiming at restoring a private market economy.

An incomes policy, especially for workers and for farmers, is a necessity. In view of the underdeveloped monetary and financial system, monetary policy is not sufficient to sustain a stabilisation programme; an incomes policy is also needed. Unusually this was also recognised for Poland by the IMF; the same principle was accepted in the CSFR, Bulgaria and—although not implemented—in Yugoslavia (December 1989) and

Hungary (1991). The Romanian and (until the Russian 1992 attempt) Soviet exceptions are a further confirmation of this principle.[2]

Contrary to the policy followed by Poland, *farmers' incomes should not be penalised but protected* on the grounds that everybody else does it. Their loans should not be taxed (see below) but subsidised; they should not be charged international prices for their inputs when they face trade obstacles in selling their output at international prices and face the competition from subsidized imports.[3] Paradoxically in Poland farmers' supply response was impeded by competition with food aid granted by the European Community and other donors in early 1990.

13.9 Monetary Policy

Anchoring a programme to real money supply can be inflationary; anchoring it to nominal money supply can be severely recessionary. Some programmes have avoided this dilemma through drastic reductions in the real money supply (Poland) or through ambiguity about whether money targets were nominal or real (as in the CSFR, and in earlier Soviet programmes which were not implemented).

Real interest rates should be raised but not necessarily to positive levels during stabilisation. It is preferable to hold down interest rates initially, introducing some credit rationing instead. In a growing economy in conditions of tranquillity, the real interest rate equilibrium has to match the positive rate of return on investment. But in the turbulent times of transition a positive real rate of interest is highly recessionary, raises the burden of government debt service, and is probably unnecessary, as even a negative real rate may be sufficient to induce the public to hold voluntarily liquid monetary assets, especially in a situation where interest differentials

[2] On the importance of incomes policy in the stabilisation of transitional economies see Coricelli and Rocha (1990).

[3] I was once asked (by Gerhard Fink): why should farmers be protected and not, say, barbers? This is a good question, but has several very good answers: because it is easier to grow longer hair and beard than to go without food; because haircuts are non-tradable and do not require tradables for their production; because haircuts are not capital-intensive services both in terms of capital/output and capital/labour ratios.

between domestic and hard currency deposits are greatly in excess of differential inflation or likely domestic devaluations. If the government expects to get inflation down during the year, it should underpin that expectation by lending over the medium term at interest rates which embody that expectation of lower inflation and therefore lower subsequent monthly rates of interest, instead of lending mostly on variable monthly rates as was done in Poland (on possible perverse real interest effects, see Kolodko 1990b, 1991).

In no circumstances should interest rates be raised on old, long-term credit contracts stipulated at fixed rates. Retroactive high interest rates are a tax on liabilities, a very bad tax which nobody has ever suggested. Assets, not liabilities, should be subject to tax. The increase in net wealth due to a drastic fall in the present value of liabilities may be subject to a capital gains tax, along with all kinds of other capital gains—not liabilities as such. Retroactive interest rises on long-term loans are also unfair and arguably unconstitutional; they were disastrous for Polish farmers and literally stopped their supply response.

The same mistake might be repeated in Bulgaria, where raising interest on old contracts has been seriously considered. Hungarians have had a much better idea, namely raising the interest rate on enterprise payment arrears *vis-à-vis* other enterprises and the banking system, up to twice the 22 per cent basic bank rate. However in Hungary in mid-1991 the marginal cost of borrowing to enterprises was of the order 30–40 per cent and therefore automatic borrowing at 44 per cent through cumulating arrears could still be preferred to negotiated borrowing at 40 per cent; twice the actual borrowing rate would be a preferable penal stipulation.

A *real wage level lower than actual (theoretical) levels, and consistent with the consumption available during stabilisation, should be strongly indexed.* This is the policy which was followed in Bulgaria. A weak indexation of the actual wage level—as was done in Poland for the determination of wage norms—produces the kind of U-shaped time pattern of real wages that occurred in Poland in 1990. The reversal of an excessive decline in real wages requires that money wages rise faster than prices, but punitive taxation of excess wages above government guidelines can amplify the resulting wage inflationary shocks by inducing a more than proportional rise in enterprise labour costs. By itself, wage indexation is neither good nor bad; its effect depends on what wage level is being protected (which should not exceed what is allowed by sustainable consumption and its distribution), on the coefficient of elasticity of money wages with respect to prices, on the lag between price and wage adjustments, on the interval between wage negotiations (when real wage protection ceases to be automatic and money wages become entirely subject to renegotiation anyway).

13.10 International Aspects

Trade liberalisation makes an important contribution to stabilisation and reform: it conveys signals of opportunities for a more efficient pattern of imports and exports; it 'imports' a system of relative prices for tradables which otherwise may be hard to settle at an equilibrium level following domestic liberalisation of prices; it enhances competition in an over-concentrated industrial system during the time it takes to partition it into smaller and competing units; it is a guarantee of decentralisation of enterprise decisions. Free trade leads to the overdue elimination of activities which would have a negative value-added at world prices (which according to recent empirical studies may be as much as one-fifth or one-quarter of industrial activities in transitional economies), and therefore facilitates the restructuring process. *However, free trade also destroys domestic activities which are unprofitable at world prices but still produce a positive value-added and make a positive contribution to national income, employment, exports and consumption.* This cost should not be neglected when deciding the degree of openness of the national economy during the process of stabilisation and transition to the market economy. Gradualism in stabilisation is not economically justified; gradualism in convertibility and trade opening until some progress is made in capacity restructuring is not necessarily unfounded—as long as the reform impetus is not lost on the way, as might happen in Hungary.

There is a contradiction between the pursuit of generalised free trade and the will to join a trading bloc such as the European Community. Inexplicably this contradiction was little understood by Central-Eastern European governments and impeded rapid progress in the negotiation of association agreements with the EC, finally concluded in November 1991 by the CSFR, Hungary and Poland. Paradoxically these countries have had to reimpose tariffs in order to be able to negotiate their reduction in trade with the EC.

Internal convertibility for current transactions is within closer reach than previously thought. One of the reasons for Polish success in this area is the pre-existence of hard currency-denominated assets and banknotes, mostly dollars, in the hands of households and firms on a scale which was unique in Eastern Europe (on 1 January 1990 of the order of $US4.5 bn for household deposits plus $US2.5 bn for enterprises, plus cash estimated at between $US4 bn to $US8 bn). The possibility of early convertibility had not been at all clear in Poland at the time; indeed many economists had warned of the dangers of capital flight and loss of reserves, whereas the opposite happened. This does not imply that, in the words of the CSFR Minister of Finance Vaclav Klaus, 'The only problem with convertibility is to declare it'; obviously there is no point in any exchange rate manoeuvre unless there are market-clearing prices, subsidies have been eliminated or very substantially reduced on tradable goods and services, and there is significant elasticity of demand and supply with respect to prices (Nuti 1991a; none of these conditions were present in Russia in early 1992). In Poland the simultaneous price liberalisation and reduction of subsidies, and the presence of a significant private sector and the hardening of budget constraints in the state sector, ensured that these preconditions were satisfied (as they were in the CSFR on 1 January 1991 when limited convertibility was also introduced, without a private sector and therefore with more limitations than in Poland).

In heavily indebted countries, the rescheduling of debt and capitalisation of interest, whether de jure or de facto, are a clear precondition for establishing convertibility. Convertibility is immensely facilitated by the lack of externally-held balances in domestic currencies (such as the sterling balances which marred British early attempts to return to convertibility). However convertibility is impossible without the freezing, or funding, or outright relief, of externally-held debt denominated in hard currencies. Poland first rescheduled unilaterally, then came to agreed rescheduling, then benefited from debt relief. Hungarians, pursuing convertibility under the burden of debt service, have faced great difficulties and have not yet established it fully.

Debt rescheduling and relief should be requested before and not after stabilisation. In the interest of the stabilising country, in order to bargain from a position of strength, the easing of the burden of debt should be made a negotiated condition for the introduction of convertibility and trade liberalisation; even after a very successful stabilisation such negotiations are held from a position of weakness. This is demonstrated by Poland's delay in obtaining debt relief and its uneven treatment by different creditors.

13.11 Exchange Rate Policy

Some undervaluation of the domestic currency and a commitment to initially support a fixed rate are necessary to establish credibility of convertibility. In Poland, through inflation continuously revaluing a nominally constant, initially undervalued zloty rate of exchange for the dollar, the real price of the dollar started high and was continuously reduced in a kind of repeated Dutch auction until it found its own equilibrium level, signaled by the nominal rate of exchange coming under pressure. Credibility of convertibility with respect to domestic holders of dollars as well as foreign and domestic firms is initially low, but grows as convertibility is maintained. This gradual credibility enhancement allowed real appreciation of the zloty in 1990–1991, which would not have occurred if the zloty had been initially set at a higher rate. Then the equilibrium rate can rise over time because of increasing confidence—up to the limits set by trade competitiveness. Yugoslavia fixed a realistic rate of exchange which however could not be maintained—among other reasons—because it was not undervalued;[4] there is no point in introducing a convertibility which cannot be maintained, especially if there is a misguided commitment to fixed rates. An initial commitment to a fixed rate also enhances credibility (Aghevli et al. 1991).

[4] In addition, of course, Yugoslavia was forced to suspend convertibility *de facto* in the autumn of 1990 because by mid-1990 it had lost control of money wages, of monetary expansion and of republican contributions to the federal budget.

Undervaluation of the domestic currency has to be fixed well below Purchasing Power Parities (PPP). PPP is not a good guidance to initial rate for three reasons: the equilibrium rate is affected by stock equilibrium, which in Polish-type conditions may require a lower rate than flow equilibrium; PPP includes non-tradables; more importantly, PPP is an average concept whereas competitiveness is a marginal one, i.e. what counts are the elasticities of supply of and demand for tradables. This is why Russian attempts in 1992 at fixing an exchange rate close to the PPP rate have floundered.

Notwithstanding the need for some undervaluation of the domestic currency for the sake of credibility, the price of hard currencies should not be pitched as high as the level prevailing in the free market. The free price in a two-tier free/controlled market is always higher than the single price which would prevail in a completely free market (due to the income effect of raising the single level above the lower-tier level). Some undervaluation is necessary but excessive undervaluation is expensive because it leads to distress exports and it worsens the terms of trade. Excessive undervaluation, such as is necessarily involved in officially adopting the free market rate, unnecessarily raises domestic inflation and, under the kind of wages policy followed in Poland, unnecessarily reduces real wages;[5] thus it is to be avoided.

The nominal exchange rate, in any case, is a bad anchor if further inflation is expected and moreover cannot be controlled. This is what happened in Poland; the ensuing progressive revaluation to the point of gross overvaluation—partly the result of inflation generated by undervaluation itself—was as unfounded as the initial excessive undervaluation and required further (still inadequate) corrections. The later then a new devaluation occurs, as it eventually must, the larger it has to be, probably raising inflation and inflationary expectations more than a series of smaller adjustments. A combination of real wage policy and floating

[5] Gomulka (1991b) rejects the notion that the January devaluation was excessive on the ground that in December 1989 in Poland nearly 60 per cent of the total money supply was dollar-denominated, and therefore devaluation did not amount to a contractionary monetary policy. However he neglects that wages were not dollar-denominated, and that the inflationary implications of the January devaluation unduly depressed real demand through real incomes if not through real balances.

exchange rate (as in the Bulgarian programme of February 1991) or, better, some kind of crawling peg, appears to be preferable.[6]

It is absurd to pre-announce devaluations. This was done in the CSFR in mid-1990 for 1 January 1991 thus forcing an earlier devaluation in September 1990, in Romania for August 1991 and in a way also in Hungary with the January 1990 devaluation which had been openly called for by government members; but prior indication of general exchange rate policy is far better than maintaining an overvalued currency until a crisis occurs.

13.12 Privatisation

Privatisation takes a great deal of time to be implemented and/or to become effective. We already know from the privatisation experience of Western countries that the preparation of state enterprises for sale and the issue of shares to the public is a lengthy process (see for instance the British experience). The transfer of ownership titles can be speeded up by the free distribution of claims to state assets to the population, as envisaged everywhere except the ex-GDR and Hungary. This in fact may eliminate or at least reduce the need for prior financial and capacity restructuring, capital valuation and share issue pricing. However the organisation of even such 'free' transfers has proven inordinately time-consuming in practice, and by mid-1992 has not yet been implemented in any of the transitional economies in spite of earlier commitments. In any case the simple transfer of ownership titles has no effect whatever—other than an undesirable inflationary wealth effect on demand—in the absence of properly

[6] Aghevli et al. (1991) discuss the relative merits of fixed and flexible exchange rate regimes in developing countries. On the one hand a commitment to manage the exchange rate flexibly may provide helpful assurances to producers of traded goods and thereby support external adjustment; on the other hand, it may undermine the credibility of the government in adopting restrictive demand policies and thus make it more difficult to lower inflation without imposing an output cost. On balance, they recommend a nominal exchange rate rule, under which the rate of crawl of the nominal exchange rate is fixed. Following this line of reasoning it was effective for Poland to maintain a fixed nominal rate for an initial extended period, to establish credibility, but the continuation of such a policy after credibility had been established will have had advantages outweighed by disadvantages with respect to exchange rate flexibility.

functioning financial markets: for managers to be subject to stockmarket discipline it is necessary for them to feel the threat of takeover in case of poor performance. Restrictions on voting and on early resale of shares, and the pulverisation of shareholdings, are actually a guarantee that financial markets will not be able to exercise a function of corporate control for a long time to come.

Privatisation, because of its necessary slowness, should not be relied upon as a means of easing the task of stabilization. 'Small-scale' privatisation (housing, catering and trade establishments, land) can be much quicker than the privatisation of state enterprises, but even that cannot soften the blow of instant price liberalisation, unless it starts beforehand and its progress is clearly and credibly announced in all its details. It follows that the Shatalin—Yavlinsky Plan of September 1990 for Soviet stabilisation in 500 days was not credible, because of its attempt to reduce the overhang through front-loaded privatisation. Soviet reform attempts of end-1990/early-1991 failed not because privatisation *per se* was not introduced, as Jeffrey Sachs argues *(Repubblica,* 8 March 1991), but because privatisation was relied upon as an instrument of stabilisation—already a tall order—and was not replaced by other stabilisation measures such as higher prices or taxes.

Property restitution to old owners is a respectable political objective but is economically costly. Restitution, introduced everywhere (except Yugoslavia) following the ex-GDR lead, is not economically necessary to build up confidence in the new institutions, since there is no expectation of policy reversals in the target system. It slows down further the process of privatisation because of the time needed to allow and process claims, especially if restitution in kind is contemplated. It also absorbs precious time to settle a large number of issues: the eligibility of nationals versus expatriates (and from what date), the fixing of ceilings and progressive scales for compensation (always confiscatory on a progressive scale—a residual of socialist egalitarianism); the fixing of arbitrary dates from which nationalised property is to be returned to old owners, and often of specific nationalising laws and types of property. Restitution to old owners, including aristocrats and the Churches, at a time when considerable sacrifices are asked of ordinary citizens and workers, is politically divisive.

These economic costs may be regarded by the governments involved as worth paying (in Hungary, restitution was a condition of the Smallholders' Party's essential participation in the government coalition), but they should not be ignored.

During the inevitable delays of privatisation the state sector, which continues to exist and to provide the bulk of productive capacity, should not be ignored, neglected and penalised. Central-Eastern European governments, particularly the Polish government, confuse their potential ability to privatise with the realisation of that potential and simply pretend that the state sector does not exist.[7] Worse, state enterprises in Poland are subject to distortionary and discriminatory taxation with respect to the private sector, such as the tax on wage payments above statutory guidelines (the so-called PPWW) and a payment of a so-called 'dividend' to the state budget calculated not on profits but on a revalued historical capital value; similar policies are followed, to a lesser extent, in the other countries. It is inappropriate to enforce incomes policy only in the state sector; a generalised progressive income tax is preferable. The argument of lack of owners' control over wage expenditures in the state enterprises is used in support of excess wage tax in Poland and Hungary but this is a case for privatisation and for the overhauling of managerial incentives in the state enterprise sector, not for tax exemption of the private sector.[8]

On the rebound from former 'soft budgets' state enterprises are indiscriminately starved of resources, whether from the reinvestment of profits or access to credit, regardless of the viability of potential investment. Under the prospect of a rapid privatisation which does not however materialise, there is hardly any reorganisation, redeployment of productive assets within the state sector, or revision of methods of assessing and rewarding managerial performance. Managerial uncertainty about the prospect, timing and terms of their enterprises' privatisation leads at best

---

[7] In this the new governments display the same kind of attitude that the old regime had with respect to inflation, confusing their potential ability to implement price stability with the realisation of that potential, and ignoring the cumulative build-up of the large monetary overhang which played such a great part in systemic failure.

[8] Polish government documents (for instance the Government Memorandum of 2nd March 1991, section IV.1) candidly recognise that the 'popiwek' tax is 'expected to provide a significant incentive' for privatisation. Surely this kind of incentive should not be needed, or less distortionary incentives could be provided.

to paralysis, at worst to de-capitalisation, anarchy and rapid decline. This kind of policy is not necessarily an improvement on the former central tutelage.[9] The only incentive for efficient managerial behaviour is the prospect of finding a foreign buyer or partner, and this is not sufficiently widespread or, apart from a few exceptions, strong enough to vitalise state enterprises.

Under the old system state enterprises were basically administrative units executing central instructions and rewarded or penalised according to the degree of fulfillment of such instructions. This, however, does not necessarily imply lack of 'entrepreneurship' on the part of managers; indeed it has been argued that the task of running a state enterprise in the face of continuous unpredictable changes in often conflicting central instructions, in conditions of endemic shortages of labour and means of production and uncertain supplies, is a much harder challenge than that faced by Western managers running a private enterprise in a market economy. The problem is not the absence of entrepreneurship but the misdirection of whatever entrepreneurship is there. There are signs that state enterprises have actually responded to some extent to the new conditions; a pilot study of Polish state enterprises conducted by the World Bank (Jorgensen et al. 1990) concludes that 'in the light of the immense and continued uncertainty and the time necessary for adjustment, the degree of response observed was high, and in most cases in the right direction'.

However, some of this response had negative side-effects (for instance, the growth of inter-firm payments arrears, which firms expected to be somehow guaranteed by the state); excess wage tax proved to be constraining output and generating distortions; firms suffered from a 'vacuum of ownership'; 'the best-placed firms are probably those with previous exposure to selling on Western markets'. It is urgent to provide new indicators of enterprise performance, budgetary constraints (e.g. cash limits) and an appropriate system of managerial incentives (rewards and penalties geared to market success).

Especially in the state sector some capacity restructuring should be effected from the start, following the kind of industrial policy which is

[9] On the negative perception of the Polish stabilisation programme by managers, from a sample of 70 state enterprises, see Maj (1991).

usually formulated and implemented in all other market economies. When, as in Poland in January—March 1991, enterprise profits are subject to 87 per cent taxation and access to credit is restricted in principle, there can be no supply response from any stabilisation programme.

13.13 Sequencing, Announcements, Contingencies

Speedy action is better than orderly procrastination. In recent literature there has been considerable discussion of the question of appropriate sequencing of reform and stabilisation steps: some have pointed out the high degree of interdependence of tasks and therefore the need to do everything at once (e.g. Dornbusch 1990); others have attempted to draw a desirable sequential critical path (e.g. Nuti 1991b). There is now, however, widespread agreement that, whatever the merits of a possibly potentially superior critical path, it is much more important to move as fast as possible, 'meandering' in the right direction than to make slower progress along a sequentially optimal path, even if it existed. Clearly stabilisation must come first, as market-clearing prices without excessive inflationary pressures are a precondition of viability of any system where markets are used at all, even if only for the distribution of resources in place of their allocation as in the traditional centrally-planned economy. Currency convertibility without price liberalisation (even solely for the tourist rate, as it was done in the Soviet Union in November 1991) unloads the monetary overhang on to that one market and leads to costly and absurd results (such as a Soviet average wage of the order of $US3 per month in the second half of 1991). It is essential that Central-Eastern European governments should not stop after stabilisation wondering what would be best to do next, but should keep going. In Poland institutional reforms practically came to a standstill in the first half of 1990 for a considerable time, while privatisation was unnecessarily delayed by political arguments and by the pursuit of facile schemes of mass privatisation. Without such gaps and delays the expected supply response might have been stronger. Of course complex and unprecedented systemic reform is bound to take time; but, confronted with such delays, it may be better to follow the line of least resistance and implement what is immediately feasible, rather than follow a rigid ideal pattern of reform sequencing: bad sequencing is costly, but may be better than no change.

Even incomplete and unsuccessful attempts at reform may have positive effects. It has been claimed that such attempts have brought about 'reform fatigue'; certainly the repeated pre-1989 aborted attempts at constructing a market socialist model must have worn out all those involved. However even failed attempts are not necessarily a waste of time. It helps stabilisation to have, beforehand, a private sector in agriculture and in manufacturing; some free trade in foreign currency, currency retentions by exporters and currency auctions (admittedly distortionary, but a powerful instrument of decentralisation and an incentive to trade); a previous banking reform, legislation of the kind already passed in Poland under Jaruzelski, even under Martial Law.

In the delay of implementation the effects of time-consuming measures can be approximated by making credible and detailed announcements. Thus, for instance, the effects of a necessarily slow privatisation programme—on saving behaviour, on incentives—can be accelerated by announcing the exact terms, schedule and procedures of the entire programme. However, this presumes that the path to be followed is clear and widely agreed, and that the government enjoys credibility when it announces what it intends to undertake next. Policy reversals or even continuous piecemeal alterations within the same general policies undermine such credibility.

Instead of adopting a single package of stabilisation measures, the government should make contingent commitments to cover possible undershooting or overshooting, and some of the possible additional external shocks. A single package could not possibly be 'robust' enough with respect to exogenous factors and to unpredictable behavioural responses. Once a package is announced, if external or domestic conditions change in an expected direction the government is paralysed, for fear of destabilising expectations by taking necessary action. For instance the Polish government could not react to the recessionary overshooting of its stabilisation plan in 1990, fearing that reflationary measures would signal the abandonment of its commitment to austerity. Only the prior announcement of contingent measures, at the same time as the stabilisation was announced, could have avoided Keynesian unemployment, which is not as justified as the unemployment generated by capacity restructuring.

13.14 System-Specific Features of Stabilisation

Post-communist countries are different from ordinary underdeveloped countries; high costs can derive from neglecting such differences. In the elation of the 1989 revolutions the prospect of an early transition to capitalism induced new rulers, international agencies, Western governments and their advisors to forget the heavy burden of the former regime's legacies. Not only were older historical legacies initially neglected—nationalist and ethnic conflicts, to name only the ones which most spectacularly manifested themselves soon afterwards—but also the more recent but deeply ingrained economic legacies of habits, institutions and expectations.

By and large, Central-Eastern European economies have been treated like ordinary developing countries, facing familiar tasks of de-regulation of economic activities, privatisation of state assets, coping with a large external debt, trying to bring down inflation and hyperinflation, opening their economies to trade, attracting new foreign investments. The skills of area studies specialists and of economists expert in centrally-planned economies and their long path to reform were, wrongly, regarded as obsolete. Knowledge of the target model was regarded as the only necessary qualification to manage the transition to that model, whereas a successful organ transplant across different species obviously requires deep knowledge of both donor and recipient.

Qualitatively the tasks of transition are the same as, or similar to, those familiar from the experience of underdeveloped countries. But one might be forgiven for quoting Engels' proposition (in Anti-During) that quantitative differences can become qualitative: the sheer scale of these tasks, as well as their simultaneous presence, reduces very greatly the relevance of the stabilisation and reform programmes of underdeveloped countries to Central-Eastern Europe. Moreover, the ultimate difference between the two groups was neglected or underestimated, namely, the extraordinary economic inertia of a centrally-planned economy no longer subject to central control but not yet fully subject or responsive to full market stimuli.

There is an inordinate difference between reducing the size of the state sector, say from 60 to 30 per cent, and reducing it from 100 to 50 per cent; for a start, one has to introduce from scratch property legislation, joint stock companies, commercial banking, financial markets, price competition, liquidation and bankruptcy; if legislation takes time, jurisprudence takes a much longer time. There is the same difference between raising unemployment, say, from 5 to 10 per cent and raising it from zero to over 10 per cent; between liberalising some price controls, and replacing with market-clearing prices a historical stratification of multiple prices varying according to agents and type of transactions; between introducing convertibility for a domestic currency and introducing a true domestic currency in place of what was essentially a unit of account or, at best, a lottery ticket. The list could go on. The neglect of these differences has led to a serious underestimation of the time-scale of transition and of the costs of a transitional economic non-system, and to a serious overestimation of the supply response that could be elicited through familiar policy instruments in an inert economy.[10]

13.15 Costs and Benefits

The benefits expected of stabilisation and reform do not have to be emphasised: the viability of markets, which for consumers means a return to 'normal life' (a theme which has frequently recurred in electoral campaigns) and for firms the elimination of the most glaring inefficiencies; the de-politicisation of economic activities; the establishment of market discipline for enterprises and personal incentives for individuals; a return to the world economy and in particular to Europe; the expectation of better standards of living.

[10] The specific features of stabilisation in post-communist economies, however, are well understood in Kolodko (1990a, 1991; see also Nuti 1991b).

The list of expected benefits is long but, when there is no alternative target available, the benefits of such a target do not even need to be mentioned, let alone quantified. There remains however a problem of cost-effectiveness of alternative ways of reaching that target (i.e. not a question of what to do but how to do it).

The stabilisation and reform plans of Central-Eastern European countries have been accompanied by inordinately high costs, in terms of employment, output, consumption, distribution of income and wealth.

Some of those costs have nothing to do with the transition to market but are simply the open manifestation of the hidden costs of the earlier system: hidden unemployment and inflation, environmental disaster, inappropriate capacity; such costs would have been openly incurred, sooner or later, whatever the target model selected.

Some of the costs have been the result of the uncoordinated nature of stabilisation and reform plans undertaken in the whole area, which have resulted in the collapse of trade within the ex-CMEA. These costs could have been at least alleviated if the countries concerned had been able to agree on establishing free trade areas or on setting up schemes for automatic trade clearing and mutual payments of the type adopted through the European Payments Union (EPU) in post-war Europe (which would have attracted Western aid just as EPU attracted Marshall aid). Keenness to undermine Soviet dominance, to make a clean break with the past, as well as fear of delaying the more desirable course of joining the European Community, have resulted in the otherwise avoidable costs of trade collapse within the ex-CMEA (although, with the benefit of hindsight, trade within the ex-CMEA would have shrunk regardless of such attempts due to the drastic decline in the Soviet or ex-Soviet area). Similar costs now are bound to be incurred if the ex-Soviet republics fail to establish a trade and payments regime capable of handling their interdependence and preserving viable trade flows.

Some of the costs of 'transition' have been the result of the sudden opening of national economies, due to (i) the lack of protection of those activities which—again, with the benefit of hindsight—we now know should not have been undertaken in the past but, being there, were still making a positive contribution to national income; (ii) the related costs of a speedy convertibility. Of course there were also benefits from opening the economy, like the expected gains in trade, competition and foreign investment, listed above; but we should not take for granted that the net result is necessarily positive, let alone positive and large.

Partly, some non-negligible costs of stabilisation and reform plans undertaken in Central-Eastern European countries have been the results of true and predictable mistakes, in the narrow sense of decisions which can be proved wrong under any circumstances, rather than plausible 'quasi-mistakes' in the sense of decisions which proved to have been inappropriate only with the benefit of hindsight and therefore can generate 'surprises'.[11] Using President Bush's language, these are 'the wrong kind of mistakes'.[12]

Thus, for instance, in Poland it was a mistake to let real wages and the real exchange rate float at random with the vagaries of inflation, to excessively over-devalue the zloty only to let it steadily overvalue, to effectively tax old loans by raising their interest rates, to neglect farmers' incomes and supply response, to neglect the state sector, to postpone further institutional changes, not to make clear announcements about further developments, and to make no provision for possible overshooting.

The inability to recognise mistakes and to learn from them, which was a main drawback of the old system, seems another legacy inherited by the new system. What is worse, Central-Eastern European governments often fail to learn not only from the mistakes of others, which is true wisdom, but even from their own.

---

[11] Recently there has been a tendency in official circles to recognise Polish overshooting and the negative phenomena associated with it, but to claim that these had been 'surprises' (Gomulka 1991a, b) and to dub economic decline and unemployment with the dubious euphemisms of 'creative destruction' (Gomulka 1991b). Moreover Gomulka also admits that 'some of the forecasts, e.g. on prices and output, were made under the pressure of policy convenience' (1991a), i.e. were actually fabricated. One might have been 'surprised', perhaps, by the results of the stabilisation plan in January 1990, but not in February 1990 (when I actually had the privilege of making these same points to Minister Balcerowicz), let alone in April–May 1991.

[12] 'As Yogi Bear used to say, I do not want to make the wrong kind of mistake.' (President George Bush discussing with journalists his cautious attitude to Soviet crackdown in Lithuania, in January 1991).

Bibliography

Aghevli, B. B., M. S. Khan and P. J. Montiel (1991). Exchange Rate Policy in Developing Countries: Some Analytical Issues. IMF Occasional Paper 78. Washington.

Angelov, L. (1991). One Year Monetary Reform in Bulgaria, Institute of Economics, Bulgarian Academy of Sciences. Sofia.

Chen, K., G. H. Jefferson and I. Singh (1990). Lessons from China's Economic Reform, World Bank, December.

Coricelli, F. and R. Rocha (1990). Stabilisation Programs in Eastern Europe: A Comparative Analysis of the Polish and the Yugoslav Programs of 1990. Conference Paper, World Bank, Poltusk (Poland), October.

Dornbusch, R. (1990). Transition to a Market Economy in Central and Eastern Europe. OECD Conference Paper. Paris.

ECE - UN (1991), *Economic Bulletin for Europe* 43.

Fry, M. J. and D. M. Nuti (1992). Monetary and Exchange Rate Policies during Eastern Europe's Transition: Some Lessons from Further East, *Oxford Review of Economic Policy.* (Forthcoming.)

Gomulka, S. (1991a). Polish Economic Reform: Principles, Policies and Surprises. Conference paper, Jerusalem, April.

Gomulka, S. (1991b). Tworcza destrukcja, *Zycie Gospodarcze* 18, 5 May, pp. 1, 6-7.

Government of Poland (1991). Memorandum on Economic Reform and Medium Term Policies, 1991-1993, Warsaw, 25 March.

Grosfeld, I. and P. Hare (1991). Privatisation in Hungary, Poland and Czechoslovakia, *European Economy*, Special edition No. 2, pp. 129-156.

Hrncir, M. and J. Klacek (1991). Stabilization Policies and Currency Convertibility in Czechoslovakia, *European Economy*, Special edition No. 2, pp. 17-39.

Jackson, M. (1991a). One Year After German Economic Union: The Impact on the German Economy. Report on Eastern Europe. 28 June, Munich, pp. 38-43.

Jackson, M. (1991b). One Year After German Economic Union: Are There Lessons to be learned?, Report on Eastern Europe, 28 June, Munich, pp. 43-48.

Jorgensen, E. A., A. Gelb and I. Singh (1990). Life for Polish Firms under the 'Big Bang': Preliminary Findings from a Field Trip. Conference Paper, World Bank, Poltusk (Poland), October.

Kolodko, G. W. (1990a). *Inflacja — reforma — stabilizacja.* Warsaw: Alma Press.

Kolodko, G. W. (1990b). Polish Hyperinflation and Stabilisation 1989-1990, Working Papers of the Institute of Finance 10, Warsaw; also in *Most-Moct: Economic Journal of Eastern Europe and the Soviet Union* 1, 1991, pp. 9-36.

Kolodko, G. W. (1991). Polish Hyperinflation and Stabilisation. A Year After, *Rivista di Politica Economica,* June, pp. 289-330.

Kolodko, G. W., D. Gotz-Kozierkiewicz and E. Skrzeszewska-Paczek (1992). *Hyperinflation and Stabilisation in Postsocialist Economies.* Boston, London and Dortrecht: Kluwer.

Maj, H. (1991). Proces dostowan mikroekonomicznych. Reakcje przedsiebiorstw w warunkach polityki stabilizacyjnej, in Kolodko, G. W. (Ed.), *Polityka finansowa-stabilizacja-transformacja.* Warsaw: Instytut Finansow.

Nuti, D. M. (1988). Perestroika: Transition Between Central Planning and Market Socialism, *Economic Policy* 7, pp. 353-389.

Nuti, D. M. (1990a). Internal and International Implications of Monetary Disequilibrium in Poland, *European Economy* 43, pp. 169-182.

Nuti, D. M. (1990b). Privatisation of Socialist Economies: General Issues and the Polish Case, in Bloomenstein, H. and M. Marrese (Eds), *The Transformation of Planned Economies.* Paris: OECD.

Nuti, D. M. (1991a). How Fast Should Convertibility Be Introduced? A Comment on F. Levcik and J. J. Polak, in Williamson, J. (Ed.), *Currency Convertibility in Eastern Europe.* Washington DC: IIE, pp. 48-55.

Nuti, D. M. (1991b). Sequencing and Credibility in Economic Reform, in Atkinson, A. B. and R. Brunetta (Eds), *Economics for the New Europe.* London: MacMillan, pp. 126-139.

Nuti, D. M. (1992). Le conseguenze economiche della rivoluzione russa d'agosto e le risposte occidentali, *Rivista di Politica Economica,* LXXXII 2, February, pp. 109-119.

Nuti D. M. and J. Pisani-Ferry (1992). Post-Soviet Issues: Stabilisation, Trade and Money, Conference on the economic consequences of the East, CEPR and Deutsche Bundesbank, March, Frankfurt, and Economic Papers 93, May 1992. Brussels: CEC-DG II.

Rosati, D. K. (1991a). Institutional and Policy Framework for Foreign Economic Relations in Poland, in UN-ECE, Reforms in Foreign Economic Relations of Eastern Europe and the Soviet Union, New York.

Rosati, D. K. (1991b). The Polish Road to Capitalism: A Critical Appraisal of the Balcerowicz Plan, *Thames Polytechnic Papers in Political Economy*, New Series 2.

Siebert, H. (1990a). The Economic Integration of Germany. Discussion Paper 160. Kiel Institute of World Economics.

Siebert, H. (1990b). The Economic Integration of Germany - An Update. Discussion Paper 160a. Kiel Institute of World Economics.

14

Economic Inertia in the Transitional Economies of Eastern Europe

Domenico Mario Nuti

"No-one said it was going to be easy... and no-one was right...".
(President George Bush, after Yogi Bear)

Published in Milica Uvalić, Efisio Espa and Jochen Lorentzen (Eds.) (1993) *Impediments to the Transition in Eastern Europe*, Florence, European University Institute, European Policy Studies no. 1. The volume included a selection of papers prepared for a conference held at the European University Institute in Florence in January 1992 organized by the EUI Working Group on East-West Policy Problems.

Acknowledgements for useful comments are due to Conference participants (in particular to discussants Marie Lavigne and Vladimir Shemiatenkov, to Stuart Holland, Miroslav Hrncir, Dariusz Rosati and Robert Waldmann) and to Joly Dixon. The views expressed in this paper do not necessarily reflect those of the Commission of European Communities.

D. M. Nuti (✉)
La Sapienza, University of Rome, Rome, Italy
e-mail: milica.uvalic@unipg.it

© The Author(s), under exclusive license to Springer Nature Switzerland AG 2023

S. Estrin, M. Uvalic (eds.), *Collected Works of Domenico Mario Nuti, Volume I*, Studies in Economic Transition, https://doi.org/10.1007/978-3-031-12334-4_14

14.1 Transition and Economic Recession

The restoration of capitalism, opened by the 1989 revolutions in Central and Eastern Europe and by the August 1991 coup/countercoup/revolution in the former Soviet Union, was expected to put those countries back onto the road to greater efficiency, technical progress, and prosperity. A "shock therapy" of price liberalisation, monetary and fiscal austerity, the opening of the economy to unrestricted free trade, and internal convertibility for residents, was understood to require initial sacrifices; however, thanks to stabilisation, privatisation and other economic and political reforms, these side effects would be short lived. In Poland, for instance, the government expected the Balcerowicz Programme to bring about a decline in national income of 5% in 1990, with a positive supply response already six months after the beginning of the Programme (Lipton and Sachs 1990). Western advisors and international organisations encouraged this expectation, in Poland and elsewhere (see Kolodko 1992a, Sect. 14.2, who reports their optimistic projections).

On the contrary, in all countries without exception, in the first two years from the beginning of stabilisation programmes—and so far in the first year in the former Soviet Union—the therapy has led to a drastic deterioration of symptoms and of general economic conditions, instead of the anticipated improvements. National income and especially industrial output, already falling in 1989, have accelerated their fall and then continued to decline at a lower rate, cumulatively by about 15% to 20% in GDP and by 25% to 30% in industrial output. Employment has fallen much more slowly, with an elasticity of 1/3 to 1/2 with respect to output,[1] though fast enough to create mass unemployment of the order of 8% to 12% of active population or more (13.8% in Poland in September 1992; in the former Soviet Union the rise of unemployment in 1992 has lagged behind output falls, but has been steady and will accelerate in 1993; see Standing 1992a, b). Initial inflation, often hyperinflation, has been

[1] This may suggest greater employment flexibility than in advanced market economies—as emphasised by Robert Waldmann—but the comparison is misleading in view of the depth of Central-Eastern European recession, which makes employment preservation there a different phenomenon from the temporary and modest labour hoarding by enterprises in market economies, facing cyclical drops in demand.

brought down but has not been defeated (with the exception of the CSFR, however thanks to draconian taxation of excess wages, reminiscent of former wage controls).

By the end of 1992 the first signs of a turnaround have appeared in Poland, with sustained industrial growth on a month to month basis since April 1992, with September 1992 industrial output being 9% higher than in September 1991, and industrial output in December 1992 expected to be 13% higher than in December 1991. In October 1992 modest industrial growth has resumed in Hungary. In November 1992 Keith Crane presented a Conference paper entitled "The end of the recession in Central and Eastern Europe", noting the Polish and Hungarian signs of recovery (though yet insufficient to reverse GDP decline for 1992 as a whole) and forecast the resumption of growth also in Bulgaria and in the Czech Republic (though the CSFR split will delay and slow down recovery; Crane 1992). The UN-ECE (1992) takes a much more pessimistic view of 1993 prospects for the whole area except for Poland. Romania, not to speak of the former Soviet Union and Albania, are still in the grips of deep recession, expected to continue well into 1993. The restructuring of productive capacity, inappropriate with respect to world and domestic demand, to technical choice and environmental protection, has hardly begun and is being delayed by drastic investment cuts (see Kolodko 1991a, b, 1992a; Nuti 1992a). In 1988–1991 gross fixed investment fell on average by about 37%, and in 1992 it continued to fall albeit at a much slower rate in Poland and the CSFR, while it fell precipitously in the former Soviet Union through 1992 (UN-ECE 1992). Such investment trends encourage a sober view of medium run sustainability of incipient recovery (Kolodko 1992b).

Production activities characterised by negative value added at current international prices, reputed to be of the order of as much as 20% to 25% of manufacturing in Poland, Hungary and the CSFR (Hughes and Hare 1991, 1992) and presumably accounting for an even higher proportion in the other economies,[2] have been cut but not eliminated and continue

[2] This is a consequence of the inefficiency of the system as a whole, due to inappropriate pricing, and not necessarily an indication of non-economic behaviour on the part of state enterprises, which had access to inputs—especially energy—priced well below world market levels relative to the price of their output.

to destroy resources, with financial losses covered no longer by subsidies but by the accumulation of tax arrears and of bad debts towards viable enterprises and the banking system. Private activities have grown fast but from too low a level to compensate for the decline recorded in the state sector, still predominant due to delays in privatisation. Changes in relative prices, including drastic falls in real wages, have created incentives for technical substitution and profitable expansion but the system has not responded to such incentives with the expected speed. Instead of the desired *supply response, supply inertia* has been the standard predicament of transitional economies.

14.2 Three Reactions: Incredulity, Complacency, Gradualism

The deep recession observed in all transitional economies has given rise to three kinds of reactions on the part of observers: incredulity (things are not as bad as they look), complacency (things are nearly as bad as they look but this is exactly how they should be), advocacy of gradualism (the course is correct but its speed is excessive).

The first reaction is exemplified by Andrew Berg (1992) and Berg and Sachs (1992): private sector growth is underrecorded, quality improvements of products are unrecorded, the living standards improvements due to the end of shortages and queues are totally excluded from national income accounting; dollar incomes—for instance in Poland where an initially over-devalued currency gradually appreciated up to overvalued levels—have actually grown.

This optimism is totally unwarranted. In order to significantly offset public sector decline the growth of the relatively small private sector would have to be massively under-recorded. On the contrary, although the *level* of private sector output may still be under-recorded, certainly it is significantly *less under-recorded now* than it was before it was legalised and encouraged, therefore the *growth* of the private sector must necessarily be, if anything, *over-recorded,* as previously illegal or unrecorded activities surface to be observed and are better counted. Moreover, the economists employed by new governments are better than their predecessors; they are also better at statistical cosmoses and index number manipulation.[3] The consumer surplus resulting from better access to markets is never recorded in national income accounting and there is no reason why it should be on this occasion, especially in view of the parallel unrecorded welfare losses due to unemployment and generalised insecurity. The growth of dollar incomes is no consolation to wage earners whose domestic purchasing power is reduced by domestic inflation being much faster than dollar inflation, and who in any case make purchases almost entirely in domestic currencies.

The second kind of reaction is exemplified by Stanislaw Gomulka (1991a, b): the recession is a disappointment and a "surprise" but what we are observing is a Schumpeterian process of "creative destruction", which is necessary to promote restructuring and subsequent growth. This argument may hold for some of the decline, namely for that due to reducing the large share of negative value added activities. But many of these activities have survived, and the observed output decline is greater than attributable to their reduction. There has been some overshooting, for instance of credit squeeze targets, with effects predictable to the point of not warranting surprises; some of the unemployment has often been Keynesian—i.e. generalised excess capacity without either excessive wages or an overvalued exchange rate. Most important, Schumpeterian "creative destruction" is the result of innovation, investment and competition, all phenomena which are scarcely present, if at all, in the transformation of post-communist economies. Destruction of the state sector has often been the result of a deliberate political design, in order to weaken the political strength of its managers as an organized interest group; "red barons"—for instance in Russia in 1992—might strain and slow down stabilisation and systemic transformation, but this is a typical ex-Soviet phenomenon not a general problem, and in any case there is no need to dress up this political strategy, costlier than more effective

[3] See for instance the treatment of the Polish 1991 budget deficit, over half of which was made invisible only to reappear at the beginning of 1992; or the prompt correction of the November 1991 Polish industrial production index to allow for the difference in working days with respect to November 1990 (both on a monthly and yearly basis)—a correction which for the construction sector reversed the direction, but which was not made on other occasions.

traditional political processes, with dubious euphemisms reminiscent of old-style propaganda.

The third reaction—advocacy of gradualism—is exemplified by Valtr Komarek in the CFSR (1992), and by the founding leader of the Russian Union of Industrialists and Entrepreneurs, Arkady Volsky (1992). In an article entitled "Economic shock therapy endangers the patients", Komarek writes: "The issue is one of time, not intent. East European economists agree on the need to establish market economies. The question is whether it should be done over two years or ten". Like many representatives of the opposition, he advocates gradualism instead; a similar position is taken in Russia by Volsky (1992), who argues for the resumption of price controls, exchange rate controls and forced surrender of export earnings, and continued though more selective ad-hoc subsidies to state enterprises: "The fundamental word is 'gradual', not 'landslide' transformation".

The range of available alternatives between gradualism and shock-therapy is significantly narrower than it is believed to be. On the one hand, a number of steps in stabilisation and reform can and must be nearly instantaneous: there is no conceivable justification for the postponement, by one single day, of the achievement of market clearing prices, a uniform exchange rate, decentralised foreign trade, the legalisation of private property and enterprise, and the beginning of privatisation. At the same time product subsidies, inflationary budget deficits, automatic credits to loss makers, and perfunctory interest rates, should come to an end as soon as possible. The dilution over time of these measures can only prolong the indignity and humiliation of queuing and shortages, inefficiency in foreign trade, the attenuation of incentives, and transform a price hike into an inflationary if not hyper-inflationary spiral; *a fortiori,* after painful measures of stabilisation, like those introduced in Russia in 1992, the reintroduction of subsidies, price and exchange rate controls (as advocated by Volsky), is a pointless and costly waste of sacrifices and time. In principle product price subsidies could be phased out gradually, in order to soften the blow of absolute and relative price changes on both producers and consumers. However for this to be a viable alternative it is necessary that: (i) the goods should be available in the quantities demanded at the subsidised prices; (ii) the budget should be in a position to finance those subsidies without higher inflationary strain due to monetisation of the budget deficit; (iii) the subsidies should not prevent at least the beginning of efficient substitution of subsidised goods in consumption and production; (iv) the unavoidable subsequent price increases should not trigger off an inflationary spiral prices/wages/prices. These considerations make a gradualist approach to the removal of subsidies somewhat problematic. Concern about the distribution effects of price increases should lead not to the preservation of product subsidies but to the introduction of more efficient income subsidies.

On the other hand, institution building can only be, and therefore must be, gradual, not out of choice but out of necessity: the process is time consuming. The counterproof of this proposition is the sheer uniqueness of the East German case, and the exceptional circumstances which have allowed East Germany to adopt at a stroke the legislation, jurisprudence, factor markets, currency, financial and monetary institutions, tax and tax collection, government administrators and government credibility—taking them from another country which happened to be nationally, linguistically and ethnically homogeneous, and to which it could surrender its sovereignty to reconstitute a previous existing national entity. The price was high,[4] but reunification was regarded as a priceless good in itself (see Siebert 1990a, b; Jackson 1991; Bryson 1992). If we seek a parallel with enterprise restructuring the German case resembles the restructuring of a weak enterprise not through internal reorganisation and rationalisation but through merger with or rather takeover by a stronger enterprise. Such instantaneous process is not repeatable except, perhaps not even in too distant a future, in the case of the two Koreas.[5] Everywhere else systemic change, no matter how fast, must necessarily be gradual: institution building and above all—the building of habits, reputations and trust—invariably takes time. Even mass privatisation i.e. the instantaneous, free of charge transfer of state assets to the population, does not and cannot lead to instantaneous capitalism, as the change in

[4] Transfers from West Germany amounted to $ 79 billion in 1991 and some $ 105 billion in 1992, more than double the amounts made available to the whole of Central-Eastern Europe and the Soviet Union (UN-ECE 1992). These large transfers were partly due to the need to rapidly bring real wages close to the West German level, in view of unrestricted labour mobility.

[5] China is a less likely occurrence, due to the marked asymmetry in the relative size of its two parts.

property titles has no effect on efficiency without the building of more complex and time-consuming institutions such as stock exchanges, bankruptcy procedures, competitive commercial banking, and the "primitive accumulation" of financial capital (see Nuti 1990).

In practice the only area where a significant choice between instantaneous or gradual transition is open to policy-makers is in the degree of protection to be granted to domestic producers. Trade decentralisation, trade opening and currency convertibility are enhanced by unrestricted free trade, but do not require it as an absolute precondition: they are achievable also with significant degrees of tariff protection. Unlike quotas and other non-tariff barriers, tariffs—like prices—are parametric instruments which do not suppress market response to changes in international demand and prices.[6] Temporary, uniform, non-discriminatory, relatively low tariffs have the advantage of raising revenue, alleviating the fiscal crisis that usually accompanies the transition. They also protect the output and employment of those enterprises which although unprofitable still produce a positive value added: many such enterprises do not cover their combined wage bill, amortisation and interest, and therefore are loss-making, but still make a positive contribution to national income and employment. Thus instant free trade, "the most liberal trade regime in the world" such as could be boasted at the inception of their programmes by Leszek Balcerowicz and Vaclav Klaus, respectively Finance Ministers of Poland and the CSFR, has a significant cost. Its main benefits are guidance in the search for new equilibrium prices in the chaotic move from macroeconomic and microeconomic disequilibrium to market clearing, and a stricter competition discipline of domestic producers, which can be important given the monopolistic and oligopolistic structure of state production and trade typical of the old system (see below, Sect. 14.5); but even tariffs allow some competitive discipline, together with the reference function of the world price system. At a time of systemic transition and capacity restructuring the net effect of unrestricted free trade, at least in the short-medium run, is not necessarily positive. Indeed there is now an increasing consensus, among academics (e.g.

[6] Even quotas, however, could be made parametric by auctioning import and export trade licences to the highest bidders.

McKinnon 1991; Williamson 1992; Portes 1992) and international organisations including the World Bank and even the IMF (see IMF 1992; Blejer and Gelb 1992), that some of the recession was the direct consequence of premature free trade. It is significant that Poland soon reintroduced some tariffs in order to be able to negotiate their reduction in its association agreement with the EC (November 1991), while in October 1992 the Polish government decided to introduce a temporary 6% import surcharge, not only with IMF blessing but apparently at IMF instigation, so as to raise additional revenue of almost 1% of GDP in order to reduce its budget deficit.

If premature free trade may have caused some of the recession, its impact has been amplified and prolonged by these economies' inability to respond quickly enough to the economic incentives and disincentives provided by greater trade opportunities, i.e. by supply inelasticity—which we have called inertia. The same inertia must account for these economies' inability to bounce back after absorbing the effects of external shocks (such as adverse terms of trade changes, reciprocal trade multiplier effects of simultaneous decline among trade partners) and of policy errors (such as initial overshooting). *Ultimately, therefore, much of the depth and persistence of the recession can be attributed to supply inertia.*

14.3 The Adjustment of Households, Private and State Enterprises

Different economic agents have different speeds of adjustment to the new incentives and disincentives activated by stabilisation and reform. Households are quickest to adjust to the new environment: they react swiftly to price increases through income and substitution effects, formulate reasonable if not rational inflationary expectations, substitute between domestic and foreign currencies, hoard or dishoard in response to relative yields of financial and real assets, and adjust labour supply and effort supply to real wages and to the changing degree of market imbalance. The end of the traditional over-valuation of the domestic currency, and of the equally traditional excess demand for goods at previously fixed prices, bring about a price rise that is compensated by money wage rises only partly and with a delay. The net impact of the households' adjustment in these conditions is negative on demand and indeterminate on their supply of labour and effort, while the potentially expansionary role of lower wages on output and exports depends on the supply response of private and state enterprises.

Private enterprises, through self-employment and old and new firms, respond to market incentives less promptly and less intensively than households. They have short time horizons due to long memories of past reversals both in government policies and in the state of market supplies; are reluctant to invest and therefore tend to favour trade, services and low capital-intensity activities, and to seek high short term returns in their pricing and investment behaviour. They are subject to rigid supply constraints especially for fixed assets (buildings, land, sometimes also capital goods); they respond more strongly to generalised contraction of demand than to relative price signals. Cooperatives may be subject to additional rigidities and even temptations of perverse response if they are at all concerned with maximisation of income per cooperative member. All private enterprises will suffer from poor access to risk capital due to lack of collateral, and from the difficulties of reaching from the start the minimum size necessary for their efficient operation, which may be quite high with respect to private agents' ability to raise and pool financial resources. In a capitalist economy most of the private sector growth comes from the growth of medium size firms, and from new firms founded by medium and large size private firms, whereas neither are available domestically in transitional economies. Hence the rather sluggish response of the domestic private sector to the new incentives provided by stabilization and reform.

This domestic vacuum can partly be filled by foreign direct investment and joint ventures; however these will be guided by the same short-term, trade-oriented, high-risk/high-mean-profit propensities of the domestic private sector, or will undertake purely "toe-in-the-water" small size strategic investments to establish a presence for their future potential expansion.[7] Private foreign capital cannot be expected to fully supplement the

[7] Foreign direct investment in five countries of Eastern Europe totalled $ 2.3 billion in 1991 and about $ 1.3 billion in the first half of 1992; most of it went to Hungary (48%) and CSFR (33%), and the flow remains very small with respect to foreign direct investment in developing countries, estimated at some $ 28 billion in 1991 (UN-ECE 1992).

sluggish response of domestic supply to the new incentives until after the transition, i.e. after the economy is stabilised and has fully implemented financial markets, ownership protection, a sound currency, and political stability (Hungarian relative success in attracting foreign investment shows that these factors are more important than formal convertibility of the domestic currency, which by the end of 1992 Hungary had not yet introduced). In other words, foreign private capital will speed up recovery once it has started, but should not be relied upon to "jump-start" the economy.

The main source of supply rigidities is the state sector. We know a great deal about state enterprise behaviour (for instance from Granick 1954, 1975; Berliner 1957, 1976; Izelt 1987; Portes 1969; Kornai 1986a, b; Hare 1990). All studies of pre-reform state enterprises stress behavioural rigidities, risk-aversion, hoarding, pursuit of physical and/or gross value indicators (*"kult vala"*; see Nove 1958), reluctance to innovate, and weakness of financial constraints. How will state enterprises respond to the replacement of commands by profit opportunities, of centralised supplies by horizontal contractual links, of softer by harder financial constraints?

A tentative answer to this question can be outlined with the help of recent empirical investigations (e.g. Jorgensen et al. 1990; Maj 1991; Schaffer 1992; Estrin et al. 1992; Pinto et al. 1992; Kotowicz-Jawor 1992; Standing 1992a, b). State enterprises will respond to tighter budget constraints, i.e. to harder money and the cuts in subsidies, by reducing activity levels; their craving for liquidity may lead them to seek export outlets, especially after substantial devaluations of the national currency, but they may be caught in a vicious circle. Namely, they need to import materials and equipment in order to promote their exports, but their import capacity is restricted by a weak domestic currency, harder money and high interest rates. The incentive to export may lead them to distress exports, i.e. characterised by low or even negative value added when inputs are valued at their replacement cost. Tight budget constraints and fear of bankruptcy, in any case, may induce managers at best to seek economic viability, i.e. a rate of return *sufficient* to service debt, not necessarily to pursue profit *maximisation.* Given the low and often negative real interest rate,[8] and the low leverage (due to past self-finance and past injections of free capital funds from the state budget), financial viability may be relatively easy to attain. Once their financial viability is ensured they may stop exploring new cost-saving opportunities generated by a change in relative prices, and continue to hold surplus employment and to waste materials and energy. Their time horizon will be short, in the turmoil of "shock treatment" stabilisation and liberalisation; the high rate of return on inventories (both financial and in terms of production flexibility) may continue to favour speculative hoarding relatively to production. At worst, managers will take advantage of their often high degree of monopoly power, holding back growth or even cutting production in line with monopoly prices; will gain command over real resources by holding back payment of deliveries, taxes, loan service; disinvest and finance higher wages by consuming their capital; and appropriate directly or indirectly the capital value of their enterprise through subcontracting, leases, sales (the so-called "wild" or "nomenklaura" privatisation). Hence the sluggish, sometimes comatose, supply response of the state sector in transitional economies.

An obvious remedy to this unfortunate state of affairs is privatisation; not, however, *nominal or cosmetic privatisation,* i.e. the facile transfer of ownership titles to private individuals and institutions, but *effective privatisation,* i.e. the additional activation of financial markets, liquidation and bankruptcy procedures, competitive commercial banking, regulatory and supervisory bodies. The trouble is that effective privatisation, even for the strongest, most stable, determined and unanimous government, takes a great deal of time. In the usual case of weak, frequently changing, undecided and divided governments, effective privatisation may take an inordinately long time. Hence the depth and persistence of recessionary trends in transitional economies.

The thesis put forward in this paper is that this state of affairs is not a necessary concomitant of transition, nor a consequence of "shock therapy" which might be eased by a more gradualist approach, but the totally unnecessary consequence of policy failures. Namely:

[8] In 1992 in Russia the point-to-point yearly rate of inflation was of the order of 2000%, while the monthly rate in November 1992 was about 25% to 30%; these rates correspond to a backward looking and forward looking real interest rate both of the order of –90%.

First, the failure to modify performance criteria and the structure of penalties and rewards for the managers of state enterprises—aggravated by the failure to announce and consistently implement a clear and coherent privatisation programme and, more generally, by uncertainty and non-credibility of government policies.

Second, the failure to speed up as a matter of absolute priority some of the measures of the reform package: anti-monopoly action, liquidation and bankruptcy discipline, financial restructuring of enterprises and banks.

Third, government mismanagement of the state sector: inappropriate, excessive, and discriminatory taxation of state enterprises; the continued redistribution of financial resources between profitable and unprofitable state enterprises though credit policy; neglect of intersectoral and inter-regional supply links (with cascade supply multiplier effects, and the real costs of *tatonnement* in search of new patterns of *recurring* supplies), including international supply links (i.e. lack of regional cooperation within ex-CMEA, ex-USSR, ex-CSFR, not to speak of ex-Yugoslavia).[9]

Some of these failures affect also the private sector directly or indirectly, i.e. through reciprocal state-private demand and supply conditions and the general economic environment; however the treatment of factors affecting specifically the supply response of the private sector is outside the scope of this paper.

To a very great extent, these failures are linked with ideological totems and taboos, namely obsession with mass free privatisation and with instant free trade, and prejudice against the state sector and any attempt at its improvement and reorganization, unchanged managerial penalties and rewards.

14.4 Unchanged Managerial Penalties and Rewards

Enterprise managers throughout the world derive direct and indirect utility from the size of their establishments, as measured by employment or capital or output, and the growth of these measures: apart from direct

[9] These propositions are developed further in Nuti and Portes (1993).

satisfaction, these variables affect status, salaries, and career opportunities. The primary difference between managers of joint stock companies and those of state enterprises (especially if operating in a centrally planned economy) is not one of organising ability, drive, initiative, and imagination, but in their incentive structure and operational environment. Managers of joint stock companies are induced to attach importance to profitability and to stock mart assesment of profitability prospects: profits are sought to self-finance and externally finance growth, to benefit from profit-linked bonuses and from the exercise of stock options, to protect managers from bankruptcy and from the potential threat of raiders who might replace them if they neglect opportunities for profits. Managers of state enterprises are not dependent on profit for their investment and growth, are safe from takeovers and bankruptcies, their incentives are geared to the degree of fulfillment of government objectives (in terms of output, employment, investment, prices, regional location, etc.). In addition, in the centrally planned economy state managers are input-constrained not demand-constrained, and have no control over prices.

Entrepreneurship, which was defined by Schumpeter (1950) as a combination of organisational skills and the ability to anticipate demand, is not absent in state enterprises, even in centrally planned economies; it is modified, oriented towards the security of supply sources rather than the penetration of market outlets, directed towards playing strategic games with central planners—anticipating *their* demands—instead of potential competitors and clients.

In the standard transitional set-up state managers are gradually liberated from central control. Their dependance from branch Ministries is loosened (in Hungary, this was already achieved in 1984–1985); direct commands are replaced first by government contracts (Russian *"goszakazy"* or Polish *"zamowienia rzadowe"*, voluntary but attractive because they involved guaranteed supplies of inputs and foreign exchange), then by contracts with suppliers and clients; their subsidies are cut but they can fix their own output prices. They have to search for new supply links and for new sales outlets; new and free market prices for inputs and outputs create opportunities for profitable input substitution and product differentiation. Their external financial resources from credit and budgetary allocations are squeezed; interest rates are raised substantially in nominal and real terms; fiscal pressure is made harsher.

State enterprise managers will certainly appreciate the new conditions and begin to adjust to them at once. But the performance of their enterprise is not judged by anyone according to their profitability, and there is no capital market to assess the value of enterprises as going concerns, nor are there potential raiders. Even if managers were concerned with bankruptcy constraints, they would continue to be motivated by preserving size—i.e. employment and output—and maintaining wage levels, far beyond the levels that would maximise the value of the enterprise, indeed right down to the point where the enterprise has zero net capital value—beyond which the bankruptcy constraint might begin to operate. In Poland and Russia managerial salaries are often a multiple of the average salary of enterprise employees; this is a clear inducement not only to pay-out after-tax value added as wages, but to consume capital, paying wages also out of amortisation funds. The bankruptcy constraint, if felt, will force the reduction of loss-making activities, but once that constraint is met those activities will continue, cross-subsidised from other parts of the same enterprise, out of concern for the size of employment. But there will not be much profit, or even amortisation funds, available for reinvestment. Hence the simultaneous maintenance of some non-viable activities and the failure to invest in new or modernised capacity. This tendency will be reinforced by general uncertainty about government policies, and by specific uncertainty about privatisation: i.e. about whether or not the enterprise will be privatised, when, whether through direct sale or free distribution, with or without a privileged treatment of employees.

The simple transfer of ownership is unlikely to induce more efficient behaviour on the part of enterprise managers until they are subject to effective control on the part of financial markets, through the exercise of shareholders' voting rights, their sale together with the sale of shares and the associated threat of hostile takeovers. Neither the dispersion of shares across a large number of private shareholders, nor the concentration of shares in investment trusts is bound to implement such effective control: diffused share ownership will leave managers still quite comfortable in the exercise of their discretionary powers, while there is no reason to expect that investment trusts owned by a large number of uninformed investors will behave differently from the state holdings which have been rejected (perhaps wrongly? see Kumar 1992) as inadequate forms of "subjectivisation" of ownership. Moreover, even if privatised state enterprises were instantly more responsive, privatisation will make those enterprises which have not been privatised even less responsive than they may have been in the past, because of additional uncertainties about the timing of further privatisation and about how managerial performance is going to be assessed and rewarded or penalised. The only managerial inducement to maximise profits in not-yet-privatised state enterprises is the hope of a merger with a joint venture or of a sale to a foreign company; even then managers' efforts may be diverted to strip assets to their own advantage rather than to maximise the return on the assets in their firm's possession. On balance, until privatisation has reached a critical mass its net effect on the bulk of former state enterprises may very well be negative rather than positive.

14.5 Slow Implementation of Essential Reform

The adverse effects of an unchanged incentive structure are amplified by the usually slow progress of essential reform steps, namely the break-up of monopoly power; the implementation of liquidation and bankruptcy procedures; the financial restructuring of enterprises and banks.

(i) Typically, centrally planned economies were characterised by extremely high industrial concentration, with single-product producers and producer associations responsible for supplying not only domestic markets but often the entire CMEA and exports to the rest of the world (see Newbery and Kattuman 1992). Once enterprises are given decisional autonomy about their pricing and output, the monopoly and oligopoly power built into such industrial concentration and specialisation is bound to exacerbate inflationary and recessionary trends. The need for competition to ensure a sizeable supply response has been emphasised by Michael Burda (1991) and has led to calls for front loaded trade liberalisation and convertibility (Newbery 1991).

The adverse impact of monopoly needs some qualifications. On the one hand, the temptation to maximise monopoly profit *per employee,* which might be present without a change in managerial performance criteria and incentives, is bound to encourage a more monopolist behaviour than that of an ordinary monopolist maximising the absolute level of profits (Meade 1972). On the other hand, once the structure of managerial incentives has been adjusted to the new system (see Sect. 14.7 below), even monopolies will still respond to changes in demand and cost conditions, economising dearer inputs and raising the level of more profitable outputs. Therefore "entrepreneurial" enterprises, though monopolistic, are more flexible than unchanged state enterprises which, though stripped of their monopoly power, remain old-style inert administrative units. However, during the process of stabilisation, if we abstract from relative price changes,[10] the move from low-profit near-full capacity output to a monopoly-profit lower-level output is undoubtedly recessionary, whereas a move to a new competitive equilibrium would have been less recessionary or possibly not recessionary at all (depending on the relative position of initial and competitive output levels). Moreover, the anti-inflationary monetary policy pursued by the government, together with the price rise involved in monopolistic behaviour, and the high wages that might be paid including an element of monopoly profit,[11] are also recessionary.

(ii) Delays in the implementation of liquidation and bankruptcy procedures[12] are responsible for enterprises being able to pursue with impunity policies of greater disinvestment than those allowed by a solvency constraint, for the purpose of maintaining higher wages

[10] I.e. we postulate that cost and demand curves remain unchanged in real terms. Relative price changes complicate the picture but do not introduce a systematic bias in the relative position of the new competitive equilibrium with respect to the initial output level.

[11] A special form of monopoly profit may be the exclusive or privileged access to under-priced non-reproducible natural resources.

[12] On the specific problems of implementing bankruptcy procedures in transitional economies see Aghion et al. (1992).

and higher, non-economic employment than otherwise would be the case. The lack of liquidation and bankruptcy procedures also enables enterprises to indefinitely postpone the payment of debt-service to banks, of goods and services to suppliers, of tax to the state budget. Arrears towards the state budget and banks are equivalent to a monetary expansion,[13] whereas inter-enterprise arrears involve a redistribution of profit from viable enterprises with a growth potential to non-viable enterprises which use it to sustain non-economic employment and output: the same process of inflationary disinvestment occurs as a result (Nuti 1992b).[14]

(iii) The enforcement of liquidation and bankruptcy procedures requires the prior financial restructuring of enterprises and banks; otherwise it might lead to the destruction of activities which, although unable to make enough profit to service past debts—incurred under a different system and therefore to be disregarded—have a present value as going concerns higher than their liquidation value. Thus inviable activities should be closed down and bankrupted, viable activities should if necessary be recapitalised through new capital injections or debt cancellation, with banks also recapitalised to make up for cancelled debt (Nuti 1992b). Recapitalisation of state enterprises and banks is a net claim on the state budget, in competition with other claims, in consideration of which it may have to be postponed; however a case ought to be made for postponement rather than for early recapitalization.[15]

[13] Of course inter-enterprise arrears do put pressure on monetary authorities to expand the money supply in order to extend credit to them: see the credit concessions granted by the Governor of the Russian Central Bank, Viktor Gerashchenko, to Russian enterprises in mid-1992. However this is not the same thing as arrears *being* automatic additions to the money supply.

[14] Not all inter-enterprise arrears are necessarily bad loans. Let us call "primary arrears" the excess, if any, of an enterprise's overdue debts over its overdue credits, and "secondary arrears" all its other overdue debts (i.e. that part of its overdue debts which is covered—or more than covered—by its overdue credits). Then only primary arrears can be bad debts, and even those may partly reflect a problem of liquidity and not one of solvency.

[15] Begg and Portes (1992) argue that recapitalisation makes no difference to the net wealth of the state "if properly accounted". Of course in a trivial sense the payment of any debt makes no difference to anybody's net wealth, whether creditor or debtor, but all the same debt repayment is a net claim on the debtor's current cash flow. Thus recapitalisation either is a net injection of liquidity into the system, or crowds out other forms of expenditure.

14.6 Government Mismanagement of the State Sector

Beside the policy omissions listed above, governments of transitional economies have undertaken active policies which account for the further promotion of state enterprise supply inertia.

(i) State enterprises have been subjected to inappropriate, excessive, discriminatory taxation. The tax basis has often been inappropriate, because unrelated to enterprise performance. Such is the nature of the Polish so-called "dividend", which is levied regardless of actual profits and of required reinvestment finance and is therefore not a dividend at all, but a tax geared to the state equity stake in enterprise capital, revalued in line with inflation—a historical accident. Another inappropriate form of enterprise taxation is that on excess wage payments over and above mildly indexed guidelines (Polish PPWW or *"Popiwek"*, and a similar tax in Hungary; the highest rates are levied in the CSFR). After the initial exaggerated and unintended real wage fall due to higher than expected inflation, the unavoidable recovery of real wages has turned excess-wage tax into an inflation-multiplier by raising money wage costs of enterprises by a multiple of the money wage increase successfully claimed by workers to recover some of the excessive initial real losses. Through this mechanism the *Popiwek* tax is bound to have sometimes amplified cost-inflation.

State enterprise taxation has also been often excessive: in the first 11 months of 1991 with respect to the corresponding period of 1990 in Poland the total tax burden as a percentage of gross profits in state enterprises had gone from 50.6% to 106.4%, i.e. absorbed more than the total gross profits; profit tax rose from 37.7% to 53.4% of gross profits, while the relative weight of both "dividend" tax and excess-wage tax had increased considerably (respectively from 7.4% to 21.5%, and from 5.6% to 29.7%). A sectoral breakdown of such tax burden gives percentages of gross profits of 200% or more in coal (291.7%), iron and steel (382.5%), electromachinery (249.0%), light industry (200.0%). It is no wonder that, in such conditions, amortisation funds become the primary source of state enterprise investment (Kotowicz-Jawor 1992). At that point a positive supply response becomes impossible not because of non-entrepreneurial behaviour of state enterprises, but because of their deliberate crippling by government policy.

State enterprise taxation has also been discriminatory: in Poland neither *Popiwek* nor capital taxes have been levied on private enterprises, which also explains the differential supply response of the two sectors. In 1991 (first eleven months) the tax burden on Polish private industrial enterprises has been 54.9% of gross profits, instead of the 126.4% burden of state enterprises (Kotowicz-Jawor 1992). Similar privileges are accorded to the private sector in other transitional economies, contributing to a generalised fiscal crisis. Of course the traditional penalisation of the private sector should have been ended, to put both sectors on an equal footing; but government policy has been reversed, with undoubted adverse effects on the efficiency of resource allocation. What is striking, however, is not only the tax differential but also the inordinately high fiscal pressure on private profits—another factor frustrating recovery.[16]

(ii) At the same time, cross subsidisation within the state enterprise sector has continued in practice, no longer through fiscal policy, i.e. lump sum and product subsidies (though enterprises have been allowed to accumulate unpaid tax bills), but through monetary policy. Namely, credit-worthy state enterprises have been subjected to indiscriminate cuts in their access to funds, while ailing state enterprises (even in the CSFR, and even notoriously unviable enterprises, for instance in the aluminium industry) have still continued to benefit from generous credits or from official acquiescence to the

[16] By comparison, in the European Community direct taxes on enterprise revenue and capital, as a percentage of gross operating surplus, averaged 12.3% in 1990 and 11.4% in 1991 (for the aggregate of state and private, financial and non-financial enterprises), ranging on average in 1991 from 6.0% in Belgium to 25.1% in the UK.

build-up of unpaid interest and amortisation on their outstanding loans.

(iii) Finally, there has been a neglect of the preservation of essential intersectoral and inter-regional supply links. Switching from direct or indirect (through government purchases) central allocation to direct contracts between enterprises, short-term profit opportunities have been pursued at the expense of longer term supply links. The initially gross under-valuation of the currency, induced to support convertibility, has diverted to exports output which could not be internationally competitive in the medium-long run, disrupting traditional supply lines and leading to either unused capacity due to input shortages or to "distress imports" of crucial components—often the same which were the object of "distress exports". While there is only anecdotic evidence of such phenomena, whose quantitative impact cannot be assessed, there is strong reason to believe that the disruption of international supply links—within ex-CMEA, ex-USSR, ex-CSFR, ex-Yugoslavia—has been a significant factor in the recession. The gains of political and economic independence have had a tangible cost in terms of mutual cumulative losses due to falls in the volume of transactions, especially with the switch to trade settlement in scarce hard currencies (see van Brabant 1992; Rodrik 1992a, b).

14.7 Policy Implications

The supply inertia deriving from the factors discussed above is a distinctive feature of the stabilisation and liberalisation experience of post-communist economies with respect to otherwise fairly similar attempts of developing countries, also undertaking stabilisation, privatisation and deregulation on a smaller scale. The costs of transition—over and above the legacy of the old system, premature free trade, deflationary overshooting—are to a great extent the result of neglecting such *"differentia specifica"*, which is only beginning to be researched by the economics profession.[17] These costs could and should have been and still may be contained, by tackling systemic inertia and tailoring economic policies to the degree of success in restoring system vitality. This involves *not slowing down or reversing the path of transition,* as argued by most of the critics of stabilisation and reform plans, *but speeding up some of it, altering some of the policies in directions which mostly have been barred by ideology, and paying more attention to the sequencing of those reform steps which necessarily take time to implement.*

On or before day 1 of the shock treatment, state enterprises could be turned into joint stock companies (which can be done overnight). Managers could be asked to attach a value to their companies at which they would be exposed to privatisation if bidders came along, and on which they would have to make a normal rate of profit thereafter (including subsequent capital growth), obtaining a prefixed share of profits above that norm (for an illustration of such procedure see Nuti 1988). Employees could be given a year's wage worth of shares at that valuation, transferable to other holders gradually over the following five years. This set up would expose managers to a discipline equivalent to that of their capitalist counterparts: they would benefit from profitability, reinvestment and growth, and they would be subject to takeover of physical assets if their own valuation was too low; employees would not have the same incentives to press for distribution of profits and assets as they have otherwise; in due course the development of a stock exchange—which could progress at the same time—would strengthen this incentive structure and bring it closer to the standards of advanced market economies. There must be a presumption that these changes would improve the performance and supply response of state enterprises, without any prejudice for

[17] See for instance Norman (1992), reviewing the Amex Bank Review Prize Essays by Richard Rose, Michael Dooley and Peter Isard, Sweder van Wijnbergen (in Dooley et al., 1992, forthcoming). Rose argues the need for constructing a "civil economy" and "the rule of law" in the region, involving legislation on property rights, enforcement of contracts, security of investments. Michael Dooley and Peter Isard argue that special care must be given to institutions, incentives and planning: "Although we have great respect for the power of markets to help countries in transition join the rest of the world in the benefits of market oriented institutions, we see great danger in overlooking the non-market institutional structure upon which markets depend"; employment contracts, banking regulations, bankruptcy laws, payments systems "typically receive little attention in discussion of macroeconomic policy design". Van Wijnbergen argues that "Eastern Europe is not well served with straight textbook advice".

either the progress of privatisation, which could still go on at the maximum practicable speed, and for the development of financial markets.

Monopolistic behaviour can be checked by external competition, even for a moderate degree of tariff protection; by splitting enterprise associations and multi-plant enterprises, which can be done fairly quickly; by setting upper price limits not administratively but with direct reference to world price levels. In the delays of implementing liquidation and bankruptcy procedures, disinvestment can be prevented by legal obligations to maintain the level of enterprise real capital (assessed as indicated above, and not on the basis of historical capital, even if revalued in line with inflation).[18] The accumulation of inter-enterprise arrears can be prevented by the automatic application of punitive interest rates on such arrears (as attempted in Hungary, though at too low a rate to make a significant difference), or by the outright imposition of a cash prepayment constraint (as established but only partially enforced in Russia in mid-1992).

Recapitalisation of state enterprises and banks—which for instance in Poland is coming to the fore only two-three years after the beginning of its stabilisation and reform programme—should be an early and urgent undertaking, worthier of Western support than the achievement of formal convertibility at fixed exchange rates.

State enterprise taxation can be levied on indicators of actual performance, at rates that allow enough reinvestable profits to enable enterprises to finance restructuring directly and through external funds, on an equal footing with the private sector. Their access to finance should neither be automatic, nor automatically barred, but based upon an evaluation of their general credit-worthiness (after the revaluation of enterprise capital and the recapitalisation mentioned above) and of the prospective present value of investment projects for which funds are being sought.

The disruption of essential intersectoral and inter-regional supply flows could be avoided domestically by the diffusion of greater information about enterprise input requirements, without reinstating any administrative planning machinery, and perhaps by giving long-standing large-scale buyers a pre-emption right to domestic supplies. Internationally,

---

[18] This kind of obligation was typical of the old-style Yugoslav enterprise; see Uvalić (1992).

the simple introduction of automatic multilateral clearing, i.e. the transferability of bilateral trade balances among trade partners within former trade blocs,[19] even without attempting anything as ambitious as a payment mechanism such as the post-War European Payments Union,[20] could help preserve or restore those trade flows which—given the sunken costs of past good and bad investments—still correspond at least temporarily to comparative advantages.

Bibliography

Aghion, Philippe, Oliver Hart and J. Moore (1992). The economics of bankruptcy reform, *Discussion Paper* no. 933, Centre for Economic Performance, LSE, London, August.

Begg, David and Richard Portes (1992). Enterprise debt and economic transformation: financial restructuring of the state sector in Central and Eastern Europe, *CEPR Working Paper* no. 695, London, June.

Berg, Andrew (1992). A critique of official data, IMF/World Bank Conference on the Macroeconomic Situation in Eastern Europe, Washington, 4-5 June.

Berg, Andrew and Jeffrey Sachs (1992). Structural adjustment and international trade in Eastern Europe: the case of Poland, *Economic Policy*, 15.

Berliner, J. (1957). *Factory and Manager in the USSR*, Harvard University Press, Cambridge, Mass.

Berliner, J. (1976). *The Innovation Decision in Soviet Industry*, MIT Press, Cambridge, Mass.

[19] Trade among former Soviet republics, in particular, has been disrupted by two totally unnecessary factors: (i) the continuation of state purchase orders for the implementation of inter-state trade agreements (prices are fixed at too low a level and orders are not fulfilled); (ii) the irrationality and instability of republican monetary regimes, amounting to a combination of roubles, rouble substitutes circulating in parallel, new republican currencies, together with the continued segmentation of monetary circulation between cash and non-cash circuits. The additional segmentation, from 1 July 1992, of rouble means of payments in republican Correspondent Accounts with the Russian Central Bank (which can be used to pay for net imports from Russia) and ordinary roubles, has effectively ended the rouble zone; see Nuti (1992c).

[20] An EPU-type mechanism would involve, in addition to automatic multilateral clearing, also mutual credits, trade partners' discipline preventing large scale surpluses and deficits, and a large scale injection of external aid.

Blejer, Mario I. and Alan Gelb (1992). The contraction of Eastern Europe's economies: introduction to a conference, IMF/World Bank Conference on the Macroeconomic Situation in Eastern Europe, Washington, 4-5 June.

Bryson, Phillip J. (1992). The economics of German reunification: a review of the literature, *Journal of Comparative Economics,* 16, pp. 118-149.

Burda, Michael (1991). Labour and product markets in Czechoslovakia and the ex-GDR: a twin study, *European Economy,* Special Issue, June.

Crane, Keith (1992). The end of the recession in Central and Eastern Europe", PlanEcon Inc., DRI/McGraw-Hill and ENI, The Economic Transition of Eastern Europe and the Former Soviet Republics: A Business Outlook Conference, Rome, 17-19 November.

Dooley, Michael et al (1992). *Finance and the International Economy — Amex Bank Review Prize Essays,* OUP, Oxford.

Estrin, Saul, Mark Schaffer and Inderjit Singh (1992). Enterprise adjustment in transition economies: Czechoslovakia, Hungary and Poland, Conference on Economic Transition in Post-communist Economies, CEP-LSE, London, 28-29 September.

Gomulka, Stanislaw (1991a). Polish economic reform: principles, policies and surprises, Conference Paper, Jerusalem, April.

Gomulka, Stanislaw (1991b). Tworcza destrukcja, *Zycie Gospodarcze,* 18, 5 May, pp. 1 & 6-7.

Granick, D. (1954). *Management of the Industrial Firm in the USSR, A Study in Soviet Economic Planning,* Columbia University Press, New York.

Granick, D. (1975). *Enterprise Guidance in Eastern Europe,* Princeton University Press, New Jersey.

Hare, Paul (1990). Reform of enterprise regulation in Hungary: from 'tutelage' to market, *European Economy,* 43, March, pp. 35-54.

Hughes, Gordon and Paul Hare (1991). Competitiveness and industrial restructuring in Czechoslovakia, Hungary and Poland, *European Economy,* Special Issue no. 2, pp. 83-110.

Hughes, Gordon and Paul Harc (1992). Industrial restructuring in Eastern Europe: policies and prospects, *European Economic Review,* 36, pp. 670-676.

IMF European Department (1992). Review of experience with programs in Eastern Europe, 30 June.

Izelt, Annamaria, Ed. (1987). *Developments in a Spiritless Age of Reform: A Case Studies of 1 Polish and 5 Hungarian Enterprises 1981-87,* Tervgdasagi Forum, Budapest.

Jackson, Marvin (1991). One year after German economic union: are there lessons to be learned?, Report on Eastern Europe, 28 June, Munich, pp. 43-48.
Jorgensen, Erika A., Alan Gelb and Inderjit Singh (1990). Life for Polish firms under the 'Big Bang': preliminary findings from a field trip, Conference Paper, The World Bank, Poltusk (Poland), October.
Kolodko, Grzegorz W. (1991a). Polish hyperinflation and stabilisation. A year after, *Rivista di Politica Economica,* June, pp. 289-330.
Kolodko, Grzegorz W., Ed. (1991b). *Polityka finansowa-stabilizacja-transformacja,* Instytut Finansow, Warsaw.
Kolodko, Grzegorz W. (1992a). Stabilisation, recession and growth in post-socialist economy, Institute of Finance, *Working Papers* No. 9, Warsaw.
Kolodko, Grzegorz W. (1992b). From output collapse to sustainable growth in transition economies - The fiscal implications, mimeo, IMF, Washington, December.
Komarek, Valtr (1992). Economic shock therapy endangers the patients, *International Herald Tribune,* 7 January.
Kornai, J. (1986a). The soft budget constraint, *Kyklos,* 39, 1, pp. 3-30.
Kornai, J. (1986b). The Hungarian reform process: visions, hopes and reality, *Journal of Economic Literature,* 24, December, pp. 1687-1737.
Kotowicz-Jawor, Joanna (1992). Ocena sytuacji finansowej predsiebiorstw przemyslowych, in IRiSS 1992, pp. 122-134.
Kumar, Anjali (1992). *Public Enterprises in Transition? The State Holding Company,* The World Bank, Washington, July; forthcoming, MacMillan 1993.
Lipton, D. and J. Sachs (1990). Creating a market economy in Eastern Europe: the case of Poland, *Brookings Papers on Economic Activity,* Washington.
Maj, Henryka (1991). Proces dostowan mikroekonomicznych. Reakcje przedsiebiorstw w warunkach polityki stabilizacyjnej, in Kolodko 1991b.
McKinnon, Ronald (1991). *The Order of Economic Liberalisation,* Johns Hopkins Press, Baltimore MD.
Meade, J.E. (1972). The theory of labour managed firms and of profit sharing, *Economic Journal,* 82, pp. 402-28.
Newbery, David M. (1991). Reform in Hungary: sequencing and privatisation, *European Economic Review,* 35, pp. 571-580.
Newbery, David M. and Paul Kattuman (1992). Market concentration and competition in Eastern Europe, *CEPR Working Paper* no. 664, London, April.
Norman, Peter (1992). Sober views of the legacy of communism, *Financial Times,* 9 November.

Nove, Alec (1958). The problem of success indicators in Soviet industry, *Economica.*

Nuti, D. Mario (1988). Competitive valuation and efficiency of capital investment in the socialist economy. *European Economic Review,* 32, 1988, pp. 2-6.

Nuti, D. Mario (1990). Privatisation of socialist economies: general issues and the Polish case, in Hans Bloomenstein and Michael Marrese, Eds., 1990, *The Transformation of Planned Economies,* OECD, Paris.

Nuti, D. Mario (1992a). Lessons from stabilisation and reform in Central and Eastern Europe, *Economic Papers* No. 92, CEC-DGII, Brussels, May.

Nuti, D. Mario (1992b). The role of the banking sector in the process of privatisation, *Economic Papers* No. 98, CEC-DGII, Brussels, November.

Nuti, D. Mario (1992c). Monetary disintegration in theory and in the ex-Soviet area, Conference on the Costs and Benefits of Independence, University of Trento, 10-12 December.

Nuti, D. Mario and Richard Portes (1993). Economic, social and political transformation of Czechoslovakia, Hungary and Poland, forthcoming as *CEPR Discussion Paper.*

Pinto, Brian, Marek Belka and Stefan Krajewski (1992) Microeconomics of transformation in Poland: a survey of state enterprise responses, *Working Papers,* The World Bank, September.

Portes, Richard D. (1969). The enterprise under central planning, *Review of Economic Studies,* 36, 2.

Portes, Richard I. (1992). Is there a better way?, *International Economic Insights,* May/June 1992, pp. 18-22.

Rodrik, Dani (1992a). Making sense of the Soviet trade shock in Eastern Europe: a framework and some estimates, IMF/World Bank, May.

Rodrik, Dani (1992b). Foreign trade in Eastern Europe's transition: early results, *CEPR Working Paper* no. 676, London, June.

Schaffer, Mark (1992). The Polish state-owned enterprises sector and the recession in 1990, *Comparative Economic Studies,* 34, 1, Spring

Schumpeter, J. A. (1950). *Capitalism, Socialism and Democracy* (3rd edition), Allen and Unwin, London.

Siebert, Horst (1990a). The economic integration of Germany, *Discussion Paper* no. 160, Kiel Institute of World Economics, May.

Siebert, Horst (1990b). The economic integration of Germany - an update, *Discussion Paper* no. 160a, Kiel Institute of World Economics, September.

Standing, Guy (1992a). Employment dynamics of Russian industry, Conference on Employment Restructuring in Russian Industry, ILO, Moscow and St Petersburg, 21-28 October.

Standing, Guy (1992b). Labour market dynamics in Russian industry in 1992: results from the second round of the RLFS, Conference on Employment Restructuring in Russian Industry, ILO, Moscow and St Petersburg, 21-28 October.

UN-ECE (1992). Overview and policy issues, *Economic Bulletin for Europe,* 44, Geneva, November.

Uvalić, Milica (1992). *Investment and Property Rights in Yugoslavia,* CUP, Cambridge.

van Brabant, Josef (1992). The new East, preferred trade regimes, and designing the transition, Arne Ryde Symposium on The Transition Problem, Rungsted Kyst, Denmark, 11-12 June.

Volsky, Arkady (1992). Prudent policy can help us curb the crisis, *Rabochaya Tribuna,* 29 September.

Williamson, John (1992). Why did output fall in Eastern Europe?, Arne Ryde Symposium on The Transition Problem, Rungsted Kyst, Denmark, 11-12 June.

15

How Quickly Should Convertibility Be Introduced? Comment

Domenico Mario Nuti

The usual role of a discussant is to stir up controversy, but the two papers in this chapter appear to take positions that are so far apart that instead I shall try to be conciliatory. When and how fast should currency convertibility be introduced in the Eastern European economies? Friedrich Levcik's answer is that it should be introduced fairly late in the process of transition to a market economy, which process should take place gradually over a period of three to five years; another five years will be needed before these countries become eligible for EC membership. According to Jacques Polak, convertibility should come early and fast, almost as fast as

Published in John Williamson (Ed.), (1991) *Currency Convertibility in Eastern Europe* (Washington D.C., Institute for International Relations) originated from a conference hosted and financed by the Austrian National Bank in Vienna in January 1991. Mario Nuti was discussant of two papers presented in the session on "How quickly should convertibility be introduced", by Jacques J. Polak, "Convertibility: An Indispensable Element in the Transition Process in Eastern Europe", and Friedrich Levcik, "The Place of Convertibility in the Transformation Process".

D. M. Nuti (✉)
La Sapienza, University of Rome, Rome, Italy
e-mail: milica.uvalic@unipg.it

© The Author(s), under exclusive license to Springer Nature Switzerland AG 2023

S. Estrin, M. Uvalic (eds.), *Collected Works of Domenico Mario Nuti, Volume I*, Studies in Economic Transition, https://doi.org/10.1007/978-3-031-12334-4_15

advocated by Czechoslovak Finance Minister Vaclav Klaus, who said in his oral presentation at the conference, "There is no convertibility problem—all there is to do is declare it."

Although the two papers appear to be far apart, they are in fact quite complementary. Polak treats the Eastern European economies as if they were ordinary less developed countries, whereas Levcik addresses precisely their system-specific features. However, there remains an irreducible difference between them: that difference concerns the costs involved in speeding the course of transition, which Polak neglects and Levcik strongly emphasizes.

Some reflections on the nature of money in the traditional Soviet-type system and on the very important consequences of its lack of convertibility should help to highlight both the need for and the difficulties involved in establishing convertibility. Three main preconditions to convertibility can be inferred, and a rush to convertibility before they are satisfied involves specific costs, which neither EPU-type arrangements (considered by Polak) nor a parallel currency (see below) can really alleviate. Convertibility, like most reforms, should be thought of as an investment—a good one, but, like all investments, in need of finance.

The nature of money in a Soviet-type system can be understood by an analogy. Imagine a lottery where tickets give a recurring entitlement to weekly prizes, with a probability p of winning a prize at each draw. The tickets are similar to British premium bonds but differ from them in three respects: they are not redeemable; winning tickets get a prize equal to their face value instead of a multiple of it; the probability p decreases over time. Only a fool would actually buy such tickets, for at best one would only recover one's stake.

Now, however, imagine an economic system in which these lottery tickets are used as money, in fact the only money for the payment of weekly incomes, with only winning tickets giving access to the purchase of goods and services, at prices that are pre-fixed in terms of the units in which the tickets are denominated. Sellers, by law but grudgingly, pass on the winning tickets they receive to the lottery organizers in exchange for new lottery tickets. People who do not have winning tickets to spend can still exchange their nonwinning tickets for goods and services at a price approximating lip of the price applied to winning tickets. Tickets may instead be deposited, in which case they do not take part in the draw but receive an interest paid in additional lottery tickets; the rate of interest is lower than the rate at which the probability p of a prize falls over time.

Lottery tickets in general, and especially those of this peculiarly unattractive kind, are very bad candidates for fulfilling the role of money. They lack all the desirable attributes of money, such as certainty of current purchasing power, stability of that power over time, and liquidity; even if they were decreed to be legal tender they would presumably be increasingly replaced by better candidates, such as nonperishable divisible objects with a more certain and stable purchasing power, from cigarettes to hard foreign exchange. Nobody ever designed such an absurd, grotesque monetary system. Yet the system described is precisely equivalent to a traditional monetary system of the Soviet type, with $p = (1 - h)$, where h is the domestic currency overhang expressed as a share (increasing over time) of the total quantity of money.[1]

Rubles, the Romanian leu, and the Bulgarian leva[2] increasingly resemble such lottery tickets, and are progressively being displaced by dollars, deutsche marks, and packages of Marlboros, with unlucky holders having to part with more notes than the lucky ones have to pay for their purchases. The Czechoslovak koruna, the East German mark, and the Hungarian forint never moved quite as far in that direction, whereas the Polish zloty—until the 1990 stabilization—went even further: in Poland repressed inflation at times coexisted with open hyperinflation.

[1] Some may regard this characterization as an exaggeration of the defects of monetary systems of the Soviet type, but in fact Soviet-type money is even worse than this analogy indicates, in several respects. First, in the actual Soviet system, enterprises can only spend money if it is accompanied by plan documents approving the transaction; it is in this sense that Joseph Berliner talks of a "documonetary" system in the socialist economies. Second, there are two separate circuits for inter-enterprise transactions and for payments to and from the population; these are, at least in theory, strictly insulated from each other. Third, on the very day this comment was presented, the Soviet authorities confiscated high-denomination (50 and 100 rubles) banknotes beyond a small personal allowance (200 rubles, although this was later raised in some of the republics). The effect of this, in terms of the lottery analogy, was to inflict large, random, negative prizes on the holders of these peculiar lottery tickets.

[2] Until the IMF-backed Bulgarian stabilization program of February 1991. In April 1991 the Romanian monetary overhang also decreased following price increases and devaluation.

The monetary arrangement just described has nothing whatever to do with socialism—it is a policy-related, not a system-related phenomenon—except that it has been associated for so long with the socialist system as to be difficult to separate from it. The policy in question is a lethal combination of monetary indiscipline, due mostly to overambition and to the lack of any prior consensus about the allocation of available resources, and to a misguided, blind, and obtuse commitment to price stability at all costs. This policy is ultimately responsible for the Soviet and Eastern European economic catastrophe: for the endemic and growing shortages; for queueing and empty shops, black markets, corruption, and the emergence of a mafia; for near-famine conditions in some areas; and for the disintegration of both the CMEA and the Soviet Union itself. None of this would have happened if the ruble had been a hard and convertible currency.

To turn a centrally planned economy, with its state enterprises executing central commands and its banks issuing the equivalent of Monopoly money, into a market economy, the peculiar lottery tickets have to be turned into ordinary money as we know it, and enterprises have to be transformed from administrative agencies into profit-maximizing, entrepreneurial entities. Levcik deals with the difficulties of consolidating money and reforming enterprises. Polak takes it for granted that in Eastern Europe "money" is money and "enterprises" are enterprises, and hurries on to the next stage, that of convertibility.

For any exchange rate policy to be effective, let alone for convertibility[3] to work, three preconditions must be satisfied: first, there must be market-clearing prices (i.e., no shortages, or what is sometimes called commodity convertibility) under nonhyperinflationary or at least not excessively

[3] I refer to convertibility by residents for current account transactions, what in Poland and Czechoslovakia is now called "internal convertibility"; this differs slightly from the IMF Article VIII definition, which includes also debt service. Here it is worth noting that the specific features of Eastern European experience have led to a change in conventional terminology, for "internal convertibility," "resident convertibility," and "commodity convertibility." Normally, countries treat nonresidents at least as favorably as residents, and therefore internal convertibility presumes external convertibility; however, in Eastern Europe nonresidents may be subject to stricter conditions than residents. Usually commodity convertibility is understood to include convertibility also into imported commodities, i.e., to imply internal convertibility other than financial convertibility; in Eastern Europe, on the other hand, the frequent presence of a monetary overhang leads to use the term "commodity convertibility" to indicate simply the lack of such an overhang and the presence of market-clearing prices. Jacques Polak uses the traditional terminology, whereas Friedrich Levcik and I follow the more recent usage peculiar to Eastern Europe.

inflationary conditions; second, there must be no generalized subsidies on tradeable goods and services; third, there must be a significant price elasticity of demand and supply. Failure to satisfy the first two conditions explains why transferable-ruble balances were never transferable even within the CMEA, let alone convertible: shortages create a sellers' market in which enterprises have no incentive to export; subsidies lead to a transfer of domestic resources abroad through the export of subsidized goods, which are all the more likely to be in shortage; thus the prospect of exporting goods that are subsidized or in short supply leads to the imposition of export bans or quotas, and the transferability of ruble balances becomes subject to negotiations over the kinds and quantities of goods that might be purchased with those balances.

The third precondition—responsiveness of demand and supply to price changes—is necessary for currency devaluations to improve the trade balance rather than merely worsen the terms of trade, under conditions in which world demand for domestic exports is not perfectly elastic. In turn, the price elasticity of supply and demand is bound to be very low when enterprises can obtain *ex post* and ad hoc compensatory subsidies and confiscatory taxes.

The first two conditions were satisfied by the price liberalization and macroeconomic stabilization plans of December 1989 in Yugoslavia, of January 1990 in Poland, and of January 1991 in Czechoslovakia; in East Germany they were satisfied by replacement of the existing currency with deutsche marks and the *de facto* unification already with West Germany on 1 July 1990. The third condition has also been partly satisfied by the stabilization plans, because the price elasticity of demand must have been enhanced by the budgetary and monetary restraint implemented through those plans. Elasticity of supply, however, has been present to a lesser degree in these four countries, but with substantial differences among them: considerable elasticity of supply exists in Poland, which has a large private sector in both agriculture and nonagricultural activities; the same is true in Yugoslavia because of a longer-standing market tradition, even though the private sector's share of the economy is lower than in Poland.[4]

[4] There is a theoretical presumption that Yugoslav worker self-management might induce supply rigidities or even perverse responses to price changes due to the temptation of value-added-per-worker maximization; however, this theoretical prediction has never been conclusively proven empirically.

Supply is less elastic in eastern Germany. In Czechoslovakia the likelihood of a strong supply response is open to question, because of the lack of both a private sector and a market tradition.

Thus, if Minister Klaus can assert that all one has to do to introduce convertibility is to declare it, without worrying about sequencing, it is because, as John Williamson quipped, Czechoslovakia has in fact already done what it takes beforehand—and, one might add, because Klaus is optimistic about the likely supply response. Hungary is progressing more slowly toward convertibility but is almost there, and has perhaps come the furthest among the four countries toward fulfilling the third precondition because of its greater progress toward freeing enterprises from central control and toward privatization.

In all of these countries this elasticity of response can be enhanced by privatization programs, by liberalization of the housing market, by increasing labor mobility, by improving transport and communications facilities, by encouraging competition, and by investment in capacity restructuring. However, these are time-consuming endeavors; even privatization, which many think could be done instantaneously by distributing state capital freely to all citizens, takes time to have an effect and cannot be expected to enhance price elasticity until financial markets are well established and functioning effectively.

In Romania, Bulgaria, and the Soviet Union, none of the three preconditions listed above are anywhere near being satisfied, although the first two might be approached soon in Bulgaria, when the stabilization plan currently under negotiation with the IMF is implemented.[5] Until recently the authorities persistently refused to raise prices, on the ground that inflation is not socially acceptable, but consumers in these countries can no more be protected from the fallout of monetary explosions than they could be protected from the fallout of the Chernobyl explosion. Quite perversely, in both the Soviet Union in 1990 and Romania in 1991, price increases were announced long beforehand, inducing panic buying, and then were withdrawn and postponed, but without also withdrawing the compensatory wage increases, which indeed took place in advance of the

[5] A Bulgarian stabilization program was in fact implemented in February 1991; some reduction of subsidies and of the monetary overhang also occurred in Romania in March–April 1991.

price hikes. The effect was to increase the monetary overhang at every step along the way. Eventually, however, any government standing between the irresistible force of monetary expansion and the immovable object of fixed prices is going to be crushed.

A distinctive feature of these three economies, which is present to a lesser extent in the other four, is the deeply rooted economic inertia in their state sectors. All studies of prereform Eastern European state enterprises stress their rigidities, their risk aversion, their hoarding, their cult of gross physical indicators *(kult vala* in Russian) and neglect of net monetary results, and their reluctance to innovate and to adjust to changing economic conditions. In the state sector—which is still extremely large everywhere in the region—this kind of behavior cannot be changed at a stroke, and indeed it may be made worse by managers' uncertainty about the timing and mode of their enterprises' privatization, or about how their performance might be assessed, penalized, or rewarded in the future. The turmoil of shock treatment will shorten their time horizon, and the high rate of return on inventories (both financial and in terms of the production flexibility they afford) may continue to favor speculative hoarding relative to production.

The only managerial inducement to maximize profits in the not-yet-privatized state enterprises is the hope of a merger or joint venture with or sale to a foreign company; even then managers' efforts may be diverted to stripping the enterprise's assets rather than to maximizing the return on those assets. It is precisely this economic inertia, visible in the conspicuously absent or weak supply response at least in the first stages of current stabilization and reform plans, that distinguishes the Eastern European countries from ordinary developing economies undertaking similar programs of stabilization, deregulation, privatization, and trade liberalization. This critical difference is well understood in Friedrich Levcik's paper, and totally neglected by Jacques Polak. This neglect is, one hopes, not terribly important in the cases of Poland, Czechoslovakia, Hungary, and Yugoslavia; it is undoubtedly unwarranted in the cases of Romania, Bulgaria, and the Soviet Union.

Ultimately, the question "How fast can convertibility be introduced?" has two answers. The first answer is that it can be introduced as fast as the three preconditions listed above—equilibrium, absence of subsidies, and a significant degree of price elasticity—can be met. In heavily indebted economies, such as Poland, Hungary, Bulgaria, and the Soviet Union, equilibrium must mean also debt rescheduling or relief (or both) and external support of the move to convertibility on a scale sufficient to allow some accumulation of hard-currency reserves instead of their depletion, and to lend credibility to the maintenance of convertibility once it is introduced. The first two preconditions can be implemented quickly through a stabilization plan; the third, especially on the supply side, is time-consuming and sensitive to the sequencing of reforms. Price inelasticity of supply is the main reason for the Polish recession and stagnation in 1990–1991 and will be, unless Klaus's optimism is right, the main reason for a Czechoslovak recession in 1991.

The second answer is that it depends on how high an adjustment cost one is willing or able to accept. The faster the rush to convertibility, the higher the cost. A relatively rapid move to convertibility increases the share of low-positive-value-added activities that have to be run down, and increases the impact on the terms of trade, price elasticities being lower in the short than in the longer term. Hence, the faster the move to convertibility, the greater the domestic currency undervaluation necessary to ensure its credibility.[6]

Could intra-Eastern European cooperation through an Eastern European Payments Union similar to the postwar European Payments Union in the West (see the paper by Jozef van Brabant, Chap. 5) reduce this cost? Jacques Polak seems to underestimate its potential. Reserve savings would be "trivial" as he suggests, only for an unchanged level of trade, but in fact trade would be expanded by such an arrangement. Intra-area trade is low only if the Soviet Union is left out. Surplus countries will have no incentive to join only if they are operating at full capacity. This is not the case with the Soviet Union (although arguably the Soviet Union does operate at full capacity of its productive system as a whole, in the sense that there is no lack of demand). The main arguments against an EPU-type arrangement are that there is no demand for it on

[6] In Poland the undervaluation was overdone by setting the nominal rate of exchange at the level prevailing in the free market; nevertheless the sustainability of that rate in spite of a point-to-point rate of inflation for 1990 as a whole of 249 percent reflects the increasing credibility of the permanence of convertibility during the year.

the part of any of its potential members, and that the external aid and finance necessary to induce the Soviet Union (as a prospective structural creditor)[7] to participate in such a scheme are unlikely to be forthcoming. Assuming that these objections can be overcome, the scheme does not deserve to be dismissed too easily; the alternative suggestion of a customs union also presumes a convertible currency and therefore is not a true alternative to convertibility with or without an EPU-type arrangement.

A much less plausible alternative is popular in the Soviet Union and is put forward in this volume by Andrei I. Kazmin and Andrei V. Tsimailo (Chap. 9). This is the introduction of a parallel convertible currency alongside the ordinary ruble, first in selected areas or sectors but eventually pervading the whole economy, gradually and painlessly replacing the old inconvertible ruble. This approach is clearly rooted in the monetary stabilization that took place under the New Economic Policy in 1922–1924, based on the chervonets (a gold- and commodity-backed monetary unit equivalent to 10 prewar gold rubles, with limited convertibility).

There is neither theoretical nor historical justification for a parallel convertible currency—as distinguished from the partial use of foreign exchange in domestic transactions, which may be a necessary evil in conditions of hyperinflation. Theoretically the case for such a device implicitly rests on the presumption that there is a positive supply response to be obtained from economic reform, but that that response is only available for a slow diffusion of reform measures via the growth of a parallel monetary circulation. Moreover, in order to wipe out the monetary overhang, that supply effect must be not only positive but greater than the current inflationary gap. Such an expectation has no foundation.

A new parallel currency with a fixed exchange rate would have the same effects as dollarization of the economy, whereas a floating parallel currency would have an arbitrary value determined solely by the monetary authorities; in any case its conditions of issue are not clear. Admittedly some resources may be derived from the resulting seignorage, but until

[7] In 1990–1991 the prospect of the Soviet Union being a substantial structural creditor has been reduced by the Soviets' inability to deliver fuels and other materials to Eastern Europe in the quantities expected (and contracted).

the economy is successfully stabilized, the national monetary authorities are bound to lack the necessary credibility.[8]

The new currency would need a one-to-one reserve backing (or more, to cover possible fluctuations in the value of hard-currency bonds, as used to be required to back the sterling convertibility of the national currencies of the British colonies). Interest-bearing liabilities denominated in convertible but not very credible rubles would have to offer an interest rate differential sufficient to induce substitutability with hard-currency deposits. These are hardly foundations for substantial seignorage.

The stabilization of the ruble through the introduction of the chervonets under the New Economic Policy was accompanied by hyperinflation and the demise of the old ruble, the sovznak, and there is no reason to suppose that this would not happen again today. There simply are no costless paths to convertibility.

The costs of speedier convertibility, and more generally of a speedier transition to a market economy, are necessarily the object of a political assessment, but they cannot be ignored. We cannot argue with people or governments that assign a low weight to such costs, but we can and must argue—joining Friedrich Levcik—with those who are prone to neglect such costs or at least the necessity of investigating them more thoroughly. The additional cost of a speedier convertibility may be regarded as an investment, if it is expected to lower the overall longer-run costs of transition to the new regime. Indeed, the whole reform process can be regarded as an investment, since the longer-term benefits of reform are not in doubt, whereas the initial economic deterioration caused by drastic reforms has been seen only too frequently. But we know from investment theory that even good investments, with large positive present values relative to the initial outlay, should not necessarily be undertaken unless there is unrestricted access to credit at the discount rate used to calculate such present values. This applies especially to indivisible projects, which systemic replacement and currency convertibility must be. Unfortunately,

[8] It is rumored that in 1990 in Leningrad, when food rationing was introduced, more coupons were distributed than were covered by current supplies, so that there was not only a ruble overhang but also a rationing coupon overhang. Given such behavior by the authorities in the recent past, would investors be indifferent between holding hard currency and holding convertible rubles, or between deposits denominated in either?

the fruits of investment in reform and in a speedy move to convertibility are not easily appropriated by investors, and therefore these projects are not easily bankable, even with the IMF, the World Bank, and the European Bank for Reconstruction and Development. However, this is not an argument against reform, or against convertibility; rather it is a strong case for aid.

16

Inflation, Interest and Exchange Rates in the Transition

Domenico Mario Nuti

16.1 Introduction

One of the most spectacular achievements of all post-communist economies has been the instant convertibility of their domestic currencies—*de facto* at least on current account and for residents—right at the very

Published in *Economics of Transition*, Vol. 4, 1, 1996, pp. 137–158.
Paper presented at the Conference on "Convertibility and Exchange-Rate Policy in Transition Economies", held in Sofia on 22–23 September 1995, by CEPR, London, and the XXI Century Foundation, Sofia. An earlier version of this paper was presented at the Polish Economic Association, Seminar on Inflation, Warsaw, 17 November 1994. Useful comments and suggestions were provided by participants in both Warsaw and Sofia meetings and in particular by Richard Portes and discussants Istvan Szekely and Garabed Minassian, as well as by Renzo Daviddi and Alan Gelb. Financial support from ACE Project 92-0101-R is gratefully acknowledged. The author is economic adviser to the Polish Minister of Finance, under a PHARE contract; however the views expressed here do not necessarily represent those of either the Minister of Finance or the European Commission.

D. M. Nuti (✉)
La Sapienza, University of Rome, Rome, Italy
e-mail: milica.uvalic@unipg.it

© The Author(s), under exclusive license to Springer Nature Switzerland AG 2023

S. Estrin, M. Uvalic (eds.), *Collected Works of Domenico Mario Nuti, Volume I*, Studies in Economic Transition, https://doi.org/10.1007/978-3-031-12334-4_16

beginning of their stabilization and systemic transformation. Foreign trade was opened to all economic agents and trade barriers were eliminated or substantially reduced: convertibility enhanced general access to trade and its impact on competition and efficiency, and encouraged foreign investment. "Trade and foreign exchange systems" are the area where transition economies score most highly in the assessment of the EBRD Transition Report (1994; see Table 16.1). Since 1994 an increasing number of countries has accepted article VIII of the IMF Articles of Agreement,

Table 16.1 Exchange rate regimes in Central Eastern Europe (April 1995)

Country	Exchange rate regime	Other exchange rate features	EBRD rating[a]
Albania	Floating lek	Restrictions on current account; heavy controls on capital account	4
Bulgaria	Floating lev	Few restrictions on current account; heavy controls on capital account	4
Croatia	Floating kuna, CB intervention	Few restrictions on current account; some controls on capital account	4
Czech Rep.	Koruna pegged to DM & US$	Current account convertibility for enterprises, some capital controls[b]	4
Estonia	Currency board, fixed kroons/DM rate	Full current account, virtual capital account convertibility	4
Hungary	Forint pegged to ECU/US$	Current account convertibility (except tourism); some residual capital account restrictions	4
Latvia	Lats informal peg to SDR	Full current and capital account convertibility	4
Lithuania	Currency board, fixed litai/US$ rate[c]	Full current and virtual capital account convertibility	4
Poland	Pre-announced daily crawling of the zloty[d]	Largely current account convertibility, limits devaluation on residents' capital account transactions	4
Romania	Floating leu[e]	Virtual current account convertibility (except tourism), but capital controls	4
Russia	Floating rouble[f]	Largely current account convertibility (capital restrictions). 50 *per cent* export surrender to interbank market	3

(*continued*)

Table 16.1 (continued)

Country	Exchange rate regime	Other exchange rate features	EBRD rating[a]
Slovak Rep.	Koruna pegged to DM/US$	Current account convertibility for enterprises; some capital controls[b]	3
Slovenia	Floating tolar	Full current account convertibility, some restrictions on capital account	4

Sources: EBRD, Transition Report, October 1994, table 8.3 and 2.1; EBRD, Transition Report Update, April 1995; Krzak (1995); official reports

[a]EBRD classification for "Trade and foreign exchange system" indicators: 4 = Few import or export quotas; insignificant direct involvement in exports and imports by ministries and state-owned former trade monopolies; almost full current account convertibility at unified exchange rate; no major non-uniformity of custom duties; 3 = Few import quotas; almost full current account convertibility at unified exchange rate; 2 = Few import quotas; almost full current account convertibility in principle but with a foreign exchange regime which is not fully transparent (possibly with multiple exchange rates); 1 = Widespread import controls or very limited access to foreign exchange.

[b]Special Czech/Slovak clearing account.

[c]Since April 1995, weekly crawling devaluation at pre-announced monthly rate (1.9 *per cent* in April-June 1995, 1.3 *per cent* thereafter).

[d]Peg to US$ from 1 January 1990 intended to last three months but maintained until 17 May 1991; then peg to a trade-weighted live-currency basket (US$ 45%, DM 35%, UK sterling 10%, FF and SF 5% each). From November 1991, daily crawling devaluation at pre-announced monthly rate falling over time (from 1.8 *per cent* to 1.2 *per cent per* month in mid-1995), and additional discrete devaluations. Since 16 May 1995, floating within a 7 *per cent* band around a baseline of daily crawling devaluation—a "seesaw" regime associated with occasional nominal revaluations. (The zloty was re-denominated in January 1995: 1 new zloty = 10,000 old zlotys).

[e]A significant spread between official and free rates has re-emerged since late 1994.

[f]Since 5 July 1995, floating within a pre-fixed band announced to be held between 4300 and 4900 roubles *per* US$.

thus introducing convertibility *de jure*: first the Baltic states, then Kyrgyzstan, the Czech Republic, Poland, to be followed by others. Capital controls, mostly on outflows and often ineffective, have also been reduced; Estonia and Latvia have abolished all restrictions to capital movements, so that their regime can be described (Hansson, 1995) as one of "extreme convertibility".

The remarkable achievement of instant convertibility has been obtained for exchange rate regimes which have differed very widely initially and have evolved in different directions over time: floating, freely or within fixed or crawling bands, with various degrees of intervention; crawling at pre-announced rates; adjustable pegs; fixed rates; forms of Currency Boards.

This paper, after a brief review of initial policies and their developments to date (Sect. 16.2), analyses some common features which do not seem to have been affected by exchange rate regime, or by speed or depth of stabilization and transformation. These are: initial gross undervaluation (Sect. 16.3); associated inflationary pressures, which in the case of fixed exchange rates impaired their intended nominal anchoring function (Sect. 16.4); the ensuing real revaluation, though with different effects on competitiveness (Sect. 16.5); while in many cases these exchange rate trends were at least partly offset by initial extreme trade liberalization and subsequent restoration of some trade barriers (Sect. 16.6). Interest rate differentials, higher (*ex post*) than domestic currency devaluations, initially simply revealed the lack of credibility of government policies, but subsequently made foreign investment in domestic financial assets particularly attractive (Sect. 16.7). Eventually such differentials have led to a surge of capital inflows on a scale that generated inflationary pressures and/or costly sterilizations (Sect. 16.8). Partly as a response to such surge, Russia and Poland have recently established exchange rate bands (respectively, fixed and crawling), though their actual policies have adverse side-effects and need to be coordinated with interest rate policy (Sect. 16.9). Section 16.10 summarizes the main arguments and conclusions.

16.2 Exchange Rate Regimes during the Transition

The very wide range of exchange rate regimes in transitional economies today is illustrated in Table 16.1. Poland started on 1 January 1991 with a fixed rate linked to the US dollar, intended to last for three months but maintained until May 1991, when the rate was devalued and linked to a trade-weighted basket of five currencies.[1] From October 1991 the zloty followed a daily crawling devaluation at a pre-announced monthly rate falling over time (from 1.8 *per cent* to 1.2 *per cent per* month), with additional discrete devaluations. Since 16 May 1995 the zloty has been floating within a 7 *per cent* band around a baseline of daily crawling devaluation—a regime which under the management of the National Bank of Poland has allowed intermittent nominal revaluations. The CSFR on 1 January 1991 adopted a fixed exchange rate for the koruna, in terms of a five-currency basket. In February 1993 following the Federal split the koruna was also split into Czech and Slovak korunas, subject respectively to occasional revaluations and devaluations; in May the Czech koruna was pegged to the DM and the US$.[2] Hungary maintained its *de facto* convertibility, with a fixed rate subject to intermittent devaluations until April 1995, since when the forint followed a weekly crawling devaluation at a pre-announced monthly rate (1.9 *per cent* in April-June 1995, 1.3 *per cent* thereafter).

Albania, Bulgaria, Croatia, Romania, Slovenia, Russia and most of the CIS republics chose a somewhat managed floating rate; in early July 1995 Russia has adopted a pre-fixed band within which the rouble was allowed to float against the US$; the band is constant instead of falling along a crawling central parity as in Poland.

Estonia adopted a Currency Board in June 1992, managing the kroon at a fixed rate in terms of DM. Latvia and Lithuania first floated then fixed their exchange rate, for lats in terms of SDR in late 1993 and for litai in terms of the US$ in April 1994, when Lithuania adopted what has been described as a "quasi-Currency Board" (Hansson, 1995).

Everywhere exchange rates have been frequently influenced by "perverse" pre-announcements, on a scale and frequency uncommon in a market economy. Thus, at the inception of any stabilization plan the prospective devaluation—if not the actual rate—was known in advance, leading to compensatory actions. In the CSFR the announcement in September 1990 of a stabilization plan that included a devaluation on 1st January 1991 led to leads and lags that forced earlier devaluations in October and November

[1] $ 45%, DM 35%, UK sterling 10%, French franc and Swiss franc 5% each.

[2] The weights were respectively 65 *per cent* and 35 *per cent.* Until then the koruna was pegged to a basket of US$, DM, Austrian schilling, Swiss and French francs.

1990. A pre-announced devaluation happened in Romania in August 1991, and, in effect, in Hungary in January 1991, when devaluation had been openly demanded by cabinet members. The split of the Czechoslovak koruna into republican korunas, announced in January 1993 with effect from 1 June, led to an immediate run on the currency that forced an immediate split already in mid-February. In Estonia a devaluation requires a parliamentary decision: while the sheer possibility undermines confidence in its Currency Board, parliamentary debate of devaluation is bound to have disastrous effects on foreign exchange markets. In Poland in mid-May 1995 the move to a band was announced by the Polish National Bank a month in advance, and was confidently and correctly expected to lead to a zloty revaluation; mass speculation followed. Clearly these pre-announcements—often due to misplaced concern about transparency of government policy—have reduced the effectiveness of these measures and dissipated public resources. Other de-stabilizing public statements—about trends in inflation, interest and exchange rates—have also occurred, whether by incompetence, carelessness or mischief, as in market economies but with much greater frequency.

With convertibility, everywhere spot markets for foreign currencies were established and/or expanded. Futures, options, other derivatives are still an exception (*e.g.* the Hungarian forward exchange market) but are being developed.

16.3 Initial Undervaluation

To a greater or lesser degree, everywhere except Hungary, instant convertibility was accompanied by a grossly undervalued exchange rate—with respect to Purchasing Power Parity (PPP) and other measures of competitiveness, to the level of domestic wages expressed in foreign currencies, to the experience of similar economies. This was already understood at the time and is now generally acknowledged: see for instance Portes (1994), Nuti (1995), de Melo et al. (1995), Halpern and Wyplosz (1995).

Exchange rates at which convertibility was introduced were everywhere well below and occasionally grotesquely below PPP rates. Except for Hungary, throughout the area US$ rose to at least 4 times its PPP value: 4–5 times in Poland and in Czechoslovakia, 9 times in Bulgaria, and about 136 times in Russia, at the inception of their respective stabilization plans (Fig. 16.1 illustrates this ratio in selected countries). De Melo et al. (1995) suggest an inverse relationship between the PPP/actual ratio and the progress of systemic transformation, which they seek to quantify by means of a "Cumulative Liberalization Index" or CLI (see Figs. 16.1 and 16.2).[3]

Of course in the short run PPP exchange rates are unlikely to prevail for at least three good reasons: (i) the weight of non-tradables; (ii) the impact of capital flows on exchange rates; and (iii) the fact that "competitiveness" is ultimately a marginal, not an average concept (a single export with sufficiently high elasticities of supply and demand—whether oil or, say, a "Rubik cube"—is in principle enough to sustain "competitiveness").[4] Yet PPP can be regarded as a proxy for trends in medium- and long-run competitiveness. It has been shown that the exchange rate of economies as developed as transition economies tends to be around twice the PPP rate (Balcerowicz & Gelb, 1994), by which standard the initial exchange rates of transition economies were grossly undervalued. Moreover, when there is significant border trade, PPP acquires a more directly relevant impact on the equilibrium exchange rate.

Gross undervaluation was signalled also by exceedingly low wage rates expressed in dollars: *e.g.* under $10 *per* month in Russia in January 1992, about $50 *per* month in Poland in January 1990, under $130 in

---

[3] This is a composite index which takes into account three dimensions of economic liberalization, cumulated over time instead of being considered at their current level: internal markets, international trade and current account convertibility, and private sector entry. See de Melo et al. (1995), Section III.

[4] Usually the PPP approach to exchange rate determination is criticized for its open or implicit assumption that the real exchange rate is constant (e.g. see Clark et al., 1994; Halpern and Wyplosz, 1995). The three factors indicated above would have an impact on the exchange rate regardless of its rate of change: because of them the exchange rate, even if constant, would not necessarily correspond to the PPP rate. Clark et al. (1994) recommend an alternative "Macroeconomic approach", whereby the equilibrium exchange rate is that consistent with the medium-term internal and external balance. "Internal balance is defined as a level of output close to potential with a low, sustainable rate of inflation. External balance is best interpreted as a current account position that reflects equilibrium levels of national saving and investment under conditions of internal balance." This undoubtedly complements the PPP approach, but is policy-contingent and probably biased towards undervaluation once the government - as in all transition economies - no longer targets national output close to potential.

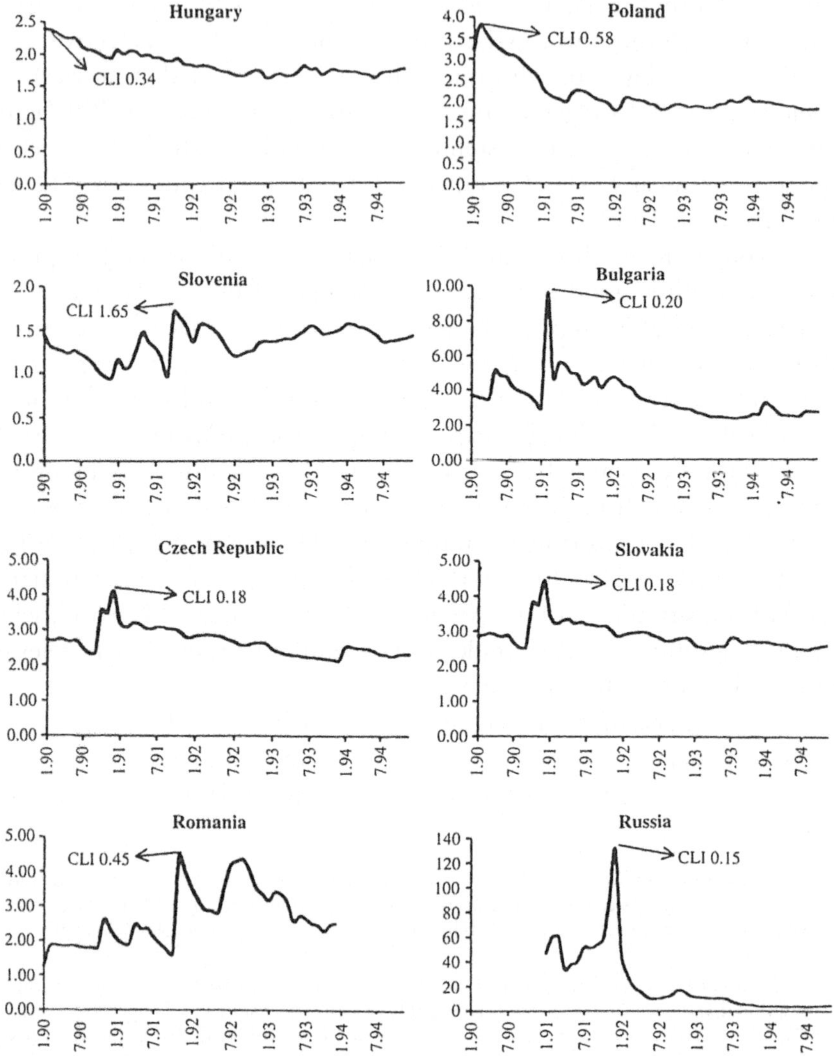

CLI = Cumulative Liberalization Index (defined in the text).
From: de Melo *et al.* (1995), Fig.6.
Source PlanEcon monthly data

Fig. 16.1 Ratio of market exchange rates to PPP rates

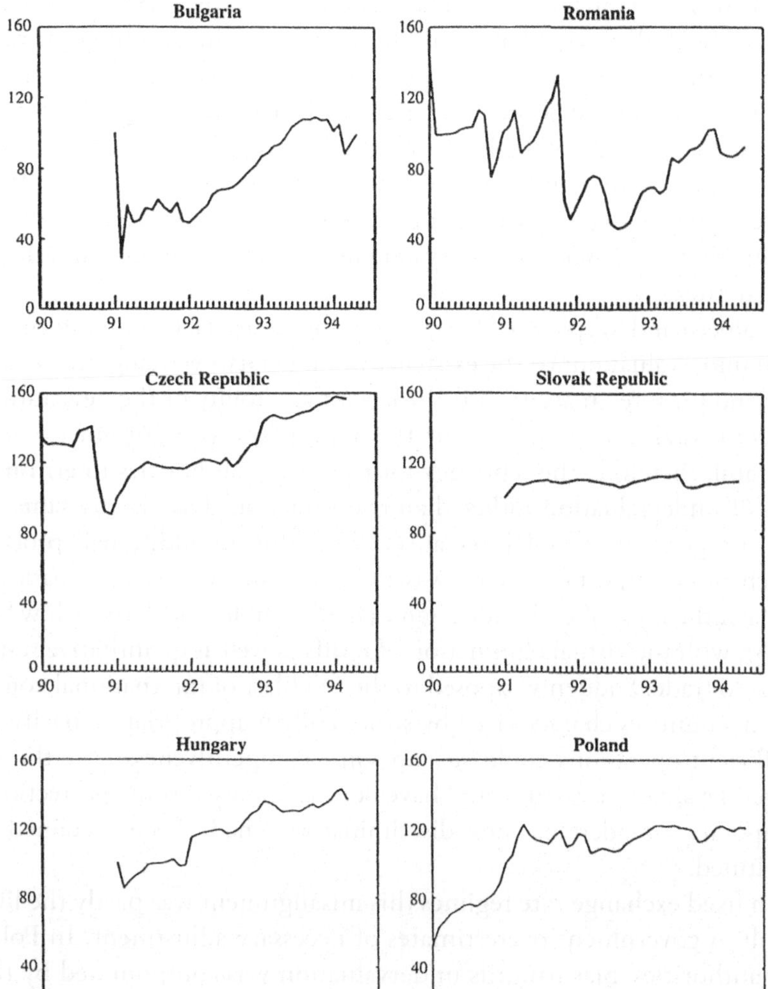

1. An increase in the index indicates an appreciation.
From: Calvo *et al.* (1995).
Source: National authorities.

Fig. 16.2 1. Central and Eastern Europe: real effective exchange rates (January 1991 = 100)

the CSFR in January 1991. Halpern and Wyplosz (1995) have estimated the dollar wage that would have prevailed in a number of transition economies on the basis of comparisons with a sample of 49 high- and middle-income countries (with five observations *per* country, in the period 1970–1990, of course excluding transition countries). They found equilibrium dollar wages ranging between $200 and $400, suggesting—apart from a possible overvaluation of the Hungarian exchange rate—a systematic significant undervaluation of actual rates.

Halpern and Wyplosz (1995) suggest four main factors accounting for such undervaluation: (i) the existence of monetary overhang; (ii) pent-up demand for foreign assets; (iii) the lack of credibility of the new authorities; iv) total uncertainty about the appropriate equilibrium exchange rate and, therefore, the tendency for risk-averse authorities to err on the side of undervaluation rather than overvaluation. Exactly the same factors are given by de Melo et al. (1995).[5] But an additional, probably much more important factor was the simultaneous instant creation of some of the most liberal trade regimes in the whole world (see below Sect. 16.5), with the virtual elimination of tariffs as well as quantitative restrictions to trade. Suddenly exposed to the full blast of international competition, countries characterized by structurally inappropriate capacity and inefficient operations could sustain some competitiveness only through larger devaluations than would have been necessary if some protection—temporary, moderate, non-discriminatory—had been retained or instituted.

In fixed exchange rate regimes this misalignment was partly the likely result of government overestimates of necessary adjustment. In Poland the authorities' bias towards undervaluation was compounded by their pitching the new nominal exchange rate at the free-market level, whereas it is well known (not least from post-War literature on price controls and black markets) that the equilibrium price prevailing in a unified market is always lower than the free price prevailing in a dual,

[5] Monetary overhang cannot have been a significant factor in the CSFR, where it was always small and where some price liberalization had already occurred in the year preceding convertibility; nor in Poland, where 1989 inflation must have virtually eliminated it.

free and regulated market: in other words, in 1990 the zloty was made cheaper than if it had been left to float.[6] This mistake was not repeated by the CSFR, which a year later introduced a rate half way between the free and the official level.

In a nutshell, devaluation had to be somewhat excessive, with respect to PPP or any other measure of competitiveness, as a price to be paid for instant convertibility by a non-credible government at a time of highly inflationary expectations. Just how much undervaluation was necessary, however, in turn depended on foreign trade policy: extra-devaluation was the price of establishing an extraordinarily open trade regime.

The implication is not that convertibility should not have been introduced on the very first day of stabilization and transition, but that (i) besides its undoubted advantages convertibility also carries the costs (discussed in the next section) of the significant undervaluation that goes with its early introduction; (ii) both costs and benefits are affected by the simultaneous pursuit of instant free trade. If convertibility had been introduced six months later, after the absorption of monetary overhang (if any), after the reduction in repressed demand for foreign assets, after the slow-down of inflation lent more credibility to government policies, and/or if some tariff protection had been temporarily kept, then the undervaluation associated with the establishment of convertibility would have been much lower. Of course free trade and instant convertibility have also brought advantages, such as greater competition, efficiency gains, attractiveness for foreign investors. It should be clear, without the benefit of hindsight, that both transition governments and the advocates of a more gradual approach have ignored this important trade-off.

---

[6] Suppose a quantity Q^ of a good is sold at a uniform equilibrium price p^. Other things being equal, if a part Q1 < Q^ is sold at a subsidized unit price p1 < p^, while the rest Q2 = Q^–Q1 is sold at a free price, consumers should be willing to pay for the residual quantity (Q^–Q1) a unit price p2 > p^. Otherwise, if they could purchase Q2 at a price p^, they would be richer by (p^–p1)*Q1 and normally would wish to spend some of this additional purchasing power on additional units of the good. Hence, the high free price in a two-tier price system is normally higher than a uniform equilibrium price at which the same total quantity is sold. If total expenditure on the good is the same under the two regimes, p^ = pl*Q1 / (Q1 + Q2) + p2 * Q2 / (Q1 + Q2), *i.e.* the uniform equilibrium price at which a given quantity is transacted is a weighted average of the free and the administered prices, using as weights the relative quantities transacted.

16.4 Associated Inflationary Pressures

Gross undervaluation distorts the short-run profitability of foreign trade with respect to longer term opportunities. Therefore, it provides no guidance for capacity restructuring; encourages distress exports (*i.e.* unprofitable in equilibrium) especially in association with restrictive monetary policy; disrupts patterns of production and trade which would be viable at a sustainable equilibrium rate. But the most damaging effect in the short run is probably its generation of inflationary pressures, under the guise of high profitability of exports and lack of competitiveness of imports: "These sharp increases [in the ratio between actual and PPP exchange rates] surely exacerbated inflationary pressures …" (de Melo et al., 1995, p. 23).

Misaligned exchange rates, once established for any reason, have a way of validating themselves through their immediate impact on the rate of inflation. This happens more frequently for an undervalued exchange rate, because an overvalued rate is much harder to sustain. Gross undervaluation must be regarded as one of the factors responsible for the initial price hike that accompanied price liberalization, and for the transformation of that price hike into an inflationary spiral, as the effects of undervaluation were diffused throughout the economic system. Once real wages (both in foreign currency and in terms of consumption) fall below medium/long-term equilibrium, their necessary recovery requires by definition money wage growth faster than inflation, thus contributing to further inflationary pressure.

When a government lacks credibility, a fixed exchange rate whose function is precisely that of a nominal anchor to bring inflation to an end, in order to be believed has to be pitched at such a low level that it becomes a source of inflation in itself, as price increases are necessary to bring the exchange rate closer to the underlying equilibrium. Bruno (1990) recommends the exchange rate as an anchor in stabilization programmes, noting that "in almost all historical hyperinflations, as well as in recent attempts at stabilization from high inflation, fixing the exchange rate was a key element of rapid stabilization" (p. 21). However Bruno neglects the specific features of transition economies indicated above:

overhang, repressed demand for foreign assets, total uncertainty about where an equilibrium rate could be, instant trade opening. He considers lack of credibility: "In practice the problem of credibility pushes relatively "soft" governments in the direction of attaching themselves to the reputation of a "stronger" government's conservative central bank through a fixed exchange rate" (p. 23)—but obviously a weak chain cannot be made strong by linking it to a strong ring. Credibility could have been enhanced by a social pact aimed at holding down inflation through wage restraint,[7] but the machinery was not in place and, in a liberal climate, governments were most reluctant to intervene in the labour market (with the notable exception of Vaclav Klaus whose market rhetoric was accompanied by central control of wages for the first four years of Czechoslovak transition).

Over time, the very maintenance of convertibility, especially at a fixed exchange rate, raises the credibility of domestic policies and gradually hardens the domestic currency in the view of the public, both domestically and abroad. However this credibility enhancement happens at the cost of prolonging inflationary tendencies.

Sachs (1995) strongly recommends that post-communist economies should "start with a pegged rate in order to end a high inflation, and then switch to a floating rate in order to preserve long-term flexibility" (p. 3), like other successful economies and against IMF preference for floating rates, which he regards as "typically more contractionary". He falls into an apparent contradiction when he recommends a fixed exchange rate both to "economies tightly linked together in an optimal currency area" (p. 15) and, in the same breath, to post-communist economies which could not conceivably be more distant from forming such an area with their main trade partners or even among themselves.

Sachs actually mentions Poland 1990 as an instance of successful nominal exchange rate anchoring, which is inexplicable in view of the Polish inflation record in 1990–1991: 586 *per cent* in 1990 alone and 70 *per cent* in 1991 for an exchange rate that remained fixed until May 1991.

[7] In Austria in the 1980s the schilling's ambitious peg to the DM could be maintained, but only thanks to considerable real wage flexibility, mainly as a consequence of the Austrian system of social partnership (Hochreiter & Winckler, 1995).

Moreover, when money and credit targets are taken—as they were in Poland—as additional nominal anchors, the higher than expected inflation induced by an undervalued exchange rate will lower the real values of these anchors and, therefore, far from avoiding contraction, will induce an unintended recessionary squeeze. Trade balance improvements such as may—and did—occur are, therefore, obtained at the cost both of worsening terms of trade and of domestic recession, raising and front-loading the costs of stabilization.

It follows that when, as typically in post-communist economies, governments have a total lack of credibility[8] the costly nominal anchor of a fixed exchange rate is ineffective: undervaluation does not "buy" credibility. It seems wiser to float initially and then, later on, lock the exchange rate into a band or a level much closer to a medium-term equilibrium, rather than immediately lock into a misalignment that is subsequently rectified by the higher inflation which it causes. This, incidentally, was the policy followed by Lithuania, which in 1994 pegged its currency to the SDR for a dollar monthly wage of $109 rather than for the initial $45 prevailing in 1992, and by Russia moving to a fixed band after the rouble/dollar floating rate had come down from 136 to about 4–5 times the PPP rate (but see below on other problems with the Russian fixed band). Alternatively, an exchange rate more appropriate to medium-/long-run competitiveness can be fixed for an initially more protected and gradually opening trade regime (see below, Sect. 16.6).

16.5 Subsequent Real Revaluation

After the initial large devaluation, exchange rates were revalued in real terms—differential inflation not being fully offset by further devaluations, if any—coming much closer to purchasing power parity: the ratio between the actual and PPP value of the dollar in 1994 fell to about 2–3 times in Poland, 5 times in Russia.

[8] Lack of credibility is consistent even with the enormous political capital enjoyed by the first post-communist governments: the population may be willing to accept unprecedented sacrifices and yet, rightly or wrongly, believe that the government will consolidate the currency more slowly than promised.

Halpern and Wyplosz (1995) estimate that in Central Eastern Europe in the early 1990s a 10 *per cent* nominal devaluation implies a parallel real devaluation of 3.6 *per cent*, which makes exchange rate policy a powerful instrument. Sometimes real revaluation was in its turn excessive, creating trade imbalances and forcing further devaluations, which by and large were successful in improving external balance. Sometimes, on the contrary, real revaluation did not adversely affect the trade balance (indeed accompanying its turnaround back into surplus in Poland and the Czech Republic in 1994, when the external balance also improved in Bulgaria, Hungary, and the Slovak Republic). In the Baltic states, since June 1992 when reforms started, real appreciation with respect to the dollar by April 1995 had reached 62 *per cent* in Latvia, 75 *per cent* in Estonia, 83 *per cent* in Lithuania, yet exports continued to expand (by a cumulative 1994/1992 growth respectively of 184 *per cent*, 21 *per cent* and 202 *per cent*, simultaneously shifting trade from an FSU share (including intra-Baltic trade) of the order of 90 *per cent* to 32 *per cent*, 45–50 *per cent* and 55 *per cent* respectively (Hansson, 1995).

Competitiveness trends for the Czech Republic, Hungary and Poland, according to a variety of alternative indices, are indicated in Table 16.2. The dollar monthly wage in manufacturing rose in 1992–1994 in the three countries (in Hungary it rose throughout the period; in Poland the fall of 1990 was already recovered in 1991, after which the dollar wage continued to rise). The unit labour cost in manufacturing fell significantly in Poland and Hungary but rose significantly in the Czech Republic in 1993–1994 where labour productivity kept falling until 1994.

One of the factors bringing exchange rates closer to PPP rates is the presence and growth of border trade, which is triggered by relative retail prices; in 1993–1994 this factor was particularly important in Poland, especially with the expansion of trade with both Germany and Ukraine.

Clearly, real revaluation was partly the reversal of earlier undervaluation, partly an adjustment towards new equilibria warranted by increasing productivity and competitiveness; if revaluation exceeded these parameters, the resulting trade deficit could be financed by capital inflows or force devaluation. Halpern and Wyplosz estimate that the initial undervaluation is bridged fairly quickly, as one half of it is corrected within ten months.

Table 16.2 Indicators of competitiveness for Czech Republic, Hungary and Poland (average percentage change), 1990–1994

	1990	1991	1992	1993	1994
Czech Republic					
Consumer prices expressed in US$[a]	-8.1	-4.6	15.9	17.1	9.9
US$ wage in manufacturing[b]	-17.6	-28.9	22.7	21.4	15.7
Labour productivity manufacturing [c,d]	-0.4	-16.6	-7.6	-3.5	5.7
Unit labour cost in manufacturing, US$[d,e]	-17.3	-14.8	32.8	25.8	9.5
Hungary					
Consumer prices expressed in US$[a]	20.5	14.2	16.4	5.3	2.0
US$ wage in manufacturing[b]	14.8	6.2	19.8	5.6	3.2
Labour productivity manufacturing [c,d]	0.6	-20.9	12.6	16.0	7.9
Unit labour cost in manufacturing, US$[d,e]	14.2	34.3	6.4	-9.0	-4.4
Poland					
Consumer prices expressed in US$[a]	3.9	53.0	11.0	1.7	2.7
US$ wage in manufacturing[b]	-28.2	46.7	6.9	4.5	7.3
Labour productivity manufacturing[c,d]	-21.1	-11.9	17.1	14.5	12.5
Unit labour cost in manufacturing, US$[d,e]	-8.9	66.5	-8.7	-8.8	-4.6

Source: EBRD (1995), table 1, p. 9. EBRD staff calculations based on data from the "OECD Short-term Economic Indicators", no.1, 1995.

[a]Measured as the local consumer price index converted into US dollars at the average exchange rate for the year.

[b]Measured as the local wage in manufacturing converted into US dollars at the average exchange rate for the year.

[c]Measured as manufacturing output *per* employee in the manufacturing sector.

[d]The entry for 1994 shows the change between Q1–Q3 of 1993 and Q1–Q3 of 1994.

[e]Measured as the cost in US dollars of labour used in manufacturing *per* unit of gross output.

16.6 Offsetting Trade and Exchange Rate Policy

Early undervaluation was accompanied—and made possible—by the drastic abolition of trade barriers. Subsequent real revaluations were accompanied by—and they were used to justify—the rise or re-imposition of tariffs and surcharges.

In 1990 Poland's average tariff fell from 18.3 to 5.5 *per cent*. In the first half of 1991, after significant real appreciation of the zloty, the average tariff was raised to 16 *per cent* (weighted average 9.4 *per cent*), with further upwards revisions in the autumn of 1991, and the end of tariff suspensions in early 1992. As a result, average weighted tariffs rose to 11 *per cent* on industrial goods and 18 *per cent* on agricultural goods (EBRD, 1994, p. 115). A "temporary" 5 *per cent* import surcharge was introduced in December 1992; it was to be reduced in 1994 and abolished in 1995 but is being phased out much more gradually.

In Russia, the abolition of tariffs in January 1992 was followed two months later by a new schedule at the prevailing rate of 5 *per cent*, raised to 15 *per cent* in September 1992—though until February 1993 imports were exempt from the 28 *per cent* VAT. In April 1993 tariffs were lowered on average to 13 *per cent*, to be raised again to 15.5 *per cent* (14.1 *per cent* if weighted, with a maximum rate of 100 *per cent*) in July 1994, and lowered again since.

In Hungary, where in 1990–1991 tariffs had undertaken a more modest reduction, non-tariff measures were taken more often in order to offset the 1990–1993 real revaluation of 31 *per cent* (77 *per cent* in Poland). In Bulgaria, the earlier liberalization has been partly offset by some later protection.

To some extent the effects of initial undervaluation were offset by those of parallel over-liberalization of trade flows, just as the effects of subsequent real revaluation were partly offset by the rise of protective barriers. The fact that the economy was heaved first in one direction than in the opposite one, while at the same time in both instances it was subjected to a countervailing force, cannot be regarded as equivalent to a state of relative tranquility in which only the net result of these forces was applied: shocks were both too many and unnecessarily large.

CSFR and Croatia, on the contrary, did much better: they introduced an import surcharge at the inception of their stabilization plans, in January 1991 and January 1993 respectively, and subsequently gradually reduced it.

16.7 Interest Rate Differentials

Real interest rates, which in the old regime were usually strongly negative (except relatively to official underestimates of inflation), were targeted by the authorities at positive levels to encourage savings and control inflation. In Poland in 1994 the Central Bank targeted a 6% real refinancing rate; in Russia in March-May 1994 the real interest rate (extrapolating current inflation) rose to inordinately high record levels of the order of 100–150 *per cent per* year, falling again to negative levels by the end of the year and rising again in 1995.

The move towards positive real rates of interest was an overdue correction with respect to earlier rates which were negative and large in absolute terms. But real rates soon exceeded sustainable levels, *i.e.* levels geared to the real rate of return obtainable on productive investment, thus becoming an undue brake on investment and sustainable growth.

After stabilization the time structure of interest rates has been unusually short, indeed truncated with respect to the yield curves prevailing in market economies: the maximum time span of loans and bonds, even for the government, was and still is of the order of six months (Russia) to 3 years (Poland). Within this short time span, there are usually higher rates for longer time periods, *i.e.* embodying expectations of rising interest rates, even in case of currently falling inflation and interest rates.

In equilibrium, interest rates (in domestic currency) will be equalized to world rates (say, in dollars) plus the expected devaluation of the domestic currency (with respect to dollars).[9] In the longer run, a PPP approach to interest rates relates interest rate differentials across currencies to their inflation rate differentials. The time patterns of inflation, exchange and interest rates are related in the same fashion.

Domestic interest rate differentials with respect to hard currency interest rates were as a rule always higher than necessary to offset the subsequent nominal devaluation of the domestic currency; indeed interest rates were higher than necessary to offset even differential inflation rates. In other words, domestic currency deposits yielded much higher rates of return than hard currency deposits. Wellisz (1995) points out that in the first three months of 1990 in Poland one could have obtained a three months' rate of return of 70 *per cent* on dollar savings. In January 1995 the real rate of return on Polish Treasury bonds was 1.5–2.4 *per cent* a

[9] Intermittent interest adjustment to continuous inflation made real rates fluctuate unnecessarily - over the short period, disturbing this relation.

year but by using dollars to purchase those bonds and switching back to dollars an investor could have realized a 10 *per cent* annual dollar return.

Interest rate differentials, higher (*ex post*) than necessary to cover domestic currency devaluations, initially simply reveal the lack of credibility of exchange rate policies. Over time, however, with continuous real (and occasionally nominal) revaluation of domestic currencies and the slow-down of inflation, interest rate differentials begin to make foreign and national investment in domestic financial assets particularly attractive,[10] thus exercising a continuous pull on foreign investment instead of exhausting its effect in a once and for all adjustment in international portfolios.

If, for the initial burst of inflation, high nominal interest rates and devalued exchange rates were necessary to offset inflationary expectations, once inflation has significantly decelerated the maintenance of high rates of interest and of currency devaluation can, on the contrary, actually generate inflationary expectations. Once built into wage negotiations and pricing behaviour, these inflationary expectations can be self-fulfilling. Arguably the quickest way to reduce inflation in a country like Poland is a simultaneous reduction of both the rate of interest and of the rate of crawling devaluation.

16.8 An *Embarras De Richesse*: The Growth of Reserves

While Central Eastern European countries as a group (the Visegrad four plus Romania and Bulgaria) exported capital in 1990–1991, in 1992–1993 a remarkable turnaround occurred, with the capital account of the area improving by about $20 billion—a trend which has continued in 1994–1995. In Central Eastern Europe this inflow has led to an accumulation of foreign reserves, both with the central bank and with the whole banking system (see Fig. 16.3). Further real and sometimes even nominal appreciation of domestic currencies has followed in an

[10] Polish experience suggests that banks are quicker off the mark than households in taking advantage of this opportunity.

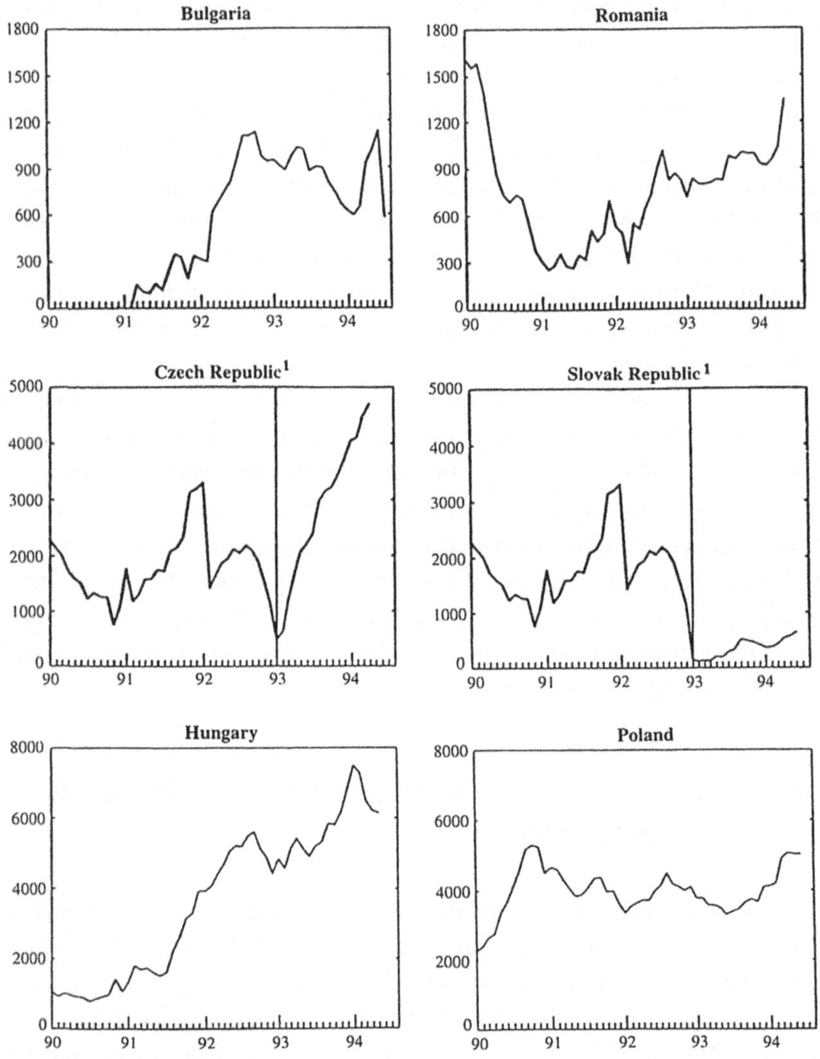

1. Czechoslovakia through end of 1992.
From: Calvo *et al.*, 1995.
Sources: IFS and National authorities.

Fig. 16.3 Central and Eastern Europe: total reserves minus gold (in millions of US$)

increasing number of countries (Poland, the Czech and Slovak Republics, Hungary, Slovenia, Croatia, the Baltic states, Russia; see Calvo et al., 1995).[11]

Discrepancies between national payments data, national customs data and mirror statistics often make it difficult to attribute reserve growth unambiguously to trade surpluses or to capital inflows. In Poland foreign exchange reserves doubled during the first half of 1995 to over $10bn, apparently (according to the National Bank of Poland) as a result not so much of capital flows but of a boom in border trade and also of competitiveness improvements obtained in spite of real (and in mid-1995 also sometimes nominal) revaluation. In the year ending September 1995 NBP acquired $5.7 bn reserves, on top of $1.4 billion repaid to the IMF.

In the Czech Republic the Central Bank's reserves almost doubled during the course of 1994 from $3.7bn to $6.2bn, rising by almost the same absolute amount in the first six months of 1995, in spite of a trade deficit, mostly thanks to foreign loans to Czech companies and to foreign investment in Central Bank bills offering attractive interest differentials. Like the Czech Republic, in 1994–1995 Estonia, Latvia and Lithuania incurred large trade and current account deficits, but experienced even larger net capital inflows and, hence, "healthy growth of foreign reserves" (Hansson, 1995): net capital inflows in 1994 amounted respectively to 9.3 *per cent*, *7.5 per cent* and *7 per cent* of GDP. The Slovakian National Bank, which at the time of the split had less than $20mn, had accumulated $2.1bn ($4.1bn in the whole banking system) by the end of April 1995.

Similar trends have been recorded also in Slovenia, Croatia, and even in Russia, especially with the prospect of rouble nominal exchange rate stabilization for a monthly interest rate of the order of 15 *per cent*.

This *embarras de richesse* has had the usual positive and adverse effects of all sudden surges of capital inflows. On the positive side, capital inflows

[11] Branson and Braga de Macedo (1995) assess macroeconomic policy in the four Visegrad countries, from the viewpoint of "convergence" to the European Union. They recommend that - once internal balance is reached - in their approach to external balance these economies adopt "a Pre-Pegging exchange rate, which essentially means no active nominal devaluation (no nominal devaluation aimed at real devaluation) as the country converges towards Union membership". In 1995, however, these countries' problem was that of containing real appreciation.

ease the external constraint and enhance potential investment and growth. Sustained, large-scale inflows, however, sooner or later pose a dilemma for monetary policy: either the surge is allowed to have an expansionary effect on the money supply with inflationary repercussions and exposure to possible sudden reversals, or countervailing measures must be taken which are directly or indirectly costly (see, Schadler et al., 1993 and Montiel, 1995), namely:

1. further real and even nominal revaluations, with subsequent loss of competitiveness and exacerbation of unemployment;
2. fiscal surpluses (to offset the growth of reserves), which may be politically painful or structurally impossible to achieve; moreover, this approach subordinates fiscal policy to monetary policy, going far beyond the call of monetary policy independence;
3. sterilization, *i.e.* central bank sales of bonds aimed at mopping up excess liquidity. This operation has two adverse side effects, namely neutralization of the beneficial effects of capital inflows and the cost of sterilization itself, which is equal to the interest rate differential over and above currency devaluation—a cost recurring over time throughout the period over which the sterilization is required. On a small scale and for a limited period this cost may be worth paying in order to avoid inflation. But Schadler et al., in a review of a broad range of recent cases, conclude that "Countries that sterilized most aggressively benefited least from the effects of inflows on investment and growth. … More generally, however, full sterilization proved unfeasible on a sustained basis: by keeping upward pressure on domestic interest rates, sterilization both perpetuated large inflows and entailed untenable *quasi-fiscal* costs" (Schadler et al., 1993, p. 30).
4. a reduction of domestic interest rates, which at the same time would reduce the inflow (through its effects on both capital and current accounts) and reduce the cost of sterilization. The pursuit of a positive real interest rate in terms of consumption becomes simply a major source of imbalance in an open economy when the corresponding dollar rate of return is significantly higher than in the international market. Regardless of possible adverse effects on savings, a reduction

of interest rates below the rate of inflation is usually unacceptable to monetary authorities.

5. direct controls on capital inflows, whether general or on short-maturity capital inflows (as in Chile), including the introduction of so-called "Tobin taxes", *i.e.* taxes on certain classes of foreign exchange transactions; alternatively, controls over capital outflows could be reduced or eliminated. Inflows may also be reduced by widening exchange rate bands in order to increase uncertainty. All these measures are directed at reducing both the total inflows and the share of "hot money", thus lowering the risk of sudden reversals. Capital controls are very much against the spirit of the transition to a market economy, but their consideration has been advocated both by the IMF and by outspoken supporters of international liberalization, such as Sachs (1995, p.23). Gros and Steinherr (1995) recommend a dual exchange rate regime, with a fixed rate for current transactions and a free rate for capital transactions: after all, Belgium had a similar system for 25 years until 1991, and South Africa scrapped the finrand (financial rand) only in March 1995.
6. trade liberalization, which can drain liquidity through import promotion, at the cost of indebtedness and short-term adverse effect on employment.
7. neutralization of the effects of growth in the monetary base, such as higher reserve requirements and quantitative credit restrictions, which however may create difficulties for an already strained banking sector.

In the affected Central Eastern European countries some sterilization has taken place, which in the Czech Republic and in Poland has been particularly costly. In the Czech Republic, due to a persistent budgetary surplus, the Central Bank has had to create a special three-month Central Bank bill, thus incurring actual losses due to interest rate differentials (in foreign exchange) instead of simply accepting a lower revenue by selling government bonds in its possession. The Bank's liabilities are increasingly dominated by these high-interest loss-making bills.[12] In Poland the cost of sterilization has been high because of the high interest rate differentials

[12] I am indebted to Chris Allen for sight of an unpublished note of his on Czech monetary policy.

(in terms of foreign exchange) and the sheer scale of the operation: $5bn in the year ending August 1995 (see Kokoszczynski and Durjasz, 1995). Otherwise, only minor steps are being undertaken or contemplated, for instance in the Czech Republic raising some reserve requirements (but lowering others) in March 1995, while Poland may allow exporters to retain foreign currency earnings without having to surrender them to the National Bank of Poland.

Basically, there is an underlying widespread disequilibrium in the exchange rate regimes of many post-communist countries, primarily due to attempts at targeting simultaneously inconsistent values of three variables: (i) nominal monetary aggregates to be held down in order to control inflation; (ii) real interest rates to be kept significantly positive in order to encourage savings, thus also contributing to holding down inflation; (iii) real exchange rates, whose increase is to be held down in order not to lose competitiveness. But something has to give: in an open economy with free trade and capital movements there is no way more than one of these variables can be set by national authorities. On the positive side, capital inflows are not only the necessary requirement of a catching-up process, and the welcome confirmation of the restoration of international confidence, but also the consequence of the increasing integration of the formerly segmented markets of transition economies into European trade and capital flows.

16.9 Exchange Rate Bands: Poland and Russia

Partly as a response to fundamentals favouring a revaluation, both Poland and Russia have recently allowed their exchange rate to float within bands: in Russia a fixed band of 4300–4900 roubles *per* dollar (announced on 5 July 1995, effective until 1 October but subsequently prolonged for another six months), in Poland a crawling band of *7 per cent* either side of a central parity which continues to be devalued at the same former monthly rate of 1.2 *per cent* (16 May 1995). This kind of regime, intermediate between floating (or loosely managed) and fixed exchange rates, has been utilized in other countries, typically with bands allowed to depreciate at a pace pre-announced a year in advance (see Helpman et al., 1994, on the experiences of Israel, Mexico and Chile).

This regime is a compromise between the advantages and disadvantages of fixed and floating rates: it affords a greater stability of the real exchange rate, though not as much as under straight floating, while still retaining some benefit from anchoring the nominal exchange rate, though not as much as under a fixed rate regime. Bands allow a response to external and internal shocks without appearing to renege on the medium- and long-term signals provided by the band's central parity, as happens with discrete realignments which reduce credibility. Moving from a fixed rate to a band gives greater autonomy to domestic monetary policy. Helpman et al. (1994) conduct a battery of tests on this intermediate system, finding no sign of loss of credibility nor increase in inflationary expectations or in customary risk premia; if this is the case, the system would be a superior alternative as it would combine the best of both worlds. Whatever the merits of the system, however, the modalities and circumstances of its application in Poland and Russia differ markedly from precedents.

In Russia the intermediate regime appears as a stage in the hardening of the rouble real exchange rate, *i.e.* a stage in the path from a floating to a fixed exchange rate, rather than the search for a compromise between the two. On 2 January 1992 the rouble began trading on the Moscow Inter-bank Currency Exchange (MICEX) at a rate of Rb220 *per* dollar. Since then, it has been depreciating in nominal terms almost continuously down to an all time low of 5130 roubles *per* dollar on 29 April 1995. In real terms, on the contrary, the rouble has been consolidating all the time as inflation significantly exceeded nominal devaluation. MICEX has been rather volatile: a 25 *per cent* devaluation on Black Tuesday (11 October 1994) was almost completely recovered within the same week. In May-July 1995 the rouble appreciated significantly in nominal terms, by over 10 *per cent* at its best; a fixed band was announced.

The sudden nominal hardening of the rouble has had adverse effects, of a kind that have nothing to do with the introduction of the band *per se*. The new Russian commercial banks (about 2500, many of them with an excessive burden of bad loans in their portfolio) traditionally have been thriving on inflation and steady nominal devaluation of the rouble. With a higher proportion of dollar assets and rouble liabilities in their portfolio, banks have lost out significantly from a more stable rouble, on average turning from net profits to losses, especially since the first signs of exchange rate hardening and stabilization were not heeded. With lower inflation and a more stable currency, it has become impossible for their debtors to achieve the kind of profitability necessary to enable them to meet interest payments at the prevailing high rates (the refinancing rate was cut in June to 15% *per* month, roughly double the rate of inflation). At the end of August the Moscow interbank market literally seized up due to fears of insolvencies, just at a time when the least performing commercial banks were seeking liquidity. The Russian Central Bank did not act promptly as expected of a lender of last resort, for fear of exceeding monetary targets. When the Bank did inject liquidity through open market operations there were technical delays in implementing monetary transfers. These circumstances created temporary panic, temporarily resolved. The lesson here is that when a Central Bank has little or no credibility, it may be better for it to gradually increase its credibility by systematically improving its performance, instead of suddenly changing its behaviour, thus totally and utterly confounding market expectations.

In Poland, the crawling band system was introduced at a time of zloty revaluation pressures, due to a combination of massive accumulation of reserves and fairly balanced trade. The introduction of a band—as correctly predicted by mass speculators—led to instant revaluation contained under 5 *per cent* only by NBP intervention. Two smaller revaluations followed within the continued slide of the band, with the zloty crawling close to its upper ceiling. Thus, the NBP could revalue without appearing to decide to do so—the market had done it—while continuing the old policy of crawling devaluation.

NBP policy is incomprehensible: what is the point of revaluing the zloty today, by as much as it was deliberately devalued at a daily crawl for the last four months, only to continue to devalue it tomorrow down against a ceiling falling at an unchanged rate of 1.2 *per cent per* month? In these circumstances clearly it would also have been feasible four months ago (i) to half the rate of crawl for at least the next eight months, or (ii) to hold the exchange rate fixed for at least four months, or (iii) to introduce a band at a time when it would not have led to a 5 *per cent* revaluation, letting the band slide thereafter but at a reduced pace. Any of these alternative policies would have defused inflationary expectations, avoided ratchet price increases triggered by devaluation, and generally created a more stable environment without affecting export competitiveness at all. In the light of these considerations, the zigzag or see-saw policy of the National Bank of Poland seems schizophrenic, while an important chance of stabilizing the economy is being wasted. Why was the zloty not allowed to consolidate, following the favourable fundamentals of very rapidly rising reserves, balanced trade, fast productivity growth and falls in unit labour costs (expressed in foreign exchange)?

According to NBP deputy President Witold Kozinski, zloty devaluation was not slowed down for fears of damaging exporters: but none of the alternatives suggested above would have damaged exporters—on average during the period considered. Besides, the case for central bank independence is precisely the ability to focus on price stability without worrying about exporters (although, understandably, their predicament must have been difficult to ignore with the nearing of a presidential election contested by the NBP President).

An additional reason for not reducing zloty devaluation is that, in such a case, the zloty interest rate targeted by the NBP would become too attractive in dollar terms, thus encouraging further capital inflows.[13] If so, the interest rate in Poland is no longer a policy instrument but has now become a primary target for its own sake. With the transition, the dogma of a positive real rate of interest in terms of consumption, regardless of its implications for external balance, appears to have replaced old communist dogmas like, say, the faster growth of output of means of production.

Clearly a crawling band deserves serious consideration in post-communist economies, both as a way of reducing the surge of capital inflows and for its own merits as a seemingly efficient compromise between floating and fixed regimes. It could also be used, as in Russia today, as a temporary stage in the hardening of the domestic currency from floating to pegged or fixed exchange rate regimes. In Poland the crawling band appears to have been a way for the NBP to implement—*sans paraître*—a revaluation made necessary by excessive nominal

[13] This became clear at the Sofia Conference in the discussion of the paper by NBP officials Kokoszczynski and Durjasz.

devaluation of the zloty, built into the earlier crawling system and continuing along the falling ceiling of the band. Given their respective exchange rate policies, both Polish and—more so—Russian interest rate policies open up attractive interest rate differentials, widening with the progress of transition and stabilization, which are bound to exacerbate rather than resolve the *embarras de richesse* of reserve accumulation.

16.10 Summary and Conclusions

Convertibility was one of the earliest achievements of transition economies, regardless of exchange rate regimes, and of the depth or speed of stabilization and institutional change. It enhanced general access to trade and its impact on competition and efficiency, and encouraged foreign investment.

Convertibility, however, was associated with initial gross undervaluation which, while it lasted, worsened terms of trade, misdirected restructuring, and above all re-kindled inflation. In fixed exchange rate regimes (notably in Poland) this misalignment was partly the likely result of government overestimates of necessary adjustment. But by and large undervaluation was the necessary implication not of convertibility as such, but of both its suddenness and the accompanying elimination of all forms of trade protection.

Convertibility could have been introduced (say) six months later, after the absorption of monetary overhang (if any), after the reduction in repressed demand for foreign assets, and after the slow-down of inflation lent more credibility to government policies. Convertibility could also have been introduced while retaining or instituting a moderate tariff barrier, temporary and non-discriminatory. Either way, the undervaluation associated with the establishment of convertibility would have been much lower—of course at the cost of losing some of its advantages such as greater competition and efficiency gains, attractiveness to foreign investors. This trade-off seems to have been ignored both by transition governments and by the advocates of a more gradual approach.

The inflationary pressures due to undervaluation impair the nominal anchor properties of a fixed exchange rate, as price increases are necessary to bring the exchange rate closer to the underlying equilibrium;

undervaluation does not "buy" credibility. It seems wiser to float initially and then later on lock the exchange rate into a band or a level much closer to a medium-term equilibrium.

Undervaluation was followed by real revaluation, which was partly the reversal of earlier misalignment, partly an adjustment towards new equilibria warranted by increasing productivity and competitiveness. Sometimes real revaluation was in its turn excessive, creating trade imbalances and forcing further devaluations.

To some extent the effects of initial undervaluation were offset by those of parallel over-liberalization of trade flows, just as the effects of subsequent real revaluation were partly offset by the rise of protective barriers. The fact that the economy was heaved first in one direction than in the opposite one, while at the same time in both instances it was subjected to a countervailing force, cannot be regarded as equivalent to a state of relative tranquility in which only the net result of these forces was applied: shocks were both too many and unnecessarily large.

Interest rate differentials were usually higher (*ex post*) than domestic currency devaluations. Initially these differentials simply reveal the lack of credibility of domestic exchange rate policies. Over time, however, with continuous real (and occasionally nominal) revaluation of domestic currencies and the slow-down of inflation, interest rate differentials begin to make foreign and national investment in domestic financial assets particularly attractive. Maintenance of interest rate differentials higher than necessary to match prospective devaluation can actually generate self-fulfilling inflationary expectations.

Basically, there is an underlying widespread disequilibrium in the exchange rate regimes of many post-communist countries, primarily due to attempts at targeting simultaneously inconsistent values of three variables: (i) nominal monetary aggregates to be held down in order to control inflation; (ii) real interest rates to be kept significantly positive in order to encourage savings, thus also contributing to holding down inflation; (iii) real exchange rates, whose increase is to be held down in order not to lose competitiveness. But something has to give: in an open economy with free trade and capital movements there is no way more than one of these variables can be set by national authorities.

The net effect of exchange rate and interest policies in Central Eastern European economies has been a remarkable improvement in their capital account, leading to an accumulation of foreign reserves (sometimes, as in Poland, due to unrecorded border trade rather than to capital inflows).

This recent surge in capital inflows or trade surpluses eases the external constraint and enhances potential investment and growth, but also poses a dilemma for monetary policy: either the surge is allowed to have an expansionary effect on the money supply with inflationary repercussions and exposure to possible sudden reversals, or countervailing measures must be taken which are directly or indirectly costly, such as revaluation, fiscal surpluses, costly sterilizations through open market operations, an interest rate reduction (rightly or wrongly unpalatable to monetary authorities), capital controls, trade liberalization, widening exchange rate bands.

Exchange rate floating within a crawling band deserves serious consideration in post-communist economies, both for its own merits as a seemingly efficient compromise between floating and fixed regimes. It could also be used, as today in Russia where the band is fixed, as a temporary stage in the hardening of their currencies from floating to pegged or fixed exchange rate regimes. In Poland the crawling band appears to have been a way for the NBP to implement—without appearing to have directly decreed it—a revaluation made necessary by excessive nominal devaluation of the zloty; excess devaluation was built into the earlier crawling system and is continuing along the falling ceiling of the band. Given their respective exchange rate policies, both Polish and—more so—Russian interest rate policies open up attractive interest rate differentials, widening with the progress of transition and stabilization, which are bound to exacerbate rather than resolve a likely surge of capital inflows and its adverse net consequences.

Bibliography

Balcerowicz, Leszek and Alan Gelb (1994). Macropolicies in transition to a market economy: a three-year perspective, World Bank Annual Conference on Development Economics, April, Washington.

Branson, William H. and Jorge Braga de Macedo (1995). Macroeconomic policy in Central Europe, London: CEPR, Discussion Paper Series No. 1195, August.

Bruno, Michael (1990). High inflation and the nominal anchors of an open economy, Cambridge, MA: NBER, Working Paper No. 3518, November.

Calvo, Guillermo A., Ratna Sahay and Carlos A. Vegh (1995). Capital flows in Central and Eastern Europe: evidence and policy options, Washington: IMF, Working Paper, May.

Clark, Peter, Leonardo Bartolini, Tanim Bayoumi and Steven Symansky (1994). Exchange rates and economic fundamentals—a framework for analysis, Washington: IMF, Occasional Paper 115.

De Melo, Martha, Cevdet Deniser and Alan Gelb (1995). From plan to market: patterns of transition, Conference paper, Dubrovnik, June.

European Bank for Reconstruction and Development (EBRD) (1994). *Transition Report 1994*. London: EBRD.

European Bank for Reconstruction and Development (EBRD) (1995). *Transition Report Update*. London: EBRD, April 1995.

Gros, Daniel and Alfred Steinherr (1995). *Winds of Change—Economic Transition in Central and Eastern Europe,* London and New York: Longman.

Halpern, Laszlo and Charles Wyplosz (1995). Equilibrium real exchange rate in transition, London: CEPR, Discussion Paper Series No. 1145, April.

Hansson, Ardo (1995). Macroeconomic stabilisation in the Baltic states, Dubrovnik Conference, June.

Helpman, Elhanan, Leonardo Leiderman and Gil Bufman (1994). A new breed of exchange rate bands: China, Israel and Mexico, *Economic Policy,* No. 19, October, pp. 259–306.

Hochreiter, Eduard and Georg Winckler (1995). The advantages of tying Austria's hands: the success of the hard currency strategy, *European Journal of Political Economy,* V 01.11, pp. 83–111.

Kokoszczynski, Ryszard and Pawel Durjasz (1995). From fixed to flexible exchange rate regime: the case of Poland, CEPR and The XXI Century Foundation, Sofia Conference.

Krzak, Maciej (1995). The experience of East European countries with different exchange rate regimes., WIIW Research Reports No. 217, April.

Montiel, Peter J. (1995). Managing economic policy in the face of large capital inflows: what have we learned?, Conference Paper, IIE and Austrian National Bank, Vienna, September.

Nuti, D. Mario (1995). Inflation, interest and exchange rates in the transition, in Polish Economic Association, Zrodla i Mechanizm Obecnej Inflacji w Polsce, Conference Proceedings, Warsaw.

Portes, Richard (1994). Transformation traps, *Economic Journal.*

Sachs, Jeffrey (1995). Do we need an international lender of last resort?, Frank D. Graham Lecture, Princeton University, 20 April.

Schadler, Susan, Maria Carkovic, Adam Bennett and Robert Kahn (1993). Recent experiences with surges in capital inflows, Washington: IMF, Occasional Paper 108.

Wellisz, Stanislaw (1995). Inflation and stabilisation in Poland, 1990–1995, Conference Paper, Dubrovnik, June.

17

The Polish Zloty, 1990–1999: Success and Underperformance

Domenico Mario Nuti

Exchange-rate regimes in transition economies over the last decade have spanned the entire spectrum of possibilities, going from freely floating to permanently fixed (currency boards, DM-ization) through managed floats, preannounced crawling rates, and bands with or without intermittent adjustments. Such extreme diversity is due to differences in available foreign reserves and in initial macroeconomic imbalances (especially the presence of a monetary overhang in some transition economies) and to differences in government preferences between inflation and unemployment. Performance of alternative exchange-rate regimes is difficult to assess, (i) because performance can be mixed, (ii) because all exchange regimes if sustained have a

Published in American Economic Review, Papers and Proceedings, May 2000, 90 (2), 53–58.

I thank Josef Brada, Padma Desai, Lucjan Orlowski, and other participants at the AEA Boston meeting and at seminars at Columbia University and the Austrian National Bank for useful suggestions and comments. I also thank Maurizio M. Habib for invaluable research assistance. Financial support from ESRC award L213-25-2003 is gratefully acknowledged.

D. M. Nuti (✉)
La Sapienza, University of Rome, Rome, Italy
e-mail: milica.uvalic@unipg.it

© The Author(s), under exclusive license to Springer Nature Switzerland AG 2023

S. Estrin, M. Uvalic (eds.), *Collected Works of Domenico Mario Nuti, Volume I*, Studies in Economic Transition, https://doi.org/10.1007/978-3-031-12334-4_17

tendency to validate themselves via their impact on inflation, and above all, (iii) because performance depends on the entire package of public policy instruments (fiscal, monetary, and structural) and on exogenous factors, as well as the exchange-rate regime itself.

Poland (1990–1999) bears out these considerations. Initially (starting 1 January 1990) a fixed exchange rate was selected, pegged to the U.S. dollar at the then-prevailing free-market rate; it was backed by a $1,000 million stabilization fund provided by the G-24 which was not used but enhanced regime credibility. Monetary overhang had been virtually eliminated by earlier rounds of price increases and of zloty devaluations in 1989. Government preferences for disinflation assigned to the exchange rate the role of nominal anchor for the entire stabilization program. The fixed rate, expected to last no more than 3–4 months, in spite of massive inflation (249 percent in 1990 alone) was maintained until May 1991, when a 17-percent devaluation occurred and the peg switched to a currency basket (full details are given in Table 17.1). Subsequently, concerns about external balance and the maintenance of trade competitiveness led to a crawling-peg regime, with intermittent additional devaluations, then to an increasingly broader band around a central parity crawling at rates progressively decreasing over time (see Table 17.1 and Figs. 17.1 and 17.2). As in every transition economy, the real exchange rate has been steadily revalued from an initial gross undervaluation. Unlike most transition economies, however, Poland gradually has been able to consolidate the exchange rate (see Fig. 17.1), stabilize the crawling regime, and even experience occasional nominal revaluations (see Fig. 17.2).

17.1 Success

In general, such an exchange-rate policy was associated with (and instrumental to) economic success. The regime was gradually made more flexible by means of orderly policy changes, instead of precipitating under duress as in the Czech crisis of 1997 or the Russian crisis of August 1998. Poland's macroeconomic performance (see Table 17.2) is enviable: after a short and sharp recession, it recovered the 1989 GDP level soonest and

Table 17.1 Polish exchange-rate regimes, 1990–1999

Date	Regime
January 1990	Peg against the US$ (after a 31.6-percent devaluation on 1 January 1990)
May 1991	Peg against a basket of 5 currencies (after a 17-percent devaluation).
	Basket: 45 percent US$, 35 percent DM, 10 percent GBP, 5 percent FRF, 5 percent CHF
October 1991	Crawling peg, preannounced crawling devaluation at a monthly rate of 1.8 percent
February 1992	10.7-percent devaluation
August 1993	7.4-percent devaluation; monthly crawling rate 1.6 percent
September 1994	Monthly crawling rate 1.5 percent
	November 1994 Monthly crawling rate 1.4 percent
February 1995	Monthly crawling rate 1.2 percent
May 1995	Crawling band, widened band (±7 percent), same crawling rate
December 1995	6-percent revaluation
January 1996	Monthly crawling rate 1.0 percent
February 1998	Band widened to ±10 percent, monthly crawl 0.8 percent
July 1998	Monthly crawling rate 0.65 percent
	September 1998 Monthly crawling rate 0.5 percent
October 1998	Band widened to ±12.5 percent
March 1999	Band widened to ±15 percent, monthly crawling rate 0.3 percent. New basket since January 1999: 55 percent EURO, 45 percent USD

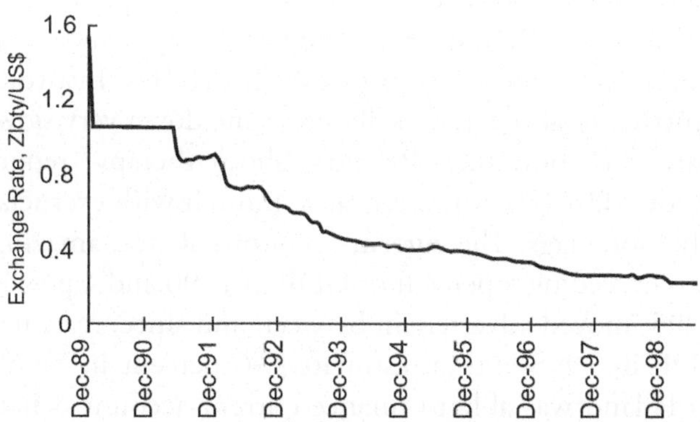

Fig. 17.1 Nominal exchange rate of the Polish Zloty against the U.S. Dollar, December 1989–July 1999. (Source: *IMF International Financial Statistics* (Datastream))

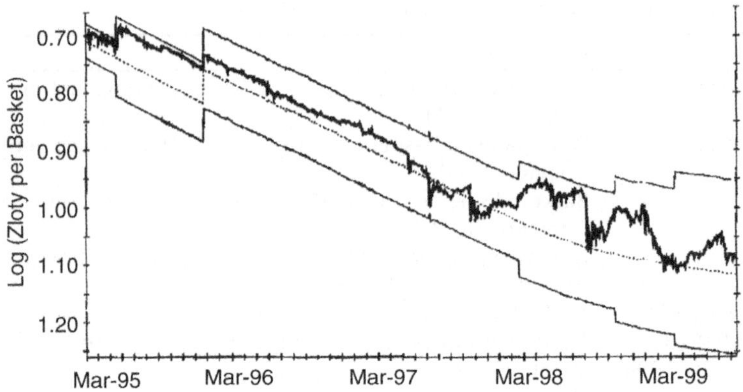

Fig. 17.2 Nominal exchange rate of the Polish Zloty, February 1995–August 1999. (Notes: Composition of the basket prior to 1999: 45 percent US$, 35 percent DM, 10 percent GBP, 5 percent CHF. Since 1999: 55 percent EUR, 45 percent US$. Note inverted y-axis scale. Source: Z. Darvas and G. Szapary (1999))

fastest and grew more rapidly than any other transition economy. Unemployment peaked at 17 percent of the labor force in 1994 but has come down fairly fast since then (until the autumn of 1999). The official exchange rate, initially grossly undervalued, was revalued in real terms for the following five years (Fig. 17.3). In January 1990, the U.S. dollar was worth almost five times its purchasing-power-parity rate, but within a year the ratio was reduced to a factor of 2, corresponding to that for countries similar to Poland in development level and structure (see Fig. 17.4; according to data from the Vienna WIIW Institute, the ratio has fallen further to about 1.6). Inflation came down very slowly (a gradualist feature that contradicts Poland's "shock therapy" reputation) but steadily, followed by lower interest rates, though with excruciatingly and unreasonably long lags. The current-account balance, amazingly recording a surplus exceeding 5 percent of GDP in 1990 and 4 percent of GDP again in 1995, moved adversely in between and since, reaching -6.7 percent of GDP in 1998 and an estimated -6 percent in 1999; however, until 2000 Poland was able to finance current-account deficits without difficulty, primarily through foreign direct investment, but also through net financial capital inflows. Foreign reserves have been accumulated fast (with a small decline in 1999), reaching the comfortable equivalent of about seven months' worth of imports.

Table 17.2 Polish macroeconomic performance

A. 1990–1994					
Variable	**1990**	**1991**	**1992**	**1993**	**1994**
GDP growth[a]	-11.6	-7.0	2.6	3.8	5.2
CPI inflation[b]	249.0	60.4	44.3	37.6	29.4
MZ growth[c]	na	37.0	57.5	36.0	38.2
Unemployment[d]	6.3	11.8	13.6	16.4	16.0
Foreign reserves[e]	na	3.6	4.1	4.1	5.8
Trade[f]	6.1	-0.9	-0.2	-2.7	-0.8
Current account[g]	5.2	-2.8	-3.7	-2.7	-1.0
Gov. balance[h]	3.1	-6.7	-6.7	-3.1	-3.1
Public debt[i]	na	na	147.3	108.6	69.0
B. 1995–1999					
Variable	**1995**	**1996**	**1997**	**1998[i]**	**1999[j]**
GDP growth[a]	7.0	6.1	6.9	4.8	3.5
CPI inflation[b]	21.6	18.5	13.2	8.6	6.5
MZ growth[c]	34.9	29.4	29.1	25.0	Na
Unemployment[d]	14.9	13.2	10.5	10.4	Na
Foreign reserves[e]	14.8	17.8	20.7	27.4	26.0
Trade[f]	-1.4	-5.7	-7.9	-8.7	-9.3
Current account[g]	4.3	-0.9	-3.0	-4.3	-6.7
Gov. balance[h]	-2.8	-3.3	-3.1	-3.0	-3.0
Public debt[i]	59.0	53.6	49.4	43.0	Na

Sources: *EBRD Transition Report*, EIU, and national statistics

[a]GDP real growth rate

[b]CPI rate of inflation (end year)

[c]MZ growth rate

[d]Unemployment, percentage of labor force, end year

[e]Foreign reserves, excluding gold ($1,000 million), end year (except in 1999, end of September)

[f]Visible trade balance (percentage of GDP)

[g]Current-account balance (percentage of GDP)

[h]General government balance (percentage of GDP). General government includes the state, municipalities, and extra-budgetary funds. General government balance excludes privatization receipts

[i]Estimated

[j]Projected

17.2 Sources of Strength

The zloty has been supported by three main sources of strength. First, there has been nominal wage restraint, relatively to high productivity growth linked to restructuring. Unit labor costs in DM (1990–1994) and

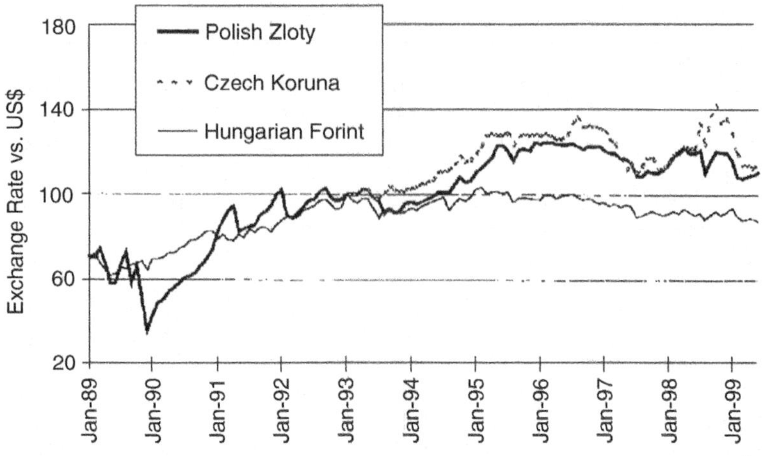

Fig. 17.3 Real exchange rates against the U.S. Dollar, CPI-based (January 1993 = 100). (Source: *IMF International Financial Statistics* (Datastream) and own calculations)

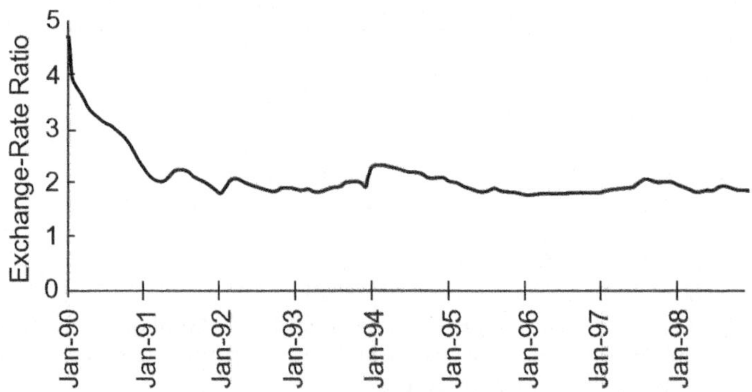

Fig. 17.4 Ratio of official to PPP exchange rates (monthly average), 1990–1998: ZLOTY/US$. (Source: PlanEcon Report (Polish Economic Monitor))

US$ (1994–1998) for Polish, Czech, and Hungarian manufacturing are given in Table 17.3, documenting the drastic loss of competitiveness of the Czech Republic, Hungary's superior performance, and Poland's sustained competitiveness since 1991.

Table 17.3 Unit labor costs, manufacturing sector (annual percentage change)

Year	Czech Republic	Poland	Hungary	Germany
A. DM, 1990–1995				
1990	-17.3	-9.8	14.4	19.0
1991	-14.8	66.5	29.4	11.6
1992	32.8	-8.7	7.6	12.2
1993	25.8	-8.8	-9.6	-2.1
1994	13.2	-7.3	-1.0	-4.1
1995	6.9	15.1	-8.7	13.0
B. US$, 1994–1998				
1994	11.3	-6.2	-3.6	–
1995	1.5	2.9	-19.1	–
1996	10.0	9.0	-3.4	–
1997	0.9	3.0	0.6	–
1998	4.3	3.2	-8.7	–

Source: *EBRD Transition Report* (updates 1997 and 1999)

Second, support has come from the appearance of a significant surplus in large-scale border trade, primarily with Germany but also with Poland's eastern neighbors (including trade in Warsaw's open-air markets), under the pull of purchasing-power parity. Such surplus was revealed by discrepancies between customs data and (higher) payments data for foreign-trade flows; at its peak in the mid-1990's this trade was of the order of \$6,000–8,000 million.

Third, there were large-scale inflows of financial capital, attracted by high interest rates (net of zloty depreciation, whether expected at the crawling rate or *ex post*). The attractive differential yield over and above the interest rate obtainable in reference currencies proved to be a mixed blessing (see Sect. 17.5).

17.3 Underperformance: Initial Undervaluation

When any market is divided into two segments, one where an administrative price is imposed below the equilibrium level corresponding to the quantity offered, and the other a free segment where a higher price is dictated by residual demand and supply, naturally the free price is higher than that which would prevail in a unified, single-price market. Thus it can be argued that when the Polish authorities on 1 January 1990 fixed the exchange rate at the level then prevailing in the free segment of the foreign-exchange market (no longer black for it had been legalized in February 1989) the zloty was undervalued. However, exchange-rate liberalization had been preceded by public debate and by wage settlements in December 1989 which took into account the inflationary effect of the forthcoming devaluation. It is possible that by 1 January 1990 the new equilibrium rate had moved to the old free rate, which simply validated itself through inflationary expectations and wage settlements.

Whatever was the case on 1 January 1990, the recession that accompanied an unintended fiscal surplus and an unintended real credit squeeze (which was aggravated, as in other transition economies, by systemic vacuum) led to a massive trade and current-account surplus and to an unintended buildup of reserves (on the order of $2,500 million). The fixed exchange rate therefore could be sustained until May 1991 (i.e. for much longer than originally anticipated), but this cannot possibly be regarded as a success, for (i) the fixed rate failed miserably as a nominal anchor, with a 1990 inflation rate of 249 percent and (ii) inflation could have been brought down much faster by allowing a nominal revaluation of the zloty such as would have necessarily occurred by floating the zloty, say, in April 1990—without adverse effects on trade flows and on employment in view of acknowledged low trade elasticities. Failure to allow a feasible zloty nominal revaluation, as well as general failure to respond to other aspects of initial overshooting, is a generally overlooked and gross mistake of Leszek Balcerowicz's management of Polish stabilization.

17.4 Underperformance: Sterilization or Inflation Costs

It is a distinguishing feature of Polish monetary policy, conducted by an independent and exceptionally powerful National Bank of Poland (NBP), that interest rates were kept high with respect to current inflation, therefore even higher with respect to expected inflation in a disinflationary environment. NBP appears to have suffered from "real illusion," targeting

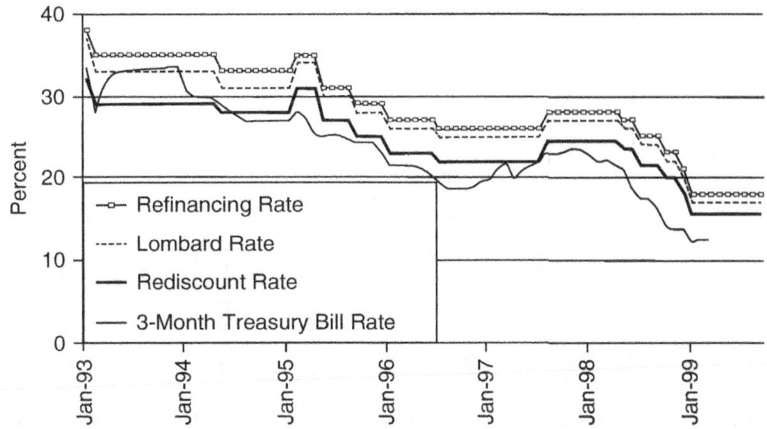

Fig. 17.5 Interest rates in Poland, 1993–1999. (Source: National Bank of Poland web site (http://www.nbp.plj and IMF International Financial Statistics (Datastream) for three-month Treasury Bill rate)

domestic real interest rates at levels no lower than in reference countries, thus neglecting the added attraction of zloty real revaluation for foreign investors. High interest rates (Fig. 17.5) maintained a strictly positive differential yield, net of preannounced devaluation (i.e. in dollar terms), with respect to U.S. Treasury Bills, averaging 5.38 percent throughout 1992–1998 (Fig. 17.6); *ex post*, the differential yield was more variable and occasionally negative but on average it was higher, at 5.73 percent (Fig. 17.7). For foreign investors, this was a one-way bet, which induced substantial net financial inflows, especially in 1995–1996. A wider band of variation, introduced to discourage capital inflows by raising the downside risk of investing in zlotys, was ineffective because, far from raising risk, it allowed nominal revaluations (see Sect. 17.5).

Net capital inflows allowed a rapid accumulation of foreign reserves, but such *embarras de richesse* posed an inescapable dilemma to the National Bank of Poland: either to allow the domestic monetary expansion brought about by reserve acquisition, at the cost of inflation, or to incur hefty costs of sterilization, equivalent to borrowing reserves at a rate corresponding to the differential yield in dollars on Polish securities, or a combination of the two. The Bank opted for both, at the same time systematically exceeding its own targets for monetary expansion and incurring sterilization costs which

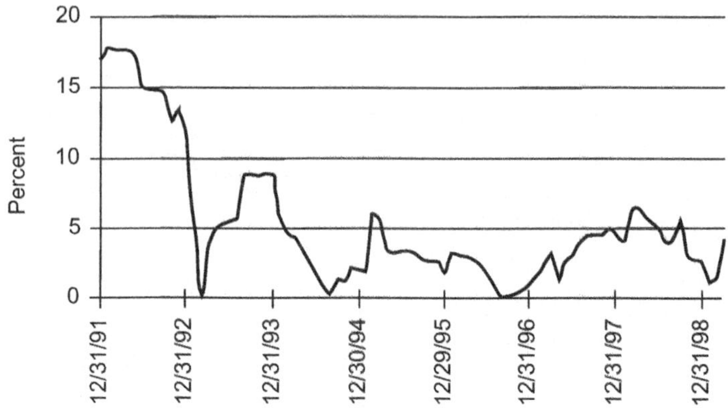

Fig. 17.6 Rate premium on Polish versus U.S. treasury bills net of preannounced crawling rate (mean = 5.38; SD = 4.75). (Source: IMF International Financial Statistics (Datastream) and own calculations)

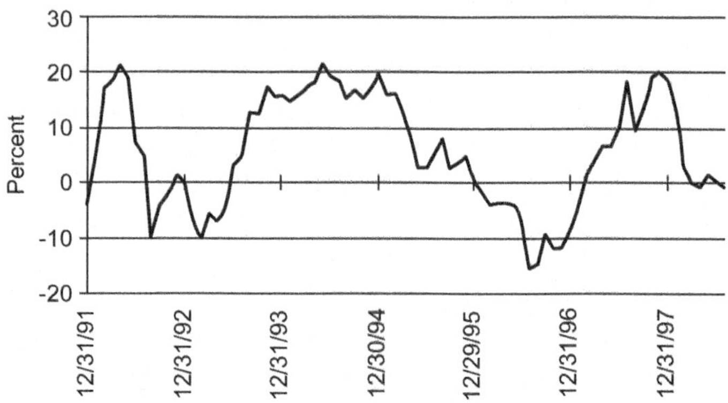

Fig. 17.7 Rate premium on Polish versus U.S. treasury bills net of subsequent actual depreciation (*ex post*) (mean = 5.73; SD = 10.09). (Source: IMF International Financial Statistics (Datastream) and own calculations)

in 1995–1997 were of the order of 1–1.5 percent of GDP. Such a cost was a hidden quasi-fiscal liability which indirectly affected the government budget, to which about 85 percent of National Bank of Poland profits are transferred. Lower interest rates would have prevented the inflationary impact of monetary overshooting, reduced fiscal imbalance, and consolidated the exchange rate without loss of competitiveness (for inflation would also have been lower).

17.5 Underperformance: The Devaluation/Revaluation Seesaw

However, the more spectacular form of underperformance of Polish exchange-rate policy is the obdurate and persistent attempt to hold the zloty on a path of crawling nominal devaluation, only for this course to be repeatedly reversed by market forces as soon as wider bands of variation allow them free play. Thus the National Bank of Poland was forced to allow a nominal revaluation of the zloty in May 1995, in December 1995, and in March 1998 (see Fig. 17.2) when the crawling band was widened. The alternative policy of lowering the rate of crawling devaluation of zloty parity (with or without a wider band) would clearly have been superior, for it would have reduced inflation and inflationary expectations and discouraged speculative inflows. In conclusion, zloty exchange-rate performance has been relatively successful not thanks to, but in spite of the policies pursued by the National Bank of Poland.

17.6 Prospects

The zloty's first two sources of strength given above (combined wage restraint and high productivity and a surplus in large-scale border trade) have now been greatly reduced if not virtually exhausted. In the medium if not already in the short run, the prospect of European Union (EU) accession and above all European Monetary Union (EMU) membership will impose a firming up of the zloty/Euro exchange rate and a gradual reduction of Polish interest rates. In the run up to EU accession, Poland will have to dismantle non-tariff trade barriers, whose growth in recent years has been a factor in containing the current-account deficit. Since the autumn of 1999 the zloty has also been weakened by fiscal slippage due to overgenerous new benefits for Polish farmers, the escalation of health expenditures, a new and unintended one-month lag in social-security payments (leading to a revenue shortfall covered by an interest-free loan from the budget to the ZUS agency). Perceived political instability (e.g., repeated threats of resignation by the Minister of Finance) have reinforced this adverse trend. On the positive side, the zloty may be strengthened by expectations of greater inflows of both foreign direct investment and budgetary transfers from the EU. The net result in the run up to accession is bound to be some exchange-rate turbulence, which is best handled in the short run by the proposed greater flexibility of the zloty exchange rate (which might go as far as straight floating in the near future). Until it is irreversibly locked onto the Euro the zloty will be increasingly vulnerable to a major currency crisis.

Bibliography

Darvas, Z. and Szapary, G. (1999). Financial contagion under different exchange rate regimes. National Bank of Hungary (Budapest) Working Paper No. 1999/10, September.

Datastream. IMF international financial statistics. Washington, DC: International Monetary Fund, various years.

EIU. Reports on Poland (quarterly and yearly). London: Economist Intelligence Unit, various years.

EBRD transition reports (and updates). London: European Bank for Reconstruction and Development, 1994–1999, various years.

Polish economic monitor. Washington, DC: Plan Econ, various years.

18

Privatisation of Socialist Economies: General Issues and the Polish Case

Domenico Mario Nuti

18.1 Introduction

Today all the socialist economies of central and eastern Europe are restoring or expanding forms of private ownership and enterprise. The process involves all these "transitional" economies, regardless of the pace and achievements of their economic reform, including the Soviet Union and excluding only Albania; differences are only speed, mode and degree. There is privatisation in a broad sense (the permission and encouragement of private enterprise and ownership), and in the narrow sense (the

Published in H. Blommestein, M. Marrese (Eds.), (1991). *Transformation of Planned Economies: Property Rights Reform and Macroeconomic Stability*. OECD, Paris, pp. 51–68.

An earlier version of this paper was presented at the OECD Conference on "The Transformation of Planned Economies", Paris, on 20th–22nd June 1990. Acknowledgements for useful comments and suggestions are due to Grzegorz Kolodko and to Conference participants, in particular to William Even as discussant, and to the Proceedings editors Hans Blommestein and Michael Marrese. Responsibility for opinions, errors and omissions rests solely with the author.

D. M. Nuti (✉)
La Sapienza, University of Rome, Rome, Italy
e-mail: milica.uvalic@unipg.it

© The Author(s), under exclusive license to Springer Nature Switzerland AG 2023

S. Estrin, M. Uvalic (eds.), *Collected Works of Domenico Mario Nuti, Volume I*,
Studies in Economic Transition, https://doi.org/10.1007/978-3-031-12334-4_18

sale, gift or rental of state assets to private individuals and companies). This paper considers the general case for privatisation in the narrow sense (Sect. 18.2) and in the light of the system-specific characteristics of socialist economies (Sect. 18.3); additional reasons are offered for the resilience of private ownership in socialist economies and the mounting pressure for its extension (Sects. 18.4, 18.5, and 18.6). Some more general issues are considered in the current process of privatisation in the transitional economies of central and eastern Europe (Sects. 18.7, 18.8, and 18.9), with a more specific focus on the privatisation process in Poland (Sects. 18.10, 18.11, and 18.12).

18.2 The General Case for Privatisation

To a great extent the drive towards privatisation in central and eastern Europe has the same basis as a similar process also seen in the last ten years in Europe, North America, Japan and the Third World (see Hemming and Mansoor 1988; Vickers and Yarrow 1988). The strongest reason for this development is the expectation that privatisation can raise efficiency through changed incentives.

This expectation is found in the recent economic literature on principal-agent relations. Company managers, as agents of owners, are subject to contractual discipline enforced by shareholders; to take-over discipline enforced by potential bidders; and to bankruptcy discipline enforced by creditors. Managers of state enterprises are not subject to any such discipline, as they are subordinated to political authority and not to economically motivated shareholders; they are not subject to take-overs; and their losses are absorbed by automatic grants from the state budget (see Vickers and Yarrow 1988). Further arguments for privatisation have been the adoption of a deflationary fiscal stance less austere than it would be if implemented through fiscal means, and the promotion of diffused ownership patterns associated with the "property-owning democracy" model as an alternative to socialism.

These arguments for privatisation may have to be modified. Public enterprises sometimes can be more efficient than their private counterparts (in practice, see South Korean state steel; in theory, see Sappington and Stiglitz 1987; Stiglitz 1989). Privatisation of management might achieve the same effects as privatisation of ownership without divesting the state of its assets (i.e. the state could hold shares in private companies; see Meade 1989). In Western market economies, privatisation has not been accompanied by significant progress towards property-owning democracy. In the case of transitional economies, however, privatisation not only raises the share of national assets held by private owners, it also extends the scope of ownership rights from absent or limited ownership to full-fledged private ownership. This qualitative aspect of privatisation in transitional economies provides additional system-specific, supportive arguments .

18.3 System-specific Arguments for Privatisation in Socialist Economies

First, there is a presumption that privatisation will inject life into the inert traditional system. With the benefit of hindsight the main drawback of central planning and state ownership has been its inability to respond to change (whether in technology, domestic demand, or world trade opportunities): the appropriation of the benefits that economic agents might obtain from faster response can only enhance the vitality and viability of those economies.

Second, privatisation is bound to weaken the opportunity for political interference in economic life, especially in those economies still dominated by the Communist Party and its all-pervasive "nomenklatura". In principle it should be possible to cut the links between the centre and enterprises by inserting an intermediate layer of independent state holdings representing state interests. In this context privatisation may not be necessary, but it is an effective, well-tested institution and therefore more appealing than more controversial and less well-tried state holdings.

Third, privatisation of enterprises and commercial banks together is bound to harden the "soft" budget constraint of enterprises, which has been one of the main sources of the endemic excess demand typical of centrally planned economies everywhere. Again, it is conceivable that the budget of a state enterprise might be hardened as a result of a change in government policy, but in the light of experience there is little—if any—support for this expectation.

Whatever the validity and strength of the general justification, these three arguments strengthen the case for the privatisation now occurring in transitional economies. But there is more: privatisation appears also as the consequence of the resilience of private ownership in socialist economies, and there is a strong case for the further extension of the limited property rights which already have existed .

18.4 The Resilience of Private Ownership

Private ownership seems to have a built-in resilience in the socialist economies, where it was never completely eradicated. Moreover, regimes of limited ownership seem to suffer from a certain institutional instability: whenever private ownership is even minimally present, the system tends naturally towards its further extension.

Let us consider what is the necessary and sufficient condition for complete abolition of private ownership. Imagine an economy where individuals have access to instant consumption of goods and services, whether freely (in unlimited amounts or within predetermined limits for each good and service) or subject to money prices and a maximum money budget per unit of time. In either case we stipulate that in this economy individuals do not have any other access to consumption and are not able to transfer their consumption claims to others or over time, i.e. they cannot save in the sense of accumulating that part of their maximum consumption entitlement which they do not actually consume. This is the kind of partial or temporary arrangement familiar from expense accounts, communal kibbutz consumption or participation in academic conferences but—with the possible though unproven exception of Stone Age economies—such an arrangement has never been a basis for the lasting economic organisation of entire communities. Free unlimited consumption, the ultimate full 'communist model',[1] belongs to this category but

[1] According to Strumilin, a sufficient condition of full communism is that free consumption should be the larger share. However in order to measure the relative shares of free and non-free goods—unless all goods are subject to a two-tier (free and non-free) regime—it is necessary to use a set of weights, i.e. actual or shadow prices. Yet it is not clear from where the necessary price system would come. In principle prices could come from a system of marginal valuations with reference to a central body, were it not for the fact that under full communism presumably central bodies "wither away" with the state.

has never been implemented anywhere; "realised socialism" has never organised consumption on that basis.

The lack of a generalised system of consumption allocation of this kind is a necessary and sufficient condition for private property to arise. Namely, it is a necessary condition because otherwise property could not be transferred, rented or used without violating our stipulations. It is a sufficient condition because a possible private property right on consumption goods arises as soon as claims to consumption can be transferred to others (creating the possibility of future reciprocity, whether through market exchange or possibly through a deferred exchange of reciprocal gifts) or to oneself over time through production or through storage of either the goods or the claims.

It is interesting to note that money is a sufficient but not a necessary condition for private ownership to arise: even in a system without either money or voucher claims and with short-lived goods only (the least favourable set up for property rights to consumption to arise), a stock of consumption goods can be carried and owned within the constraints set by the rate of durability and by the storage space available, the actual stock being determined possibly as the result of an optimisation process leading to the equalisation of rates of time preference and expected rates of return on each consumption good accumulated.[2] Once there is money—at least in the limited role of a means of distributing

[2] If I consume a quantity c(i) of good i per unit of time and that good has durability T(i), I can carry a revolving stock of c(i)*T(i); if v(i) is the storage volume required per unit of consumption good i and I have a maximum storage space V, then I will have a maximum command on a stock of consumption goods given by a vector c with elements c(i)*T(i) subject to the scalar product of c and v (the corresponding vector of storage requirements per unit of consumption) being equal to or less than V. Here "durability" means 100 per cent conservation for a period of time T(i), which is equivalent to a zero real own rate of return on storage; this already gives rise to an optimisation problem, in that the rational consumer, given his expected future claims to consumption c(i, t) will equate his real rate of time preference, implicit in his rate of intertemporal substitution, to the zero own rate of return on storage. As a result of this maximisation problem actual stocks of goods C(i, t) may well be lower than the maximum allowed by storage space and durability characteristics. In practice the consumption goods stored have a rate of decay d(i) which is a function of storage time, i.e. d(i)=d[i, T(i)], giving rise to a more complex optimisation problem, simultaneously determining d(i) and T(i) as well as C(i, t); now there can be different real rates of time preferences for each good, being equated to the rate of decay which is an implicit negative rate of (own) real interest.

consumption goods—and this money is non-perishable,[3] the possibilities of amassing potential command over a stock of consumption goods become virtually unlimited even if all goods were perishable and no storage space were available. The actual stock of money held will be limited, though, by the same optimisation process, whereby the real rate of time preference is set equal to the real rate of return on money holdings, i.e. the percentage cost of money storage[4] minus the expected rate of money price increase, for all goods.

This reasoning presumes that "markets" clear, though it does not necessarily imply a supply schedule, only that given quantities of dated consumption goods are available and distributed at state-fixed prices. Market clearing is an inappropriate assumption for traditional socialist economies, which are inordinately prone to permanent excess demand due to the unreasonable overambition of planned targets, combined with an unsustainable commitment to stable prices. However, a claim to a stock of consumption goods can be held in real terms and (through money) even in conditions of persistent shortages except that the relevant prices are official money prices plus a premium for queuing or for random access to goods. Secondary retrading of shortage goods, whether it exists legally or illegally, will necessarily tend toward this relevant price level.

It follows from these reflections on theoretical consumption behaviour that, when we discuss private property under models of socialism other than the (unrealised) full communist model, we cannot bring into question the possibility of private property, which is always there at least in the form of some property rights to a stock of consumption goods, nor the existence of a rate of return (negative though it may be in real terms) on that stock. We can only discuss the scope of those property rights and the way that rate of return is determined. Namely we can discuss who can own what for what purpose, the unbundling of property into its

[3] Even paper money could be made perishable if an early enough date were fixed by which it had to be spent, or its liquidity could be reduced if its validity as legal tender were subject to some inconvenient procedure of official validation. Keynes (1936), for instance, suggested that cash should be stamped at frequent intervals; for a history of the idea of money "melting" or "reabsorbing", see Morley-Fletcher (1980–1981).

[4] This cost is virtually equal to zero, or a small amount taken with a negative sign; if interest-earning liquid deposits are possible, they are treated here as financial assets different from money.

constituent rights (as simultaneous *jus utendi, fruendi ac abutendi* in Roman law, with possible finer distinctions in modern times), their yield and their transferability to whom, and how the efficiency implications of private property respond to progressively increasing extensions of the scope of private property. We can also discuss the set of possible limitations or obligations which may be attached to property rights. Finally, we can discuss whether and to what extent the effects of private property might be simulated by alternative arrangements .

18.5 The Case for Extension of Limited Property Rights

The presence of property rights to consumption goods is an apparently harmless consequence of permitting individual choice of how to allocate consumption over time, an arrangement which is both efficient and—arguably—a basic freedom. However, once this limited scope of property rights is established there are very strong logical arguments on efficiency grounds, and in response to actual economic pressures, for their extension to a full-fledged capitalist regime of property rights—where anybody can own and trade anything except drugs and slaves, and rights can be unbundled and transferred at will.[5]

In fact, if I am allowed to save real consumption and retain its ownership at a real rate of interest implicit in storage conditions, obviously I should be given the opportunity to save instead in the form of cash and interest-yielding deposits and bonds at a nominal monetary rate of interest equivalent to the same real rate, thus releasing real resources for productive use. Indeed, if I am willing to save more and more at progressively higher interest rates, and there are correspondingly profitable productive uses for those resources, I should be given that opportunity for the sake of efficiency. This multiplies the possibility of accumulating private

[5] Except for contracts involving the delivery of future labour services, which would not be capitalistic but feudal, as they would imply the compulsory subjection of individuals to other individuals or firms.

property by relaxing storage and perishability constraints and of receiving a rentier income.

Any investment in consumption goods has an element—albeit small—of risk-taking, depending on current conditions (should I invest in an umbrella or in sunglasses?) affecting the course of relative prices. Financial claims broaden the scope of potential exposure to risk and to its rewards or penalties; loans can be at fixed or variable interest rates; borrowers' creditworthiness will be reflected in their cost of finance. Even in the absence of risk-taking in financial markets, lotteries may and usually do exist in any socialist economy.[6] Moreover employment contracts even under socialism often carry performance-related bonuses, uncertain and lottery-like, broadening further the scope of risk-taking. But now, if I am allowed to draw an interest on financial claims and to expose myself to risk for the sake of a higher expected return, why should I be barred from owning a stake in the present value of an "enterprise" (defined broadly as a set of productive activities and contractual rights and obligations). In a world where there are interest rates and risk premia the introduction of private shares and capital markets does not involve a qualitative change. At first shares may be issued to workers of the same enterprise and may not carry a vote; risk-spreading however suggests a reshuffling of stock across enterprises through generalised trade in a stock exchange, and managerial discipline requires the objection of managers to the threat of an adverse majority vote (and the take-over threat of vote-acquiring bidders).

Finally, once I am allowed to hold an equity stake in an enterprise, and share in its success and failure, there is no qualitative change involved in my being allowed to directly found and run an enterprise and employ workers directly rather than through the mediation of managers.[7] Down the slippery slope of property rights, through small Pareto-improving steps, one may quickly revert to full-fledged traditional capitalism.

[6] China appears to have been an exception, at least until recently.

[7] The March 1990 Soviet legislation on property prohibits one-man-owned enterprises employing wage labour, but allows joint-stock companies, somehow regarded as "collective" forms of ownership. This is an absurd distinction, co-ownership being no less private than one-man ownership of a whole asset. Soviet legislators literally are preventing "exploitation of man" by one other man but allow it when it is done by several men together.

Over time, the case for privatisation mounts implacably with the accumulation of successive monetary gaps between income and expenditure, due to the excess demand systematically present in the socialist economy and the stubborn commitment to maintain stable prices in spite of it. The overhang takes the form of excess liquid assets and abnormally high levels of stocks, both by households and enterprises.[8] In the end the domestic overhang becomes so large as to suggest the selling of state assets to the population instead of alternatives which may be more unpalatable (currency confiscation, hyperinflation) or simply not available (additional domestic or international borrowing) .

18.6 Ownership and Entrepreneurship

An interesting question is whether there is a natural breaking point in this chain, i.e. where—if anywhere—do decreasing returns set in on the road to full capitalist ownership. According to Mises, private ownership of capital is a necessary precondition of capital markets and therefore of markets in general: without ownership markets cannot even be simulated (see Mises 1951; Hanson 1989). Mises was certainly right in that private appropriability (including potential transferability and use/abuse) of at least a share of enterprise profits and capital gains must be essential to the very existence of ownership;[9] however this does not necessarily imply the private ownership of any of the actual means of production. In fact one could imagine a state ownership system in which state assets are leased on competitive leasing markets to private entrepreneurs, who appropriate at least part of any residual income and who by selling their leases to others, can realise the present value of their entrepreneurial activities, without ever acquiring ownership of capital goods or, technically, of any enter-

[8] In the Soviet economy in 1990 excess liquid assets in the hands of the population are estimated to be of the order of an average four months' wage bill; enterprises' inventories were 82 per cent of national income in 1985, compared with 31 per cent in the United States (Shmelev and Popov 1989, p. 305).

[9] In this respect my own views have radically altered with respect to Nuti (1974), where the possibility of group entrepreneurship in the traditional socialist model was considered with excessive optimism.

prise. In such a system investment could remain a state function, whose efficiency would be monitored by comparing, *ex post*, the return on investment obtained from the rentals determined in competitive leasing markets, to the interest rates prevailing at the time of investing.

It is tempting to conjecture that there can be no markets without private property, nor economic planning with private property: however this conjecture, though not rejected by experience, is still unproven on theoretical grounds. Once entrepreneurial rewards are at least partly appropriable it is possible to conceive a replication of competitive capital markets with or without the participation of private individuals but without private ownership of capital assets as such (see Nuti 1988, 1989). These kinds of arrangements (which could be actual markets and not just simulations), however, are not a case against private ownership but a case for economic reform; ideological obstacles against reform could be side-stepped, even if they were not to disappear, as now seems the case. In practice leasings of state property (as in the Soviet "arenda" and the Polish "dzierzawa", and on an even larger scale in China) are one of the possible ways of implementing privatisation of state assets especially in special sectors such as agriculture, catering and small-scale production, but cannot represent a general exclusive alternative to the sale of assets and shares .

Another interesting question is whether entrepreneurship could be associated with forms of ownership other than state and private, such as municipal or cooperative. In the Soviet Union a great deal of emphasis has been placed on the growth of the co-operative sector, which in the 30 months since June 1987 has grown from 55 000 to 5.5 million employees (including members, full- and part-time dependent workers), and raised turnover from 29 million to 40 billion rubles. Soviet co-operatives are not subjected to the income and capital sharing restrictions typical of traditional co-operatives, and very often serve as shells for private enterprises. Therefore their growth is an indication of the potential role that might be played by ownership forms other than state or private under special conditions, but this growth cannot be taken at face value or simply extrapolated to other countries or periods. However it is conceivable that privatisation of state assets could help to transform dependent workers into partial entrepreneurs. This process seems to be making some progress in modern Western capitalism with the introduction of income and capital sharing and worker participation in enterprise decision-making (see Nuti 1990c) .

18.7 General Issues: Subjectivisation

In the current privatisation experience of central and eastern European economies three general issues have arisen. The first is the danger that, in the early steps towards economic reform, decentralisation of decision-making from central bodies to enterprises might divest the state of its assets without transferring ownership rights to other subjects. In that case it is as if state ownership became "*res nullius*", and before privatisation can take place it is necessary to undertake and complete a process of "resubjectivisation", re-uniting property rights under the same public holder before actually privatising. This is what happened in Hungary with the 1984–1985 legislation on state enterprises, which *de facto* acquired most of the rights associated with ownership on the unprecedented and nonsensical theory that "enterprises belong to themselves" (as officially stated by the Ministry of Justice). This unusual state was not remedied by the first attempts at privatisation (Act VI 1988; Act XIII 1989; see Hare 1989).

A similar problem arises in those countries where workers have gained a measure of self-management: some of the new shares may have to be sold or granted to enterprise employees, in order to trade off their full management rights (incompatible with shareholders' rights) with fuller ownership rights on a smaller scale (therefore embodying a smaller voice in enterprise management). Regardless of this argument, or beyond the limits of this kind of "conversion", shares may be sold to workers in order to strengthen popular support and to promote a property-owning democracy as an alternative system. Forms of workers' ownership abound in a capitalist economy: Employee Stock Ownership Plans (ESOPs, where workers acquire shares held collectively before they are distributed after a period or at retirement or departure) or Trusts (ESOTs, where workers are temporary co-owners and only enjoy a share of the revenue while they are employed), Personal Equity Plans (for regular savers, attracting tax exemption up to a maximum limit), Equity Holding Cooperatives, Additional Pension Funds, Swedish-type collective investors, and so forth (see Uvalic 1990).

The new shares can be partly managed by state holdings and new pension funds. State holdings—as noted above—are often regarded with suspicion, as bearers of central interests, dependent on and ultimately answering to the centre. There is however no reason why they should not respond to a policy commitment to make profits instead of being responsible for the achievement of government targets (the Italian state holding IRI, for instance, has responded to policy changes and has rapidly turned from an endemic loss maker into a profit-oriented and profit-making entity, presiding over privatisation). Pension funds (new, for there are none in Eastern European economies) are also credible collective investors, but they should only be given as much stock as they can reasonably need to take over pension liabilities; there is no justification in profits funding the consumption of pensioner rentiers, instead of being channelled to self-financed investment .

It is conceivable that the banking system might exercise control over companies through direct and indirect (namely on behalf of clients) shareholdings and the associated voting rights. Such a role is typical of the German-Japanese model of financial markets and has been advocated for Poland by Gomulka (1989). However, banks in that model rely on a full-fledged stock exchange and do not replace it. Thus the ability of the banking system to hold and administer state ownership should not be overestimated.[10]

18.8 Private Appropriation of State Property

A phenomenon often practised and sometimes advocated in our "transitional" economies is the private appropriation of state property, either as a public policy of free distribution or as the result of spontaneous, "wild" auto-appropriation (in Polish "*samouwlaszczenie*").

[10] Gomulka envisages a special role for banks in the privatisation process: public shareholdings in state enterprises would be entrusted to the management of banks, which would earn a share of dividends and realised capital gains; Gomulka regards privatisation of those banks as equivalent to the privatisation of the public assets entrusted to them but this is a misconception: if I buy shares in Merrill Lynch I do not acquire a stake in the portfolio of their clients. Moreover, emphasis on realised capital gains rather than on the increase of portfolio evaluation is bound to unduly inflate turnover (by encouraging a special case of so-called "bed and breakfast" transactions, i.e. sales followed by quick repurchases).

It has been suggested (for instance by Attila Soos in Hungary, Dusan Triska in Czechoslovakia, Jan Szomburg and Janusz Lewandowski in Poland) that shares in state enterprises or holdings may be given away freely to all citizens, directly or in the form of vouchers. This policy seems to have the advantage of creating an instant capital market, as well as the political advantage of generating instant capitalism and popular support for it. The needs of budgetary balance and monetary discipline, however, should strictly limit any privileged access to shares, as well as their free distribution (apart from the need of "converting" self-management rights into ownership stakes, discussed in the previous section). Free distribution of shares would be costly (as it was in the only known case to date, in British Columbia in 1979).[11] It would add a wealth effect to consumption demand, worsening inflationary pressure whether open or repressed. It would have an urban bias (of a kind that would not be present in case of free distribution of the profits of state enterprises as citizens' income): peasants in remote rural areas would be unlikely to benefit as much as the inhabitants of the capital city. As soon as potential limits to disposal lapsed, free distribution would also likely lead to rapid retrading and concentration of assets in the hands of a few better-informed people with access to liquid means (if this is not a preoccupation, perhaps a lottery with large bundles of shares would be preferable and cheaper to administer). The state is not withering away in the course of transition and will continue to tax "Daddy state… is alive and well", as Kornai (1990, p. 82) graphically puts it; privatisation revenues could replace taxes, thereby avoiding their distortionary effects on economic efficiency (Newbery 1990).

Free share issues are often advocated on grounds of lack of sufficient domestic capital. However—depending on the policy towards debt-equity swaps—domestic credit may be granted on a large scale for the population to take part in privatisation; as long as this credit is sterilised and is not recycled to government expenditure, it can create a useful buffer against possible subsequent loss of macroeconomic control, when the government might sell its credits rather than raise additional taxes. In a

[11] In early 1979 the provincial government of British Columbia set up a new Crown Corporation, the British Columbia Resources Investment Corporation, with $151.5 million in assets, and distributed five free shares to any citizen who asked for them, plus additional shares at $6 each; 170 000 persons were involved. However the new company made some bad investments and soon incurred substantial losses; the operation is not judged to have been a success (see Stanbury 1989, pp. 282–283, in MacAvoy et al. 1989) .

country like Poland, state revenue from privatisation could be used to retire hard currency credits of enterprises and households via the state banking system, which are not backed by hard currency reserves and therefore limit central control over the money supply. Finally, the free gift of state assets seems an out-of-place largess on the part of governments heavily indebted to international creditors, who would be justified in asserting a prior claim to those assets.[12]

The other form of private appropriation—spontaneous, or "wild" auto-appropriation—is worse because it is selective: privatisation without publicity and competition may result at least partially in divestiture, rather than sale, and in the parallel appropriation of state property by a few well-informed people in positions of power. In the early stages of privatisation in Hungary and Poland (Hare 1989; Grosfeld 1990; Chilosi 1990), then elsewhere, managers and party officials often converted their position into a share of state capital, through semi-legal outright illegal transactions tolerated because of their large scale and the offenders' positions. This type of transaction includes: subcontracting of profitable activities, reciprocal disposals between state enterprise managers to their personal advantage, personal deals in joint ventures with foreign partners, artificial liquidation of viable activities transferred to internal bidders, etc.[13] There is no conceivable justification for condoning these practices, which are equivalent to the worst cases of insider trading in western markets .

[12] The loss of potential collateral on the part of creditors may be thought to be overcompensated by the greater potential productivity which could derive from privatisation and the further impulse to economic reform. Certainly no international creditor has publicly argued against free distribution of state assets in debtor countries.

[13] The auto-appropriation of state assets by the nomenklatura has been facilitated in Poland by the extraordinary growth of joint stock and limited liability companies founded in Poland, which were almost 30 000 in 1989. Some transactions, in which managers appeared on both sides as sellers on behalf of their state enterprises and as buyers for their own companies or even joint ventures naturally have been declared void by the Supreme Court, but the bulk of this kind of transaction are unlikely to be challenged especially when foreign buyers are also involved (Chilosi 1990). A famous case is that of Igloopol, the largest Polish agro-industrial complex, valued at 145 billion zlotys and artificially liquidated and transferred for 55 billion zlotys to a joint stock company with the same board of directors, whose shares—transferable at their discretion—were sold mostly to Party organisations and activists. The Ministry of Agriculture (of which the Igloopol Managing Director was Deputy Minister) approved the liquidation procedure in spite of a Ministry of Finance report which declared it illegal and economically unjustified (Grosfeld 1990). A recent decree of the Mazowiecki Government has now made illegal the participation of state enterprise managers and workers' councils in the companies founded by their own enterprise (Chilosi 1990).

18.9 Privatisation in the Reform Sequence

A crucial general question is the position of privatisation in the sequence of reform measures, i.e. whether it should occur during or after stabilisation, before or after de-monopolisation, and financial and productive restructuring.

It seems most inappropriate to sell off shares in state enterprises before stabilisation and fiscal reform. Here stabilisation is understood as domestic market equilibrium in non-hyperinflationary or excessively inflationary conditions, at uniform prices; fiscal reform is understood as the termination of *ex-post, ad hoc*, enterprise-specific taxes and subsidies levelling profitability throughout the economy. Without these prior achievements, trends in product and input prices and therefore enterprise profitability would be impossible to assess, and as a result assets would be underpriced and yet unattractive in conditions of uncertainty. Thus privatisation cannot really contribute directly to the stabilisation process (see Nuti 1990a, b). An exception can be the privatisation of housing (where the stream of future services is directly consumed by the owner), small plots of land and small scale services (where future benefits are more strictly dependent on the owner-worker's effort supply). This kind of "small" privatisation can contribute to stabilisation .

The very announcement of a firm decision to proceed with privatisation on a clearly predetermined schedule and procedure can itself make a contribution to stabilisation (the opposite happened in the USSR where announcement of future price increases destabilised domestic markets and aggravated shortages). The announcement can be particularly effective if it is followed by the issue of special bonds, at low or zero nominal interest but carrying an option to purchase without restriction any state asset which will be privatised subsequently—pending the determination of asset prices. In Poland in November 1989 this instrument was used but bonds redeemable through privatisation were indexed and the timing and pattern of privatisation were not specified; thus the bonds cost the government much more than other forms of bond financing and even so, in the uncertainty about privatisation terms, were not very attractive to the public at the time of issue.[14]

De-monopolisation is also a necessary precondition of privatisation: without it asset prices would include a capitalisation of monopoly power, which would be either unduly validated or—from the viewpoint of buyers—unfairly removed later on. A firm commitment to subsequent de-monopolisation still leaves a strong element of uncertainty; foreign trade liberalisation may alleviate the problem by raising the degree of competition.

The transformation of state enterprises into joint stock companies presupposes the valuation of their net assets and their recapitalisation (as the Czechs put it, "the bride has to be endowed before being given away…"). Or, if necessary, excess liquid resources may be drained away before privatisation; at least some rationalisation of output structure and input outlays (including labour employment) must take place. To proceed otherwise implies the likely underselling of state assets. If, before privatisation, an active capital market has been organised, valuation and financial restructuring can be left to competitive mechanisms; otherwise some competitive redeployment of assets has to be stimulated among state enterprises. In any case it seems important that labour redundancies and redeployments should be handled before, rather than after, privatisation, both to ensure fair compensation of workers and to make assets more attractive to potential alternative users .

18.10 The Polish Economic Framework

In the ten years preceding 1990 Poland experienced stagnation in real output, while consumption levels fell by 10 per cent over the ten years (to end-1989). Polish external debt reached $42 billion (of which $28 billion was owed to other governments), too large an amount to be fully serviced

[14] Kolodko (1990) reports that a million zlotys invested in these bonds at the end of 1989 were worth by the end of the first quarter of 1990 2.5 million zlotys, compared with 1.3 million zlotys if invested in three-month deposits at the National Savings Bank (PKO) and 1.06 million zlotys if invested in dollar-denominated deposits. This is an indication of the lack of credibility of government policies.

in spite of recurring trade surpluses (about $1 billion per year in 1985–1989). Shortages were endemic and inflation accelerated reaching the yearly rate of 740 per cent in 1989, when output declined by 1.7 per cent (see Kolodko 1989) .

The economic framework of the 1990 drive towards privatisation is that of a drastic stabilisation programme, launched by the new Mazowiecki Government on 1 January 1990, aimed at restoring market equilibrium, introducing resident convertibility for current transactions, and promoting net exports, while at the same time making progress towards reform and restructuring (see Kolodko 1990; Frydman et al. 1990; Nuti 1990c).

The stabilisation package envisaged the abolition of subsidies and the reduction of the budget deficit to 1 per cent of GNP (down from 8 per cent in the previous year); monetary discipline and an increase in real interest rates to positive levels (the interest rate was raised also on old contracts, amounting to a tax); almost complete price liberalisation (except for energy, pharmaceuticals and fertilisers, whose price increases were diluted in subsequent months); very mild wage indexation of wage guidelines (at 30 per cent of inflation in January, 20 per cent in February to April, 60 per cent in May to December except for July when indexation was 100 per cent to compensate for energy price increases) and penal taxation over that level; trade liberalisation; 32 per cent devaluation of the zloty, made convertible and held at 9 500 zlotys per dollar, with the backing of external assistance provided by international agencies and the Group of 24 (a $700 million International Monetary Fund (IMF) stand-by credit, a $1billion stabilisation fund, $300 million from the World Bank, EC-coordinated assistance under the PHARE programme, and credits and gifts by individual countries) and the rescheduling of debt service .

The programme was successful in establishing domestic market equilibrium: net exports rose to $1.7 billion over the first seven months; inflation exploded going up to the monthly (point-to-point) rate of 105 per cent in January 1990 then settled down to 4–6 per cent per month, which is still much too high on a yearly basis; and the exchange rate was held at the target rate, in spite of hyperinflation and continued inflation differentials with hard currency countries (which just goes to show how grossly undervalued it must have been in January 1990). However, the real purchasing power of wages (formerly overestimated by statistics because of permanent shortages) fell by a third; output in mid-year stagnated after a fall of over one-third; and unemployment, around 10 000 at the end of 1989, grew fast and at the end of July 1990 had reached 700 000, rising at a rate of over 25 000 per week—government forecasts expect 1.3 million unemployed by the end of 1990.

In brief, the stabilisation programme has overshot its output, employment and real wages targets, and yet there is hardly a sign of "supply response". Against this background the advantages expected of privatisation—demand deflation, efficiency, entrepreneurship—become particularly important .

18.11 Polish Privatisation: Debates and Practice

In Poland there is a long-standing tradition of private enterprise both in agriculture (following the de-collectivisation of 1956, with about 4 million employees today) and outside agriculture as well, especially in the last six years (private manufacturing, transport and other services, including joint ventures, with over 1 million employees). This makes up almost one-third of the labour force and grew in 1988 at 11 per cent while state employment was falling at 1–2 per cent; these trends have accelerated in 1989–1990. By early 1990 there were 845 677 private enterprises (though mostly of very small size) attracting the best employees away from the public sector (Chilosi 1990). Official forecasts for 1990 expect state industrial output to fall by 28 per cent and private output to grow by 5 per cent, bringing the relative shares of the two sectors in industry from 92 to 87–88 per cent and from 8 to 12–13 per cent, respectively.

The privatisation of Polish state assets and the setting up of a stock exchange where they could be sold and retraded were already under consideration by the last communist-dominated Polish Government, and naturally were revamped by the Mazowiecki-led coalition (see Grosfeld 1990). Finance Minister Leszek Balcerowicz, speaking at the IMF assembly in Washington in October 1989, stated that: "The government of

Poland intends to transform the Polish economy to a market economy. This process is to be accompanied by a gradual change in the pattern of ownership towards that which prevails in countries with advanced economies." (Balcerowicz 1989)

Privatisation has been generally regarded as a deflationary instrument to avoid or reduce hyperinflation, a guarantee of enterprise independence from central organs and most importantly, a way of enhancing productivity and entrepreneurship.

The main difficulty faced by both the former and the present government has been the reconciliation of privatisation schemes with the self-management institutions set up in Polish enterprises by the legislation of September 1981 (see Nuti 1981 for a comparison of the legislation with the more militant draft law submitted by Solidarity at that time). This legislation gave workers collectively some, indeed most, of the rights usually exercised by shareholders (such as managerial appointments and dismissals, verification of current performance, distribution of profit, and investment plans). Therefore the transformation of state enterprises into joint stock companies to be sold off to the public implies the cancellation or substantial dilution of those rights which, especially at times of drastic reductions in real wages, has to be compensated and negotiated. But there were also other difficulties, in part indirectly related to the modification of self-management.

The starting position of workers before privatisation is that of part entrepreneurs—not having ownership rights but having extensive decision-making rights and some profit-related benefits—for 100 per cent of the enterprise. An obvious trade off is that of giving workers the position of full entrepreneurs—i.e. 100 per cent owners, decision-makers and residual claimants—as shareholders in the enterprise with a much smaller stake. But how much smaller? And should it not be an equal absolute stake in all enterprises rather than a percentage which would unduly favour capital intensive sectors? But then how are shares to be valued, before a capital stock is set up? Should one start with the ailing enterprises or with the viable ones? And why limit the share-out to workers in state enterprises, excluding for instance workers in government services, or the unemployed; should everybody not have an equal share of state assets financed by past consumption sacrifices on the part of the whole population? Current savings could not afford to buy more than a small fraction of the whole national capital anyway. Why not give everybody a free share in all state enterprises, or rather in a number of state holding companies, thus solving at a stroke problems of capital valuation, equality and small size of the market? Or perhaps free equal vouchers should be offered to the whole adult population to convert into a portfolio of their choice as privatisation proceeds. But then, why dilapidate state assets when the state budget deficit must be eliminated and there are pressing welfare needs, not to speak of the burden of external debt? Should sales and debt-equity swaps not be explored first? Could workers in state enterprises be satisfied by a combination of lesser involvement in decision-making and stronger participation in enterprise profit, instead of having to be paid off with a capital stake?

These questions were hotly debated in Poland and arguments somewhat impeded the progress of privatisation .

18.12 The New Polish Law on Privatisation (July 1990)

The office of the Government Plenipotentiary for questions of Property Transformations—a new ministerial post in the new government, held by Krzystof Lis - prepared a number of successive versions of draft laws on "The Privatisation of State Enterprises" and on "The Council of National Capital and the Agency for Ownership Transformations" (Biuro 1990a, b). In April 1990 the 15th version was presented to the Polish Parliament, with a counter-draft law being submitted by a group of Trade Union deputies close to Andrzej Milkowski of OKP (Solidarity's Citizen Parliamentary Committee; see OKP 1990). The government project, somewhat modified to take into account suggested amendments, was approved in July 1990 by impressive majorities (328 votes to two with 39 abstentions in the lower house; 60 votes to seven with two abstentions in the Senate), but it left many issues still unresolved.

The Law establishes a Ministry of Property Transformation, to oversee the transformation of state enterprises into share companies initially held by the Treasury as single shareholder, followed within two years by the sale of shares to domestic and foreign investors, mostly by public offer at a prefixed price. The initiative to privatise a given enterprise can be taken by management, workers or the "founding organs" (i.e. the central body or bodies exercising authority on the enterprise to date) and is subject to governmental authorisation.

Up to 20 per cent of shares are reserved for workers of the privatised enterprise at a 50 per cent discount on the price of issue; the discount however cannot exceed half of the buyer's salary over the last six months. This is an ingenious constraint which broadly equalises access to capital by employees in enterprises characterised by different amounts of capital per person.

This reserve creates a potential class of 4 million small investors but excludes from the discount the other 13 million working in state agencies other than enterprises and in the private sector; however a portion (expected to be 10–20 per cent) of the shares of companies undertaking privatisation is to be distributed freely and equally to the general public. Moreover, access to capital ownership is facilitated by the fact that shares can be purchased on credit, if so decided by the Minister of Property Transformation and the Minister of Finance. In order to limit nomenklatura acquisitions only individuals can acquire shares at the time of privatisation. As long as an enterprise is in state hands, one-third of the board of directors is to be elected by workers.

Foreign investors can freely purchase state company shares subject to an overall ceiling of 10 per cent, which can be raised by the Agency for Foreign Investments (transferred to the Ministry of Property Transformations from the Foreign Trade Ministry). Dividends and the proceeds of subsequent share sales may be repatriated abroad without special permits.

An alternative form of ownership transformation is through liquidation, i.e. selling or leasing all or part of the enterprise assets to employees or external entrepreneurial groups, preferably at public auction, with a view to facilitate the creation of new private enterprises.

Several hundred enterprises are expected to close in the next year, and their assets will be sold or leased. Privatisation of some companies (out of over 7 000 potential candidates) started in September 1990; some leading enterprises will be included, e.g. the Kielce construction conglomerate Exbud and a cable factory in Czechowice. Foreign assistance is providing funds to pay the fees of Western consultants and banks involved in this operation.

Opposition to earlier government plans had been voiced primarily on the grounds of infringement of workers' self-management rights, neglect of workers' ownership schemes and excessive concentration of power in the hands of the CNC President. The proposed counter-project left greater scope for ESOP-type schemes of employee ownership and for access to finance by domestic investors, and envisaged greater social control over privatisation, at the risk however of bureaucratising the process. The Law approved in July 1990 made some concessions in this direction, introducing some free shares and the possibility of purchases on credit.

A central question remains: what role foreign capital might play in Polish privatisation, and therefore the weight of implicit or explicit "debt-equity swaps". Capital inflows to date have been fairly small (a cumulative amount of $200 million to March 1990 for joint ventures—over one-third from West Germany—compared with a Soviet total of $600 million). On the one hand foreign participants are needed to secure competition, to provide know-how and fresh hard currency capital; on the other hand Poland has little incentive to repay the extant debt ($41.4 billion at end—1989, or 4.8 times total Polish yearly exports) out of national capital assets, other than as part of an international exercise in debt relief or at a discount comparable to that at which Polish commercial debt retrades today in secondary markets (over 80 per cent). In any case, the result of any privatisation targeted to foreign buyers is indeterminate without stipulating the associated credit policy (determining the zloty credit available to domestic buyers for the purchase of state assets) and exchange rate policy (determining the domestic value of foreign bids) .

The Law leaves to governmental discretion the scale and time schedule of privatisation; Parliament is to set only "basic directions" for privatisation once a year and decides on the uses to which sales revenues are to be put. The law also leaves to future governmental decisions the scale of free distribution, the scale of credit sales and the size of foreign acquisitions; it also leaves to subsequent legislation the institution and regulation of financial markets—a step which is obviously out of sequence. Until these questions are resolved, the progress of privatisation is bound to continue to be controversial and to be delayed .

Bibliography

Act VI (1988) on *Economic Associations* [companies], HungaroPress, Special issue, October, Budapest.

Act XIII (1989) on the *Transformation of Organizations carrying on economic activity and Economic Associations,* June, Budapest.

Balcerowicz, Leszek (1989). *Economic reforms in Poland and the role of financial aid,* Ministry of Finance. Warsaw (mimeographed).

Biuro Pelnomocnika Rzadu do Spraw Przeksztalcen Wlasnosciowych (1990a). Zalozenia rzadowego programu prywatyzacji przedsiebiorstw panstwowych. Warsaw.

Biuro Pelnomocnika Rzadu do Spraw Przeksztalcen Wlasnosciowych (1990b). Ustawa (Projekt) o prywatyzacji przedsiebiorstw panstwowych. April, Warsaw.

Chilosi, Alberto (1990). L'economia polacca tra stabilizzazione e trasformazione istituzionale. Conference Paper, Pisa.

Frydman, Roman, Grzegorz W. Kolodko and Stanislaw Wellisz (1990). Stabilisation in Poland: a Progress Report. Second International Monetary Conference, FU and Landeszentralbank Berlin, Berlin, 10–12 May.

Gomulka, Stanislaw (1989). How to create a capital market in a socialist country and how to use it for the purpose of changing the system of ownership. Conference paper, LSE Financial Markets Group, 13 December.

Grosfeld, Irena (1990). Prospects for privatisation in Poland. *European Economy* No. 43, CEC Brussels, March.

Hanson, Phil (1989). Von Mises' revenge. Paper for the *Conference on Perestroika: a socioeconomic survey.* Radio Free Europe/Radio Liberty, Munich, 7–10 July.

Hare, Paul G. (1989). Reform of enterprise regulation in Hungary—from 'tutelage' to market. Seminar Paper, PHARE Group, EC-DG-II, Brussels, November.

Hemming, Richard and Ali M. Mansoor (1988). Privatisation and Public Enterprise. *IMF Occasional Paper No. 56,* Washington, D.C., January.

Keynes, J. M. (1936). *The General Theory of Employment, Interest and Money.* London.

Kolodko, Grzegorz W. (1989). Reform, stabilisation policies, and economic adjustment in Poland. *WIDER Working Papers* No. 51, Helsinki, January.

Kolodko, Grzegorz W. (1990), Polish hyperinflation and stabilisation 1989–1990. *Working Papers of the Institute of Finance* No. 10, Warsaw.

Kornai, Janos (1990). *The Road to a Free Economy—Shifting from a Socialist System: the Example of Hungary.* W.W. Norton & Co., New York and London.

MacAvoy, Paul W., et al. (1989). *Privatisation and state owned enterprises.* Kluwer Academic Publishers, Boston.

Meade, James (1989). *Agathotopia: the economics of partnership.* The Hume Institute, London.

Mises, Ludwig von (1951). *Socialism—An Economic and Sociological Analysis.* Translated by J. Kahane, Liberty Classics, Indianapolis.

Morley-Fletcher, Edwin (1980–1981). Per una storia dell'idea di 'minimo sociale garantito'. *Rivista Trimestrale,* Nos. 64–66, October-March, pp. 297–321.

Newbery, David M. (1990). Reform in Hungary: sequencing and privatisation. Paper presented at the EEA Fifth Annual Conference, Lisbon, September.

Nuti, D. Mario (1974). Socialism and ownership. *The Socialist Idea.* Eds. L. Kolakowski and S. Hampshire. Proceedings of a Conference at Reading University, 1973, Weidenfeld and Nicholson, London.

Nuti, D. Mario (1981). Poland: socialist renewal and economic collapse. *New Left Review*, November.

Nuti, D. Mario (1988). Competitive valuation and efficiency of capital investment in the socialist economy. *European Economic Review* 32, pp. 2–6.

Nuti, D. Mario (1989). Feasible financial innovation under market socialism. Eds. Christine Kessides, Timothy King, Mario Nuti, Kathy Sokil, *Financial Reform in Centrally Planned Economies*, EDI-World Bank, Washington, pp. 85–105.

Nuti, D. Mario (1990a). Internal and international implications of monetary disequilibrium in Poland. *European Economy* No. 43, March, CEC Brussels, pp. 169–182.

Nuti, D. Mario (1990b). Stabilisation and reform sequencing in the Soviet Economy. *Recherches Economiques de Louvain,* Vol. 56, No. 2, pp. 1–12.

Nuti, D. Mario (1990c). Alternative employment and payment systems. Forthcoming in a DG-V volume on Profit-sharing, Commission of European Communities, Brussels.

OKP (1990). Kontr-Ustawa (Projekt) o przeksztalceniach wlasnosciowych przedsiebiorstw panstwowych. Warsaw, Polish Ministry of Finances (Holding companies as a means of accelerating privatisation in Poland), Warsaw, 7 March.

Sappington, D., and J. E. Stiglitz (1987). Privatisation, information, and incentives. *Journal of Policy Analysis and Management,* Vol. 6, No. 4, pp. 567–82.

Shmelev, Nikolai and Vladimir Popov (1989). *The turning point: revitalising the Soviet Economy.* Doubleday, New York.

Stanbury, W.T. (1989). Privatisation in Canada: ideology, symbolism or substance?. In MacAvoy *et al.,* pp. 272–329.

Stiglitz, Joseph E. (1989). On the economic role of the state. In Stiglitz *et al.*, *The Economic Role of the State*, Blackwell, Oxford.

Uvalic, Milica (1990). *The PEPPER Report: Promotion of Employee Participation in Profits and Enterprise Results in the Member States of the European Community*, EUI and CEC, Florence and Brussels.

Vickers, John and George Yarrow (1988). *Privatisation: an Economic Analysis*. The MIT.

[illegible]

19

Mass Privatization: Costs and Benefits of Instant Capitalism

Domenico Mario Nuti

19.1 An Unprecedented Experiment

A striking feature of post-1989 systemic transition in Central and Eastern Europe is the widespread, almost universal reliance—to greater or lesser extent—on *mass privatization*, understood as *offering the free or very*

Published in R. Daviddi (Ed.),(1995). *Property rights and privatization in the transition to a market economy: A comparative review*, pp. 103–132. European Institute of Public Administration (EIPA), Maastricht.

Earlier drafts of this paper were presented at various Conferences: EUI, Florence, December 1993; AEA, Boston, January 1994; BASEES, Cambridge, March 1994. Acknowledgements for useful comments are due to Wladimir Andreff, Horst Brezinski, Alberto Chilosi, Renzo Daviddi, Staszek Gomulka, Kaz Poznanski, Ajit Singh, Milica Uvalic, Hans Wagener and especially to Saul Estrin.

D. M. Nuti (✉)
La Sapienza, University of Rome, Rome, Italy
e-mail: milica.uvalic@unipg.it

© The Author(s), under exclusive license to Springer Nature Switzerland AG 2023

S. Estrin, M. Uvalic (eds.), *Collected Works of Domenico Mario Nuti, Volume I*, Studies in Economic Transition, https://doi.org/10.1007/978-3-031-12334-4_19

heavily subsidized transfer of a large proportion of state assets to the whole population.[1]

The only exception has been East Germany, where it was originally intended to distribute to the population not state assets directly but, eventually, the net receipts from their sales, initially (in 1990) estimated at DEM 180 billion. By the time *Treuhandanstalt* closed its operations in 1994 its net worth was negative: accumulated debts in the order of DEM 270 billion were taken over by the Unwelcome Legacy Repayment Fund set up in 1990 after unification (Financial Times, 26 July 1994). This does not imply that state assets have a negative market value everywhere else. In East Germany their negative worth was due to exceptional circumstances, namely real wage growth towards parity with West Germany due to free labour mobility, whereas East German labour productivity was of the order of one third of the West German level. Moreover *Treuhandanstalt* gave up much potential revenue from asset sales in exchange for employment and investment guarantees by buyers; it honoured domestic and external liabilities of state enterprises which might have been rejected through bankruptcy procedures; and incurred the burden of large-scale loan guarantees (see Dodds and Wachter 1993; Carlin 1994).

In Hungary, mass privatization has taken the form of citizens' access to free or subsidized credit. At some point there was even talk of 'credit card' privatization, but in the end a less radical scheme was preferred. At the end of 1992, Finance Minister Tamas Szabo announced the Small Investors Share Purchase Programme, elaborated with the help of Shroeder Wagg (UK) and approved by the Hungarian Government in April 1993. Under the scheme any citizen can purchase vouchers up to 100,000 forints (equivalent to about $1,000, or five times the average monthly wage) for a registration fee of 1 per cent of the total value, repayable without interest over five years (dividends being used for automatic repayment); about a third of the population are expected to

[1] In 1989 Phil Hanson gave a paper on Soviet restoration of private property under the title 'Von Mises' Revenge' (see Hanson, 1989). This paper could be entitled 'Proudhon's Revenge': this most misquoted reformer regarded as theft not property as such but the exclusion from property of the mass of the population; moreover he objected to idle owners but strongly favoured worker-owners (Proudhon 1970).

avail themselves of this opportunity (see Canning and Hare 1994).[2] In the first instance 70 enterprises valued at 120 billion forints are included (over $1 billion), thus involving at least 1.2 million people, beginning in April 1994.[3]

Everywhere else in the area, mass privatization has taken the form of distribution to the population of privatization vouchers, free or subject to a token registration fee. In different countries there were different provisions for their conversion into property titles (see Sect. 19.3 below; for general overviews of the progress of privatization throughout the area, see Bolton and Roland 1992; UN-ECE 1993; Daviddi 1994; Estrin 1994).

Strictly speaking these mass privatization schemes have nothing in common with a number of apparently similar phenomena which however have a different rationale, such as:

(a) so-called 'small privatization', i.e. the often privileged sale of small items of state property, such as houses, catering establishments, retail shops or small plots of land. These are assets directly used by buyers, which reduces both valuation problems and the importance of control mechanisms over the efficient use of the assets after privatization; privileged buyers are invariably the present users, i.e. the sale is targeted and not open to the whole population;
(b) the privileged sale or lease of part or whole of a state enterprise to its employees and/or managers. This mode of ownership diffusion, which has often occurred independently of government policies (see Sect. 19.5 below), is another striking feature of the transition. However, this is either a form of compensation to employees for the loss of self-management rights and of employment security, both necessary to make enterprises commercially saleable; or a necessity, where enterprise viability depends so much on employees' efforts and low pay that there are no external competitors bidding to acquire the enterprise.

[2] The scheme is a move in the direction of 'entrepreneurial socialism' advocated by Hungarian radical reformer Tibor Liska (see Liska 1963; Barsony 1982; Kornai 1982; Nuti 1991b). In addition, Hungarian citizens have access to so-called 'E' credit (where 'E' stands for 'existence') to buy an enterprise, or shares in the company where one is employed or in other companies, with no upper limit on credit.

[3] The programme includes profitable enterprises (consumer goods, retail trade, hotels, utilities); the first candidates already have foreign investors as majority or controlling shareholders.

(c) restitution of state assets nationalized after the last World War to their original owners, first allowed by Germany (where, by the end of 1993, 2,171 million often conflicting claims had been made by former owners and their successors for restitution or compensation, of which over two thirds were still being processed) and rapidly extended—where applicable—to the whole area.

Frequently, however, mass privatization has been mixed up with these other schemes. Thus, for instance, whenever it was not possible or desired to restitute the original physical asset, former owners have been given vouchers instead (in Hungary, vouchers have been used not only for property restitution but also to compensate the victims of political persecutions; in Lithuania, vouchers were also distributed in exchange for roubles over and above the amounts convertible into the new republican currency—the Lit). In Lithuania, and even more so in Estonia, vouchers originally intended for the mass privatization of state enterprises have been diverted towards the purchase of houses. Russian privatization vouchers can be used for the acquisition of any state asset.

It should be stressed that mass privatization is totally unprecedented. There have been Western attempts at implementing a project of 'people's capitalism', or 'property owning democracy', granting privileged treatment to smaller individual investors relative to institutional and larger investors. But no capitalist country has ever matched the scale, speed and size of the discount granted to investors or number of recipients of the privatization schemes under discussion. All previous and subsequent instances elsewhere involve the privatization of one state enterprise at a time, out of a much smaller total stock, only part of which is transferred at a modest discount to a tiny section of the population.[4]

There is a single exception whose very insignificance confirms the extraordinary nature of the operation: in 1979, the provincial government of British Columbia set up a new Crown Corporation, the British Columbia Resources Investment Corporation, with $151.5 million in

[4] British privatizations, for instance, have favoured the small investor but have raised very substantial revenue: Leipold (1990) notes that between 1979 and 1989 the gross privatization proceeds for the British Treasury amounted to GBP 27 billion, plus GBP 15 billion from the sale of council flats (net proceeds were lower at most by 9 per cent); this allowed a temporary substantial reduction in both public debt and tax burden.

assets, and distributed five free shares to any citizen who asked for them, plus additional shares at $6 each; 170,000 persons were involved. Transaction costs were high; the new company made some bad investments and soon incurred substantial losses; the operation was not judged to have been a success (see Stanbury 1989, pp. 282–283). What the post-communist governments attempted was an unprecedented experiment which took them into totally uncharted territory—which is *per se* no criticism: the tasks of transition were equally unprecedented.

19.2 Common and Distinctive Features

In general the restoration of private property is expected to put an end to the undue appropriation of state property by insiders (whether nomenklatura, managers or employees); to de-politicize the economy by removing direct political interference in managerial appointments and enterprise policies; to harden soft-budget constraints, especially when state banks as well as other state enterprises are privatized; to raise efficiency already in the short run through the appropriation of gains from improved inputs and outputs levels and structure, thus activating a supply response; to promote capacity restructuring in the medium/long-run; to alleviate the fiscal crisis typical of the transition by raising sales revenue for the state budget (see Nuti 1991a).

Mass privatization shares most of these general aims of privatization but sacrifices to some extent two of them, while pursuing three additional aims. On the negative side, it reduces privatization revenue by the extent of the usually large discount granted to the population. It is also likely to favour insiders more than alternative methods involving greater scrutiny of managerial behaviour (restructuring plans before privatization, subsequent control by concentrated shareholdings). On the positive side, mass privatization has three expected advantages which the new governments regard as overwhelming:

(a) it represents a form of restitution of state capital to a population that has already paid for it over time by sacrificing current consumption. This argument was specifically spelled out in the Introduction to the Shatalin-Yavlinsky '500 days' plan (September 1990); it was also implicit in Lech Walesa's electoral promises in his presidential campaign ('I will make you all rich'). '[Mass privatization] is simply the proper culmination of the demise of a communist fiction. Ownership of the means of production will now at least partially truly be vested in the people' (Dusan Triska, while Czechoslovak Minister of Privatization 1992, p. 101). Also, in Hungary, mass privatization is understood partly as 'compensation for four decades of economic injustice'; 'As one satirical cartoonist has put it: for 40 years they said that the means of production were owned by the people; now they'll have the papers to prove it' (Canning and Hare 1994).

(b) in principle, mass privatization can be much faster than conventional methods. On the demand side, it overcomes the inadequacy of financial capital, both domestic and foreign, with respect to the requirements of the speed and scale of the privatization task. It is a paradox that at the inception of transition and stabilization there should usually be a monetary overhang which causes a large-scale price hike and cannot be absorbed by time-consuming traditional privatization, whereas soon after macroeconomic equilibrium is re-established there is not enough liquid capital to fund commercial privatization on the desired scale. This 'capitalism without capital' resolves the so-called stock/flow problem (Bolton and Roland 1990), i.e. the high ratio between the target capital stock to be privatized and the flow of current savings per unit of time, whose inverse defines the maximum speed of commercial privatization per unit of time. Conversely, rejection of mass privatization of East German state assets was accompanied by access to West German and international savings and capital, which practically eliminated the stock/flow problem. On the supply side, greater speed appears to be obtainable because enterprises can be subjected to simple tests of economic viability (positive gross present value of productive activities) and financial net worth (with some recapitalization, if negative) before being slated for mass privatization, instead of undergoing the lengthy and costly valuation procedures necessary for one-by-one privatization, whether through public offers of their shares or buy-outs or direct external sale.

High speed—if implemented—has the added attraction of reaching all that sooner the point of no return, i.e. the point beyond which privatization of state assets can be regarded as irreversible; it may also stop sooner the more glaring inefficiencies of the state sector, and the more scandalous forms of insiders' 'spontaneous' undue appropriation of state assets.

(c) mass privatization generates political support for the whole transition and a built-in insurance against systemic reversals, by giving the whole population an immediate tangible gain expected to appreciate over time, and an opportunity to be directly involved in shaping the transition; both benefits would be lost in case of policy reversals.[5] The sheer fragmentation and dispersal of state assets, achieved by mass privatization, makes a system reversal all that harder. Probably Vaclav Klaus would have been elected and become Czech Premier anyway, but his chances were certainly enhanced by the handing out of assets valued at $7 billion to the population beforehand; the Hungarian credit scheme of mass privatization was also launched just before the May 1994 elections.

In sum, mass privatization has been seen as a method for implementing *instant, irreversible, politically self-supporting, large-scale capitalism.*

On reflection, it should have been clear from the outset that the net advantages of mass privatization had been over-estimated, perhaps grossly so. While restitution of nationalized assets to old owners involves a redistribution in their favour from the rest of the population, under mass privatization gainers and losers are the same; universal restitution is a delusion, as the whole population cannot redistribute equally to itself.[6] In any case, the population will have to pay for the hand-out either in higher taxes or lower public expenditure (or a combination of both) than otherwise would have been possible. Paraphrasing Milton Friedman, we can say confidently that 'There is no such a thing as a free asset'.[7] Moreover, the case against mass privatization—in a well-established market economy—is that

[5] Political support may be enhanced by the egalitarian nature of most forms of mass privatization, which therefore tend to be less controversial than other privatization tracks. However, mass privatization is perfectly compatible with inegalitarian policies implemented by diversifying individual claims to free state assets according to any number of alternative criteria (see below, Sect. 19.3, points (c) and (d)).

[6] Only if ownership of state enterprises is regarded as vested *de facto* in their managers and employees can mass privatization be regarded as effective redistribution to the whole population (as suggested by Saul Estrin).

[7] However, apparently Milton Friedman untypically advocated free distribution of state enterprise shares in Israel (Sachs 1993).

against the government provision of any non-public goods in kind, the re-establishment of Pareto efficiency conditions is bound to require re-trading among recipients, involving transaction costs which would be avoided if cash was distributed (or not taxed away) instead.

The shortage of financial capital could be handled by means of automatic credits for the purchase of privatized assets, preferably at the going interest rate but also at a subsidized rate. Privatization receipts of sales funded out of such credit would have to be sterilized, for their immediate use by government would be inflationary; but the government could use repayments and interest in later years to fund its expenditure, including the cost of capacity restructuring. This is the approach followed by Hungary (see above, Sect. 19.1), though it has not yet taken off: interest in the scheme, and indeed in any form of privatization, has been reduced by the widespread expectation that eventually free vouchers will be distributed. Mass privatization on credit is also the proposal put forward by President Walesa and his coalition in the campaign for the Polish September 1993 elections: instead of the hand-out promised in his Presidential campaign, he then proposed a $15,000 investment credit, repayable over twenty years at an interest rate of 3 per cent (instead of the going rate of around 40–45 per cent) for the lower paid and old-age pensioners.

The potential speed associated with mass privatization is not the same as actual speed, as obstacles other than lack of finance may—and will—slow down the process, and/or divert it to unintended directions, and/or impair its effectiveness, possibly reducing it below that of slower privatization methods. Mass privatization is sooner said than done: it sounds simplicity itself, but it involves an exceptionally complex set of decisions which are unavoidably controversial even in the presence of overwhelming, universal consensus for privatization, with endless opportunities for mistakes, delays, diversions, reversals, at almost every step. It competes with other privatization tracks and it is affected by their progress; like other transition processes, once set in motion it acquires a life of its own.

These considerations should not be taken as criticism of privatization, which is an unstoppable necessary aspect of the transition, nor of mass privatization as such, which may very well turn out to be the necessary track for such privatization and therefore part of an optimal strategy for transition. What an investigation of the problems indicated above can offer is an understanding of what may have gone wrong in the experience of particular countries, a dampening of over-optimistic expectations of the likely effects of mass privatization, and an indication of additional actions that might have to be taken in order to make mass privatization more successful (it is no accident that, for instance, in Russia in 1993–1994 the emphasis should have shifted somewhat on to post-privatization policies).

19.3 Complex Multiple Choices

A simple idea such as the free transfer of state assets to the population presents a large number of complex multiple choices, grouped here under different headings.

(a) *Size of the Scheme*

The government could (should) decide beforehand what proportion of state assets to devote to mass privatization, together with an indication of the target residual share (if any) of the state sector; or proceed with a first round (see below) leaving further developments indeterminate; or put for sale a sequel of assets one by one with an indicative time schedule (as in Russia, where long after the start of mass privatization a target was announced of 80 per cent of state assets for July 1994).

(b) *Gift Versus Credit*

The same result can be achieved through sales on credit (or by instalments) or through free/subsidized vouchers. Loans can be secured by the assets which they are used to purchase, so that there is no lending risk. Asset property can be obtained gradually as the loan is repaid, but rights of vote or control could be exercised at once; transferability could also be immediate, either transferring also the residual liability and the lien on the assets or giving the lending agency a prior claim on the price of the asset so as to extinguish residual liability. (On the relative merits of the two methods, see above Sect. 19.2). While being cheap relative to their capital entitlement, the registration fee can vary; it was in the order of one week's average wages in Czechoslovakia and in Russia; in Poland, a

June 1990 opinion poll indicated that 80 per cent of respondents preferred shares to be sold commercially, against 9 per cent in favour of free distribution (Kolarska-Bobinska 1994).

(c) *Recipients*

Free or credit vouchers could be issued to the whole resident population, or only to nationals (excluding or including expatriates and, if so, from a cut-off date to be decided); also to children (thus favouring rural areas and Catholics) or only to adults. In Poland, the first round of mass privatization, originally designed for the general public but, following an amendment of the April1993 Mass Privatization Law, was reserved to civil servants and old-age pensioners as compensation for the loss—decreed by the government but declared illegal by the Constitutional Court—of earlier indexation provisions.

(d) *Proportions*

Allocations could be equal or diversified, for instance according to age or nationality. In Lithuania in 1991, for instance, people aged 35 years or older received vouchers with a nominal value of 5,000 roubles, people under 18 years received 1,000 roubles and in between the amount was stepped down gradually. In Estonia, the number of vouchers per person depended on the years of employment. In Latvia, at the beginning of 1993, citizens were given one voucher for each year of post-War residence, plus 15 for pre-War citizens and their descendants, minus 5 vouchers for post-War immigrants (in payment for 'the use of Latvian infrastructure'); anybody connected with the Soviet Army or the KGB received none; thus 87 per cent of the vouchers went to Latvian citizens, i.e. the people with voting rights in the June 1993 elections (Mygind 1993). In the CSFR, a special problem arose with the Czech and Slovak split of 1 January 1993: access to vouchers had been equal in the two republics but after the split the Czech government claimed compensation for the excess of Slovak citizens' acquisition of Czech assets over Czech citizens' acquisitions of Slovak assets; eventually the claim was withdrawn but the dispute delayed the distribution of financial assets against vouchers for several months.

(e) *Denomination*

Whether in special units or in money terms, in which case it can be special money or—if it can be used at its nominal value without restrictions—ordinary money. In the Czechoslovak privatization, vouchers were denominated in investment points; the price of assets in terms of investment points could, in principle, be found through a Walrasian tatonnement process, with transactions not taking place until equilibrium prices in terms of points are reached which match demand and supply. In the Czechoslovak practice, shares were put up for sale at an initial price of 100 investment points per 3 shares; shares in excess supply were distributed at that price and unsold shares were offered in a following round at reduced prices; shares in excess demand by less than 25 per cent of the amount available were distributed in amounts proportionately scaled down; shares whose excess demand was above 25 per cent were not distributed at all but were offered in an extra round at a higher price; firms whose price rose over 1,000 points would be withdrawn altogether (see Takla 1994). There were four or five rounds and the iteration was closed without the process converging. This amounts to what Edgeworth called 'trading at false prices', i.e. with transactions taking place at different prices other than the price structure that would have equilibrated demand and supply, involving wealth effects along the line which are bound to affect the end results.[8] This unnecessary complication turns the

[8] For instance, in Czechoslovakia, Investment Funds bought too early and at too high a price relatively to private individuals (see Takla 1994). An even worse scheme was considered by Dusan Triska (1992) while Czechoslovak Minister for Privatization, namely a 'pro rata allocation system' whereby investors would allocate a specified number of vouchers to each of the companies in which they wished to invest. The price of a company's shares would then be determined by the total vouchers invested in that company divided by the number of shares; the number of a company's shares allocated to each investor would depend on the purchasing power—at that price—of the points allocated to that company. The chances of the resulting investors' portfolio being in equilibrium would be zero. This method, rejected in Czechoslovakia, was adopted in Russia instead, but with the welcome correction of bidders being able to indicate the minimum number of shares that they are prepared to accept for their bid, i.e. a reservation price (Lissovolik 1993). Triska (1992) considered the use of investment points in an auction of state enterprises to be privatized, a method also advocated by Frydman and Rapaczynski (1991). This is rather naive: enterprises will have to be auctioned in a sequence, at the beginning of which bidders have to formulate expectations about the prices (in investment points) of enterprises to be auctioned later, and at the end of which bidders will have to rush to dispose of residual investment points which have no other use, without at any time having any notion of how an investment point might relate to the monetary value which they attribute to enterprise assets. Frydman and Rapaczynski advocate 'institutional innovation' in the transition, but this kind of innovation is a non-starter; moreover, the time of systemic crisis and transition is no time for experiments. 'It is perhaps unavoidable that, in the process of rediscovering the market and market institutions, people might rediscover the wheel. But the introduction of special vouchers [i.e. denominated in special units] is a square wheel' (Nuti 1992a).

distribution process into a kind of lottery; indeed a straight lottery would have been simpler and therefore preferable, especially since it would allow the desired degree of share ownership concentration to be reached immediately. The justification for denominating vouchers in special units is the uncertainty about the market value of the assets to be so privatized (Triska 1992); but this can be handled by having more than one wave of mass privatization (see next point) or—as in Poland—by distributing to recipients certificates in investment funds to which all the enterprises covered by the scheme are allocated.

Vouchers could be denominated in money (in Russia, for instance, vouchers had a nominal value of 10,000 roubles). The implications differ according to whether vouchers are allowed to compete freely with ordinary money. If they are, but their total value is lower than that of assets offered for privatization, cash will also be used and they will have an actual value corresponding to their face value. If they are in excess, as they cannot be used for anything else, they will be worth less than their nominal value regardless of whether money can also be used in the privatization process. If mass privatization is reserved to vouchers, their value will depend on the value of assets to be privatized in this way, and may be higher or lower than the nominal value (the same problem arising with Czechoslovak investment points arises here). If vouchers must be used in certain pre-fixed proportions with money, or maximum proportions (as they were in Russia), the value of vouchers will be determined by such proportions as well as by the value of assets to be privatized.[9] The problem of 'vouchers' overhang—i.e. a total nominal value of vouchers greater than that of assets to be privatized—arose in Lithuania but was resolved by allowing the conversion of excess vouchers into state bonds.

(f) *Number of Mass Privatization Rounds*

Two rounds have taken place in Czech Republic (the first involved over 1,000 companies valued at $7 billion; the second and final round started at the end of September 1993, offering shares in 861 companies

[9] The market value of Russian vouchers rose fast from a large discount (greater than 50 per cent) to a 200 per cent premium, thus falling drastically in real or in dollar terms; by the end of 1993, the entire stock of Russian vouchers could have been bought for just over $700 million (Lissovolik 1993).

worth an estimated $5.3 billion); several rounds are envisaged in Poland. There was only one round in Mongolia, which achieved an 80 per cent privatization of all state assets. Even in those countries where no second round has been announced, there are expectations of more than one round. In Russia, a single round of voucher distribution has been used to privatize state enterprises put up for sale continuously one by one (see Lissovolik 1993; Bim et al. 1994).

(g) *Transferability of Vouchers*

Vouchers could be nominative (Lithuania, Poland) or transferable (Czechoslovakia, Russia). If transferable, the distribution of vouchers is equivalent to a distribution of cash (even if, as in Russia, they cannot be used directly for the purchase of goods and services), though—as we have seen above—not necessarily in the same amount as their nominal value. Therefore their issue is inflationary; it is no accident that on the day when voucher distribution began in Russia (1 October 1992) the rouble rate of exchange plummeted. Such an effect is bound to be all that greater if—as in Russia—voucher distribution begins well before state assets are put on sale. Transferability also involves the strong probability of an immediate process of concentration of ownership, as in Russia where vouchers were soon traded in the budding exchanges in bundles of 2,000; it also involves an opportunity to launder cash obtained from illegal transactions (as also happened in Russia on a large scale). Transferability, in turn, may be extended to foreigners or limited to nationals.

Beside limits on transferability, other limits have been considered or imposed on other share rights namely dividends and voting rights (e.g. Romanian holders of privatization funds certificates receive no dividends for the first three years and have no vote for five years; see Ben-Ner and Montias 1994).

(h) *Voucher Conversion*

Vouchers can be used directly to acquire state assets or shares, and/or certificates in investment funds. Investment funds, in turn, could be set up privately and acquire state assets with the vouchers obtained in exchange for certificates (as they were set up in large numbers in the

Czechoslovak privatization;[10] private investment funds have also been set up in Kazakhstan, where citizens cannot convert their vouchers directly into company shares, and in Lithuania and Romania). Or, as in Poland, national investment funds could be set up by the government and be given the ownership of state assets to manage and re-trade among themselves and on the stock exchange, with vouchers being exchanged for certificates of these funds. The Polish procedure raises additional choices: how many funds? Where to find the expertise? What degree of discretion in their portfolio selection? What incentive structure for fund managers? What distribution of state assets among the funds? We shall see in the next section how the need to settle these questions literally paralyzed and brought mass privatization in Poland to a standstill for over four years.

The important question also arises of whether privatization vouchers should be convertible only into specified assets (such as the Polish national investment funds) or into any state asset offered for sale, as in Russia or in all Baltic countries, thus mixing mass privatization with 'small privatization' and with the sale of state enterprises or their shares to employees (see Sect. 19.5).

(i) *Transferability of Assets*

The assets acquired with the vouchers, in turn, may have to be held for a certain period—in which case asset ownership fails to allow the kind of stock exchange discipline over managers which is essential to obtain the efficiency expected from private ownership. Or they may be immediately transferable, with the same effects (noted above) of immediate concentration of ownership and inflationary impact.

(j) *Local Versus Central Issues*

It is reported that in Tatarstan local vouchers for mass privatization with a face value of 30,000 roubles were issued in addition to those issued centrally (Lissovolik 1993).

---

[10] Initial apathy among Czechoslovak investors was won over by the aggressive advertising campaign launched by the Harvard Capital and Consulting Investment Fund, which promised a tenfold return on the initial cost of the vouchers within a year (the promise was kept).

(k) *Time Validity of Vouchers*

When vouchers are issued for a specific single round of mass privatization their value lapses *de facto* if they are not used; when, as in Russia, assets are continuously offered for sale, a validity term is usually fixed; it was of course extended beyond the first deadline, thus giving rise to expectations of further extensions that may or may not be fulfilled but which affect the course of privatization.

(l) *Interest*

In Montenegro, interest was paid on mass privatization vouchers (Uvalic 1993). In Lithuania, no interest was paid but the nominal value of vouchers was intermittently indexed, thus yielding their holders a nominal rate of return equal to the rate of inflation for the goods basket of the price index used for indexation.

(m) *Recycling*

One would expect that vouchers would be withdrawn and destroyed after redemption; in Russia, they were supposed to be destroyed within three days but there have been reports of their being illegally recycled (Lissovolik 1993).

(n) *Voluntary or compulsory enterprise participation in the mass privatization scheme*

The government can simply slate a given enterprise for privatization by decree, as in Czechoslovakia where quantitative targets for mass privatization were decided centrally and implemented with methods reminiscent of central planning heydays (Andreff 1993). Or, as decided in an amendment to the April 1993 Polish Law on Mass Privatization, participation in mass privatization schemes may be left to negotiations between the government and state enterprise managers: as a result, out of 200 state enterprises slated for the first round of privatization about 50 requested to withdraw and 32 succeeded, mostly on the grounds that they were in the process of negotiating joint ventures or sales with foreign buyers.

In an ideal world the government should address all these questions beforehand: settle them once and for all, avoiding the more outlandish or plainly silly solutions, and making sure that the trade-offs between government objectives implicit in those decisions are consistent with government policy; announce the decisions and their implementation schedule; and stick to it thereafter.

In the actual experience of post-communist economies, as it should be abundantly clear from the instances quoted above, none of this has happened. Solutions have been improvised under the pressure of predictable but non-anticipated problems. Questionable solutions have been adopted, moreover without consideration for the internal consistency of government policy. Debates about the more controversial aspects of mass privatization programmes have delayed implementation. Successive governments have bid different emphasis on mass privatization relative to other privatization methods. Policies have been modified or reversed in mid-course. Technical times of implementation have revealed themselves to be longer than expected. *As a result, mass privatization has been delayed, diverted, impaired.*

19.4 Delays

The most spectacular delay has occurred in Poland. First, there were long debates on many of the controversial issues indicated above (see Nuti 1991a; Gomulka and Jasinski 1994). Five successive ministers in charge of privatization, with the second—Janusz Lewandowski, co-author of the first Polish proposal (Lewandowski and Szomburg 1990)—returning as fourth, took different views about the scope, methods and importance of mass privatization. The frequent opposition of employees, who still had residual self-management powers, had to be won over first by the prospect of higher wages, as excess wage tax was no longer levied on enterprises where the state held a minority ownership stake, then through employees' privileged access to ownership in their enterprise.

The ensuing shift of emphasis onto other privatization methods was probably a blessing in disguise since, as a result, privatization followed a multi-track approach, but held up mass privatization. The first draft Law specifically regulating mass privatization was rejected by Parliament (March 1992). The second draft was approved in April 1993 only after very substantial amendments demanded by the former Communist Party in exchange for its external support to the divided government coalition headed by Ms. Suchocka. The amendments introduced on that occasion gave state enterprises the opportunity to withdraw from the schemes, placed limitations on the management powers of the national investment funds, gave a privileged position to civil servants and old-age pensioners in the first round of mass privatization (see above).

Beside the difficulties and delays in formulating government policies, there were unavoidable technical delays due to specific features of the adopted solutions. Two dozen or so national investment funds were to be set up by the government; in view of the recognized lack of domestic expertise, initially they were to be managed by foreign management groups approved by the government. Shares in 2,000 state enterprises after 'commercialization' (i.e. conversion into joint-stock companies initially owned by the Treasury) would be transferred to these funds, which would trade them freely among themselves and on the stock exchange, obtaining a flat fee covering their overheads plus a bonus related to their certificates' performance on the stock exchange. State enterprises would be allocated to the various funds by the same method used to select football teams out of a pool of potential players, with funds taking turns in selecting one state enterprise at a time out of the available pool. A non-transferable 1/3 participation in each enterprise would be entrusted to one of the funds, which would be the leading fund for that enterprise and would then be expected to take an active interest in the enterprise' s financial and physical restructuring and to exercise control on managerial behaviour (a 1/3 stake can plausibly be regarded as a controlling interest; if not, the fund responsible could always acquire a controlling interest on the market; this arrangement should be contrasted with the 20 per cent ceiling imposed on Czechoslovak investment funds for their holdings in any company). Each citizen participating in the scheme would be given one certificate in each of the funds—a method which makes it totally unnecessary to assign a value to vouchers, in money or in special currency. After ten years, certificate holders would decide whether the funds should be liquidated, or continue, and on what terms.

The search for suitable fund managers (merchant banks, brokers, existing funds, etc.) had to wait until all these questions—defining the role of the funds, their responsibilities and rewards—were settled and then it took rather longer than anticipated. The activity of the committee in charge of the selection had to be suspended in view of the May 1993 government crisis and the dissolution of Parliament until after the September 1993 elections. The new government confirmed its commitment to go ahead at least with the first round of mass privatization in the first instance but gave it a lower degree of priority; a new selection committee was set up at the end of 1993. Premier Pawlak's procrastination beyond reason became counterproductive. Approval for fifteen funds involving between 300 and 460 firms had to wait until early 1995; the management fee had become an expensive commission on the total value of the funds' portfolio and not just on its increment; a large number of Polish and joint management groups were also admitted to the selection.

As a result of all these circumstances, by mid-1995, i.e. four years after the first Privatization Law (June 1990) which paved the way to mass privatization was passed by the Polish Parliament, not one single state enterprise has been privatized through this method.

19.5 Diversions

We have already noted that in some countries mass privatization has been mixed with small privatization (e.g. in Russia) thus diverting vouchers away from their original use; in some cases, as a result, mass privatization of state enterprises has all but stalled (e.g. in Estonia, where in 1992–1993 there was a switch towards *Treuhand*-type privatization). But the most significant diversion of mass privatization is the use of vouchers for the purchase of shares by employees and managers in their own enterprises, thus financing partial or total manager/employee buy-outs (MEBOs).

The last thing that the new post-communist leaders—from Balcerowicz to Gaidar—wished to promote was the emergence of significant forms of employee ownership, reminiscent of Yugoslav self-management, Western socialist programmes and the search for a 'Third Way', which they firmly rejected.[11] Wage employment was one of the few features of a market economy that was already in place under the old system: all that was needed to turn the existing near-market for labour[12] into a genuine market was to remove *de-facto* 'job rights protection' (i.e. entitlements to existing jobs, which were never a legal right and therefore could be removed without any change in legislation) and create large scale unemployment in order to discipline wage demands and introduce flexibility in labour redeployment. In spite of free trade unions, collective bargaining, income policies and social pacts, this was no sooner said than done.

Yet employee ownership emerged almost everywhere. This was partly the result of public policy measures forced on the new governments by the need to implement a quick and smooth transition, and partly it happened purely by default (see also Smith 1993; Schaffer 1993).

Employee ownership had to be introduced for a variety of reasons:

(a) to reverse the effects of earlier attempts at reforming the old system that had introduced employee self-management, notably in Poland and to a smaller extent in Hungary (of course, in addition to Yugoslavia; in Romania self-management was formally introduced but remained a dead letter). Paradoxically, these attempts at reform became an obstacle to transition, which could only be overcome by

[11] In 1990 the Polish Privatization Minister Krzystof Lis actually wrote to the British Embassy complaining that the support given by the British Know-How Fund to employees' companies was against Polish government policy (Kowalik 1994). In June 1991, Leonid Grigoryev and Evgeny Yasin regarded the birth of an employee-controlled economy as one of the dangers of voucher privatization (quoted by Sutela 1994). The Russian Privatization Minister Anatoly Chubais (1993) stressed that the Russian government was strongly opposed to any privatization procedures that would imply a give-away of enterprise shares to insiders.

[12] Even at the height of Stalinism, state enterprises had to offer a wage level and structure matching their labour demands; they were subject to wage-bill ceilings, but had a fair amount of flexibility in their wage policy through the grading of jobs and of employees and through fringe benefits as well as in wage-fixing. The difference with respect to capitalism was primarily in the state of the labour market, i.e. the full and often over-full employment which prevailed in the centrally planned economy. While undoubtedly consistent with government policies, this was obtained as a by-product of 'tight' or 'taut' planning, i.e. endemic excess demand for goods and services at administered prices fixed below market-clearing levels, rather than as a result of specific measures of employment creation and protection. Apart from full/over-full employment, the wage contract in the traditional Soviet-type economy was basically the same as in the market economy.

converting self-management into co-ownership. Privatization of state enterprises with self-management provisions required employees to surrender their 100 per cent entitlement to, say, 20 per cent of property rights (i.e. that part of property rights that involved the right to appoint and dismiss managers, to use and control capital, and the right to appropriate some of the results). For them to do so willingly employees had to be given instead, say, 20 per cent of full property rights (i.e. including the entitlement to any increase in capital value and the free disposal of capital, which they did not have before);

(b) as a natural consequence of transition, employee ownership was also introduced with the transformation of former pseudo-cooperatives, i.e. public sector cooperatives, into genuine cooperatives run by elected officials and independent of central organs;

(c) to win over employee support for the transition in spite of concern for its short-run adverse effects on real wages and on mass unemployment.

In addition, unintended employee ownership also happened, by default, given:

(a) the low and often negative value (at the prevailing fixed wage rates but not for more flexible participatory earnings) of some state enterprises for which there could not have been other takers;

(b) the shortage of domestic capital, which placed employees (especially in view of their inside information) in a good position with respect to domestic outsiders, while alternative external buyers frequently evoked xenophobic reactions;

(c) employees' and managers' natural inclination, in the absence of information about other enterprises and other localities, simply to select automatically the one which they knew best and was most important for their livelihood, or at most enterprises in the same locality—what Peter Murrell (1994) calls the 'balkanization of ownership'.

Partial or complete MEBOs occurred in Germany (2,400 cases accounting for just under one-fifth of the total number of sales, though *Treuhandanstalt* 'did not initiate the MEB0 route as a deliberate strategy'

(Carlin 1994)); in Poland, MEBOs turned out to be the single fastest privatization track, with over 1,300 buy-outs by mid-1993 through what is known as 'liquidation' privatization, applicable to viable enterprises and not to be confused with liquidation of insolvent enterprises (Gomulka and Jasinski 1994). Buy-outs are an important element of privatization in Ukraine and in Romania (where discounts for employees and managers buying up to 10 per cent of the shares in their firms were not mentioned in the original privatization law but have evolved as the primary privatization track; see Ben-Ner and Montias 1994). In Hungary, out of an estimated value of 2,000 billion forints of socially-owned capital stock, an estimated 100 billion are to be given to employees under the various schemes in operation similar to standard Employee Stock Ownership Plans or Trusts (ESOPs/ESOTs) and MEBOs (see Canning and Hare 1994).

Mass privatization was instrumental in the promotion of employee ownership either as a result of investment decisions by vouchers holders, even in the absence of favourable terms for the purchases of employee shares, or as a result of government policy. Thus, in Mongolia, insiders ended up owning 45 per cent of enterprises (Murrell 1994). In Russia, under the so-called 'Option 2' of the state enterprise privatization up to 51 per cent of the voting shares could be purchased by employees/managers at a price corresponding to 1.7 times the enterprise book-value which, in view of rampant inflation, was a most generous concession in spite of often inappropriate productive capacity.[13] It is reported that this option was taken up in about 80 per cent of Russian privatizations (Lissovolik 1993); Sutela (1994) reports widespread acquisition by insiders of equity stakes much higher than the 51 per cent allowed by Option 2, through additional purchases and re-purchases. Thus at the Davos Forum of March 1994, Grigory Yavlinsky could refer to Russian mass privatization as 'a form of socialization'.

---

[13] Option 1 was the concession of 25 per cent free shares, non-voting unless and until sold, plus an option of a further percentage of voting shares (10 per cent for workers and 5 per cent for administrative officers). Option 3 was the concession of 20 per cent voting shares at book value for a group of workers and managers undertaking to restructure the enterprise in a year according to a plan, if successful, in which case all workers and managers could acquire a further 20 per cent of the shares at a highly concessional rate. With all three options, the rest of the shares was to be sold at public auctions to nationals and foreigners (Bim et al. 1994).

In general the acquisition of a non-controlling interest by managers and employees in their own enterprises can be regarded as a positive development, which encourages productivity, better labour relations, economic democracy; the diffusion of employee ownership is encouraged in the European Community (Uvalic 1991). The acquisition of a *controlling* interest is, however, capable of having devastating effects on earnings, employment, efficiency, restructuring.[14]

First, employees may use their controlling power to maintain employment levels higher than those compatible with profit maximization at the going wage-rate. Workers will be dismissed only if their wages are higher than the value of their average product, instead of the value of their marginal product.

Second, employees may use their controlling power to raise earnings (including fringe benefits in kind, individual and collective) above the going wage-rate to the point of bringing profits down to zero profits or even incurring losses, eating up equity capital right down to the point of bare solvency, i.e. of zero capital value of the enterprise, even if budget constraints are hard. Other shareholders can be effectively disenfranchised and expropriated. No additional equity capital will be available from outside on that basis; the enterprise will have to rely on internal

[14] We presume here that the controlling equity stake is held fairly equally among employees, so that they each gain more from higher earnings or stable employment as employees than they lose as shareholders. There is no need for collusion; self-interest will induce them to back individually whatever decisions/measures promote the interests of their group. Of course the same risks arise whenever a controlling equity stake in a company is held by a major supplier, customer or competitor of that company, either of which may pursue their own private benefits at the expense of the other shareholders (respectively, by enforcing a higher price for the input supplied, or a lower price from the enterprise bought out, or a combination of higher product price or lower investment in the case of a competitor). However, customers, competitors, or suppliers, other than labourers, are invariably companies, and this conflict of interest can be avoided through mergers which they will have an incentive to undertake, or through outsiders acquiring a controlling interest in both the company under consideration and in the company which is a major supplier/customer/competitor. In the case of a controlling equity stake held by employees/managers, however, such an opportunity to avoid a conflict of interest does not arise simply because employees cannot be owned by a company (see Nuti 1994). 'Firms where employees are major shareholders have different objectives than firms owned by outside investors and therefore experience different agency-managerial and technical administrative problems. Their organizational structure, the way decision-making rights are allocated, the extent to which employees should be monitored, and the way in which incentives should be structured, ought to be adapted to those different objectives' (Ben-Ner and Montias 1994). Frydman et al. (1993) recognize the problem but fail to distinguish between a controlling and a non-controlling interest, expressing general hostility to any form of employee-ownership.

finance for its growth, and naturally its viability will be limited to the sectors or techniques with less than average risk, size or capital per man.[15]

In the course of time the employee-controlled enterprise might easily revert to an ordinary company, when a sufficient number of employees-shareholders cease to be employees or shareholders.[16] But as long as employees/managers hold a controlling equity stake this is bound to have some effects. On the positive side there will be a lower unemployment level than otherwise, as a result of what is effectively a form of work-sharing within workers-controlled enterprises. On the negative side: a) such work-sharing at the microeconomic level will be less efficient than economy-wide work-sharing, because there will be no tendency for the value of labour's marginal product to be equalized throughout the economy; and indeed employees might be kept on even when their marginal product is negative; b) capacity restructuring, if any, will be much slower than otherwise, in the short run because of obstacles to labour shedding, in the medium-long run because of lower self-financed investment, lower access to loans and no access to external equity capital.

If the resulting trade-offs between employment, efficiency and capacity restructuring—which ultimately involve a trade-off between lower short-term social costs and higher costs and longer duration of necessary restructuring—were actually acceptable to governments, all would be well in the best of all possible worlds. The trouble is that such trade-offs are uncontrollable and unpredictable, and therefore unlikely to coincide with government preferences; they are the result of an absence of government policy, without the justification of a *laissez-faire* approach because such phenomena are policy-induced and interfere with market processes rather than being their natural result.

---

[15] In this respect the enterprise with a controlling ownership stake by employees resembles the standard cooperative or self-managed firm, where members are not full co-owners but only share the right to use enterprise capital and to appropriate net value added (see Nuti 1994). But enterprises which are co-owned by employees, unlike self-managed enterprises, do not have an incentive to restrict employment, over-exploit a monopoly position, respond sluggishly and possibly 'perversely' to price changes, distribute rather than reinvest profits, and exhibit a bias for labour-saving projects.

[16] Unless they sell their stock to new or existing employees, thus maintaining a controlling equity stake in the hands of a group whose members individually have a lower share in enterprise capital than in enterprise labour.

19.6 Corporate Control

For some of the protagonists of mass privatization, 'The main purpose of privatization is privatization' (Vladimir Dlouhy, in 1992, while Czechoslovak Minister of the Economy); '...in a purely economic sense, privatization must be viewed as an end in itself rather than as a process with an efficiency-oriented objective' (CSFR Privatization Minister, Dusan Triska 1993, p. 287). Politically, in a post-communist economy this is unquestionably the case; but 'in a purely economic sense' it must be presumed that the purpose of privatization is that of raising efficiency, entrepreneurship, market discipline, thus achieving greater prosperity.

This purpose of privatization is inordinately harder to achieve than the sheer transfer of ownership titles from the state to the private sector because it presumes that the new holders of shares and fund certificates are in a position to exercise effective control over resource allocation in the joint stock companies of which they are ultimate owners.

This problem of 'corporate control' or 'corporate governance' is due to the separation of shares ownership from direct control over the assets they incorporate. In a broad sense, the problem includes the pursuit of private benefits by groups of shareholders to the detriment of other shareholders, which we have considered in the previous section. Here we are concerned with corporate control in a stricter sense, as shareholders' control over managerial discretion. This is particularly important for mass privatization, in view of its alleged speed and of the dominance of shares and certificates ownership relative to other privatization tracks; paradoxically, mass privatization would be much more effective in a capitalist economy where mechanisms of corporate control are already operational.[17]

In developed market economies, in principle, a degree of corporate control is obtained through the discipline exercised on managerial discretion either directly by a shareholder (or coalition of shareholders) endowed with a controlling equity stake; or indirectly by the threat that such a controlling equity stake might be acquired on the stock

[17] See Milton Friedman's proposal for mass privatization in Israel (Sachs 1993) mentioned above. Nuti (1992c) recommended mass privatization in Italy using as vouchers the receipts of a special surtax levied on capital in order to reduce public debt.

exchange—cheaply, when managers depress the value of shares below their potential by neglecting profit opportunities. The first mode of control is typical of continental Europe, especially Germany, and Japan; the second is typical of the UK and the US (see de Cecco 1989; Franks and Mayer 1993).

The Nippo-German model is characterized by: 'few listed companies, an illiquid capital market where ownership and control [are] infrequently traded, a complex system of intercorporate holdings' (Franks and Mayer 1993, p. 3). Thus, in 1990, in Germany almost 85 per cent of companies had at least one shareholder (a single family in one third of the cases) with at least 25 per cent of shares (Mayer 1993), and banks also exercise control both as shareholders and as proxy-voters on behalf of their clients; in Japan cross-participations are much more important.

The Anglo-Saxon model is characterized by 'a large number of listed companies, a liquid capital market where ownership and control rights are frequently traded, few inter-corporate equity holdings' (Franks and Mayer 1992, pp. 2–3); shareholdings are much less concentrated but control can be acquired much more easily than in the Nippo-German model. Franks and Mayer (1992) talk of 'insider' and 'outsider' corporate control respectively: 'The outsider system [of the UK and US] relies on the market for corporate control; the insider system of control [of Continental Europe and Japan] uses committees'.

In recent literature there is a frequent presumption that the German model is more suited to the undeveloped state of financial markets in Central Eastern Europe (see de Cecco 1989; Lipton and Sachs 1990; Corbett and Mayer 1992). Fischer (1991) argues that, given the large scale indebtedness of enterprises towards banks, involvement in enterprise management might induce banks to throw good money after bad (see also Perotti 1994); Frydman et al. (1993) stress that in any case this control role could not be played by state banks. All these drawbacks associated with the Nippo-German model could be avoided with the financial restructuring and re-capitalization of both enterprises and banks and the subsequent privatization of both (see Nuti 1992b).

Polish mass privatization is decidedly inspired by the German model, given the statutory minimum 1/3 shareholding by a leading national investment fund in each of the participating enterprises (see above,

Sect. 19.4). A similar important role in corporate control has been assigned in Romania to private ownership funds (POF). Excessive weight seems to have been attached to the possible disciplining role of these financial intermediaries (Frydman and Rapaczynski 1990; Blanchard et al. 1991; Frydman et al. 1993). In Romania, for instance, holders of POF certificates 'have very limited ability to influence the Councils [of Administration] and thus the performance of the fund. According to the Statutes, no shareholders' meetings will be held during the first five years of operation (under the rationale that meetings with 16.5 million participants are infeasible)'; during this period limited control can be exercised only by sufficiently large groups of certificate holders (Earle and Sapatoru 1993, p. 19). If corporate control can be exercised by investment funds whose certificates—with or without a vote—are anyway dispersed among the population, it is not clear why these funds might not have exercised the same autonomous function if they had been given the same degree of independence by the Treasury as owner—without privatization.

At the other extreme, Czechoslovak mass privatization was decidedly inspired by the Anglo-Saxon model, seeing that instead of a minimum 1/3 stake by a leading fund, as in Poland, there is a 20 per cent maximum ceiling in any single fund's holdings in any company (40 per cent applicable to any group of funds set up by the same founders; though there are complaints of a concentration process sometimes exceeding these limits through cross-shareholdings). In practice banks—including state banks—with government acquiescence ended up acquiring holdings which were fairly large (on average of the order of 15 per cent) but not large enough to exercise corporate control. In Russia investment funds (which have been growing fast from about 100 in February 1993, to 550 in August 1993) have also been placed under a maximum limit of a 5 per cent shareholding in any one enterprise (Sutela 1994).

In other countries, no specific model of corporate control seems to have been explicitly or implicitly adopted and will gradually emerge in actual practice; while stock exchanges have been growing in the Czech Republic, Poland and Hungary, where they were booming in 1993–1994, the far more undeveloped nature of financial markets in other countries needs to be stressed.[18]

Empirical evidence of the impact of privatization on corporate control, efficiency and restructuring is still scant. Pinto et al. (1992) found winners and losers, i.e. instances of successful restructuring and of persistent loss-making, both among state enterprises and in the private sector, regardless of the branch of activity. A study of Russian privatization (KPMG 1993) found that 12 out of a sample of 27 privatized enterprises had made no changes in their operations; employment and welfare provisions were being strongly defended; in no cases had incumbent management changed; there were no plans for nor commitment to restructuring and commercialization following the transfer of ownership; the effects of privatization were 'disappointing': 'living off the past allows the system to continue but there is little evidence of enterprises building a foundation for the future'. Estrin et al. (1994) find that 'The emphasis on privatization … seems to explain much of the considerable and somewhat surprising progress towards enterprise adjustment observed in the CSFR as well as the Hungarian cases … On the other hand, the sustained lack of any effective Polish strategy towards privatization was clearly an important explanatory factor in the failure of much of the state-owned sector to adjust adequately to the new market conditions' (p. 29).

So far in the emerging financial markets of post-communist economies neither of the corporate control mechanisms discussed above seem to be in operation. On the one hand, those markets are not sufficiently large, active, efficient, liquid, to pose a threat to managerial discretion through hostile takeover bids—which are unheard of to date anywhere in the area. On the other hand, share ownership is not sufficiently concentrated for existing shareholders to be able to exercise direct control over managers. Moreover, markets for managerial skills are also somewhat undeveloped, thus assigning less importance to managers' reputation for the

[18] For instance, Romania has been plagued by a large-scale fraudulent scheme ('Caritas') swindling millions of depositors of over $1 billion with the impossible promise of real rates of return of the order of 600 per cent a year. Kiev's stock exchange transacts the shares of two companies once a week. Even in Poland, people awaiting registration for taking part in stock exchange dealings have formed queues longer than those which used to be formed for shortage commodities under the former system.

determination of their earnings. It follows that managers of privatized and other private companies enjoy a degree of decisional power much higher than their counterparts in advanced market economies, which enables them to get away with inefficiency in spite of privatization. Instead of implementing standard models of modern capitalism, the new systems resemble an early version of pure 'managerial' capitalism *à la* Berle and Means (1932), not to say a 'proto-managerial' version of it. Independence from capital owners makes managers more vulnerable to employees' wage claims, to some extent potentially replicating some of the problems discussed in the previous section with respect to employee-owned firms.

19.7 Conclusions

Mass privatization has attractive features, such as restitution of collective sacrifice to citizens, potential speed, political expediency. But these advantages may have been overstated, while there are also disadvantages—such as the loss of budgetary revenue and the privileged position of insiders. It is not a superior method of privatization, but one whose costs and benefits have to be assessed with respect to government preferences.

It is important to avoid some of the more damaging features of specific mass privatization programmes and to put mass privatization in a more sober perspective, lowering expectations about how quickly it can be implemented and what it can achieve, especially to avoid dangerous disillusionment. Rather than giving a dominant role to mass privatization, a multi-track approach to privatization should be followed, including liquidation and redeployment of the assets of bankrupt enterprises; employees' and managers' buy-outs; sale at auctions or tenders of whole enterprises or their parts; public offers of shares; acquisitions by investment funds selling certificates to the public. Most of all, it would be wise to shift emphasis away from the transfer of state enterprises to the private sector, towards the redeployment of their physical assets and the 'organic' growth of entirely new private enterprises.

Faced with the complexity of multiple choices in mass privatization, the government should address all these questions beforehand: settle them once and for all, avoiding the more outlandish or plainly silly solutions, and making sure that the trade-offs between government objectives implicit in those decisions are consistent with government preferences; announce the decisions and their implementation schedule; and stick to it thereafter .

The danger of delays and disappointment should be considered and avoided. Mass privatization schemes should not be mixed up with small privatization, property restitution and, above all, the establishment of employee ownership which, when pushed to a controlling equity stake, represents an inefficient diversion potentially slowing down capacity restructuring, though reducing the short-run social costs of transition.

Finally, ownership changes should be accompanied by those additional institutional changes required to establish corporate control over managerial discretion, whether through actual or potential control over company equity or through other means. Otherwise, instead of representing the most rapid, direct and efficient route to the restoration of capitalism, mass privatization is bound to be delayed, diverted, and made ineffective through lack of corporate control.

Bibliography

Aslund, Anders and Richard Layard (Eds.) (1993). *Change of Economic System in Russia*, London.

Andreff, Wladimir (1993). Planning private ownership: Is the Czechoslovak solution a model? Conference paper, Kopint-Datorg-UNCTAD, Budapest, 21–22 May.

Barsony, J. (1982). Tibor Liska's concept of socialist entrepreneurship. *Acta Oeconomica,* Vol. 28, No. 13–14, pp. 424–455.

Ben-Ner, Avner and John Michael Montias (1994). Economic system reforms and privatisation in Romania. In: Estrin (Ed.) (1994).

Berle, Adolf Jr. and Gardiner Means (1932). *The Modern Corporation and Private Property,* Macmillan, New York.

Bim, Alexander S., Derek C. Jones and Thomas Weisskopf (1994). Privatisation in the former Soviet Union and the new Russia, in: Estrin (Ed.) (1994).

Blanchard, Olivier, Rudiger Dornbusch, Richard Krugman, Richard Layard and Laurence Summers (1991). *Reform in Eastern Europe*, MIT Press, Cambridge, Mass.

Blommenstein, Hans and Michael Marrese (Eds.) (1991). *Transformation of Planned Economies: Property Rights Reform and Macroeconomic Stability*, OECD, Paris.

Bolton, P. and R. Roland (1990). Privatisation policies in Central and Eastern Europe. *Economic Policy*, 13, pp. 275–309.

Bolton, P. and R. Roland (1992). The economics of mass privatisation: Czechoslovakia, East Germany, Hungary and Poland. Discussion Paper No. 155, LSE Financial Markets Group.

Canning, Anna and Paul Hare (1994). The privatisation process—economic and political aspects of the Hungarian approach, In: Estrin (Ed.) 1994.

Carlin, Wendy (1994). Privatisation and deindustrialisation in East Germany, in: Estrin (Ed.), 1994.

Chubais, Anatoly (1993). Main issues of privatisation in Russia. In: Aslund and Layard (Eds.) 1993.

Clarke, Thomas (Ed.) (1993). *International Privatisation: Strategies and Practices*, Walter de Gruyter, Berlin.

Corbett, Jenny and Colin Mayer (1992). Financial Reform in Eastern Europe: Progress with the Wrong Model. *Oxford Review of Economic Policy*.

Daviddi, Renzo (1994). Property Rights and Privatisation in the Transition to a Market Economy: A Comparative Review. Conference paper, EIPA, Maastricht.

De Cecco, Marcello (1989). Alternative modes of financial organization, in: Kessides et al. (Eds.), 1989, pp. 196–204.

Dodds, Paul and Gerd Wachter (1993). Privatisation contracts with the German Treuhandanstalt: an Insiders' Guide. *The International Lawyer*, Vol. 27, No. 1, spring, pp. 65–90.

Earle, John and Dana Sapatoru (1993). Incentive contracts, corporate governance and privatisation funds in Romania. Seminar Papers No. 22, Cracow Academy of Economics.

Estrin, Saul (Ed.) (1994). *Privatisation in Central and Eastern Europe*, Longman Group UK, Harlow.

Estrin, Saul, Mark E. Shaffer and Inderjit Singh (1992). Enterprise adjustment in transition economies: Czechoslovakia, Hungary & Poland. Conference Paper, IMF/World Bank, Washington, June.

Fischer, Stanley (1991). Privatisation in East European transformation, causes and consequences. NEBR Working Paper, No. 3703, May.
Franks, Julian and Colin Mayer (1992). Corporate control: a synthesis of the international evidence. LBS and University of Warwick, November.
Frydman, Roman and Andrzej Rapaczynski (1990). Markets and institutions in large scale privatisations. *New York University Research Report,* No. 90–42.
Frydman, Roman and Andrzej Rapaczynski (1991). Evolution and design in the East European Transition. C.V. Starr Center for Applied Economics, *Economic Research Reports,* No. 91–53.
Frydman, Roman, Edmund S. Phelps, Andrzej Rapaczynski and Andrei Schleifer (1993). Needed mechanisms of corporate governance and finance in Eastern Europe. *Economics of Transition,* Vol. 2, June 1993, pp. 171–208.
Gomulka, Staszek and Piotr Jasinski (1994). Privatisation in Poland, in: Estrin (Ed.), 1994.
Hanson, Phil (1989). Won Mises' 'revenge'. Paper for the Conference on 'Perestroika: A Socio-Economic Survey', Radio Free Europe/Radio Liberty, 7–10 July, Munich.
Kessides, Christine, Timothy King, Mario Nuti, Kathy Sokil (Eds) (1989). *Financial Reform in Socialist Economies,* EDI-World Bank, Washington.
Kolarska-Bobinska, Lena (1994). *Privatisation in Poland: the evolution of opinions and interests, 1988–1993.* CBOS, Warsaw.
Kornai, J. (1982). Comments on Tibor Liska's concept of entrepreneurship. *Acta Oeconomica,* Vol. 28, No. 13–14, pp. 455–460.
Kowalik, Tadeusz (1994). The social costs of liberalisation and privatisation in Poland (mimeo), Warsaw.
KPMG Management Consultants (1993). A study of the Russian privatisation process: changing enterprise behaviour, CERT, Edinburgh.
Leipold, Helmut (1990). Die Politik der Privatisierung unde Deregulierung: Lehren fur die Wirtschaftsreformem im Sozialismus, in: Schuller and Krusselberg (Eds.), 1990.
Lewandowski, Janusz and Jan Szomburg (1990). The strategy of privatization. *Economic Transformation Papers* No. 7, The Gdansk Institute for Market Economics, Warsaw-Gdansk.
Lipton, D. and J. Sachs (1990). Privatisation in eastern Europe: the case of Poland. *Brookings papers on economic activity,* 2, pp. 293–333.
Liska, Tibor (1963). Kritika es Konceptio. Tezisek a gazdasagi mechanizmus reformjahoz (Critique and construction. Theses for a reform of the economic mechanism), *Kozgazdasagi Szemle,* No. 9.

Lissovolik, Bogdan (1993). Special features of Russian privatisation: causes and consequences. Conference Paper, European University Institute, Florence, December.

MacAvoy, Paul W. et al. (1989). *Privatisation and state owned enterprises*. Kluwer Academic Publishers, Boston.

Mayer, Colin (1993). Ownership—An Inaugural Lecture. *Warwick Economic Research Papers* No. 402, Department of Economics, Warwick University, February.

Murrell, Peter (1994). Peremptory privatization. AEA Annual Conference, Boston, 3–5 January.

Mygind, Niels (1993). A comparative analysis of the economic transition in the Baltic countries—barriers, strategies, perspectives. Copenhagen Business School, September.

Nuti, D. Mario (1991a). Privatisation of socialist economies: general issues and the Polish case, in: H. Blommestein and M. Marrese, 1991.

Nuti, D. Mario (1991b). On Tibor Liska's entrepreneurial socialism. In: Marguerite Mendell and Daniel Salee (Eds.), *The Legacy of Karl Polanyi—Market, State and Society at the End of the Twentieth Century*, St. Martin's Press, New York, 1991, pp. 215–230.

Nuti, D. Mario (1992a). Free distribution?, in: A. Stadler and J. Poshl (Eds.), 1992, pp. 42–44.

Nuti, D. Mario (1992b). The role of the banking sector in the process of privatization. *Economic Papers* No. 98, CEC-DGII, Brussels, November; forthcoming in T. Clarke (Ed.), 1994.

Nuti, D. Mario (1992c). Come far comprare ai privati una parte del debito pubblico. *Politica ed Economia*, XXIII, No. 12, December, pp. 49–54.

Nuti, D. Mario (1994). The economics of participation. IRTI-Islamic Development Bank, *Eminent Scholars Lectures Series*, No. 3, Jeddah (forthcoming).

Perotti, Enrico C. (1994). Corporate governance in mass privatisation programs, in: Estrin (Ed.), 1994, pp. 54–68.

Pinto, Brian, Marek Belka and Stefan Krajewski (1992). Microeconomics of transformation in Poland: a survey of state enterprise responses. *Working Papers*, The World Bank, September.

Proudhon, Pierre-Joseph (1970). *What is Property? An enquiry into the principle and right of government*, New York.

Rowthorn, R. E. (1994). Participation and cooperation in economic enterprises, CUP, Cambridge (forthcoming).

Sachs, Jeffrey (1993). Poland's Jump to the Market Economy. *Lionel Robbins Lecture Series,* The MIT Press, Cambridge (Mass.) and London.

Schaffer, Mark (1993). Worker participation in socialist and transitional economics, forthcoming in: R. E. Rowthorn, 1994.

Schuller, Alfred and Hans-Georg Krusselberg (Eds.) (1990). Zur Transformation von Wirtschaftssystemen: von der Sozialistischen Planwirtschaft zur Sozialen Markwirtschaft. *Arbeitsberichte zum Systemvergleich* No. 15, Marburg University, Marburg, July.

Smith, Stephen C. (1993). Employee ownership in privatisation in developing and reforming countries. George Washington University, April.

Stadler, Andreas and Jozef Poschl (Eds.) (1992). *Privatisation in Eastern Europe,* Friederich Ebert Foundation-Karl Renner Institute, Vienna.

Stanbury, W. T. (1989). Privatisation in Canada: ideology,e symbolism or substance?, in: MacAvoy et al. (1989), pp. 272–329.

Sutela, Pekka (1994). Insider privatisation in Russia: speculations on systemic change. *Review of Economies in Transition-Idantalouksien Katsauksia,* No. 1, Bank of Finland, pp. 5–26, forthcoming in *Europe-Asia Studies,* 1994 No. 3.

Takla, Lina (1994). The relationship between privatisation and the reform of the banking sector: the case of the Czech Republic and Slovakia, in: Estrin (Ed.), 1994, pp. 154–175.

Triska, Dusan (1992). A voucher scheme of privatization, in: A. Stadler and J. Poschl (Eds.), 1992, pp. 101–115.

Triska, Dusan (1993). Comment, in: Winkler (Ed.) 1993, pp. 286–293.

UN-ECE (1993). *Economic Survey of Europe in 1992–93,* Geneva.

Uvalic, Milica (1991). The PEPPER Report: Promotion of Employee Participation in Profits and Enterprise Results in the Member States of the European Community. Revised edition, *Social Europe,* Supplement No. 3.

Uvalic, Milica (1993). Privatisation in a disintegrating country: the case of former Yugoslavia. EACES-ACES-AEA Annual Conference, Boston, 3–5 January.

Winkler, G. (1993). Central and Eastern Europe: roads to growth. IMF, Washington.

20

The Impact of Investment Funds on Corporate Governance in Mass Privatization Schemes: Czech Republic, Poland and Slovenia

Saul Estrin, Domenico Mario Nuti, and Milica Uvalic

20.1 Introduction

In 1990–1997, in the vast majority of central and eastern European countries, the "transition" to the market economy has been accompanied by mass privatisation schemes, i.e. the free or subsidised distribution of

Published in *MOCT-MOST* 1, 2000, pp. 1–26. An earlier version of the paper ("The impact of privatization funds on corporate governance in mass privatisation schemes: Czech Republic, Poland, Slovenia") was published in Marko Simoneti, Saul Estrin and Andreja Bohm (Eds.) (1999), *The Governance of Privatisation Funds: Experiences of Czech Republic, Poland and Slovenia*, Ljubljana, Cheltenham: Edward Elgar, pp. 137–162; and in Negoslav P. Ostojić, Norman Scott (Eds), *Recent Lessons from Transition and Privatisation—Problems of Institutions and Corporate Governance*, ECPD, Belgrade 1999, pp. 135–166.

The authors gratefully acknowledge financial support from ACE Project P-95-2110-R, "Corporate Governance of Privatisation funds. The Case of Czech Republic, Poland and Slovenia". Advice and comments from participants in the project, especially Marko Simoneti, are also acknowledged with thanks, though any remaining errors are our own.

S. Estrin
London School of Economics and Political Science, London, UK

© The Author(s), under exclusive license to Springer Nature Switzerland AG 2023

S. Estrin, M. Uvalic (eds.), *Collected Works of Domenico Mario Nuti, Volume I*, Studies in Economic Transition, https://doi.org/10.1007/978-3-031-12334-4_20

state assets to citizens, through vouchers or equivalent means (see Nuti, 1995). This was a major track for the privatisation of large state enterprises, usually labelled large scale privatisation, but in some countries, vouchers could be used also for the "small" privatisation of flats, shops, restaurants, small plots of land.[1] The few exceptions to date are Hungary; Azerbaijan, Turkmenistan and Uzbekistan in the former Soviet Union; Bosnia and Herzegovina, the FYR of Macedonia and Serbia in the former Yugoslav Federation (see Estrin and Stone, 1996).

Apart from the political advantage of raising popular support for the transition, mass privatisation had a number of clear advantages:

- overcoming the lack of domestic liquid assets, which had been pulverised in the stabilisation that accompanied the early stage of transition;
- avoiding the difficulties of assessing the present value of enterprise assets in a period of changing relative prices and large-scale restructuring of output and trade flows;
- distributional fairness: mass privatisation was viewed as a kind of restitution to the entire population for their past consumption sacrifices; and
- above all speed, relatively to other privatisation methods.

[1] These definitions of mass, large scale and small privatisation appear to be both widespread and sensible and will be adopted here, though there is some confusion in the literature. Mass privatisation is sometimes used as a synonym for large-scale privatization, while voucher privatisation is used to indicate what we call mass privatisation (e.g. Kotrba et al., 1997). With reference to the Czech case, Takla (1994) uses large scale privatisation to indicate voucher privatisation. The World Development Report 1996 includes under Czech mass privatisation also assets sold for cash (IBRD, 1996, Table 3.2, note c, p. 53); this reflects original government policy, for in 1991 CSFR large scale privatisation was supposed to coincide with voucher privatisation, but then additional methods were introduced—hence the confusion.

D. M. Nuti (✉)
La Sapienza, University of Rome, Rome, Italy
e-mail: milica.uvalic@unipg.it

M. Uvalic
Department of Political Science, University of Perugia, Perugia, Italy

The loss of potential revenue, with respect to asset sales at prices closer to market valuation, was not—perhaps wrongly—perceived as a significant disadvantage. It was felt that state enterprises would be stripped or run down in the delays of privatisation and, in any case, speedy privatisation was regarded as indispensable to put an end to state interference in the enterprise sector and to de-politicise the economy (Boycko et al., 1996).

Mass privatisation had also a major disadvantage, namely inadequate discipline of "corporate governance", i.e. effective control by enterprise owners over managerial decision-making. Through share ownership diffusion, and in many cases also significant insiders' ownership (e.g. Russia, Slovenia), in combination with thin and still undeveloped financial markets, mass privatisation has in most cases disabled traditional mechanisms of corporate governance, whether by actual or potential controlling ownership stakes as respectively in the German-Japanese or in the Anglo-Saxon model. Weak governance leaves old managers unchallenged and inhibits the willingness of financial markets to provide risk capital. Therefore governance is crucial to improving efficiency and promoting capacity restructuring of newly privatized enterprises; it ultimately determines the effectiveness of privatization itself (Uvalic, 1997b).

In the course of mass privatisation, investment funds have emerged. Such funds range from special "national investment funds" (NIFs) with a centrally given role in the privatisation process, as typically in Poland, to spontaneous and decentralised investment funds as typically in Slovenia and in the Czech Republic. All such funds are often called "privatisation investment funds", or PIFs, although—except for the Polish case—the association is purely incidental and the term is not always used in the relevant legislation (see Simoneti and Triska, 1994). In ordinary market economies investment funds do not normally play a significant role in enhancing or inhibiting corporate governance (OECD, 1996). Fund managers usually diversify their portfolio without accumulating controlling stakes in any single company, and if they disapprove of managerial policies they tend to sell rather than force change through a takeover bid. In turn an investor would choose among funds according to their stated policy (e.g. investing in small companies, giving priority to income or capital, etcetera) and track record, and also would tend to use an "exit" rather than a "voice" strategy if dissatisfied with performance. In transition economies, on the contrary, investment funds which have become involved in mass privatisation have played important roles in corporate governance, both positive and negative.

In some cases, as in Poland, the promoters of mass privatisation have relied on forms of investment funds in order to eliminate or at least alleviate both the potential loss of corporate governance and other disadvantages such as reduced access to capital and management. This has been achieved by specifically assigning to a particular "lead" fund a large minimum stake (one third) of each enterprise subjected to mass privatisation.

Reliance on investment funds for the activation of corporate governance of privatised enterprises, in turn, raises the additional question of governance within the funds: "who monitors the monitors?" (Stiglitz, 1994). Thus the agenda is extended from first level governance—of firms—to second level governance—of funds; transforming the problem rather than solving it. This problem arises also in those investment funds which have not been given a "lead" and indeed have been prevented from taking a lead by the imposition of maximum ceilings to their shareholdings in any single enterprise. It turns out that Czech funds are themselves often subject to control by leading investors, in the guise of state banks which are still bearers of those interests and behaviours that the mass privatisation intended to eradicate.

By and large, actual experience with investment funds to date, though short-lived, is sufficiently heterogeneous, problematic, and different from initial expectations, to justify detailed scrutiny and investigation. The purpose of this paper is that of providing a comparative overview of these countries' experience (Sect. 20.2 on general features of mass privatisation schemes; Sect. 20.3 on specific features of investment funds) and drawing implications for both corporate governance and enterprise performance (Sects. 20.4 and 20.5 respectively), as well as some general conclusions (Sect. 20.6).

20.2 A Comparative Overview of Mass Privatization

General differences between the mass privatisation schemes in the Czech Republic, Poland, and Slovenia concern primarily their timing and speed; size relatively to state-owned assets, GDP, or other indicators; and their mode of implementation. These general differences are reviewed in this section, whereas Sect. 20.3 compares more specific features of investment funds design.

Timing and Speed

Mass privatisation was always presumed to be much faster than conventional methods, but in the end it was implemented with delays in all three countries (particularly in Poland), due to a series of problems—intense debates about some of the controversial issues, times of implementation longer than expected, unanticipated technical problems, complicated and long procedures of approval of privatisation programmes, and so forth (see Nuti, 1995).

In the Czech Republic, mass privatisation was part of the overall privatisation strategy adopted in the early stage of transition by the former Czechoslovak government, to be implemented immediately after small-scale privatisation and the restitution of property to former owners was terminated in 1991. The basic legal framework for mass privatisation was provided in the February 1991 *Law on large-scale privatisation*, which envisaged the use of various methods for privatising medium and large-scale firms, including privatisation via vouchers.[2] However, the law failed to specify a number of technical details regarding the vouchers scheme, which was done only in amendments and additional laws adopted in 1991–1992. As initially conceived by the Czechoslovak government, mass privatisation was to be implemented in two waves, and this provision was maintained by the Czech Republic after the split (in Slovakia, on the contrary, there was only one wave, with already distributed vouchers for the second wave redeemed for government bonds). The two waves were supposed to be completed over a two-year period but were somewhat delayed: the first was implemented in 1992, the second only in

[2] According to initial proposals, large-scale privatisation was supposed to coincide with vouchers privatisation, but then the government decided not to use vouchers privatisation as the exclusive method for privatising large-scale firms. This is the main reason why, in the literature on Czech privatisation, there is confusion in the terminology as large-scale, vouchers, and mass privatisation are sometimes used as synonyms.

1994. It turned out that the whole process of compiling, processing, and approving privatisation projects, as well as the transfer of property to the new owners, was rather lengthy (Kotrba et al., 1997). In this way speed in implementation, which was one of the main goals of voucher privatisation, was greatly compromised.

Mass privatisation (and privatisation in general) has taken even longer in Slovenia. A vouchers scheme was not part of the first privatisation programme launched by the former Yugoslav government, implemented also in Slovenia for a brief period in 1990, but was included as one of the methods only in the new privatisation law adopted after the Yugoslav split (see Uvalic, 1997a). The strong initial opposition to mass privatisation by some major political parties had prolonged the privatisation debate, and after several draft laws which were rejected in Parliament, a new privatisation law was finally adopted in November 1992. The law was again amended in June 1993 and effectively started being implemented in the second half of 1993, when further delays were caused by the long and complicated procedure of preparing, submitting, and approving enterprise privatisation programmes, including problems linked to unsettled restitution claims and procrastination by management in the expectation of more favourable legislative changes. Out of a total of 1543 enterprises planned for privatisation, by the end of 1994 as many as 90% had submitted their privatisation programmes, and by February 1997, 92% (1347) had also obtained approval, but by the end of 1996 only 58% (900) of privatising firms had actually completed the entire privatisation procedure (see Jaklin and Heric, 1997, p. 473). Because of the slow pace of privatisation, the validity of ownership certificates distributed in 1993 to Slovene citizens has been extended several times, but they should have definitely expired in mid-1997. A major problem emerged in the meantime in Slovenia known as the "privatisation gap" or a vouchers overhang (a huge discrepancy between capital disposable for privatisation and ownership certificates distributed to the population). The problem arose because the authorities initially took the book value of enterprise property to be privatised as the basis for calculating the value of vouchers to be distributed to citizens; but after their distribution they revised the value of property downwards.[3] Consequently, contrary to initial intentions of implementing mass privatisation in one wave as part of the global privatisation programme, a "second wave" is expected in the near future. The government has recognised its legal obligation to provide additional property in exchange of excess ownership certificates, but by mid-1997 had not yet decided which sectors or enterprises to add to the privatisation list.

The longest delays in implementing mass privatisation have occurred in Poland (see Nuti, 1995). The debate on mass privatisation started during the early phase of the transition in 1990–1991, but its actual implementation incurred substantial delays due to long controversies about a number of specific issues. The first law enabling mass privatisation was passed in June 1991, but only on 30 April 1993 was a law specifically dealing with the details of mass privatisation adopted by Parliament ("*Law on national investment funds and their privatisation*"). Thereafter, due to a combination of technical and political problems, it took another twenty months for the national investment funds to be created, effectively established only in December 1994, while the other provisions of the law were not implemented until 1996–1997. In particular, the actual privatisation of the national investment funds has been taking much longer than expected. The passage from the first phase of the programme "of single shareholder", during which the funds are owned by the State Treasury, to the second phase of conversion of certificates distributed to the population into shares of national investment funds, started only in June-July 1997. The deadline for converting certificates into shares was prolonged several times and expired at the end of 1998. It was expected that the first shareholders meetings would be held only at the beginning of 1998. Thus contrary to the other two countries' experience, mass privatisation in Poland is being implemented in a rather late phase of transition. Several rounds of mass privatisation were initially planned, but the Polish government has decided that residual state assets will be devoted to funding pension system reform, rather than to further mass privatisation.

[3] The problem could have been avoided had the value of vouchers not been determined in advance in national currency, and had the calculations of the supply and demand side of the programme been more accurate and coordinated in time. In Czechoslovakia the denomination of vouchers was in investment points, which had the advantage of eliminating expectations of redeeming vouchers at face value.

Size of the Mass Privatisation Programme

In all three countries mass privatisation was not the exclusive method of privatisation, but was used along with other techniques within a multi-track privatisation strategy; it had a much more important role in the Czech Republic than in both Slovenia and Poland, in terms of the most important indicators (enterprise number and value, their share in total state-owned and national assets or relative to GDP, proportion of enterprise capital privatised through vouchers).

In the Czech Republic, the large-scale privatisation programme involved around 70% of the then 4800 state-owned enterprises in Czechoslovakia. The programme was implemented through a combination of different methods, but vouchers privatisation was quantitatively the most important. During the first wave, mass privatisation involved the offer of some 1491 joint-stock companies (988 Czech and 503 Slovak), of a nominal value of CSK 299 billion; and during the second wave, of 861 joint-stock companies (only Czech) of which 676 were new and 185 were from the first wave, of a nominal value of CSK 155 billion (Cermak 1997, p. 100). The actual amount of property privatised through vouchers privatisation was somewhat lower than the amount initially offered: over the whole period 1991–1996, the nominal value of shares privatised through the vouchers method amounted to CSK 342 billion, which corresponds to 55% of the value of all property privatised within the large-scale privatisation programme (Cermak, 1997, p. 99). In terms of total state assets, around 25% was privatised through voucher privatisation (Takla, 1994, p. 161).

In addition to these global indicators, confirming the importance of mass privatisation for property transformation of the Czech economy, for individual firms vouchers privatisation was not only one of the most frequently used methods but in many cases involved a very high percentage of total enterprise capital. Contrary to the regulations in Poland or Slovenia, where the proportion of enterprise capital to be privatised via vouchers was fixed for all firms in advance (60% in Poland and 20–40% in Slovenia, see below), in the Czech Republic it was up to the enterprise to propose the desired combination of different methods, including the portion of equity to be privatised through vouchers.[4] Apart from 3% of equity that had to go to the restitution fund, an enterprise could in principle propose to be privatised using the vouchers scheme for all remaining 97% of its equity. This seems to have been indeed a frequent practice: during the first wave, 39.7% of projects used vouchers as the only privatisation method (see Kotrba et al., 1997). On average, during the first wave, enterprises used voucher privatisation as a method to distribute 81% of their shares, representing 63.5% of the total stock value; while in the second wave, the corresponding figure was almost 70% of stock value (Coffee, 1996, p. 120).

The mass privatisation scheme was of more limited importance in Slovenia, although it automatically involved, unlike the Czech or Polish case, all 1543 enterprises planned for privatisation. These firms in 1992 represented around 30% of total capital of the Slovene economy, 40% of revenues, 50% of employment and 40% of GDP (the private sector already accounted for 30%, and the state sector for another 40% of GDP; see Uvalic, 1997a, Rems and Jasovic, 1997, p. 2). However, mass privatisation as a method was quantitatively much less important in Slovenia than in the Czech Republic, due to a very different general privatisation procedure. According to the 1992 privatisation law, each enterprise had to transfer 20% of its shares to the Development Fund, which was to offer them at auctions to investment funds in exchange for ownership certificates they had collected from citizens. This was obligatory for all privatising firms,[5] but an enterprise could decide to distribute, in addition, up to 20% of its shares to employees (past, present, or their relatives) in exchange for their ownership certificates.[6] Thus within a single

[4] The differences in these regulations have crucially determined the proportion of capital that ended up being transferred, directly or indirectly, to investment funds, and consequently also the distribution of capital among different categories of new owners after privatisation. Therefore they have fundamental implications also for corporate governance of privatised firms and of investment funds (see the next two sections).

[5] There was an exception to this general rule: if a firm was privatised through cash sales, it could decide to transfer, instead of shares, 20% of the proceeds to the Development Fund. However, since this option was hardly ever used by firms in practice, it can be disregarded.

[6] According to the general privatisation scheme, another 20% had to be transferred to two government funds (the Pensions Fund and the Compensation Fund), whereas the remaining 40% could be privatised through an internal buy-out at privileged terms or using other methods based on conventional sales.

enterprise, only 20% of the shares actually had to be allocated to mass privatisation (via the Development Fund), another 20% being optional. Mass privatisation therefore involved a relatively low percentage of total capital or GDP of the Slovenian economy.[7]

In Poland, mass privatisation was less important than in Slovenia in terms of several global indicators, although generally involving a larger proportion of an individual enterprise's capital. Some 512 large and medium-scale enterprises were included in the mass privatisation programme. These firms represent around 10% of sales of the Polish industrial sector, while their book value is around 7 billion zloty (or US$ 2.8 billion; see Lewandowski and Szyszko, 1997, p. 4). Enterprises which entered the mass privatisation programme are also reported to control 10% of the production potential of all Polish state-owned companies, to account for about 4.5% of GDP, and for 8% of total assets of the Polish economy (Lawniczak, 1996, p. 3). At the same time, as much as 60% of total capital of enterprises included in the mass privatisation programme had to be transferred to national investment funds, to be later exchanged for ownership certificates distributed to the whole population.

Mode of Mass Privatization

Mass privatisation was based on the same basic principle—the transfer at a low nominal fee of state property to the population at large—but the mode of implementing this unprecedented privatisation method was actually very different in the three countries under consideration, in several respects: the general approach and procedure; compulsory versus voluntary inclusion of enterprises; denomination, distribution, conversion, tradability, and other features of vouchers.

The general approach followed in the Czech large-scale privatisation was centrally organised (in contrast to small privatisation), as the government prepared and published a detailed list of companies to be privatised during the first and second privatisation wave. At the same time, an

[7] Considering that privatising enterprises in Slovenia represent 40% of GDP, and that 20–40% of their shares went in exchange for vouchers, mass privatisation actually involved no more than 8–16% of Slovene GDP, and even less in terms of total capital.

enterprise's management (and other interested buyers) had the right to propose alternative privatisation projects, based on a combination of five different methods (of which voucher privatisation was one), but the project had to be evaluated and approved by specific government institutions. No fixed proportion of capital had to be set aside for vouchers, but whatever was not privatised through other methods usually was privatised through the vouchers scheme (see Takla, 1994, p. 173). Thus the inclusion of enterprises in mass privatisation was "semi"-voluntary: the government decided which firms were to be privatised within the large-scale privatisation programme, but since an enterprise could propose its own privatisation methods, privatisation through vouchers was not obligatory.

In Poland the mass privatisation programme was directly sponsored and organised by the government. By ordinance of the Council of Ministers, the enterprises selected for mass privatisation were formally included in the National Investment Funds Programme, and their shares were transferred to the 15 funds in the following proportions: 33% was transferred to a lead fund, another 27% in equal proportions to the other 14 funds, 15% was given to enterprise employees (and in certain cases a further 15% to entitled individuals, like farmers and fishermen, who had contractual relations with the company concerned), and 25% to the State Treasury. However, the selection of firms to be included in the programme was again "semi"-voluntary, although in a different sense than in the Czech Republic. The government decided which enterprises to include in the mass privatisation programme, to which an open invitation was sent to enter the programme, but within 45 days the enterprise director or workers council could raise objections. While the voluntary basis of enterprise inclusion was regarded a serious constraint on the supply-side of the programme, it was also a condition for having parliamentary majority in favour of the programme in 1993 (see Lewandowski and Szyszko, 1997) and a recognition of employee stakeholder power under the old system and in the transition.

In Slovenia the government decided which sectors were to be excluded from privatisation, while all the other enterprises were automatically included in the general privatisation programme. All enterprises slated for privatisation were obliged to privatise a fixed proportion of their capital through the vouchers scheme (i.e. through the transfer of 20% of shares to the Development Fund, to be later sold to investment funds in exchange for ownership certificates). Another 20% had to be transferred to two other government funds (the Pensions fund and the Compensation fund). For the remaining 60% of capital, enterprises could propose their own privatisation methods where, given the long tradition of self-management, a strong preference was given to employee buy-outs: 20% could be given to employees freely in exchange of their ownership certificates, another 40% could be sold to workers at preferential terms (a 50% discount and deferred payment), or otherwise privatised using conventional methods based on sales to outside owners.

In the three countries the general procedure of mass privatisation consisted of a combination, in different proportions, of a centralised approach based on government regulations and a certain degree of decentralisation delegating some decisions to enterprises. Other characteristics of mass privatisation varied, particularly regarding various features of vouchers and the design of investment funds (see Sect. 20.3 below).

Vouchers had very different specific features, from their label—vouchers in the Czech Republic, ownership certificates in Slovenia and share certificates in Poland—to more substantial features such as their denomination, nominal fee, recipients, distribution mechanism, tradability, conversion options.[8]

In the Czech Republic a 14-page book of vouchers was offered at a nominal fee of US$ 30 to all adult citizens, entitling them to 1000 investment points, to be invested in a maximum of 10 enterprises or in newly-established investment funds. In Poland, share certificates were offered at a nominal fee of 20 zloty (US$ 7–8) to all adult permanent resident citizens in the form of a single share certificate, which could be converted into shares of national investment funds. In Slovenia, all citizens (not only adults) had a special account opened with the Social Accounting Service, entitling them to a nominal value of ownership certificates between 150,000 and 400,000 tolars per person (between DM 2000 and DM 6400) depending on age, for which a small charge in tolars (corresponding to about DM 2) had to be paid upon registration.

[8] These characteristics of vouchers schemes are only discussed briefly, as they are not directly relevant for issues of corporate governance.

Vouchers were also denominated differently: in the Czech Republic in investment points, where each of the 1000 investment points had a predetermined value at the start of the first round of bidding, in Poland and Slovenia in national currencies, zlotys and tolars respectively. Vouchers were bearer instruments (and therefore immediately tradable) in Poland, but not in the Czech Republic and Slovenia where they normally become tradable only after having been converted into enterprise shares, or investment fund equity (though in the Czech Republic they could be transferred to heirs).

In both the Czech Republic and Slovenia, ownership certificates could be used for acquiring shares of either privatising enterprises or PIFs, but not in Poland where their use was limited to conversion into shares of national investment funds. A specific feature of the Slovenian model was that vouchers could also be invested under special terms in the employing enterprise (and therefore similarly to the Russian model).[9] However, there are also specific restrictions in Slovenia on shares acquired by employees in exchange for ownership certificates through the internal distribution scheme, as these shares are not tradable for a period of two years (whereas all shares transferred to the Development Fund are immediately tradable). In Poland, where certificates were immediately tradable, a large percentage (around 50%) of citizens sold them at once, at a significant profit (see Lewandowski and Szyszko, 1997, p. 29). Another feature of Polish certificates is that during the first phase of the mass privatisation programme (i.e. of state ownership of funds), all dividends are allocated to a fiscal account for the benefit of certificate holders, who are entitled to receive them at a later stage, at the latest once share certificates have been converted into national investment funds' shares.

These differences in general features of mass privatisation programmes in the Czech Republic, Poland and Slovenia are summarised in Table 20.1. Further details on specific features of investment funds are discussed in Sect. 20.3.

[9] Through the so-called internal distribution scheme, 20% of shares could be given to employees in exchange for their ownership certificates; in addition, certificates in excess of internal distribution could also be used in employee-management buy-outs.

Table 20.1 General features of mass privatisation programmes (MPP) in the Czech Republic, Poland and Slovenia

	Czech Republic	Poland	Slovenia
Period of implementation	1992 (1st wave) 1994 (2nd wave)	1991–present	1993–present
Role of MPP in privatisation strategy	Part of the large-scale privatisation programme	Implemented as a separate programme	Part of the global privatisation programme
Size			
Number of firms	1491 (1st wave): 988 (Czech R.) 503 (Slovakia), 861 (2nd Czech wave)	512 medium and large-scale firms	All 1543 firms planned for privatisation
– *Nominal value of firms*	299 bln CSK (1st wave) 155 bln CSK (2nd wave) Value of shares privatised via vouchers, 1991–1996: 342 bln CSK	7 bln zloty (USD 2.8 bln)	887 bln tolars (book value of 1,370 approved projects)
– *Other indicators*	55% of property privatised within the large-scale programme; 25% of all state-owned assets	4.5% of GDP; 10% of sales of industrial sector	40% of GDP 30% of capital
Inclusion of firms	Semi-voluntary for a selected group	Semi-voluntary for a selected group	Obligatory for all privatising firms
General share allocation scheme	Up to 97% could be auctioned to general public in exchange for vouchers	60% transferred to funds (33% to lead fund and 27% to other funds); 15% to employees; 25% retained by state	20% transferred to Development Fund, obliged to sell them to PIFs; another 20% to employees (optional)

(continued)

Table 20.1 (continued)

	Czech Republic	Poland	Slovenia
Auction process	Pre-fixed prices (in investment points), but changing to match supply and demand; voucher holders bid for shares	None; no pre-fixed prices, PIFs do not bid for vouchers but are given firms' shares	No pre-fixed prices, PIFs bid for shares offered by Development Fund
Main features of vouchers			
– *Fee*	US$ 30	US$ 8	DM 2
– *Denomination*	Investment points	Not expressed in monetary form	National currency (tolars)
– *Nominal value*	Not predetermined	Not predetermined	Fixed in tolars (DM 2000–6400), depending on age
– *Tradability*	Not tradable	Immediately tradable	Not tradable
– *Conversion options*	Shares of firms or of PIFs	Shares of only PIFs	Shares of firms or PIFs

Source: Compiled by the authors, mainly on the basis of the Project's Country Reports

20.3 Investment Funds Compared

In all the three countries under consideration, new financial institutions, usually referred to as privatisation investment funds[10] (PIFs), were intended to play a fundamental role as financial intermediaries in the post-privatisation period. Since the implementation of mass privatisation had usually resulted in a high dispersion of ownership in the hands of numerous small shareholders, PIFs were expected to provide an

[10] In the literature on the Czech Republic, these funds are most frequently referred to as 'investment privatisation funds' (though officially called 'investment funds'); in Slovenia, as 'privatisation investment funds' (though officially called 'authorised investment companies'); while in Poland, 'national investment funds' (corresponding to their official name). For convenience, we will refer to all these funds as privatisation investment funds (PIFs).

opportunity for portfolio diversification, but without excessive fragmentation of individual holdings. While the rationale for their creation was similar, the design of PIFs was rather different in many respects, including the mode of their creation, legal form, management, and portfolio restrictions. These differences in legal regulations have resulted in national differences with respect to the number of PIFs and of management companies, their dominant sponsors, distribution of vouchers, concentration of ownership.

Legal Regulations of PIFs

The general approach to the creation of PIFs was basically the same in the Czech Republic and Slovenia, in both countries in net contrast with the one adopted in Poland. The first two countries have relied on the free entry of investment funds to be market driven and created spontaneously by independent legal entities,[11] which were themselves most frequently established by other legal or physical persons (whether state of private banks, private enterprises, other existing or new financial intermediaries, individuals), while the government was to provide only the basic regulatory framework (the so-called bottom-up approach). In Poland the government directly organised the whole process—from the creation of funds[12] and selection of funds' management boards, to determining the allocation of enterprise assets to different funds, stipulating minimum holdings for "lead" funds, fixing remuneration schemes, and other details (the so-called top-down approach).

PIFs' legal form also differed. In Poland, Slovenia, and initially also in the Czech Republic, PIFs could only be established as joint stock companies, and thus as closed-end investment funds. In the Czech Republic, the 28 April 1992 *Law on investment companies and investment funds* allowed, in addition, the form of a closed-end and open-end mutual fund

[11] The terminology is complicated further by the fact that companies which create and manage PIFs are referred to as 'investment companies' in the Czech Republic, and as 'authorised management companies' in Slovenia.

[12] All funds were created by the Ministry of Privatisation, acting on behalf of the State Treasury as the official founder, which following state enterprise corporatisation initially owned all the enterprises included in the mass privatisation programme.

or unit trust, the main difference with respect to a joint stock company being that individuals investing their voucher points in these funds (trusts) are not given voting rights (see Mladek, 1995[13]). This change in the legislation had a major impact on the legal form of PIFs established during the second wave, when a number of open-end and closed-end mutual funds were also created (see below). Further legal changes were adopted in the Czech Republic in early 1996, as it became possible to convert PIFs into holding companies, enabling them to by-pass regulations covering investment companies and investment funds altogether; the government reacted by adopting new regulations, which came into effect on July 1, 1996, requiring funds to obtain the permission of the Securities Office of the Ministry of Finance for any change in their status (Hashi, 1997, p. 14).

The main features of PIF certificates, and therefore also voting and other rights of individual investors, depend directly on the legal form of funds.[14] In Slovenia and Poland, where PIFs can only be established as joint stock companies, citizens that have converted their vouchers into PIF shares normally have voting rights, and PIF shares are tradable once they are registered on the stock exchange. In Slovenia, PIF shares have to be registered and they are not tradable until they are listed on the stock exchange, which means that at least initially, fund managers are safe from the implications of shareholders dissatisfaction and exit (which indeed has been the case).[15] In Poland, once citizens certificates are converted into PIF shares, they are freely tradable (as shares of any ordinary joint-stock company listed on the stock exchange). In the Czech Republic PIFs can be created either as joint stock companies or as mutual funds. If a PIF

[13] A unit trust is a closed-end fund, which does not give its investors voting rights. A mutual fund is an open-end investment fund, which gives investors' the right to redeem the shares, but not voting rights. These forms are therefore similar with respect of investors lack of voting rights.

[14] As a joint stock company a PIF is owned by its shareholders, i.e. individuals investing their vouchers in the fund; this implies that they have voting rights and must be consulted on all important issues (mergers, acquisitions, etc.). If a PIF is founded as a mutual fund or unit trust, individual investors are unit holders without voting rights.

[15] Indeed, Slovenian companies managing PIFs have jointly been resisting quotation of funds' shares, imposing informal rules which effectively hamper any competitive action (see Bohm, 1997b, pp. 22–23). The main excuse for not registering PIF shares is the existence of the 'privatisation gap' (i.e. vouchers overhang). Until this problem is resolved, it is clear that registering PIF shares would imply a low market price.

is created as a joint-stock company its shares give shareholders voting rights and are tradable but with some delay with respect to shares of normal companies, since PIFs have to apply to the Ministry of Finance to obtain public tradability status for their shares (see Triska, 1995). If a PIF is registered as a mutual fund/unit trust, a frequent practice during the second wave, individuals investing their vouchers in PIFS are unit holders but without voting rights; it is reported that there is no liquid market in these units, and thus the unit holders' ability to sell their units is quite limited (see Hashi, 1997, p. 23).

The management of PIFs is also regulated differently. In Slovenia and initially also in the Czech Republic, a contract between the PIF and an external management company, normally its founder, was compulsory. In the Czech Republic the 1992 law abolished this obligation, and thus some funds created during the second wave are self-managed.[16] In Poland, an investment fund is not obliged to have an external manager, though self-managed funds have been strongly discouraged through both formal and informal channels.[17] Another important difference regards the actual selection of PIF managers. In the Czech Republic and Slovenia usually the company founding a PIF automatically becomes its management firm; in Poland PIFs could conclude management contracts exclusively with management companies selected through competitive tender by the Selection Commission, according to publicly announced selection criteria.[18]

Regulations on PIFs holdings and portfolio diversification also vary widely, partly revealing different perceptions of governance role. In the Czech Republic a fund cannot invest more than 10% of its assets in one

[16] According to the April 1992 Law on Investment Companies and Investment Funds, new investment funds are no longer required to be managed externally (see Hashi, 1997, p. 6).

[17] The programme was designed to discourage supervisory boards of funds from managing the funds on their own. A fund which would not employ a management firm was "punished" for being unaware of a special World Bank loan available only for the "good" funds participating in the programme. In addition, according to the 1993 Law on Investment Funds, funds managing their assets without the help of a management firm are not eligible for a performance fee, unlike the externally managed funds (see Lawniczak, 1996, p. 5).

[18] Nevertheless, it is reported that there was little competition among management companies, as the number of those companies that participated in the tender was only marginally higher than the number of funds (Lewandowski and Szyszko 1997, p. 21).

enterprise and cannot hold more than 20% of shares of a single firm. Thus PIFs are loosely regulated on the standard model of institutional investors with diversified portfolio, expected to primarily engage in "passive" portfolio management (i.e. trading of enterprises shares); however, they were also occasionally, as major shareholders or in coalition with other shareholders, active on supervisory boards of enterprises (Simoneti, 1996). In Slovenia, PIFs are more loosely regulated with similar standard requirements for portfolio diversification, since a fund cannot invest more than 10% of its assets in a single company; but contrary to the Czech regulations, a PIF in Slovenia can hold a 100% equity in an individual enterprise (only exceptionally a limit of 20% is imposed);[19] thus the choice between a passive portfolio management or more active involvement in management of enterprises is left to the funds (Simoneti, 1996). In Poland portfolio diversification is subject to detailed rules: each fund as "lead" fund would hold at least 33% of shares of about 30 firms at all times, and about 2% of shares in the remaining 450 firms (see Lawniczak, 1996, p. 2). For each privatising enterprise the "lead fund" is not only encouraged but effectively induced to play a significant role in raising finance, monitoring performance, managing and promoting restructuring (while another 27% of the shares are initially held by the other 14 funds). Thus PIFs in Poland are given a special governance role, similar to that of financial institutions in the German model.

Partly due to their differences in legal design, actual experience with PIFs has also been very different in the three countries considered, with respect to their creation, functioning, and later developments during the post-privatisation period.

PIFs in Practice

During the first wave of Czechoslovak mass privatisation, reliance on private initiative led to the creation of some 429 PIFs (over 260 in the Czech Republic); a total of 354 funds participated in the second wave (both new funds and those established during the first wave; see Mladek, 1995). As

[19] The limit of 20% of a fund's shareholding in a single company applies only to companies which are at the same time at least 10% owners of the fund's management company.

already mentioned, a major development in the second wave was the appearance of a number of open-end and closed-end mutual funds or unit trusts, while some of the formerly created PIFs also changed their status to mutual funds (see Mejstrik, 1997).[20] Thus out of the 354 funds participating in the second wave, 133 were old investment funds established during the first wave; 63 were newly established investment funds; 120 were closed-end mutual funds; and 38 were open-end mutual funds (Mladek, 1995, p. 84). The large majority of investment companies in both waves created only one fund, but several of the most powerful investment groups established a large number of funds. During the first wave, 336 investment companies had created a total of 428 funds; but whereas 301 investment companies created only one fund each, the remaining 35 companies created the other 127 funds.[21] Similarly, during the second wave, 238 investment companies created a total of 349 funds; again, 191 investment companies created only one PIF each, while the remaining 47 companies created the other 158 funds (calculated from Kotrba et al., 1997, Table 3.3). After the early 1996 legal changes enabling PIFs to by-pass existing regulations (in particular, the 20% maximum limit of any company's shares), several PIFs transformed themselves into holdings and were exempted from the 20% limit (Hashi, 1997, p. 14).[22]

Multiple funds are frequent also in Slovenia. Some 23 management companies established a total of 72 PIFs, mostly during 1994 and 1995 (Rems and Jasovic, 1997, p. 11). The formal reason for multiple funds in Slovenia is the legal restriction imposing a maximum limit on a fund's capital (10 billion SIT, or around DM 115 million), not present in the other two countries. The Slovenian Securities Exchange Commission, also in charge of supervising investment funds, is now considering the possibility of merging PIFs which are managed by the same management company.

[20] Investment companies setting up and running PIFs had discovered that a joint stock company was expensive to administer, exposed them to the threat of hostile take-overs, and denied them full autonomy and discretion in the decision making process (see Hashi, 1997).

[21] The largest 14 investment groups created a total of 71 funds, where the extreme case was Agrobanka, setting up 17 funds (see Mladek, 1995, p. 76).

[22] Thus by the time the new July 1996 regulations came into effect requiring statutory changes to be approved by the Ministry of Finance, 121 investment funds and 9 investment companies had already changed their status; and by April 1997, a further 32 funds changed their status after obtaining permission (Hashi, 1997, p. 14).

In Poland management companies are also less numerous than PIFs, but for different reasons; namely, Polish PIFs are not obliged to make a contract with an external manager (though self-managed funds were strongly discouraged). Of the 15 PIFs established by the government, 14 had a contract with a management company.[23] In the meantime, however, there were disputes in three cases between management companies and the funds; two ended with the cancellation of the management contract, while in the third case the Minister of Privatisation dismissed most members of the supervisory board (Lewandowski and Szyszko 1997, p. 15).

The initial allocation of vouchers differed. Only in Poland were all ownership certificates invested directly in PIFs (as this was the only option available). In the Czech Republic and Slovenia, where citizens could choose whether to invest in PIFs or in enterprises directly, funds were very active in their promotion campaigns, which proved to be successful. In the Czech Republic, PIFs managed to attract, out of all citizens' vouchers, 72% during the first wave and 63.5% during the second. Ownership was highly concentrated, however, especially during the first wave, when the top 5 founders with their 10 funds attracted over 50% of all vouchers; during the second wave, the top 10 founders with their 48 funds attracted 50% of all vouchers (Kotrba et al., 1997). In Slovenia out of the total nominal value of issued certificates (567 billion tolars, or DM 9.3 billion), by the beginning of 1997 PIFs had collected some 310 billion tolars worth of certificates, or almost 55% (Rems and Jasovic, 1997, pp. 6–7). Employees of Slovenian firms being privatised have invested their certificates mainly directly in the employing enterprise (as part of the internal distribution scheme or an internal buy out), while around 10% of ownership certificates which have not been utilised have expired in June 1997.

Who Controls PIFs?

A similar pattern of control of PIFs emerged in the three countries under consideration. Though PIFs are owned by private individual shareholders—citizens who have exchanged their vouchers for PIF shares—financial

[23] The national investment fund number 9 (the Eugeniusz Kwiatkowski Fund) has been managed without a management firm from the very beginning.

institutions, mainly banks as the main and dominant owners of companies managing PIFs, *de facto* control them, thus generating potential conflicts of interest.

In the Czech Republic, of the 13 largest investment companies in each of the two waves, 11 were created by financial institutions in the first wave, and 6 in the second (Hashi, 1997, p. 11).[24] The four largest banks (Ceska Sporitelna, Investicni a postovni banka, Komercni banka and Ceskoslovenska obchodni banka), all with significant state ownership stakes (40–45%), were prominently represented in this group of 13, as they are the parent institutions of the largest investment companies setting up PIFs (Hashi, 1997, p. 11). Consequently a number of investment companies have large state-owned stakes, though private investment companies were also represented (3 in the first wave and 7 in the second wave) (Hashi, 1997, p. 11). Extensive cross-ownership between PIFs, their sponsoring investment companies and banks is another major problem. In principle banks' shares could not be held by their subsidiary investment companies, but by setting up PIFs which were only managed by their investment companies, banks could by-pass this regulation; thus many PIFs are under the direct control of banks and hold shares of their founding 'grandparents' (see Hashi, 1997, p. 24).

Similarly, in Slovenia, banks have been the most important indirect actors in the setting up of PIFs. The dominant owners of the 23 management companies are domestic legal entities (foreigners own minority shares in only two management companies), mainly banks which indirectly control 48% of PIFs and 62% of PIF assets, and insurance companies which control 19% of PIFs and 17% of PIF assets (Rems and Jasovic, 1997, p. 12). Thus over three fourths of total PIF assets are indirectly controlled by domestic banks and insurance companies, some of which have still not been privatised. These financial institutions also have the majority stake in banking and insurance services, with potential conflicts of interest between PIFs, their management companies, and banks sponsors and owners of management companies (Rems and Jasovic, 1997,

[24] Harvard Capital and Consulting Investment Company was the third largest investment company in both waves and the only large private investment company without an apparent financial institution behind it.

p. 12). However, the state has indirect ownership shares in only two management companies while another two are owned by socially owned sponsors (Rems and Jasovic, 1997, p. 11), which suggests that non-privatised financial institutions may not have as important a role as in the Czech Republic.

In Poland, large financial groups are also the main players controlling PIFs, but the situation differs in several respects. First, contrary to the situation in the Czech Republic or Slovenia, where managing companies setting up and running PIFs are the key actors, in Poland it seems to be the other way round, given that a PIF's supervisory board can cancel a contract with a management company if it so decides (Lewandowki and Szyszko 1997, p. 22).[25] Second, foreign financial institutions have a much greater role in Poland than in the Czech Republic or Slovenia. In the majority of cases, PIFs are managed by a management company sponsored by a consortium of domestic and international banks and consulting companies, foreign managers and consultants (see Lewandowski and Szyszko 1997, pp. 10–12). While in the Czech Republic PIFs are frequently controlled by semi-privatised banks in which the state still has an important stake, in Poland in several cases the majority stake is in the hands of foreign institutions. Out of the 14 funds that had concluded a contract with an external managing company, in 9 cases the management company has a single majority shareholder (with a 50% or larger stake), of which in 7 cases the owner of the majority stake of the management company is a foreign entity (usually a bank), and in 2 cases only, a Polish entity (a commercial bank and a consulting firm; see Lewandowski and Szyszko, 1997, p. 12). Finally, it seems that in Poland there are no significant opportunities for cross-ownership between management companies, their sponsors and PIFs, since banks, as the main sponsors of management companies, are either already private or are too large to be object of significant investment by PIFs, while limits on PIFs borrowing make such cross-ownership unfeasible. Polish authorities have also tried to

[25] Management contracts are concluded for a period of 10 years but can be terminated at 180 days' notice.

impose a number of regulations which are supposed to reduce (if not eliminate) the possibility of cross-ownership.[26]

The specific features of PIFs in the three countries under consideration are summarised in Table 20.2.

20.4 Implications for Corporate Governance

Corporate governance in a broad sense includes both governance in the strict sense defined in our Introduction, as effective control by enterprise owners over managerial decision-making, and in addition equality among owners regardless of their being insiders or outsiders, or otherwise bearing an interest (stake) other than ownership (see Nuti, 1998). In transition economies this broader notion can be important, in view of the unexpected dominant role of insiders in the privatisation of state enterprises. In this paper, however, we shall refer to corporate governance in the stricter sense, for two basic reasons. First, ownership by insiders (or other stakeholders), however introduced, can only be expected to adversely affect corporate governance—through inside owners appropriating indirectly more than their fair share of profits and ultimately of capital—in a special case, i.e. when a controlling interest is in the hands of insiders (or stakeholders) who individually hold a smaller share in equity than in factor supply (or other stake; see Nuti 1997). Second, the Czech Republic does not exhibit insider ownership, while in Slovenia and Poland insider ownership, though significant, is the result of managerial and employee buy-outs in the absence of alternative takers, rather than the result of mass privatisation. In any case, there is no clear evidence that in these countries insider ownership has prevented or delayed enterprise restructuring.

In a normally functioning financial market, corporate governance as shareholders' control over managerial discretion relies on two major mechanisms usually associated respectively with the German-Japanese and the Anglo-Saxon models. The first is the direct monitoring and

[26] E.g. a management company is not allowed to own shares of any fund to which it is providing management services, without prior approval by the Anti-Monopoly Office.

Table 20.2 Features of investment funds in the Czech Republic, Poland and Slovenia

	Czech Republic	Poland	Slovenia
Basic legislation	In 1991 no specific legislation; April 1992 Law on Investment Companies and Investment Funds. New legislation adopted in July 1996	April 1993 Law on National Investment Funds and their Privatisation	Special provisions of the December 1994 Law on Investment Funds and Management Companies
General approach	Spontaneously created market driven funds ("bottom-up")	Created and sponsored directly by the government ("top-down")	Spontaneously created market driven funds ("bottom-up")
Founder	Any legal entity ('investment company'). Minimum capital requirement: US$ 33,000	State Treasury	Any legal entity ('authorised management company'). Min. capital SIT 10 mln, max. SIT 10 bln (DM 115 mln)
Legal form	Joint stock company; and since 1992 also closed-end and open-end mutual fund	Joint stock company	Joint stock company
Portfolio regulations	A fund cannot invest more than 10% of its assets in one firm, and of shares of a single firm	Each fund as lead fund initially has a 33% holding in some 30 firms, which cannot be reduced	A fund cannot invest more than 10% of its assets in one firm, but can hold up to 100% (exceptionally limited to 20%)
Management	After adoption of 1992 law, contract with external management company no longer compulsory	Contract with external management company not compulsory, although strongly encouraged	Contract with external management company (founder) compulsory

(*continued*)

Table 20.2 (continued)

	Czech Republic	Poland	Slovenia
PIF certificates	Not always assuring voting rights; tradable with some delay	Certificates tradable, but gave no voting rights; became voting shares once exchanged for PIF shares	Voting shares; not tradable until listed on the stock exchange
Number of PIFs	429 (1st wave, CSSR) (1) 354 (2nd wave, CR only) (1)	15	72
Number of management companies (MC)	336 (1st wave, CSSR) (2) 238 (2nd wave) (2)	Initially 14, reduced to 12 by mid-1996	23
Major owners of MCs	Domestic banks (mainly semi-privatised)	Domestic and foreign banks	Domestic banks and insurance companies
Vouchers invested in PIFs	1st wave: 72% 2nd wave: 63.5%	100% (obligatory for all voucher holders)	Almost 55% of total
Concentration of ownership	1st wave: top 5 founders with their 20 funds attracted 50% 2nd wave: top 10 founders with their 48 funds attracted 50%	Initially equally distributed, but getting concentrated	Major banks control 34 funds and 62% of total PIF assets

Source: Compiled by the authors, mainly on the basis of the Project's Country reports, except for (1) Mladek (1995), p. 84; and (2) Calculated from Kotrba et al. (1997), Table 3.3.

control exercised by one or several large shareholders, indirectly benefiting also other shareholders; in 1990 in Germany 80 per cent of companies had at least one shareholder with at least 25 per cent of the equity; additional control is exercised—especially in Japan—by banks and cross-ownership. The second is the threat posed to managers by the potential rise of a controlling interest—through a successful takeover bid—even in a situation of highly fragmented shareholding; this requires market liquidity and developed financial institutions, as in the Anglo-Saxon model.

Within such a developed and well-functioning financial market, the corporate governance role for investment funds is fairly limited. It is true that some role is suggested by corporate governance and finance literature. Namely, the concentration of ownership in investment funds can be seen as a mechanism to overcome the co-ordination costs of small shareholders, enabling them to internalise the economies of scale of collective action and to overcome the agency problems in monitoring management associated with highly dispersed ownership (see Blair 1995 and Shleifer and Vishny 1995).[27] The relevance of this advantage for mass privatisation schemes is clear, since by definition these lead to highly dispersed ownership structures, thus needing new structures to monitor firms and motivate managers.

However, ownership concentration by a fund does not necessarily amount to control; and in any case monitoring managers by funds does not necessarily involve funds in forcing managers to change their ways, even when they might be able to do so if they tried. Funds are more likely—as we already indicated—to choose "exit", i.e. the sale of shares with less than satisfactory performance, rather than "voice", i.e. fight to change managerial policy or even managers. If this is the case, investment funds will only improve company performance if capital markets are fully developed and well-functioning, so that the share price of non-satisfactory companies drops, raising the probability of a takeover. Indirect methods of governance—through funds—therefore may work well only in the context of effective financial markets.

In transition economies, however, financial markets are still not fully developed; they tend to have a low capitalisation with respect to GDP, a relatively low turnover—even in those countries such as the Czech Republic where mass privatisation has been used extensively and capitalisation is relatively high—with respect to both capitalisation and GDP (see the EBRD Transition Report 1995, 1997; in 1996, for instance,

---

[27] The literature has also explored conflicts among owners, notably concerning securities with different combinations of control and cash flow claims (see e.g. Grossman & Hart, 1988), while the private benefits of control by a dominant owner have been studied empirically by Barclay and Holderness (1989), with reference to the premium paid for a large block of shares.

market capitalisation was 43.5% of GDP in the Czech Republic, 8.8% in Slovakia, 5.9% in Hungary and 5% in Slovenia; with a turnover/capitalisation ratio respectively of 0.23, 0.11, 0.13 and 0.53).

In this situation, there is something to be said both against and for investment funds. First, the classic governance problem arises from the asymmetries of information inherent in the relationship between distant owners and operational management. But this is not the key problem in transition economies, where the real issues concern how to generate rents in the first place, not the allocation of those rents. The governance problem in transition economies is therefore the provision of additional capital for investment, and investment funds, whose funding has come in the form of mass privatisation vouchers, are not in a good position to bring real capital to bear on restructuring. Slovenian funds appear to be particularly under-capitalized, their assets apparently still consisting predominantly of vouchers, illiquid and practically worthless until the next round of mass privatisation.[28]

Second, not necessarily in terms of importance, the problem arises of corporate governance once removed, i.e. governance of the funds themselves. Presumably fund managers—even in the Polish case, where they are partly rewarded according to performance—should maximise the funds' yield to investors. However in some cases, notably in the Czech Republic and in Slovenia, state owned banks appear to have had a major role in the creation of funds and still retain substantial residual ownership. Whether this is an obstacle to restructuring, i.e. whether banks are still bearers of government interests in sustaining employment at the cost of efficiency, remains to be seen. When there is no substantial ownership, fund investors are exposed to the risk of managers "tunnelling" companies, i.e. creaming off profits to their own advantage, as it is frequently reported in the Czech Republic—though this is more a question of inadequate supervision, typical of the Czech approach to state regulation, than a problem of governance as such. More generally, we can detect conflicts of interest behind the disputes between the Management and Supervisory Boards, which appear more frequent in Poland.

[28] Slovenian funds, incidentally, decide when they will be quoted on the stock exchange.

Third, well managed Funds may be able to generate a good rate of return for their investors by selling stock in bad firms and concentrating on high return stock (e.g. monopolies, utilities, etcetera). But this will do nothing to resolve the problem that the funds are often expected to tackle, namely to ensure that the previously poorly returning enterprises improve their performance.

Fourth, even the tangible risk of takeover will not have a significant effect on managerial behaviour, if the managerial market is so thin or tight that reputation has no impact on managerial remuneration in the future. Peiperl and Estrin (1997) stress precisely such thinness of the managerial market in transition economies, which combined with current and future expected significant excess demand lowers the prospects for reputational factors being significant in the short to medium run.

On the positive side, there seem to be three main redeeming features of the experience with investment funds in mass privatisation in the three countries under consideration. The first is the Polish experience which relies on a fund's large shareholding, presumably amounting to a controlling interest or more easily extended to reach a controlling interest, to establish corporate governance, inject management and capital, promote restructuring—relying on the ownership incentives of a normal market economy, though in a way "forcing" to some extent the portfolio policy of investment funds. The Polish approach embodies some kind of industrial policy, especially seeing that three of the funds have holdings concentrated in specific branches.

Second, some of the problems indicated above should be alleviated both by supervision of funds and by appropriate remuneration schemes for fund management boards. Supervisory Boards differ very considerably in the three countries: for instance, in Slovenia the Supervisory Board consists of only three members, appointed by the management companies themselves, thus being effectively controlled by their supervisees. In Poland, on the contrary, there appear to be five to nine members on supervisory boards, and one to seven members on the management board (appointed by the supervisory board); the very fact that conflicts with management boards are reported indicates a degree of checks and balances; amidst controversy, the management contracts of three of the funds have been terminated by their supervisory boards. Fund managers fees appear to be excessively high relatively to western standards. In Slovenia Management Boards obtain a yearly fee corresponding to 3 per cent of the value of the assets (1% in shares and another 2% in cash), plus a flat fee to cover fixed costs. Management fees are also very high in Poland, with an equivalent formula and a slightly higher rate. It would seem much better to reward management boards according to the increase in the value of fund assets instead of their total value, indeed according to the increase in the value of fund assets relatively to the stock exchange index, in order to reward only differential performance, making up with a higher percentage for the lower basis. However, the volatile nature of stock exchanges in transition economies should be taken into account.

Third, the role of investment funds must be seen as an alternative possibly preferable to a greater role for insider ownership, for the risks specified above. Indeed Slovenian investment funds were set up precisely in order to be a countervailing power to insiders, though this does not seem to have happened: from the questionnaires in a country study it appears that investment funds actually support enterprise managers. Investment funds are emerging as the major outside institutional shareholders in all countries relying on mass privatization programmes—though they are very specific institutions, a combination of holding companies and mutual funds (Ellerman, 1997), whose performance therefore requires detailed empirical study.

20.5 Implications for Economic Performance

The material in the previous sections highlights that, in an environment of perfectly functioning capital and management markets, investment funds may not be ideal institutions for the exercise of corporate governance by outsider owners; but the question remains whether this is a relevant point of comparison. The capital and financial markets of transition economies are particularly weak and almost all private ownership which is not in the hands of investment funds is instead controlled by insiders, either workers or managers. It is not clear whether the particular governance problems raised by insider ownership are more or less serious than those discussed in this study. This section is concerned with the evidence to date about the impact of ownership by investment funds on enterprise performance.

In brief, early studies on private versus state ownership, which lump together all private firms—e.g. insider owned, investment funds owned and foreign direct investments—find little evidence of differential performance in the first years of transition. The standard interpretation is that the hardening of budget constraints motivated such an improvement in performance among state owned firms that they could not be distinguished from their privatised counterparts. Note that these studies do typically find better performance in *de novo* firms, and sometimes in particular cases in foreign owned firms. In that sense, these studies may confirm that all forms of privatisation have not been particularly successful in stimulating improved performance.

All these empirical studies are bedevilled by the problem of endogeneity of ownership form; that is to say that the choice of form of privatisation was not independent of the performance of the firm in the first place. In particular, it seems likely that insiders managed to obtain ownership of the best firms for themselves, except in the case of very large firms where they were unable to raise enough capital to purchase the assets from their own resources. Thus if one observes poor performance of firms owned by investment funds, relative to the group of all privatised firms, this may be explained by the fact that only the worse firms were made available to investment funds. A similar problem may apply to studies which suggest a better performance in firms taken over by foreign multinationals. In many cases, these were already the best firms in the economy, and the foreign multinationals therefore had a sound basis upon which to build with their investments.

There have been a number of studies which compare privatised and state-owned firms, but only recently have convincing results about the positive effects of privatisation begun to emerge. The first major study was by Pinto et al. (1993), who used a survey of 75 large state-owned firms to explore the relationship between privatisation prospects and restructuring. Theory suggests that the prospect of future privatisation may be sufficient to induce good managers to reveal their abilities by successfully restructuring their state-owned firms. Pinto et al. confirmed that existing managers expected to keep their jobs post-privatisation.

Most of the early studies failed to isolate any relationship between ownership form (private versus state) and the performance of firms. This finding emerges for example in Belka et al. (1994), Earle et al. (1996) and Balcerowicz et al. (1998). The standard approach has been to include ownership type in regressions explaining productivity, the change in productivity or enterprise growth. The dummy variables for private ownership have almost always proved to be statistically insignificant. However, a few recent studies suggest privatisation may be beginning to have an effect. Earle and Estrin (1997) find that privately owned firms have a greater increase in productivity than state owned firms in Russia in 1994. In Frydman et al. (1997), there is evidence from mid-sized firms in the Czech Republic, Hungary and Poland between 1990–1994 that private ownership does improve company performance in terms of increasing revenue and reducing costs.

There are several interpretations of this very mixed evidence on the impact of privatisation. One is that it is simply too early to make a judgement—the full effects of privatisation may take many years to become established. The point is reinforced when one realises that other aspects of the economic environment formed by firms were also changing rapidly, most notably the hardness of budget constraints. Several studies show that the hardening of budget constraints may have been a major source of improved corporate performance and productivity increases (see in particular Estrin et al. (1995), Basu et al. (1996), Alfaranderi et al. (1996)).

An alternative interpretation is that privatisation did not have the desired effects because ownership went into the hands of insiders, and that group cannot be expected to deliver significantly improved economic performance, relative to the state. The comparative performance of insider and state ownership is analysed in Earle and Estrin (1996), who suggest insiders may be equivalent to the state as owner, particularly in the areas of investment, and restructuring via employment reduction. Evidence is accumulating that the form of dominant ownership matters at least as much as whether the state or private agent own firms. Earle and Estrin (1997) report that in Russia insider owned firms increase productivity faster than outsider owners or the state, though it is managers rather than workers as dominant owners who play the significant role. However, outsiders appear to play a more positive role in Central Europe. A study by Zemplinerova et al. (1995) highlights superior economic performance in firms which were foreign owned, or owned by a dominant investor, while Djankov and Pohl (1997) find that strategic domestic investors are effective owners in the Czech Republic, Poland and Slovakia. Frydman et al. (1997) also find improved performance to stem primarily from outside owners for their sample of Central European economies. Finally, a study by Classens et al. (1997) explains the impact of institutional owners, notably Investment Funds. They looked at the relationship between ownership concentration and two outcome variables—profitability and Tobin's q (the ratio between market valuation and replacement cost of capacity)—in Czech privatised firms. They found that ownership concentration was increasing strongly over time, and that the significance of the concentration was increasing over time. Bank related funds raised Tobin's q over and above the concentration variable, though it had no significant independent effect on profitability.

In conclusion, there have been a number of studies of the relationship between ownership and corporate performance in transition, but the results have so far been weak and rather mixed. Only in very recent studies are we beginning to see some evidence that privatisation improves performance, and that outsider owned firms perform better than insider owned ones. The likely reason is the subject matter of this paper, namely the weak governance mechanisms and capital market structures associated with insider ownership via mass privatisation.

20.6 Conclusions

Large-scale ownership by investment funds, generated in the course of mass privatisation, may be less than ideal. Once a large, deep, liquid and efficient financial market is instituted, investment funds involvement in corporate governance is neither likely nor necessary. Until then, with the exception of Poland where each enterprise privatised on the mass track is specifically assigned to the responsibility of a "lead" fund, one should not expect investment funds to play a major role in the corporate governance of companies in which they invest, thus leaving greater scope for managerial discretion than it was originally intended. Moreover, the unintended, residual leading role of state banks in the creation and ownership of investment funds might well exercise an adverse impact on the governance of funds and, indirectly, on the governance of companies.

At the same time, neither ideal solutions nor instant financial markets were available at the beginning of the transition. There is a theoretical presumption—until proven otherwise—that ownership by investment funds is probably better than insider ownership, and there is some evidence for this empirically. Moreover, the very limited evidence that is now emerging suggests that investment fund ownership may be associated with some improvement in enterprise performance, at least relative to other privatised firms.

Bibliography

Alfaranderi, Giles et al. (1996). Arrears in the Russian enterprise sector, in S. Commander, Q. Fan and M. Schaffer (Eds.), *Enterprise Restructuring and Economic Policy in Russia*, World Bank—EDI Development Studies, Washington, D.C.

Balcerowicz, Leszek, Cheryl Gray, Iraj Hashi (1998). Exit processes in transition economies: downsizing, workouts and liquidation, Budapest, Central European University Press.

Barclay M. J. and Holderness, C.G. (1989). Private Benefits from the Control of Public Corporations, *Journal of Financial Economics*, vol. 25, 371–97.

Basu, Swati, Saul Estrin and Jan Svejnar (1996). Employment and wage behaviour of enterprises in transitional economies, University of Trento, Centre on the Evolution in Eastern European Countries Discussion paper B-96/1; forthcoming in *Economics of Transition.*

Belka, Marek, Saul Estrin, Mark Schaffer and I. J. Singh (1994). Enterprise adjustment in Poland: Evidence from a survey of 200 privatized, private and state owned firms, LSE Centre for Economic Performance Working Paper no. 658.

Blair M. M. (1995). *Ownership and Control: Rethinking Corporate Governance for the 21st Century*, Brookings Institution, Washington DC.

Bohm, Andreja (Ed.) (1997a). Economic Transition Report 1996, C.E.E.P.N., Ljubljana.

Bohm, Andreja (1997b). Supervisory Boards and Issues of Corporate Governance of Privatisation Funds, Part III of Draft Country Report: Corporate Governance of Privatisation Investment Funds in Slovenia, Ljubljana, mimeo, June.

Boycko, Maxim, Andrei Shleifer and Robert Vishny (1996). A Theory of Privatization, *Economic Journal*, 106, 309–319.

Cermak, Petr (1996). Economic transition in the Czech Republic—1996, in Andreja Bohm (Ed.), 1997, pp. 96–112.

Classens, Stijn, Simeon Djankov and Gerhard Pohl (1997). Ownership and Corporate Governance: Evidence form the Czech Republic, World Bank, Washington, mimeo.

Coffee John C. Jr (1996). Institutional investors in transitional economies—Lessons from the Czech experience, in R. Frydman, C. Gray and A. Rapaczynski (Eds), 1996.

Djankov, Simeon and Gerhard Pohl (1997). Restructuring of large firms in Slovakia, mimeo, March.

Earle John S. and Saul Estrin (1996). Workers self-management in transition economies, mimeo, forthcoming in *Advances in the Economic Analysis of Participatory and Labor-Managed Firms*, 1998, JAI Press, Greenwich and London.

Earle John S. and Saul Estrin (1997). After voucher privatization: The structure of corporate ownership in Russian manufacturing industry, mimeo, June.

Earle John S., Saul Estrin and L. Leshchenko (1996). Ownership structures, patterns of control and enterprise behaviour in Russia, in S. Commander, Q. Fan and M. Schaffer (Eds.), *Enterprise Restructuring and Economic Policy in Russia*, World Bank—EDI Development Studies, Washington, D.C.

EBRD—European Bank for Reconstruction and Development (1995, 1997). *Transition Report*, London.

Ellerman, David (1997). Voucher privatization with investment funds: A reappraisal, Washington, mimeo.

Estrin, Saul, Alan Gelb and I. J. Singh (1995). Shocks and adjustment by firms in transition: A comparative study, *Journal of Comparative Economics*, Vol. 21, No. 2, 131–153.

Estrin, Saul and Robert Stone (1996). A taxonomy of Mass Privatization, *Transition*, Vol. 7, No. 11–12, The World Bank, Washington, pp. 8–9.

Frydman, Roman, Cheryl W. Gray and Andrzej Rapaczynski (Eds) (1996). *Corporate Governance in Central Europe and Russia*, CEU, Budapest, London and New York.

Frydman, Roman, Cheryl W. Gray, Marek Hessel and Andrzej Rapaczynski (1997). Private ownership and corporate performance: some lessons from transition economies, Economic Research Report 97–28, C.V. Starr Center for Applied Economics.

Grossman, G. and Oliver Hart (1988). One share one vote and the market for corporate control, *Journal of Financial Economics*, Vol. 20, 2203–35.

Hashi, Iraj (1997). Mass privatisation and corporate governance in the Czech Republic, Staffordshire University, mimeo, July.

International Bank for Reconstruction and Development (1996). *From Plan to Market—World Development Report 1996*, New York, Oxford University Press.

Jaklin, Joze and Bostjan Heric (1997). Economic transition in Slovenia—1996, in A. Bohm (Ed.), 1997a, pp. 466–501.

Jasovic, Bozo (1997). Management companies and issues of corporate governance of privatisation funds, part II of Draft Country Report: Corporate Governance of Privatisation Investment Funds in Slovenia, Ljubljana, June.

Kotrba, Josef, Evzen Kocenda and Jan Hanousek (1997). Corporate governance of investment privatization funds, Draft Country Report: Corporate Governance of Privatization Investment Funds in the Czech Republic, August.

Lawniczak, Ryszard (1996). A Polish experiment in corporate governance of the National Investment Funds (NIFs), Poznan University of Economics Working Paper and Reprint Series.

Lewandowski, Janusz and Roman Szyszko (1997). Corporate governance of privatization investment funds—Poland, Draft Country Report: Corporate Governance of Privatization Investment Funds in Poland, Gdansk, February.

Mejstrik, Michal (1997). The emergence of institutional owners: The role of banks and non-banking financial institutions in the privatization of the economy and the banks, in M. Mejstrik (Ed.) 1997, *The Privatization Process in East-Central Europe—Evolutionary Process of Czech Privatization*, Kluwer, Dordrecht, Boston, London, pp. 145–169.

Mladek, Jan (1995). Voucher privatisation in the Czech Republic and Slovakia, in OECD (1995), pp. 61–86.

Nuti, D. Mario (1995). Mass privatisation: costs and benefits of instant capitalism, in Renzo Daviddi (Ed.) *Property Rights and Privatization in the Transition to a Market Economy. A Comparative Review*, Maastricht, EIPA, 1995, pp. 103–132.

Nuti, D. Mario (1997). Employeeism: Corporate governance and employee share ownership in transition economies, in Mario I. Blejer and Marko Skreb (Eds.), *Macroeconomic Stabilisation in Transition Economies*, C.U.P., Cambridge, pp. 126–154.

Nuti, D. Mario (1998). Stocks and stakes: the case for protecting stakeholders' interests, *Economic Analysis*, Vol. 1, No. 1, 7–16.

OECD—Centre for Co-operation with the Economies in Transition (1995). *Mass Privatization—An Initial Assessment,* Paris.

OECD (1996). *Corporate governance in transition economies: Lessons from recent development in OECD member countries,* Paris.

Peiperl, Maury and Saul Estrin (1997). Managerial markets in transition in central and eastern Europe, mimeo, March.

Pinto, Brian, Marek Belka and Stefan Krajevski (1993). Transforming state enterprises in Poland: Evidence on adjustment by manufacturing firms, *Brookings Papers on Economic Activity*, No. 1, pp. 213–270.

Rems, Marko and Bozo Jazovic (1997). The role of privatisation funds in privatisation and post-privatisation, Part I of Draft Country Report: Corporate Governance of Privatisation Investment Funds in Slovenia, Ljubljana, June.

Shleifer, Andrei and R.W. Vishny (1995). A survey of corporate governance, Harvard Institute of Economic Research, *Discussion Paper* No. 1741, October.

Simoneti, Marko (1996). Corporate governance of privatization funds: Experiences of Czech Republic, Poland and Slovenia, mimeo, Ljubljana.

Simoneti, Marko and Dusan Triska (Eds.) (1994). *Investment Funds as Intermediaries of Privatization,* Ljubljana, CEEPN.

Stiglitz, Joseph (1994). *Whither Socialism?,* MIT Press, Cambridge, MA.

Takla, Lina (1994). The relationship between privatization and the reform of the banking sector: the case of the Czech Republic and Slovakia, in S. Estrin (Ed.) (1994), pp. 154–175.

Triska, Dusan (1995). Post privatisation securities markets in the Czech Republic, in OECD (1995), pp. 87–106.

Uvalic, Milica (1997a). Privatization in the Yugoslav successor states: converting self-management into property rights, in M. Uvalic and D. Vaughan-Whitehead (Eds.), 1997, *Privatization Surprises in Transition Economies—Employee Ownership in Central and Eastern Europe*, ILO and Edward Elgar, Cheltenham, pp. 266–300.

Uvalic, Milica (1997b). Corporate governance in transition economies, in Faculty of Economics Split (Ed.) (1997), *Enterprise in Transition—Second International Conference*, Split, Faculty of Economics and Vienna, DAAAM International, pp. 203–208.

Zemplinerova, A., R. Lastovicka and A. Marcincin (1995). Restructuring of Czech manufacturing enterprises: An empirical study, *Working Paper Series* No. 74, CERGE-EI, Prague.

21

The Privatization of Financial Institutions

Domenico Mario Nuti

The privatization of state financial institutions is partly the same as for other state enterprises, namely the expectation—backed by recent literature on principal agent relations—of higher efficiency, through the subjection of state managers to bankruptcy rules and stock market discipline; the raising of budget revenue to contain or pay off government debt, or to allow a less severe deflationary stance than otherwise might be necessary; and the search for a model of property-owning democracy. However, the privatization of state financial institutions raises special issues, and, in particular, issues in the transformation of centrally planned socialist economies into private property market economies (see Nuti 1991). Alongside privatization of state assets and institutions, the growth of a private financial sector in any system is further increased by newly founded private activities.

Published in P. Newman, M. Milgate and J. Eatwell (Eds.) (1993). *The New Palgrave Dictionary of Money and Finance*, Vol 3, The Macmillan Press and Stockton Press, London and New York, pp. 212–214.

D. M. Nuti (✉)
La Sapienza, University of Rome, Rome, Italy
e-mail: milica.uvalic@unipg.it

© The Author(s), under exclusive license to Springer Nature Switzerland AG 2023

S. Estrin, M. Uvalic (eds.), *Collected Works of Domenico Mario Nuti, Volume I*, Studies in Economic Transition, https://doi.org/10.1007/978-3-031-12334-4_21

Like other state enterprises, state financial institutions in general are used as instruments of economic policy, through direct control of their output and prices. In their case, this means direct control of the level and sectoral and regional structure of credits and interest rates. Thus state financial institutions do not lend themselves to the kind of capacity restructuring of production enterprises, through plant closures and redeployment of assets. Before privatization, bad loans and guarantees, most of which would not have been granted on purely commercial considerations, have to be identified, swapped for equity or written off partly or totally. Any likely shortfall of net assets, which might be inadequate to sustain current activities or even be negative, has to be offset by re-capitalization—that is, by an injection of state equity capital possibly in the form of state bonds, or by a cancellation of extant liabilities of the financial institution in question towards the state sector. Only after such financial restructuring can the institution, like other state enterprises, be transformed into a joint-stock company whose shares can be transferred to public investors (like pension funds, or state holdings which might in turn be privatized later), sold to the general public including foreign investors, and perhaps partly transferred to employees on favourable terms. The net financial result of the operation (re-capitalization cost minus revenue from privatization) should strictly be included in the state budget capital transactions, although it might be no more than the delayed manifestation or costs incurred in a distant past.

In centrally planned socialist economies, financial institutions were (1) totally owned by the state, perhaps with the exception of small-scale cooperative credit; (2) totally concentrated within a monolithic state banking system, consisting of the central bank—dubbed Monobank, not only the lender of last resort but the only lender, mixing commercial banking with functions of issue—and a small number of specialized banking segments directly controlled by the central bank; (3) subject to the authority of the Ministry of Finance and conducted in such a way as to fit centrally planned transactions and to control their execution; (4) strictly segmented between cash transactions involving payments to and from the population, and bank money transactions involving only state agencies. Central planning included foreign trade and therefore was made easier by an inconvertible currency. Ideology restricted the use of interest charges—at low, almost symbolic, nominal rates—to enterprise working capital and time deposits (see Arnold 1937; Garvy 1966; Grossman 1968; Nuti 1986). The system was expected to yield price stability and domestic and external macroeconomic balance; in practice—apart from roughly 1950–70—it was broadly characterized by widespread excess demand at controlled prices (i.e. repressed inflation visible through generalized shortages) and/or external imbalances financed through external debt.

In these economies, such as those of central-eastern Europe, financial innovation might have been introduced within the framework of a new model of market socialism (see Nuti 1989), but was not. Thus there are additional, system-specific reasons for the privatization of state enterprises and financial institutions (see Nuti 1991): (1) there is a presumption that privatization will inject life into the inert traditional system; (2) privatization is bound to weaken the opportunity for political interference in economic life, especially in those economies still dominated by the old elite; and (3) privatization of enterprises and of commercial banks together is bound to harden the 'soft' budget constraint of enterprises, which has been one of the main sources of the endemic excess demand typical of centrally planned economies everywhere, and a major cause of their collapse.

From the starting conditions of centrally planned socialist economies, privatization of financial institutions requires the prior implementation of a long list of formidable tasks. These are (in a roughly sequential but often overlapping order): preliminary consolidation of the domestic currency, through stabilization programmes involving price liberalization and fiscal and monetary austerity; the restructuring and possibly partial relief of external debt; the unification of the two monetary segments of cash and bank money; the rise of nominal interest rates to positive or nearly positive real levels; the separation of commercial credit functions from the central banking functions of the Central Bank, and their attribution to independent sections of the Bank in competition between themselves; authorization of new financial institutions founded with domestic and foreign capital participation; the creation of a payments clearing system; the replacement of automatic credit for planned tasks by discretionary credit on a contractual basis; the replacement of direct controls of financial institutions by ordinary instruments of monetary policy, such as reserve requirements, the scale and rate of refinancing, open market operations; the decentralization of economic decisions to enterprises, and their subjection to financial discipline and procedures for liquidation and bankruptcy; and the setting up of financial markets for state and enterprise bonds and for equities.

After the completion of the essential tasks specific to former centrally planned economies, the privatization of financial institutions can proceed as in ordinary market economies, in parallel with the privatization of other state enterprises.

This process was undertaken first in Hungary in 1984–91 (see Blejer and Sagari 1991; Hungarian State Banking Supervision 1991). In 1984, a government decree authorized the issue of bonds to the public by government, local authorities, financial institutions and all enterprises. In 1987 the National Bank of Hungary hived off its credit activities by transforming its lending directorates and some local branches into associated but separate banks, soon joined by other banks with substantial foreign participation. An obligatory reserve ratio of 20 percent was established for demand deposits and 10 percent of time deposits; the discount rate, which until the end of 1984 was decided by the government, was put under the control of the President of the Central Bank. A law on bankruptcy (1986) gave initiative to creditors and established rapid proceedings. A market for share issues by private and state enterprises to the general public was set up from 1 January 1989. The 1988 Law on the Transformation of Enterprises and subsequent legislation laid the foundation for the privatization of state enterprises (which had occurred spontaneously since the mid-1980s); in June 1991 a bank privatization plan was announced, which may permit foreign ownership of up to 20 percent of even the largest commercial banks. However the growth of the private sector, especially in banking and financial activities, has proceeded mostly through new institutions rather than through privatization of the state sector.

The Hungarian road to banking reform and privatization of financial institutions was later followed in Poland and Czechoslovakia in 1990–92, where it was facilitated by the introduction of domestic currency convertibility for current account transactions by residents; it is still in progress in other central and eastern European countries in 1992. An early starter but slow developer of financial reform was China. In Yugoslavia, especially since 1971, a plurality of commercial banks, investment banks and other financial institutions have been in existence; however, they were primarily founded and owned by enterprises towards which they channelled private savings on favourable terms, acting as a decentralized form of collectivization of enterprise losses (see Dimitrijevic and Macesich 1983), so that their privatization involves problems similar to those of other central and eastern European economies.

The cleaning up of the balance sheets of financial institutions, through the identification and writing off of bad loans and guarantees, has the important role of activating liquidation and bankruptcy proceedings for state enterprises. However in Soviet-type economics, a substantial share of enterprise credit was used to fund enterprise payments to the state budget in excess of current profits. Thus the cleansing of financial institutions' balance sheets brings to the surface the hidden burden of financing past state budget deficits.

As soon as the traditional prohibition of inter-enterprise credits (introduced in the USSR around 1930 and later in all other Soviet-type economies) is lifted, there is a tendency for state enterprises to build up a large stock of payments arrears in their reciprocal transactions. This cannot be regarded—as it sometimes is—as monetary expansion or quasi-money, since it cancels out in the consolidation of the state sector accounts and cannot be used for the payment of incomes (except in Yugoslavia where inter-enterprise credits mostly took the form of bills of exchange rediscounted by the banking system). However the buildup of payments arrears involves a forced redistribution of liquidity across firms regardless of their viability, and therefore the elimination of arrears through liquidation and bankruptcy proceedings and/or additional credits to viable enterprises is a precondition of orderly privatization of all state enterprises including slate financial institutions.

The implicit model of financial reform in central eastern Europe is the UK-USA system, where in general equity is not held by banks, but by a large number of private investors (USA) or non-bank intermediaries (UK), with corporate control exerted indirectly by outsiders through takeover bids. It has been suggested that a model more appropriate to the centralized and undeveloped financial systems of central eastern Europe would have been the German-Japanese system of control by insiders, with banks' direct and indirect holdings and involvement in the control of industry (Corbett and Mayer 1992). This view is supported by the slow progress of privatization throughout the area, given the lower dependence of the German-Japanese model, compared with the UK-USA model, on the completion of privatization.

Bibliography

Arnold, A. Z. (1937). *Banks, Credit and Money in Soviet Russia.* New York: Columbia University Press.

Blejer, M. and Sagari, S. (1991). Hungary: financial sector reform in a socialist economy. Policy Research and External Affairs Working Paper, WPS 595, World Bank, Washington DC, February.

Corbett, J. and Mayer, C. (1992). Financial Reform in Eastern Europe: progress with the Wrong Model. *Oxford Review of Economic Policy,* forthcoming.

Dimitrijevic, D. and Macesich, G. 1983. *Money and Finance in Yugoslavia.* New York: Praeger.

Garvy, G. (1966). *Money, Banking and Credit in Eastern Europe.* New York: Federal Resent Bank of New York.

Grossman, G. (ed.) (1968). *Money and Plan.* Berkeley and Los Angeles: University of California Press.

Hungarian State Banking Supervision (1991). Banks in Hungary 1991. Occasional Paper, Budapest.

Nuti, D. M. (1986). Hidden and Repressed Inflation in Soviet-Ape Economies: definitions, Measurements and Stabilization. *Contributions to Political Economy* 5: 37-82.

Nuti, D. M. (1989). Feasible financial innovation under market socialism, in *Financial Reform in Centrally Planned Economies,* Eds. C. Kessides, T. King, D.M. Nuti and K. Sokil, Washington DC: EDI - World Bank.

Nuti, D. M. (1991). Privatisation of socialist economies: general issues and the Polish case, in *Transformation of Planned Economies: Property Rights Reform and Macroeconomic Stability,* Ed. H. Blommestein and M. Marrese, Paris, OECD.

22

A Counter-Factual Alternative for Russia's Post-Socialist Transition

Domenico Mario Nuti

22.1 Introduction

On Sunday 18 June 1815, at the Battle of Waterloo, Napoleon Bonaparte was decisively defeated by the Duke of Wellington and the forces of the "Seventh Coalition", marking the end to his rule as French Emperor. Wellington is reported to have declared that the battle was "*the nearest-run thing you ever saw in your life*" (to Thomas Creevey, see Maxwell 1903, p. 236). In 1965 Dr Jerry Koehl, a History Lecturer at Oxford, having resigned to take up a lucrative job in commercial television, ended his last lecture with the words: "*And this is how Napoleon won the battle of Waterloo*".

Paper originally presented at the International Conference on *The Great Transformation: 1989-2029*. TIGER Institute at Kozminski University, Warsaw, 3–4 April 2009 and later published under a somewhat different title in G. W. Kolodko and J. Tomkiewicz (Eds), *20 years of Transformation: Achievements, Problems and Perspectives,* (2011), Nova Science Publishers, New York.

I thank Grzegorz W. Kolodko and Vladimir Popov for their valuable comments; I am solely responsible for the contents of this paper.

D. M. Nuti (✉)
La Sapienza, University of Rome, Rome, Italy
e-mail: milica.uvalic@unipg.it

© The Author(s), under exclusive license to Springer Nature Switzerland AG 2023

S. Estrin, M. Uvalic (eds.), *Collected Works of Domenico Mario Nuti, Volume I*, Studies in Economic Transition, https://doi.org/10.1007/978-3-031-12334-4_22

On Wednesday 25 December 1991 Mikhail Sergieyevich Gorbachev, General Secretary of the Communist Party of the Soviet Union (CPSU, 11 March 1985–24 August 1991) and first and only President of the USSR (from 15 March 1990), gave a televised 10-minutes "Address to the Soviet Citizen" resigning from the Presidency. This happened almost immediately after the Presidents of 11 Soviet Republics, at a meeting in Alma Ata on 21–22 December 1991, agreed the dissolution of the USSR and its replacement with a looser Commonwealth of Independent States (CIS, excluding the three Baltics and initially Georgia). That meeting confirmed the decision already taken on 9 December, at Viskulia-Belovezha near Minsk, by the Presidents of Russia, Ukraine and Belarus (respectively Boris Yeltsin, Leonid Kravchuk and Stanislav Shuskievich).

Gorbachev's resignation marked the final defeat of his project of *perestroika* (restructuring) and *glastnost* (transparency) launched at the 27th Party Congress in February 1986. Like Napoleon's Waterloo, Gorbachev's defeat was *"the nearest-run thing you ever saw in your life"*.

In a vein similar to Dr Koehl's reconsideration of Napoleon's Waterloo, my paper illustrates how Mikhail Gorbachev *won* the battle of *perestroika*—how he *succeeded* (or rather *might have succeeded*) in achieving the radical reform of the Soviet political and economic system, the construction of market socialism, the re-structuring and acceleration (*uskoreniye*) of the Soviet economy, and the possible though unlikely continued existence of the USSR.

I should stress that this is not, or at least is not meant to be, an exercise in 20/20 hindsight. Alternative courses can be formulated without the possession of perfect foresight of the state of the world in 1985–1991. Nor is a change in Gorbachev's initial conditions required, of the kind "If only he had come to power in 1974, at the height of the fourfold rise in the oil price ...". This exercise is meant as a *genuine counterfactual* alternative. Its purpose is that of damning Gorbachev's disastrous economic strategy and showing that he and his economic policies, more than anybody else's doings, are ultimately responsible for the collapse of socialism in the Soviet Union, for the failure of an alternative design of market socialism, and for the immense human cost of Soviet transition. A similar exercise, considering counter-factual alternatives to the actual course of transition in Cental-Eastern Europe, is only outlined to suggest that transition might have been handled at a lesser human cost.

22.2 Actual Perestroika

Gorbachev gave priority—in terms of timing as well as importance—to political over economic reform, to *demokratizatsiya* (January 1987) originally understood as multi-candidate choice in local Party and the Soviets elections. In June 1988, at the first Party conference held since 1941, steps were taken to reduce party control over the administration. There were major personnel changes at the top of the Party hierarchy: Gorbachev became Chairman of the Presidium of the Supreme Soviet (1988). A new legislative body, the Congress of People's Deputies, was decided on in December 1988 and elected in March 1989; it first met in May and during the summer the first opposition group formed, the Interregional Group including among others, Boris Yeltsin. In 1990 CPSU supremacy (art. 6) was abolished. In March 1990 Gorbachev's authority was strengthened further by his election by the Congress as President of the Soviet Union (1990). The Supreme Soviet became increasingly like a Parliament.

These developments weakened the CPSU, whose republic branches began to split between factions supporting republic independence and those supporting the Union; nationalists gained ground in republic elections. Pressure for republic independence grew particularly in the Baltic Republics—Estonia, Latvia and Lithuania (which had been annexed by the Union only in 1940) as well as in other Soviet Republics such as

Ukraine, Georgia and Azerbaijan. Ethnic clashes flared (for instance in 1988 involving Armenian and Azeri groups). In the new climate, political repression and censorship were greatly reduced; arts and social sciences were liberalised and thrived.

Initially Gorbachev's economic measures were not market oriented. He wanted to improve central planning in order to obtain growth acceleration (*uskoreniye,* first mentioned on 20 April 1985). For instance, in May 1986 *Measures to radically improve the quality of output* established centralised quality control by a state body, *Gospriemka*, instead of promoting decentralised choices of price/quality by producers. *Gospriemka* was to raise the quality of 95% of Soviet goods to international standards by 1990; by January 1988 officials controlling 2300 factories rejected about 15% of output; its impact simply petered out. In November 1986 a small step towards private enterprise was taken with the Law on Individual Labour Activity, that allowed individual and family activities in handicraft or consumer services.

In June 1985 an aggressive anti-alcohol campaign was conducted not through prices and taxes but by reducing imports and production of spirits and wine (including uprooting Georgian vineyards). This raised temporarily life expectancy (from 68.2 to 70 years) but greatly undermined budget revenue and therefore aggravated the monetary imbalances that wrecked the system, thus contributing to the subsequent drop in life expectancy during the transition (down to 64 years in 1994).

Gorbachev presented the "basic theses" of *perestroika* at the June 1987 CPSU Central Committee meeting, over two years after coming to power. In July 1987 the Law on State Enterprise was approved by the Supreme Soviet. It enabled state enterprises to determine output based on demand; negotiate input purchases directly with suppliers; state targets took the form of state "orders" (in the sense of purchase orders, not of commands). Once these orders were fulfilled, enterprises could dispose of the remaining output as they wished, as long as they were self-supporting, i.e. their revenues had to cover costs (the old *khozraschet* principle of accounting autonomy, or commercialisation), otherwise they could face bankruptcy. Control over enterprise operations was decentralised from ministries to elected workers' collectives. Instead of formulating detailed production plans in physical terms, *Gosplan* was to prepare only general guidelines and a national investment programme.

In May 1988 the Law on Cooperatives introduced very radical changes, enabling the operation of cooperative restaurants, retail and wholesale trade, banks, small scale manufacturing of consumer goods, foreign trade; although capital could be raised only from state enterprises and from other cooperatives. Initial high taxes and employment restrictions were later reduced. The sector thrived; by June 1989 there were 5.9 million members working in 133,000 cooperatives. In theory these cooperatives were to be forms of Marx's "independent commodity production" (Kotz and Weir 2007); in practice they were shells for private enterprise, often set up to work with state enterprises. Sub-contracting state enterprise activities became a way to practically "privatise" their more profitable operations.

In 1988 the state monopoly of foreign trade, conducted through large FTO (Foreign Trade Organisations) specialised in import-export operations by commodity groups, was reduced by allowing branch Ministries (as well as some state enterprises, and regional and local organisations—though not private economic subjects) to conduct foreign trade directly. The foreign currency necessary for imports was increasingly made available through export earnings retentions, transferable to other enterprises, and through foreign exchange purchases at auction from *Gosbank* (the State Central Bank) as well as the usual direct allocations of currency.

Foreign Direct Investment was encouraged through the formation of Joint Ventures, by foreign companies with Russian Ministries, enterprises, cooperatives. The Law of June 1987 limited foreign shares to a maximum of 49 percent and required the chairman and general manager to be Soviet citizens; soon these restrictions were eliminated, to allow foreign majority ownership and control.

Gorbachev was aware that the decentralisation of economic decisions to enterprises required a price reform: "Radical reform of *price formation* is the most important component of economic restructuring" (quoted by Cook 1993, emphasis added). The quote is revealing: it betrays thinking in terms of cost-based formulas for administrative price fixing, consistent with *khozraschet*, instead of looking also at demand conditions and therefore at market-clearing prices. Cost-based price formulas can be fine *if and only if* at the resulting prices all demands are satisfied, but market clearing was such an exceptional event in Soviet and Soviet-type systems, that it was referred to as demand "saturation".

In June 1987 the Price Commission (*Goskomtsen*) had been asked to prepare a new price system for the 13th Five Year Plan, but nothing happened. There were talks of raising input prices and reducing subsidies but concerns about the impact of inflation on workers' living standards were said to be paramount—without realising that living standards depended on total supply, and—within broad bounds—the price level affected not actual consumption but only the degree of excess demand. "We have always stressed it is a merit of socialism that goods are so cheap in our country"—said Deputy Premier and main reformer Leonid Abalkin (quoted by Cook 1993)—obtusely and absurdly, for nobody, no matter how politically and economically powerful, can determine both the quantity and the price of anything. There were references to the need for compensatory income payments and tax relief, in order to offset the impact of likely price rises, but this possibility did not allay worries about the impact of price rises on the distribution of income.

In 1989–90 reform and stabilisation plans proliferated. In 1989 Leonid Abalkin produced a reform much more radical than any previous package, but exceedingly gradual in its proposed implementation, especially in achieving stabilisation, delayed until 1993–95, with partial and gradual price liberalisation, nullified by wage indexation. Soviet Premier Nikolai Ryzhkov backed a diluted version of the Programme, presented in December 1989. In 1990 Grigory Yavlinsky and Stanislav Shatalin proposed an ambitious *Transition to the Market* document, known as the *500 days Programme*, calling for the creation of a modern competitive market economy, market-determined prices, mass privatisation, integration with the world economy, Republic decentralisation, and other radical reforms. Instead of operating through Joint Ventures, foreign companies could acquire up to 100% ownership of Soviet firms. "Within two years, 70% of the nation's industrial enterprises would be privatized, with stock markets in Moscow and Leningrad trading shares in competitive firms. An even larger proportion—perhaps 90%—of businesses in the service and retail trading sectors would be put in private hands. A version of the Shatalin plan circulating in Moscow … put it bluntly:

'Mankind has not succeeded in creating anything more efficient than a market economy' " (Cohan 1990).

The Yavlinsky-Shatalin Programme was delayed by the Supreme Soviet. Ryzhkov and Abalkin warned that trying an unsuccessful form of "shock treatment" might leave "the populace and the government allergic to the market idea for decades." Ryzhkov expressed concern that by giving free rein to market forces, the Gorbachev-Yeltsin group plan might set off a "staggering surge of prices, destabilize economic life and disorient enterprises." A watered-down version was mediated by Abel Aganbegyan, entitled *Basic Guidelines for Stabilization of the Economy and Transition to a Market Economy*; it lacked an implementation schedule and it left undetermined the division of power between Union and Republics (Gorbachev was apparently keen to postpone the question of Republican powers of taxation, Cohan 1990). In the end the *Basic Guidelines* package was approved.

A stabilisation plan required the reform of the State Bank of the USSR (*Gosbank*), i.e., the ending of its role as the only lender—leaving only its Central Bank role as Lender of Last Resort—and delegating commercial and investment lending to independent banks (other than its dependent Savings Bank *Sberbank*; the Construction Bank *Stroybank*, and Foreign Trade Bank *Vneshtorgbank*.) In 1987–88 this reform was accomplished, but the system retained two separate circuits for monetary circulation, cash and non-cash money (*nalichnye* and *nienalichnyie*, respectively for wage payments and purchases of consumption goods, and for inter-enterprise transactions), although the separation was increasingly eroded in practice.

As a result of the Gorbachev-Yeltsin conflict, in November 1991, on the eve of USSR disintegration, the Russian branch of *Gosbank* was transformed into the independent Central Bank of Russia (CBR), in order to establish direct control over republican monetary policy. The other republics followed. On 1 January 1992, the CBR took over *Gosbank*'s assets in Russia. Its Republic subsidiaries turned themselves into Republic Central Banks: they continued to issue non-cash rouble credits, usable in Russia and equivalent to about 8% of Russian GDP, until July 1992 when the CBR stopped honouring those credits. In turn the Russian monopoly of cash issue and the accompanying cash rouble scarcity forced

Republic Central Banks to issue first rouble substitutes then their own republican currencies.

All these reforms—many of which were announced and only partly implemented—naturally were unsuccessful in realising the hoped-for stabilisation and systemic transformation. Instead of *uskoreniye,* decline set in. The proposed policies could not succeed because not only did prices continue to be subject to administrative controls but continued to be fixed at artificially low levels at which an excess demand persisted. "The stock of un-capitalised personal savings (cash plus saving banks deposits including time deposits) at the end of 1988 stood at 93 per cent of total annual consumption and 84 per cent of annual disposable income"; in 1989 and 1990 such a stock rose to a whole year disposable income (Smith 1993, pp. 110–111). The Shatalin Plan envisaged the absorption of excess cash in the hands of the population via the privatisation of state assets, but this was not implemented. In addition, there was a vast non-cash monetary overhang in the hands of state enterprises. Liberalising prices before the excess demand was drained would have led to large-scale inflation, regarded as politically infeasible. According to Gorbachev chief economic advisor, Nikolai Petrakov, "Soviet citizens would rather stand in long lines than confront a rise in prices." (Cohan 1990). Anyway, the rouble continued to be inconvertible, and a large proportion of the means of production was still subject to direct allocation (instead of the wholesale trade advocated by various reform proposals).

Two other obstacles to the construction of market socialism were present. First, the Soviet leadership's reluctance to liberalise foreign trade, unifying exchange rates, making the currency convertible on current account (of course only after having reached a market clearing structure of domestic prices, to prevent all excess demand concentrating on foreign exchange), the end of quantitative restrictions on imports and exports, the end of state monopoly of foreign trade exercised through Foreign Trade Organisations. Second, the Soviet leadership's reluctance to allow private ownership of land—instead of implementing at least the kind of long-term rental agreements (*arenda*) introduced in Russia in the 1920s *New Economic Policy* period and in China after 1978. More generally there was resistance to the formation of new private enterprises; deep-rooted ideological objections were in the way, though paradoxically hostility towards share stock companies was being mollified by considering them as forms of "collective" ownership (sic).

The reforms did not amount to a market system but were successful in reducing government control over economic conditions, both macroeconomic (with a sharp increase in government spending) and microeconomic (with *ad hoc* state support to enterprises and product subsidies). The weakening of the state reduced tax collection. The fiscal deficit rose from 2.3% of GDP to 10%; its monetisation raised monetary overhang, and shortages increased. Enterprise autonomy broke the traditional supply *linkages* without replacing them with contractual links, thus disrupting production. "The old system tumbled down before the new one could begin functioning" (Gorbachev 1996, p. xxxvi). There were significant lay-offs, on a scale of 3 million workers "released" by late 1999, though mostly re-deployed. In 1991 GDP fell by 17 per cent and retail prices rose 140%. Shortages affected an increasing range of goods, causing widespread discontent. Food shortages, due more to supply disorganisation than to genuine shortfalls, became serious. Income distribution became more unequal, some individuals amassed large-scale wealth through privileged access to scarce commodities and credit at artificially low prices and interest. Organised criminality (*mafiya*) thrived. Foreign trade accounts deteriorated and Soviet hard-currency debt rose significantly, piling up arrears in debt service. Centrifugal forces created increasing pressure for republican independence.

The failures of *perestroika* led Hanson (1992) to refer to it as *catastroika* (a label he attributes to Alexander Zinovyev) and *perestrelka* (a shootout). On 7 October 1989 Gorbachev visited Berlin for the celebration of the GDR 40th-anniversary and said: "History punishes those who come too late" (Childs 2000): the statement criticised Honecker but was best suited as his own epitaph.

Such failures are often compared with the successful transition of China and Vietnam, usually attributed to their gradualist approach in place of Russian shock therapy. Chinese economic reform was, indeed, gradual by comparison, but China started in 1978 and could afford the time that Russia no longer had in the late 1980s. China was a less developed country, mostly agricultural, and was not burdened by a hypertrophic heavy industry and military complex; growth from a lower level was easier to promote. China had developed private farms on long-term, transferable land leases, within state ownership of land; farmers were allowed to produce for the market, once they had fulfilled their quotas of state procurement. China developed special locally-based cooperatives, the Town and Village Enterprises, neither state nor private but still in the public sector, which were particularly successful. Foreign trade and exchange regimes were more liberal than in Russia; foreign direct investment was promoted and directed to Special Economic Zones. Large regions had considerable administrative autonomy. Most importantly, China managed to contain open inflation without incurring repressed inflation and shortages. A "dual pricing" system, state-controlled and free, was gradually unified. Enterprise autonomy was validated by bank credit and fiscal instruments. At the same time, China maintained the totalitarian grip of the Party on the economy, outlawed Trade Unions and strikes, repressed dissidents, right to the 4 June 1989 Tiananmen Square massacre—which undoubtedly played an important role in making communist leaders in Central and Eastern Europe undertake a peaceful transition. On the same day the first (partially) contested political elections since the last War took place in Poland, bringing down the regime, and the socialism realised there.

22.3 Back to the Future

In February 2008 *The New Scientist* reported that two Russian scientists, Professor Irina Arefeva and Dr Igor Volovich of Moscow's Steklov Mathematical Institute, claimed to have discovered time travel. The Large Hadron Collider (LHC), a vast atom-smashing machine at CERN—the European Particle Physics Centre near Geneva—could use a blend of colliding particles and "phantom energy" to create a time tunnel to the past, a "wormhole" through spacetime, enabling time travel. A similar "vehicle" for time travel had been proposed in 1988 by Professor Kip Thorne and colleagues at the California Institute of Technology in Pasadena (Brooks 2008).

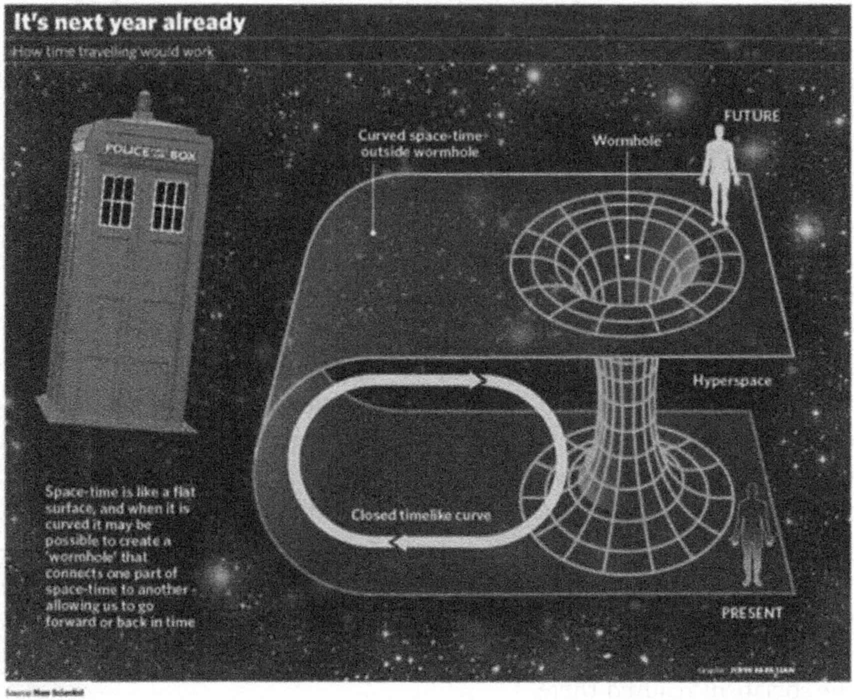

Suppose a time travel machine along these lines had been perfected and let us ignore familiar problems such as the extension of subatomic time travel to a human scale; keeping the maw of the wormhole open to allow two-way travel; the end of cause-and-effect principles; the incongruence of a time traveller killing his own mother before he was born, and the like. Suppose that Mikhail Sergieyevich could be persuaded to go back to 11 March 1985 or, better, 11 March 1984 in order to give him also the time to develop, alongside the New Political Thinking that he did develop, a New Economic Thinking to enable him to do a blitz on the Soviet economy immediately in the first 100 days after his appointment. And why not, he has nothing to lose from reality but his own past failure and occasional jobs in advertising. Gorbachev was a great statesman, a true democrat, a first-rate politician, a generous man, but he was a lawyer,[1] completely untrained—indeed illiterate—in basic economics, and was surrounded by economists who understood neither basic macro nor microeconomics. Our parallel Gorbachev must at once hire a team of competent and reliable economists, with socialist commitment but versed in market economics.

At least three major tasks were required for the implementation of a market version of socialism, while retaining a dominant or at least a significant socialist ownership—which is what Gorbachev intended to achieve. First, the end of repressed inflation, i.e., endemic excess demand at the current administered prices. Second, the break-up of state monopoly of foreign trade, which in turn involved a measure of rouble convertibility (only on current account for some time) and trade liberalisation. Third, an overhauling of the enterprise system from the viewpoint of ownership, competition and incentives.

We can argue whether these measures were best taken simultaneously, or in a sequence. It is not clear whether a single large-scale shock is preferable to three smaller but still large-ish shocks. What is clear is that the first step, ending repressed inflation, on its own would achieve little; the second step, trade opening and currency convertibility, could not possibly work without the first, a market clearing system with internal, free convertibility of the currency into goods. And that the third step of market-driven enterprises, could not possibly work without both the first and second steps. Sequencing the three steps in this order was an alternative, but not truly gradualist. Steps would have to be taken, if not simultaneously, then in rapid succession, in order not to allow what Edgeworth (1881), p.17) called "trading at false prices" in the sequence of steps towards a final "true" equilibrium. It was imperative that both market clearing prices and foreign trade reform be introduced without advance notice of timing or details. The reform of the enterprise system could be pre-announced but, if introduced on its own, as attempted in countless "experiments" since Stalin's death in 1953, could not and would not ever work.

[1] Incidentally, this is a bad omen for Barack Obama, also a lawyer, who has surrounded himself with some of the economists responsible for the crisis he now tries to resolve, from Larry Summers to Robert Rubin and his creature Timothy Geithner.

22.4 Perestroika Economic Foundations: A) Market Clearing Prices

The first political moves made by Gorbachev after appointment were excellent; they will be replicated by the parallel Gorbachev: democratisation, multi-candidate elections to Party offices, freedom of speech and of association, de-monopolisation of politics. But in his new parallel world he will wait for some tangible economic improvements before going any further, to enable organised opposition and encourage republic independence.

In the economy, the Law on Individual Labour, a harmless new step, will also be replicated. The anti-alcohol campaign as well, but only using higher prices and taxes, and applied also to tobacco. The *Gosbank* reform of 1987 was necessary to eliminate its monopoly of credit, but granted excessive discretion to the Bank President; this time Gorbachev would retain some control over *Gosbank*, but would also go further in the integration of cash and noncash monetary circuits. If he had wanted to keep the Union together, he should have opposed the 1991 *Gosbank* disintegration into republic Central Banks and devised something like the European System of Central Banks that manage the euro. And before even suggesting a move towards a market economy, parallel Gorbachev would confront the one stumbling block that he never did confront in his first life: the elimination of repressed inflation, i.e., the widespread and endemic shortages, queues, waiting lists, black markets.

On 26 April 1986, the fourth reactor of the Chernobyl nuclear power plant exploded, due to a massive power excursion that destroyed it during a cooling experiment; this released a large amount of radioactivity into the environment over an extensive area. Sixty per cent of the fallout landed in Belarus; large areas of Ukraine and Russia were also affected, causing the evacuation and resettlement of over 336,000 people. Other parts of the western Soviet Union, western and northern Europe, were involved. Some of the fallout fell on me, as I was in Poland at the time; but even the honey produced by the bees in our Florence garden was contaminated and had to be thrown away. The explosion released four hundred times more fallout than that of Hiroshima. It was the worst nuclear plant disaster in history, at a large—though hard to estimate—human cost and $200bn (OECD-NEA 2002).

"Don't waste a good crisis"—Hilary Clinton in March 2008 said of the global financial crisis, speaking to the European Parliament in Brussels—though it sounds even more cynical if referred to Chernobyl. But our parallel Gorbachev would have made history if, immediately after the explosion, he had taken the opportunity, in a big public speech, to draw two important economic lessons from the Chernobyl catastrophe.

First, the accident was a direct result of the Soviet planning system of enterprise management incentives. A crucial safety test, that was supposed to be carried out before the reactor came into operation in March 1984, had not been completed successfully but the Chernobyl station director Viktor Bryukhanov on 31-12-1983 had signed that it had, in order to enable thousands of workers, engineers and functionaries to obtain their bonuses; records were falsified. Moreover, there had been a total lack of information exchange and co-ordination.[2] Clearly the Soviet management and rewards system needed to be radically changed.

Second, the nuclear fall-out could not be stopped or avoided by claiming that it was "socially unacceptable". Similarly, neither could the inflationary impact of past monetary explosions be stopped or avoided. Commenting on Chernobyl, our parallel Gorbachev would take the opportunity to drive home the inescapable fact that—whatever the reasons for it, whether it had been over-ambition, indiscipline, bad luck or bad judgement; and whoever was responsible, individuals at the top or low-down the system—there simply *is* inflationary fallout in the economy, the result of earlier monetary explosions, which cannot be "repressed" anymore than nuclear fallout can be repressed. The time had come for restoring market balance between planned prices and delivered quantities of goods and services. Until then, markets cannot be activated, the

[2] "It was decided to carry out a test of the capability of the plant equipment to provide enough electrical power to operate the reactor core cooling system and emergency equipment during the transition period between a loss of main station electrical power supply and the start up of the emergency power supply provided by diesel engines...Unfortunately, this test, which was considered essentially to concern the non-nuclear part of the power plant, was carried out without a proper exchange of information and coordination between the team in charge of the test and the personnel in charge of the operation and safety of the nuclear reactor." OECD-NEA (2002 [1995]), p. 1.

currency cannot be made convertible, enterprise activities cannot be disciplined and regulated automatically.

Quantities being fairly rigid at least in the short run, balance could be restored by raising money prices, whether administratively or via liberalisation. Alternatively, the government would have to make a stock adjustment (see McKinnon 1993), i.e., to confiscate the excess purchasing power in the hands of households and enterprises, through the kind of monetary conversion that was implemented in the 1950s throughout eastern Europe and China. Cash and savings would be converted at a less favourable rate than wages and prices, moreover progressively, and verifying the origin of large cash holdings. Unless economic agents surrendered their excess cash in exchange for government bonds and other state assets, or could, somehow, be persuaded to hold liquid assets not by default but voluntarily: i.e., via high interest rates; or the credible announcement of an early future privatisation of government assets, including physical assets.

Clearly any such price increase or confiscatory currency reform would have to be introduced by stealth and in secret, without prior announcements. Instead, announcements of forthcoming extra supplies (e.g. imports, if feasible) and of future privatisations, could be used to reduce the size of monetary overhang, together with, say, privatisation bonds indexed to foreign exchange.

I would have advised Gorbachev to go for a currency reform, in order to be able both to make it progressive, and to force the surfacing and destruction of illegal cash holdings. Indeed, this is what I did recommend to Gorbachev's Chief Economic Advisor Nikolai Petrakov in September 1990, when I visited him in his office at the Presidential Administration in Novaya Ploshchad, while I was an official of the European Commission. Petrakov had been involved in the preparation of the 500 days Programme; I told him that he did not have 500 days. I suggested a conversion of roubles into new heavy roubles at par for prices and wages, and at 10:1 ratio for cash and savings, thus confiscating 9/10 of the country's liquid assets plus any cash of dubious provenance. I would have left only *kopek* coins in circulation as a progressive small measure, a token psychological message, and a practical way to reduce the cost of changeover. Petrakov rehearsed his argument that neither currency conversion nor price rises were "socially acceptable" or "politically feasible". I rehearsed my comparison between Chernobyl fallout and inflationary fallout, mentioned above. We parted friends but in complete disagreement.[3]

Only after, or together with, the establishment of equilibrium prices could rouble convertibility on current account be contemplated (see next section). If it was done after the end of repressed inflation, then relative prices would need a second round of adjustment in line with international prices. Any stabilisation of the absolute price level would have to be set against the cost of squeezing economic activity. Income subsidies to the population, more efficient than product price subsidies, would best cover the impact of price rises on their standard of living; they had been discussed in stabilisation proposals but had remained dead letter.

Slightly fewer than 500 days after my meeting with Nikolai Petrakov the Soviet system and the Union itself collapsed. In January 1992 monthly inflation in Russia was 245 per cent, 1992 yearly inflation was 2520 per cent—equivalent to a rate of confiscation of Russian liquid assets over two and a half times higher that would have been involved at the time of our meeting by a currency conversion of 10:1. So much for the "social unacceptability" of inflation.

The shock of hidden inflation surfacing into the open has been criticised by the supporters of a gradualist transition, but the move to a market economy inescapably required, on day 1, market-clearing prices. There were three gradual alternatives, all of them inferior to a one-step instantaneous change.

First, sequential price rises initially short of equilibrium. This is the worst of all possible worlds, with the persistence of disequilibrium and the rise of actual and expected inflation, as duly happened when it was tried out for instance in the late 'eighties in the Soviet Union and at the

[3] Petrakov had a special telephone on his desk, a direct hotline to Gorbachev; he spoke to his boss during my visit but did not relay my suggestion… I only spoke to Gorbachev on 11 March 1995, at the celebration of the tenth anniversary of his coming to power, organised by the communist-led provincial administration of Genova (sic). I meant to criticise his failure to eliminate hidden inflation, but the occasion was unsuitable and he and Raissa were so charming that I could not bring myself to do it, neither privately nor in my presentation at the conference that followed. Incidentally, on his return from Moscow around the same time (autumn 1990), Grzegorz W. Kolodko immediately organised a seminar at the Warsaw Institute of Finance, on "500 days to hyper-inflation".

beginning of Romanian transition in 1990–91 (what Kolodko and McMahon 1987, call *shortageflation*).

Second, a two-track price system as in China in the 1980s, with a controlled price for a fixed part of planned supply, and a free price for the rest. There was too large an imbalance and too much urgency and too little administrative capacity in the Soviet Union and central eastern Europe in the late 'eighties for this approach to succeed; it had been tried without success on a small scale for instance in Poland.

The third gradual alternative was a sequential price liberalisation of successive groups of commodities, as in the post-War gradual relaxation of rationing and price controls in the United Kingdom. This is inefficient because of forced substitution effects due to demand spill-over from products still subject to control to newly liberalised products; and again, time was short.

Thus, a move to price clearing at a stroke was necessary, regardless of system transformation—even simply to improve central planning. And at that point, straight liberalisation seemed preferable to the uncertain guesswork of an arbitrary system of market-clearing administered prices, which would also have preserved the inefficiency of being out of line with foreign trade opportunities. With foreign trade still not liberalised, price liberalisation might generate price changes some of which will be reversed by subsequent necessary foreign trade liberalisation; hence simultaneous price and trade liberalisation had the tangible advantages of not requiring the possible reversal of price changes.

22.5 Perestroika Economic Foundations: B) Foreign Trade Opening and Rouble Convertibility

Endemic excess demand killed any attempt to introduce convertibility and, thus, opening trade. Foreign trade was conducted all the same, by large Foreign Trade Organisations (FTOs) exercising state monopoly on imports and exports by commodity groups, implementing trade plans on their own account and not on behalf of producers and importers, transferring their profits to the price equalisation account in the state budget. Their breakup had been envisaged but not implemented. Customs duties lowered their profits but also ended up in the state budget and therefore the split between trade profit and duties did not matter at all. Most hard currency was requisitioned by the Central Bank and allocated for planned tasks, just like coal or steel; this generated an autarkic bias.

The socialist trade bloc, the Council of Mutual Economic Assistance or Comecon, traded at prices geared to a five-year average of international prices, in dollars translated into transferable roubles at a conventional rate. The average was taken at first every five years then, after the oil price rise of 1974, every year. A star-pattern of trade with the USSR at the centre was planned at an overall balance; any bilateral imbalance was carried over at zero interest in terms of "transferable" roubles, a unit of account which actually was neither transferable to third countries without their consent, nor indeed a rouble seeing as a surplus could not be spent in the Soviet Union even when it corresponded to a Soviet deficit. In the late 1980s bilateral trade balances began to be settled in dollars (see Lavigne 1985, 1999).

The first step in foreign trade reform is the breakup of the state monopoly of trade. This can be done at a stroke, instantly, by a decree enabling all economic subjects, private and public, to trade with currency acquired freely in the market from any economic agents who happen to have some, thus abolishing any administrative allocation and multiple exchange rate provision. It cannot be done before market clearing prices prevail, because otherwise the entire excess demand in the market for goods would spill over into the market for foreign exchange. (A large spill-over effect, of price liberalisation for goods on the foreign exchange rate, is unavoidable even if foreign trade was liberalised with a delay after market-clearing, in view of the low elasticity of supply of domestic industry). In turn, opening to foreign trade is the only way to rapidly establish market competition, and to break the monopoly position involved in the high industrial concentration typical of the planned economy. Convertibility initially would be confined to current account transactions—as was the case in post-War market economies for a considerable time; capital account convertibility would be the last step in the transition, its coronation. For

Gorbachev there were not enough foreign exchange reserves to target a fixed exchange rate, so convertibility at a floating rate was imperative. All these changes were introduced, together with price liberalisation, by the Russian government in January 1992. *Could Gorbachev have done anything different earlier?*

There had been an original proposal, for a gradual, simultaneous reform of both internal and foreign trade, but it was a non-starter. In 1988–89 George Soros, Wassily Leontief, Ed Hewett and Ivan Ivanov (Deputy Chairman of the State Foreign Economic Committee, GVK) launched their "Open Sector" project, with the participation of many Soviet, western, and east-European economists (see Hanson 1998). It was a plan, initially surrounded by secrecy, for both wiping out monetary overhang and promoting foreign trade by introducing a new convertible currency, paid to Soviet exporters and then circulating in parallel with domestic roubles. The plan was inspired by the Soviet *chervonets* introduced in 1922–24 by Lenin (after Peter the Great's gold coinage, see Barnett 1994) and circulating next to the inflated *sovznak*. Although I took part in the project, I never believed it could work. Clearly the rate of conversion between the two currencies had to be floating, for the new currency at an under-valued fixed rate would be displaced by Gresham's law, while an overvalued rate would be pointless and rouble-inflationary. But if the two currencies were exchanged freely in the market the old currency would gradually disappear through higher and accelerating rouble-inflation and hyperinflation, which is what I understand happened in the early 1920s, leaving a single sound currency. Effectively what Soros-Leontieff-Hewett-Ivanov were recommending was a slow-motion currency stabilisation through accelerating rouble inflation, instead of a single inflationary shock to reach immediate market balance. Not a very effective or attractive measure, and it was shelved, like other radical plans, without being taken seriously into consideration.

If price and trade liberalisation were the only options open to Gorbachev in implementing his market socialist design, what are the differences, between what he should have done and what was actually done in Russia by Yeltsin's government in 1992?

First, Gorbachev could and should have eliminated repressed inflation in 1986 (shortly after Chernobyl), when the monetary overhang was far more manageable. Second, he should have done it through confiscatory, progressive currency conversion rather than through open inflation (as argued above), lessening the impact of stabilisation on actual open inflation and on income distribution. Third, he could have waited, say, a few months after price stabilisation before trade liberalisation. Fourth, most important, the adverse impact of stabilisation on incomes and employment could have been cushioned by a *controlled monetary easing* and *fiscal support of employment through wage subsidies.*

This fourth step requires justification. Unlike the Latin American countries that inspired the "Washington Consensus" package of stabilisation, liberalisation and privatisation, Russia and all transition economies suffered from repressed, not open inflation, were not open economies to start with, and had dominant state enterprises. In Latin American countries, stabilisation took only the form of an instant higher equilibrium price level. In Russia and other transition economies stabilisation had two additional effects. First, necessary over-shooting; second the shock of a change in relative prices and not just in price level.

Over-shooting was a mathematical necessity. Moving from repressed inflation with a market segment at artificially low prices, and a segment at free prices, to single prices and open inflation, the new free equilibrium price is necessarily lower than the old black-market price (which was boosted by the income effect of having access to some supplies at a price lower than the equilibrium level). However, in the search for the new equilibrium consumers and suppliers, and officials knew and took seriously only the old black-market prices as guidance. Also, consumers suddenly experiencing goods availability at equilibrium prices lower than the old black-market prices are likely to demand more than they did earlier, also on the expectation that market clearing might not last and/or prices will rise again.

Thus, real monetary balances fall below their new equilibrium level, and need to be replenished. This would be easy if prices could fall, but prices tend to be downwards inflexible, now as ever. Monetary and fiscal policy need easing, to rebuild real balances, but are increasingly restrictive instead. Predictably, demand and capacity utilisation fall, a recession sets in that could have been avoided by an accommodating monetary policy (Nuti 1986). In 1992 the President of the Central Bank of Russia, Viktor

Gerashchenko, engaged in just this kind of an accommodation, but he used his independence perversely and went overboard, destroying Gaidar's entire fiscal stabilisation package of January-April 1992. Better advised, and facing a quantitatively much less serious imbalance, Gorbachev would have avoided this over-shooting of the stabilisation programme.

Latin American countries after stabilisation in the 1980s ended up with a higher price level but their *relative* prices did not undertake significant change. Russia and transition economies, instead, moved from a below-market-clearing to a market-clearing price level, but also from administered to free prices; therefore relative prices must change, a move which represents an "*adverse supply shock*" (Popov 2007). This is not an argument in favour of gradualism, as Popov suggests. Some enterprises that are unprofitable at the new prices and must contract output, either were producing negative value added at international prices and their immediate closure is advantageous, or their value added was positive but insufficient to pay wages, and their wage bill ought to be subsidised. The CSFR Finance Minister Vaclav Klaus subsidised wage bills in the early 1990s, in spite of his liberal rhetoric, as it was done on a larger scale in Eastern Germany after re-unification, thus containing income decline and the rise of unemployment.

While Latin American had an inefficient state sector, transition countries had been centrally planned, their state-owned enterprises were dominant and they had no experience of adjusting to internal and international prices. Thus, transition economies—unlike Latin American economies—needed to change fast the entire system of ownership, management and incentives; here again Gorbachev might have chosen a different course. Before tackling these questions in the next section, consider the implications of the existing trading blocs of both the USSR and Comecon.

There were advantages from retaining *both* blocs: the maintenance of high trade volumes through the use of a single currency (the rouble; the transferable rouble); sustainability of inter-republic and intra-Comecon imbalances, via central transfers and credits.

However, the international socialist division of labour had a bad name, in spite of Soviet subsidisation of its Comecon partners since 1974, by supplying oil and raw materials at below world prices. Memories and accusations of earlier Soviet exploitation through trade, at prices different from world prices, were still deeply ingrained; and indeed even trade with the USSR at world prices can be exploitative if, at those prices, quantities traded were not voluntarily transacted.

Comecon efficiency could have been improved, as a lot of intra-Comecon trade was already taking place at world prices and settled in dollars. In 1990–91 centrifugal forces were at their maximum not only for considerations of national independence but simply because the USSR was changing at a slower pace than desired by other Comecon members. Had Gorbachev accelerated Soviet transition much earlier, liberalised foreign trade and come to terms politically with the other leaderships, it is conceivable that he might have been able to continue a form of looser trade integration within Comecon, say a Free Trade Area (FTA). He would have had to soften the impact of moving to world prices by compensatory subsidies to trade partners, or by granting credits. The bizarre construction of the transferable rouble—a mere unit of account—would have had to be either fleshed out as something like the European Currency Unit or replaced by a hard currency. But even maintaining Comecon in existence as an FTA the shock of moving to international prices and the consequent disruption of traditional backwards and forwards links could have not been avoided.

By the beginning of 1990 Soviet trade partners within the bloc decided that they would rather not trade at all within the Comecon framework, in the belief that the continuation of a system which they regarded as inefficient and detrimental was too high a price for access to cheap Soviet natural resources. The roots of Comecon disintegration dated from before Gorbachev: the economics and politics of Comecon were not sustainable. By September 1991 Comecon was officially extinct—and its disintegration was a major factor in the transition recession of the whole area (Mundell 1997).

Would Gorbachev have been able to hold the Soviet Union together? The same arguments for maintaining Comecon in existence applied to the Soviet Union, in a stronger form. Inter-republic trade within the Union was on average over 60% of total trade, sustained by All-Union budgetary transfers and central credits. At the turn of the 'nineties the IMF was being accused by radical reformers of trying to prevent USSR dis-integration; if this was the case, it must have been for these economic advantages, but the attempt failed. Again, if Gorbachev had moved in the early stages of his mandate, and had been economically successful, he would have lessened centrifugal forces within the Union. If the rouble had been made convertible both internally and externally, the move towards a market economy had begun to give some fruits, and some autonomy granted to republics, the probability of retaining the Union would have been greater than zero, but not significantly greater.

22.6 Perestroika Economic Foundations: C) Enterprises, Ownership, Incentives

When Gorbachev came to power in 1985 there were in the USSR various types of enterprises: state enterprises and associations of enterprises (mostly sectoral, rather than conglomerates); state and collective farms (*sovkhozy* and *kolkhozy*); individual and family enterprises mostly in crafts and services, which Gorbachev encouraged with the 1986 Law; co-operatives in a variety of sectors, which he promoted with the 1988 Law; enterprises leased to their own workers; Joint Ventures with foreign enterprises, whose scope was broadened in 1987–88. Such a range of enterprises was not sufficient, in types, numbers and composition, for the full functioning of a market economy.

Undoubtedly *perestroika* required a reduced, indeed minority role for the state sector; by 1990 there were plans for reducing it to 40% (Hanson 1992). The "small" privatisation of apartments, small plots of land, shops, restaurants, hotels, was part of this design and should have been implemented long beforehand. Chinese-style land leases, long-term and transferable, were contemplated in 1990 but not introduced before Gorbachev's fall; they were needed as the first ownership transformation element in his programme, based on the land leases (*arenda*) tradition of the New Economic Policy of 1921–26.

It was essential, in addition, to legalise and promote the setting up of private enterprises of any size, engaged in any legal activity, their private ownership and that of their means of production, their full and unconditional transferability—without fictional arrangements such as those of cooperatives. The size of the state sector would thus be reduced through the "organic" growth of the private sector, regardless of whatever was done in the state sector. *De novo* enterprises would be the engine of growth, the vehicles of capacity restructuring, the vitality and response of production to the new domestic and international prices. Empirical studies (such as Richter and Schaffer 1996) confirm that such *de novo* firms, neither state nor privatised enterprises, are responsible for capacity restructuring, investment and growth in Russia and other transition economies. Such organic growth of private enterprises has been the main component of private sector growth in several transition economies, especially Hungary and Poland.

In the state sector, regardless of privatisation, it was essential first to remove enterprises from the clutches of branch ministries, placing them under Treasury ownership and responsibility. Second, to "commercialise" them by replacing central commands with managerial responsibility for their viability, profitability and self-finance (from profit reinvestment and credits), with salaries and bonuses dependent on achieved results in these areas, in a competitive environment. Domar (1974), for instance, shows that managerial bonuses geared to both revenue and profit, with parameters adjusted by trial and error, can lead the manager of a state enterprise to maximise profits as if she was operating in perfect competition; this type of bonuses was familiar in Russian industry from Brezhnev's times in the late sixties, though of course not with a trial and error determination of parameters nor, more importantly, in a market-clearing environment. Third, it was essential to transform those "commercialised" enterprises into share stock companies so as to allow the spreading of ownership within the rest of the public sector and, sooner or later, among private investors.

Instead, the Enterprise Law of 1987 gave workers' collectives—at least on paper—control powers which might be exercised in their own interest rather than those of their enterprise. Worse, the Law gave managers of state enterprises not only some independence in running them, but also a first opportunity to directly *loot* state assets, subcontracting or selling off non-competitively the more profitable assets or parts of their enterprises to their own advantage. Trade opening in commodities sold internally at prices below world prices, and privileged credit at negative real interest rates at times of hyperinflation is another form of *looting* state assets. Again, market-clearing at single prices, and competition among producers, are missing ingredients that need to be introduced and strengthened before granting managerial autonomy.

Mass privatisation—the virtually free distribution to the population of *vouchers* convertible into state assets—is a bad idea. It is a political gimmick to give everybody something to lose if the transition went wrong; an experiment in institutional engineering, unprecedented apart from one case of the subsidised privatisation of a single company in British Columbia in 1974, which promptly went bust. I own one privatisation *voucher* from Belarus, given to me by a friend in 1999 at a time when there was a *voucher* overhang (sic!) and nothing to get in exchange; one Russian privatisation *voucher* which I exchanged for half a litre of vodka with a sailor in Tallin in 1995; one Polish privatisation *voucher* presented to me in 1995 during the long lag between their distribution and possible redemption. Speed was supposed to be the main advantage of mass privatisation, but in Poland it took five years for implementation to begin, delayed by discussion of programme details and of the role of the state in the process, especially in view of the involvement of foreign management companies. In 1995 mass-privatised enterprises represented 10% of the book value of Polish state enterprises. In 2008, twelve years after completion of the programme, the assets of all the state-authorised Polish Investment Funds whose certificates were acquired with *vouchers*, and in which the ownership of mass-privatised enterprises was vested, represented less than 1 per cent of the capitalisation of all Polish industrial enterprises (Kempiak 2009), and falling. *Much ado about nothing.*

The initial equalisation of access to mass-privatised assets (involving 94% of adult population in Poland) was followed by rapid and extreme concentration of either the *vouchers*, as in Russia (where they soon changed hands in packets of 4000 *vouchers*) or, when these were non-transferable, of the assets into which they were converted. Mass privatisation did not improve management, which remained unchanged, nor access to fresh investment as it did not bring new capital, nor technology, nor market access—unlike company sales to private investors especially foreigners. Nor did corporate governance improve, due to the fragmentation of shareholdings involved in mass privatisation (World Bank 1996).

Indeed in Russia the frequent, unexpected acquisition of a majority stake by the employees of privatised enterprises, created the possibility of other shareholders being damaged by over-generous wage and employment policies adopted by managers answering to shareholding employees (a possibility that could materialise when a controlling interest is in the hands of employees all holding a smaller share of capital than their share in total enterprise employment, see Nuti 1997). Mass privatisation appears to have been pursued not as a policy instrument but as an aim in itself (Kolodko 2002).

Moreover, Stuckler-King-McKee 2009 argue that rapid mass privatisation (defined as a transfer of at least 25% of state assets in two years from the issue of *vouchers*) in transition economies was associated with an average increase in short-term adult mortality rates of 12.8%. Similar results hold for the privatisation indices from the EBRD Transition Reports; one mediating factor could be male unemployment rates, raised by privatisation. (Incidentally, Stuckler-King-Basu 2008 find that IMF reform programmes are associated with significantly worsened tuberculosis incidence, prevalence, and mortality rates in central-eastern European and former Soviet Union countries, independent of other political, socioeconomic, demographic and health changes in these countries). One could object that if people who have undertaken major open-heart surgery turn out to have a higher mortality rate than those who have not, this does not *necessarily* imply that the operation has on average shortened their lives. But staunch supporters of the Washington Consensus, while criticising Stuckler-King-McKee findings, recognise that future studies might examine whether the disruption of social services caused by privatisation is an important mechanism of increased mortality (*The Economist*, various issues, January 2009).

In Russia privatisation via the *loans for shares* scandalous process of 1995–96, whereby banks are given grossly under-valued shares as a guarantee for loans to the government that are known beforehand will never be repaid, was a particularly bad idea. Anatoly Chubais, privatisation Minister at the time, candidly recognises that this was done only in order to finance Boris Yeltsin's 1996 re-election against his communist challenger Gennady Zyuganov (Desai 2006). In addition to the enrichment techniques indicated above (through privileged access to the purchase of under-priced tradables, and to subsidised credit), privatisation was another major instrument of looting national resources. In these ways inequality in income distribution in Russia increased drastically, with a Gini coefficient (the index of inequality going from 0 for absolute equality to 100% for total concentration in a single subject) rising from 28.9% in 1991 to 40% in 2000 and 42.7% in 2007. According to *Forbes*, in 2008 Russia had 87 billionaires, second only to the United States. This is an adverse development because it is *inefficient* inequality, not justified by entrepreneurial success and productive accumulation but due to straight looting. *Gorbachev's market economy and ownership changes would have avoided these adverse impacts on income and wealth distribution.*

The radical policies implemented in market economies as a response to the global financial crisis of 2008–2009 put a new complexion on the policies and processes of transition economies. Many observers in the world press have talked of such a crisis as "the end of capitalism"; some have made a direct comparison between the Berlin Wall collapse and the Wall Street collapse, suggesting that we are now in the middle of a New Transition. The end of capitalism has been grossly exaggerated, but we certainly are in the middle of a transition, whether temporary or permanent, from hyper-liberal capitalism to state financial capitalism. There is no alternative to the market system of production and exchange of goods and services, but financial markets have failed spectacularly and macroscopically, as witnessed in many countries by large scale government bailouts, re-capitalisations, nationalisations, not only of banks but also of production enterprises, at taxpayers' expense.

In this perspective, the neophyte enthusiasm with which post-socialist transition economies privatised banks and insurance companies, established stock exchanges and developed derivatives markets, set up a capitalised pension system lately destroyed by stock exchange collapse, appears as a naïve and ill-advised policy. In particular, reliance on foreign-owned financial institutions, now rapidly repatriating their capital in difficult times, leaving national enterprises starved of credit, seems particularly disastrous not only for the Russian billionaires (now reduced to 32, *The Economist*, 13 March 2009), but for all Russian firms and the Russian population. The well advised, parallel Gorbachev, whose hypothetical feats we are considering here, would not have been caught in the particularly profound crisis in which Russia and all central eastern European economies find themselves today (with the exception of Euro-zone new members). Their vulnerability to a great extent is the direct result of their adoption of a hyper-liberal target model of capitalism rather than, say, the European Social Model.

22.7 Subsequent Challenges, in Russia and Other Transition Economies

In our parallel world, by 1991 Gorbachev in Russia has largely implemented economic *perestroika*. Russia is now neck and neck with most other transition economies, indeed slightly ahead; it is facing exactly the same problems as they do. Therefore it is useful to consider now those policies that went wrong or could go wrong in post-socialist economies in the course of their transition to a market economy—regardless of the relative size of their public/private sector.[4] We have already mentioned some policies regarded as inappropriate, such as mass privatisation; and premature unilateral trade liberalisation and its reversals, instead of retaining a uniform non-discriminatory temporary moderate tariff barrier (as recommended even by the IMF authoritative fiscal specialist Vito Tanzi 1997); we will not go back to them.

If Gorbachev had initiated the transition, Central-Eastern Europe might have followed his lead. Instead of accompanying price liberalisation with deflationary monetary and fiscal policies—often resulting in an unwanted credit squeeze and an unexpected budgetary surplus, as in Poland in 1990—the other transition economies might have implemented monetary easing and wage subsidisation, thus softening the shocks of the change in absolute and relative prices, and of the change of enterprise incentives.

In turn Russia and other countries might have learnt from each other. For instance, that fast disinflation is unnecessarily costly: Poland took over ten years to gradually disinflate down to one-digit inflation, thus

[4] Necessarily this section is largely a reasoned checklist of what not to do, and a programme for further research.

shortening the depth and duration of transition recession, and so the output loss involved in the fast reduction of inflation would be avoided once the operationally reasonable two-digit rate had been reached. Unfortunately countries have learnt very little in the course of transition, whether from other countries' experience or even from their own. Suffice to look at how Russia in 2008–2009 is replicating its own 1997–1998 exchange rate policies that led straight to the 1998 crisis (Popov 2009).

An alternative strategy, different from the traditional shock-therapy Washington Consensus that prevailed throughout post-socialist countries especially in the first years of transition, was proposed in Poland in 1994–97 by the First Deputy Premier and Minister of Finance Grzegorz W. Kolodko, and outlined in three official policy documents, *Strategia dla Polski* (1994), *Polska 2000* (1996) and *Euro 2006* (1997). In this approach it was noted that unnecessary shocks, plus a therapy overdose, had led to overshooting with respect to important original targets, such as the fiscal stance, the trade balance and the unplanned acquisition of reserves, and to real wage falls. The new S*trategy*, as the Finance Minister stressed in a speech to the IMF annual meeting in Madrid in October 1994,

> does not involve any change in target model, nor in transition speed, nor in fiscal stance... The target remains a modern capitalist mixed economy, though with emphasis on equality and partnership between private and public sectors, rather than the previous discrimination and antagonism between the two. The speed of transition is, in some respects, accelerated... In other respects (it) continues to be dictated by the technical delays of effective institution-building... The overall fiscal stance does not leave much scope for manoeuvre by any government. The differences are in actual policies, in the choice and calibration of policy instruments, in the trade-offs between alternative targets selected by the government in preference to other possible trade-offs—as is normally the case in the theory and practice of economic policy.

This *Strategy* emphasises also the reform of central administration, the need for a participatory process in institution-building, public and private investment promotion, greater security in economic transactions, the combination of fiscal austerity with a measure of monetary relaxation and an anti-inflationary social pact on wages. It relies on privatisation to raise revenue and to improve governance and competition, and on the commercial management of the residual state sector. Industrial and agricultural policy guides restructuring, avoiding direct or indirect favour for individual enterprises and the softening of budget constraints. Greater openness to trade integration and to foreign direct investment was to prepare an early Polish accession to the EU and the eventual early adoption of the euro. For a full discussion of these policies and the official documents, see Kolodko and Nuti (1997).

As an illustration of macroeconomic policies that made the "realised transition"[5] more costly than need be, we give three typical examples here (see also Nuti 2007, 2008): 1) the misuse of Central Bank independence; 2) lack of coordination between monetary and fiscal policy; 3) the changeover from a re-distributive to a funded pension system, under extreme pressure from the World Bank.

Misuse of Central Banks Independence

Transition economies have instituted—also due to pressure from international organisations—independent Central Banks pursuing exclusively inflation targets, following the German model rather than the milder British, Japanese or even US model of Central Bank independence, and in an even stronger version (Cukierman et al. 2002).

This model has not always performed well in the transition. Some Central Bank governors look independent, but they are not; in Belarus president Lukaschenko replaced four Central Bank governors in five years (1994–98), one of whom was imprisoned for a month and one of whom was the former Finance Minister actually responsible for financial imbalance. Other governors are truly independent of the government but are not politically independent technicians: when in 1997 Leszek Balcerowicz was appointed as governor of the Polish National Bank he was the leader of Freedom Union, a political party defeated in the preceding parliamentary elections. His predecessor Gronkiewicz-Waltz had stood as a

[5] The expression is used by Gorga (2004), mirroring the "realised socialism" label usually attached to the traditional system.

candidate in the presidential elections without stepping down from her office, which she continued to hold after defeat. Some independent central bankers have pursued policies manifestly contrary to the pursuit of price stability (Russia 1992).

Real interest rates have been pushed to inordinately high levels (Russia 1994, Poland throughout its transition) with respect to the requirements of domestic and external balance. Inflation targets have been treated not as something to hit but to over-fulfil, as if they were central planning targets, and without adjusting nominal rates accordingly. After all, the principle of Central Bank independence is a recent fashion (from the late 'eighties), has shaky foundations in the theory of rational expectations, and has been suspended in practice to enable governments to cure the current global financial crisis.

Lack of Coordination of Monetary and Fiscal Policies

A consequence of extreme Central Bank independence is the lack of fiscal-monetary coordination. Failure to coordinate leads to higher fiscal deficits, higher interest rates and stronger exchange rates than otherwise would be the case, thus adversely affecting exports, investment, output and therefore employment and growth (Castren 1998). In many transition economies the sterilisation of Central Bank reserve acquisition has lost the state budget significant fractions of GDP, of up to 2–3 per cent, as reserves earned foreign interest rates lower (expressed in any common currency) than those paid out in sterilisation issues of Central Bank Bonds.

The Perverse Reform of the Pension System

In most transition economies, under pressure from the World Bank, there has been a pension reform from the traditional Pay As You Go (PAYG) system to a funded system. PAYG is unfunded and re-distributive, in that pensions are paid, at a rate of pre-defined benefits, out of the pension contributions made by current employees. A funded pension system, instead, accumulates defined contributions while benefits depend on the yield earned on the accumulated individual contributions over time.

There are three presumed advantages from the changeover: 1) the reduction or elimination of the PAYG "pension debt", i.e. the present value of today's pensioners' pensions for the rest of their lives, which is not matched by current government assets and may get worse for an ageing population; 2) the exercise of individual choice in the investment of individual contributions; 3) the positive impact of a funded scheme on the development of financial markets.

These presumed advantages are overestimated or non-existent. In a universal and permanent PAYG system future current pensions continue to be paid out of future current contributions; as long as the number of old age pensioners multiplied by their individual average pension is no greater than the number of current employees multiplied by their individual average pension contribution, the system is balanced and sustainable. The "pension debt" as defined above is there but never comes to the surface.[6] Only if current pensions exceed current contribution (for instance due to population ageing) does *that* deficit fall on the government budget and raise government debt. Then pensions must be reduced, or contributions raised, or retiring age raised, or a combination of all three, until total current contributions and total current pensions balance, or their imbalance is a bearable burden on the government budget.

The changeover to a funded system, instead, makes the entire pension debt surface instantly into government accounts—an unnecessary open burden at a time when the transition faces intense budgetary needs. Individual choice and financial market developments are normally advantages but turn into individual losses and vulnerability at a time of financial turmoil like that of 2008–2009, when insurance companies and banks go bust and stock exchange values fall by over a half. Then funded schemes end up with disappearing yields and capital values, i.e. pensions tend to vanish. Ultimately the government will have to look after pensioners no longer covered by their "funded" schemes. The pension

[6] If an unfunded system was balanced, and was offered for privatisation, there should be no shortage of takers without paying the purchaser the value of the buried pension debt.

burden then falls entirely on the public budget—inexorably and regardless of whether pensions are funded or unfunded. From these viewpoints, the pension reform favoured by the World Bank in transition economies and elsewhere is a bad idea (see Eatwell et al. 2000, Chap. 5).

It is extremely difficult to estimate the *quantitative impact* of all the measures that we have classified as mistaken on the welfare of populations in transition. We are discussing not only general policies, but also single policy instruments, indeed the numerical value of policy parameters such as interest or exchange rates. After a structural break one must compare what actually happened not with the past but with what plausibly would have happened without that needed break. The application of different economic theories will put a different complexion on whether or not some measure is mistaken, or how serious is the mistake. Different policy measures will involve different categories of winners and losers, and often the relative desirability of those measures involves arbitrary weights assigned to distribution among groups. It is impossible for observers not to bring to bear their own moral and political values in the relative assessment of what did happen in the transition and what might have happened instead. Thus *there will never be a unanimous, or even a broad consensus view about the transition.*

It is reasonable and respectable to consider several of the policy "mistakes" discussed in this paper as negligible or dependent on a particular set of theories and values, just as it is reasonable and respectable to consider them all as mistakes. The belief that all or almost all went well in "realised" transition, in the best or one of the better possible worlds—or that, if anything went wrong, it was not because different policies should have been applied, but because the actual policies followed were not applied with sufficient vigour and speed—this is neither reasonable nor respectable. Worse, the belief that the same policies should be replicated in the transition of countries that are lagging behind, or repeated in countries where they have already failed once, is unforgivable. Errare humanum est, perseverare diabolicum.

22.8 Conclusions

A Successful Perestroika?

Retrospectively, it is conceivable that Gorbachev might have succeeded in implementing his economic *perestroika*—the combination of a market system with a continued high share of public ownership, whether majority or significant minority—and the resulting economic acceleration of income and consumption.

In order to succeed, Gorbachev would have had to act swiftly, instead of practically wasting his first two years in power (1985–87), and lay down sound economic foundations for *perestroika*: eliminate repressed inflation, preferably through a confiscatory currency conversion; break state monopoly of foreign trade, introduce rouble convertibility on current account, liberalise trade, foster competition. By 1991 he would have also legalised private ownership and enterprise, given state managers bonuses geared to market performance, implemented small privatisation, commercialised state enterprises, begun some privatisation of large enterprises and banks. On Christmas Day 1991, instead of resigning as President of the Union, he could have celebrated the victory of economic *perestroika*.

What Next?

There are still thorny choices and therefore possible mistakes to be made, before completing transition and after. Gorbachev would have needed continued vigilance and sound economic advice, for instance to avoid too rapid disinflation at inordinately high real interest rates, as happened in 1994–95, and the consequent recession; to avoid an unsustainable combination of overvalued exchange rate, high interest rate to support it, and a public debt increasing as a result of high debt service, as happened in 1998 under the IMF's watch; to avoid the unnecessary cost to the budget of switching the pension system from PAYG to a funded system.

The Economic Gains

As a result of the good economic foundations of economic *perestroika*, and the avoidance of these kinds of subsequent pitfalls, income losses from the transition recession would have been lower, and growth would have accelerated earlier and faster than it actually was and did. The welfare of Russians would have improved significantly and continuously as a result. The same reasoning applies to all other transition economies that to a greater or lesser extent followed stabilisation and transition paths out of sequence or to excess. It is impossible to have unanimity about whether the measures taken were or were not mistakes, and how serious, let alone quantify the gains. But pretending that there were no serious unnecessary mistakes in the transition is neither reasonable nor respectable.

The Serious Political Cost of Market Socialism

The improved economic performance generates political consensus, but not necessarily to the point of providing *permanent* democratic support for a political regime associated with significantly large state ownership and associated political values (of equality, solidarity, participation, etc.). In some transition countries post-communist parties were returned to power in democratic elections (e.g. Poland, Hungary, Slovakia) after being defeated, but only intermittently, not permanently; some party alternation in power is an integral part of democracy. But *non-persistent, intermittent* market socialism cannot deliver its expected economic and social advantages. When democratic support for an economic system is lacking or is not *permanent*, then its maintenance over time requires necessarily forms of political repression. *There is a high political price to pay for an economically successful and persistent market socialism*—as confirmed by "market socialist" countries such as China, Vietnam, Belarus, Uzbekistan.

Would an Economically Successful Gorbachev Have Been Able to Hold Together the Soviet Union?

There would be some economic advantages to be shared out, from holding it together. A continued Union would maintain and promote intra-Union trade volumes thanks to the single currency, and sustain inter-republic imbalances through transfers within the All-Union budget and inter-republic credits. An early initiative and widespread economic success, including internal and external convertibility of the rouble, would have lessened centrifugal forces. If some political and administrative autonomy was granted to the 15 republics as well, the chances of retaining the Union would have improved. But the Soviets had seldom solved ethnic conflicts, mostly they had only suppressed them (just as they had done with inflation). Independence aspirations would have made it difficult for Russia to retain close ties even with republics that economically had most to gain from continued integration, like Ukraine. *The probability of holding together the Union would have been greater than zero, but not significantly greater.*

Would a Successful Market-Socialist Russia Have Been Able to Hold Together CMEA/Comecon?

Arguments similar to those for holding together the Soviet Union would apply, but would be much weaker. The international socialist division of labour had a bad name, in spite of Soviet subsidisation of its Comecon partners since 1974, by supplying oil and raw materials at below world prices. Memories and accusations of earlier Soviet exploitation through trade were still deeply ingrained. In January 1990 Comecon partners *de facto* destroyed it by trading freely rather than continue the old trade arrangements, even at the cost of paying higher prices for oil and materials. By September1991 Comecon was officially dissolved. Comecon Soviet trade partners were already negotiating European Association Agreements and aid programmes with the European Community (now the European Union).

Gorbachev's hypothetical successful perestroika would not have led to Comecon survival. At most, perhaps, a couple of years earlier he might have been able to extract economic assistance from the West in exchange for his acquiescence to the re-unification of Germany—for which he got nothing at all—and for the Finlandisation of Eastern Europe—a prospect overtaken by events in 1989.

What Difference Would Gorbachev's Hypothetical Successful Perestroika Have Made in Russia?

Only an alleviation of the pains of transition in the 1990s; there would have been not very much difference in the 2000s, considering that in his second presidential term Putin had already reversed enterprise ownership trends, re-acquiring greater state control in many sectors and a majority stake in energy (Hanson 2008). By comparison with the sensitivity of Russian performance to the price of oil, probably Gorbachev's success would have been equivalent to a ten-year-long rise of $10 on the price of a barrel. (According to the Bank of Finland Research Department a $10 permanent increase raises Russia's growth rate by 1%). The recent implosion of the US and global financial system had a far greater effect on Russia's prospects.

What Difference Would Gorbachev's Hypothetical Successful Perestroika Have Made to Modern Geopolitics?

An earlier economically stronger Russia would have probably contained USA bids for the "American Century", thus sparing them the humiliation of their century ending so soon after it had barely begun. Certainly Georgia would not have responded to encouragement by George W. Bush and Dick Cheney to attack Russia. But the Twin Towers had nothing to do with Russia, and it is impossible to tell whether the major armed conflicts that followed their attack—in Afghanistan and Iraq—would have been prevented by an economically stronger Russia. Most probably not.

Gorbachev's and the whole Transition's economic *débacle* clearly reduced the demand for socialism on a world scale, but his success would have made no difference for European social-democracy, as it would not have prevented the disintegration of the Italian left or the degeneration of British Labour into New Labour, nor favoured Zapatero's victory in Spain. Probably both the European Union and NATO would have been smaller.

A Russian economy made stronger by an efficient Transition would have been less vulnerable to the contagion of global financial turmoil, both in the South East Asian crisis of 1997 (that was an important factor in the Russian crisis of 1998), and today. But a stronger Russia would have neither prevented such global financial crises, nor contributed much to their resolution.

Russia 2029

Our Conference time horizon daringly extends to 2029, a daunting task. We know how the Russian government looks at the future today. In March 2008 the Russian Ministry of Economic Development published an ambitious *Conception of Long-term Socio-Economic Development to 2020,* with targets for diversification and modernisation to 2030 (see Russian Ministry of Economic Development 2008; Hanson 2008). This *Conception* envisaged three alternatives for 2020: 1) *inertia,* with a continued dominance of the energy sector and raw materials but with a marked slowdown of their export growth, a GDP yearly growth rate of 3–3.5% in 2011–2020 and the maintenance of R&D investment at a constant 1% of GDP; 2) *concentration on energy and raw materials,* with the "full exploitation of Russian comparative advantages" in this sector, a yearly growth rate of 5–5.5% in 2011–2020 and a gradual growth of R&D investment up to 2% in 2020; 3) *innovation*, equivalent to the second scenario plus a greater development of high and medium technology, with a yearly growth rate of 6.4–6.5% in 2011–2020 and higher investment (raised from 20% to 35% of GDP by 2020) and R&D expenditures up to 2.8% in 2015, 4% in 2020 and 4.7% in 2030. This scenario was supposed to ensure in 2020 a per capita income of about $30,000 (in PPP) with respect to $13,000 in 2007, a life expectancy at birth of 72 years (from 65.6 in 2006), a population growing to 145 million (from 142 million in 2008).

After a great deal of discussion the last, most ambitious scenario, was approved in January 2009—a particularly bad timing in view of the Russian economic performance nosedive. Informed analysts, such as Cooper (2008) and Hanson (2008), consider this scenario unrealistic: in its demographic forecasts; the expectation of successful measures to raise productivity, without the incentive of a competitive environment favouring innovation; the hypothesis—already resoundingly falsified by recent trends—of a continuous rise in the price of energy and raw materials. In the circumstances of the global financial crisis and its contagion, with falling prices of Russian exports, instead of the third, innovative option Russia is likely to find itself in an intermediate position between options 1 and 2, with maximum extraction of oil and materials, exported at low prices, at a relatively modest growth rate of income.

The future of Russia in the world economy has also been explored by Goldman Sachs (2007) and PricewaterhouseCoopers (Howksworth and Cockson 2008; discussed by Cooper 2008). The latter investigate 20 emerging economies and in a recent update covering 2007–2050 place Russia in 19th place, at a yearly 4.3 per cent in US$ terms (only 2.5% in rouble terms: thus they implicitly expect continuous appreciation of the rouble *vis-à-vis* the US$, a trend drastically reversed since September 2008). Goldman Sachs (2007) give a somewhat more optimistic assessment of Russia's prospects (Cooper 2008).

Our Future

We should leave the future to futurologists. In 1989 Fukuyama's conjecture about *The End of History* was falsified before the ink had dried. Kolodko (2008) might do better. All we know for sure, whether Gorbachev had or had not been successful in implementing economic *perestroika*, is that—as prophesised by a wall graffiti in London in 1991: "*The future is not what it used to be*".

Bibliography

Barnett, Vincent (1994). As Good as Gold? A Note on the *Chervonets*, *Europe-Asia Studies*, Vol. 46, No. 4, 663-669.

Blejer, Mario I. and Marko Skreb (Eds) (1997). *Macroeconomic Stabilisation in Transition Economies*, Cambridge University Press, Cambridge.

Brooks, Michael (2008). Does time travel start here?, *The New Scientist*, Issue 2642, 9 February.

Castren, Olli (1998). *Fiscal-Monetary Policy Coordination and Central Bank Independence*, Central Bank of Finland, Scientific Monographs E:12.

Childs, David (2000). *The Two Red Flags: European Social Democracy and Soviet Communism since 1945*, Routledge, London.

Cohan, John (1990). Soviet Union beyond *Perestroika*, *Time Magazine*, 24 September.

Cook, Linda (1993). *The Soviet Social Contract and why it Failed – Welfare policy and workers' politics from Brezhnev to Yeltsin*, Harvard Russian Research Center Studies, HUP.

Cooper, Julian (2008). Russia as a Populous Emerging Economy: A Comparative Perspective, Conference Paper, CREES, Birmimgham University.

Cukierman, Alex, Geoffrey P. Miller and Bilin Neyapti (2002). Central bank reform, liberalization and inflation in transition economies — an international perspective, *Journal of Monetary Economics*, Vol. 49, 2, March, 237-264.

Desai, Padma (2006). *Conversations on Russia,* Cambridge, CUP.

Domar, Evsey. (1974). On the Optimal Compensation of a Socialist Manager, *Quarterly Journal of Economics*, February 1974, 1-18.

Eatwell, John, Michael Ellman, Mats Karlsson, D.M. Nuti, Judith Shapiro (2000). *Hard Budget and Soft States: social policy in Central and Eastern Europe*, IPPR, London.

Edgeworth, Francis Ysidro (1881). *Mathematical Psychics, An Essay on the Application of Mathematics to Moral Sciences*, Kegan Paul, London.

Ellman, Michael and Vladimir Kontorovich (1998). *The Destruction of the Soviet Economic System – An Insiders' History*, M.E. Sharpe, Armonk – New York.

Fukuyama, Francis (1989). The End of History?, *The National Interest*, Summer.

Goldman Sachs Global Economics Department (2007). *BRICs and Beyond*, November.

Gorbachev, Mikhail S. (1996). *Memoirs*, Doubleday, Randon House Inc.

Gorga, Beatrice (2004). *Realities in Transformation: from Realised Socialism to Realised Transition,* PhD thesis, Faculty of Economics, University of Rome "La Sapienza".

Hanson, Philip (1992). *From Stagnation to Catastroika: Commentaries on the Soviet Economy, 1983-1991*, Washington Papers, CSIS.

Hanson, Philip (1998). Foreign Advice, in Ellman and Kontorovich, 1998, pp. 238-255.

Hanson, Philip (2008). The economic development of Russia: between state control and liberalization, ISPI Working Papers, Issue 32, Rome.

Hawksworth, John and Gordon Cookson (2008). *The World in 2050. Beyond the BRICs: a broader look at emerging market growth prospects*, Pricewaterhouse Coopers, London.

Kempiak, Dorota Inga (2009). *Efficienza della privatizzazione di massa nella Polonia post-socialista* (dissertation), Faculty of Economics, University of Rome "La Sapienza".

Kolodko, Grzegorz W. (2002). *Globalization and Catching-up in Transition Economies*, Un. of Rochester Press, Rochester and Woodbridge.

Kolodko, Grzegorz W. (2008). *Wędrujący świat*, Prószyński i S-ka, Warsaw.

Kolodko, Grzegorz W. and Walter W. McMahon (1987). Stagflation and Shortageflation: A Comparative Approach, *Kyklos*, Vol. 40, Fasc. 2, 176-197.

Kolodko, Grzegorz W. and D. Mario Nuti (1997). The Polish Alternative. Old Myths, Hard Facts and New Strategies in the Successful Transformation of the Polish Economy, *Research for Action*, 33, UN-WIDER, Helsinki.

Kotz, David M. and Fred Weir (2007). *Russia's path from Gorbachev to Putin: The Demise of the Soviet System and the New Russia*, Routledge, London and New York.

Lavigne, Marie (1985). *Economie internationale des pays socialistes*, Arman Collin Collection U, Paris.

Lavigne, Marie (1999). *The Economics of Transition: From Socialist Economy to Market Economy*, Macmillan, London.

McKinnon, Ronald I. (1993). *The order of Economic Liberalisation- Financial Control in the Transition to a Market Economy*, Johns Hopkins Un. Press, Baltimore.

Maxwell, Herbert (Ed), (1903). *Creevey Papers*, London.

Mundell, Robert A. (1997). The great contractions in Transition economies, in Blejer and Skreb (Eds), 1997, pp.73-99.

Nuti, D. Mario (1986). Hidden and repressed inflation in Soviet-type economies: definitions, measurements and stabilisation, *Contributions to Political Economy*, Vol. 5, pp. 37-82.

Nuti, D. Mario (1997). Employeeism: corporate governance and employee share ownership in Transition economies, in Blejer and Skreb (Eds), 1997, Cambridge University Press, pp. 126-154.

Nuti, D. Mario (2007). Managing Transition Economies, in White, Batt and Lewis (2007), Ch. 15.

Nuti, D. Mario (2008). Alternative targets, paths and speed in Post-Socialist Transition, EACES Conference paper, Higher School of Economics, Moscow, 28-30 August 2008.

OECD-NEA Nuclear Energy Agency (2002). *Chernobyl: Assessment of Radiological and Health Impacts - 2002 Update of Chernobyl: Ten Years On[1995]* http://www.nea.fr/html/rp/chernobyl/allchernobyl.html (accessed March 2009).

Popov, Vladimir (2007). Shock therapy versus gradualism: lessons from Transition economies after 15 years of reforms, *Comparative Economic Studies*, 49, 1-3.

Popov, Vladimir (2009). Memories about the Future: The second edition of the 1998 crisis, *Russian Analytical Digest*, 54/9, 3 February, pp. 7-12.

Richter, Ann and Mark Schaffer (1996). The Performance of De Novo Private Firms in Russian Manufacturing, *DERT Discussion Papers n. 9610*, Heriot Watt University.

Russian Ministry of Economic Development (2008). *Kontseptsiya dolgosrochnogo sotsial'no-ekonomicheskogo razvitiya Rossiiskoi Federatsii, Proekt*, Moscow, March.

Smith, Alan, (1993). *Russia and the World Economy – Problems of Integration*, Routledge, London.

Stuckler, David, Lawrence King and Martin MacKee (2009). Mass privatisation and the post-Soviet mortality crisis, *The Lancet*, published on line 15 January, www.thelancet.com.

Stuckler, David, Lawrence King and Sanjay Basu (2008). International Monetary Fund Programs and Tuberculosis Outcomes in Post-Communist Countries, *PLoS Medicine*, 5 (7).

Tanzi, Vito (1997). Economic transformation and the policies for long-term growth, in Blejer and Skreb (Eds), 1997.

White, Stephen, Judy Batt and Paul Lewis (Eds) (2007). *Developments in Central and East European Politics*, Palgrave/Duke UP.

World Bank (1996). *World Development Report 1996: From Plan to Market*, New York: Oxford University Press.

23

Did We Go about Transition in the Right Way?

Domenico Mario Nuti

23.1 The Transformation Recession

The post-socialist transition that began in 1990–1992 in central-eastern Europe and the former Soviet Union (FSU) was widely expected to lead to early significant improvements in the level and growth of people's consumption and income.

It was a plausible expectation: leaving aside its authoritarian drawbacks, the old system—with dominant state ownership and enterprise, central planning and broad insulation from foreign trade and investment—was notoriously inefficient. It neglected consumers' preferences, input substitutability in production, and the opportunities and stimuli of the international division of labour. The system had an autarkic bias,

Published in Paul Hare and Gerard Turley (Eds) (2013), *Handbook of the Economics and Political Economy of Transition,* Routledge, London and New York, Ch. 3, pp. 46-58.

D. M. Nuti (✉)
La Sapienza, University of Rome, Rome, Italy
e-mail: milica.uvalic@unipg.it

© The Author(s), under exclusive license to Springer Nature Switzerland AG 2023

S. Estrin, M. Uvalic (eds.), *Collected Works of Domenico Mario Nuti, Volume I*,
Studies in Economic Transition, https://doi.org/10.1007/978-3-031-12334-4_23

which facilitated central planning but was a source of gross inefficiency, even within Council for Mutual Economic Assistance or Comecon (CMEA), the bloc of socialist countries engaged in a process of planned integration since the end of the 1950s (Lavigne, 1991). For instance, Hare and Hughes (1991) showed that on the eve of transition in Czechoslovakia, Hungary and Poland, between one-fifth and one-quarter of manufacturing production exhibited negative value added at world prices (using 1988–1989 data on inputs, outputs and exchange rates). Japan bought Soviet machinery for scrap, and aluminium from the socialist bloc was sold internationally at less than the international price of the energy it embodied.

The Soviet-type system (for short, leaving aside national differences and repeated incomplete attempts at reform, only partly successful) was also unstable and imbalanced, marred by internal and external imbalances, both open and repressed. Endemic excess demand, for both consumption and production goods, prevailed at administered prices artificially held below market-clearing levels and disconnected from opportunity costs in production and trade. Excess monetary balances in the hands of the population resulted in shortages, queues, waiting lists and black markets. So much so that Kornai (1980) could entitle his two-volume treatise on that system, *Economics of Shortage*. Such repressed inflation had doomed to failure the frequent attempts at reform of the system in the direction of 'market socialism'.

The system had achieved rapid industrialization and growth, built military might and conquered space, but in the end it was unable to provide basic necessities to the population, had wasted the windfall of price increases enjoyed by its vast natural resources in the 1970s, accumulated unsustainable foreign debt, and in the 1980s stagnated and often declined. The new system would generate market-clearing prices in domestic and international transactions, revive the incentives to follow them thanks to the appropriation of profits by owners of private enterprises, and unleash and discipline entrepreneurship. The few practitioners of the transition who did contemplate some disruption (e.g. Leszek Balcerowicz in Poland in 1990), anticipated at most a one-digit temporary decline followed by accelerated growth and catching up with other market economies.

Instead of that, the transition process was accompanied by a deep and often protracted 'transformation recession' (Kornai's label). Poland experienced the shortest and smallest fall in income (17 per cent of 1989 GDP in just under three years) recovering its 1989 level in 1996 and moving rapidly ahead, while Georgia had the largest and most prolonged fall (75 per cent by 1994 before reversing, and still below the 1989 level in 2011)—leaving aside the transition countries that experienced war (with Bosnia and Herzegovina at over 80 per cent GDP decline and by 2012 still not fully recovered).

23.2 Three Reactions: Denial, Necessity, Cock-up

This unexpected statistical record provoked three contrasting reactions: disbelief to the point of denial, belief coupled with acceptance of its necessity, belief coupled with rejection of its necessity.

The initial response, which to this day is still held by a few observers (e.g. Aslund, 2000) is that the transformation recession was by and large a statistical illusion, owing to changes in conventions and enterprise behaviour. In the old system there was universal reporting by enterprises that had an incentive to exaggerate gross production achievements, to avoid penalties involved by failure to reach planned targets and to reap the bonuses deriving from plan over-fulfilment. In the new system there was incomplete sample coverage of producers under-reporting net results in order to avoid tax. Also, a significant amount of production activity took place in the black or grey economy, simply going unreported. And people benefited from an increase of their consumer surplus, simply from having access to a broader range of goods, while price increases were to some extent justified by quality increases.

These considerations cannot be dismissed but can easily be overplayed. There was a grey/black economy, though illegal, already under central planning; its newly found legality in the transition led to at least some of it surfacing, thus unduly boosting the performance of the new system. Consumer surplus is not and has never been included in national income accounting anywhere in the world, and there is no reason to begin accounting for it in the post-socialist transition. Parallel price and quality increases were not necessarily an improvement for all consumers. The availability and quality of public services plummeted. Transition performance was boosted to a great extent by the growth in formerly underprovided and underpriced services, and by real revaluation of the currency from initial gross undervaluation (see below). A single, exceedingly long queue for jobs replaced the many former queues for goods. Both inequality and poverty increased significantly in most transition economies (World Bank, 2000).

The second response to the transformation recession was that it was indeed real, but unavoidable. It was said that the transition was like 'turning a fish soup back into an aquarium', it had to be costly. In Poland the transition was likened to 'turning vodka back into potatoes'. Except that there had been no actual capacity destruction as there had been in wartime to justify this proposition. Others referred to the recession as a form of Schumpeter's 'creative destruction', also implausible since destruction of value-subtracting activities like those mentioned above should have *boosted* national income instead of reducing it, while competition and investment in innovation were missing anyway. Shleifer and Treisman (2000) justify the recession as due to the unprecedented nature of the transition: they entitle their book on Russian transition, *On the Road without a Map*. On uncharted territory we can all easily get lost, but this was not the case. We knew very well where we were, and all the conceivable advantages and drawbacks of the Soviet-type system; we knew what was going increasingly wrong with that system; we had—unlike any earlier transition—complete maps of the alternative points of arrival of the transition, i.e. the various versions of available models of capitalism—from Scandinavian type social-democracy to French indicative planning, from German *Mitbestimmung* to the Japanese neo-corporative model. Therefore we knew what had to be changed to implement the transition from where we were to the target model. What we did not know was the desirable speed of the transition and therefore, in case of a non-instantaneous transition, the appropriate sequencing of the necessary moves.

In one respect, however, the politics of transition rather than its economics necessarily involved disruption and recession to some extent. International trade was greatly disrupted by the economic and monetary disintegration associated with the transition in central-eastern Europe and the FSU. In 1991 the socialist trade bloc, CMEA, disintegrated; the transferable rouble, its purely accounting unit used to register planned trade flows at planned prices and carry over trade imbalances within the bloc for later consensual corrections, was replaced by trade at international prices settled in hard currencies. In 1992 the Soviet Union split into its 15 component Republics, with the rouble being replaced by 15 republican currencies, first as rouble substitutes then as proper domestic currencies. Mundell (1997), who regards the transformation recession as the worst ever, more serious than the 1929–1932 recession and even the Black Death recession in the fourteenth century (when population also fell, thus preserving living standards), attributes it to a great extent to such monetary disintegration.

Suddenly, next to the Russian rouble there were Belorussian roubles, Lithuanian litas, Latvian lats, Estonian kroons, Ukrainian hryvnas, Uzbek soms and Kyrgyz soms, Georgian laris, Tajik roubles later followed by the somonis, Azeri manats and Turkmen manats, Kazak tenges, Moldovan leus and Armenian drams—a veritable Babel of currencies. The move to republican currencies, initially with limited convertibility and liquidity, restricted trade to bilateral transactions of balanced barter, or to deficits liquidated in scarce hard currencies. The changeover to international prices, and the end of cross transfers within the trading bloc, were other factors depressing trade and therefore employment and GDP. Should the current eurozone crisis eventually lead to its split into national currencies, the same kind of devastating recession should be expected as a result.

The IMF tried to prevent the FSU monetary disintegration and was actually accused of holding back the transition. The different target models and stages of transition reached and intended by different republics made the preservation of the Union politically impossible. The same can be said of CMEA: early in 1990 Central-Eastern European members of CMEA had refused to continue planned integration within the trade bloc even if that involved loss of access to oil and raw materials from the Soviet Union at subsidized prices.

Having said that the recession was to some (not very large) extent overstated by national statistics, partly (significantly) the consequence of the politically unavoidable split of CMEA and of the Soviet Union (as well as of the Czecho-Slovak Federation and the Yugoslav Federation), a large residual of the recession was indeed real and due to 'having gone about transition the wrong way', to give a summary answer to the question raised by this volume's Editors.

More precisely, much of what did go wrong was owing to (1) the uncritical acceptance of a particular and controversial model of capitalist market economy, namely hyper-liberalism; (2) the extension to transition economies of the Washington Consensus policies applied in the 1980s in Latin America (price liberalization, trade opening, privatization); (3) misplaced emphasis on the relative merits of gradualism versus 'shock therapy', neglecting actual policy trade-offs and governments' preferences; (4) 'state desertion' of public enterprises and more generally of its role even in a market economy, and, in particular, the neglect of institutions in the naive belief that they would establish themselves, develop and regulate themselves automatically; (5) various policies that can be regarded as mistakes even without the benefit of hindsight, mostly rooted in ideological dogmatism; (6) eventually, sooner or later, most transition economies especially those that joined the European Union (in 2004 and 2007, and the current candidates) completed the transition and accelerated their catching up with the rest of Europe, but the same factors mentioned here caused a vulnerability to the global crisis of 2007—to date, and a stronger (though later and shorter) fall (with the exception of Poland, Albania and Azerbaijan) than in other European economies and, above all, a marked deceleration of their growth. The same factors are now standing these countries in good stead for the subsequent recovery.

23.3 Hyper-Liberalism

The target model adopted almost everywhere in the transition countries was that of an open and liberal (in the European sense) market economy that would reap the benefits of markets and private ownership and enterprise. However, the timing of the post-socialist transition coincided with the general domination of a particular and controversial model of capitalist market economy, namely hyper-liberalism, typical of the Reagan-Thatcher era. Under the strong influence of this ideology, the instigation of most foreign advisors, the conditionality imposed by the IMF and the World Bank, and the acquiescence of the European Union, the most widespread model in the transition was a hyper-liberal model that was more fundamentalist than any modern capitalist model in existence, including American capitalism.

The hyper-liberal character of the post-socialist transition model is confirmed by the dominant adoption of the following policies:

- Immediate unilateral opening of foreign trade, frequently revoked and therefore premature.
- Exceptionally rapid liberalization of capital flows, in contrast to the experience of other European economies after the Second World War.
- An unprecedented mass privatization (a notable exception was Hungary), through the distribution to the population of free or symbolically priced vouchers, convertible into state assets or shares in state enterprises—a macroscopic experiment in social engineering of debatable effectiveness.
- The demotion of the state, that led to delays or gaps in market regulation, especially in financial markets (see the disastrous diffusion of banking pyramids in Russia, Romania, Albania, Serbia, Macedonia and elsewhere), for the protection of shareholders and more generally for corporate governance.
- The dismantling of the welfare state, which in these economies was to a large extent the responsibility of state enterprises, without reconstructing it at the central level.
- A costly reform of the pension system from a Pay As You Go, defined benefits, distribution system (whereby pensioners are funded by the contributions of current employees), to a capitalization, defined contributions or funded system (with pensions paid out of the revenue earned on accumulated past contributions).

- A low and uniform rate of direct taxation (flat tax), therefore mildly progressive, on households and companies, mostly without taxation of capital gains but with higher indirect taxation.
- A flexible labour market, with weak trade unions and a low incidence of collective bargaining; the principle of market sovereignty was not applied to the labour market, frequently subjected to widespread wage ceilings enforced through punitive taxes.
- Lack of consultation and concertation between social partners and with the government.
- A central bank not only independent but exceptionally independent and free from any controls, without co-ordination with fiscal policy, pursuing a strict policy of inflationary containment and high interest rates, aiming at positive real rates even in the presence of currency appreciation (therefore attracting foreign capital but making the sterilization of the ensuing monetary expansion very costly).
- In general, a dominant weight of markets as against institutions.

This list could continue. Usually the IMF and the World Bank have been either praised or blamed for their part in imposing economic policies and institutional transformations in extreme forms, through the conditionality of their financial assistance, whose effects were multiplied by other public and private institutions in turn making their assistance conditional on an IMF programme. Sometimes Western advisors have been blamed for recommending policies that they would not have dared propose to their own governments. However, the ultimate responsibility for the policies actually adopted must be attributed to the sovereign governments that adopted those policies, and that were often only too pleased to conform to the requests of international institutions and the advice of some Western consultants.

The hyper-liberal victory in central-eastern Europe has involved a watering down of the European Social Model (ESM) as a result of EU enlargement to the East that began in 2004 and 2007 and is still in progress. A model somewhat closer to the ESM was adopted in Slovenia and Estonia, while Belarus and a few Asian republics adopted a model still close to an etatist one and to the old system, while under Putin's leadership since 2000, especially during his second mandate, Russia has moved somewhat in the same direction, of something approaching a *developmental state*. In view of the bitter reconsideration of hyper-liberalism that followed the global crisis of 2007-to date, we can say that, had the transition taken place 20 years later, post-socialism would have certainly adopted a very different model and policies.

23.4 The Washington Consensus

The IMF, the World Bank and the US Treasury applied to transition economies the policies implemented in the 1980s in Latin America with relative success: rapid macroeconomic stabilization, liberalization of prices and foreign trade, privatization. The notion that these policies might be replicated in transition economies in the 1990s ignored fundamental differences between the two groups of countries. Latin America in the 1980s suffered from open inflation and hyper-inflation, state enterprises were a minority and were familiar with the market economy including international markets. Transition economies, on the contrary, suffered from repressed inflation (see above); state enterprises were dominant and were not used to a market environment; the bulk of foreign trade was planned and the preserve of state monopoly.

These differences had profound implications. In the transition economies the price increase towards market-clearing level—which was the first necessary step towards a market economy, and indeed would have been necessary for the orderly and efficient running of a planned economy—was naturally bound to overshoot. Faced with a sudden new, unusual state of market balance, at uniform prices higher but necessarily lower than those previously prevailing in the black market, and with expectations of accelerating inflation, economic subjects were bound to reduce their demand for money below its equilibrium level at the new prices. The successive replenishment of liquid resources therefore had to depress the current demand for goods and services. Latin American consumers, instead, faced with a slowing down of open inflation were induced to maintain higher monetary resources than they would have done otherwise.

Looking at it in another way, repressed inflation could be deconstructed, as was usual in Polish literature, into: an inflationary gap (*luka inflacyjna*), i.e. the price increase that would make the current flow of real goods equivalent to the current flow of monetary incomes; and the stock (*nawis*) of accumulated past inflationary gaps. In theory there were ways to eliminate both, in the necessary advance to market clearing. For instance, a confiscatory currency reform at different rates for prices, incomes and cash (as in the late 1950s in the Soviet Union, many central-eastern European countries and China); but this was not politically feasible. Alternatively, a burst of imported consumption financed by foreign loans and aid, but this was not available at the time. Or a front-loaded privatization of state assets, but this was still controversial and a simple announcement would have been hardly credible before the start of the transition.

The choice of price liberalization was the simplest, fastest and most expedient way to clear markets, as a by-product of changing relative prices.[1] However, it necessarily involved overshooting: price rises that were practically irreversible had to absorb both the current inflationary gap and its past cumulation; in the following period (defined as the weighted average of the intervals at which markets were restocked) there would be lower demand than sustainable and consequent unemployment (Nuti, 1986).

Overshooting in price liberalization from a repressed inflationary state appears as unplanned fiscal surpluses and massive exchange-rate devaluations with respect to purchasing power parity (PPP) (with the US dollar worth 32 times its Russian rouble PPP equivalent, 20 times its Polish zloty equivalent, eight times its Hungarian forint equivalent when prices were first liberalized). Supply elasticities being low, these devaluations did not always work, but sometimes produced unplanned trade surpluses and reserves accumulation (e.g. in Poland).

[1] There were three gradual alternatives, all of them inferior to instant change. First, sequential price rises initially short of equilibrium (involving lower inflation but persistent disequilibrium and expectations of further inflation). Second, a two-track price system (China 1980s, part-controlled part free, but in transition economies imbalances were too large, there was no time and too little administrative capacity). Third, sequential price liberalization of groups of commodities (which would have led to adverse forced substitution). Price liberalization was preferable to the uncertain guesswork of an arbitrary and inefficient system of market-clearing administered prices.

This is not a good reason not to undertake price liberalization, for a market economy cannot exist without market clearing. But it makes a strong case for subsequent fiscal and/or monetary stimulus, and parallel price and wage subsidies of the sort introduced in Czechoslovakia and in the early stages of German unification, instead of wage controls and punitive taxation on wage rises (the Polish *popiwek tax*) and the abolition of price subsidies.

Both Latin American and transition economies had inefficient state enterprises, but in transition economies, moreover, they had a dominant position and were centrally planned, without the experience of adjusting to internal and international prices. Thus, the organic growth of new enterprises and the restructuring and commercialization of state enterprises were more important than their instantaneous privatization, and it was unlikely that liberalization could stimulate a rapid supply response, although it was important as a source of greater competition.

Neglect of the *repressed* nature of their inflation caused transition economies significant losses in terms of employment and output, in an economy shifting from supply-side constraints to Keynesian lack of effective demand. The overshooting implied by this approach was aggravated by fiscal and monetary policies more restrictive than intended, and by central controls over wages. The transformation recession was not, or should not have been, a surprise, but a mathematical certainty, although only a Kaleckian economist such as Laski (1990) was able to anticipate it, forecasting correctly a range of 15–20 per cent GDP fall in Poland.

23.5 Gradualism Versus Shock Therapy

Since the early stages of the transition there have been endless and lively debates on the relative merits of gradualism versus 'shock therapy' (Kolodko, 2000; Popov, 2007). In truth the scope for government choice in the transition is rather narrow in this respect, and the emphasis on this issue was misplaced. In the transition there are measures that can and must be introduced instantaneously and simultaneously, such as:

- Raise prices to market-clearing levels (see above).
- Legalize private ownership and enterprise.
- Allow all economic subjects—individuals and enterprises—free access to international trade.
- Eliminate quantitative restrictions on imports and exports.
- Unify exchange rates.
- Establish convertibility for current account transactions (not yet for capital account transactions) by residents.

All these changes can and should be made by decree, literally from one day to the next, at a stroke. Temporizing is counterproductive. At the other extreme there are measures that need time for their realization and therefore they should be given all the time that they reasonably require. Such measures include to (i) draft and introduce legislation; (ii) establish a properly functioning legal/judicial system separated from politics; (iii) break-up monopolies and establish competition; (iv) restructure productive capacity; (v) create financial markets; and (vi) establish relations of reputation and trust between government and private sector agents. It does not make sense, indeed it is counterproductive, to pretend that these changes could be accelerated, let alone be instantaneous.

The cases where there is a possible choice between shock therapy and gradualism can literally be counted on the fingers of one hand, namely trade liberalization; the elimination of subsidies; privatization; convertibility on capital account; and, especially, disinflation. I consider this an exhaustive list of policy areas where there is no absolute superiority of either gradualism or shock. Their relative merits depend on their respective costs and benefits, i.e. the trade-offs that the economy offers between government objectives, and the actual government preferences between those objectives.

For instance, alternative methods of privatization have costs and benefits (World Bank, 1996); mass privatization can be rapid and equitable, but with some associated costs: losing the fiscal revenue that would result from the sale of state assets, establishing weak corporate governance, leaving an unchanged management and poor access to new investment funds. Privatization via sales to employees and managers is less rapid and obtains some additional revenue for the budget, at the cost of less equity, here as well without managerial improvements and access to investment funds (provided not only by buyers but also through credit). Privatization via sales to the public is slower but involves greater revenue for the state budget, better governance, better management and greater access to investment funds. Sales to foreigners have the advantages of a capital inflow, better access to new technologies and investment funds, trade outlets, at the cost of losing national control and the risk of future capital losses via profit repatriation and capital sales at times of crisis. On the other hand, delaying privatization often creates unprecedented opportunities for self-appropriation of state assets by managers and party officials, and straight corruption (see for instance the 'loans for shares' scheme that gave a few Russian banks a large stake in privatization at rock-bottom prices).

Similar considerations—of costs and benefits subject to government valuation—apply also to the other four areas indicated above. Thus, dis-inflation, from hyperinflationary rates to single-digit inflation, can be tackled gradually or rapidly; the benefits of price stability must be offset against the costs of associated unemployment. External tariffs can be eliminated rapidly and unilaterally or negotiated more slowly; the positive impact on competition and prices must be offset against the possible adverse effect on government revenues and unemployment; it is no accident that countries that opened trade fast, as did Poland, Czechoslovakia and Hungary, subsequently backpedaled and reintroduced tariffs and surcharges. Subsidies can be eliminated gradually (as in the Czech Republic, in spite of Vaclav Klaus's hyper-liberal rhetoric) or quickly (as in Poland); the benefits in term of inflation control must be offset against the claim on government expenditure. Currency convertibility on capital account can be introduced quickly, gaining from capital inflows but risking their volatility, or slowly, avoiding both benefits and risks.

There is perhaps a presumption against instantaneous privatization (in comparison to the birth and growth of *de novo* enterprises), against the rapid introduction of convertibility on capital account (see the Czech koruna crisis of 1997 and the Russian rouble crisis of 1998), against the rapid lowering of trade tariffs (for the resulting loss of government revenue, as lamented even by the then head of IMF Fiscal Affairs, Vito Tanzi, in 1997). And against rapid dis-inflation: Poland's star performance is probably owing among other things to its particularly slow dis-inflation, taking 10 years to go from three digits to single-digit inflation in spite of its shock rhetoric; Slovenia also benefited from slow dis-inflation.

'Clearly a generalised and unconditional "shock therapy" approach is facile and superficial. Just as for Lenin in December 1920, *communism = electrification + Soviet power*, we can say that for the initial Washington Consensus, *transition = liberalization + privatization*. Both equations have a doubtful theoretical foundation and have borne poor results' (Nuti, 2007).

23.6 State and Institutions

On the rebound from the experience of a totalitarian state, transition leaders went to the opposite extreme of wanting to contain state activity to the minimum and destroy state institutions in order to allow the free play of market forces. Policy interventions appeared as undue interferences with market forces: in 1990 the Polish Minister for Industry and Trade, Tadeusz Syryjczyk, argued that 'The best industrial policy is no industrial policy' (Kolodko and Nuti, 1997). In the still large public sector, pending privatization, 'state desertion' of public enterprises occurred and led to continued inefficiency and to the appropriation of state assets by managers and *apparatchiks*. The weakening of state institutions made it possible for private subjects and enterprises to benefit from 'state capture', effectively a form of corruption.

In particular, the role of the state in the establishment, monitoring and regulation of institutions was neglected, in the naive belief that institutions would establish themselves, develop and regulate themselves automatically. Sachs (1993) typically asserts that 'markets spring up as soon as central planned bureaucrats vacate the field'. Markets are self-regulating (homeostatic) mechanisms in the sense of adjusting prices to demand, supply to prices, actual to desired capacity; but they are not generated automatically, nor are they self-disciplined. They are social artefacts that rely on state authority for their validation and regulation, and often for their very existence. The kind of markets that moved in when central planners left at the beginning of the transition were the wretched people who lined up in Moscow streets to offer a few individual items for sale or barter, not the fabric of a market economy. When central planners move out, unless the state creates and controls markets, they leave a vacuum, and what moves in is disorganization and chaos (Blanchard and Kremer, 1997): former backward and forward planned linkages are broken, and a supply multiplier leads to chain losses of output and unemployed inputs. Unfortunately the importance of institutions (stressed by North, 1990) came too late to influence transition policy-making.

Ellman (2012) stresses 'The need for an effective and accountable state', compared with the Friedmanite notion that 'the state is not the solution but the problem'. He quotes the World Bank's 1997 *World Development Report* recognizing that 'An effective state is vital for the provision of the goods and services—and the rules and institutions—that allow markets to flourish and people to lead healthier, happier lives. Without it, sustainable development, both economic and social, is impossible' (p. 1). And the 2002 *World Development Report* was entitled *Building institutions for markets*. Ellman regards the official acceptance of these principles, that were not new, as one of the lessons of the transition, and reviews a number of adverse effects of their earlier neglect, such as the accumulation of payment arrears in the Russian economy, a new institution generated in the transition but actually incompatible with a market economy.

23.7 The Quality of Policies

The quality of transition policies is usually judged by the speed and intensity with which a country has followed the prescriptions of the Washington Consensus, or by the indices of transition progress assessed by the EBRD in their annual *Transition Reports*, or their cumulation over time. It seems necessary, however, to consider instead the consistency and feasibility of policy targets; the choice and intensity of qualitative and quantitative policy instruments and packages with respect to those targets, the co-ordination of policies delegated to different agencies; the continuity of policies, in the sense of their inter-temporal consistency, the possible undesirable side-effects. We have already discussed the necessary overshooting of price liberalization without subsequent fiscal or monetary stimuli. Two other examples are given here: central bank independence and pension reform.

Central Bank Independence

The principle of Central Bank independence rests on very shaky theoretical foundations, namely rational expectations. These are supposed to eliminate the trade-off between unemployment and inflation, to the point that inflation can be targeted by an independent Central Bank while the government is supposed to take care of unemployment.

In the transition this principle was implemented with mixed results. Some central bank governors were not really independent (Belarus 1994–1998); others followed their own personal political agenda (in Poland in 1995 the Central Bank governor stood for election as President without resigning beforehand and resumed her position after a resounding defeat); others aimed at targets different from price stability, such as the support of state enterprises (Russia 1992).

In the fight against inflation, the Central Bank sometimes fixed real interest rates at usurious levels (Russia 1994, with a real annual rate of the order of magnitude of 200 per cent, or Poland towards the end of the 1990s and early 2000s). Such rates became a residual form of central planning that necessarily caused deflation. There was no co-ordination with fiscal policies, which involved interest rates, exchange rates and fiscal deficits all higher, with less inflation but higher unemployment and lower net exports and lower incomes, than would otherwise have been possible and desirable.

In Russia in 1998 the containment of inflation led to overvalued exchange rates, maintained thanks to high interest rates which were not consistent—given the burden of public debt—with fiscal balance. The bubble exploded in August 1998: the Russian government defaulted in spite of the massive financial support of the IMF, the World Bank and the G8; the banks that had sold credit default swaps to cover investors against the risk of devaluation were unable to meet their obligations; those investors who were not favoured by the government with the early redemption of government bonds lost most of their investment; and the rouble was massively devalued.

A policy of excessively high real interest rates naturally encouraged the postponement of payments of purchases, wages and taxes on the part of enterprises, and eventually the postponement of all payments (including salaries and pensions) on the part of the government, also in view of the IMF unwisely setting limits on the government deficit in cash instead of on an accruals basis. This form of de-monetization and accumulation of payment arrears, which in Russia reportedly reached something like 40 per cent of industrial transactions, was an unnecessary recessionary factor.

Pension Reform

Imagine that a PAYG pension system is introduced where there was none before. Pensions begin to be paid instantly, out of the current contributions of those currently employed, while making sure, however, that the following condition is continuously satisfied:

$$p.P = a.w.L,$$

where p is the average pension, P are the old age pensioners, w is the average wage, L are those currently employed, and a is the fraction of their wage that they contribute to the pension system. As long as:

$$a = p.P / w.L = (p / w).(P / L),$$

the system is balanced, does not absorb any resources from the state budget and can be deemed to 'yield' pensioners a rate of return equal to the growth rate of the wage bill. Certainly it is like a Ponzi scheme, in that payments out are funded by payments in. However, it is a viable Ponzi scheme, in that there are always new depositors (as long as there are some current employees), withdrawals are restricted (to pensioners, monthly) and are orderly (i.e. not exceeding new payments in). Population ageing can be anticipated, dealt with by prior accumulation of reserves, or by raising pension contributions, by lowering pensions or extending the retirement age.

A capitalized, fully funded, defined contributions system, by definition, does not cost anything to the budget—until there is a serious financial crisis in which the state cannot leave the elderly destitute. It yields whatever rate of return is earned by the investment of employee contributions; it promotes 'choice' and the development of financial markets. However, the switch from the first to the second pension system has an *unnecessary cost*, i.e. the emergence of a pension debt that—as long as the equilibrium condition mentioned above is satisfied—could otherwise remain conveniently buried forever, until the end of the world.

A PAYG system has an implicit hidden debt, equal to the present value of the pension rights already matured by current employees and pensioners, but such a debt only has to be paid if there is a transition to a capitalized, fully funded, defined contribution system (see Chap. 9 of Eatwell et al., 2000; Barr and Diamond, 2008).

Paradoxically, the reversal of such a reform, with a return to PAYG (partial or full, temporary or permanent), would free fiscal resources equivalent to the pension contributions of those currently employed for the entire period during which the reversal lasts (see the recent examples of Poland, Hungary, and other transition economies), without resorting to unnecessary and illegal confiscation of pension funds already accumulated.

23.8 The Current Crisis

The global crisis of 2007 to date struck transition economies in the middle of a process of rapid growth and robust catching up with the rest of Europe. In 2000–2007, central-eastern Europe grew at an average yearly rate of 6.3 per cent, south-eastern Europe at an average of 5.0 per cent, and the CIS at 8.3 per cent, while the EU-15 grew at an average of 2.6 per cent, thus leading to progress in convergence towards average EU-15 income levels, from 39 per cent in 1995 to 57 per cent in 2005 (Connolly, 2010). The crisis hit them: (1) *with a 1-year delay* compared to the global economy, in the last quarter of 2008 after the collapse of Lehman Brothers (simply because of the relative under-development of their financial systems, for they were not involved in the sub-prime crisis); (2) *with particular intensity*, not so much compared to other country groups but rather with respect to their earlier performance before the crisis and especially contrasting with previous forecasts of their performance. Against this background, therefore, the actual income falls (with the exception of Poland in the EU, Albania and Azerbaijan, with positive though slow growth in 2009) are an under-estimate of the impact of the global crisis in the region. What counts is the *deceleration* (i.e. the growth rate decrease) involved; and (3) was followed by a *more rapid recovery* compared to the rest of Europe (though not as fast as other emerging countries), resuming the earlier convergence process with the EU-15 but still with modest and intermittent progress. There has been a great diversity among these countries, depending on their economic policies and in particular their exchange rate regime, their dependence on foreign trade, and their integration in global financial markets.

The Bruegel-WIIW (2010) report gives great importance to the exchange rate regime: floating rates have fared better than fixed. This is true—with two qualifications. First, a floating exchange rate can maintain international competitiveness through devaluation—up to a point, for competitive devaluations make every competitor worse-off. If trade flows are sufficiently elastic and there is appropriate spare capacity, this improves trade balances. However, devaluation raises the value of all debt denominated in foreign exchange—which is most of it in these countries, in view of higher interest rates in a fairly stable domestic currency and the difficulty of borrowing in domestic currency. Thus, devaluation may turn private and public loans into sub-primes, raising both the risk of default and interest rates.

A fixed exchange rate does not have this negative impact on debt, but loses international competitiveness and causes unemployment, and is still exposed to the risk of sudden devaluation, all the more damaging as it is less expected; the very prospect of a possible devaluation may raise interest rate spreads and the price of Credit Default Swaps. Every exchange rate regime has both costs and benefits, but there is no regime that protects a country fully from a crisis.

Second, the orthodox 'bi-polar' view of exchange rates typified by Fischer (2001), namely that a fixed or adjustable peg should be avoided in favour of either a flexible or hyper-fixed regime (Currency Boards, or the unilateral adoption of a foreign currency), has been falsified by the transition countries in the economic crisis. In particular the Baltic states have suffered greatly—from the straitjacket of a hyper-fixed misaligned parity—in terms of output and interest rates, and from the alternative 'internal' devaluation in the form of a severe deflation, which was forced upon them as the only remedy to restore competitiveness.

The EU has not allowed its members and accession candidates to adopt unilateral euroization, but has allowed Currency Boards (e.g. Bulgaria, Latvia), inexplicably because their success is subject to the achievement of at least the fiscal and monetary convergence conditions required before adopting the euro. A Currency Board simply reduces the probability of a crisis at the very considerable cost of making the crisis catastrophic if and when it occurs (as in Argentina in 2002).

The adoption of a hyper-liberal economic system, which had partly contributed to the transformation recession, subsequently facilitated their integration in the European economy, their growth and convergence. Openness to trade and dependence on external finance made them particularly vulnerable in 2009, with the collapse of world trade (the first episode of de-globalization since global integration resumed its course after the last War) and the slowdown and often the reversal of capital flows (often referred to as their 'sudden stop'). There was also the impact of worsening terms of trade, which on average was almost as large as that of the reduction in trade volume, and worse for primary products exporters (primarily Russia, Azerbaijan and Kazakhstan).

Financial integration promoted growth and convergence, but in the crisis, it became a channel for contagion. Large capital inflows (flowing 'downhill' in this case, not 'uphill' from emerging to advanced economies as is often the case globally, reaching 11 per cent of their GDP before the crisis) made these countries vulnerable to flow reversals. Moreover, the composition of capital inflows in many transition economies was often inappropriate, focusing on real estate and financial services rather than on manufacturing tradeables.

Transition economies on average had a high share of foreign ownership of banks, growing especially in 1999–2001 from an average 40 per cent to over 70 per cent (except Slovenia), mostly by EU-15 groups, approaching 100 per cent in some countries of Central-Eastern Europe. Foreign banks provided personnel, know how, funds, credibility and expanded the volume of credit. At the beginning of the global crisis, however, in a framework of lower capital inflows, these countries suffered initially from the frequent capital repatriation by foreign banks, also because national government support for EU-15 banks was not extended to their eastern operations. This was a typical prisoner's dilemma, i.e. there was a collective advantage if all banks kept lending, an individual advantage for one bank that did not while all the others did, and a collective loss if all banks withdrew. However, the EBRD and the IMF provided funds and incentives that kept this adverse development under control through the European Bank Co-ordination Initiative (the so-called 'Vienna Initiative') between international banking groups, home and host-country authorities, IFIs and the EU (see the EBRD's *Transition Report*, 2009). The Initiative is being replicated in 2012, with lower prospects of success.

The Bruegel-WIIW (2010) report stresses the need for regulation and supervision of financial markets, such as constraints on leverage, regulation of derivatives, better capitalization, counter-cyclical macroeconomic policies, Glass-Steagall-type legislation, consumer protection, transaction taxes, provisions for systemic risk. That all this was needed was already well known before the crisis, except that the hyper-liberal approach that had dominated the global economy since the late 1980s shaped the financial systems of transition countries even more forcefully than those of advanced countries.

Those transition economies that joined the EU did not—with the exception of Slovenia and to some extent Estonia—adopt the institutions of the European Social Model; it was not part of the institutional convergence required by the EU of new members. This resulted in the inadequacy of social safety nets, to protect the population from unemployment, poverty, illness and old age. Such inadequacy raised the social cost of the economic crisis when it happened and disabled some of the mechanisms that dampen economic decline (they are usually called 'automatic stabilizers', improperly because they can slow down the decline but cannot reverse it on their own).

On the positive side, the same deep and possibly premature integration with the global real and financial economy is bound to lead to economic recovery in these countries if and when—sooner or later—the global economy bounces back.

Bibliography

Aslund, A. (2000). *The Myth of Output Collapse after Communism*, Washington, DC: Carnegie Institute.

Barr, N. and Diamond, P. (2008). *Reforming Pensions: Principles and Policy Choices*, New York and Oxford: Oxford University Press.

Blanchard, O. and Kremer, M. (1997). Disorganization, *The Quarterly Journal of Economics*, Vol. 112(4), 1091–1126.

Bruegel-WIIW Expert Group on Central-Eastern Europe (2010). *Whither Growth in Central and Eastern Europe? Policy lessons for an integrated Europe*, Brussels and Vienna, June.

Connolly, R. (2010). The determinants of the economic crisis in emerging Europe, CREES, University of Birmingham, December.

Eatwell, J., Ellman, M., Karlsson, M., Nuti, D.M. and Shapiro, J. (2000). *Soft Budgets, Hard Choices: the Future of the Welfare State in Central Eastern Europe*, London: IPPR.

EBRD (2009, various years). *Transition Report*, London: European Bank for Reconstruction and Development (annual publication since 1994).

Ellman, M. (2012). What did the study of transition economies contribute to mainstream economics?, JACES Conference Paper, June.

Fischer, S. (2001). Exchange Rate Regimes: Is the Bipolar View Correct?, *Journal of Economic Perspectives*, Vol. 15(2), Spring.

Hare, P. and Hughes, G. (1991). Competitiveness and Industrial Restructuring in Czechoslovakia, Hungary and Poland', *CEPR Discussion Paper* No. 543, London, April.

Kolodko, G.W. (2000). *From Shock to Therapy. The Political Economy of Postsocialist Transformation*, Oxford and New York: Oxford University Press.

Kolodko, G.W. and Nuti, D.M. (1997). The Polish Alternative—Old myths, hard facts and new strategies in the successful Polish economic transformation, *UNU/WIDER Research for Action series* no. 33, Helsinki, May.

Kornai, J. (1980). *Economics of Shortage*, 2 Vols, Amsterdam: North Holland Pub Co.
Laski, K. (1990). The stabilisation plan for Poland, *Wirtschaftpolitische Blotter* No. 5, 37 Jg., 444–57.
Lavigne, M. (1991). *International Political Economy and Socialism*, Cambridge: Cambridge University Press.
Mundell, R.A. (1997). The great contractions in transition economies, in Blejer, Mario I. and Skreb, Marko (eds), *Macroeconomic Stabilisation in Transition Economies*, Cambridge: Cambridge University Press, pp. 73–99.
North, D.C. (1990). *Institutions, Institutional Change and Economic Performance*, Cambridge: Cambridge University Press.
Nuti, D.M. (1986). Hidden and repressed inflation in Soviet-type economies: definitions, measurements and stabilization, *Contributions to Political Economy*, 5, 37–82.
——— (2007). Managing Transition Economies, in White, Stephen, Batt, Judy and Lewis, Paul (Eds), *Developments in Central and East European Politics*, No. 4, Durham, NC: Duke University Press.
Popov, V. (2007). Shock therapy versus gradualism: lessons from transition economies after 15 years of reforms, *Comparative Economic Studies*, 49, 1–31.
Sachs, J. (1993). *Poland's Jump to the Market Economy*, Cambridge, MA: MIT Press.
Shleifer, A. and Treisman, D. (2000). *On the Road without a Map, Political Tactics and Economic Reform in Russia*, Cambridge, MA: MIT Press.
World Bank (1996). *From Plan to Market. World Development Report*, Oxford and New York: Oxford University Press.
——— (1997). *The State in a Changing World.* World Development Report, Vol. 1, Washington, DC: World Bank.
——— (2000). *Making Transition Work for Everyone: Poverty and Inequality in Europe and Central Asia*, Washington, DC: World Bank.
——— (2002). *Building Institutions for Markets.* World Development Report, Washington, DC: World Bank.

Selected Bibliography of Domenico Mario Nuti[1]

Monographs and Multi-Authored Books

Report on Poland, The World Bank, Washington DC, 1988 (main author).

The Economics of Participation, IRTI-Islamic Development Bank, Eminent Scholars' Lectures Series, No. 11, Jeddah, 1995.

Transformation and Integration: Shaping the Future of Central Eastern Europe (with John Eatwell, Michael Ellman, Mats Karlsson, Judith Shapiro), IPPR, London 1995. Slovenian Edition, *Iz Tranzicije v Evropsko Povezovanje*, Ljubljana, 1996.

Not 'Just Another Accession' - Political Economy of EU Enlargement to the East (with John Eatwell, Michael Ellman, Mats Karlsson, Judith Shapiro), IPPR, London 1997. Bulgarian Edition, Friedrich Ebert Stiftung, Sofia, 1998. Czech and Polish editions, 1999.

Employee Ownership in Privatisation: Lessons from Central and Eastern Europe (with Felix FitzRoy, Derek Jones, Mark Klinedinst, Gyorgy Lajtai, Niels Mygind, Charles Rock, Milica Uvalic, Daniel Vaughan-Whitehead), Experts' Policy Report, ILO-CEET, Budapest, 1998. Russian Edition, Budapest, 1999.

[1] The Bibliography was originally prepared by Mario Nuti and was available on his Blog. However, there were some missing papers or publications that have been added. The Bibliography does not include Nuti's early papers on economic development and some written only in Polish.

© The Author(s), under exclusive license to Springer Nature Switzerland AG 2023

S. Estrin, M. Uvalic (eds.), *Collected Works of Domenico Mario Nuti, Volume I*, Studies in Economic Transition, https://doi.org/10.1007/978-3-031-12334-4

Soft Budgets, Hard Choices: the Future of the Welfare State in Central Eastern Europe (with John Eatwell, Michael Ellman, Mats Karlsson, Judith Shapiro), IPPR, London 2000. Bulgarian (2001) and Estonian (2002) translations.

Edited Volumes

Socialist Economics: Selected Readings (with Alec Nove), Baltimore, Penguin Books, 1972, reprinted in 1974, 1977.

V. K. Dmitriev: Economic Essays on Value, Competition and Utility. Translated from Russian (V. K. Dmitriev, *Ekonomicheskie Ocherki,* Moscow, 1904) by D. Fry. Edited with an Introduction, A Biographical Note and an Editorial Note by D. M. Nuti (pp. 7 – 35). Cambridge, Cambridge University Press, 1974. Re-published in Russian, with the original text, Moscow 2001.

Il paradigma polacco della transizione (in Italian, *The Polish Paradigm of the Transition*), Special issue of *Europa Europe*, Fondazione Gramsci, vol. III, no. 2, 1994.

Post-Communist Transition to a Market Economy. Lessons and Challenges (with Milica Uvalic), Ravenna, Longo Editore, 2003.

La transizione in Europa orientale e in Russia e l'integrazione europea, Editor of the monographic part of the Report (pp. 21-228); in Roberto Gualtieri e José Luis Rhi-Sausi (Eds), (2009). *L'Europa e la Russia a vent'anni dall'89,* Rapporto 2009 sull'Integrazione Europea, Fondazione Istituto Gramsci e CeSPI, 2009.

Journal Articles, Book Chapters, Working Papers

1967–1980

Material incentive schemes and the choice of techniques in Soviet industry, *Australian Economic Papers,* Vol. 5, No. 8, June 1967, 183-198.

On incomes policy, *Science and Society*, Vol. 33, No. 4 (Fall-Winter) 1969, 415-425.

The degree of monopoly in the Kaldor-Mirrlees growth model, *Review of Economic Studies*, Vol. 35, No. 2, 1969, 257-260.

Investment reforms in Czechoslovakia, *Soviet Studies*, Vol. 21, No. 3, January 1970, 360-70.

Capitalism, socialism and steady growth, *Economic Journal*, 1970, Vol. 80, 32-57.
The evolution of Polish investment planning, *Jahrbuch der Wirtschaft Osteuropas*, 1971, Band 3, 395-438.
On the truncation of production flows, *Kyklos*, 1973, Vol. 26, No. 3, 485-496.
On the rates of return on investment, *Kyklos*, 1974, Vol. 27, No. 2, 345-369.
The wage-interest frontier, *Zeitschrift fur Nationalekonomie*, 35 (Heft 1-2), 1975, 177-186.
Large corporations and the reform of Polish industry, *Jahrbuch der Wirtschaft Osteuropas*, Band 7, 1977, 345-405.
The transformation of labour values into production prices and the Marxian theory of exploitation, in J. Schwartz (Ed.), *The Subtle Anatomy of Capitalism*, Santa Monica, California, Goodyear, 1977. In Italian: "La trasformazione dei valori in prezzi di produzione e la teoria Marxiana dello sfruttamento", in R. Panizza e S. Vicarelli (Eds), *Valori e Prezzi nella Teoria di Marx*, Einaudi, Torino, 1981, pp. 211-263.
Price and composition effects and the pseudo-Production Function, *Revue d'Economie Politique*, Vol. 2 (March-April) 1977, 232-243.
Investment, interest and degree of centralization in Maurice Dobb's theory of the socialist economy, *Cambridge Journal of Economics*, Vol. 2, No. 2, Maurice Dobb Memorial Issue, 1978, 191-202.
The contradictions of socialist economies. A Marxian interpretation, in R. Miliband and J. Saville (Eds.), *The Socialist Register 1979*, London, The Merlin Press, 1979, pp. 228-73. Reprinted in Italian (as a shorter paper): Le contraddizioni delle economie socialiste: una interpretazione marxiana, in *Quaderni dell'Istituto di Economia dell'Universita' di Siena*, No. 3, May 1979; in *Dissenso e Democrazia nei Paesi dell'Est*, Vallecchi, Florence, 1980; and in Mario Telò (Ed.), *Crisi e piano*, De Donato, 1981, pp. 171-190; as a book in Swedish, *Motsattningar i de Socialistiska Ekonomierna*, Kristianstad, Zenit Haften, 1981; partly reprinted in K. Martin (ed.), *Strategies of Economic Development: Readings in the Political Economy of Industrialisation*, Macmillan 1991, London and Basingstoke, pp. 233-262.

1981–1990

Socialism on earth, *Cambridge Journal of Economics*, Vol. 5, No. 4 (December 1981), 391-403.
Poland: socialist renewal and economic collapse, *The New Left Review*, I/130, November-December 1981, 23-36.

The Polish crisis: economic factors and constraints, in R. Miliband and J. Saville (Eds) (1981), *The Socialist Register 1981*, London, The Merlin Press, 104-43.

Polish Projects for Economic Reform 1980-81, *Socialist Economic Review*, 1981.

Industrial Enterprises in Poland, 1973-80: Economic Policies and Reforms, in: Ian Jeffries (Ed.), *The Industrial Enterprise in Eastern Europe*, Eastbourne and New York, Praeger, 1981, pp. 39-62.

Outlook for Socialist Economies - A Roundtable Discussion (Wladimir Brus, Julian Cooper, Michael Ellman, Domenico Mario Nuti, chair M. Johnstone), *Marxism Today*, February 1982, 22-28.

Poland's Economic Mess, *Marxism Today*, March 1982, 28-29.

Economic crisis in Eastern Europe: prospects and repercussions, EUI Working Paper No. 26, European University Institute, Florence, 1984a.

Mergers and disequilibrium in labour-managed economies, EUI Working Paper No. 113, European University Institute, Florence, 1984b. Also in *Jahrbuch der Wirtschaft Osteuropas*, 1984, Vol. 11, No. 1, 73-90.

Political and economic fluctuations in the socialist system, EUI Working Paper No. 156, European University Institute, Florence, 1985.

Economic and financial evaluation of investment projects: general principles and EC procedures, EUI Working Paper No. 119, European University Institute, Florence 1984; also in Giancarlo Gandolfo and Ferruccio Marzano (Eds), *Keynesian Theory, Planning Models and Quantitative Economics: Essays in Memory of Vittorio Marrama*. Vol. I, Milan, Giuffre, 1987a, Pubblicazioni della Facoltà di economia e commercio 44, pp. 457-478.

A critique of Orwell's oligarchic collectivism as an economic system. EUI Working Paper No. 161, European University Institute, Florence 1985; also in *Coexistence: A Review of East-West and development issues*, Vol. 22, July 1985, pp. 151-163.

Economic planning in market economies: scope, instruments, institutions, EUI Working Paper No. 180, European University Institute, Florence, 1985; also in P. Nolan and Susy Paine (Eds.), *Rethinking Socialist Economics*, London, Croom Helm, 1986, pp. 83-98.

The share economy: plausibility and viability of Weitzman's model, EUI Working Paper No. 194, European University Institute, Florence, 1985; also in S. Hedlund (Ed.), *Incentives and Economic Systems*, London and Sidney, Croom Helm, 1987, pp. 267-290.

Systemic aspects of investment and employment in Soviet-type economies, in D. Lane (Ed.), *Labour and Employment in the USSR*, London, The Harvester Press, 1985, pp. 112-121.

Commercio estero, integrazione e aggiustamento macroeconomico nei paesi dell'Europa Orientale, *Moneta ed Economia Internazionale*, Torino, Cassa di Risparmio di Torino, 1985, pp. 165-182.

Hidden and repressed inflation in Soviet-type economies: definitions, measurements and stabilisation, EUI Working Paper No. 200, European University Institute, Florence, 1985. Re-published in *Contributions to Political Economy*, Volume 5, No. 1, March 1986, 37-82; and in Christopher Davis and Wojciech Charemza (Eds), *Models of Disequilibrium and Shortage in Centrally Planned Economies*, London and New York, Chapman and Hall, 1989, pp. 101-146.

Michal Kalecki's contributions to the theory and practice of socialist planning, EUI Working Paper No. 227, European University Institute, Florence, 1986. A shorter version re-published under the same title in *Cambridge Journal of Economics*, Vol. 10, 1986, 333-353. Reprinted in Malcolm C. Sawyer (Ed.), *The Legacy of Michal Kalecki*, Intellectual Legacies in Modern Economics 5, Vol 2, Cheltenham, Edward Elgar, 2000, pp. 137-157.

Codetermination, profit-sharing and full employment, EUI Working Paper No. 228, European University Institute, Florence, 1986. Also in Derek Jones and Jan Svejnar (Eds), *Advances in the Economic Analysis of Participatory and Labor-Managed Firms*, Vol. 3, Greenwich and London, JAI Press, 1988, pp. 169-183.

Information, expectations and economic planning, EUI Working Paper No. 240, European University Institute, Florence, 1986.

Profit-sharing and employment: claims and overclaims, EUI Working Paper No. 245, European University Institute, Florence 1986; also in *Industrial Relations*, Vol. 26, No. 1, Berkeley, Winter 1987b, 18-29.

Financial innovation under market socialism, EUI Working Paper No. 285, European University Institute, Florence, 1987; also as "Feasible financial innovation under market socialism" in C. Kessides, T. King, D. Mario Nuti and K. Sokil (Eds), *Financial Reform in Socialist Economies*, Washington DC, EDI-World Bank, 1989, pp. 85-105.

Cycles in socialist economies, in John Eatwell, Murray Milgate and Peter Newman (Eds), *The New Palgrave: A Dictionary of Economics*, Vol. I, Macmillan, London, 1st edition, 1987, pp. 744 – 746; also in Palgrave Macmillan (Ed.), 1987, *The New Palgrave Dictionary of Economics*.

Perestroika: transition between central planning and market socialism, *Economic Policy*, Vol. 3, No. 7, 1988, 353-389.

On traditional cooperatives and James Meade's labour-capital discriminating partnerships, EUI Working Paper No. 337, European University Institute, Florence, 1988; also in Derek Jones and Jan Svejnar (Eds.), *Advances in the Economic Analysis of Participatory and Labor-Managed Firms*, Vol. 4, Greenwich and London, JAI Press, 1992, 1-26.

Competitive valuation and efficiency of capital investment in the socialist economy, *European Economic Review*, Vol. 32, No. 2–3, March 1988, pp. 459–464.

Economic relations between the European Community and CMEA, EUI Working Paper No. 360, European University Institute, Florence, 1988.

Remonetisation and capital markets in the reform of centrally planned economies, EUI Working Paper No. 361, European University Institute, Florence 1988; also in *European Economic Review*, Vol. 33, No. 2–3, March 1989, pp. 427–438.

Poland: Economic Problems and Prospects of Institutional Change, CREES-Birmingham University, Annual Conference, Cumberland Lodge, Windsor Great Park, 24-26 June 1988.

The new Soviet cooperatives: advances and limitations, EUI Working Paper No. 362, European University Institute, Florence, 1988; also in *Economic and Industrial Democracy*, 1989, Vol. 10, No. 3, 311-327, and in *Revue d'Etudes Comparatives Est-Ouest*, Vol. 20, No. 3, 93-109.

The enterprise between central planning and market socialism: a discussion, in *Economic Reforms in the European Centrally Planned Economies*, Proceedings of a Symposium conducted in association with The Vienna Institute for Comparative Economic Studies, United Nations Economic Commission for Europe (UNECE), 1989, Economic Studies No. 1, New York, pp. 145-153.

The case for Western aid to Central Eastern Europe, paper presented at the Conference "An East European Recovery Programme" held at the EUI, Florence, on 19-20 February 1990.

Basic Income: Costs and Benefits of Alternative Approaches, Conference on "Economic Democracy and Citizenship Income", European University Institute, Florence 19-22 September 1990. Italian version published as Reddito di Base: Costi e Benefici di alcuni approcci alternativi, in *Politiche del Lavoro*, No. 14 (Special Issue on Economics of Participation), Milan, Franco Angeli, 1991, pp. 199-212.

1991–2000

Progress in trade reforms, missing links, convertibility: A discussion, in UN-Economic Commission for Europe, *Reforms in Foreign Economic Relations of Eastern Europe and the Soviet Union*, Economic Studies No. 2, New York 1991, pp. 49-52.

Contribution to a Round Table on *Five Years of Perestroika: Results, Problems, Prospects,* in UN-Economic Commission for Europe Discussion Papers, Vol. 1 (1991), No. 2, pp. 11-15, 31.

Sequencing and credibility in economic reform; in A. B. Atkinson and R. Brunetta, *Economics for the New Europe*, MacMillan, 1991.

How quickly should convertibility be introduced? Comment, in John Williamson (Ed), *Currency Convertibility in Eastern Europe*, Washington D.C., Institute for International Economics, September, pp. 48-55.

Privatisation of socialist economies: general issues and the Polish case, in Hans Blommestein and Michael Marrese (Eds), *Transformation of Planned Economies: Property Rights Reform and Macroeconomic Stability*, OECD, Paris, 1991, pp. 51-67; also in Thomas Clarke and Christos Pitelis (Eds), *The Political Economy of Privatisation*, London, Routledge, 1993, pp. 373-390.

A comment on Yugoslavia, in Michael Bruno, Stanley Fischer, Elhanan Helpman, Nissan Liviathan (Eds), *Lessons of Economic Stabilisation and its Aftermath*, Boston, MIT Press, 1991, pp. 389-392.

Limiti e potenziale dell'impresa cooperativa, Two unpublished conference papers combined, Lega Nazionale Cooperative e Mutue, Rome 13 March 1991 and AGCI Toscana, Florence 6 April 1991.

Tibor Liska's entrepreneurial socialism, in Marguerite Mendell and Daniel Sallee (Eds.), *The Legacy of Karl Polanyi. Market, State and Society at the End of the Twentieth Century*, New York, St. Martin's Press, 1991, pp. 215-230.

Stabilization and sequencing in the reform of socialist economies, in Simon Commander (Ed.), *Managing Inflation in Socialist Economies in transition,* EDI Seminar Series, World Bank, Washington DC, 1991, pp. 155-174. French version, 1992.

Monetary and exchange rate policies during Eastern Europe's transition: Some lessons from further East (with Maxwell J. Fry), *Oxford Review of Economic Policy*, Vol. 8, No. 1, Macroeconomics of Transition in Eastern Europe, Spring 1992, 27-43.

On Stanislaw Lem's model of populist localism, French version published in *Economies et Sociétés*, No. 4-5-6, Série G (Economie Planifiée), Special issue on "Transition en Europe de l'Est", No. 44, 1992, 367-381.

Market socialism: the model that might have been - but never was, in A. Aslund (Ed.) *Market Socialism or the Restoration of Capitalism?*, Cambridge, Cambridge University Press, 1992, pp. 17-31; Italian version: "Il socialismo di mercato: Il modello che avrebbe potuto esserci, ma che non c'e' mai stato", in Alberto Chilosi (Ed.), *L'economia del periodo di transizione - Dal socialismo di tipo sovietico all'economia di mercato*, Il Mulino, 1992, pp. 143-158.

Privatisation of Socialist Economies: General Issues, in *Privatization in Eastern Europe*, Vienna 1992, Proceedings of the Conference "Privatization: How to Use This Instrument for Economic Reform in Eastern Europe", Friedrich Ebert Stiftung and Renner Institut, Vienna, 17-18 November 1990, pp. 21-35, including "Free Distribution?", "Discussion", pp. 42-44; "Conclusion", pp. 198-202.

The role of the banking sector in the process of privatisation, *Economic Papers* No. 98, Commission of the European Communities - DGII, Brussels, 1992; also in T. Clarke (Ed.), *International Privatization: Strategies and Practices*, 1994, Chapter 10, Walter de Gruyter, pp. 187-202.

Privatization in Hungary, in Michael Keren and Gur Ofer (Eds), *Trials of Transition - Economic Reform in the Former Communist Bloc,* Boulder-San Francisco-Oxford, Westview Press, 1992, pp. 193-202.

Post-Soviet issues: stabilisation, trade and money (with Jean Pisani-Ferry), *Economic Papers* No. 93, Commission of the European Communities - DGII, Brussels, May 1992, pp. 1-31

Economic Consequences of the Soviet August Revolution and Western Response, *Rivista di Politica Economica*, 1992.

Lessons from stabilisation and reform in central and eastern Europe, *Economic Papers* No. 92, Commission of the European Communities - DGII, Brussels, May 1992; also as "Lessons from the stabilization programmes of Central and Eastern European Countries, 1989-1991" in L. Somogyi (Ed.), *The Political Economy of the Transition Process in Eastern Europe*, Edward Elgar, Aldershot and Brookfield, 1993, pp. 40-66.

Alternative employment and payment systems, as "Profit-sharing" entry in Gyorgy Szell, *Concise Encyclopedia of Participation and Co-Management*, Berlin, New York, Walter de Gruyter, 1992, pp. 680-686; also in S. Bowles, H. Gintis and B. Gustafsson (Eds), *Democracy and Markets: Participation,*

Accountability and Efficiency, Cambridge, Cambridge University Press, 1993, pp. 40-47.

Dallo Stato del Benessere allo Stato del Lavoro, National Seminar of PDS-Area lavoro e riforme sociali on "Le ragioni dell'equità - Principi e politiche per lo stato sociale", Rome, 6-8 May 1993.

Central Europe: the way forward (with Richard Portes), in Richard Portes (Ed.), *Economic Transformation in Central Europe. A Progress Report*, European Communities Official Publications and CEPR, Brussels and London, 1993, pp. 1-20.

Monetary Dis-integration: Ex-Yugoslavia, Ex-CSFR and Ex-USSR, Invited Lecture, Annual meeting of the Nationalokonomische Gesellschaft - Austrian Economic Association, Karl Franzen University, Graz, 14-16 April 1993.

Privatization of financial institutions, in Peter Newman, Murrey Milgate and John Eatwell (Eds.), *The New Palgrave Dictionary of Money and Finance*, Vol. 3, 1993, London and New York, The Macmillan Press and Stockton Press, pp. 212-214.

Socialist banking, in Peter Newman, Murrey Milgate and John Eatwell (Eds.), *The New Palgrave Dictionary of Money and Finance*, Vol. 3, London and New York, The Macmillan Press and Stockton Press, 1993, pp. 474-479.

Stabilizzazione e transizione: il prototipo polacco (in Italian, Stabilisation and transition: the Polish prototype) in Domenico M. Nuti (Ed.), *Il paradigma polacco della transizione* (in Italian, *The Polish Paradigm of the Transition*), Special issue of *Europa Europe*, Fondazione Gramsci, vol. III, no. 2, 1994, pp.17-46.

The Restoration of Markets in East-Central Europe, in Marguerite Mendell and Klaus Nielsen (Eds), *Europe: Central and East,* Vol 6, *Critical Perspectives on Historic Issues,* 1995, pp. 74-89.

Riflessioni sulla disoccupazione: che fare?, *Il Nuovo Osservatore*, Year X, No. 4, April 1993, 3-8.

Economic inertia in the transitional economies of central eastern Europe, in Milica Uvalić, Efisio Espa and Jochen Lorentzen (Eds.), *Impediments to the Transition in Eastern Europe*, European Policy Studies, No. 1, European University Institute, Florence, 1993, pp. 25-49.

Lessons from stabilization and reform in central and eastern Europe, in L. Somogyi (Ed.) *The Political Economy of the Transition Process in Eastern Europe*, 1993, Aldershot and Brookfield: Edward Elgar, pp. 40-66.

L'allargamento dell'Unione Europea verso l'Est, *Europa/Europe*, Vol. III, No. 1, pp. 113-150.

Indicizzazioni e scala mobile: costi e benefici (Costs and benefits of wage indexation, in Italian), in F. Roberto Pizzuti (Ed.), *L'economia italiana dagli anni Settanta agli anni Novanta - Pragmatismo, Disciplina, Saggezza convenzionale*, Milano, McGraw-Hill Libri Italia srl, 1994.

The impact of systemic transition on the European Community, CIS-ME London Business School Discussion Papers No. 10, May 1994; also in Stephen Martin (Ed.), *The Construction of Europe. A Festschrift in Honour of Emile Noel*, Kluwer Academic, Dortrecht, 1994, Chapter 8, pp. 143-181; reprinted in Paul G. Hare and Junior R. Davis, *Transitions to the Market Economy - Critical Perspective on the World Economy* Vol. 4, Taylor and Francis, 1997.

Employeeism: corporate governance and employee share ownership in transition economies, Conference paper, 1995; published in Mario I. Blejer and Marko Skreb (Eds.), *Macroeconomic Stabilization in Transition Economies*, Cambridge, Cambridge University Press, 1997, pp. 126-154; Italian translation: Employeeism: il governo aziendale e la proprietà azionaria dei dipendenti nelle economie di transizione, in *Cooperative ed Economia Sociale a 150 Anni da Rochdale*", Atti di un Convegno del 4-6 maggio 1995, Reggio Emilia, *Unipolis* No. 1, 1996, pp. 194-229.

Mass privatisation: costs and benefits of instant capitalism, in Renzo Daviddi (Ed.), *Property Rights and Privatization*, EIPA, Maastricht, 1995, pp. 103-132.

The role of the state in post-communist economies, in: C. W. M. Naastepad and Servaas Storm (Eds), *The State and the Economic Process*, Cheltenham and Brookfield, Edward Elgar, 1996, pp. 159-176.

Efficiency, equality and enterprise democracy, in Ugo Pagano and Robert Rowthorn (Eds.) *Democracy and Efficiency in the Economic Enterprise*, WIDER and Routledge Studies in Business Organization and Networks, London and New York, Routledge, 1996, pp. 184-206.

Inflation, interest and exchange rates in the transition, *Economics of Transition*, Vol. 4, No. 1, 1996, 137-158.

European Community Response to the Transition: Aid, Trade Access, Enlargement, *Economics of Transition*, Vol. 4, No. 2, 1996, 503-511.

Post-communist mutations, *Emergo*, 7 (Winter 1996), 7-15.

Comparative Economics after the Transition, ACE Bulletin, 1997; also in *Economic Systems*, Vol. 23, No. 2, 1999, pp. 155-159.

Transitions ou Moutations - Pour une nouvelle economie politique de la transformation postcommuniste, *Revue Economique*, Vol. 48, No. 3, 1997, 719-730.

The Polish Alternative: Old Myths, Hard Facts and New Strategies in the Successful Polish Transformation (with Grzegorz W. Kolodko), *UN-WIDER Research for Action* No. 33, Helsinki, 1997; enlarged Polish version: *Polska Alternatywa: stary mity, twarde fakty, nowe strategie*, Poltext, Warsaw 1997.

Employee ownership in Polish privatisations, in Milica Uvalic and Daniel Vaughan-Whitehead (Eds), *Privatisation Surprises in Transition Economies - Employee Ownership in Central and Eastern Europe*, Aldershot, Edward Elgar, 1997, pp. 165-181.

Euro 1999? Costi e benefici dell'unificazione monetaria, *Europa-Europe*, Vol. VI, 0, 1997, 9-18

Riflessioni sull'Euro e dintorni, *Europa-Europe,* Vol. VII, 3, 1998, 45-58.

Stock and Stakes: the case for protecting stakeholders' interests, *Economic Analysis - Journal of Enterprise and Participation*, Vol. 1, No. 1, February 1998, 7-16.

Alternative pension systems: generalities and reform issues in transition economies, Conference paper, revised version published in Stephany Griffith-Jones et al., *Reforms of the Pension System and National Savings,* Working paper No. 84, Prague, 1998, Institut Ekonomie, Ceska Narodni Banka, pp. 25-41.

Making sense of the Third Way, *Business Strategy Review*, Vol. 10, No. 3, Autumn 1999, pp. 57-67; shorter Italian version: "Le nuove vie del socialismo", Europa/Europe, No. 3, 1999, 89-97.

Alternative pension systems – A comment to John Eatwell, in UN-ECE, Economic Survey of Europe, No. 3, Geneva 1999, pp. 64-66.

The Belarusian Alternative: Transition or Solely Reform, *Belarus Economic Trends*, *Quarterly Report* No. 2, April-June 1999, pp. 14-20.

The impact of privatization funds on corporate governance in mass privatisation schemes: Czech Republic, Poland, Slovenia (with Saul Estrin and Milica Uvalic), in Marko Simoneti, Saul Estrin and Andreja Bohm (Eds.) (1999), *The Governance of Privatisation Funds: Experiences of Czech Republic, Poland and Slovenia,* Ljubljana, CEEPN, Cheltenham: Edward Elgar, pp. 137-162; also as "The impact of investment funds on corporate governance in mass privatisation schemes: Czech Republic, Poland, Slovenia" in Negoslav P. Ostojić, Norman Scott (Eds.), *Recent Lessons from Transition and Privatisation – Problems of Institutions and Corporate Governance*, ECPD, Belgrade 1999, pp. 135-166; and in *MOCT-MOST*, Vol. 1, 2000, pp. 1-26.

The Polish Zloty, 1990-99: Success and Under-Performance, *American Economic Review,* May 2000, Papers and Proceedings, Vol. 90, No. 2, 53-58.

Employee Participation in Enterprise Control and Returns: Patterns, Gaps and Discontinuities, in Vojmir Franičević and Milica Uvalić (Eds), *Equality, Participation, Transition - Essays in Honour of Branko Horvat,* London and New York, Macmillan and St Martin's Press, 2000; also as Discussion Paper No. 4, CNEM-LBS, September 2000.

The Costs and Benefits of Euro-isation in Central-Eastern Europe before or instead of EMU Membership, in Sven Arndt, Heinz Handler and Dominick Salvatore (Eds), *Eastern Enlargement: The Sooner, The Better?* MPRA Paper No. 44943, Austrian Ministry for Economic Affairs and Labour, July 2000.

2001–2010

Not 'Just Another Accession', Leon Kozminski Academy of Entrepreneurship and Management (WSPiZ), Warsaw *& TIGER Distinguished Lectures Series* No.3, Warsaw, 26 April 2001.

Globalizzazione e Regionalismo, *Europa-Europe*, Vol. X, No. 8, 2001, pp. 11-23.

Belarus: a command economy without central planning, in Mario I. Blejer and Marko Skreb (Eds), *Transition: The First Decade*, Cambridge Ma., MIT Press, 2001; also in *Russian and East European Finance and Trade,* Vol. 36, No. 4 (July-August) 2000, pp. 45-79.

Albania and the euro: Economic implications of unilateral euroization, Conference Paper, Central Bank of Albania, Tirana, December 2001.

Symposium on *Exchange rate regimes in transition economies – the euroization debate.* Introduction, Guest Editor. *Economics of Transition*, Volume 10 (2) 2002, 339–342.

Costs and benefits of unilateral euroization in central eastern Europe, *The Economics of Transition*, Vol. 10, No. 2, 2002, 419-444 (Guest-Editor of Symposium on *Exchange rate regimes in transition economies – the euroization debate*, same issue); also as RECEP Working Paper, Moscow 2002. Earlier versions: The costs and benefits of Euro-isation in central-eastern Europe before or instead of EMU membership, in Mario I. Blejer and Marko Skreb, Proceedings of the 6th Dubrovnik Economic Conference, June 2000; Discussion Paper No. 8, CNEM-LBS, September 2000; Working Paper No. 340, The William Davidson Institute, University of Michigan Business School, October 2000.

Governing Incomplete Globalisation, Leon Kozminski Academy of Entrepreneurship and Management (WSPiZ) and *TIGER Working Papers*

Series No. 25, Warsaw, 2002; also in Grzegorz W. Kolodko (Ed.), *Emerging Market Economies. Globalization and Development*, Aldershot, England and Burlington, VT, USA: Ashgate Publishing Ltd, 2005.

A Comment on Leszek Balcerowicz, 'Post-communist Transition in a Comparative Perspective', Washington DC, World Bank, 8-11-2003; unedited official transcript of the event available at: http://info.worldbank.org/etools/bspan/PresentationView.asp?PID=955&EID=328

L'euro 2002: gioie e dolori, in Giuseppe Vacca (Ed.), *L'unità dell'Europa. Rapporto 2003 sull'integrazione europea*, Edizioni Dedalo, Rome 2003, pp. 9-20, and guest editor of section on "Il ruolo e la potenzialità dell'euro sul piano globale", pp. 7-168; also as a supplement to *L'Unità*, 2003.

Twelve years of transition to a market economy (with M. Uvalic), in D.M. Nuti and M. Uvalic (Eds), *Post-Communist Transition to a Market Economy. Lessons and Challenges*, Longo Editore, Ravenna, 2003, pp. 9-19.

Adopting the Euro in an Enlarged Union: An Obstacle Course, *TIGER Working Papers Series No. 38*, Warsaw, March 2003.

The Belarus economy – Suspended animation between state and markets, in Stephen White, Elena A. Korosteleva and John Lowenhardt (Eds), *Postcommunist Belarus*, Rowman and Littlefield, Lanham MD, 2004.

I sistemi economici post-comunisti, ovvero 2001 odissea nella transizione, in Bruno Jossa (Ed.), *Sistemi Economici Comparati*, Bologna, Il Mulino, 2004, pp. 167-207.

Kalecki and Keynes revisited: Two original approaches to demand-determined income – and much more besides, in Zdzislaw L. Sadowski and Adam Szeworski (Eds), *Kalecki's Economics Today*, London and New York, Routledge, 2004; paper presented at a Conference "The work of Michal Kalecki from the perspective of contemporary macroeconomics", Polish Economic Association, Warsaw, 29 September 1999.

L'introduzione dell'euro nell'Unione allargata: tempi, processi, ostacoli, in Fabio Sdogati (Ed.), *L'unificazione dell'Europa: Opportunita' dell'Unione allargata*, Bari, Progedit, 2005.

Efficiency and Distribution in the Global Economy (in Italian), *Lezioni Federico Caffè*, University of Rome La Sapienza, 2006; condensed English version Globalization Today: Incomplete, Distorted and Unfair, in Pompeo della Posta, Milica Uvalic and Amy Verdun (Eds), *Globalisation, Development and Integration*, London, Palgrave-Macmillan, 2009, pp. 326-329.

Alternative fiscal rules for the EU new members, CESifo Workshop on Euro-Area Enlargement, Munich, 26 November 2006; and TIGER-WSPiZ Discussion Papers, No. 84, Warsaw 2006.

Exchange rate policy and economic performance in the transition, Scientific Conference in Honor of Padma Desai on "Russia: Soviet Past; Present Performance and Future Prospects", Columbia University, New York, 26-27 April 2007.

The European Social Model and its Dilution as a Result of EU Enlargement (with Marilena Giannetti), *TIGER Working Papers Series No. 105*, Warsaw, July 2007; a revised and enlarged version as "The European Social Model: Is There a Third Way?", PECOB's Paper Series, No. 7, 2011.

Managing Transition Economies, in Stephen White, Judy Batt and Paul Lewis (Eds), *Developments in Central and East European Politics*, No. 4, Palgrave-Duke University Press, 2007.

Belarus: Market Socialism Prototype?, in David Lane (Ed.), *The Transformation of State Socialism: System Change, Capitalism, or Something Else?*, Basingstoke, Macmillan, 2007.

Post-socialist Transition and the Resources of Economic Thought. Keynote Address, ESHET-European Society for the History of Economic Thought, Prague, 15-15 May 2008.

Alternative Targets, Paths and Speed in Post-Socialist Transition, EACES-European Association for Comparative Economic Systems, 10th Bi-Annual Conference on "Patterns of Transition and New Agenda for Comparative Economics", Higher School of Economics, Moscow, 28-30 August 2008.

Exit Strategies, *Est-Ovest*, No. 3, 2009.

Akerlof & Shiller, Animal Spirits: A misnomer for their sound economics, 2009, *Short Notes* No. 1, Department of Public Economics, University of Rome La Sapienza.

The Former Soviet Union After Dis-Integration and Transition, International Conference "Twenty Years after the Fall – A Reconsideration of the End of Communism", Gramsci Foundation Institute, Rome 9-10 October 2009; also in: Joanna Dzwonczyk and Jerzy Kornas (Eds), *Transformacja polska - ochekiwania i rzeczywistosc* [*Polish Transformation - Expectations and Reality*], University of Economics Publishing House, Krakow, 2010, pp. 149-178.

The Impact of the Global Crisis on Transition Economies, International Conference on "Reflections on Transition: Twenty Years after the Fall of the Berlin Wall", UNU-WIDER, Helsinki, 18-19 September 2009; a shorter version published in *Economic Annals*, Faculty of Economics, University of

Belgrade, Vol. LIV, No. 181, April – June 2009, pp. 7-20; also in Italian in Giovanni Bonifati and Annamaria Simonazzi (Eds), Il ritorno dell'economia politica. Saggi in ricordo di Fernando Vianello, Donzelli, Roma 2010.

La transizione nell'economia russa, *XXI Secolo*, Enciclopedia Treccani, Rome, 2009, pp. 309-317.

A counter-factual alternative for Russia's post-socialist transition, International conference on "The Great Transformation: 1989-2029", TIGER Institute at Kozminski University, Warsaw, 3-4 April 2009; published in Polish in Grzegorz W. Kolodko and Jacek Tomkiewicz (Eds) *20 Lat Transformacji* (20 Years of Transformation), Wydawnictwa Akademickie i Profesjonalne Warsaw 2009, pp. 49-83; also as Counter-factual alternative scenarios for postsocialist transition in Grzegorz W. Kolodko and Jacek Tomkiewicz (Eds), *20 years of Transformation: Achievements, Problems and Perspectives* (2011), New York, Nova Science Publishers, pp. 165-192.

Venti anni dopo: ragioni, processi, risultati della transizione post-socialista, in Roberto Gualtieri e José Luis Rhi-Sausi (Eds), *L'Europa e la Russia a vent'anni dall'89,* Rapporto 2009 sull'Integrazione Europea, Fondazione Istituto Gramsci e CeSPI, 2009.

2011–2018

Industrial Relations at FIAT: Dr. Marchionne's Class War, *Transfer: European Review of Labour and Research,* 2011, Vol. 17, No. 2, 251-54.

Scenari possibili dopo la crisi globale, *Democrazia e Diritto*, Vol. XLIX, 2012, No. 3-4, 98-127.

Euroarea: Premature, Diminished, Divergent, Paper presented at a Conference on "Economic and Political crises in Europe and the United States", 7-9 November 2013, University of Trento

Austerity versus Development, Paper presented at the International Conference on "Management and Economic Policy for Development", Kozminski University, Warsaw, 10-11 October 2013.

Did we go about transition in the right way?, in Paul Hare and Gerard Turley (Eds), *Handbook of the Economics and Political Economy of Transition*, London and New York, Routledge, 2013, Ch. 3, pp. 48-58.

Kornai: Shortage Versus Surplus Economies, Paper presented at the Conference on "Institutions that change the World", WINIR (World Interdisciplinary

Network for Institutional Research), Greenwich, London, 11-14 September 2014, published in *Acta Oeconomica,* Vol. 68, 2018, pp. 155-159.

An Overview of the Transition, Founding Conference, Centre for Research of Economic and Socio-cultural Development of CIS Countries, Central and Eastern Europe, St. Petersburg, 26-27 June 2014.

Seismic Faults in the European Union, 2016, Conference paper, Rome, revised in 2017.

Sul Ristagno Secolare (On Secular Stagnation, in Italian), in Felice Roberto Pizzuti (Ed.), *Il Rapporto Sullo Stato Sociale 2017,* Sapienza Università Editrice, Rome, 2017.

The Rise and Fall of Socialism, DOC-RI (Dialogue Of Civilisations - Research Institute), Conference on "Inequality: Economic Models and Russian October 1917 Revolution in Historical Perspective", Berlin 23-24 October 2017, published in May 2018 at: https://doc-research.org/2018/05/rise_and_fall_of_socialism/; also in Italian: "Ascesa e Caduta del Socialismo", May 2018.

The Chinese alternative, *Acta Oeconomica,* Vol. 69, 2019, pp. 31-47.

Miscellaneous

Domenico Mario Nuti (1937-), in Philip Arestis and Malcolm C. Sawyer (Eds.) *A Biographical Dictionary of Dissenting Economists.* London, Elgar Publishing, 1992, pp. 401-409.

Blaug M. (1983, 1986, 1999). *Who's Who in Economics. A Biographical Dictionary of Major Economists.* Cambridge, Mass: MIT Press.

Teaching materials, Types of capitalism and socialism, La Sapienza, University of Rome.

Blog, Transition: April 2009 – 2018 (Collected Posts).

Index[1]

[1] Note: Page numbers followed by 'n' refer to notes.

© The Author(s), under exclusive license to Springer Nature Switzerland AG 2023

S. Estrin, M. Uvalic (eds.), *Collected Works of Domenico Mario Nuti, Volume I*, Studies in Economic Transition, https://doi.org/10.1007/978-3-031-12334-4

The manufacturer's authorised representative in the EU is Springer Nature Customer Service Centre GmbH, Europaplatz 3, 69115 Heidelberg, Germany. If you have any concerns regarding our products, please contact ProductSafety@springernature.com

Printed and bound by CPI Group (UK) Ltd, Croydon, CR0 4YY

30/09/2026

02225243-0019